Where to Stay
in Britain

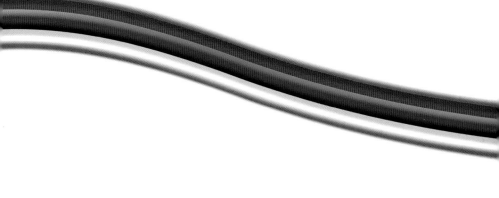

BRITAIN

Contents

Further information

Useful Indexes

VisitBritain

VisitBritain is the organisation created to market Britain to the rest of the world, and England to the British.

Formed by the merger of the British Tourist Authority and the English Tourism Council, its mission is to build the value of tourism by creating world-class destination brands and marketing campaigns.

It will also build partnerships with – and provide insights to – other organisations which have a stake in British and English tourism.

Guernsey

Jersey

Guernsey and Jersey are not drawn to scale

Welcome to Britain

Unique, traditional, cutting edge, refreshing, imaginative, surprising – Britain is all this and more. Come and discover it for yourself. This official VisitBritain guide is packed with information to help you plan your trip, from where to stay and what to see and do, to essential travel information.

Wherever you visit in England, Scotland, Wales, Northern Ireland or the Channel Islands, you'll find a warm welcome and a great choice of quality accommodation, whatever your budget. Take a look through this guide and you'll find something to suit your needs, from city hotels and farmhouse B&Bs, to coastal holiday homes and rural camp sites. All accommodation has been rated for quality to nationally agreed standards, so you can book with the confidence that it will meet your expectations.

If you're looking for inspiration take a look through our Great Ideas pages and regional sections. Lively cities, heritage towns, stately homes and great family attractions are here to be discovered. And don't forget our diverse natural heritage – spectacular coast and stunning countryside. Explore our national parks, the flat waterscapes of the east of England, ancient woodlands and rolling downland in the south, and jutting peaks in Scotland, Wales and the Lake District. There's scenery and breathing spaces to suit every activity and mood.

From Wimbledon to Ascot, the Proms to the Edinburgh Tattoo and the Llangollen Eisteddfod, there are many exciting events throughout the year to plan your holiday around. So, what are you waiting for? Explore Britain your way...

GB, UK, British Isles?

Do you think that Great Britain, the United Kingdom and the British Isles are the same? Well, they're not! Here's a brief explanation:

GREAT BRITAIN
Great Britain is the largest island of the British Isles, and includes the greater parts of England, Scotland and Wales. Sometimes people refer to Britain or GB instead of Great Britain.

UNITED KINGDOM
The United Kingdom of Great Britain and Northern Ireland is the official name referring to England, Scotland, Wales and Northern Ireland. People refer to the United Kingdom or the UK.

BRITISH ISLES
The British Isles includes Great Britain, the whole of Ireland and numerous smaller islands.

OTHER ISLANDS
The Channel Islands and the Isle of Man are British Crown Dependencies with their own parliament and laws. Together with the United Kingdom they are collectively known as the British Islands – not to be confused with the British Isles!

This guide includes accommodation in England, Scotland, Wales, Northern Ireland and the Channel Islands.

Accommodation

Places to visit

Tourist information

Living heritage

Marvel at the ancient stone circle of Stonehenge. Watch royal pageants like Trooping the Colour in London. Hop aboard a steam train and journey through time. Varied, vibrant heritage is part of daily life in Britain.

You can visit over 25 World Heritage Sites and they come in all shapes and sizes. Join a yeoman warder for a guided tour through nearly 1,000 years of history at The Tower of London and see the precious Crown Jewels. Wander the evocative waterfront of Liverpool, Maritime Mercantile City. In Wales, mighty castles like 13th-century Caernarfon and Beaumaris recall a tumultuous past.

Follow in the footsteps of royalty all around the nation, to fairytale Leeds Castle in Kent, the dramatic medieval fortress of Warwick Castle in Warwickshire, Windsor Castle – official residence of The Queen, or battlefields such as Bosworth in Leicestershire. Stately homes are a particular glory, including treasure-filled Castle Howard in North Yorkshire. You might even bump into the dukes or lords who live in these stunning historic houses, at Chatsworth in Derbyshire, Blenheim Palace in Oxfordshire, or Beaulieu in Hampshire.

Heritage Cities are equally fascinating, from walled Chester and Oxford with its 'dreaming spires', to the Roman spa of Bath – try the modern spa, too. Then get to know the world's most-performed playwright, William Shakespeare, at his birthplace in Stratford-upon-Avon. Or admire the architectural splendours of the cathedrals in St Davids, Canterbury and Durham. Winchester Cathedral is Europe's longest medieval cathedral and took some 300 years to build!

You'll also come across lots of exciting legends that add spice to any exploration. Follow in the footsteps of folk hero Robin Hood in Sherwood Forest, Nottinghamshire, or King Arthur in Cornwall and Somerset. Look for the Loch Ness Monster in Scotland, and visit scenes countrywide where modern hero Harry Potter was filmed.

Great British Heritage Pass

Planning to visit historical or heritage attractions on your trip to Britain? Buy the Great British Heritage Pass before you leave. For an affordable one-off price, it gives you free entry to more than 580 UK castles, gardens, stately homes and properties. It really is the key to unlocking Britain's secrets!

For more information, or to buy a pass, go to visitbritaindirect.com

For lots more great ideas go online to visitbritain.com

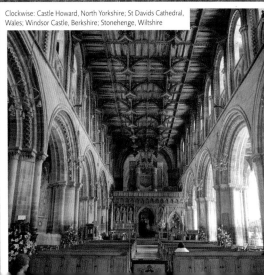

Clockwise: Castle Howard, North Yorkshire; St Davids Cathedral, Wales; Windsor Castle, Berkshire; Stonehenge, Wiltshire

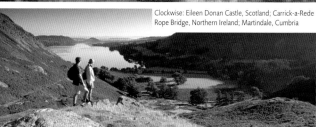

Clockwise: Eileen Donan Castle, Scotland; Carrick-a-Rede Rope Bridge, Northern Ireland; Martindale, Cumbria

Outdoor Britain

Discover the UK's astonishing diversity of landscapes: from England's heather-covered North York Moors to the dramatic mountains of Scotland's Cairngorms. From the exhilarating beaches of Cornwall, to the grassy hills of the Brecon Beacons in Wales.

Once you're here, they're all so easy to reach. Walk and admire panoramic views, picnic overlooking the sea, cycle beside rivers and peaceful canals. Within minutes you're totally relaxed.

Britain's National Parks, Heritage Coasts and Areas of Outstanding Natural Beauty safeguard the countryside for all to enjoy. Explore the Lake District where romantic peaks reflect in mirror-still waters. Wander with ponies in the ancient woodlands of southern England's New Forest. Watch the sun set over Porlock Bay, Exmoor. There's scenery to suit every mood.

If you like walking, you'll find plenty of trails, both long and short. Dorset and East Devon's Jurassic Coast is rich with fossils and wildlife. Gentle riverside routes thread through the Wye Valley. Follow Hadrian's Wall, the great ancient boundary running across northern England. Or for a different experience saunter

the footpaths and cycleways to East Lancashire's Panopticons: imaginative landmarks like the Singing Ringing Tree that lead to magnificent landscapes.

And do remember to bring your camera to capture some memorable scenes, like the Giant's Causeway World Heritage Site on Northern Ireland's rugged Antrim coast. Did the massive black basalt columns form naturally, or did the giant Finn McCool put them there as stepping-stones? The iconic White Cliffs of Dover never fail to impress either – they were created over 80 million years from billions of crushed shells, sea-dwelling plants and animals. Come and be inspired.

For lots more great ideas go online to visitbritain.com

8

Glorious gardens

Gardening in Britain is a national pastime – in fact it's a passionate art form! You'll find every type of design, from grand parks to quaint cottage gardens filled with roses, from mazes to dazzling water features.

Stately homes and manor houses lead the way with beautiful grounds. Stroll the outdoor 'rooms' of Mount Stewart, County Down in Ireland, including flamboyant Italian and Spanish Gardens. Discover England's largest restoration project at Trentham in Staffordshire – look out for the mile-long lake. Samarès Manor in Jersey features exotic specimens, living willow tunnels and a herb garden. Contrast all this with tiny cottage gardens planted in bright, higgledy-piggledy ways: learn the secrets of this typical British fashion at East Lambrook Manor Gardens in Somerset, the 'Home of the English Cottage Garden'.

Amazing botanic gardens at Kew, its sister garden Wakehurst Place in West Sussex, and at Llanarthne in Wales span continents with their lush exhibits. Walk through a tropical rainforest and Mediterranean plant world in the giant biomes (greenhouses) of the Eden Project in Cornwall. And what is more restful than the sight and sound of water? Elegant ornamental lakes, canals, temples and cascades create eye-catching views at Studley Royal Water Garden in North Yorkshire. Children love the Grand Cascade and giant tree house of the imaginative 21st-century Alnwick Garden, Northumberland. Everyone loves mazes – tackle the famous one at Hampton Court Palace, Surrey.

Britain's gardens flourish in different ways all year round, from spring snowdrops to winter gardens of evergreens. Come in autumn and arboreta burst with rich colours. Make a date, too, for stunning shows like May's Chelsea Flower Show and seasonal floral festivals in the Channel Islands.

For lots more great ideas go online to visitbritain.com

Clockwise from left: Eden Project, Cornwall; The Alnwick Garden, Northumberland; Wakehurst Place, West Sussex

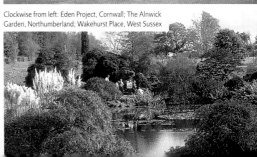

Museums and galleries

Priceless treasures, groundbreaking contemporary art, even the odd dinosaur skeleton or two – they're all kept safe in Britain's museums and galleries. And another wonderful surprise is that entry is free to the outstanding National Collections!

Britons are great collectors – just visit any museum or gallery and you'll agree. Every period is covered, from pre-history to glimpses into the future. Every theme is explored, from science and technology to toys.

One of the best places to start is with the National Collections – they're spread across the country. In London alone they include the British Museum, which features over 90 galleries and spans civilizations from ancient Assyria to modern Japan. The National Gallery displays world-famous paintings through the centuries, while the Victoria and Albert Museum boasts rich collections of art and design. Drop into Tate Modern to browse inspirational 20th-century art – there are also Tate galleries of modern art in Liverpool and St Ives, Cornwall. The National Museums of Scotland range from Scottish history to rural life and costume. The National Museums of Wales showcase top art, Welsh heritage, coal and slate mining – don a hard hat and take a trip underground!

Sometimes state-of-the-art buildings are breathtaking exhibits in themselves: the shiny aluminium Imperial War Museum North in Manchester, designed by Daniel Libeskind, is just one 'must-see' example.

Visiting museums and galleries in Britain is also lots of fun. Ironbridge Gorge in Shropshire was at the heart of the Industrial Revolution and its ten museums offer all sorts of activities: from decorating a ceramic tile to observing objects with a giant x-ray machine. Whilst in Bristol, At-Bristol is a thrilling interactive science centre, and The Roald Dahl Museum and Story Centre in Buckinghamshire, dedicated to the popular children's author, even hosts storytelling and cookery classes!

For lots more great ideas go online to visitbritain.com

Clockwise from bottom: At-Bristol, Bristol; Imperial War Museum North, Manchester; Victoria and Albert Museum, London

Make your break memorable with traditional British fayre and fresh local flavours

Food and drink

You're in for a treat! British food has undergone a quiet revolution in recent years. Fresh, local and organic ingredients have become the order of the day. Global influences and regional specialities combine adventure and tradition.

Get to know the country through its scrumptious food. Start with the famous Ludlow Food Festival and follow the Sausage Trail – you'll find everything from organic rare-breeds sausages to the Shropshire Sizzler, a rich blend of local pork, peaches and blue cheese. Scotland, of course, is renowned for its whisky. Visit a distillery to find out how it's made and sample a 'wee dram'. The Speyside Malt Whisky Trail journeys through beautiful Speyside taking in seven working distilleries. Somerset and Herefordshire are 'Cider country' and everywhere has its own cheese, from mellow Cheshire to classic Cheddar. Wales, too, has many award-winning cheeses. Britain also now boasts over 400 vineyards and wineries, many producing award-winning tipples.

Fancy lunch while out exploring? Look around a farmers' market where artisan pies, freshly baked bread, meat and juices provide all you need for a tasty picnic. Or drop into a village

pub for hearty fare and real ales at reasonable prices. New-breed gastropubs serve high-quality bistro meals, adding modern flair to a great British institution. Or try a themed eaterie like a waffle house, or an authentic curry in a multicultural city like Leicester. In the Channel Islands you'll find the best of French and English style.

And, while you're out and about, do make the most of British teatime – cakes and scones oozing with jam and clotted cream, in tearooms from Yorkshire to Devon and Cornwall.

For lots more great ideas go online to visitbritain.com

Finding accommodation is easy...

Choose from a wide range of quality-assessed accommodation to suit all budgets and tastes. Whatever your destination, there's a wide choice of quality accommodation to choose from in Britain.

Look through this guide and book a place to stay with confidence – accommodation must participate in a national quality assessment scheme to be included. Each property is visited annually by a professional assessor who applies nationally agreed standards of quality. An explanation of ratings and awards can be found on the following pages.

Detailed accommodation entries include descriptions, prices and facilities. You'll also find special offers, and if you want something a little different look out for the themed breaks in some entries. Remember, you can find out even more about each property online.

Regional sections

The guide is divided into regions (see page 3). Accommodation is listed alphabetically by place name within each region. If you know which part of the country you wish to visit, start your search for accommodation in these sections.

Colour maps

Use the colour maps, starting on page 30, to pinpoint the location of all accommodation featured in the regional sections.

Then refer to the place index at the back of the guide to find the page number.

Place index

If you know the city, town or village where you want to stay, use the place index at the back of the guide. The index also includes tourism areas such as the New Forest and the Cotswolds to help you with your search.

Property index

If you're looking for a specific property, turn to the Property Index where you will find an alphabetical list of all accommodation within the regional sections of this guide.

Further information

If you need more information before you make your choice contact one of the regional tourism organisations or a tourist information centre in your chosen destination. Contact details can be found within each regional section. And for invaluable travel information, turn to the back of the guide.

A special welcome

To help make your selection of accommodation easier VisitBritain has four special Welcome schemes which accommodation in England can be assessed to. Owners participating in these schemes go the extra mile to welcome walkers, cyclists, families or pet owners and provide additional facilities and services to make your stay even more comfortable.

Families Welcome

If you are searching for a great family break look out for the Families Welcome sign. The sign indicates that the proprietor offers additional facilities and services catering for a range of ages and family units. For families with young children, the accommodation will have special facilities such as cots and highchairs, storage for push-chairs and somewhere to heat baby food or milk. Where meals are provided, children's choices will be clearly indicated, with healthy options available. They'll also have information on local walks, attractions, activities or events suitable for children, as well as local child-friendly pubs and restaurants. Not all accommodation is able to cater for all ages or combinations of family units, so do check when you book.

Welcome Pets!

Want to travel with your faithful companion? Look out for accommodation displaying the Welcome Pets! sign. Participants in this scheme go out of their way to meet the needs of guests bringing dogs, cats and/or small birds. In addition to providing water and food bowls, torches or nightlights, spare leads and pet washing facilities, they'll buy in food on request, and offer toys, treats and bedding. They'll also have information on pet-friendly attractions, pubs, restaurants and recreation. Of course, not everyone is able to offer suitable facilities for every pet, so do check if there are any restrictions on the type, size and number of animals when you book.

Walkers Welcome

If walking is your passion seek out accommodation participating in the Walkers Welcome scheme. Facilities include a place for drying clothes and boots, maps and books for reference and a first-aid kit. Packed breakfasts and lunch are available on request in hotels and guesthouses, and you have the option to pre-order basic groceries in self-catering accommodation. A wide range of information is provided including public transport, weather, local restaurants and attractions, details of the nearest bank and all night chemists.

Cyclists Welcome

If you like to explore by bike seek out accommodation displaying the Cyclists Welcome symbol. Facilities include a lockable undercover area and a place to dry outdoor clothing and footwear, an evening meal if there are no eating facilities available within one mile, and a packed breakfast or lunch on request. Information is also provided on cycle hire and cycle repair shops, maps and books for reference, weather and details of the nearest bank and all night chemists and more.

For further information go online at enjoyengland.com/quality

Accommodation entries explained

Each entry contains detailed information to help you decide if it is right for you. This has been provided by proprietors and our aim is to ensure that it is as objective and factual as possible.

① ② ③ ④   ⑤   ⑥   ⑦ ⑧

BUXTON, Derbyshire Map ref 4B2   **SELF CATERING**

★★★★
SELF CATERING

Units **8**
Sleeps **2–5**

LOW SEASON PER WK
£340.00–£467.00

HIGH SEASON PER WK
£488.00–£651.00

Contact us for special deals on late availability. 5% discount if you arrive by public transport.

Wheeldon Trees Farm, Earl Sterndale, Buxton
contact Deborah & Martin Hofman, Earl Sterndale, Buxton SK17 0AA **t** +44 (0) 1298 83219
e stay@wheeldontreesfarm.co.uk

wheeldontreesfarm.co.uk GUEST REVIEWS · SPECIAL OFFERS · REAL-TIME BOOKING

open All year
payment Credit/debit cards, cash, cheques
nearest pub 1 mile
nearest shop 2.5 miles

Relax and explore unspoilt landscapes, picturesque villages and lively market towns. 18thC dairy barn conversion, in quiet and secluded valley with fabulous views. Seven self-catering holiday cottages sleeping up to 28 (4 singles, 8 twins, 4 doubles). Newly refurbished with consideration to the environment. Communal dining and leisure facilities.

SAT NAV *SK17 0AA* **ONLINE MAP**

Unit 🖵 📷 💻 🛁 🔥 🍳 🍽 📼 ✂ ❄ General 🛋 🏠 🅿 Ⓢ 🐕 Leisure 🔍 🚲

Sample enhanced entry

⑨ ⑩ ⑪   ⑫   ⑬

1   Listing under town or village with map reference

2   Star rating plus Gold, Silver or Rose Award where applicable

3   Classification

4   Prices
    Hotels – per room for bed and breakfast (B&B) and per person for half board (HB)
    Bed and breakfast – per room for bed and breakfast (B&B) and per person for evening meal

    Self catering – per unit per week for low and high season
    Caravanning – per pitch per night for touring pitches, per unit per week for caravan holiday homes

5   Establishment name and booking details

6   Website information (web addresses are shown without the prefix www.)

7   Indicates when the establishment is open

8   Accommodation details and payment accepted

9   Accessible rating where applicable (see page 24)

10 Walkers, cyclists, pets and families welcome where applicable (see opposite)

11 Special promotions and themed breaks

12 Travel directions

13 At-a-glance facility symbols (see overleaf)

Key to symbols

Information about many of the accommodation services and facilities is given in the form of symbols.

Hotels and Guest Accommodation

Rooms

- Bedroom (s) on ground floor
- Four-poster bed(s)
- Telephone in all bedrooms
- TV in all bedrooms
- Satellite/cable channels in all bedrooms
- Tea/coffee facilities in all bedrooms
- Hairdryer in all bedrooms
- Smoking rooms available

General

- Children welcome (a number following gives minimum age)
- Cots
- Highchairs
- P Parking on site
- Wi-Fi
- Internet access
- Bar
- Evening meals served [2]
- Special diets by arrangement
- Night porter [1]
- Lift [1]
- Air-conditioning throughout [1]
- Games console available
- Laundry facilities
- Conference/meeting facilities [1]
- Garden/patio
- Pets welcome by arrangement

Self Catering Accommodation

Unit

- TV
- SC Satellite/cable channels
- Telephone
- DVD player
- Games console
- Microwave
- Dishwasher
- Freezer
- Hairdryer
- Washing machine in all units
- Linen provided
- Linen available for hire
- Towels provided
- Smoking units available
- Daily servicing of unit
- Garden/patio
- Barbecue
- Real log/coal fire

General

- Children welcome (a number following gives minimum age)
- Cots
- Highchairs
- P Parking next to unit
- Laundry facilities
- S Weekend/mid-week bookings
- Pets welcome by arrangement

16

Camping, Caravan and Holiday Parks

Pitches

🚐 Caravans (number of pitches and rates)

🚐 Motor caravans (number of pitches and rates)

⛺ Tents (number of pitches and rates)

🏠 Caravan holiday homes (number of pitches and rates)

🏠 Log cabins/lodges (number of units and rates)

🏠 Chalets/villas (number of units and rates)

General

🚐 Overnight holding area

🚐 Motor home pitches reserved for day trips off-site

🔌 Electrical hook-up points

🔥 Calor Gas/Camping Gaz purchase/exchange service

🚽 Chemical toilet disposal point

WP Motor home waste disposal point

🚿 Showers

📞 Public telephone

🧺 Laundry facilities

🛒 Food shop on site

✕ Restaurant on site

🐕 Pets welcome by arrangement

☼ Prior booking recommended in summer

((•)) Wi-Fi

🖥 Internet access

Leisure facilities
(all accommodation)

🏊 Swimming pool - indoor

🏊 Swimming pool - outdoor

♨ Sauna[1]

🤸 Gym[1]

⊗ Health/fitness/beauty facilities[1]

🎾 Tennis court(s)

U Riding/pony-trekking nearby

🎣 Fishing nearby

► Access to golf

🚲 Cycle hire nearby

● Games room[3]

🍸 Clubhouse with bar[4]

♫ Regular evening entertainment[4]

🎠 Outdoor play area[4]

---

[1] Hotels only

[2] Guest accommodation only (hotels must serve dinner at least five days a week).

[3] Self catering and camping, caravan and holiday parks only.

[4] Camping, caravan and holiday parks only.

National Accessible Scheme

The National Accessible Scheme includes standards for hearing and visual impairment as well as mobility impairment – see pages 24-25 for further information.

Welcome schemes

Walkers, cyclists, families and pet owners are warmly welcomed where you see these signs – see page 14 for further information.

Ratings and awards at a glance

Reliable, rigorous, easy to use – look out for the following ratings and awards to help you choose with confidence.

Star ratings

Establishments are awarded a rating of one to five stars based on a combination of quality of facilities and services provided. Put simply, **the more stars, the higher the quality and the greater the range of facilities and level of service.**

The process to arrive at a star rating is very thorough. National tourist board professional assessors visit establishments annually and work to strict criteria to check the available facilities and service. A quality score is awarded for every aspect of the experience.

Ratings made easy

★
Simple, practical, no frills

★★
Well presented and well run

★★★
Good level of quality and comfort

★★★★
Excellent standard throughout

★★★★★
Exceptional, with a degree of luxury

For full details of the quality assessment schemes, go online at
enjoyengland.com/quality

For hotels and bed and breakfast accommodation this includes the comfort of the bed, the quality of the breakfast and dinner and, most importantly, the cleanliness. For self-catering properties the assessors also take into consideration the layout and design of the accommodation, the ease of use of all appliances, the range and quality of the kitchen equipment, and the variety and presentation of the visitor information provided. They also score the warmth of welcome and the level of care that each establishment offers its guests.

From January 2006, most national assessing bodies (VisitBritain, VisitScotland, Visit Wales, Jersey Tourism, VisitGuernsey and the AA) have operated to a common set of standards, giving a clear guide on exactly what to expect at each level (see page 412). The Northern Ireland Tourist Board operates to a different set of rating standards. To find out more visit discovernorthernireland.com/information.

For information on awards see overleaf

Gold and Silver Awards

If you want a superior level of quality guaranteed seek out accommodation in England with a Gold or Silver Award. They are only given to properties offering the highest levels of quality within their star rating (see page 23).

National Accessible Scheme

Establishments with a National Accessible Scheme rating have been thoroughly assessed to set criteria and provide access to facilities and services for guests with visual, hearing or mobility impairment (see page 24).

Welcome schemes

VisitBritain runs four special Welcome schemes in England: Cyclists Welcome, Walkers Welcome, Welcome Pets! and Families Welcome. Scheme participants actively encourage these types of visitors and make special provision to ensure a welcoming, comfortable stay (see page 14).

Caravan Holiday Home Award Scheme

VisitBritain and VisitScotland run award schemes for individual holiday caravan homes on highly graded caravan parks. In addition to complying with standards for Holiday Parks, these exceptional caravans must have a shower or bath, toilet, mains electricity and water heating (at no extra charge) and a fridge (many also have a colour TV).

Award-winning parks listed in this guide show 'Rose Award' in their entry.

Visitor Attraction Quality Assurance

Attractions participating in this scheme are visited every year by a professional assessor and must achieve high standards in all aspects of the visitor experience. The assessment focuses on the nature of the welcome, hospitality, services and presentation as well as the standards of toilets, shop and café where provided.

Classifications explained

The following classifications will help you decide which type of establishment is right for you, whether you are seeking a non-stop, city-buzz holiday, a quiet weekend away or a home-from-home break for all the family.

Hotels

Hotel
A minimum of six bedrooms, but more likely to have over 20.

Small Hotel
A maximum of 20 bedrooms and likely to be more personally run.

Country House Hotel
Set in ample grounds or gardens, in a rural or semi-rural location, with the emphasis on peace and quiet.

Town House Hotel
In a city or town-centre location, high quality with a distinctive and individual style. Maximum of 50 bedrooms, with a high ratio of staff to guests. Possibly no dinner served, but room service available. Might not have a dining room, so breakfast may be served in the bedrooms.

Metro Hotel
A city or town-centre hotel offering full hotel services, but no dinner. Located within easy walking distance of a range of places to eat. Can be of any size.

Budget Hotel
Part of a large branded hotel group, offering limited services. A Budget Hotel is not awarded a star rating.

Northern Ireland
Northern Ireland has separate classifications for hotels, guest accommodation, bed and breakfasts and self catering properties. For more information visit discovernorthernireland.com/information.

Bed and Breakfast

Guest Accommodation

Encompassing a wide range of establishments from one-room bed and breakfasts to larger properties, which may offer dinner and hold an alcohol licence.

Bed and Breakfast

Accommodating generally no more than six people, the owners of these establishments welcome you into their home as a special guest.

Guest House

Generally comprising more than three rooms. Dinner is unlikely to be available (if it is, it will need to be booked in advance). May possibly be licensed.

Farmhouse

Bed and breakfast, and sometimes dinner, but always on a farm.

Restaurant with rooms

A licensed restaurant is the main business but there will be a small number of bedrooms, with all the facilities you would expect, and breakfast the following morning.

Inns

Pubs with rooms, and many with restaurants as well.

Self Catering

Self Catering

Choose from cosy country cottages, smart town-centre apartments, seaside villas, grand country houses for large family gatherings, and even quirky conversions of windmills, railway carriages and lighthouses. Most take bookings by the week, generally from a Friday or Saturday, but short breaks are increasingly offered, particularly outside the main season.

Serviced Apartments

City-centre serviced apartments are an excellent alternative to hotel accommodation, offering hotel services such as daily cleaning, room service, concierge and business centre services, but with a kitchen and lounge area that allow you to eat in and relax when you choose. A telephone and Internet access tend to be standard. Prices are generally based on the property, so they often represent excellent value for money for families and larger groups. Serviced apartments tend to accept bookings for any length of period, and many are operated by agencies whose in-depth knowledge and choice of properties makes searching easier at busy times.

Approved Caravan

Approved caravan holiday homes are let as individual self-catering units and can be located on farms or holiday parks. All the facilities, including a bathroom and toilet, are contained within the caravan and all main services are provided. There are no star ratings, but all caravans are assessed annually to minimum standards.

Camping and Caravan Parks

Camping Park

These sites only have pitches available for tents.

Touring Park

If you are planning to travel with your own caravan, motor home or tent, then look for a Touring Park.

Holiday Park

If you want to hire a caravan holiday home for a short break or longer holiday, or are looking to buy your own holiday home, a Holiday Park is the right choice. They range from small, rural sites to larger parks with all the added extras, such as a swimming pool.

Many parks will offer a combination of these classifications.

Holiday Village

Holiday villages usually comprise a variety of types of accommodation, with the majority in custom-built rooms, chalets for example. The option to book on a bed and breakfast, or dinner, bed and breakfast basis is normally available. A range of facilities, entertainment and activities are also provided which may, or may not, be included in the tariff.

Holiday Villages must meet a minimum entry requirement for both the provision and quality of facilities and services, including fixtures, fittings, furnishings, decor and any other extra facilities. Progressively higher levels of quality and customer care are provided at each star level.

Forest Holiday Village

A holiday village which is situated in a forest setting with conservation and sustainable tourism being a key feature. It will usually comprise a variety of accommodation, often purpose built; and with a range of entertainment, activities and facilities available on site free of charge or at extra cost.

Gold and Silver Awards

Enjoy England's unique Gold and Silver Awards are given in recognition of exceptional quality in hotel and bed and breakfast accommodation in England.

Enjoy England professional assessors make recommendations for Gold and Silver Awards during assessments. They will look at the quality provided in all areas, in particular housekeeping, service and hospitality, bedrooms, bathrooms and food, to see if it meets the highest quality for the star level achieved.

While star ratings are based on a combination of quality, range of facilities and level of service offered, Gold and Silver Awards are based solely on quality. You may therefore find that a two-star Gold Award hotel offering superior levels of quality may be more suited to your needs if, for example, enhanced services such as a concierge or 24-hour room service are not essential for your stay.

Here we list hotels and bed and breakfast accommodation with a Gold Award featured in this guide. Use the property index starting on page 432 to find their page numbers.

Award-winningestablishments listed in this guide show the relevant award in their entry.

Gold Awards 2009

Hotels

Ashdown Park Hotel
Forest Row, *East Sussex*

Calcot Manor Hotel & Spa
Tetbury, *Gloucestershire*

Combe House
Honiton, *Devon*

Gilpin Lodge Country House Hotel
Windermere, *Cumbria*

The Grand Hotel
Eastbourne, *East Sussex*

The Grange Hotel
York, *North Yorkshire*

Linthwaite House Hotel
Windermere, *Cumbria*

Hotel Riviera
Sidmouth, *Devon*

Swinton Park
Masham, *North Yorkshire*

Tides Reach Hotel
Salcombe, *Devon*

Tylney Hall Hotel
Hook, *Hampshire*

Bed and breakfast accommodation

Arundel House Restaurant & Rooms
Arundel, *West Sussex*

Athole Guest House
Bath, *Somerset*

The Ayrlington
Bath, *Somerset*

Bays Farm
Stowmarket, *Suffolk*

Giffard House
Winchester, *Hampshire*

Grassington Lodge
Grassington, *North Yorkshire*

Magnolia House
Canterbury, *Kent*

Old Bakery
Pulham Market, *Norfolk*

Old Pump House
Aylsham, *Norfolk*

The Old Vicarage
Pickering, *North Yorkshire*

The Summer House
Penzance, *Cornwall*

Tor Cottage
Tavistock, *Devon*

National Accessible Scheme

The criteria VisitBritain and national/regional tourism organisations have adopted do not necessarily conform to British Standards or to Building Regulations. They reflect what the organisations understand to be acceptable to meet the practical needs of guests with mobility or sensory impairments and encourage the industry to increase access to all.

Finding suitable accommodation is not always easy, especially if you have to seek out rooms with level entry or large print menus. Use the National Accessible Scheme to help you make your choice.

Proprietors of accommodation taking part in the National Accessible Scheme have gone out of their way to ensure a comfortable stay for guests with special hearing, visual or mobility needs. These exceptional places are full of extra touches to make everyone's visit trouble-free, from handrails, ramps and step-free entrances (ideal for buggies too) to level-access showers and colour contrast in the bathrooms. Members of staff may have attended a disability awareness course and will know what assistance will really be appreciated.

Appropriate National Accessible Scheme symbols are included in the guide entries (shown opposite). If you have additional needs or special requirements we strongly recommend that you make sure these can be met by your chosen establishment before you confirm your reservation.

For a wider selection of accessible accommodation, order a copy of the *Easy Access Britain* guide featuring almost 500 places to stay. It is available from Tourism for All for £9.99 (plus P&P). Alternatively, visit tourismforall.org.uk for a directory of National Accessible Scheme and Tourism for All members.

tourismforall

The National Accessible Scheme forms part of the Tourism for All campaign that is being promoted by VisitBritain and national/regional tourism organisations. Additional help and guidance on finding suitable holiday accommodation can be obtained from:

Tourism for All
c/o Vitalise, Shap Road Industrial
Estate, Kendal LA9 6NZ

t +44 (0) 1539 814683

f +44 (0) 1539 735567

e info@tourismforall.org.uk

w tourismforall.org.uk

Scotland

Category 1
Accessible to a wheelchair user travelling independently.

Category 2
Accessible to a wheelchair user travelling with assistance.

Category 3
Accessible to a wheelchair user able to walk a few paces and up a maximum of three steps.

Wales
Owners of all types of accommodation in Wales should have an Access Statement available to visitors.

England

Mobility Impairment Symbols

Typically suitable for a person with sufficient mobility to climb a flight of steps but who would benefit from fixtures and fittings to aid balance.

Typically suitable for a person with restricted walking ability and for those who may need to use a wheelchair some of the time and can negotiate a maximum of three steps.

Typically suitable for a person who depends on the use of a wheelchair and transfers unaided to and from the wheelchair in a seated position. This person may be an independent traveller.

Typically suitable for a person who depends on the use of a wheelchair and needs assistance when transferring to and from the wheelchair in a seated position.

Access Exceptional is awarded to establishments that meet the requirements of independent wheelchair users or assisted wheelchair users shown above and also fulfil more demanding requirements with reference to the British Standards BS8300:2001.

Visual Impairment Symbols

Typically provides key additional services and facilities to meet the needs of visually impaired guests.

Typically provides a higher level of additional services and facilities to meet the needs of visually impaired guests.

Hearing Impairment Symbols

Typically provides key additional services and facilities to meet the needs of guests with hearing impairment.

Typically provides a higher level of additional services and facilities to meet the needs of guests with hearing impairment.

Country ways

The Countryside Rights of Way Act gives people new rights to walk on areas of open countryside and registered common land.

To find out where you can go and what you can do, as well as information about taking your dog to the countryside, go online at countrysideaccess.gov.uk.

And when you're out and about...

Always follow the Country Code

- Be safe – plan ahead and follow any signs
- Leave gates and property as you find them
- Protect plants and animals, and take your litter home
- Keep dogs under close control
- Consider other people

enjoyEngland ™

official tourist board guides

Hotels, including country house and town house hotels, metro and budget hotels and serviced apartments in England 2009

£10.99

Guest accommodation, B&Bs, guest houses, farmhouses, inns, restaurants with rooms, campus and hostel accommodation in England 2009

£11.99

Self-catering holiday homes, including serviced apartments and approved caravan holiday homes, boat accommodation and holiday cottage agencies in England 2009

£11.99

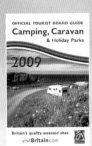

Touring parks, camping holidays and holiday parks and villages in Britain 2009

£8.99

informative, easy to use and great value for money

Pet-friendly hotels, B&Bs and self-catering accommodation in England 2009

£9.99

Great Places to Stay Four and five star accommodation in Britain

£17.99

Great ideas for places to visit, eat and stay in England

£10.99

Accessible places to stay in Britain

£9.99

Now available in good bookshops.
For special offers on VisitBritain publications,
please visit **visitbritaindirect.com**

ALNWICK CASTLE
NORTHUMBERLAND

the RHYTHMS of LIFE
A guide to the gallery of musical instruments at the Horniman Museum and highlights of the collection.
HORNIMAN MUSEUM

Haddon Hall
Bakewell Derbyshire

BOUGHT

St P
CATH

CASTLE
GARDENS OF
THE QUEEN MOTHER'S HOME

RENISHAW HALL
D THE SITWELLS

DERBY CATHEDRAL

WOBURN ABBEY

Sulgrave Manor

HEVER CASTLE
& GARDEN

BLENHEIM PALACE

LOSELL
a stately home

EASTNOR CASTLE

WORLD HERITAGE SITE

TIME & TIDE

SCONE PALACE
THE CROWNING PLACE OF SCOTTISH KINGS

A HISTORY OF ALNWICK PARKS
AND PLEASURE GROUNDS
Colin Shrimpton

PASHLEY MANOR GARDENS
through the seasons

SquerryeS
SINCE 1731

HATFIELD HOUSE

HERITAGE MOTOR CENTRE

Lasting memories of Britain's finest
All guidebooks available from giftshops

THE ALNWICK GARDEN

ELBURN
LE & COUNTRY CENTRE

GLAMIS CASTLE

STEAM
MUSEUM OF THE GREAT WESTERN RAILWAY
THE BRISTOLIAN
6000

TISSINGTON HALL
Home of the FitzHerbert family for 500 years

Westminst
Cathedra

Map 1

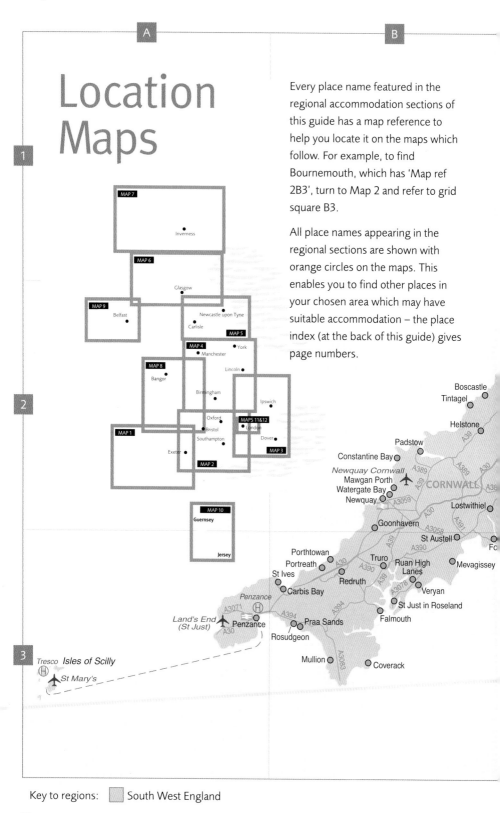

Location Maps

Every place name featured in the regional accommodation sections of this guide has a map reference to help you locate it on the maps which follow. For example, to find Bournemouth, which has 'Map ref 2B3', turn to Map 2 and refer to grid square B3.

All place names appearing in the regional sections are shown with orange circles on the maps. This enables you to find other places in your chosen area which may have suitable accommodation – the place index (at the back of this guide) gives page numbers.

Key to regions: ░░░ South West England

Map 1

Orange circles indicate accommodation within the regional sections of this guide

Map 2

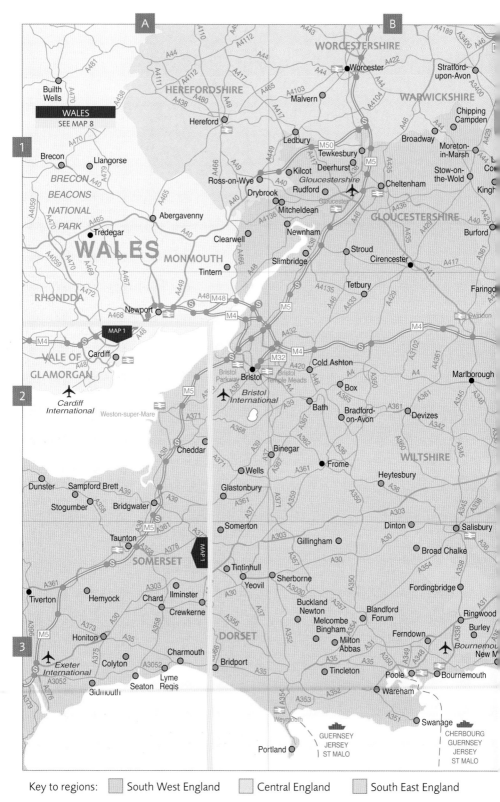

Key to regions: ▢ South West England ▢ Central England ▢ South East England

Map 2

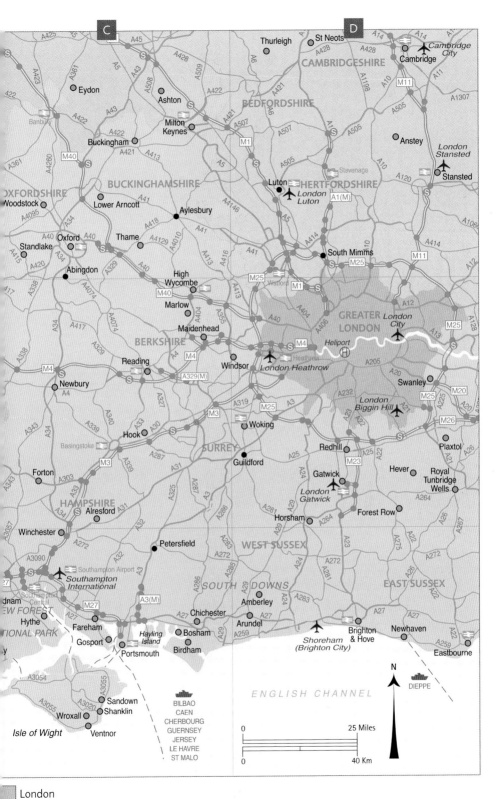

London

Orange circles indicate accommodation within the regional sections of this guide

Map 3

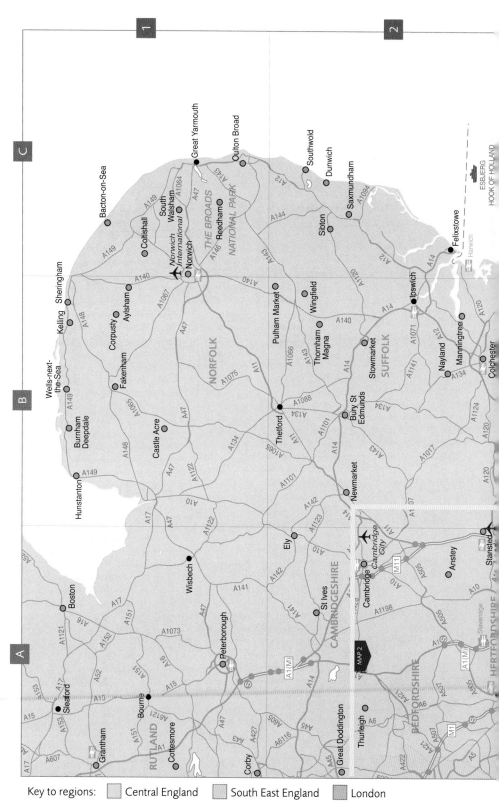

Key to regions: ☐ Central England ☐ South East England ☐ London

Map 3

Orange circles indicate accommodation within the regional sections of this guide

Map 4

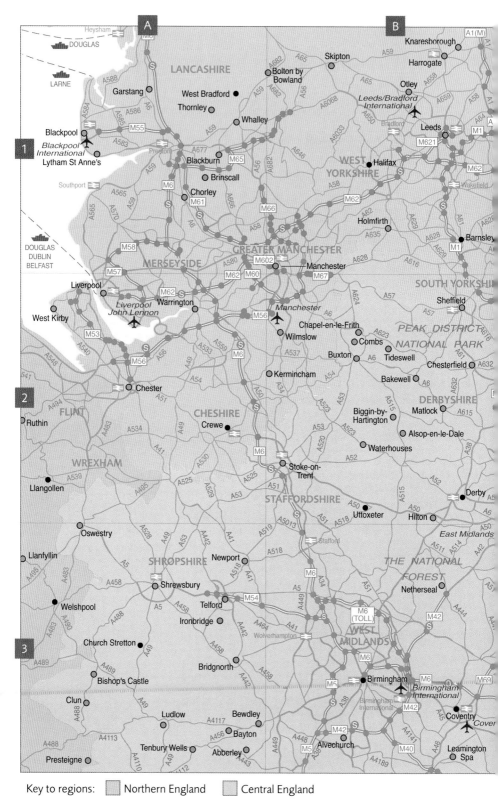

Key to regions: ▢ Northern England ▢ Central England

Map 4

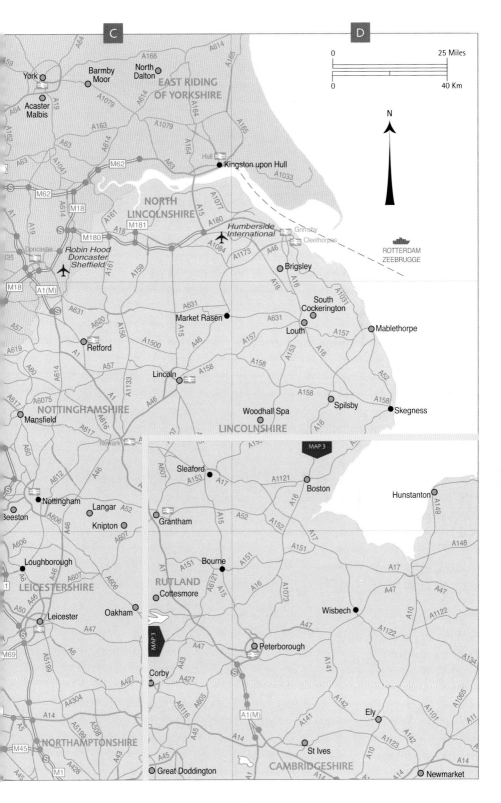

Map 5

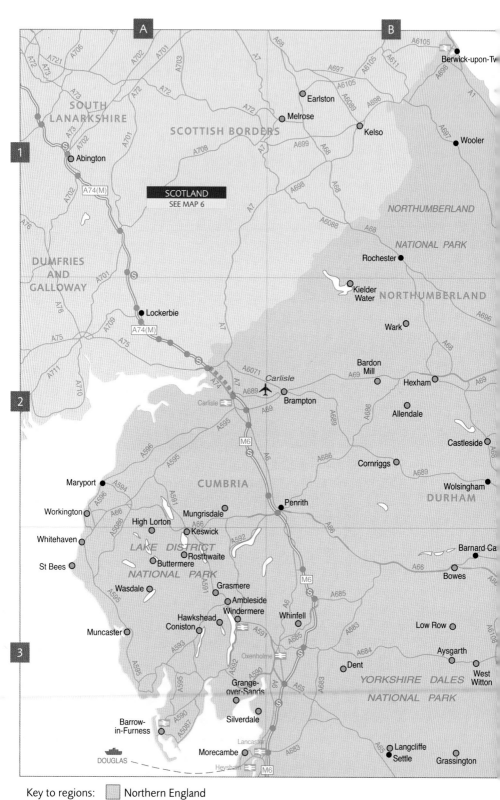

Key to regions: ⬛ Northern England

Map 5

Map 6

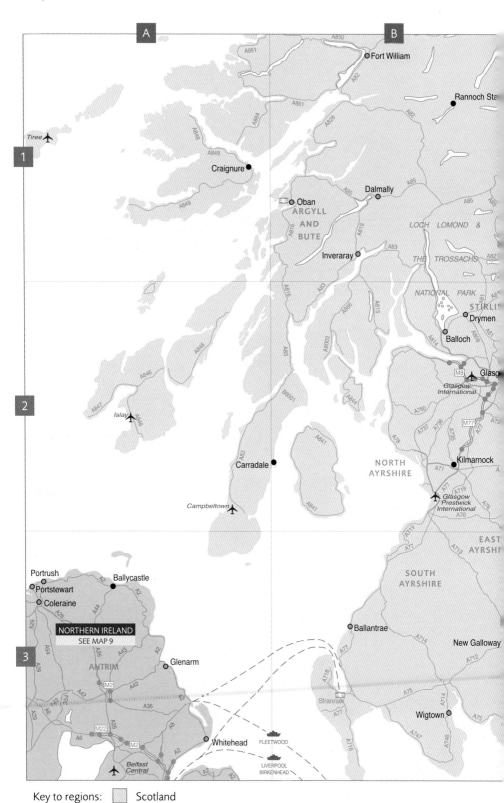

Key to regions: Scotland

Map 6

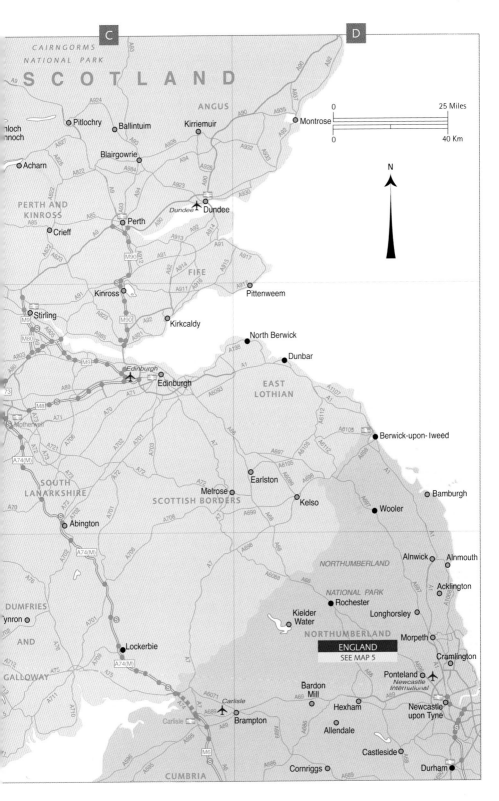

Map 7

Key to regions: ▨ Scotland

Map 7

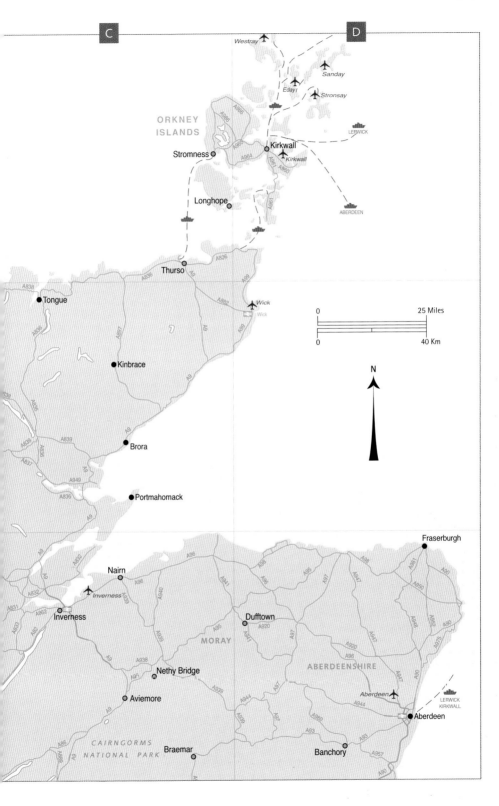

Map 8

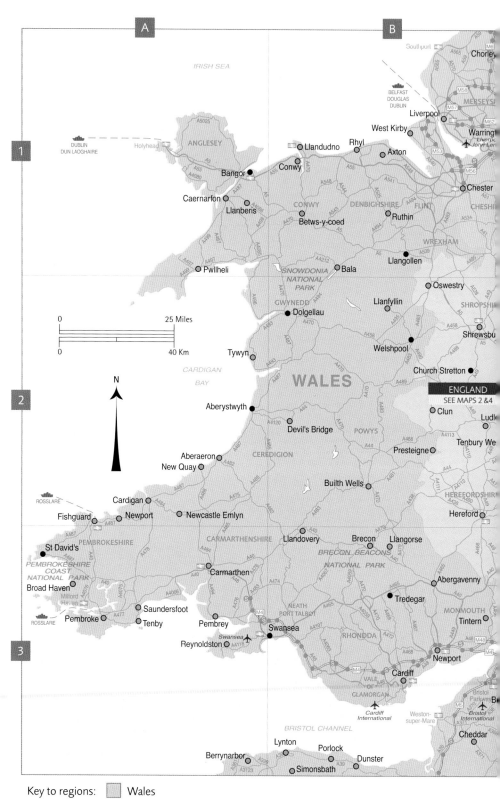

Key to regions: ▢ Wales

Orange circles indicate accommodation within the regional sections of this guide

Map 9

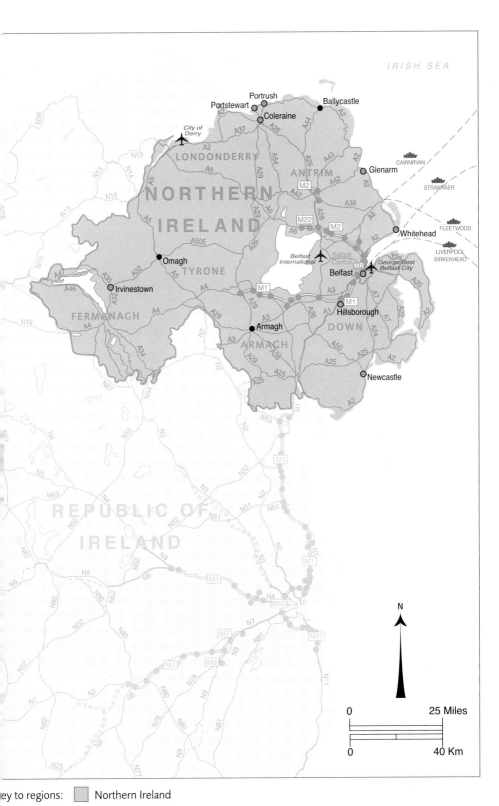

Map 10

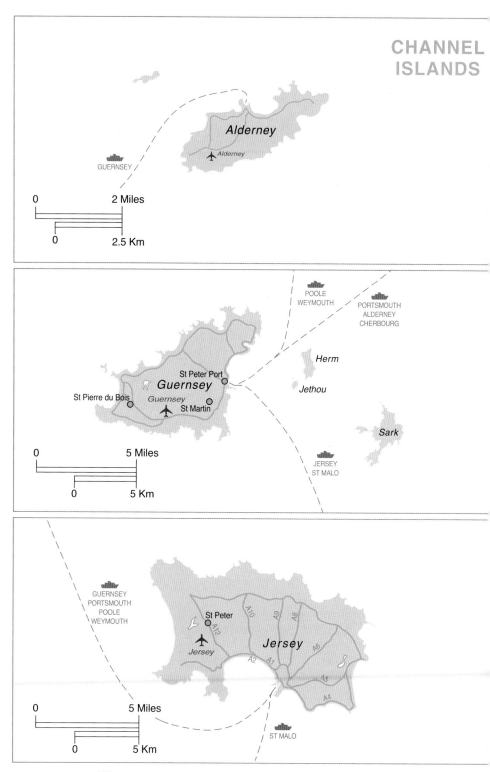

CHANNEL
ISLANDS

Alderney

GUERNSEY

🛩 Alderney

0   2 Miles

0   2.5 Km

POOLE
WEYMOUTH

PORTSMOUTH
ALDERNEY
CHERBOURG

Herm

Jethou

St Peter Port

Guernsey

St Pierre du Bois   Guernsey

St Martin

Sark

JERSEY
ST MALO

0   5 Miles

0   5 Km

GUERNSEY
PORTSMOUTH
POOLE
WEYMOUTH

St Peter

A12
A10
A9
A8
A6
Jersey
A2   A1
A4

Jersey

ST MALO

0   5 Miles

0   5 Km

Key to regions: ░░░ Channel Islands

Orange circles indicate accommodation within the regional sections of this guide

Map 11

ntral London

Map 12

Greater London

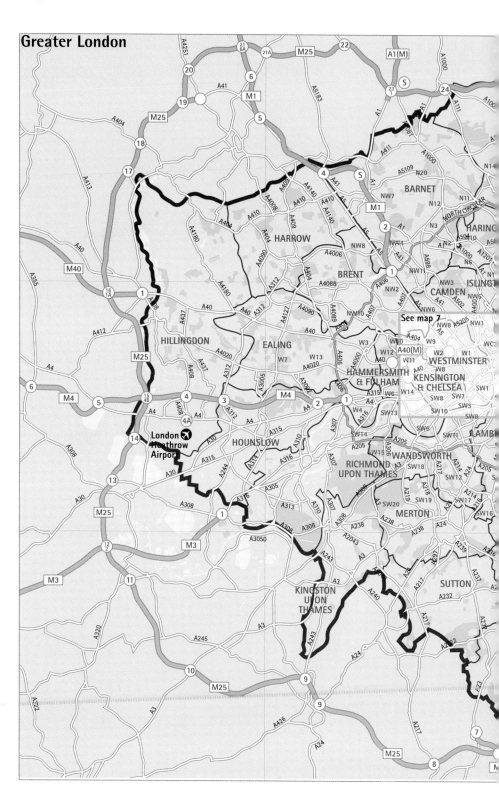

Map 12

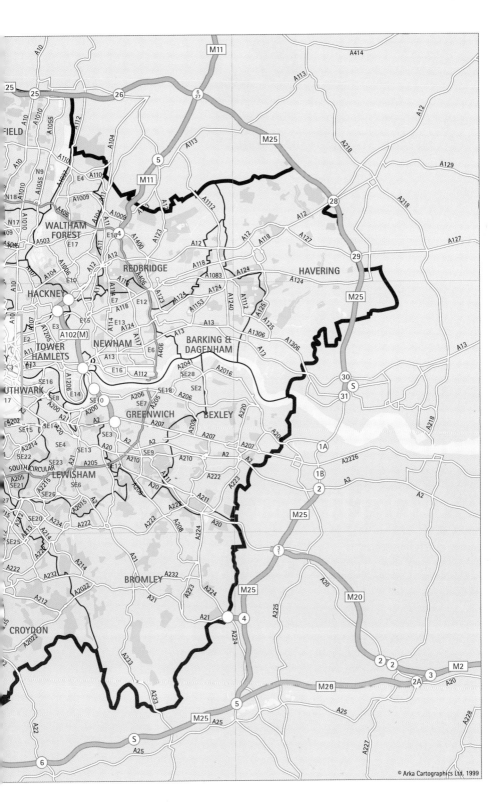

Northern England

Cheshire, Cumbria, Durham, Greater Manchester, Lancashire, Merseyside, Northumberland, Tees Valley, Tyne and Wear, Yorkshire

Clockwise: Bamburgh Castle, Northumberland; Liverpool; North Yorkshire Moors Railway

Great days out

Explore windswept moors and breathtaking coastlines. Admire mirrored-glass lakes and magnificent cathedrals. Discover pioneering industrial heritage and cutting-edge cities. Northern England is a proud fusion of history, dramatic landscapes and modern culture – not forgetting fun-filled seaside resorts!

Relive the revolution

Where did the Industrial Revolution gather pace? In Northern England, of course! Experience its legacy in so many ways. At **Beamish Museum**, a town, colliery village and farm have been recreated using authentic early 19th and 20thC buildings – get around by tramcar and chat to costumed interpreters. Children love living history this way. Hear vivid tales at the **National Coal Mining Museum for England** at Wakefield, put on hat, belt and battery and tour underground with an experienced miner. Clamber onto historic craft at **The National Waterways Museum**, Ellesmere Port. Or maybe trains are more your style? Go spotting at **Locomotion, The National Railway Museum** in Shildon, one of the oldest railway towns in the world. Steaming Days get dads as excited as the kids.

Natural highs

Wide-open spaces abound in the National Parks – Yorkshire alone has over 1,000 square miles to explore. Escape and hear your laughter in the breeze as you fly a kite from high on the **North York Moors**. You can always pick up tips from the professionals at Sunderland International Kite Festival. **The Lake District and Cumbria** have inspired poets, painters and climbers, and Wastwater was recently voted 'Britain's favourite view'. Enjoy it at ground level or hike up Scafell Pike, England's highest peak, for a stunning aerial picture. You'll also feel on top of the world cycling or walking to **East Lancashire's Panopticons**, a series of innovative structures pointing the way to panoramic countryside: Halo, illuminating the Rossendale night sky, is simply breathtaking.

For more firsts and highs, ramble the **North Pennines Area of Outstanding Natural Beauty**, Britain's first geopark. Weardale and Teesdale are renowned for dazzling waterfalls – aptly named **High Force** is England's

Wastwater, Cumbria

highest. Build castles along rippled-sand beaches, such as Spittal and St Aidans, in the North East. Board a boat to **Holy Island** to learn the secrets of the Lindisfarne Gospels. And remember the binoculars on the **Farne Islands** – home to hundreds of thousands of puffins and dewy-eyed grey seals.

Join the Romans

Pace along **Hadrian's Wall** in the footsteps of soldiers nearly two millennia ago. Built in just six years, it runs for an amazing 73 miles. **Chesters** is Britain's best-preserved Roman cavalry fort and you can find out more about Romans in the region at **Tullie House**

Left to right: Alnwick Castle, Northumberland; York Minster

why not... cycle the shoreline of Coniston Water, perfect for easygoing family rides?

Museum and Art Gallery, Carlisle. In the walled city of Chester, Britain's best-preserved Roman town, visit the partially excavated amphitheatre or the **Dewa Roman Experience** where you can step aboard a Roman galley, stroll a reconstructed street and handle 'dig' discoveries.

Grand designs

Northern England has more than its fair share of remarkable buildings. Please the children with a visit to **Alnwick Castle**, aka Hogwarts in the first Harry Potter films. They'll be enthralled by one of the world's largest treehouses, too. **Tatton Park** in Cheshire is among the most complete historic estates, featuring a mansion, gardens, farm, Tudor Old Hall, deer park and speciality shops. And **Castle Howard**, near York, sets an impressive standard In home décor with its Canalettos, Holbeins and Gainsboroughs. Seek green-fingered inspiration at **Sheffield's Winter Garden**, which grows more than 2,500 plants from around the world in a huge temperate glasshouse the size of 5,000 domestic greenhouses!

Tiptoe beneath the towering vaulted ceilings of **York Minster**, the largest medieval Gothic cathedral in Northern Europe and home to glittering stained glass collections. Durham City's medieval cobbled streets are crowned by the magnificent towers of **Durham Castle and Cathedral** – 'the best cathedral on planet earth', according to travel writer Bill Bryson. And now's the time to discover the twin **Anglo-Saxon monasteries at Wearmouth and Jarrow**, the UK's nomination for World Heritage Status in 2009.

Young hearts and minds

Candyfloss and sticky rock, thrills and spills – **Blackpool** is your dream ticket for family fun. Book ringside seats at the **Tower Circus**, and gasp in amazement as international artists

Blackpool

perform superhuman feats. Hop onto sock-popping rides at **Camelot Theme Park** near Chorley or **Go Ape!** in Grizedale Forest on rope bridges and Tarzan swings. Then stimulate the brain cells at **Rotherham's Magna** on an elemental interactive adventure through fire, earth, air and water. Or take the plunge at **The Deep** in Hull and come nose to nose with sharks in the submarium.

Modern city culture

There's also plenty to keep pulses racing in Northern England's dynamic cities where regeneration is the name of the game. Enjoy the renaissance of **NewcastleGateshead**, highlighted by the stunning architecture of the **Gateshead Millennium Bridge**. New artists at the **Baltic Centre for Contemporary Art**

why not... join a ghost walk around York, claimed as Europe's most haunted city?

keep pushing the boundaries. Explore **Liverpool** and **Manchester**, both vibrant club scenes – of the soccer and night-time variety. Liverpool, revered birthplace of The Beatles, is still sparking from its European Capital of Culture 2008 status. Tour the revitalised **Albert Dock** along the World Heritage waterfront and sample the contemporary art of **Tate Liverpool**.

In **Manchester** head for **Salford Quays** and **The Lowry**, the inspirational waterfront centre for the visual arts and entertainment. The daring aluminium **Imperial War Museum North** designed by Daniel Libeskind is a showstopper, one of Manchester's many free museums. Next up: **Leeds** has a new must-see **City Museum** featuring an astounding Treasures Gallery. Middlesbrough, though not a city, also beckons with the recently opened **Middlesbrough Institute of Modern Art** housing works by Tracey Emin and other headline names.

Clockwise: NewcastleGateshead; The Deep, Hull; The Lowry, Manchester

Destinations

Berwick-upon-Tweed

England's northernmost town guards the mouth of the River Tweed. Marvel at some of the finest 16thC city walls in Europe, built by Elizabeth I to protect the town. Visit Bamburgh Castle and the beautiful gardens at Alnwick. Roam magnificent Heritage coastline and see Holy Island and the fairytale Lindisfarne Castle.

Bamburgh near Berwick-upon-Tweed

Blackpool

Britain's favourite holiday resort. Experience thrills and excitement at the Pleasure Beach, take tea in the magnificent Tower Ballroom, or stroll the seven miles of sandy beaches. Blackpool offers you world-class shows, cosmopolitan restaurants, vibrant nightlife, an active sports scene and breathtakingly beautiful scenery on the doorstep.

Chester

Experience one of Europe's top heritage cities. Walk the unique city walls, then visit the famous Rows, unique two-tiered galleries, to shop for everything from antiques to high fashion. Stroll along the banks of the beautiful River Dee, explore the Roman amphitheatre, and spend a day at Chester's famous Roodee Racecourse.

Cumbria – The Lake District

With breathtaking mountains and sparkling lakes, the unsurpassed scenery of Cumbria – The Lake District has inspired writers and poets across the ages. Explore the best walking and climbing routes that England has to offer, and see for yourself 'Britain's favourite view'. Take a lake cruise, visit wonderful homes and gardens or simply enjoy the views.

Durham

Described by Bill Bryson as 'a perfect little city.' Explore majestic Durham Cathedral, a World Heritage Site, and thought by many to be the finest Norman church architecture in England. Visit the tombs of St Cuthbert and the Venerable Bede. Take a coffee in the cobbled Market Place and enjoy the stunning floral displays, or walk down to the riverbank for magnificent views.

Hull

Enjoy the invigorating yet relaxing atmosphere that only a waterfront city can offer. Visit the Museum Quarter linking four of Hull's eight free museums. Don't miss 'The Deep', home to 40 sharks and one of the most spectacular sea-life attractions in the world. Marvel at the engineering of the Humber Bridge and, after dark, experience Hull's very own café bar culture.

Leeds

Rich local history, world-class sport, outstanding museums and galleries, and diverse year-round entertainment, that's Leeds. It's a shopaholic's dream, from the elegant Corn Exchange to the exquisite Victoria Quarter, not to mention the only Harvey Nichols outside London. See opera and dance at the Opera North and Northern Ballet and explore the Yorkshire Dales right on the doorstep.

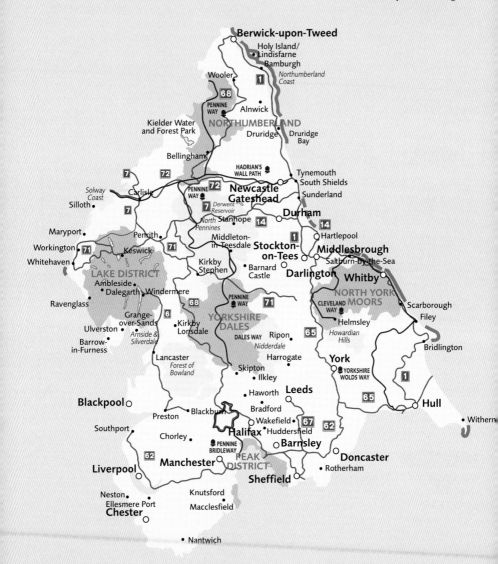

National Park

Area of Outstanding Natural Beauty

Heritage Coast

National Trails
nationaltrail.co.uk

3 **Sections of the**
National Cycle Network
nationalcyclenetwork.org.uk

Berwick-upon-Tweed
Holy Island/
Lindisfarne
Bamburgh
Wooler
Northumberland
Coast
68
PENNINE
WAY
Alnwick
Kielder Water
and Forest Park
NORTHUMBERLAND
Druridge
Druridge
Bay
Bellingham
7 **72**
HADRIAN'S
WALL PATH
72
Tynemouth
South Shields
Carlisle
PENNINE
WAY
Newcastle
Gateshead
Sunderland
Solway
Coast
Silloth
7
7
Derwent
Reservoir
Durham
North Stanhope
Pennines
14
14
Maryport
Penrith
Middleton-
in-Teesdale
Hartlepool
Workington
71
71
Keswick
Stockton-
on-Tees
Middlesbrough
Whitehaven
Kirkby
Stephen
Barnard
Castle
Saltburn-by-the-Sea
LAKE DISTRICT
Ambleside
Dalegarth Windermere
Darlington
Whitby
Ravenglass
PENNINE
WAY
NORTH YORK
MOORS
Grange-
over-Sands
68
71
CLEVELAND
WAY
Scarborough
Ulverston
6
Kirkby
Lonsdale
YORKSHIRE
DALES
Helmsley
Howardian
Hills
Filey
Barrow-
in-Furness
Arnside &
Silverdale
DALES WAY
Ripon
65
Bridlington
Lancaster
Forest of
Bowland
Nidderdale
Skipton
Harrogate
York
YORKSHIRE
WOLDS WAY
1
Blackpool
Haworth
Ilkley
Leeds
65
Hull
Preston
Blackburn
Bradford
Southport
Chorley
Halifax
PENNINE
BRIDLEWAY
Wakefield
Huddersfield
67
62
Withern
62
Manchester
PEAK
DISTRICT
Barnsley
Doncaster
Liverpool
Rotherham
Neston
Knutsford
Sheffield
Ellesmere Port
Macclesfield
Chester

Nantwich

0   50 miles

0   75 kms

Durham

Liverpool

Experience the unique atmosphere of Liverpool. The birthplace of the Beatles and European Capital of Culture 2008 offers you more theatres, museums and galleries than any UK city outside London. Its history as one of the world's great ports has left a remarkable legacy of art and architecture to explore, not forgetting, the city's famous sporting pedigree. So if it's Strawberry Fields, Premiership football or Europe's finest culture you're looking for, it has to be Liverpool.

Manchester

Explore a city that has reinvented itself as a truly contemporary metropolis. You'll find modern landmark buildings, a wealth of art and culture, great bars and world-class hospitality. There's every experience imaginable, from fine dining and top-class theatre, to major sporting events and year-round festivals. It's a shopping destination in its own right, rivalling that of the capital, with top stores and chic boutiques.

NewcastleGateshead

Must-see attractions including the award-winning Gateshead Millennium Bridge, the Baltic Centre for Contemporary Art and the magnificent new Sage Gateshead, a stunning Sir Norman Foster building, with billowing curves of glass and steel catering for every genre of music. Rich in culture, architecture and history and with a great reputation for style, shopping and nightlife, the variety of life in NewcastleGateshead surprises even the most well travelled visitor.

Whitby

With its quaint cobbled streets and picturesque houses standing on the steep slopes of the River Esk, Whitby is dominated by its cliff top Abbey. Explore one of Britain's finest stretches of coastline. Climb the steps to the parish church of St Mary, whose churchyard inspired Bram Stocker's 'Dracula'. Then down to the historic quayside of this 1,000-year-old port and celebrate the town's seafaring tradition at the Captain Cook Festival, named in honour of Whitby's most famous son.

York

Visit award-winning attractions including the magnificent York Minster, and the world's biggest and best railway museum. Let 21stC technology transport you back to the Viking age at Jorvik, and wander through the terrifying York Dungeon. Pedestrianised streets make York an ideal city to explore on foot. Follow the city's specialist shopping trails '5 Routes to Shopping Heaven', or browse the specialist antique and book dealers.

Clockwise: Chester; Leeds; Martindale, Cumbria

For lots more great ideas visit visitbritain.com/destinations

Visitor attractions

Family and Fun

Aquarium of the Lakes
Lakeside, Cumbria
+44 (0) 15395 30153
aquariumofthelakes.co.uk
Freshwater aquarium complete with underwater viewing tunnel.

Beamish, The North of England Open Air Museum
Beamish, Durham
+44 (0) 191 370 4000
beamish.org.uk
Award-winning open-air museum of working life.

Blackpool Tower & Circus
Blackpool, Lancashire
+44 (0) 1253 622242
blackpooltower.co.uk
Entertainment for all ages, night and day.

Blue Planet Aquarium
Ellesmere Port, Cheshire
+44 (0) 151 357 8804
blueplanetaquarium.com
Underwater adventure in the UK's largest aquarium.

Chester Zoo
Chester, Cheshire
+44 (0) 1244 380280
chesterzoo.org
Meet over 7,000 animals and 500 species.

Darlington Railway Centre and Museum
Darlington, Durham
+44 (0) 1325 460532
drcm.org.uk
See, touch and feel living railway heritage.

The Deep
Hull, East Yorkshire
+44 (0) 1482 381000
thedeep.co.uk
One of the world's most spectacular aquariums.

Hartlepool's Maritime Experience
Hartlepool, Durham
+44 (0) 1429 860077
hartlepoolsmaritimeexperience.com
Authentic reconstruction of an 18thC seaport.

JORVIK Viking Centre
York, North Yorkshire
+44 (0) 1904 543400
jorvik-viking-centre.co.uk
Meet the Vikings, face-to-face.

Killhope, The North of England Lead Mining Museum
Cowshill, Durham
+44 (0) 1388 537505
durham.gov.uk/killhope
Award-winning underground experience.

Liverpool Football Club Museum and Stadium Tour
Liverpool
+44 (0) 151 260 6677
liverpoolfc.tv
Touch the famous 'This is Anfield' sign!

Locomotion: The National Railway Museum at Shildon
Shildon, Durham
+44 (0) 1388 777999
locomotion.uk.com
Historic buildings and vehicles celebrate railway heritage.

Magna Science Adventure Centre
Rotherham, South Yorkshire
+44 (0) 1709 720002
visitmagna.co.uk
An unforgettable, interactive science adventure.

Manchester United Museum & Tour
Manchester
+44 (0) 870 442 1994
manutd.com
Official tour of the 'Theatre of Dreams'.

Merseyside Maritime Museum
Liverpool
+44 (0) 151 478 4499
merseysidemaritimemuseum.org.uk
Liverpool's seafaring heritage brought to life.

MOSI (Museum of Science and Industry)
Manchester
+44 (0) 161 832 2244
mosi.org.uk
Five historic buildings packed with fascinating displays.

The National Waterways Museum
Ellesmere Port, Cheshire
+44 (0) 151 355 5017
nwm.org.uk
Britain's largest collection of inland waterway craft.

Nature's World
Middlesbrough
+44 (0) 1642 594895
naturesworld.org.uk
Pioneering eco-garden of the future.

Saltburn Smugglers Heritage Centre
Saltburn-by-the-Sea, Tees Valley
+44 (0) 1287 625252
redcar-cleveland.gov.uk/leisure
Meet costumed characters in ancient fishermens' cottages.

Seven Stories, The Centre for Children's Books
Newcastle upon Tyne, Tyne and Wear
+44 (0) 845 271 0777
sevenstories.org.uk
Britain's first centre dedicated to children's literature.

Yorkshire Waterways Museum
Goole, East Yorkshire
+44 (0) 1405 768730
waterwaysmuseum.org.uk
Museum, adventure centre and nature trail.

Heritage

Alnwick Castle
Alnwick, Northumberland
+44 (0) 1665 510777
alnwickcastle.com
Dazzling medieval castle with glorious state rooms.

Arley Hall & Gardens
Northwich, Cheshire
+44 (0) 1565 777353
arleyhallandgardens.com
Charming stately home and award-winning gardens.

Bamburgh Castle
Bamburgh, Northumberland
+44 (0) 1668 214515
bamburghcastle.com
Imposing castle in dramatic coastal setting.

Beeston Castle
Beeston, Cheshire
+44 (0) 1829 260464
english-heritage.org.uk
13thC castle with views over eight counties.

Belsay Hall, Castle and Gardens
Newcastle upon Tyne, Tyne and Wear
+44 (0) 1661 881636
english-heritage.org.uk
Medieval castle, 17thC manor and gardens.

Brodsworth Hall and Gardens
Doncaster, South Yorkshire
+44 (0) 1302 724969
english-heritage.org.uk
Italianate house with marvellous labyrinthine gardens.

Castle Howard
York, North Yorkshire
+44 (0) 1653 648444
castlehoward.co.uk
Magnificent 18thC house in stunning parkland.

Chester Cathedral
Chester, Cheshire
+44 (0) 1244 324756
chestercathedral.com
Medieval cathedral with spectacular carved choir stalls.

Durham Castle
Durham
+44 (0) 191 334 3800
durhamcastle.com
Superb Norman castle in World Heritage Site.

Fountains Abbey and Studley Royal Water Garden
Ripon, North Yorkshire
+44 (0) 1765 608888
fountainsabbey.org.uk
12thC monastic ruin with captivating landscaped gardens.

Harewood House
Harewood, West Yorkshire
+44 (0) 113 218 1010
harewood.org
Stunning architecture and exquisite Adam interiors.

Holker Hall and Gardens
Cark in Cartmel, Cumbria
+44 (0) 15395 58328
holker-hall.co.uk
Magnificent Neo-Elizabethan mansion and award-winning gardens.

Levens Hall & Gardens
Levens, Cumbria
+44 (0) 15395 60321
levenshall.co.uk
Elizabethan mansion and world-famous topiary gardens.

Lyme Park
Disley, Cheshire
+44 (0) 1663 766492
nationaltrust.org.uk
Tudor house transformed into an Italianate palace.

National Coal Mining Museum for England
Wakefield, West Yorkshire
+44 (0) 1924 848806
ncm.org.uk
Award-winning museum of the English coalfields.

Newby Hall & Gardens
Ripon, North Yorkshire
+44 (0) 845 450 4068
newbyhall.com
One of England's renowned Adam houses.

North Yorkshire Moors Railway
Pickering, North Yorkshire
+44 (0) 1751 472508
nymr.co.uk
Nostalgic steam excursions through spectacular landscapes.

Ripley Castle
Ripley, North Yorkshire
+44 (0) 1423 770152
ripleycastle.co.uk
Medieval castle set in a delightful estate.

Sewerby Hall and Gardens
Sewerby, East Yorkshire
+44 (0) 1262 673769
sewerby-hall.co.uk
Country house and gardens in cliff-top location.

Speke Hall, Garden and Estate
Speke, Merseyside
+44 (0) 151 427 7231
nationaltrust.org.uk
Wonderful, rambling Tudor mansion with Victorian interiors.

Indoors

1853 Gallery
Shipley, West Yorkshire
+44 (0) 1274 531163
saltsmill.org.uk
Works by Hockney in historic mill buildings.

BALTIC Centre for Contemporary Art
Gateshead, Tyne and Wear
+44 (0) 191 478 1810
balticmill.com
Dynamic international art.

The Bowes Museum
Barnard Castle, Durham
+44 (0) 1833 690606
thebowesmuseum.org.uk
Outstanding European fine and decorative arts.

Captain Cook Birthplace Museum
Middlesbrough
+44 (0) 1642 311211
captcook-ne.co.uk
Learn about Cook's life.

Discovery Museum
Newcastle upon Tyne, Tyne and Wear
+44 (0) 191 232 6789
twmuseums.org.uk/discovery
The history of Tyneside brought to life.

Imperial War Museum North
Manchester
+44 (0) 161 836 4000
iwm.org.uk
Dynamic displays reflecting the impact of war.

Jodrell Bank Visitor Centre
Holmes Chapel, Cheshire
+44 (0) 1477 571339
jb.man.ac.uk/scicen
Home of the world-famous Lovell Telescope.

Leeds City Art Gallery
Leeds, West Yorkshire
+44 (0) 113 247 8256
leeds.gov.uk/artgallery
Remarkable collection of 20thC British art.

The Lowry
Salford, Manchester
+44 (0) 161 876 2000
thelowry.com
World-renowned art gallery, exhibitions and theatre.

Millennium Galleries
Sheffield, South Yorkshire
+44 (0) 114 278 2600
sheffieldgalleries.org.uk
Vibrant galleries of arts, craft and design.

mima, Middlesbrough Institute of Modern Art
Middlesbrough
+44 (0) 1642 726720
visitmima.com
Inspiring modern and contemporary art.

National Glass Centre
Sunderland, Tyne and Wear
+44 (0) 191 515 5555
nationalglasscentre.com
Stunning displays and live glass-blowing.

National Media Museum
Bradford, West Yorkshire
+44 (0) 870 701 0200
nationalmediamuseum.org.uk
Seven-floor gallery featuring giant IMAX screen.

Royal Armouries Museum
Leeds, West Yorkshire
+44 (0) 113 220 1916
royalarmouries.org
Thrilling entertainment and world-famous arms collection.

Tullie House Museum and Art Gallery
Large Visitor Attraction of the Year - Silver
Carlisle, Cumbria
+44 (0) 1228 618718
tulliehouse.co.uk
Jacobean house, Pre-Raphaelite art and interactive fun.

South Shields Museum and Art Gallery
South Shields, Tyne and Wear
+44 (0) 191 456 8740
twmuseums.org.uk/southshields
Explore the history of South Tyneside.

Sunderland Museum and Winter Gardens
Sunderland, Tyne and Wear
+44 (0) 191 553 2323
twmuseums.org.uk/sunderland
Stunning winter gardens and imaginative galleries.

Tate Liverpool
Liverpool
+44 (0) 151 702 7400
tate.org.uk/liverpool
Housing the National Collection of Modern Art.

Thackray Museum
Leeds, West Yorkshire
+44 (0) 113 244 4343
thackraymuseum.org
Experience Victorian slums, explore the human body.

The Whitworth Art Gallery
Manchester
+44 (0) 161 275 7450
whitworth.man.ac.uk
Internationally famous collection of British watercolours.

World Museum Liverpool
Liverpool
+44 (0) 151 478 4393
liverpoolmuseums.org.uk
Featuring the award-winning Natural History Centre.

The World of Glass
St Helens, Merseyside
+44 (0) 1744 22766
worldofglass.com
Live glass-blowing and multi-media shows.

Outdoors

Chesters Roman Fort (Hadrian's Wall)
Chollerford, Northumberland
+44 (0) 1434 681379
english-heritage.org.uk
The best-preserved Roman cavalry fort in Britain.

Go Ape! High Wire Forest Adventure – Grizedale
Grizedale, Cumbria
+44 (0) 845 643 9215
goape.co.uk
High-adrenaline adventure in the trees.

Go Ape! High Wire Forest Adventure – Dalby
Low Dalby, North Yorkshire
+44 (0) 845 643 9215
goape.co.uk
Exhilarating course of bridges, swings and slides.

Hadrian's Wall Path National Trail
Hexham, Northumberland
+44 (0) 1434 322002
nationaltrail.co.uk/hadrianswall
84-mile trail stretching from coast to coast.

Kielder Castle Forest Park Centre
Kielder, Northumberland
+44 (0) 1434 250209
forestry.gov.uk
Visitor centre for England's largest forest.

National Wildflower Centre
Liverpool
+44 (0) 151 738 1913
nwc.org.uk
A peaceful haven with seasonal wildflower displays.

RHS Garden Harlow Carr
Harrogate, North Yorkshire
+44 (0) 1423 565418
rhs.org.uk/harlowcarr
Spectacular 58-acre garden with year-round interest.

RSPB Blacktoft Sands Nature Reserve
Whitgift, East Yorkshire
+44 (0) 1405 704665
rspb.org.uk
Spot avocets, bitterns and marsh harriers.

Windermere Lake Cruises
Lakeside, Cumbria
+44 (0) 15394 43360
windermere-lakecruises.co.uk
Sail the Lakes on launches and steamers.

WWT Washington Wetland Centre
Washington, Tyne and Wear
+44 (0) 191 416 5454
wwt.org.uk
100-acre conservation site with diverse wildlife.

Yorkshire Sculpture Park
Wakefield, West Yorkshire
+44 (0) 1924 832631
ysp.co.uk
Browse art alfresco on beautiful 18thC parkland.

 ASSURANCE OF A GREAT DAY OUT
Attractions with this sign participate in the Visitor Attraction Quality Assurance Scheme which recognises high standards in all aspects of the visitor experience.

Events 2009

Bradford International Film Festival
Bradford
bradfordfilmfestival.org.uk
Feb - Mar

Jorvik Viking Festival
York
jorvik-viking-centre.co.uk
18 - 22 Feb

John Smith's Grand National
Liverpool
aintree.co.uk
2 - 4 Apr

Chester Food and Drink Festival 2009
Chester
chesterfoodanddrink.com
10 - 13 Apr

Arley Horse Trials and Country Fair 2009
Northwich
arleyhallandgardens.com
16 - 17 May

Great Yorkshire Show
Harrogate
greatyorkshireshow.co.uk
Jul

Sunderland International Air Show
Sunderland
sunderland-airshow.com
25 - 26 Jul

Stockton International Riverside Festival
Stockton
sirf.co.uk
29 Jul - 2 Aug

St Leger Festival
Doncaster
doncaster-racecourse.co.uk
Sep

Regional contacts and information

For more information on accommodation, attractions, activities, events and holidays in Northern England, contact one of the following regional or local tourism organisations. Their websites have a wealth of information and many produce free publications to help you get the most out of your visit.

England's Northwest

There are various publications and guides about England's Northwest available from the following Tourist Boards or by logging on to **visitenglandsnorthwest.com** or calling **+44 (0) 845 600 6040**:

Visit Chester and Cheshire
Chester Railway Station, 1st Floor, West Wing Offices, Station Road, Chester CH1 3NT
t +44 (0) 1244 405600
t +44 (0) 845 073 1324 (accommodation booking)
e info@visitchesterandcheshire.co.uk
w visitchester.com or visitcheshire.com

Cumbria Tourism
Windermere Road, Staveley, Kendal LA8 9PL
t +44 (0) 15398 22222
e info@cumbriatourism.org
w golakes.co.uk

The Lancashire and Blackpool Tourist Board
St George's House, St George's Street Chorley PR7 2AA
t +44 (0) 1257 226600 (Brochure request)
e info@visitlancashire.com
w visitlancashire.com

Visit Manchester – The Tourist Board For Greater Manchester
Carver's Warehouse, 77 Dale Street Manchester M2 2HG
t +44 (0) 161 237 1010
t +44 (0) 871 222 8223 (information and brochure request)
e touristinformation@visitmanchester.com
w visitmanchester.com

The Mersey Partnership – The Tourist Board for the Liverpool City Region
12 Princes Parade, Liverpool L3 1BG
t +44 (0) 151 233 2008 (information enquiries)
t +44 (0) 844 870 0123 (accommodation booking)
e info@visitliverpool.com (accommodation enquiries)
e 08place@liverpool.gov.uk (information enquiries)
w visitliverpool.com

Clockwise: Arley Hall and Gardens, Cheshire; Ilkley Moor, Yorkshire; Beamish, Durham

Yorkshire

The following publications are available from the Yorkshire Tourist Board by logging on to **yorkshire.com** or calling **+44 (0) 844 888 5123**:

- **Yorkshire Accommodation Guide 2009**
  Information on Yorkshire, including hotels, self catering, camping and caravan parks.

- **Make Yorkshire Yours Magazine**
  This entertaining magazine is full of articles and features about what's happening in Yorkshire, including where to go and what to do.

North East

Log on to the North East England website at **visitnortheastengland.com** for further information on accommodation, attractions, events and special offers throughout the region. A range of free guides are available for you to order online or by calling **+44 (0) 870 160 1781**:

- **Holiday and Short Breaks Guide**
  Information on North East England, including hotels, bed and breakfast, self-catering, caravan and camping parks and accessible accommodation as well as events and attractions throughout the region.

- **Cycling Guide**
  A guide to day rides, traffic-free trails and challenging cycling routes.

- **Gardens Guide**
  A guide to the region's most inspirational gardens.

- **Walking Guide**
  Circular trails and long distance routes through breathtaking countryside.

Tourist Information Centres

When you arrive at your destination, visit an Official Partner Tourist Information Centre for quality assured help with accommodation and information about local attractions and events, or email your request before you go. To search for attractions and Tourist Information Centres on the move just text INFO to 62233, and a web link will be sent to your mobile phone. To find a Tourist Information Centre by region visit enjoyEngland.com/find-tic.

Accrington	Town Hall, Blackburn Rd	+44 (0) 1254 872595	tourism@hyndburnbc.gov.uk
Alnwick	2 The Shambles	+44 (0) 1665 511333	alnwicktic@alnwick.gov.uk
Altrincham	20 Stamford New Road	+44 (0) 161 912 5931	tourist.information@trafford.gov.uk
Ashton-under-Lyne	Wellington Road	+44 (0) 161 343 4343	tourist.information@tameside.gov.uk
Aysgarth Falls	Aysgarth Falls National Park Centre	+44 (0) 1969 662910	aysgarth@ytbtic.co.uk
Barnard Castle	Flatts Road	+44 (0) 1833 690909	tourism@teesdale.gov.uk
Barnoldswick	Fernlea Avenue	+44 (0) 1282 666704	tourist.info@pendle.gov.uk
Barrow-in-Furness	Duke Street	+44 (0) 1229 876505	touristinfo@barrowbc.gov.uk
Batley	Bradford Road	+44 (0) 1924 426670	batley@ytbtic.co.uk
Beverley	34 Butcher Row	+44 (0) 1482 391672	beverley.tic@eastriding .gov.uk
Blackburn	50-54 Church Street	+44 (0) 1254 53277	visit@blackburn.gov.uk
Blackpool	1 Clifton Street	+44 (0) 1253 478222	tic@blackpool.gov.uk
Bolton	Le Mans Crescent	+44 (0) 1204 334321	tourist.info@bolton.gov.uk
Bowness	Glebe Road	+44 (0) 15394 42895	bownesstic@lake-district.gov.uk
Bradford	Centenary Square	+44 (0) 1274 433678	tourist.information@bradford.gov.uk
Bridlington	25 Prince Street	+44 (0) 1262 673474	bridlington.tic@eastriding.gov.uk
Brigg	Market Place	+44 (0) 1652 657053	brigg.tic@northlincs.gov.uk
Burnley	Croft Street	+44 (0) 1282 664421	tic@burnley.gov.uk
Bury	Market Street	+44 (0) 161 253 5111	touristinformation@bury.gov.uk
Carlisle	Greenmarket	+44 (0) 1228 625600	tourism@carlisle-city.gov.uk
Chester (Town Hall)	Northgate Street	+44 (0) 1244 402111	tis@chester.gov.uk
Cleethorpes	42-43 Alexandra Road	+44 (0) 1472 323111	cleetic@nelincs.gov.uk
Cleveleys	Victoria Square	+44 (0) 1253 853378	cleveleystic@wyrebc.gov.uk
Clitheroe	12-14 Market Place	+44 (0) 1200 425566	tourism@ribblevalley.gov.uk
Congleton	High Street	+44 (0) 1260 271095	tourism@congleton.gov.uk
Coniston	Ruskin Avenue	+44 (0) 15394 41533	mail@conistontic.org
Danby	Lodge Lane	+44 (0) 1439 772737	moorscentre@northyorkmoors-npa.gov.uk
Darlington	13 Horsemarket	+44 (0) 1325 388666	tic@darlington.gov.uk
Doncaster	38-40 High Street	+44 (0) 1302 734309	tourist.information@doncaster.gov.uk

Durham	2 Millennium Place	+44 (0) 191 384 3720	touristinfo@durhamcity.gov.uk
Ellesmere Port	Kinsey Road	+44 (0) 151 356 7879	cheshireoaks.cc@visitor-centre.net
Filey*	The Evron Centre, John Street	+44 (0) 1723 383637	fileytic@scarborough.gov.uk
Fleetwood	The Esplanade	+44 (0) 1253 773953	fleetwoodtic@wyrebc.gov.uk
Garstang	High Street	+44 (0) 1995 602125	garstangtic@wyrebc.gov.uk
Grassington	Colvend, Hebden Road	+44 (0) 1756 751690	grassington@ytbtic.co.uk
Guisborough	Church Street	+44 (0) 1287 633801	guisborough_tic@redcar-cleveland.gov.uk
Halifax	Piece Hall	+44 (0) 1422 368725	halifax@ytbtic.co.uk
Harrogate	Crescent Road	+44 (0) 1423 537300	tic@harrogate.gov.uk
Hartlepool	Church Square	+44 (0) 1429 869706	hpooltic@hartlepool.gov.uk
Hawes	Station Yard	+44 (0) 1969 666210	hawes@ytbtic.co.uk
Haworth	2/4 West Lane	+44 (0) 1535 642329	haworth@ytbtic.co.uk
Hebden Bridge	New Road	+44 (0) 1422 843831	hebdenbridge@ytbtic.co.uk
Helmsley	Helmsley Castle	+44 (0) 1439 770173	helmsley@ytbtic.co.uk
Hexham	Wentworth Car Park	+44 (0) 1434 652220	hexham.tic@tynedale.gov.uk
Holmfirth	49-51 Huddersfield Road	+44 (0) 1484 222444	holmfirth.tic@kirklees.gov.uk
Hornsea*	120 Newbegin	+44 (0) 1964 536404	hornsea.tic@eastriding.gov.uk
Huddersfield	3 Albion Street	+44 (0) 1484 223200	huddersfield.tic@kirklees.gov.uk
Hull	1 Paragon Street	+44 (0) 1482 223559	tourist.information@hullcc.gov.uk
Humber Bridge	Ferriby Road	+44 (0) 1482 640852	humberbridge.tic@eastriding.gov.uk
Ilkley	Station Rd	+44 (0) 1943 602319	ilkley@ytbtic.co.uk
Kendal	Highgate	+44 (0) 1539 725758	kendaltic@southlakeland.gov.uk
Keswick	Market Square	+44 (0) 17687 72645	keswicktic@lake-district.gov.uk
Knaresborough	9 Castle Courtyard	+44 (0) 845 389 0177	kntic@harrogate.gov.uk
Knutsford	Toft Road	+44 (0) 1565 632611	ktic@macclesfield.gov.uk
Lancaster	29 Castle Hill	+44 (0) 1524 32878	lancastertic@lancaster.gov.uk
Leeds	The Arcade, City Station	+44 (0) 113 242 5242	tourinfo@leeds.gov.uk
Leeming Bar	The Yorkshire Maid, The Great North Road	+44 (0) 1677 424262	leeming@ytbtic.co.uk

Left to right: Holker Hall and Gardens, Cumbria; Locomotion: The National Railway Museum, Durham

Leyburn	Railway Street	+44 (0) 1969 623069	leyburn@ytbtic.co.uk
Liverpool 08 Place	Whitechapel	+44 (0) 151 233 2459	contact@liverpool.08.com
Liverpool John Lennon Airport	Speke Hall Avenue	0906 680 6886**	info@visitliverpool.com
Lytham St Annes	67 St Annes Road West	+44 (0) 1253 725610	touristinformation@fylde.gov.uk
Macclesfield	Town Hall	+44 (0) 1625 504114	informationcentre@macclesfield.gov.uk
Malham	National Park Centre	+44 (0) 1969 652380	malham@ytbtic.co.uk
Malton	58 Market Place	+44 (0) 1653 600048	maltontic@btconnect.com
Manchester Visitor Information Centre	Lloyd St	+44 (0) 871 222 8223	touristinformation@marketing-manchester.co.uk
Morecambe	Marine Road Central	+44 (0) 1524 582808	morecambetic@lancaster.gov.uk
Morpeth	Bridge Street	+44 (0) 1670 500700	tourism@castlemorpeth.gov.uk
Nantwich	Market Street	+44 (0) 1270 537359	touristi@crewe-nantwich.gov.uk
Newcastle-upon-Tyne	8-9 Central Arcade	+44 (0) 191 277 8000	tourist.info@newcastle.gov.uk
Northwich	1 The Arcade	+44 (0) 1606 353534	tourism@valeroyal.gov.uk
Oldham	12 Albion Street	+44 (0) 161 627 1024	ecs.tourist@oldham.gov.uk
Otley	Nelson Street	+44 (0) 1943 462485	otleytic@leedslearning.net
Pateley Bridge*	18 High Street	+44 (0) 845 389 0177	pbtic@harrogate.gov.uk
Pendle Heritage Centre	Park Hill	+44 (0) 1282 661701	heritage.centre@pendle.gov.uk
Penrith	Middlegate	+44 (0) 1768 867466	pen.tic@eden.gov.uk
Pickering	The Ropery	+44 (0) 1751 473791	pickering@ytbtic.co.uk
Preston	Lancaster Road	+44 (0) 1772 253731	tourism@preston.gov.uk
Redcar	Esplanade	+44 (0) 1642 471921	redcar_tic@redcar-cleveland.gov.uk
Reeth	Hudson House, The Green	+44 (0) 1748 884059	reeth@ytbtic.co.uk
Richmond	Victoria Road	+44 (0) 1748 828742	richmond@ytbtic.co.uk
Ripon	Minster Road	+44 (0) 1765 604625	ripontic@harrogate.gov.uk
Rochdale	The Esplanade	+44 (0) 1706 924928	tic@link4life.org
Rotherham	40 Bridgegate	+44 (0) 1709 835904	tic@rotherham.gov.uk
St Helens	The World of Glass	+44 (0) 1744 755150	info@sthelenstic.com
Salford	The Lowry, Pier 8	+44 (0) 161 848 8601	tic@salford.gov.uk
Saltburn-by-the-Sea	3 Station Buildings	+44 (0) 1287 622422	saltburn_tic@redcar-cleveland.gov.uk
Scarborough	Brunswick Shopping Centre	+44 (0) 1723 383636	tourismbureau@scarborough.gov.uk
Scarborough (Harbourside)	Sandside	+44 (0) 1723 383636	harboursidetic@scarborough.gov.uk
Settle	Cheapside	+44 (0) 1729 825192	settle@ytbtic.co.uk
Sheffield	14 Norfolk Row	+44 (0) 114 2211900	visitor@sheffield.gov.uk
Skipton	35 Coach Street	+44 (0) 1756 792809	skipton@ytbtic.co.uk
Stockport	30 Market Place	+44 (0) 161 474 4444	tourist.information@stockport.gov.uk
Sunderland	50 Fawcett Street	+44 (0) 191 553 2000	tourist.info@sunderland.gov.uk
Sutton Bank	Sutton Bank Visitor Centre	+44 (0) 1845 597426	suttonbank@ytbtic.co.uk

Thirsk	49 Market Place	+44 (0) 1845 522755	thirsktic@hambleton.gov.uk
Todmorden	15 Burnley Road	+44 (0) 1706 818181	todmorden@ytbtic.co.uk
Wakefield	9 The Bull Ring	+44 (0) 845 601 8353	tic@wakefield.gov.uk
Warrington	Academy Way	+44 (0) 1925 428585	informationcentre@warrington.gov.uk
Wetherby	17 Westgate	+44 (0) 1937 582151	wetherbytic@leedslearning.net
Whitby	Langborne Road	+44 (0) 1723 383637	whitbytic@scarborough.gov.uk
Whitehaven	Market Place	+44 (0) 1946 598914	tic@copelandbc.gov.uk
Wigan	62 Wallgate	+44 (0) 1942 825677	tic@wlct.org
Wilmslow	Rectory Fields	+44 (0) 1625 522275	i.hillaby@macclesfield.gov.uk
Windermere	Victoria Street	+44 (0) 15394 46499	windermeretic@southlakeland.gov.uk
Withernsea*	131 Queen Street	+44 (0) 1964 615683	withernsea.tic@eastriding.gov.uk
York (De Grey Rooms)	Exhibition Square	+44 (0) 1904 550099	info@visityork.org
York (Railway Station)	Station Road	+44 (0) 1904 550099	info@visityork.org

*seasonal opening

**UK number only, charged at premium rate

Clockwise: High Force, Durham; Royal Armouries Museum, Yorkshire; Manchester United Museum and Tour

Finding accommodation
is as easy as 1 2 3

VisitBritain's official guides to quality accommodation make it quick and easy to find a place to stay. There are several ways to use this guide.

1

PROPERTY INDEX

If you know the name of the establishment you wish to book, turn to the property index at the back where the relevant page number is shown.

2

PLACE INDEX

The place index at the back lists all locations with accommodation featured in the regional sections. A page number is shown where you can find full accommodation and contact details.

3

COLOUR MAPS

All the place names next to orange circles on the colour maps at the front have an entry in the regional sections. Refer to the place index for the page number where you will find one or more establishments offering accommodation in your chosen town or village.

where to stay in
Northern England

All place names in the blue bands are shown on the maps at the front of this guide.

Accommodation symbols

Symbols give useful information about services and facilities. On pages 16 to 17 you can find a key to these symbols.

ACASTER MALBIS, North Yorkshire Map ref 4C1   SELF CATERING

★★★★
SELF CATERING

Units   **1**
Sleeps   **1–6**

LOW SEASON PER WK
Min £400.00

HIGH SEASON PER WK
Max £700.00

10% discount for multiple-week bookings.

Orchard Lodge, Acaster Malbis, York

contact Ms Bridget Karn, Mount Pleasant House, Acaster Malbis YO23 2UP **t** +44 (0) 1904 700924 & +44 (0) 7766 352049 **e** bridget@orchardlodgeyork.co.uk

orchardlodgeyork.co.uk REAL-TIME BOOKING

open All year
payment Cash, cheques
nearest pub 1 mile
nearest shop 3 miles

Scandinavian log cabin offering a high specification with double and twin bedrooms, both with en suite (bathroom and shower room). There is also a double sofa bed in the lounge, allowing six people to stay comfortably. The cabin is designed for relaxation and leisure, sitting in a secluded landscape of fields and orchard.

ONLINE MAP

Unit 📺 🖥 📀 🎦 📼 🔲 🗄 🗒 🍽 🔔 🎮 ☀ 🏔 General 🛏 🏛 🛁 P 🅾 🆂
Leisure ∪ 🏊 ► 🚲

ACKLINGTON, Northumberland Map ref 5C1   SELF CATERING

★★★★
SELF CATERING

Units   **11**
Sleeps   **2–8**

LOW SEASON PER WK
£200.00–£550.00

HIGH SEASON PER WK
£400.00–£1,152.00

Bank House Holiday Cottages, Guyzance, Acklington

contact Mr Steven Stone, 1 Whalton Park, Morpeth NE61 3TU **t** +44 (0) 7525 615411
e info@bankhouseholidaycottages.co.uk

bankhouseholidaycottages.co.uk GUEST REVIEWS - SPECIAL OFFERS - REAL-TIME BOOKING

open All year except January
payment Credit/debit cards, cash, cheques
nearest pub 3 miles
nearest shop 3 miles

A range of one, two, three and four-bedroom beautifully converted stone buildings, complete with original farmhouse, set in a natural woodland setting close to beautiful Northumbrian coastline.

SAT NAV *NE65 9AP* **ONLINE MAP**

Unit 📺 🖥 🔲 🗄 🗒 🗄 🗒 🍽 💡 General 🛏 🏛 🛁 P 🅾 🆂 🐦

ALLENDALE, Northumberland Map ref 5B2 — GUEST ACCOMMODATION

★★★★
FARMHOUSE

B&B PER ROOM PER NIGHT
S £35.00–£40.00
D £60.00–£70.00

EVENING MEAL PER PERSON
£15.00–£25.00

High Keenley Fell Farm

Allendale NE47 9NU t +44 (0) 1434 618344 e camaclean@btinternet.com

highkeenleyfarm.co.uk

Traditional, recently refurbished Northumbrian farmhouse built round a courtyard with stunning views around Allendale and up to the Cheviots and Scottish Borders.

open All year
bedrooms 2 double, 1 twin
bathrooms All en suite
payment Cash, cheques

Room 🛗 📺 👜 ☕ General 🕳 🎬 P ⚒ ✕ 🍽 ⊙ ✣ 🐾 Leisure ∪ ♪ ▸

ALNMOUTH, Northumberland Map ref 5C1 — SELF CATERING

★★★★★
SELF CATERING

Units   **1**
Sleeps   **1–7**

LOW SEASON PER WK
Min £550.00

HIGH SEASON PER WK
Max £1,275.00

Low-season short breaks available by arrangement, within one month of booking.

Paradise Lodge, Alnmouth, Alnwick

contact Ms Sandra MacDonald, Heavenly Holiday Homes, Durham House, 33a Old Elvet, Durham DH1 3HN t +44 (0) 191 384 3904 & +44 (0) 7971 538316 e sa@heavenlyholidayhomes.co.uk

heavenlyholidayhomes.co.uk GUEST REVIEWS · SPECIAL OFFERS · REAL-TIME BOOKING

open All year
payment Credit/debit cards, cash, cheques
nearest pub less than 0.5 miles
nearest shop less than 0.5 miles

Exceptional and individual Victorian renovation in Alnmouth's prime seaside location. Light-filled and spacious, this fabulous property's bay windows have window seats and comfy chairs to take full advantage of the fantastic panoramic sea and estuary views. Furnished and equipped to the highest standards. Welcome hamper. True luxury.

ONLINE MAP

Unit 📺 SC 🖵 📀 🖥 🗜 🗄 ⊙ 🗑 🗐 ⌂ ✣ ⛏ General 🕳 🎬 ⚿ P Leisure ∪ ♪ ▸ 🚲

ALNWICK, Northumberland Map ref 5C1 — GUEST ACCOMMODATION

★★★
GUEST ACCOMMODATION

B&B PER ROOM PER NIGHT
S £45.00
D £70.00–£120.00

EVENING MEAL PER PERSON
£15.00–£20.00

Alnwick Lodge

West Cawledge Park, Alnwick NE66 2HJ t +44 (0) 1665 604363 & +44 (0) 1665 603377
e bookings@alnwicklodge.com

alnwicklodge.com REAL-TIME BOOKING

open All year
bedrooms 3 double, 2 twin, 2 single, 2 family, 1 suite
bathrooms All en suite
payment Credit/debit cards, cash, cheques

A unique creation AD1650-2007. Alnwick Lodge at West Cawledge Park is a combination of history and rural charm with an air of sophistication, whilst linked to technology. Fascinating and incomparable accommodation set in beautiful Northumberland, one mile south of Alnwick, off the A1. For business or pleasure, conferences, functions, parties. Antique galleries and log fires.

SAT NAV *NE66 2HJ* **ONLINE MAP**

Room 🛗 🚪 📺 👜 ☕ General 🕳 🎬 ⚿ P ⚒ ✕ 🍽 ⊙ ✣ 🐾 Leisure ∪ ▸

Do you have access needs?

Look for the National Accessible Scheme symbols if you have special hearing, visual or mobility needs. An index of accommodation participating in the scheme can be found at the back of this guide.

★ ★ ★
**HOTEL
SILVER AWARD**

Rothay Manor

Rothay Bridge, Ambleside LA22 0EH **t** +44 (0) 15394 33605 **e** hotel@rothaymanor.co.uk

rothaymanor.co.uk SPECIAL OFFERS

B&B PER ROOM PER NIGHT
S £90.00–£140.00
D £140.00–£215.00
HB PER PERSON PER NIGHT
£103.00–£175.00

Special short-break rates available. Special-interest holidays Oct-May: antiques, music, painting, gardening, walking, bridge, Scrabble, chess and Lake District heritage.

bedrooms 6 double, 4 twin, 1 single, 5 family, 3 suites
bathrooms All en suite
payment Credit/debit cards, cash, cheques

Cumbria for Excellence Small Hotel of the Year 2006. Regency country-house hotel standing in its own grounds a short walk from the centre of Ambleside and the head of Lake Windermere. Renowned for its comfortable, friendly atmosphere and excellent food and wine. Free use of nearby leisure centre. Closed 3-23 January.

SAT NAV *LA22 0EH* **ONLINE MAP**

Room 🔌 📺 ⛲ ☕ General 🛎 🏛 ⛪ P 🛜 🍽 🎱 ☀ Leisure ∪ ♩ ► 🚲

★ ★ ★ ★
GUEST ACCOMMODATION

The Old Vicarage

Vicarage Road, Ambleside LA22 9DH **t** +44 (0) 15394 33364 **e** info@oldvicarageambleside.co.uk

oldvicarageambleside.co.uk

B&B PER ROOM PER NIGHT
S Min £100.00
D £100.00–£150.00

open All year except Christmas
bedrooms 4 double, 4 twin, 2 family, 4 suites
bathrooms All en suite
payment Credit/debit cards, cash, cheques, euros

Quiet central situation. Car park. Pets welcome. Heated indoor swimming pool, sauna and hot tub. Quality accommodation with TV/DVD/VCR, hairdryer, fridge, en suite. Some four-posters, spa baths and some ground-floor rooms.

SAT NAV *LA22 9DH*

Room 🔌 📺 📺 SC ⛲ ☕ General 🛎 🏛 ⛪ P 🛜 🍽 ☀ 🐕
Leisure ♨ ∪ ♩ ► 🚲

★ ★ ★ ★ ★
**BED & BREAKFAST
SILVER AWARD**

Red Bank

Wansfell Road, Ambleside LA22 0EG **t** +44 (0) 15394 34637 **e** info@red-bank.co.uk

red-bank.co.uk SPECIAL OFFERS

B&B PER ROOM PER NIGHT
D £70.00–£90.00

open All year
bedrooms 2 double, 1 twin
bathrooms All en suite
payment Cash, cheques, euros

Elegant, traditionally built Lakeland house in residential fringes of Ambleside. Three tastefully furnished en suite rooms offering spacious, deluxe accommodation. Village centre five minutes. An ideal base for discovering the grandeur of the Lake District National Park. We will do our very best to make your stay as relaxing and comfortable as possible. Private parking.

SAT NAV *LA22 0EG* **ONLINE MAP**

Room 📺 ⛲ ☕ General 🛎 9 P 🛜 🍽 ☀ Leisure ♩ ► 🚲

AYSGARTH, North Yorkshire Map ref 5B3
GUEST ACCOMMODATION

★★★★★
GUEST ACCOMMODATION
SILVER AWARD

B&B PER ROOM PER NIGHT
D £80.00–£120.00

EVENING MEAL PER PERSON
£15.00–£20.00

Thornton Lodge
Thornton Rust, Leyburn DL8 3AP t +44 (0) 1969 663375
e enquiries@thorntonlodgenorthyorkshire.co.uk

thorntonlodgenorthyorkshire.co.uk REAL-TIME BOOKING

open Easter to mid-October
bedrooms 2 double, 2 twin, 2 single, 2 family, 1 suite
bathrooms All en suite
payment Credit/debit cards, cash, cheques, euros

Thornton Lodge is a beautiful Edwardian country house with something for everyone. Its setting, within acres of landscaped grounds, woodlands and pasture, offers peace and tranquillity, which visitors find difficult to draw away from. Located in the National Park, there are walks and cycle routes from the doorstep. Available for house parties in winter.

SAT NAV DL8 3AP

Room ♿ 🛏 📺 ☕ 🍷 General 🐕 ♨ ⚐ P ✕ 🍽 ❄ Leisure ∪ ⚓ ► ☆

BAMBURGH, Northumberland Map ref 5C1
SELF CATERING

★★★★
SELF CATERING

Units   16
Sleeps   2–6

LOW SEASON PER WK
£259.00–£466.00

HIGH SEASON PER WK
£420.00–£776.00

Outchester & Ross Farm Cottages, Belford
contact Mrs Shirley McKie, 1 Cragview Road, Belford NE70 7NT t +44 (0) 1668 213336
e enquiry@rosscottages.co.uk

rosscottages.co.uk

open All year
payment Cash, cheques
nearest pub 3 miles
nearest shop 3 miles

Outchester and Ross are both in unique, secluded coastal locations in one of the most beautiful areas of Northumberland between Bamburgh and Holy Island. Our cottages are warm, comfortable and well equipped – each double glazed and with its own private garden. Relax completely and just enjoy being here.

Unit 📺 🎧 📀 🖥 📷 🔊 🍴 🗑 📱 📁 ❄ General 🐕 ♨ ⚐ P Leisure ∪ ► ☆

BAMBURGH, Northumberland Map ref 5C1
SELF CATERING

★★★
SELF CATERING

Units   5
Sleeps   2–5

LOW SEASON PER WK
£210.00–£275.00

HIGH SEASON PER WK
£520.00–£700.00

Point Cottages, Bamburgh
contact Mrs Sanderson, 30 The Oval, Benton, Newcastle upon Tyne NE12 9PP
t +44 (0) 191 266 2800 e info@bamburgh-cottages.co.uk

bamburgh-cottages.co.uk

Cluster of cottages with fine sea views to Lindisfarne, the Farne Islands and Bamburgh Castle. Adjacent to golf course. Furnished to a high standard. Large garden.

open All year
payment Cash, cheques
nearest pub 1 mile
nearest shop 1 mile

Unit 📺 🖥 🍴 ❄ General 🐕 ♨ ⚐ P ◯ Ⓢ 🐾 Leisure ∪ ⚓ ► ☆

Check the maps for accommodation locations
Colour maps at the front pinpoint all the places where accommodation is featured within the regional sections of this guide. Pick your location and then refer to the place index at the back to find the page number.

BAMBURGH, Northumberland Map ref 5C1 — SELF CATERING

★★★★–★★★★★★
SELF CATERING

| Units | 3 |
| Sleeps | 2–28 |

LOW SEASON PER WK
£221.00–£1,666.00

HIGH SEASON PER WK
£394.00–£2,362.00

Short breaks available all year. Weekend breaks, 3 nights, Fri-Mon. Midweek breaks, 4 nights, Mon-Fri.

Waren Lea Hall, Bamburgh

contact Carolynn Croisdale-Appleby, Abbotsholme, Hervines Road, Amersham HP6 5HS
t +44 (0) 1494 725194 & +44 (0) 7901 716136 **e** croisdaleappleby@aol.com

selfcateringluxury.co.uk

open All year
payment Cash, cheques
nearest pub 1.5 miles
nearest shop 1.5 miles

Imposing, spacious country house on shore of Budle Bay at Waren Mill near Bamburgh in two acres of waters-edge parkland. Breathtaking views of Lindisfarne and Cheviots. Holiday homes can be booked individually or together and sleep 14, 10 and 4 guests. Waren Lea Hall enjoys an unrivalled location with easy access for walking, golf, fishing etc.

Unit 📺 ⬛🖭 ⬛.⬛ ♨🗑 ❑📶 ⬛🗑 ❂◿ General 🐎 🏬🛗P🅿️ⓈS Leisure ∪♪▸🚲

BARDON MILL, Northumberland Map ref 5B2 — GUEST ACCOMMODATION

★★★
INN

B&B PER ROOM PER NIGHT
S £30.00–£35.00
D £50.00–£80.00

EVENING MEAL PER PERSON
£8.00–£15.50

Bridge weekends held first weekend in Mar and first weekend in Nov. 1 Nov – end Feb: 3 nights for 2 B&B (excl Christmas period).

Twice Brewed Inn

Bardon Mill, Hexham NE47 7AN **t** +44 (0) 1434 344534 **e** info@twicebrewedinn.co.uk

twicebrewedinn.co.uk SPECIAL OFFERS

open All year except Christmas
bedrooms 6 double, 6 twin, 2 single
bathrooms 6 en suite
payment Credit/debit cards, cash, cheques

Family-run inn situated 0.5 miles from Hadrian's Wall offering accommodation, a warm welcome, good food, real ales, breathtaking views and wide-open spaces. Centrally placed for visits to Scotland, Cumbria and the North East (all within one hour's drive).

SAT NAV NE47 7AN **ONLINE MAP**

Room 🛏 General 🐎 🏬🛗P🅿️🔌🍽✕🎱❂ Leisure ∪▸🚲

BARMBY MOOR, East Riding of Yorkshire Map ref 4C1 — SELF CATERING

★★★★
SELF CATERING

| Units | 1 |
| Sleeps | 1–6 |

LOW SEASON PER WK
£375.00–£400.00

HIGH SEASON PER WK
£440.00–£600.00

Short breaks (3 days), bookable 28 days in advance, 60% normal weekly rate.

Northwood Coach House, York

contact Ann Gregory, Northwood Coach House, St Helens Square, Barmby Moor YO42 4HF
t +44 (0) 1759 302305 **e** annjgregory@hotmail.com

northwoodcoachhouse.co.uk

open All year
payment Cash, cheques, euros
nearest pub less than 0.5 miles
nearest shop less than 0.5 miles

This pretty, three-bedroomed, converted Victorian coach house overlooks open countryside. Warm and cosy in winter, it is ideally situated in a picturesque village on the edge of the Wolds, only 12 miles from York and convenient for the coast and moors. Pubs, shops and restaurants nearby.

Unit 📺 ⬛ ⬛.⬛ ♨🗑 ❑📶 ⬛🗑 ❂ General 🐎 🏬🛗P🅿️ⓈS 🐕
Leisure ∪♪▸🚲

BARROW-IN-FURNESS, Cumbria   Map ref 5A3 — GUEST ACCOMMODATION

★★★★
BED & BREAKFAST
SILVER AWARD

November House B&B

Hawcoat Lane, Barrow-in-Furness LA14 4HE   **t** +44 (0) 1229 827247   **e** november-house@tiscali.co.u

novemberhouse.co.uk

B&B PER ROOM PER NIGHT
D £50.00–£55.00

EVENING MEAL PER PERSON
£15.00–£25.00

We offer guests quality B&B accommodation and aim to provide genuine hospitality, making your stay enjoyable and memorable.

open All year except Christmas
bedrooms 2 double, 1 family
bathrooms All en suite
payment Cash, cheques

Room 💿 🕿   General 🛏 🖿 🕭 P ✕ 🍽 🖂

BLACKBURN, Lancashire   Map ref 4A1 — HOTEL

★★★
COUNTRY HOUSE HOTEL
SILVER AWARD

Northcote Manor Hotel

Northcote Road, Blackburn BB6 8BE   **t** +44 (0) 1254 240555   **e** sales@northcotemanor.com

northcotemanor.com SPECIAL OFFERS · REAL-TIME BOOKING

B&B PER ROOM PER NIGHT
S £150.00–£195.00
D £180.00–£225.00

Gourmet Breaks available from £290, based on 2 people sharing – includes: champagne, 5-course gourmet dinner, overnight stay and stunning Lancashire breakfast.

open All year except Christmas and New Year
bedrooms 8 double, 4 twin, 2 family
bathrooms All en suite
payment Credit/debit cards, cash, cheques, euros

Northcote Manor is an award-winning restaurant with highly individual rooms offering total luxury and comfort. Elegant wood panelling, warm welcoming lounges with sumptuous leather sofas and impressive staircases add to the atmosphere. Enjoy the gardens and grounds, with breathtaking views of the Ribble Valley.

SAT NAV *BB6 8BE* ONLINE MAP

Room 🛏 🖿 📞 TV SC 💿 🕿 ♿   General 🛏 🖿 🕭 P 📶 🍷 🍽 🌑 🎮 🖂 🍴 ✲
Leisure 🏊 ▶

BLACKPOOL, Lancashire   Map ref 4A1 — GUEST ACCOMMODATION

★★★
GUEST ACCOMMODATION

Hadley

225 Promenade, Blackpool FY1 5DL   **t** +44 (0) 1253 621197   **e** admin@hadley-hotel.com

hadley-hotel.com REAL-TIME BOOKING

B&B PER ROOM PER NIGHT
S £23.00–£30.00
D £46.00–£60.00

EVENING MEAL PER PERSON
£10.00

Friendly, family-run hotel, recently refurbished. Twenty en suite bedrooms. Situated on Central Promenade overlooking the Irish Sea.

open All year
bedrooms 11 double, 6 twin, 1 single, 2 family
bathrooms All en suite
payment Credit/debit cards

Room 🛏 TV 💿   General 🛏 🖿 🕭 🍷 ✕ 🍽 ✲

BLACKPOOL, Lancashire   Map ref 4A1 — GUEST ACCOMMODATION

★★
GUEST HOUSE

The Manor Grove

24 Leopold Grove, Blackpool FY1 4LD   **t** +44 (0) 1253 625577   **e** themanorgrove@blueyonder.co.uk

themanorgrove.co.uk

B&B PER ROOM PER NIGHT
D £44.00–£56.00

Lovely, bright, clean, modern rooms. Family-run guesthouse, central location behind the Winter Gardens. All rooms en suite, TV, hairdryers, tea/coffee.

open All year
bedrooms 2 double, 4 single, 3 family
bathrooms All en suite
payment Credit/debit cards, cash, cheques

Room TV 💿 🕿   General 🛏 🖿 🕭 P 📶 ♿ 🍽

Need some ideas?

Big city buzz or peaceful panoramas? Take a fresh look at England and you may be surprised at what's right on your doorstep. Explore the diversity online at enjoyengland.com

★★★★
GUEST ACCOMMODATION

B&B PER ROOM PER NIGHT
S £31.00–£36.00
D £62.00–£72.00

EVENING MEAL PER PERSON
£8.95–£10.50

3 nights for the price of 2, Mon-Fri (excl Bank Holidays), Jan-Aug.

The Raffles Guest Accommodation

73-77 Hornby Road, Blackpool FY1 4QJ   t +44 (0) 1253 294713
e enquiries@raffleshotelblackpool.fsworld.co.uk

raffleshotelblackpool.co.uk

open All year
bedrooms 12 double, 3 twin, 1 single, 1 family, 3 suites
bathrooms All en suite
payment Credit/debit cards, cash, cheques

Excellent central location for promenade, shopping centre, Winter Gardens, theatres. All rooms en suite. Licensed bar, English tea rooms, parking and daily housekeeping. Imaginative choice of menus. Listed in the Good Hotel Guide and the Which? Guide to Good Hotels. Three new family apartments each sleeping up to four people.

SAT NAV FY1 4QJ

Room 🛏 📺 🕯   General 🛋 🏚 🅿 🌿 ❢ ✕ 🍴 🐎

★★★
GUEST ACCOMMODATION

B&B PER ROOM PER NIGHT
S £25.00–£50.00
D £40.00–£80.00

The South Beach

367 Promenade, Blackpool FY1 6BJ   t +44 (0) 1253 342250   e info@southbeachhotel.co.uk

southbeachhotel.co.uk GUEST REVIEWS · SPECIAL OFFERS · REAL-TIME BOOKING

Above-average, friendly family-run licensed bed and breakfast situated in the main holiday area on Blackpool's South Promenade. Great for families and couples.

open All year
bedrooms 10 double, 4 twin, 2 single, 12 family
bathrooms All en suite
payment Credit/debit cards, cash

Room 🛏 📺 🕯   General 🛋 🏚 🅿 ❢

★★★★
GUEST HOUSE

B&B PER ROOM PER NIGHT
S £40.00–£50.00
D £60.00–£75.00

EVENING MEAL PER PERSON
£25.00–£35.00

Middle Flass Lodge

Forest Becks Brow, Clitheroe BB7 4NY   t +44 (0) 1200 447259   e middleflasslodge@btconnect.com

middleflasslodge.co.uk

open All year
bedrooms 4 double, 2 twin, 1 family
bathrooms All en suite
payment Credit/debit cards, cash, cheques

Tastefully converted barn/cow byre, set in idyllic countryside location of Forest of Bowland. Ideal touring base on Lancashire/Yorkshire border. Always personal and professional attention with neat and cosy bedrooms. Lounge with stove, dining room with chef-prepared cuisine. Licensed. Gardens and ample parking.

SAT NAV BB7 4NY

Room 📺 🕯   General 🛋 🏚 🅿 ❢ ✕ 🍴   Leisure 🚶 🚲

Where can I get help and advice?

Tourist Information Centres offer friendly help with accommodation and holiday ideas as well as suggestions of places to visit and things to do. You'll find contact details at the beginning of each regional section.

BOWES, Durham Map ref 5B3

★★★★
SELF CATERING

Units **5**
Sleeps **2–4**

LOW SEASON PER WK
£165.00–£220.00

HIGH SEASON PER WK
£270.00–£360.00

Short breaks (3 nights) available from £125 for a 2-bedded cottage to £260 for a 4-bedded cottage.

Mellwaters Barn, Bowes, Barnard Castle

contact Mr Andrew Tavener, East Mellwaters Farm, Stainmore Road, Barnard Castle DL12 9RH
t +44 (0) 1833 628181 **e** mellwatersbarn@aol.com

mellwatersbarn.co.uk

open All year
payment Cash, cheques
nearest pub 1 mile
nearest shop 5 miles

Wake up to wildlife on the edge of England's last wilderness, with quiet country roads and magnificent scenery. These spacious and airy cottages are fully equipped and are designed to give maximum possible access. Some cottages can be joined together for larger parties. Prices include everything except food.

Unit 📺 🔲 🔳 🔌 🔧 🍴 🛁 📱 General ♘ 🏛 ⅋ P ⊙ S Leisure ∪ ♪ ⊢

BRAMPTON, Cumbria Map ref 5B2

★★★★
BED & BREAKFAST

B&B PER ROOM PER NIGHT
S £40.00–£50.00
D £64.00–£80.00

EVENING MEAL PER PERSON
£20.00–£25.00

Scarrowhill House

Scarrow Hill House, Denton Mill, Brampton CA8 2QU **t** +44 (0) 1697 746759 & +44 (0) 7789 950322
e ianmac2949@aol.com

scarrowhillhouse.co.uk GUEST REVIEWS

open All year except Christmas and New Year
bedrooms 1 double, 1 twin
bathrooms All en suite
payment Credit/debit cards, cash, cheques, euros

Scarrow Hill House is a Victorian gamekeeper's dwelling set in secluded grounds on the Naworth Castle estate. It offers first-class accommodation and food, fine hospitality and relaxation in its own extensive gardens. It is close to Hadrian's Wall, the Scottish Borders and the Lake District.

SAT NAV *CA8 2QU* **ONLINE MAP**

Room 📺 SC ⅋ 🍴 General ♘ P 🛎 🔧 ✗ 🍽 ▣ ❊ ✚ Leisure ∪ ♪ ⊢ ♣

BRIDLINGTON, East Riding of Yorkshire Map ref 5D3

★★★★
BED & BREAKFAST

B&B PER ROOM PER NIGHT
S £45.00–£50.00
D £50.00–£60.00

7 nights for the price of 6.

Lincoln House

43 Wellington Road, Bridlington YO15 2AX **t** +44 (0) 1262 679595 **e** lincolnhousebrid@fsmail.net

lincolnhousebridlington.co.uk GUEST REVIEWS

open All year except Christmas and New Year
bedrooms 3 double
bathrooms All en suite
payment Cash, cheques

Lincoln House, built c1892, is recently renovated and offers three tastefully decorated and spacious bedrooms with en suite facilities and is ideally situated to take advantage of all that Bridlington has to offer. Just a ten-minute stroll to the town centre, promenade, theatres, historic harbour, bus and rail stations.

SAT NAV *YO15 2AX* **ONLINE MAP**

Room 📺 SC ⅋ 🍴 General ❊

BRIDLINGTON, East Riding of Yorkshire   Map ref 5D3 — GUEST ACCOMMODATION

★★★★
GUEST HOUSE

B&B PER ROOM PER NIGHT
S Min £25.00
D Min £56.00

EVENING MEAL PER PERSON
Min £8.00

Providence Place

11 North View Terrace, Bridlington YO15 2QP   t +44 (0) 1262 603840
e enquiries@providenceplace.info

providenceplace.info

Fully accessible, family-run establishment, home-from-home atmosphere. Ground-floor rooms. Quiet location close to sea and all amenities. Licensed guest lounge, attractive garden. Ample on-site parking.

open All year
bedrooms 1 double, 3 twin, 1 single, 1 family
bathrooms 5 en suite, 1 private
payment Credit/debit cards, cash, cheques

Room ♿ 📺 ☕   General 🐴 P ♟ ✕ ⛺ ❀ 🐾   Leisure 🎵 ►

BRINSCALL, Lancashire   Map ref 4A1 — SELF CATERING

★★★
SELF CATERING

Units   **1**
Sleeps   **5–8**

LOW SEASON PER WK
£375.00

HIGH SEASON PER WK
£475.00

Part- and midweek bookings accepted.

Moors View Cottage, Chorley

contact Mrs Sheila Smith, Moors View Cottage, Four Seasons Guest House, Thornton FY5 1EP
t +44 (0) 1253 853537 & +44 (0) 7747 808406   e fourseasonsguesthouse@talktalk.net

open All year
payment Cash, cheques, euros
nearest pub less than 0.5 miles
nearest shop less than 0.5 miles

Situated amid lovely countryside adjacent to canal, motorways, market towns and coast, this fully equipped cottage comprises two bedrooms and excellent bed-settee, luxury bathroom, separate shower and toilet, large through lounge and dining area, oak kitchen, off-road parking, large rear garden and sun room. Fuel, power and linen included.

Unit 📺 💿 📀 📻 🍴 🍳 ⛄ 🎮 ✂   General 🐴 ⛰ P 🅂 🐾   Leisure 🎵 ►

BUTTERMERE, Cumbria   Map ref 5A3 — HOTEL

★★★
COUNTRY HOUSE HOTEL
SILVER AWARD

B&B PER ROOM PER NIGHT
S £45.00–£69.00
D £90.00–£138.00
HB PER PERSON PER NIGHT
£70.00–£105.00

Any reservations of 4 or more nights DB&B receive a further night free on the same basis. Please refer to website for last-minute offers.

Bridge Hotel

Buttermere, Nr Keswick CA13 9UZ   t +44 (0) 1768 770252   e enquiries@bridge-hotel.com

bridge-hotel.com SPECIAL OFFERS

open All year
bedrooms 13 double, 6 twin, 2 single
bathrooms All en suite
payment Credit/debit cards, cash, cheques

18thC coaching inn, beautifully situated between two lakes. Superb, unrestricted walking country and breathtaking scenery. Two antique four-poster rooms available. Afternoon tea served in our very comfortable residents' lounge. Two well-stocked bars, fine range of malt whiskies and hand-pulled ales. Wide variety of bar meals served throughout the day.

SAT NAV CA13 9UZ

Room 📺 📞 ☕ 🍳 ✂   General 🐴 ⛰ 🏃 P 🎱 ♟ ⛺ 🖥 🍴 ❀   Leisure ∪ 🎵 ► 🚴

It's all quality-assessed accommodation

Our commitment to quality involves wide-ranging accommodation assessment. Ratings and awards were correct at the time of going to press but may change following a new assessment. Please check at time of booking.

CASTLESIDE, Durham Map ref 5B2

GUEST ACCOMMODATION

★★★★
GUEST HOUSE

B&B PER ROOM PER NIGHT
S £45.00–£48.00
D £70.00–£76.00

EVENING MEAL PER PERSON
£20.00

Special prices for 3-day breaks and winter breaks. DB&B. See website.

Bee Cottage Guesthouse

Castleside, Nr Consett DH8 9HW **t** +44 (0) 1207 508224 **e** beecottage68@aol.com

beecottage.co.uk SPECIAL OFFERS

open All year
bedrooms 2 double, 2 twin, 3 family, 1 suite
bathrooms All en suite
payment Credit/debit cards, cash, cheques, euros

Situated on the edge of the Durham Dales with stunning views. A wonderful place to relax. Peaceful walking and cycling (next to C2C). Ideal base for Beamish, Durham, Newcastle, Hadrian's Wall, Hexham and Corbridge. Some ground-floor rooms, all en suite. Home-cooked evening meals. Licensed. You will be most welcome.

SAT NAV *DH8 9HW* **ONLINE MAP**

Room 🔥 📺 🍴 🍵 General 🛏 🏭 🏋 P 🍽 ✕ 🎱 🎯 ❄ 🐕 Leisure ∪ ♪ ▶ 🚴

CHESTER, Cheshire Map ref 4A2

HOTEL

★★
HOTEL

B&B PER ROOM PER NIGHT
S £70.00–£95.00
D £95.00–£130.00
HB PER PERSON PER NIGHT
£70.00–£85.00

Deva Break: any 2 nights' DB&B from £70pppn. Winter Warmers (from Dec): third night's DB&B half price. Special breaks our speciality.

The Curzon Hotel

52-54 Hough Green, Chester CH4 8JQ **t** +44 (0) 1244 678581 **e** curzon.chester@virgin.net

curzonhotel.co.uk

open All year except Christmas and New Year
bedrooms 8 double, 3 twin, 1 single, 2 family, 2 suites
bathrooms All en suite
payment Credit/debit cards, cash, cheques

The Curzon is a family-run, Victorian townhouse hotel. Unwind in the lounge bar and sample our excellent cuisine in the splendid restaurant. Sleep peacefully in one of the individually designed guest rooms. There is ample private parking, and we are within easy reach of the city centre.

SAT NAV *CH4 8JQ*

Room 🔥 🛋 📞 📺 🍴 🍵 General 🛏 🏭 🏋 P 🍷 🍽 ❄ Leisure ▶

CHESTER, Cheshire Map ref 4A2

HOTEL

★★★★
HOTEL

B&B PER ROOM PER NIGHT
S £95.00–£130.00
D £130.00–£160.00

Romantic Break £195 per executive room – £20 dinner allowance per person, Champagne and chocolates, breakfast, use of leisure facilities.

Grosvenor Pulford Hotel & Spa

Wrexham Road, Pulford, Chester CH4 9DG **t** +44 (0) 1244 570560
e reservations@grosvenorpulfordhotel.co.uk

grosvenorpulfordhotel.co.uk GUEST REVIEWS · SPECIAL OFFERS · REAL-TIME BOOKING

open All year
bedrooms 50 double, 13 twin, 1 single, 8 family, 1 suite
bathrooms All en suite
payment Credit/debit cards, cash, cheques

Winner of Visit Chester and Cheshire's Large Hotel 2007. Seventy-three bedrooms, Mediterranean-themed restaurant, gastro-style bar, and luxurious spa including six indulgent treatment suites, VIP couple's suite, three relaxation rooms, Turkish Hammam, Arabian Rasul, Rejuvenation Skin Clinic, Roman-style swimming pool, jacuzzi, steam room, sauna, Technogym gymnasium, tennis court, Spa Boutique and Spa Eatery.

SAT NAV *CH4 9DG* **ONLINE MAP**

Room 🔥 🛋 📞 📺 SC 🍴 🍵 ♿ 🛗 General 🛏 🏭 🏋 P 🍷 🍽 🎱 ♨ 🎯 🎱 🍴 ❄ 🐕
Leisure 🎣 ♨ ⛳ 🎾 🏊 ∪ ♪ ▶

CHESTER, Cheshire Map ref 4A2
SELF CATERING

★★★
SELF CATERING

Units 1
Sleeps 1–4

LOW SEASON PER WK
£150.00–£200.00

HIGH SEASON PER WK
£200.00–£250.00

Kingswood Coach House, Chester

contact Mrs C Perry, Kingswood Coach House, Kingswood, Parkgate Road, Chester CH1 6JS
t +44 (0) 1244 851204 **e** caroline.m.perry@btopenworld.com

Ideal for couples. Large bedroom, fitted kitchen, living room, toilet and shower. Garden and patio, off-road parking. Close to bus route. Near Wales and Wirral.

open All year
payment Cash, cheques
nearest pub less than 0.5 miles
nearest shop 2 miles

Unit 📺 🔲 General P Leisure ▶

CHESTER, Cheshire Map ref 4A2
SELF CATERING

★★★★
SELF CATERING

Units 1
Sleeps 1–4

LOW SEASON PER WK
Min £400.00

HIGH SEASON PER WK
Min £570.00

Wharton Lock Apartment & Balcony, Chester

contact Mrs Sandra Jeffrey, Chester Canalside Holidays, Chester CH2 3DH **t** +44 (0) 1244 312788
e rentals@stayinchester.com

stayinchester.com GUEST REVIEWS · SPECIAL OFFERS · REAL-TIME BOOKING

Luxury apartment with private canalside balcony in Chester, five minutes' walk to city centre. King-size and twin bedrooms, two bathrooms, parking, Wi-Fi. Romantic breaks, family holidays, business trips.

open All year
payment Credit/debit cards, cash, cheques, euros
nearest pub less than 0.5 miles
nearest shop less than 0.5 miles

Unit 📺 🔲 General P 🅾️ ⑤ Leisure

CHORLEY, Lancashire Map ref 4A1
GUEST ACCOMMODATION

★★★★
GUEST ACCOMMODATION

B&B PER ROOM PER NIGHT
S £40.00–£50.00
D £70.00–£80.00

Parr Hall Farm

Parr Lane, Eccleston, Chorley PR7 5SL **t** +44 (0) 1257 451917 **e** enquiries@parrhallfarm.com

parrhallfarm.com

open All year
bedrooms 7 double, 2 twin
bathrooms All en suite
payment Credit/debit cards, cash, cheques

Georgian farmhouse built in 1721 and tastefully restored. Quiet, rural location within easy walking distance of good public houses, restaurants and village amenities. Conveniently situated for Lancashire coast and countryside, Lake District and Yorkshire Dales. Manchester Airport 45 minutes, Liverpool Airport 45 minutes.

SAT NAV PR7 5SL

Room 📺 General P Leisure

CONISTON, Cumbria Map ref 5A3
CAMPING, CARAVAN & HOLIDAY PARK

★★★★
TOURING &
CAMPING PARK

🚐 (280) £12.20–£25.10
🚐 (280) £12.20–£25.10
⛺ on application
280 touring pitches

Park Coppice Caravan Club Site

Park Gate, Coniston LA21 8LA **t** +44 (0) 15394 41555

caravanclub.co.uk

open March to November
payment Credit/debit cards, cash, cheques

Landscaped site set in 63 acres of National Trust woodland. Lake for watersports, on-site play areas, orienteering courses and Red Squirrel Nature Trail.

SAT NAV LA21 8LA

Special member rates mean you can save your membership subscription in less than a week. Visit our website to find out more.

THE
CARAVAN
CLUB

General ☀ Leisure

CORNRIGGS, Durham Map ref 5B2 — SELF CATERING

★★★★★
SELF CATERING

Units **2**
Sleeps **2–6**

LOW SEASON PER WK
£310.00–£380.00

HIGH SEASON PER WK
£450.00–£560.00

Cornriggs Cottages, Cowshill in Weardale, Bishop Auckland

contact Mr & Mrs Harry and Janet Elliott, Cornriggs Cottages, c/o Low Cornriggs Farm, Cornriggs, Cowshill DL13 1AQ **t** +44 (0) 1388 537600 & +44 (0) 7818 843159 **e** cornriggsfarm@btconnect.com

britnett.net/lowcornriggsfarm SPECIAL OFFERS · REAL-TIME BOOKING

open All year
payment Credit/debit cards, cash, cheques, euros
nearest pub 1 mile
nearest shop 4 miles

Two beautiful, large, luxury cottages in the heart of Weardale. Working hill farm with wildflower meadows, spectacular views, quiet roads. Wake up to the sound of birdsong. Each cottage has three bedrooms, two en suite bathrooms and an accessible wc and shower, fitted kitchen and dining area, lounge, patio, garden and safe play area.

SAT NAV DL13 1AQ **ONLINE MAP**

Unit 📺 🖥 📀 🔌 ♨ 🍳 🔲 ❄ ⛰ General 🏇 🛏 P 🅂 Leisure ∪ ⌁

CRAMLINGTON, Northumberland Map ref 5C2 — SELF CATERING

★★★★
SELF CATERING

Units **9**
Sleeps **2–36**

LOW SEASON PER WK
£290.00–£590.00

HIGH SEASON PER WK
£430.00–£870.00

3-4-night stays welcomed, all year round.

Burradon Farm Houses & Cottages, Cramlington

contact Mrs Judith Younger, Burradon Farm Houses & Cottages, Burradon Farm, Cramlington NE23 7ND **t** +44 (0) 191 268 3203 **e** judy@burradonfarm.co.uk

burradonfarm.co.uk REAL-TIME BOOKING

open All year
payment Credit/debit cards, cash, cheques
nearest pub 0.5 miles
nearest shop 0.5 miles

Burradon Farm is located only a few miles from the spectacular Northumbrian coastline and within easy reach of the cultural heritage and dynamic centre which is Newcastle-upon-Tyne. The new barn conversions have become characterful, high-quality houses and cottages boasting every amenity and facility to ensure an enjoyable visit. Dishwasher in houses. Wi-Fi internet connection.

ONLINE MAP

Unit 📺 📱 🖥 📀 🔌 ♨ 🍳 🔲 ❄ ⛰ General 🏇 🛏 P 🅾 🅂 🐾 Leisure ⌁ ⮕

DANBY, North Yorkshire Map ref 5C3 — GUEST ACCOMMODATION

★★★★
INN

B&B PER ROOM PER NIGHT
S £45.00–£60.00
D £75.00–£90.00

The Fox & Hounds Inn

45 Brook Lane, Ainthorpe, Whitby YO21 2LD **t** +44 (0) 1287 660218
e info@foxandhounds-ainthorpe.com

foxandhounds-ainthorpe.com

open All year except Christmas
bedrooms 3 double, 3 twin, 1 family
bathrooms All en suite
payment Credit/debit cards, cash, cheques

16thC former coaching inn, now a high-quality residential country inn and restaurant. Set amidst the beautiful North York Moors National Park. Enjoy freshly prepared dishes, cask ales or selected quality wines in our restaurant or oak-beamed bar.

SAT NAV YO21 2LD

Room 📺 ♨ 🍳 General 🏇 🛏 P 📶 🔥 ⁉ ✕ ❄ 🐾 Leisure ⚲ ∪ ⌁ ⮕ 🚴

DANBY, North Yorkshire Map ref 5C3

SELF CATERING

★★
SELF CATERING

Units **1**
Sleeps **1–7**

LOW SEASON PER WK
£190.00–£290.00

HIGH SEASON PER WK
£220.00–£330.00

Clitherbecks Farm, Danby, Whitby

contact Mrs Catherine Harland, Clitherbecks Farm, Danby YO21 2NT t +44 (0) 1287 660321
e nharland@clitherbecks.freeserve.co.uk

clitherbecks.freeserve.co.uk

open All year
payment Cash, cheques
nearest pub 1 mile
nearest shop 2 miles

Neil and Cathy Harland welcome you to Clitherbecks Farm, one mile from Danby and directly north from the National Park Moors Centre. Accommodation for seven people in two bedrooms in the farmhouse. You have your own entrance through a fenced garden. Seasonal produce available from this traditional hill farm.

SAT NAV YO21 2NT

Unit 📺 🖥 ⚙ 🍽 💷❄🌿 General 🐴 P 🐕 Leisure 🎣

DARLINGTON, Tees Valley Map ref 5C3

HOTEL

★★★
COUNTRY HOUSE HOTEL
SILVER AWARD

B&B PER ROOM PER NIGHT
S £90.00–£160.00
D £110.00–£185.00
HB PER PERSON PER NIGHT
£74.00–£109.00

Winter, Easter and summer breaks. Plus website offers and golf/spa breaks.

Headlam Hall Hotel, Spa and Golf Course

Headlam, Darlington DL2 3HA t +44 (0) 1325 730238 e admin@headlamhall.co.uk

headlamhall.co.uk GUEST REVIEWS · SPECIAL OFFERS · REAL-TIME BOOKING

open All year except Christmas
bedrooms 26 double, 6 twin, 4 family, 4 suites
bathrooms All en suite
payment Credit/debit cards, cash, cheques

Charming Jacobean mansion in picturesque hamlet, surrounded by its own 9-hole golf course and farmland. Beautifully appointed, luxurious bedrooms, and restaurant serving freshly prepared food using local ingredients. The superb new spa offers a pool, thermal zone, outdoor spa pool, gym, treatment rooms and informal brasserie bar.

SAT NAV DL2 3HA ONLINE MAP

Room 🛁🖥📞📺🆂♨🍽🎵 General 🐴🏛🍴P🎤🍽🎵🌙🍽⚙🐕🐾🐎
Leisure 🎣♨🏹⊗🔍♨🚴▶🚲

DENT, Cumbria Map ref 5B3

SELF CATERING

★★★
SELF CATERING

Units **2**
Sleeps **4**

LOW SEASON PER WK
£220.00–£265.00

HIGH SEASON PER WK
£265.00–£350.00

Short breaks from Oct-Mar, weekend or midweek. Any combination, subject to availability.

Middleton's Cottage and Fountain Cottage, Dent, Sedbergh

contact Mr & Mrs Ayers, Middleton's Cottage and Fountain Cottage, The Old Rectory, Polegate BN26 5RB t +44 (0) 1323 870032 e candpayers@mistral.co.uk

dentcottages.co.uk

open All year
payment Cash, cheques
nearest pub less than 0.5 miles
nearest shop less than 0.5 miles

Modernised mid-17thC cottages in centre of small quaint village, comfortably furnished and decorated to high standards. Quiet, unspoilt Dentdale offers a good base for walking, touring and exploring the Yorkshire Dales or the Lake District, with Kendal and Hawes nearby. Brochure available.

Unit 📺 📀 🖥 🗄 🔲 ⚙❄ General 🐴🏛P🆂

DURHAM Map ref 5C2 — GUEST ACCOMMODATION

★★
GUEST ACCOMMODATION

B&B PER ROOM PER NIGHT
S £24.00–£27.00
D £24.00–£27.00

St Johns College

3 South Bailey, Durham DH1 3RJ t +44 (0) 191 334 3877 e s.l.hobson@durham.ac.uk

durham.ac.uk/st-johns.college

Located in the heart of Durham City alongside the cathedral, St John's offers accommodation in distinctive, historic buildings with riverside gardens.

open All year except Christmas and New Year
bedrooms 9 twin, 36 single
payment Credit/debit cards, cash, cheques

Room ♿ ♿ General ♿ ♨ ⁽ᵖ⁾ ♿ ♿ ✕ ▦ ▣ ❀

DURHAM Map ref 5C2 — GUEST ACCOMMODATION

★★★★
GUEST ACCOMMODATION
SILVER AWARD

B&B PER ROOM PER NIGHT
D £60.00–£75.00

The Victorian Town House

2 Victoria Terrace, Durham DH1 4RW t +44 (0) 5601 459168
e thevictoriantownhouse-durham@yahoo.co.uk

durhambedandbreakfast.co.uk

Victorian terraced family home. Three en suite rooms. City centre, train, bus all five minutes' walk. Private and nearby parking.

open All year
bedrooms 1 double, 1 twin, 1 family
bathrooms All en suite
payment Credit/debit cards, cash, cheques

Room ♿ TV ♿ ⁋ General ♿5 P ⁽ᵖ⁾ ▦ ❀

GARSTANG, Lancashire Map ref 4A1 — GUEST ACCOMMODATION

★★★★
GUEST ACCOMMODATION

B&B PER ROOM PER NIGHT
S £51.56–£74.00
D £56.12–£80.00

EVENING MEAL PER PERSON
£5.00–£30.00

Champagne weekend from £165. Sunday saver only £65 for 2 people, DB&B.

Guys Thatched Hamlet

Canalside, St Michael's Road, Bilsborrow, Preston PR3 0RS t +44 (0) 1995 640010
e info@guysthatchedhamlet.com

guysthatchedhamlet.com SPECIAL OFFERS · REAL-TIME BOOKING

open All year except Christmas
bedrooms 48 double, 10 twin, 7 family
bathrooms All en suite
payment Credit/debit cards, cash, cheques

A canalside haven of thatched-roof buildings, just off the A6 at Bilsborrow near Garstang. Featuring Guy's Lodge, Owd Nell's Tavern, Guy's Restaurant and Pizzeria, craft shops, bowling green and cricket ground. Guy's Lodge offers rooms from only £52.00. Executive spa rooms and deluxe rooms available. All have Sky TV, tea/coffee etc.

SAT NAV PR3 0RS **ONLINE MAP**

Room ♿ ☎ TV ⓢⓒ ♿ ⤵ General ♿ ▦ ♨ P ⁽ᵖ⁾ ♿ ♿ ✕ ▦ ▣ ❀
Leisure ∪ ♪ ▸ ᵭ

GARSTANG, Lancashire Map ref 4A1 — SELF CATERING

★★★
SELF CATERING

Units   **2**
Sleeps   **2–5**

LOW SEASON PER WK
£220.00–£320.00

HIGH SEASON PER WK
£290.00–£420.00

Knotts Hey Cottages, Bilsborrow, Preston

contact Mr Collinson, Knotts Hey Cottages, Stanzaker Hall Drive, Catterall, Preston PR3 0PB
t +44 (0) 1995 640519 e holidays@brockcottages.co.uk

brockcottages.co.uk

Secluded Knotts Hey Cottages in the heart of north west Lancashire within easy access of Lakes, Dales, Bowland, and Fylde Coast. Open-plan cottages, two double bed and one double bed, all en suite.

open All year
payment Cash, cheques, euros
nearest pub 2 miles
nearest shop 1 mile

Unit TV ⓢⓒ ⊠ ▣ ▤ ▦ ⁋ ▣ ▣ ♿ ❀ ♨ General ♿ ▦ ♨ P Leisure ♪ ▸ ᵭ

Do you have access needs?

Look for the National Accessible Scheme symbols if you have special hearing, visual or mobility needs.

GRANGE-OVER-SANDS, Cumbria Map ref 5A3 — HOTEL

★★★
HOTEL

B&B PER ROOM PER NIGHT
S £40.00–£100.00
D £60.00–£150.00

HB PER PERSON PER NIGHT
£50.00–£120.00

Free child places 0-4 years. Half-price 5-14 years. Murder Mystery and tribute weekends. Christmas and New Year breaks.

The Cumbria Grand Hotel

Lindale Road, Grange-over-Sands LA11 6EN t +44 (0) 15395 32331
e salescumbria@strathmorehotels.com

strathmorehotels.com SPECIAL OFFERS · REAL-TIME BOOKING

open All year
bedrooms 28 double, 70 twin, 12 single, 9 family, 1 suite
bathrooms All en suite
payment Credit/debit cards, cash, cheques

Set in 20 acres of private gardens and woodlands, and overlooking the stunning Morecambe Bay, you will receive a warm and friendly welcome at this charming Victorian hotel. Only six miles from Lake Windermere, there is much to see and do in the beautiful surrounding area.

SAT NAV LA11 6EN ONLINE MAP

Room 👥 🛏 📞 TV SC ♿ 🔔   General 🐕 🏛 🛎 P ♟ 🎱 ◐ 🖼 🏆 ❄ 🐎
Leisure 🎾 U 🎵 ►

GRANGE-OVER-SANDS, Cumbria Map ref 5A3 — GUEST ACCOMMODATION

★★★★
GUEST ACCOMMODATION

B&B PER ROOM PER NIGHT
S £36.00–£39.00
D £39.00–£45.00

EVENING MEAL PER PERSON
£10.50–£19.95

Competitive rates available for 4 nights or more.

The Lymehurst

Kents Bank Road, Grange-over-Sands LA11 7EY t +44 (0) 15395 33076 e enquiries@lymehurst.co.uk

lymehurst.co.uk GUEST REVIEWS · SPECIAL OFFERS · REAL-TIME BOOKING

open All year
bedrooms 5 double, 2 twin, 3 single
bathrooms All en suite
payment Credit/debit cards, cash

A beautiful Victorian building with a welcoming and peaceful atmosphere retaining many original features, in the centre of Grange-over-Sands, a charming town with many individual shops and cafes. Lymestone restaurant on the lower ground floor open for lunch every day with seasonal menus prepared by Master Chef of Great Britain Kevin Wyper.

SAT NAV LA11 7EY ONLINE MAP

Room 👥 🛏 TV SC ♿ 🔔   General 🐕 🏛 P 📶 ♟ ✕ 🎱 ❄   Leisure 🎵 ► 🚲

GRASMERE, Cumbria Map ref 5A3 — SELF CATERING

★★★★
SELF CATERING

Units   3
Sleeps 2–5

LOW SEASON PER WK
£303.00–£340.00

HIGH SEASON PER WK
£502.00–£670.00

A week booked in the year allows 10% off a second week booked in Mar (excl Easter holidays).

Broadrayne Farm Cottages, Grasmere

contact Mr Bev Dennison & Mrs Jo Dennison Drake, Broadrayne Farm, Grasmere, Ambleside LA22 9RU t +44 (0) 15394 35055 e jo@grasmere-accommodation.co.uk

grasmere-accommodation.co.uk

open All year
payment Cash, cheques
nearest pub 0.5 miles
nearest shop 1.3 miles

With dramatic mountains, rolling fells, glorious lakes and peaceful valleys, Broadrayne Farm is at the heart of the Lake District, superbly located for wonderful views. The traditional farm properties have been lovingly renovated with today's creature comforts, including open coal fires, central heating and off-street parking. Pets welcome by arrangement.

SAT NAV LA22 9RU ONLINE MAP

Unit TV SC 📼 📀 🖥 🍳 🔲 🍽 ❄ ♨ ◐   General 🐕 🏛 🛎 P ◐ S 🐎
Leisure U 🎵 🚲

For **key to symbols** see pages 16 and 17

GRASSINGTON, North Yorkshire Map ref 5B3 GUEST ACCOMMODATION

★★★★★
**GUEST ACCOMMODATION
GOLD AWARD**

B&B PER ROOM PER NIGHT
D £85.00–£100.00

Grassington Lodge

8 Wood Lane, Grassington, Skipton BD23 5LU t +44 (0) 1756 752518
e relax@grassingtonlodge.co.uk

grassingtonlodge.co.uk

open All year
bedrooms 6 double, 5 twin, 1 suite
bathrooms 11 en suite, 1 private
payment Credit/debit cards, cash, cheques, euros

Grassington Lodge is a contemporary-styled, comfortable Victorian guesthouse in a quiet setting less than 100yds from the centre of Grassington, the capital village of Upper Wharfedale.

SAT NAV BD23 5LU

Room ♿ 📺 💧 ✎ General ♿12 P 📶 ❄ Leisure ∪ ♪ ► ⚲

HARROGATE, North Yorkshire Map ref 4B1 HOTEL

Rating Applied For
HOTEL

B&B PER ROOM PER NIGHT
S £50.00–£130.00
D £80.00–£180.00
HB PER PERSON PER NIGHT
£60.00–£150.00

Free child places 0-4 years. Half-price 5-14 years. Christmas and New Year breaks available. Special last-minute breaks. See website.

Cairn Hotel

Ripon Road, Harrogate HG1 2JD t +44 (0) 1423 504005 e salescairn@strathmorehotels.com

strathmorehotels.com SPECIAL OFFERS · REAL-TIME BOOKING

open All year
bedrooms 36 double, 74 twin, 16 single, 4 family, 1 suite
bathrooms All en suite
payment Credit/debit cards, cash, cheques

Built during Harrogate's period as a spa town, stylish and comfortable decor goes hand in hand with gracious hospitality to offer a welcome that is second to none. This charming hotel is only five minutes' walk from the town centre – ideal for leisure breaks, meetings/conferences and exhibitions.

SAT NAV HG1 2JD **ONLINE MAP**

Room 🖼 📞 📺 🆂🅲 💧 ✎ General ♿ ▥ ♣ P 📶 ♟ 🍴 ◖ ▣ ♂ ❄ 🐾 Leisure 🏃

HARROGATE, North Yorkshire Map ref 4B1 GUEST ACCOMMODATION

★★★★
GUEST HOUSE

B&B PER ROOM PER NIGHT
S £38.00–£45.00
D £65.00–£70.00

Alamah Guest House

88 Kings Road, Harrogate HG1 5JX t +44 (0) 1423 502187 & +44 (0) 1423 502187
e alamahguesthouse@btconnect.com

An ideal base from which to explore North Yorkshire. A short walk to Harrogate's stylish shops, restaurants, theatre, gardens and Harrogate International Conference Centre. Yorkshire's breathtaking countryside within a short drive.

open All year
bedrooms 2 double, 2 twin, 2 single, 1 family
bathrooms 6 en suite, 1 private
payment Credit/debit cards, cash, cheques

Room 📺 💧 ✎ General ♿5 P 📶 ♨ 🍴

Remember to check when booking

Please remember that all information in this guide has been supplied by the proprietors well in advance of publication. Since changes do sometimes occur it's a good idea to check details at the time of booking.

HARROGATE, North Yorkshire Map ref 4B1 · SELF CATERING

★★★★
SELF CATERING

Units **3**
Sleeps **2–5**

LOW SEASON PER WK
£240.00–£325.00

HIGH SEASON PER WK
£395.00–£580.00

Dinmore Cottages, Burnt Yates, Harrogate

contact Denise Wales, Dinmore Cottages, Dinmore House, Pateley Bridge Road, Burnt Yates HG3 3ET **t** +44 (0) 1423 770860 **e** aib@dinmore-cottages.freeserve.co.uk

dinmore-cottages.co.uk

open All year
payment Credit/debit cards, cash, cheques, euros
nearest pub 1 mile
nearest shop 3 miles

Award-winning Dales cottages converted from 17thC farmstead. Peaceful situation, breathtaking views over Nidderdale, a protected Area of Outstanding Natural Beauty. Only seven miles to spa town of Harrogate, close to York and Herriot Country. Ideal for walkers and birdwatchers and for touring and sightseeing in the Yorkshire Dales.

Unit 📺 🖥 🗝 🍳 💷❄ General 🛋 🎢 🍴 P 🅿 Leisure ∪ ♪

HARROGATE, North Yorkshire Map ref 4B1 · SELF CATERING

★★★★★
SELF CATERING

Units **2**
Sleeps **2–4**

LOW SEASON PER WK
£1,155.00

HIGH SEASON PER WK
£1,155.00

Rudding Gates, Follifoot

contact Jan Mackaness, Rudding Park Estate Ltd, Haggs Farm, Haggs Road, Follifoot HG3 1EQ **t** +44 (0) 1423 844844 **e** info@rudding.com

rudding.com/gates GUEST REVIEWS · SPECIAL OFFERS · REAL-TIME BOOKING

open All year
payment Credit/debit cards, cash, cheques
nearest pub less than 0.5 miles
nearest shop less than 0.5 miles

These award-winning gatehouse apartments in Follifoot, just three miles from central Harrogate, provide the very latest in luxury self-catering accommodation. Decorated and equipped to the highest standard, they are the perfect destination for special holidays and indulgent weekend breaks. Each apartment has two en suite bedrooms, private parking and pretty walled gardens.

SAT NAV HG3 1DT **ONLINE MAP**

Unit 📺 SC 🍳 DVD 🖥 🗝 🍳 🖥 💷❄ General P S Leisure ∪▶

HAWKSHEAD, Cumbria Map ref 5A3 · GUEST ACCOMMODATION

★★★★
FARMHOUSE

B&B PER ROOM PER NIGHT
S £32.00–£38.00
D £27.00–£32.00

EVENING MEAL PER PERSON
£14.00

Crosslands Farm

Rusland, Hawkshead LA22 8JU **t** +44 (0) 1229 860242 **e** enquiries@crosslandsfarm.co.uk

crosslandsfarm.co.uk

open All year except Christmas
bedrooms 2 double, 1 twin
bathrooms 2 en suite, 1 private
payment Cash, cheques

Crosslands is a 17thC farmhouse with original features in the unspoilt valley of Rusland between the lakes of Windermere and Coniston. Perfect base for walking and cycling. Lots of lovely walks from the farm. Near Hawkshead, Grizedale Forest and all the lakeland hills. Plenty of parking. Great breakfast. Lovely views.

SAT NAV LA22 8JU

Room 📺 ♨ 🗝 General 🛋 🎢 🍴 P ✕ 🍲❄ 🐕 Leisure ∪ ♪ 🚴

HEXHAM, Northumberland Map ref 5B2   SELF CATERING

★★★★★
SELF CATERING

Units **1**
Sleeps **5**

LOW SEASON PER WK
£700.00

HIGH SEASON PER WK
£700.00

Any number of nights available (minimum 2).

Chapel House, Steel, Hexham

contact Mrs Joan Liddle, Chapel House, Peth Head Cottage, Juniper, Hexham NE47 0LA
t +44 (0) 1434 673286 e info@chapel-house.info

chapel-house.info

open All year
payment Credit/debit cards, cash, cheques, euros
nearest pub 2 miles
nearest shop 4 miles

Lovely secluded detached cottage with wonderful views and sunny south-facing garden. Spacious open plan living area featuring oil-fired Aga and inglenook fireplace with woodburning stove. Any number of nights available (minimum two).

Unit 📺 📠 🖥️ 🔌 🍴 🔲 🧺 ⚙️ ❄️ ⛏️   General 🐎 P 🅿️   Leisure ∪ ⚓ ▶ 🚴

HEXHAM, Northumberland Map ref 5B2   SELF CATERING

★★★★
SELF CATERING

Units **2**
Sleeps **2–4**

LOW SEASON PER WK
£280.00–£380.00

HIGH SEASON PER WK
£380.00–£480.00

Special-price weeks available Nov-Mar.

Sammy's Place/Broadway Apartment, Hexham

contact Mr & Mrs Ian and Susan Sibbald, 9 Charlton Close, Beaumont Park, Hexham NE46 2QF
t +44 (0) 1434 604143 & +44 (0) 7903 038623 e sammys-place@hotmail.com

sammyshideaway.com

open All year
payment Cash, cheques
nearest pub less than 0.5 miles
nearest shop less than 0.5 miles

Beautifully appointed self-catering apartments, ideal for couples, individuals and families. Situated in and around the heart of Hexham, Hadrian's Wall Country. Single level, one double, one twin, both en suite. Linen, towels, Sky TV, cooker, microwave, dishwasher, washer/dryer, fridge/freezer. Cot and highchair available. No pets/smoking.

SAT NAV *NE46 2EA*

Unit 📺 📠 🖥️ 🔌 🍴 🔲 🧺   General 🐎 🏠 ♿ P 🅿️ Ⓢ   Leisure ▶ 🚴

HIGH LORTON, Cumbria Map ref 5A3   SELF CATERING

★★★
SELF CATERING

Units **3**
Sleeps **2–8**

LOW SEASON PER WK
£210.00–£560.00

HIGH SEASON PER WK
£320.00–£820.00

High Swinside Holiday Cottages, High Lorton

contact Mr Jacques Hankin, High Swinside Holiday Cottages, High Swinside Farm, High Lorton, Cockermouth CA13 9UA t +44 (0) 1900 85206 e bookings@highswinside.demon.co.uk

highswinside.demon.co.uk

open All year
payment Cash, cheques
nearest pub 2 miles
nearest shop 2 miles

Former hill farm, overlooking Lorton Vale with stunning views and offering peace and tranquillity. Well-equipped cottages. Large groups (up to 14) can be catered for. Children welcome. Beams and log fires, together with meal service, make for a wonderful stay. Full details on our website.

ONLINE MAP

Unit 📺 🖥️ 🔌 🍴 🧺 ❄️ ⛏️   General 🐎 🏠 ♿ P 🅿️ Ⓢ   Leisure ∪ ⚓

HOLMFIRTH, West Yorkshire Map ref 4B1   **SELF CATERING**

★★★★
SELF CATERING

Units **1**
Sleeps **6**

LOW SEASON PER WK
Min £400.00

HIGH SEASON PER WK
Max £650.00

Book 2 weeks and get a 5% discount.

Manor Farm Cottage, Upper Denby, Huddersfield

contact Mrs C E Crossland, 37 Bank Lane, Huddersfield HD8 8UT **t** +44 (0) 1484 864722
e manorfarmcottage@btinternet.com

manorfarmcottage.com GUEST REVIEWS · SPECIAL OFFERS

open All year
payment Cash, cheques
nearest pub less than 0.5 miles
nearest shop 1.5 miles

This beautiful Grade II Listed 17thC farmhouse cottage provides high quality accommodation combining original features with new fixtures and fittings. Sleeps up to six people in one double bedroom and one family bedroom. Secure parking. Garden with patio and barbecue. Excellent walking country. Many places of interest within easy reach.

ONLINE MAP

Unit 📺 📀 💻 🛏 🍳 🔥 🍽 💷 ☀ ⛰ General 🐴 🏠 🚶 P ☐ Leisure ∪ ♪ ►

HOLMFIRTH, West Yorkshire Map ref 4B1   **SELF CATERING**

★★★★
SELF CATERING

Units **1**
Sleeps **1–5**

LOW SEASON PER WK
£200.00–£270.00

HIGH SEASON PER WK
£220.00–£400.00

Mytholmbridge Studio Cottage, Holmfirth

contact Sue Clay, Luke Lane, Holmfirth HD9 7TB **t** +44 (0) 1484 686642
e sue@mytholmbridge.co.uk

mytholmbridge.co.uk

Secluded 250-year-old stone barn situated in 'Last of the Summer Wine' country. Original beams retained within the contemporary open space. Light, spacious living area. Garden, large car park, close to local amenities.

open All year
payment Credit/debit cards, cash, cheques, euros
nearest pub less than 0.5 miles
nearest shop less than 0.5 miles

Unit 📺 📀 💻 🛏 🍳 🔥 🍽 ☀ ⛰ General 🐴 🏠 🚶 P Ⓢ Leisure ♪

KERMINCHAM, Cheshire Map ref 4B2   **GUEST ACCOMMODATION**

★★★★
FARMHOUSE

B&B PER ROOM PER NIGHT
S £35.00–£40.00
D £70.00–£80.00

EVENING MEAL PER PERSON
£12.00–£25.00

The Fields Farm

Forty Acre Lane, Crewe CW4 8DY **t** +44 (0) 1477 571224

theenglishdiningroom.co.uk GUEST REVIEWS

Quality accommodation in English country house. Ideal for business people, families and small groups. Cordon bleu evening meal available. Ideally located for opera, market towns and attractions.

open All year
bedrooms 2 double, 1 twin, 1 single
bathrooms 2 en suite, 2 private
payment Cash, cheques, euros

Room 🛏 📺 🍵 🍴 General 🐴 P ✕ 🖥 💷 ☀ Leisure ∪ ♪ ►

Don't forget www.

Web addresses throughout this guide are shown without the prefix www. Please include www. in the address line of your browser.
If a web address does not follow this style it is shown in full.

KESWICK, Cumbria Map ref 5A3 — HOTEL

★ ★
HOTEL

B&B PER ROOM PER NIGHT
S £40.00–£45.00
D £80.00–£99.00
HB PER PERSON PER NIGHT
£55.00–£70.00

3 or 5 nights' DB&B breaks available all year.

Crow Park Hotel

The Heads, Keswick CA12 5ER   t +44 (0) 1768 772208   e enquiries@crowpark.co.uk

crowpark.co.uk REAL-TIME BOOKING

open All year except Christmas
bedrooms 17 double, 7 twin, 4 single
bathrooms 26 en suite, 2 private
payment Credit/debit cards, cash, cheques

Centrally located, but quiet hotel overlooking Crow Park, Derwent Water and Catbells. Hope Park, with its golf course, is 30m away and the Theatre on the Lake 500m. Private parking for 23 cars. The hotel has some of the best views in Keswick.

SAT NAV CA12 5ER **ONLINE MAP**

Room 🛗🖨📺👘🍽   General 🛋🚪P🍽🍵❄🐾   Leisure ∪♦▶🚴

KESWICK, Cumbria Map ref 5A3 — GUEST ACCOMMODATION

★ ★ ★ ★ ★
**GUEST HOUSE
SILVER AWARD**

B&B PER ROOM PER NIGHT
S £72.00–£86.00
D £90.00–£106.00

Special rates are normally available for a stay of three or more nights, please contact us to find out more.

The Grange Country House

Manor Brow, Ambleside Road, Keswick CA12 4BA   t +44 (0) 17687 72500
e info@grangekeswick.com

grangekeswick.com GUEST REVIEWS · SPECIAL OFFERS · REAL-TIME BOOKING

open All year except mid-December to early February
bedrooms 6 double, 3 twin, 1 single
bathrooms All en suite
payment Credit/debit cards, cash, cheques

Spacious rooms, beautifully decorated, furnished with quality bedding, flat-screen televisions, Fairtrade beverage trays, mineral water and super toiletries. Superb freshly prepared Cumbrian breakfast, free 24-hour Wi-Fi access, lounge and scenic outdoor terrace. Ample off-street parking.

SAT NAV CA12 4BA **ONLINE MAP**

Room 📞📺🆂🅲👘🍽   General 🛋10 P👘🍽🍵❄   Leisure ∪♦▶🚴

KESWICK, Cumbria Map ref 5A3 — CAMPING, CARAVAN & HOLIDAY PARK

★ ★ ★ ★
**HOLIDAY, TOURING
& CAMPING PARK**

🚐(53) £15.00–£21.00
🚐(53) £14.00–£21.00
⛺(120) £13.00–£16.00
🏕(7) £220.00–£470.00

10% discount on your stay for all ANWB, ACSI, ADAC cardholders.

Castlerigg Hall Caravan & Camping Park

Castlerigg Hall, Keswick CA12 4TE   t +44 (0) 17687 74499   e info@castlerigg.co.uk

castlerigg.co.uk SPECIAL OFFERS

open 20 March to 9 November
payment Credit/debit cards, cash, cheques

Situated 1.5 miles south east of the pretty market town of Keswick, our elevated position commands wonderful panoramic views of Derwentwater and the surrounding fells. Formerly a Lakeland hill farm, Castlerigg Hall has been sympathetically developed into a quality touring park. Many scenic walks are available directly from the park.

SAT NAV CA12 4TE

General 🔌🗑🚿🆆🅿🍴📲📟🧺🐕☀🍵   Leisure 📶∪♦🚴

KIELDER FOREST

See under Kielder Water, Wark

KIELDER WATER, Northumberland Map ref 5B2

★★★★★
SELF CATERING

Units **4**
Sleeps **1–6**

LOW SEASON PER WK
£200.00–£300.00

HIGH SEASON PER WK
£500.00–£800.00

Short breaks, golf, riding, pamper, fine dining, special celebrations/ weddings. Sleeps 14 if rented as a whole.

Falstone Barns, Nr Kielder Water and Forest Park, Hexham

contact Mrs Nicolette Forster, Falstone Barns, Falstone Farm, Falstone, Hexham NE48 1AA
t +44 (0) 1434 240251 & +44 (0) 7891 817185 **e** info@falstonebarns.com

falstonebarns.com SPECIAL OFFERS · REAL-TIME BOOKING

open All year
payment Credit/debit cards, cash, cheques
nearest pub less than 0.5 miles
nearest shop less than 0.5 miles

Barn conversions near Kielder Water offering luxurious themed holiday apartments; set in 38 acres of private estate, offering tailor-made holidays.

SAT NAV NE48 1AA

Unit 📺 SC 🎬 📷 🖥️ 🍽️ 🔌 🔥 💡 🧺 ❄️ 🛁 ⚬ General 🛋️ 🏠 🅿️ 🅾️ Ⓢ 🐕
Leisure ⚓ ∪ ♪ ♦ 🚴

KIRKBY MALZEARD, North Yorkshire Map ref 5C3

★★★★
SELF CATERING

Units **1**
Sleeps **6**

LOW SEASON PER WK
£300.00–£370.00

HIGH SEASON PER WK
£430.00–£580.00

Alma Cottage, Kirkby Malzeard, Ripon

contact Mrs Janet Barclay, 12 St Stephen's Road, Cold Norton, Chelmsford CM3 6JE
t +44 (0) 1621 828576 **e** janet@lbarclay.demon.co.uk

almacottage.co.uk GUEST REVIEWS

Comfortable three-bedroom period cottage in stone terrace of friendly Nidderdale village. Ideal for dales, moors, walking, cycling, riding, sightseeing and birdwatching. Walled garden, secure garage, one double, two twins.

open All year
payment Cash, cheques
nearest pub less than 0.5 miles
nearest shop less than 0.5 miles

Unit 📺 🎬 🖥️ 🍽️ 🔌 🔥 💡 ❄️ 🛁 ⚬ General 🛋️ 🏠 🅿️ 🅾️ Ⓢ Leisure ⚓ ∪ ♪

KNARESBOROUGH, North Yorkshire Map ref 4B1

★★★★
SELF CATERING

Units **1**
Sleeps **1–2**

LOW SEASON PER WK
£295.00–£325.00

HIGH SEASON PER WK
£260.00–£295.00

Short breaks available. 3-night stays Oct-Mar.

The Granary, Knaresborough

contact Mrs Rachel Thornton, Gibbet House Farm, Farnham Lane, Knaresborough HG5 9JP
t +44 (0) 1423 862325 & +44 (0) 7970 000068

open All year
payment Cash, cheques, euros
nearest pub 1.5 miles
nearest shop 1.5 miles

Traditional, converted granary adjacent to farmhouse. Situated in 30 acres of parkland with stunning views of the Nidderdale Valley. Furnished to a high standard. Five miles Harrogate, two miles Knaresborough. Central for Dales, Yorkshire coast, Herriot and Heartbeat Country. The perfect setting for a peaceful and comfortable holiday.

Unit 📺 🖥️ 🔌 🔥 💡 🧺 ❄️ General 🅿️ 🅾️ Ⓢ Leisure ∪ ♪ ♦

LANGCLIFFE, North Yorkshire Map ref 5B3 — SELF CATERING

★★★
SELF CATERING

Units **1**
Sleeps **4**

LOW SEASON PER WK
£160.00–£200.00

HIGH SEASON PER WK
£270.00–£300.00

Bear Cottage, Langcliffe, Nr Settle
contact Mr D Widdop, 1 St Johns Row, Langcliffe BD24 9NJ t +44 (0) 1729 824363
e jayne.craig2@btopenworld.com

bear-cottage.com

An early 19thC terraced cottage in a small picturesque village overlooking Langcliffe village green. It has a warm, cosy feel, tucked away to the side of the old chapel.

open All year
payment Cash, cheques
nearest pub 1 mile
nearest shop 1 mile

Unit TV SC DVD ▣ 🖥 🖪 ☀ ⚒ ∅ General ⚄5 P S Leisure 🎣 ⚲ U ♪ ► 🚴

LEEDS, West Yorkshire Map ref 4B1 — HOTEL

★★
HOTEL

B&B PER ROOM PER NIGHT
S £35.00–£45.00
D £55.00–£65.00
HB PER PERSON PER NIGHT
£45.00–£55.00

5% discount for 6 or more days and group bookings.

Ascot Grange Hotel
126-130 Otley Road, Leeds LS16 5JX t +44 (0) 113 293 4444 e ascotgrangehotel@hotmail.com

ascotgrangehotel.com GUEST REVIEWS · REAL-TIME BOOKING

open All year except Christmas and New Year
bedrooms 7 double, 7 twin, 10 single, 3 family
bathrooms All en suite
payment Credit/debit cards, cash, cheques

In the heart of Far Headingley, two miles from city centre. A walk away from bars, restaurants, public transport and the university. Private parking for all hotel residents. All bedrooms en suite, with Freeview TV, telephones and internet. Bar and restaurant in the hotel. A warm welcome from friendly staff.

SAT NAV LS16 5JX ONLINE MAP

Room ♿ 🛏 ☎ TV 🍴 ⚲ ⚑ General ⚄ 🏛 ♨ P ⚟ 🍷 ☀

LEEDS, West Yorkshire Map ref 4B1 — GUEST ACCOMMODATION

★★
GUEST ACCOMMODATION

B&B PER ROOM PER NIGHT
S £34.00–£44.00
D £48.00–£60.00

EVENING MEAL PER PERSON
£6.00–£10.00

Special three-night weekend stay. Double en suite £54pn incl breakfast.

The Moorlea
146 Woodsley Road, Leeds LS2 9LZ t +44 (0) 113 243 2653 e themoorleahotel@aol.com

open All year
bedrooms 3 double, 1 twin, 5 single, 2 family
bathrooms 6 en suite
payment Credit/debit cards, cash, cheques

Five minutes from the university and 15 minutes from the city centre. Friendly atmosphere and fully licensed bar. Quality cooked English breakfasts. Two miles from Test Match cricket ground in Headingley.

SAT NAV LS2 9LZ

Room ♿ 🍴 ⚲ General ⚄ 🏛 🍷 ✕ 🍳 ☀ ⌂

LEEDS, West Yorkshire Map ref 4B1 — GUEST ACCOMMODATION

★★★
GUEST HOUSE

B&B PER ROOM PER NIGHT
S £27.00–£37.00
D £40.00–£50.00

St Michael's Guest House
5 St Michael's Villas, Cardigan Road, Leeds LS6 3AF t +44 (0) 113 275 5557
e stmichaels-guesthouse@hotmail.co.uk

stmichaels-guesthouse.co.uk

Well-presented B&B, 1.5 miles from city centre and close to Headingley Cricket Ground and university. Easy access to Headingley and the city centre. Warm welcome from friendly staff.

open All year except Christmas and New Year
bedrooms 8 double, 6 twin, 8 single, 2 family
bathrooms 13 en suite
payment Credit/debit cards, cash, cheques

Room ♿ TV 🍴 General ⚄ 🏛 ♨ P ✕

LEEDS BRADFORD INTERNATIONAL AIRPORT

See under Leeds, Otley

LIVERPOOL, Merseyside Map ref 4A2

★★★
GUEST ACCOMMODATION

B&B PER ROOM PER NIGHT
S £21.00–£28.00
D £48.00–£59.00

Holme-Leigh Guest House

93 Woodcroft Road, Wavertree, Liverpool L15 2HG t +44 (0) 151 734 2216 e info@holmeleigh.com

holmeleigh.com GUEST REVIEWS · SPECIAL OFFERS · REAL-TIME BOOKING

Victorian, red-brick, three-storey corner guesthouse, just 2.5 miles from city centre, two miles from M62 and close to Sefton Park.

open All year
bedrooms 2 double, 9 twin, 2 single, 2 family
bathrooms All en suite
payment Credit/debit cards, cash, cheques

Room 🛏 📺 🍴 General 🐾 🛏

LIVERPOOL, Merseyside Map ref 4A2

★★★★
SELF CATERING

Units   2
Sleeps   4–6

LOW SEASON PER WK
£500.00

HIGH SEASON PER WK
£600.00

Port Sunlight Village Trust, Port Sunlight, Wirral

contact Mrs Sandra Nicholls, 95 Greendale Road, Port Sunlight, Wirral CH62 4XE
t +44 (0) 151 644 4801 e s.nicholls@portsunlightvillage.com

portsunlightvillage.com

open All year
payment Credit/debit cards, cash, cheques
nearest pub 0.5 miles
nearest shop 0.5 miles

Grade II Listed cottages located in the heart of Port Sunlight garden village amid picturesque surroundings. Within easy reach of Chester, Liverpool and North Wales.

Unit 📺 🖥 💻 🔲 📷 🍽 📱 ☼ General 🐾 P Ⓢ Leisure ∪ ⤵ ▶

LONGHORSLEY, Northumberland Map ref 5C1

★★★★
SELF CATERING

Units   1
Sleeps   8

LOW SEASON PER WK
£500.00–£850.00

HIGH SEASON PER WK
£975.00–£1,250.00

West Moor Farm Cottage, Longhorsley

contact Mrs Carolyn Raven, West Moor Farm Cottage, West Moor Farm, Longhorsley NE65 8QX
t +44 (0) 7816 245678 e info@westmoorfarm.co.uk

westmoorfarm.co.uk

open All year
payment Cash, cheques, euros
nearest pub 1.5 miles
nearest shop 1.5 miles

This four-bedroom cottage with views over the Cheviots has been described as having the wow factor! On site is a livery/trekking yard. We welcome pets and encourage horse-owners to bring their animals on holiday too. Many bridleways/footpaths and beaches, plus golf courses. Please take a look at the virtual tour on our website.

Unit 📺 🖥 💻 🖨 🍽 📷 🍽 📱 ☼ ⚒ ✎ General 🐾 🛏 ⚿ P ◎ Ⓢ 🐕
Leisure ▶ 🚲

Do you like walking?

Walkers feel at home in accommodation participating in our Walkers Welcome scheme.
Look out for the symbol. Consider walking all or part of a long-distance route – go online at nationaltrail.co.uk.

★★★★
SELF CATERING

Units **1**
Sleeps **1–2**

LOW SEASON PER WK
£250.00–£265.00

HIGH SEASON PER WK
£330.00–£410.00

Curlew Cottage, Low Row, Richmond

contact Mrs Rachel Browning, 8 Hyperion Drive, Rochester ME2 3RG t +44 (0) 1634 725273
e hillsr1@hotmail.com

curlew-cottage.org.uk

Curlew Cottage is a delightful one-bedroom
Grade II Listed 18thC former lead miner's cottage,
commanding spectacular views over Swaledale in
the heart of the Yorkshire Dales National Park.

open All year
payment Cheques
nearest pub 0.5 miles
nearest shop 4 miles

Unit 📺 🖥 💻 📠 🍴 🔘 🍽 🗄 ❄ General 🎠 P Ⓢ 🐎 Leisure ∪

★★★★
HOTEL

B&B PER ROOM PER NIGHT
S £90.00–£150.00
D £100.00–£200.00
HB PER PERSON PER NIGHT
£60.00–£125.00

*All our special offers
are to be found on
our website –
updated daily!*

The Grand Hotel

South Promenade, St Annes-on-Sea, Lytham St Annes FY8 1NB t +44 (0) 1253 643424 &
+44 (0) 1253 721288 e book@the-grand.co.uk

the-grand.co.uk GUEST REVIEWS · SPECIAL OFFERS · REAL-TIME BOOKING

open All year except Christmas
bedrooms 43 double, 2 family, 10 suites
bathrooms All en suite
payment Credit/debit cards, cash

55 superbly appointed bedrooms, all individually
designed and all with fine linen bedding. The hotel's
Cafe Grand is a modern bar/restaurant with a wide
range of beers and wines from around the world.
Local specialist suppliers provide most of the
ingredients that create the menu's innovative dishes.

SAT NAV FY8 1NB ONLINE MAP

Room 🔧 📞 📺 👤 🍴 🌿 General 🎠 P 🔫 🍷 🍴 🌙 🛗 ⊜ 🍽 🌸
Leisure 🎣 🏊 ⛱ ➤

★★★★
SELF CATERING

Units **1**
Sleeps **1–5**

LOW SEASON PER WK
£225.00–£380.00

HIGH SEASON PER WK
£380.00–£520.00

*Ribble Way walking,
Ribble Estuary
birdwatching,
Christmas and New
Year.*

Lytham Holiday Cottage, Lytham

contact Mr & Mrs Llewellyn, 5 Rosewood Close, Lytham St Annes FY8 4PE t +44 (0) 1253 739598 &
+44 (0) 7941 866447 e cottage@llewellyns.freeserve.co.uk

freewebs.com/lytham-holiday-cottage SPECIAL OFFERS

open All year
payment Cash, cheques, euros
nearest pub less than 0.5 miles
nearest shop less than 0.5 miles

Modern mews cottage, two bedrooms, one king-
double, one twin (sleeps four/five with cot or
foldaway bed), lounge, dining/kitchen, jacuzzi
bathroom, cot, highchair. Freeview TV, DVD
recorder. Electric cooker, gas hob. Dishwasher,
fridge-freezer, microwave, washing machine.
0.25 miles Lytham Green, 0.5 miles town centre.
Rear garden, barbecue and furniture. Parking.

SAT NAV FY8 5AU

Unit 📺 🖥 💻 🖨 📠 🍴 🔘 🍽 🗄 ❄ 🍳 General 🎠 🛏 🐾 P 🔲 Ⓢ

PETS! WELCOME
WELCOME PETS!

Where is my pet welcome?

Want to take your cherished companion with you on holiday? Proprietors participating
in our Welcome Pets! scheme go out of their way to make special provision for you and
your pet. Look out for the symbol.

MALTON, North Yorkshire Map ref 5D3 — SELF CATERING

★★★★
SELF CATERING

Units **1**
Sleeps **1–4**

LOW SEASON PER WK
£204.00–£249.00

HIGH SEASON PER WK
£283.00–£442.00

£25 discount for stays of 2 weeks or longer.

Walnut Garth, Nr Malton
t +44 (0) 7766 208348 e cas@walnutgarth.co.uk

walnutgarth.co.uk GUEST REVIEWS

open All year
payment Cash, cheques
nearest pub less than 0.5 miles
nearest shop less than 0.5 miles

Tastefully decorated, two-bedroom cottage furnished to a high standard with all modern conveniences. Walnut Garth is set in the grounds of owner's property at edge of village, yet only two miles from market town of Malton and excellent selection of local amenities and attractions. Easy access to York and coast.

ONLINE MAP

Unit 📺 ▦ 🎦 💻 🖨 🖳 🔌 🧺 🛒 ✂️ ✳️ General 🦮 🏚 ♿ P 🅿 🐕 Leisure 🎣

MANCHESTER, Greater Manchester Map ref 4B1 — GUEST ACCOMMODATION

★★★
GUEST ACCOMMODATION

B&B PER ROOM PER NIGHT
S **£55.00–£60.00**
D **£58.00–£65.00**

EVENING MEAL PER PERSON
£5.00–£14.00

Stay Inn – Manchester
55 Blackfriars Road, Salford, Manchester M3 7DB t +44 (0) 161 907 2277 e info@stayinn.co.uk

stayinn.co.uk GUEST REVIEWS · REAL-TIME BOOKING

open All year
bedrooms 41 double, 12 twin, 12 family
bathrooms All en suite
payment Credit/debit cards, cash, euros

Modern, purpose-built hotel offering excellent value for money. Free car parking, city-centre location, close to railway station. Five minutes' walk from the MEN Arena, and further five minutes from GMEX and MICC. Residents' bar open until 0100. Breakfast from £5.95 to £7.25 for a full English.

SAT NAV M3 7DB **ONLINE MAP**

Room 🛗 📺 🆂🅲 🧴 🔌 🍵 General 🦮 🏚 ♿ P 🅿 📶 🎥 🍽 ✕ 🖥 ✳️

MANCHESTER AIRPORT

See under Manchester, Wilmslow

MASHAM, North Yorkshire Map ref 5C3 — HOTEL

★★★★
HOTEL
GOLD AWARD

B&B PER ROOM PER NIGHT
S **£160.00–£350.00**
D **£160.00–£350.00**
HB PER PERSON PER NIGHT
£115.00–£210.00

Swinton Park
Ripon HG4 4JH t +44 (0) 1765 680900 e enquiries@swintonpark.com

swintonpark.com GUEST REVIEWS · SPECIAL OFFERS · REAL-TIME BOOKING

A family home since the late 1800s, Swinton Park has played host to country-house parties of legendary style and grandeur. Mark and Felicity Cunliffe-Lister are proud to welcome you to join them to continue this tradition.

open All year
bedrooms 26 double, 4 suites
bathrooms All en suite
payment Credit/debit cards, cash, cheques, euros

Room 🛏 📞 📺 🧴 🔌 🛗 General 🦮 🏚 ♿ P 🅿 📶 🍽 🎱 ♨ 📺 ⚒ ✳️ 🐕
Leisure 🏊 🎯 🎾 U 🎣 🚶 🚴

Looking for an ideal family break?

For accommodation offering additional facilities and services for a range of ages and family units, look out for the Families Welcome symbol. Owners of these properties will go out of their way to welcome families.

MIDDLEHAM, North Yorkshire Map ref 5C3 — SELF CATERING

★★★★
SELF CATERING

Units **1**
Sleeps **1–5**

LOW SEASON PER WK
Min £322.00

HIGH SEASON PER WK
Min £491.00

Middle Cottage, Middleham, Leyburn

contact Mrs Jennie Perren, 2 North Park Grove, Roundhay, Leeds LS8 1JJ t +44 (0) 113 237 1817
e jennifer.perren@btinternet.com

yorkshire-dales-holiday-cottage.co.uk

Sitting room with dining area, kitchen, three bedrooms, bathroom with shower. Electric heating, garden to the rear, parking 200yds.

open All year
payment Cash, cheques
nearest pub less than 0.5 miles
nearest shop less than 0.5 miles

Unit 📺 ⬛⬛ 💿 ⬛ ⬛⬛ 🍳 ⬛⬛ ✳️ ⛺ ∅   General 🛏 Ⓢ 🐕   Leisure ∪ ♪

MORECAMBE, Lancashire Map ref 5A3 — GUEST ACCOMMODATION

★★★
GUEST ACCOMMODATION

B&B PER ROOM PER NIGHT
S Min £30.00
D £58.00–£60.00

EVENING MEAL PER PERSON
Min £9.00

The Clifton

Marine Road West, Morecambe LA3 1BZ t +44 (0) 1524 411573 e clifton.hotel@btinternet.com

hotel-clifton.co.uk

Family-run seafront guesthouse with 45 en suite rooms, bar and dance floor. Comfortable, with great service. Groups welcome.

open All year except January and February
bedrooms 18 double, 11 twin, 9 single, 7 family
bathrooms All en suite
payment Credit/debit cards, cash, cheques

Room 🔓 📺 ☕   General 🏛 🔥 P 🍷 ✕ 🍴 ✳️

MORECAMBE, Lancashire Map ref 5A3 — GUEST ACCOMMODATION

★★★
GUEST HOUSE

B&B PER ROOM PER NIGHT
S £21.00–£25.00
D £40.00–£50.00

EVENING MEAL PER PERSON
£6.00–£12.00

Silverwell

20 West End Road, Morecambe LA4 4DL t +44 (0) 1524 410532 e svlerwll@aol.com

silverwellguesthouse.co.uk

Victorian terraced guesthouse 100yds from promenade. Within easy reach of shops and amenities. Ideal as base for the Lakes and dales.

open All year
bedrooms 4 double, 2 twin, 7 single, 1 family
bathrooms 6 en suite
payment Credit/debit cards

Room 🔓 📺 ☕ 🍳 🍽   General 🛏8 🍷 ✕ 🍴

MORPETH, Northumberland Map ref 5C2 — GUEST ACCOMMODATION

★★
GUEST HOUSE

B&B PER ROOM PER NIGHT
S £35.00–£40.00
D £55.00–£60.00

Child discounts available.

Cottage View Guesthouse

6 Staithes Lane, Morpeth NE61 1TD t +44 (0) 1670 518550 e bookings@cottageview.co.uk

cottageview.co.uk REAL-TIME BOOKING

open All year
bedrooms 10 double, 6 twin, 6 single, 3 family
bathrooms 19 en suite, 6 private
payment Credit/debit cards, cash, cheques

Centrally situated, family-run guesthouse. Private car parking, reception bar, two lounges (one private), email and fax facilities (small charge made). Night porter available for late arrivals/early departures. We can accommodate over 50 people – ideal for wedding guests. So don't delay, book today!

SAT NAV NE61 1TD **ONLINE MAP**

Room 🔓 📺 ☕   General 🛏 🏛 🔥 P 📶 🍷 🐕

Using map references

The map references refer to the colour maps at the front of this guide. The first figure is the map number, the letter and figure that follow indicate the grid reference on the map.

★★★★
GUEST ACCOMMODATION

B&B PER ROOM PER NIGHT
S Max £45.00
D £75.00–£100.00

Muncaster Coachman's Quarters

Muncaster Castle, Muncaster, Ravenglass CA18 1RQ t +44 (0) 1229 717614 e info@muncaster.co.uk

muncaster.co.uk

open All year
bedrooms 4 double, 4 twin, 2 family
bathrooms 9 en suite
payment Credit/debit cards, cash, cheques

The Coachman's Quarters are within the stable yard of the magnificent Muncaster Gardens. One room has facilities for people with disabilities. The Granary is a large bedroom with lounge area and kitchenette. Tariff includes admission to the Gardens, World Owl Centre, MeadowVole Maze, Darkest Muncaster when operational, and reduced entry to the Castle.

SAT NAV CA18 1RQ

Room 🛏 📺 🕯 🍵 General 🐎 🏛 🛏 P ⚐ ✳ 🐕 Leisure ∪ ►

★★★★
SELF CATERING

Units   5
Sleeps   2–7

LOW SEASON PER WK
£275.00–£450.00

HIGH SEASON PER WK
£350.00–£650.00

Near Howe Cottages, Penrith

contact Steve & Jill Woolley, Near Howe Cottages, Near Howe, Mungrisdale, Penrith CA11 0SH
t +44 (0) 17687 79678 e enquiries@nearhowe.co.uk

nearhowe.co.uk GUEST REVIEWS · REAL-TIME BOOKING

open All year
payment Cash, cheques, euros
nearest pub 2 miles
nearest shop 5 miles

The ideal answer for a stress-free, away-from-it-all holiday, set amidst 350 acres of open moorland. All cottages have spectacular views over the Cumbrian Fells. Large garden with relaxation areas. Easily accessible, yet isolated enough to ensure peace and tranquillity.

ONLINE MAP

Unit 📺 🖥 💻 🗄 🍴 ✳ 🍳 General 🐎 🏛 🛏 P ⚐ 🐕 Leisure ∪ ♪ ► 🚴

★★★
GUEST ACCOMMODATION

B&B PER ROOM PER NIGHT
S £29.00–£40.00
D £69.00–£72.00

EVENING MEAL PER PERSON
£12.50–£20.00

Clifton House

46 Clifton Road, Off Grainger Park Road, Newcastle upon Tyne NE4 6XH t +44 (0) 191 273 0407
e cliftonhousehotel@hotmail.com

cliftonhousehotel.com

Comfortable, elegant country-style house with private grounds and car park. Close to the city, central for travel, sightseeing and shopping. Evening meals by arrangement.

open All year except Christmas
bedrooms 2 double, 2 twin, 4 single, 3 family
bathrooms 9 en suite
payment Credit/debit cards, cash, cheques

Room 📺 🕯 General 🐎 🏛 🛏 P 🦽 ♟ ✗ ✳ 🐕

What if I need to cancel?

It is advisable to check the proprietor's cancellation policy in case you have to change your plans at a later date.

NORTH DALTON, East Riding of Yorkshire Map ref 4C1

SELF CATERING

★★★
SELF CATERING

Units **1**
Sleeps **3–4**

LOW SEASON PER WK
£200.00–£315.00

HIGH SEASON PER WK
£330.00–£410.00

Short breaks available, 2 nights (excl Christmas, New Year, Easter and Bank Holidays).

Old Cobbler's Cottage, Driffield, North Dalton

contact Chris Wade, Waterfront Cottages, 2 Star Row, North Dalton, Driffield YO25 9UX
t +44 (0) 1377 217662 & +44 (0) 7801 124264 e chris.wade@adastra-music.co.uk

waterfrontcottages.co.uk

open All year
payment Credit/debit cards, cash, cheques
nearest pub less than 0.5 miles
nearest shop 1.5 miles

19thC, mid-terraced, oak-beamed cottage overlooking picturesque pond in a peaceful and friendly farming village, between York and Yorkshire's Heritage Coast. Ideally located for walking, visiting the coast, historic houses, races at York and Beverley or just relaxing. Excellent inn/restaurant adjacent, shops 1.5 miles. Pets welcome

Unit 📺 🎞️ 📀 💻 ▪️ 🔌 🔲 🍳 🧺 🚿 ⛺ 🪆 🍃 General 🐕 🏛️ ♿ P 🅾️ S 🐾 Leisure ▶

OTLEY, West Yorkshire Map ref 4B1

SELF CATERING

★★★★
SELF CATERING

Units **1**
Sleeps **13**

LOW SEASON PER WK
£700.00–£900.00

HIGH SEASON PER WK
£800.00–£1,200.00

The Birches, Otley

contact Liz Burrows, The Old Rectory, The Green, Guiseley LS20 9BB t +44 (0) 7799 142745
e lzburrows@aol.com

chevinvista.co.uk

open All year
payment Cash, cheques
nearest pub 1 mile
nearest shop 1 mile

Large seven-bedroomed detached property. Four doubles, two singles, one bunk room, each with LCD TV and Sky link. Property has two lounges, large kitchen/diner with spectacular views and balcony off, and games room with full-size pool table. Located next to Chevin Forest.

Unit 📺 SC 📀 📷 ▪️ 🔲 🍳 🔌 🔲 🍳 🚿 ⛺ General 🐕 🏛️ ♿ P 🅾️ S 🐾
Leisure 🎣 ∪ ▶ 🚴

PICKERING, North Yorkshire Map ref 5D3

GUEST ACCOMMODATION

★★★★★
GUEST ACCOMMODATION
GOLD AWARD

B&B PER ROOM PER NIGHT
S £60.00–£80.00
D £75.00–£95.00

The Old Vicarage

Toftly View, Pickering YO18 8QD t +44 (0) 1751 476126 e oldvic@toftlyview.co.uk

toftlyview.co.uk

The Old Vicarage at Toftly View offers stylish accommodation in a stunning location with wonderful south-facing views towards the Wolds. You will find a warm welcome and a high standard of comfort.

open February to October
bedrooms 4 double
bathrooms All en suite
payment Credit/debit cards, cash, cheques

Room 🛏️ 📺 🍴 🔌 General 10 P 🕸️ 🔥 🍽️ 🔆

Place index

If you know where you want to stay, the index by place name at the back of the guide will give you the page number listing accommodation in your chosen town, city or village. Check out the other useful indexes too.

PONTELAND, Northumberland Map ref 5C2   **SELF CATERING**

★★★
SELF CATERING

Units **2**
Sleeps **4**

LOW SEASON PER WK
£206.00–£398.00

HIGH SEASON PER WK
£358.00–£500.00

The Old Stables and The Old Tack Room,
Newcastle upon Tyne

contact Miss Clare Stephenson, The Old Stables and The Old Tack Room, North Road, Newcastle upon Tyne NE20 9UR **t** +44 (0) 1661 822188 & +44 (0) 7786 537424 **e** elandgreen@msn.com

elandfarm.co.uk

Conversion of farm buildings. Both sleep four – one double and one twin in each. On 200-acre grassland farm.

open All year
payment Cash, cheques
nearest pub 0.5 miles
nearest shop 0.5 miles

Unit 📺 🔲 💻 🗄 🍳 🗑 ⚙ ❄ ⛺ General 🔥 🛏 🅿 🆂 Leisure ● 🔍 ⛵ 🎣

RIBBLE VALLEY

See under Whalley

RICHMOND, North Yorkshire Map ref 5C3   **GUEST ACCOMMODATION**

★★★★★
BED & BREAKFAST
SILVER AWARD

B&B PER ROOM PER NIGHT
S £40.00
D £60.00

3rd night half price.

New Skeeby Grange
Sedbury Lane, Skeeby, Richmond DL10 5ED **t** +44 (0) 1748 822276 **e** gandmf@tiscali.co.uk

newskeebygrange.co.uk GUEST REVIEWS

open All year except Christmas and New Year
bedrooms 1 double, 1 family
bathrooms All en suite
payment Cash, cheques

We welcome you to our lovely, luxury accommodation, peaceful and quiet, surrounded by farmland. Both attractive en suite bedrooms overlook our garden, full of birds; watch our woodpecker family feeding whilst you enjoy a hearty English breakfast of locally produced bacon, sausage and free range eggs to set you up for a day's sightseeing!

SAT NAV DL10 5ED **ONLINE MAP**

Room 📺 ♿ 🍳 General 🔥5 🅿 🍴 ❄ Leisure U 🎣 🚲

RICHMOND, North Yorkshire Map ref 5C3   **GUEST ACCOMMODATION**

★★★★
GUEST ACCOMMODATION

B&B PER ROOM PER NIGHT
S £60.00–£70.00
D £70.00–£80.00

Nuns Cottage
5 Hurgill Road, Richmond DL10 4AR **t** +44 (0) 1748 822809 **e** the.flints@ukgateway.net

nunscottage.co.uk

Nuns Cottage is an 18thC house set in secluded gardens. Comfortable bedrooms. Five minutes from the centre of Richmond. Easy access to the A1 and the beautiful Yorkshire Dales.

open All year except Christmas and New Year
bedrooms 1 double, 1 twin
bathrooms 2 private
payment Cash, cheques, euros

Room 📺 ♿ 🍳 General 🔥12 ❄ Leisure U 🎣 ⛵

Where can I find accessible accommodation?

If you have special hearing, visual or mobility needs, there's an index of National Accessible Scheme participants featured in this guide. For more accessible accommodation buy a copy of Easy Access Britain available online at visitbritaindirect.com, and from Tourism for All on 0845 124 997 or visit tourismforall.org.uk.

RICHMOND, North Yorkshire Map ref 5C3

★★★★
SELF CATERING

Units **1**
Sleeps **2–4**

LOW SEASON PER WK
Max £250.00

HIGH SEASON PER WK
Max £370.00

Bookings taken for 3-7nights out of season if available. Price from £50 per night.

Coach House, Whashton, Richmond

contact Mrs Fairlie Turnbull, Coach House, New Skeeby Grange, Skeeby, Richmond DL10 5ED
t +44 (0) 1748 822276 e gandmf@tiscali.co.uk

newskeebygrange.co.uk

open All year
payment Cash, cheques
nearest pub 1.5 miles
nearest shop 3 miles

Oak-beamed coach house on our family working farm three miles from historic Richmond, gateway to Swaledale. Both bedrooms have a wonderful view over our farmland and the hills beyond. A small patio opens out from the sitting room, where you can dine and enjoy a glass of wine in the sunshine!

SAT NAV DL11 7JS

Unit 📺 🖥 💻 🗄 🍴 🔥 🍽 🛁 ✳ General 🐾 🏠 🅿 Ⓢ Leisure ∪ ♪ 🚲

RIPON, North Yorkshire Map ref 5C3

★★★★★
GUEST ACCOMMODATION

B&B PER ROOM PER NIGHT
S £35.00–£45.00
D £69.00–£89.00

Check out our website for offers/ promotions.

The Old Coach House

2 Stable Cottages, North Stainley, Ripon HG4 3HT t +44 (0) 1765 634900
e enquiries@oldcoachhouse.info

oldcoachhouse.info

open All year
bedrooms 5 double, 1 twin, 2 single
bathrooms All en suite
payment Credit/debit cards, cash, cheques

The Old Coach House is an accommodation jewel and one of Yorkshire's best kept secrets. The 18th coaching house stands proud in the grounds of North Stainley Hall in the picturesque village of North Stainley just north of Ripon. All eight rooms are en suite and designed with modern living in mind.

SAT NAV HG4 3HT **ONLINE MAP**

Room 🛁 📞 📺 ♦ 🍴 General 🅿 🍽 ✳ Leisure ∪ ♪ ►

ROSEDALE ABBEY, North Yorkshire Map ref 5C3

★★★★
SELF CATERING

Units **1**
Sleeps **2–8**

LOW SEASON PER WK
£300.00–£550.00

HIGH SEASON PER WK
£550.00–£850.00

Woodlea, Pickering

contact Pauline Belt, PO Box 63, Tadcaster LS24 9WN t +44 (0) 1937 831290
e p.belt@daviscoleman.com

rosedaleholidaycottage.co.uk

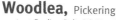

open All year
payment Cash, cheques
nearest pub 0.5 miles
nearest shop 0.75 miles

Delightful house with stunning views. Three twin bedrooms and one double. Beautiful, well-maintained garden. New kitchen recently fitted. Log fire in the lounge. Village shop, pubs and restaurants within five minutes' walk. Many places of interest within easy reach.

Unit 📺 🖥 💻 🗄 🍴 🔥 🍽 🛁 ✳ General 🐾 🏠 🅿 Ⓢ 🐕 Leisure ∪

ROSTHWAITE, Cumbria Map ref 5A3 HOTEL

★★★
COUNTRY HOUSE HOTEL

B&B PER ROOM PER NIGHT
S £38.00–£65.95
D £76.00–£131.90
HB PER PERSON PER NIGHT
£49.95–£87.50

Spring, summer, autumn and winter breaks available throughout the year. Please call or check the website for details.

Scafell Hotel

Rosthwaite, Borrowdale, Keswick CA12 5XB t +44 (0) 1768 777208 e info@scafell.co.uk

scafell.co.uk GUEST REVIEWS · SPECIAL OFFERS

open All year
bedrooms 9 double, 8 twin, 3 single, 2 family, 1 suite
bathrooms All en suite
payment Credit/debit cards, cash, cheques, euros

The Scafell Hotel is situated in the heart of Borrowdale Valley, considered by many to be England's finest valley. Situated almost at the foot of Great Gable and the Scafell Massif, the hotel is an excellent centre for walking. Recently refurbished, the Scafell boasts great food, great service and a great atmosphere.

SAT NAV *CA12 5XB* **ONLINE MAP**

Room ⬚ 📞 📺 ⬚ ⬚ ⬚ General ⬚ ⬚ ⬚ P ⬚ ⬚ ⬚ ⬚ ⬚ ⬚ Leisure ⬚ ⬚

RUNSWICK BAY, North Yorkshire Map ref 5D3 GUEST ACCOMMODATION

★★★★
GUEST HOUSE

B&B PER ROOM PER NIGHT
S £48.00
D £75.00

EVENING MEAL PER PERSON
£19.50

The Firs

26 Hinderwell Lane, Runswick Bay, Nr Whitby TS13 5HR t +44 (0) 1947 840433
e mandy.shackleton@talk21.com

the-firs.co.uk

In a coastal village, eight miles north of Whitby. All rooms en suite with colour TV, tea/coffee facilities. Private parking. Children and dogs welcome.

open April to October
bedrooms 3 double, 2 twin, 1 single, 5 family
bathrooms All en suite
payment Cash, cheques, euros

Room ⬚ ⬚ 📞 📺 ⬚ ⬚ General ⬚ P ⬚ ⬚ ✕ ⬚ ⬚ ⬚ Leisure U

ST BEES, Cumbria Map ref 5A3 GUEST ACCOMMODATION

★★★★
FARMHOUSE

B&B PER ROOM PER NIGHT
S £30.00–£35.00
D £60.00–£65.00

Stonehouse Farm

133 Main Street, St Bees CA27 0DE t +44 (0) 1946 822224 e csmith.stonehouse@btopenworld.com

stonehousefarm.net

150-acre livestock farm. Modernised, Georgian, listed farmhouse, conveniently and attractively situated next to station, shops and hotels. Start of coast-to-coast walk. Golf course, long-stay car park.

open All year except Christmas
bedrooms 2 double, 1 twin, 1 single, 2 family, 1 suite
bathrooms All en suite
payment Credit/debit cards, cash, cheques, euros

Room ⬚ 📺 ⬚ ⬚ General ⬚ ⬚ ⬚ P ⬚ ⬚ ⬚ ⬚ Leisure U ▶

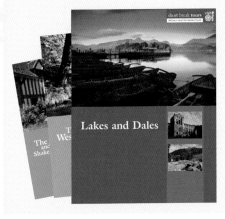
For **key to symbols** see pages 16 and 17

ST BEES, Cumbria Map ref 5A3
SELF CATERING

★★★
SELF CATERING

Units **2**
Sleeps **4–5**

LOW SEASON PER WK
£250.00–£350.00

HIGH SEASON PER WK
£400.00–£600.00

Springbank Farm Lodges, St Bees

contact Carole Woodman, Springbank Farm, High Walton, St Bees CA22 2TY **t** +44 (0) 1946 822375
e stevewoodman@talk21.com

springbanklodges.co.uk GUEST REVIEWS · SPECIAL OFFERS · REAL-TIME BOOKING

open All year
payment Credit/debit cards, cash, cheques, euros
nearest pub 1 mile
nearest shop 1 mile

New luxury two-bedroomed log cabins, en suite, fully fitted kitchen, open-plan lounge/dining area, separate wet room. Balcony with spectacular open views. Tranquil farm setting. Rare breeds, farm walks, children's play area. Close to beach and the mystical Western Lakes. Wheelchair-friendly with ample parking.

SAT NAV CA22 2TY **ONLINE MAP**

Unit 📺 🎛 💻 🔲 🍳 🎛 🔲 🔲 ❄ ♨ General 🛏 🎫 ♿ P S Leisure ∪ ⚓ ► 🚲

SANDSEND, North Yorkshire Map ref 5D3
SELF CATERING

★★★★–★★★★★★
SELF CATERING

Units **9**
Sleeps **2–9**

LOW SEASON PER WK
£320.00–£505.00

HIGH SEASON PER WK
£585.00–£1,095.00

Short breaks available from Sep–May. We offer a 10% reduction for last-minute bookings and recommendations.

Raithwaite Hall, Whitby

contact Amanda Pearson, Raithwaite Hall, Sandsend, Whitby YO21 3ST **t** +44 (0) 1947 893284
e admin@raithwaite.co.uk

raithwaite.co.uk SPECIAL OFFERS

open All year
payment Credit/debit cards, cash, cheques
nearest pub less than 0.5 miles
nearest shop less than 0.5 miles

Luxury stone cottages in a secluded woodland retreat just a short walk from three miles of golden sands. These extremely comfortable cottages have been converted to the highest standard offering well-equipped modern facilities, making this the idea location for a peaceful and relaxing holiday.

SAT NAV YO21 3ST **ONLINE MAP**

Unit 📺 SC 🎛 💿 🔲 🍳 🎛 🔲 🔲 ♨ ✿ General 🛏 🎫 ♿ P S 🐕
Leisure ⚓ ► 🚲

SCARBOROUGH, North Yorkshire Map ref 5D3
GUEST ACCOMMODATION

★★★★
**FARMHOUSE
SILVER AWARD**

B&B PER ROOM PER NIGHT
S £35.00–£40.00
D £60.00–£70.00

Sawdon Heights

Scarborough YO13 9EB **t** +44 (0) 1723 859321 **e** info@sawdonheights.com

sawdonheights.com

A warm welcome awaits on our family farm adjacent to forest. Quiet location, stunning views. Cycle hire and storage, walks and pack-ups available. Ideal location for exploring east coast and moors. Extra bed available.

open All year except Christmas
bedrooms 2 double, 1 twin
bathrooms All en suite
payment Cash, cheques

Room 🛏 📺 ♨ ⬜ General 🛏 10 P 🍽 🎛 ❄ Leisure ∪ ⚓ ► 🚲

Fancy a cycling holiday?

For a fabulous freewheeling break, seek out accommodation participating in our Cyclists Welcome scheme. Look out for the symbol and plan your route online at nationalcyclenetwork.org.

★★★★
GUEST ACCOMMODATION

B&B PER ROOM PER NIGHT
S £37.00–£39.00
D £32.00–£34.00

Smugglers Rock Country House

Staintondale Road, Ravenscar, Scarborough YO13 0ER   **t** +44 (0) 1723 870044
e info@smugglersrock.co.uk

smugglersrock.co.uk REAL-TIME BOOKING

open Easter to mid-October
bedrooms 3 double, 1 twin, 1 single, 3 family
bathrooms All en suite
payment Credit/debit cards, cash, cheques

Georgian country house in Ravenscar with panoramic views over surrounding National Park and sea. Ideal country holiday area, with wonderful walks in all directions, located at southern end of Robin Hood's Bay. Whitby, Scarborough and 'Heartbeat' Country within easy reach. Friendly farm animals. Self-catering cottages also available.

SAT NAV YO13 0ER **ONLINE MAP**

Room 🖼 📺 ☕ 🍳   General 🛏5 P 🍴✳   Leisure ∪ ♪ ⛵ 🚴

★★★–★★★★★
SELF CATERING

Units   **3**
Sleeps   **1–4**

LOW SEASON PER WK
£240.00–£305.00

HIGH SEASON PER WK
£460.00–£580.00

3-night and last-minute breaks available Oct-Mar.

Smugglers Rock Cottages, Ravenscar, Scarborough

contact Mrs Sharon Gregson, Staintondale Road, Ravenscar YO13 0ER   **t** +44 (0) 1723 870044
e info@smugglersrock.co.uk

smugglersrock.co.uk REAL-TIME BOOKING

open All year
payment Credit/debit cards, cash, cheques
nearest pub 2 miles
nearest shop 2 miles

Beautiful cottages in Ravenscar (southern end of Robin Hood's Bay) furnished to a very high standard with panoramic views of the National Park and sea. Fully equipped for maximum comfort and relaxation. The cottages are an ideal base for country and coastal holidays. Friendly farm animals. Bed and breakfast also available.

SAT NAV YO13 0ER **ONLINE MAP**

Unit 📺 🖥 💻 🖨 🔔 🍲 🍽 🧺 ✳ ⛺   General 🛏 🍴 P Ⓢ 🐕
Leisure ∪ ♪ ⛵ 🚴

★★★★★
HOLIDAY, TOURING
& CAMPING PARK
ROSE AWARD

🚐 (220) £18.00–£28.50
🚛 (30) £22.50–£28.50
⛺ (50) £14.00–£19.00
🚐 (20) £230.00–£595.00
300 touring pitches

Early-booking discount: £25 off full week's hire. 10% discount off full week's pitch fees, booked by post in advance.

Flower of May Holiday Parks Ltd

Lebberston, Scarborough YO11 3NU   **t** +44 (0) 1723 584311   **e** info@flowerofmay.com

flowerofmay.com

open Easter to October
payment Credit/debit cards, cash, cheques

Excellent facilities on family-run park. Luxury indoor pool, adventure playground, golf course. Ideal for coast and country. Prices based per pitch, per night, for four people with car. Luxury hire caravans. Serviced seasonal touring pitches.

SAT NAV YO11 3NU

General 🚿 🔌 🚻 ☎ ♿ 🏧 🗑 ⚓ 🐕 ☀   Leisure 🎣 🍴 🎵 🎮 🎡 ∪ ♪ ⛵

SHEFFIELD, South Yorkshire Map ref 4B2 — SELF CATERING

★★–★★★★
SELF CATERING

Units **5**
Sleeps **2–6**

LOW SEASON PER WK
£150.00–£350.00

HIGH SEASON PER WK
£200.00–£400.00

Short breaks and special promotions, please call for details.

Foxholes Farm, Low Bradfield, Sheffield

contact Rachel Hague, Foxholes Farm, Sheffield S6 6HY **t** +44 (0) 114 285 1383 & +44 (0) 7917 030602 **e** foxholes.farm@tiscali.co.uk

foxholesfarm.co.uk

open All year
payment Cash, cheques
nearest pub 0.5 miles
nearest shop 0.5 miles

The converted Grade II Listed buildings house the cottages, three of which have a double room and a twin room, one a double room and a single room, and the other a double room. All units have fitted kitchens, lounge area, bathroom and some also have a double sofa bed.

SAT NAV *S6 6HY*

Unit 📺 🖥 📼 🍳 📱 ✳ General 🐴 P ○ S Leisure ∪ 🎵

SILVERDALE, Lancashire Map ref 5A3 — SELF CATERING

★★★★–★★★★★★
SELF CATERING

Units **2**
Sleeps **1–8**

LOW SEASON PER WK
£365.00–£595.00

HIGH SEASON PER WK
£395.00–£675.00

Short breaks available Nov–Mar (weekends and midweek).

Wolf House Cottages, Silverdale, Nr Arnside

t +44 (0) 1524 701573 **e** enquiries@wolfhousecottages.co.uk

wolfhousecottages.co.uk

open All year
payment Cash, cheques
nearest pub 1 mile
nearest shop 1 mile

Detached, beautifully furnished cottages with private gardens and stunning views over fields or Morecambe Bay in an Area of Outstanding Natural Beauty. Owners have lifetime interest in the arts, crafts and environment. Walks and cycle rides from the doorstep, close to RSPB reserve, Lake District, Yorkshire Dales and Forest of Bowland.

Unit 📺 🖥 📼 🍳 🔌 📼 📱 ✂ ✳ 🎣 🔥 General 🐴 🏢 ⚑ P S Leisure ∪ 🎵 ►

SKIPTON, North Yorkshire Map ref 4B1 — GUEST ACCOMMODATION

★★★★
RESTAURANT WITH ROOMS

B&B PER ROOM PER NIGHT
S Max £69.50
D Max £79.50

EVENING MEAL PER PERSON
£10.00–£30.00

Book 3 nights and receive 10% discount on accommodation.

Napier's Restaurant & Accommodation

Chapel Hill, Skipton BD23 1NL **t** +44 (0) 1756 799688 **e** info@accommodation-skipton.co.uk

restaurant-skipton.co.uk

open 14 January to 31 December
bedrooms 4 double, 2 twin
bathrooms All en suite
payment Credit/debit cards, cash, cheques, euros

Originally a large farmhouse dating back to the 13th century, offering relaxed and friendly accommodation. Come away and stay with us in the most picturesque corner of Skipton.

SAT NAV *BD23 1NL* **ONLINE MAP**

Room 🛏 ☎ 📺 🍴 🔌 General 🐴 🏢 ⚑ P 🌐 🔥 ♨ ✕ 🍴 ○ ✳ Leisure ∪ 🎵 ► 🚲

What do the star ratings mean?

Detailed information about star ratings can be found at the back of this guide.

STAITHES, North Yorkshire Map ref 5C3 — SELF CATERING

★★★
SELF CATERING

Units **1**
Sleeps **5**

LOW SEASON PER WK
£265.00–£365.00

HIGH SEASON PER WK
£355.00–£595.00

Pennysteel Cottage, Staithes

contact Chris Wade, Waterfront Cottages, 2 Star Row, North Dalton, Driffield YO25 9UX
t +44 (0) 1377 217662 & +44 (0) 7801 124264 **e** chris.wade@adastra-music.co.uk

waterfrontcottages.co.uk

open All year
payment Credit/debit cards, cash, cheques
nearest pub less than 0.5 miles
nearest shop less than 0.5 miles

Old fisherman's cottage of unique character with beamed ceilings, wood-panelled walls and wood-burning stove. All windows and terrace overlook the picturesque harbour of Staithes. Ideal for the coast and walking. Top-quality restaurant, pub serving food, cafes, art gallery and craft and local shops all within a few yards.

Unit 📺 ▨ ▣ ⬛ ▤ ▤ ▤ ▥ ▦ ✳ ♨ ⬦ General ⌂ ▥ ♣ ◉ 🐕 Leisure ♪

THIRSK, North Yorkshire Map ref 5C3 — GUEST ACCOMMODATION

★★★★
**GUEST ACCOMMODATION
SILVER AWARD**

B&B PER ROOM PER NIGHT
S £47.50–£49.50
D £70.00–£75.00

EVENING MEAL PER PERSON
£21.50–£22.50

In spring and autumn we run courses in all types of embroidery. Please ask for our brochure.

Borrowby Mill, Bed and Breakfast

Borrowby, Nr Thirsk YO7 4AW **t** +44 (0) 1845 537717 **e** markandvickipadfield@btinternet.com

borrowbymill.co.uk

open All year except Christmas and New Year
bedrooms 1 double, 2 twin
bathrooms All en suite
payment Credit/debit cards, cash, cheques

Tastefully converted 18thC flour mill in a secluded location between Thirsk and Northallerton. Convenient for touring North Yorkshire Moors and Dales. Cosy en suite rooms, excellent breakfasts and dinners prepared by chef/proprietor. Relax in our drawing room with library or explore our woodland gardens.

SAT NAV YO7 4AW

Room 📺 ⬥ ▥ General ⌂ ♣ P ⦾ ♨ ✕ ▥ ✳ 🐕 Leisure ∪ ♪ ▶ ☆

THIRSK, North Yorkshire Map ref 5C3 — GUEST ACCOMMODATION

★★★★
GUEST ACCOMMODATION

B&B PER ROOM PER NIGHT
S £40.00–£55.00
D £50.00–£65.00

EVENING MEAL PER PERSON
£12.95–£15.95

Manor House Cottage

Hag Lane, South Kilvington, Thirsk YO7 2NY **t** +44 (0) 1845 527712
e info@manor-house-cottage.co.uk

manor-house-cottage.co.uk REAL-TIME BOOKING

open All year
bedrooms 2 double, 1 twin
bathrooms 2 en suite, 1 private
payment Cash, cheques

Superior accommodation in quiet rural location, three minutes from town centre, close to the dales and the North York Moors.

SAT NAV YO7 2NY

Room 📺 ⬥ ▥ General ⌂ P ✕ ▥ ◻ ✳ 🐕 Leisure ∪ ♪ ▶

Using map references

Map references refer to the colour maps at the front of this guide.

THIRSK, North Yorkshire Map ref 5C3
GUEST ACCOMMODATION

★★★★
FARMHOUSE

B&B PER ROOM PER NIGHT
S £35.00–£40.00
D £50.00–£65.00

Town Pasture Farm

Thirsk YO7 2DY t +44 (0) 1845 537298

Comfortable farmhouse in picturesque Boltby village within the North York Moors National Park. Views of the Hambleton Hills. Excellent walks. Horse-riding available in village. Central for east coast, York and the Dales. Colour TV in lounge.

open All year except Christmas
bedrooms 1 twin, 1 family
bathrooms All en suite
payment Cash, cheques

Room ♦ ⚲ General ⛤ ⛺ ✿ ♈ Leisure ∪

THORNLEY, Lancashire Map ref 4A1
SELF CATERING

★★★★
SELF CATERING

Units **2**
Sleeps **4–10**

LOW SEASON PER WK
£260.00–£510.00

HIGH SEASON PER WK
£415.00–£760.00

Loudview Barn, Preston

contact Mr & Mrs Oliver & Ness Starkey, Loudview Barn, Rams Clough Farm, Thornley, Preston PR3 2TN t +44 (0) 1995 61476 e loudview@ic24.net

open All year
payment Cash, cheques, euros
nearest pub 2 miles
nearest shop 4 miles

Stone barn conversion in peaceful location on fellside in Forest of Bowland, enjoying exceptional views across unspoilt countryside. Accommodation in two units that can be combined. Unit 1 comprise one double, one twin and pair of bunk beds. Unit 2 comprises one double and one twin.

Unit 📺 🎛 💻 📷 ⚲ 🔔 🍽 📠 ✿ General ⛤ ⛺ ♈ P ♈ Leisure ♫ ♿

WARK, Northumberland Map ref 5B2
GUEST ACCOMMODATION

★★★★
INN
SILVER AWARD

B&B PER ROOM PER NIGHT
S £55.00–£60.00
D £90.00–£110.00

EVENING MEAL PER PERSON
£8.50–£18.50

Changing offers throughout the year. Please see website.

Battlesteads Country Inn & Restaurant

Wark, Hexham NE48 3LS t +44 (0) 1434 230209 e info@battlesteads.com

battlesteads.com

open All year
bedrooms 7 double, 7 twin, 1 single, 2 family
bathrooms All en suite
payment Credit/debit cards, cash, cheques

18thC inn, formerly a farmhouse, in the heart of rural Northumberland, close to the Roman Wall and Kielder Water. An ideal centre for exploring Border country and for relaxing, walking or cycling. Ground-floor bedrooms available. Excellent restaurant using fresh, local produce. Five cask ales.

SAT NAV NE48 3LS

Room ♿ ☎ 📺 🆂 ♦ ⚲ General ⛤ ⛺ ♈ P ⚲ ❢ ✕ 🍽 ✿ ♈ Leisure ∪ ♫ ▶

WARRINGTON, Cheshire Map ref 4A2
GUEST ACCOMMODATION

★★
BED & BREAKFAST

B&B PER ROOM PER NIGHT
S Min £37.00
D Min £52.00

EVENING MEAL PER PERSON
Min £7.00

New House Farm Cottages

Hatton Lane, Hatton, Warrington WA4 4BZ t +44 (0) 1925 730567
e newhousefarmcottages@google.com

newhousefarmcottages.co.uk

Fully modernised farm-workers' cottages which still retain their original features. Fields surround the cottages. Organic fruit sold from garden. Close to motorways. Evening meals available. Pick-ups arranged.

open All year
bedrooms 1 double, 1 twin, 1 single, 1 family
bathrooms 2 en suite, 2 private
payment Cash, cheques, euros

Room ♿ General ⛤ P 🛜 ⚲ ✕ 🍽 ✿ ♈ Leisure ∪ ♫ ▶ ♿

WASDALE, Cumbria Map ref 5A3 — SELF CATERING

★★★★
SELF CATERING

Units **1**
Sleeps **1–10**

LOW SEASON PER WK
Min **£350.00**

HIGH SEASON PER WK
Max **£550.00**

Bleng Barn, Gosforth, Seascale

contact Thomas Ostle, Bleng Farms, Mill House Farm, Wellington, Seascale CA20 1BH
t +44 (0) 7801 862237 & +44 (0) 7775 512918 **e** info@blengfarms.co.uk

blengfarms.co.uk GUEST REVIEWS · SPECIAL OFFERS

This newly converted rural property on a large working farm has many traditional features and modern conveniences, providing a base for a leisurely break or a variety of activity holidays.

open All year
payment Cash, cheques, euros
nearest pub 0.6 miles
nearest shop 1 mile

Unit [symbols] General [symbols]
Leisure [symbols]

WEST KIRBY, Merseyside Map ref 4A2 — GUEST ACCOMMODATION

★★★★
**GUEST HOUSE
SILVER AWARD**

B&B PER ROOM PER NIGHT
S Min **£65.00**
D Min **£85.00**

Winter breaks available.

At Peel Hey

Frankby Road, Frankby, Wirral CH48 1PP **t** +44 (0) 151 677 9077 **e** enquiries@peelhey.co.uk

peelhey.co.uk SPECIAL OFFERS · REAL-TIME BOOKING

open All year
bedrooms 4 double, 2 twin, 1 single, 2 family
bathrooms All en suite
payment Credit/debit cards, cash, cheques

Award-winning country house offering luxury, en suite accommodation, a warm welcome and excellent breakfasts and cream teas. Located in picturesque village, yet minutes from Hoylake, British Open Championship venue 2006 and West Kirby for restaurants and bars. Close to M53 for Chester and 15 minutes from Liverpool – European Capital of Culture 2008. Wi-Fi.

SAT NAV CH48 1PP

Room [symbols] General [symbols] Leisure [symbols]

WEST WITTON, North Yorkshire Map ref 5B3 — GUEST ACCOMMODATION

★★★
GUEST ACCOMMODATION

B&B PER ROOM PER NIGHT
S **£26.00–£38.00**
D **£48.00–£54.00**

We offer a price reduction for stays of 3 or more nights and a further reduction for a week or more.

The Old Star

Main Street, West Witton, Leyburn DL8 4LU **t** +44 (0) 1969 622949 **e** enquiries@theoldstar.com

theoldstar.com

open All year except Christmas
bedrooms 4 double, 1 twin, 2 family
bathrooms 5 en suite
payment Cash, cheques

Seventeenth-century, stone-built former coaching inn set in the Yorkshire Dales National Park with uninterrupted views of Wensleydale from the rear of the property. Oak beams, log fire and a friendly atmosphere, The Old Star is an excellent centre for exploring the Dales. West Witton has two excellent pubs for food.

SAT NAV DL8 4LU

Room [symbols] General [symbols] Leisure [symbols]

Check the maps for accommodation locations

Colour maps at the front pinpoint all the places where accommodation is featured within the regional sections of this guide. Pick your location and then refer to the place index at the back to find the page number.

WHALLEY, Lancashire Map ref 4A1 — GUEST ACCOMMODATION

★★★★
GUEST ACCOMMODATION

B&B PER ROOM PER NIGHT
S £35.00
D £70.00

Whalley Abbey

The Sands, Whalley, Clitheroe BB7 9SS t +44 (0) 1254 828400 e office@whalleyabbey.org

whalleyabbey.co.uk SPECIAL OFFERS

Whalley Abbey Conference House offers en suite accommodation with TV, phone and free internet connection. The 14thC Cistercian Abbey ruins, gardens and coffee shop are open daily.

open All year except Christmas and New Year
bedrooms 1 double, 9 twin, 6 single, 1 family
bathrooms 16 en suite, 1 private
payment Credit/debit cards, cash, cheques

Room 🛏🔌📺♿ General 🛎🏫🅿🔔♨✕📶☼ Leisure 🎣🚴

WHINFELL, Cumbria Map ref 5B3 — SELF CATERING

★★★
SELF CATERING

Units **2**
Sleeps **6–9**

LOW SEASON PER WK
£300.00–£450.00

HIGH SEASON PER WK
£500.00–£750.00

Topthorn Holiday Cottages, Nr Kendal

contact Mrs Diane Barnes, Topthorn Holiday Cottages, Topthorn Farm, Whinfell, Nr Kendal LA8 9EG
t +44 (0) 1539 824252 e info.barnes@btconnect.com

topthorn.com SPECIAL OFFERS

open All year
payment Credit/debit cards, cash, cheques
nearest pub 4 miles
nearest shop 4 miles

Two new 18thC barn conversions. Outstanding views, ideal area for walking. Large garden area, patios, barbecue, wheelchair-friendly, children and pets welcome. Peaceful location yet only four miles to the market town of Kendal. Windermere and the Lakes 25 minutes away. Horse-riding centre two miles. Climbing wall, leisure centre, cinema and pub in Kendal.

Unit 📺 🆂 📀 🖥 🍽🍳🔌🍴☼♨ General 🛎🏫🅿🆂🐾 Leisure ♨🎣

WHITBY, North Yorkshire Map ref 5D3 — GUEST ACCOMMODATION

★★★★
BED & BREAKFAST
SILVER AWARD

B&B PER ROOM PER NIGHT
D £60.00–£85.00

Gramarye Suites B&B

15 Coach Road, Sleights, Whitby YO22 5AA t +44 (0) 1947 811656 e gramaryesuites@btinternet.com

gramaryesuites.co.uk

open All year
bedrooms 2 double, 1 family
bathrooms All en suite
payment Cash, cheques

Three-bedroom, luxury bed and breakfast in a former village shop in Sleights, Whitby. Ideally suited for the North York Moors and the Yorkshire coast. The rooms have king-size four-poster/high-post beds, satellite LCD TVs, free Wi-Fi, irons, hairdryers fridges, room safes, very generous beverage trays and high-quality en suites.

SAT NAV YO22 5AA **ONLINE MAP**

Room 🛏🛋📺🆂🔌🍵 General 🛎🏫🅿📶♨📶 Leisure ♨🎣

Do you like visiting gardens?

Discover Britain's green heart with this easy-to-use guide. Featuring a selection of the most stunning gardens in the country, The Gardens Explorer is complete with a handy fold-out map and illustrated guide. You can purchase the Explorer series from good bookshops and online at visitbritaindirect.com.

★★★★★
**HOLIDAY, TOURING
& CAMPING PARK**
ROSE AWARD

🚐 (20)   £12.50–£20.00
🚗 (20)   £12.50–£20.00
⛺ (80)   £8.00–£20.00
🏕 (30) £150.00–£595.00
100 touring pitches

Middlewood Farm Holiday Park

Middlewood Lane, Fylingthorpe, Robin Hood's Bay, Whitby YO22 4UF t +44 (0) 1947 880414
e info@middlewoodfarm.com

middlewoodfarm.com

open 1 March to 4 January
payment Credit/debit cards, cash, cheques

Peaceful, award-winning family park. A walker's
paradise with magnificent, panoramic coastal and
moorland views! Level, sheltered hardstandings,
luxury heated facilities, private bathroom, children's
play area. Ten-minute walk to pub/shops/beach and
Robin Hood's Bay. Superb caravans for hire. A
friendly welcome awaits!

SAT NAV YO22 4UF **ONLINE MAP**

General 🐕 🛁 🍴 WP 📶 🎮 🐾 Leisure ⛰ ∪ ⚓ 🚴

★★★★
SELF CATERING

Units   **1**
Sleeps   **1–5**

LOW SEASON PER WK
£160.00–£380.00

HIGH SEASON PER WK
£390.00–£470.00

Snowdrop Cottage, Mountain View, Whitehaven

contact Mr Mark Warbrick, Wild Acre, Summergrove, Hensingham, Whitehaven CA28 8XZ
t +44 (0) 1946 814194 & +44 (0) 7773 052960 e markwarbrick@aol.com

tranquilakescottages.co.uk SPECIAL OFFERS

open All year
payment Cash, cheques
nearest pub 1 mile
nearest shop 1 mile

Snowdrop Cottage is situated high above the
surrounding countryside. Panoramic views to the
Western Lake District and also towards Scotland and
the Isle of Man. Internally, the holiday cottage is very
cosy. Exposed beams, Sky TV and DVD. The lounge
is tastefully furnished and decorated to a high
standard.

SAT NAV CA28 8UN **ONLINE MAP**

Unit 📺 🆂 🖥 💻 📀 📻 🍳 🧺 🍴 ❄ 🍳 General 🐕 🛏 P ⬜ S
Leisure ♨ ∪ ⚓ ⛵ 🚴

★★★★
HOTEL
SILVER AWARD

B&B PER ROOM PER NIGHT
D £70.00–£145.00
HB PER PERSON PER NIGHT
£60.00–£97.50

Park and fly – £65pp
sharing (room only)
including 15 days'
free car parking,
plus courtesy coach
to airport between
0800 and 2300.

Stanneylands Hotel

Stanneylands Road, Wilmslow SK9 4EY t +44 (0) 1625 525225 e enquiries@stanneylandshotel.co.uk

stanneylandshotel.co.uk SPECIAL OFFERS · REAL-TIME BOOKING

open All year
bedrooms 36 double, 15 twin, 1 single, 1 family,
2 suites
bathrooms All en suite
payment Credit/debit cards, cash, cheques

Exclusive country-house hotel set in several acres of
beautiful gardens. All rooms en suite with satellite
TV, radio, trouser-press and telephone. Rosettes for
fine cuisine, in addition to many awards for
excellence. Ideal base for exploring Cheshire and the
Peak District. Twenty minutes from Manchester city
centre and three miles from airport.

SAT NAV SK9 4EY **ONLINE MAP**

Room 📶 🍳 📞 📺 🆂 🌀 🍵 🦽 General 🐕 🛏 🍴 P 📶 🍷 🍽 🌙 🈺 🍴 ❄
Leisure ∪ ⛵

★★★★
COUNTRY HOUSE HOTEL
GOLD AWARD

Gilpin Lodge Country House Hotel

Crook Road, Windermere LA23 3NE **t** +44 (0) 15394 88818 **e** hotel@gilpinlodge.co.uk

gilpinlodge.co.uk REAL-TIME BOOKING

B&B PER ROOM PER NIGHT
S £155.00
D £230.00–£350.00
HB PER PERSON PER NIGHT
£135.00–£195.00

Year-round breaks
from £315pp for
3 nights' DB&B, plus
3 nights and 2
games of golf
(Windermere) from
£396pp.

open All year
bedrooms 7 double, 7 twin, 6 suites
bathrooms All en suite
payment Credit/debit cards, cash, cheques

An elegant, friendly, and relaxing hotel, privately owned and run by the Cunliffe family. The 20 sumptuous rooms have crisp white linen and luxurious bathrooms, each of the six Garden Suites has its own garden and hot tub. A Relais & Chateaux hotel with award-winning food. Year-round golfing breaks.

SAT NAV LA23 3NE ONLINE MAP

Room ⌂ 🛏 ☎ 📺 🆂🅲 🖐 ⌨ ♿ General 7 P 🛜 ☂ ⌗ 🌙 ☺ ☀ Leisure ⊗ ∪ ♪ ▸ 🚲

★★★
COUNTRY HOUSE HOTEL
GOLD AWARD

Linthwaite House Hotel

Crook Road, Bowness-on-Windermere, Windermere LA23 3JA **t** +44 (0) 15394 88600
e stay@linthwaite.com

linthwaite.com GUEST REVIEWS · SPECIAL OFFERS · REAL-TIME BOOKING

B&B PER ROOM PER NIGHT
S £130.00–£150.00
D £154.00–£330.00
HB PER PERSON PER NIGHT
£92.00–£190.00

Special offers
updated monthly on
website.

open All year
bedrooms 19 double, 4 twin, 2 single, 1 family,
1 suite
bathrooms All en suite
payment Credit/debit cards, cash, cheques

Spectacular views over Lake Windermere, friendly, unstuffy staff, award-winning food and eclectic wine list all make Linthwaite a great place to unwind. Attractions include the Lake District, Muncaster and Sizergh Castles, Levens and Holker Halls. Antiques, galleries and quality shopping widely available. Fourteen acres of peace and tranquillity, including private tarn for fishing.

SAT NAV LA23 3JA ONLINE MAP

Room ⌂ 🛏 ☎ 📺 🖐 ⌨ ♿ General 🛎 🎹 ♿ P 🛜 ☂ ⌗ 🌙 ☺ ☀ 🐕
Leisure ⊗ ∪ ♪ ▸ 🚲

★★★★
GUEST HOUSE
SILVER AWARD

Fairfield House and Gardens

Brantfell Road, Bowness Bay LA23 3AE **t** +44 (0) 15394 46565 **e** relax@the-fairfield.co.uk

the-fairfield.co.uk GUEST REVIEWS · SPECIAL OFFERS · REAL-TIME BOOKING

B&B PER ROOM PER NIGHT
S £45.00–£60.00
D £66.00–£140.00

EVENING MEAL PER PERSON
Min £27.50

Reduced prices for
3 nights during
weekdays, or
extended weekends
in low season. DB&B
available Nov–Mar.

open All year except Christmas
bedrooms 4 double, 2 twin, 1 family, 3 suites
bathrooms All en suite
payment Credit/debit cards, cash, cheques, euros

Secluded Georgian house set in own grounds with beautiful garden and private car park. Informally run D&B with exceptional breakfasts. King-size four-poster and spa-bath bedrooms available. All rooms en suite, some with state-of-the-art, deluxe bathrooms. Guest lounge with internet access. Located central Bowness – close to Lake Windermere, restaurants, shops and pubs.

SAT NAV LA23 3AE ONLINE MAP

Room ⌂ 🛏 📺 🖐 ⌨ General 🛎 10 P 🛜 ♿ ☂ ✕ ⌗ ☀ 🐕 Leisure ∪ ♪ ▸ 🚲

★★★★
GUEST HOUSE

B&B PER ROOM PER NIGHT
S £45.00–£60.00
D £55.00–£90.00

Special off-peak offer: 3 nights for £165 per en suite double. Discount from high-season prices available all year for 3-night stays.

Tarn Rigg Guest House

Thornbarrow Road, Windermere LA23 2DG **t** +44 (0) 15394 88777
e info@tarnrigg-guesthouse.co.uk

tarnrigg-guesthouse.co.uk GUEST REVIEWS · SPECIAL OFFERS

open All year except Christmas
bedrooms 3 double, 2 family
bathrooms All en suite
payment Credit/debit cards, cash, cheques, euros

Welcome to the Lake District. Built in 1903, Tarn Rigg is situated in an ideal position midway between Windermere and Bowness. Panoramic Langdale Pike views. Quiet, convenient location, ample parking, beautiful 0.75-acre grounds. Spacious, en suite rooms with excellent modern facilities. Rooms with lake views available.

SAT NAV *LA23 2DG*

Room 📺 👤 🍽   General 🛋 🏢 🏧 P 🎱 👤 ✱ 🐕   Leisure ∪ 🏌 🚲

★★★★
SELF CATERING

Units   **4**
Sleeps   **2–6**

LOW SEASON PER WK
£210.00–£450.00

HIGH SEASON PER WK
£300.00–£680.00

Heaning Barn Cottages, Heaning, Windermere, Windermere

contact Mrs Jenny Truch, Heaning Barn Cottages, Heaning, Windermere, Cumbria LA23 1JW
t +44 (0) 1539 766107 **e** info@heaning.com

heaning.com GUEST REVIEWS · SPECIAL OFFERS · REAL-TIME BOOKING

Four newly refurbished cottages in converted 19thC Lakeland barn. Tranquil countryside location 1.5 miles from Windermere town. Walking/cycling from door. Central heating, new kitchens, courtyard garden, cycle store, private parking.

open All year
payment Credit/debit cards, cheques
nearest pub 1 mile
nearest shop 1 mile

Unit 📺 📷 📼 🖥 📻 🍽 ✱   General 🛋 🏢 🏧 P ◻ S   Leisure ∪ 🏌 ▶ 🚲

WIRRAL

See under West Kirby

★★★
COUNTRY HOUSE HOTEL

B&B PER ROOM PER NIGHT
S Max £89.00
D Max £120.00

Hunday Manor Country House Hotel Ltd

Hunday, Winscales, Workington CA14 4JF **t** +44 (0) 1900 61798
e reception@hunday-manor-hotel.co.uk

hunday-manor-hotel.co.uk

open All year except Christmas and New Year
bedrooms 19 double, 2 twin, 2 single, 1 family
bathrooms All en suite
payment Credit/debit cards, cash, cheques

With probably the finest facilities in West Cumbria, we have recently undergone major expansion and refurbishment. We offer facilities for weddings, business conferencing and functions of any type, for approximately 200+ people.

SAT NAV *CA14 4JF* **ONLINE MAP**

Room 🛏 📞 📺 👤 🍽 ♿   General 🛋 🏧 P 👤 🍽 🍴 ✱ 🐕   Leisure ∪ 🏌 ▶

Has every property been assessed?

All accommodation in this guide has been rated for quality, or is awaiting assessment, by a professional national tourist board assessor.

★★★★
INN

B&B PER ROOM PER NIGHT
s £55.00–£65.00
D £70.00–£110.00

Old Ginn House

Moor Road, Great Clifton, Workington CA14 1TS t +44 (0) 1900 64616
e enquiries@oldginnhouse.co.uk

oldginnhouse.co.uk

The Old Ginn House has been successfully converted from a 17thC farm into a charming village inn offering quality accommodation, great food and a warm welcome. Ideal for exploring the Western Lake District.

open All year except Christmas
bedrooms 11 double, 3 twin, 4 family, 1 suite
bathrooms All en suite
payment Credit/debit cards, cash, cheques

Room ⬧ ☎ 📺 ⚓ General ⌘ 🛏♿P⚑✕⚒✿ Leisure ∪♪▶

★★
HOTEL

B&B PER ROOM PER NIGHT
s £40.00–£52.00
D £60.00–£84.00
HB PER PERSON PER NIGHT
£44.00–£66.00

Blakeney Hotel

180 Stockton Lane, York YO31 1ES t +44 (0) 1904 422786 e reception@blakeneyhotel-york.co.uk

blakeneyhotel-york.co.uk SPECIAL OFFERS · REAL-TIME BOOKING

20% discount for 7 or more nights. Special rates for 3 nights' DB&B (excl Bank Holidays).

open All year except Christmas
bedrooms 4 double, 4 twin, 3 single, 6 family
bathrooms 15 en suite, 2 private
payment Credit/debit cards, cash, cheques, euros

We offer a warm welcome, free parking, comfortable en suite rooms, relaxing lounge, cosy bar, spacious restaurant, hearty English breakfasts, fine evening dining and pleasant friendly service. Ideally located within 20 minutes' walk of historic city centre. No smoking throughout. Wi-Fi access.
'...Excellent as always – room, bed, food, staff – fantastic! Will recommend and return...'

SAT NAV YO31 1ES **ONLINE MAP**

Room ⬧ 📺 ⚓ 🍵 General ⌘1 🛏♿P⚡⚑✿⚒ Leisure ∪▶🚴

★★★
HOTEL
SILVER AWARD

B&B PER ROOM PER NIGHT
s £85.00–£120.00
D £120.00–£225.00
HB PER PERSON PER NIGHT
£110.00–£145.00

Dean Court Hotel

Duncombe Place, York YO1 7EF t +44 (0) 1904 625082 e sales@deancourt-york.co.uk

deancourt-york.co.uk SPECIAL OFFERS · REAL-TIME BOOKING

Sunday Dine & Wine break. Champagne Lovers' break. Food & Wine Lovers' break.

open All year
bedrooms 24 double, 5 twin, 3 single, 4 family, 1 suite
bathrooms All en suite
payment Credit/debit cards, cash, cheques

Superbly appointed hotel opposite York Minster. All the historic attractions of York are within easy walking distance. All public areas have been tastefully refurbished in recent years along with the Two AA Rosette-awarded restaurant, re-launched as DCH, plus a new addition: The Court Café-Bistro & Bar. The new decor is contemporary with magnificent design features.

SAT NAV YO1 7EF **ONLINE MAP**

Room 🖥 ☎ 📺 💾 ⚓ 🍵 ✍ General ⌘🛏♿P⚡⚑✿⚒●▤🎮⚓ Leisure ∪▶🚴

Need some ideas?

Big city buzz or peaceful panoramas? Take a fresh look at England and you may be surprised at what's right on your doorstep. Explore the diversity online at enjoyengland.com

★ ★ ★
HOTEL
GOLD AWARD

The Grange Hotel

1 Clifton, York YO30 6AA **t** +44 (0) 1904 644744 **e** info@grangehotel.co.uk

grangehotel.co.uk GUEST REVIEWS · SPECIAL OFFERS · REAL-TIME BOOKING

B&B PER ROOM PER NIGHT
S £117.00–£188.00
D £130.00–£225.00
HB PER PERSON PER NIGHT
£75.00–£130.00

Award-winning Regency town house hotel, offering luxurious accommodation, stylish rosetted restaurant serving modern brasserie classics, Cellar Bar and car park. Comfy sofas, fresh flowers and blazing fires create the perfect ambience in which to relax and unwind.

open All year
bedrooms 14 double, 18 twin, 3 single, 1 suite
bathrooms All en suite
payment Credit/debit cards, cash, cheques

Room   General   Leisure

★ ★ ★
HOTEL

Mount Royale Hotel

119 The Mount, York YO24 1GU **t** +44 (0) 1904 628856 **e** stuartoxo@mountroyale.co.uk

mountroyale.co.uk SPECIAL OFFERS

B&B PER ROOM PER NIGHT
S £85.00–£120.00
D £97.50–£180.00

open All year
bedrooms 12 double, 3 twin, 1 single, 8 suites
bathrooms All en suite
payment Credit/debit cards, cash, cheques

The Mount Royale Hotel is a privately owned, tastefully restored William IV building with individually furnished bedrooms. The restaurant overlooks fine English gardens. Heated swimming pool open May to September. Outdoor hot tub and new Scandinavian log cabin housing steam room and sauna (open all year round).

SAT NAV YO24 1GU **ONLINE MAP**

Room   General   Leisure

★ ★ ★ ★
GUEST HOUSE
SILVER AWARD

23 St Marys

Bootham, York YO30 7DD **t** +44 (0) 1904 622738 **e** stmarys23@hotmail.com

23stmarys.co.uk GUEST REVIEWS · SPECIAL OFFERS · REAL-TIME BOOKING

B&B PER ROOM PER NIGHT
S £45.00–£55.00
D £70.00–£90.00

3rd night at 50% reduction (excl peak periods).

open All year except Christmas
bedrooms 6 double, 1 twin, 1 single, 1 family
bathrooms All en suite
payment Credit/debit cards, cash, cheques, euros

Large Victorian terraced house peacefully set within five minutes' stroll of city centre. Spacious rooms, antique furnishings, en suite bedrooms of different sizes and character. Extensive breakfast menu in elegant surroundings. Julie and Chris will offer you a warm welcome to their home.

SAT NAV YO30 7DD **ONLINE MAP**

Room   General   Leisure

Where can I get help and advice?

Tourist Information Centres offer friendly help with accommodation and holiday ideas as well as suggestions of places to visit and things to do. You'll find contact details at the beginning of each regional section.

YORK, North Yorkshire Map ref 4C1 — GUEST ACCOMMODATION

★★★★
GUEST ACCOMMODATION
SILVER AWARD

B&B PER ROOM PER NIGHT
S £55.00–£70.00
D £70.00–£80.00

Ascot House

80 East Parade, York YO31 7YH **t** +44 (0) 1904 426826 **e** admin@ascothouseyork.com

ascothouseyork.com

open All year except Christmas
bedrooms 8 double, 2 twin, 3 family
bathrooms 12 en suite, 1 private
payment Credit/debit cards, cash, cheques

A family-run Victorian villa, built in 1869, with en suite rooms of character and many four-poster or canopy beds. Delicious English, continental and vegetarian breakfasts served. Fifteen minutes' walk to historic walled city centre, castle museum or York Minster. Residential licence and residents' lounge, sauna and private, enclosed car park.

SAT NAV YO31 7YH

Room 🛏🖨📺🚿🍴 General 🛋🏢🛗P📶🔥🍷🍽🐾

YORK, North Yorkshire Map ref 4C1 — GUEST ACCOMMODATION

★★★★
GUEST ACCOMMODATION

B&B PER ROOM PER NIGHT
S £30.00–£35.00
D £60.00–£70.00

Single-night price reduction for 2 or more nights' stay.

Ascot Lodge

112 Acomb Road, York YO24 4EY **t** +44 (0) 1904 798234 **e** info@ascotlodge.com

ascotlodge.com

open All year
bedrooms 1 twin, 4 single, 5 family
bathrooms 7 en suite
payment Cash, cheques

Receive a warm welcome at this beautiful mid-Victorian guesthouse on the west side of York. Peaceful, yet near to the city centre – 25 minutes' walk or 5-10 minutes by regular bus service. Luxurious, en suite double, family and single rooms. Non-smoking throughout. Secure, private car park. Vegetarians catered for.

SAT NAV YO24 4EY

Room 🛏📺🚿🍴 General 🛋🏢🛗P🍽❄🐾 Leisure ▶

YORK, North Yorkshire Map ref 4C1 — GUEST ACCOMMODATION

★★★★
GUEST ACCOMMODATION

B&B PER ROOM PER NIGHT
S £35.00–£40.00
D £60.00–£80.00

The Ashberry

103 The Mount, York YO24 1AX **t** +44 (0) 1904 647339 **e** kevlyon@ashberryhotel.co.uk

ashberryhotel.co.uk

The Ashberry is a double-fronted Victorian town house, only five minutes from the town centre, Minster, railway station and racecourse. Enjoy an award-winning breakfast.

open All year except Christmas
bedrooms 3 double, 2 twin, 1 family
bathrooms All en suite
payment Credit/debit cards, cash, cheques, euros

Room 📺🚿🍴 General 🛋🏢🛗❄

★★★★
**GUEST ACCOMMODATION
SILVER AWARD**

B&B PER ROOM PER NIGHT
S £68.00–£84.00
D £78.00–£92.00

Discount on stays of 3 or more days (excl Fri and Sat). See website for details.

Barbican House

20 Barbican Road, York YO10 5AA **t** +44 (0) 1904 627617 **e** info@barbicanhouse.com

barbicanhouse.com GUEST REVIEWS · SPECIAL OFFERS · REAL-TIME BOOKING

open All year except Christmas and New Year
bedrooms 6 double, 1 twin, 1 family
bathrooms All en suite
payment Credit/debit cards, cash, cheques

Welcome to our wonderful restored Victorian villa overlooking the medieval city walls. Delightful bedrooms, each individually decorated to complement the charm and character of the period. All rooms are en suite and non-smoking. Full English breakfast using local, free-range produce. Free private parking available.

SAT NAV YO10 5AA **ONLINE MAP**

Room ⚿ 📺 ☕ ☏ General ⛹10 P ⌖ ⚐ ⚒ ❄ Leisure ♪

★★★★
GUEST ACCOMMODATION

B&B PER ROOM PER NIGHT
S £38.00–£45.00
D £70.00–£82.00

Why not book our celebrations package too? Please call or visit the website for details.

The Bentley Guest House

25 Grosvenor Terrace, Bootham, York YO30 7AG **t** +44 (0) 1904 644313
e enquiries@bentleyofyork.com

bentleyofyork.com

open All year except Christmas
bedrooms 3 double, 1 twin, 1 single
bathrooms All en suite
payment Credit/debit cards, cash, cheques

Steve and Margaret Bradley look forward to welcoming you to The Bentley, an elegant Victorian town house situated close to York's historic centre. All our rooms are en suite and prettily decorated with colourful linen and interesting pictures. A highlight of a stay here is a superb breakfast.

SAT NAV YO30 7AG **ONLINE MAP**

Room 🛏 📺 ☕ ☏ General ⛹10 ⌖ Leisure ▶

★★★★
GUEST HOUSE

B&B PER ROOM PER NIGHT
S £50.00–£65.00
D £60.00–£85.00

Dairy Guest House

3 Scarcroft Road, York YO23 1ND **t** +44 (0) 1904 639367 **e** stay@dairyguesthouse.co.uk

dairyguesthouse.co.uk REAL-TIME BOOKING

A lovingly restored and upgraded Victorian town house with original features, situated just 300yds from the medieval city walls and within an easy stroll of York's many attractions and museums.

open All year
bedrooms 4 double, 1 twin, 1 family
bathrooms All en suite
payment Credit/debit cards, cash, cheques

Room ⚿ 🛏 📺 ☕ ☏ General ⛹ ⌖ ❄

enjoyEngland.com

Get in the know – log on for a wealth of information and inspiration. All the latest news on places to visit, events and quality-assessed accommodation is literally at your fingertips. Explore all that England has to offer.

YORK, North Yorkshire Map ref 4C1

Fourposter Lodge

★★★
GUEST HOUSE

B&B PER ROOM PER NIGHT
S £28.00–£70.00
D £45.00–£95.00

Reduction for 3 nights or more, all year round.

68-70 Heslington Road, York YO10 5AU **t** +44 (0) 1904 651170 **e** fourposter.lodge@virgin.net

fourposterlodge.co.uk SPECIAL OFFERS · REAL-TIME BOOKING

open All year except New Year
bedrooms 7 double, 1 twin, 1 single, 1 family
bathrooms 8 en suite, 2 private
payment Credit/debit cards, cash, cheques

Your hosts Shirley and Gary welcome you to their Victorian villa. Enjoy the comfort and luxury of our four-poster beds. Start the day with the house speciality – 'a hearty English breakfast'. Ten minutes walk to the city centre, close to Fulford Golf Course and York University. Licensed. Car park.

SAT NAV YO10 5AU **ONLINE MAP**

Room 🛏🗄📺☕🍳 General 🎠🏛🔥P🌐🍷🍽❄🐴 Leisure 🎵

YORK, North Yorkshire Map ref 4C1

Heworth Court

★★★★
GUEST ACCOMMODATION

B&B PER ROOM PER NIGHT
S £58.00–£118.00
D £69.00–£129.00

10% discount to guests booking online. See also 'Sunday Saver', stay 5 nights arriving Sunday, get Sunday at half price.

Heworth Green, York YO31 7TQ **t** +44 (0) 1904 425156 **e** hotel@heworth.co.uk

heworth.co.uk GUEST REVIEWS · SPECIAL OFFERS · REAL-TIME BOOKING

open All year except Christmas and New Year
bedrooms 22 double, 2 twin, 2 single, 2 family
bathrooms All en suite
payment Credit/debit cards, cash

Heworth Court offers guests bed and full English breakfast. Twelve minutes from York Minster and York's numerous restaurants. Free parking. Our 'Minster Bells' bar features over 30 malt whiskies as well as draught beers and soft drinks. Superking-size, king-size with rolltop bath, four-poster, executive, VIP chandelier and standard rooms.

SAT NAV YO31 7TQ **ONLINE MAP**

Room 🛏🗄📞📺☕🍳 General 🎠🔥P🌐🍷🍽❄ Leisure 🚲

YORK, North Yorkshire Map ref 4C1

Manor Guest House

★★★★
GUEST ACCOMMODATION

B&B PER ROOM PER NIGHT
S £45.00–£55.00
D £65.00–£80.00

EVENING MEAL PER PERSON
£12.50–£25.00

Book full week and pay for 6 nights. Various seasonal and midweek offers. Excellent dinners available on request from £12.50.

Main Street, Linton-on-Ouse YO30 2AY **t** +44 (0) 1347 848391 **e** manorguesthouse@tiscali.co.uk

manorguesthouse.co.uk

open All year
bedrooms 2 double, 2 twin, 1 single, 2 family, 1 suite
bathrooms All en suite
payment Credit/debit cards, cash, cheques, euros

Award-winning en suite accommodation in a listed Georgian manor house. Period oak-beamed rooms and ground-floor family suite. Ideal for Yorkshire Dales and Moors and picturesque towns, yet only 10 minutes York 'park and ride'. Lovely village location, river walks, pubs/restaurants. Spacious grounds with ample private parking. Dogs welcome.

SAT NAV YO30 2AY

Room 🛏🗄📺☕🍳 General 🎠🏛🔥P🌐✖🍽📺❄🐴 Leisure ⛵🎵🎣🚲

Where are the maps?

Colour maps can be found at the front of the guide. They pinpoint the location of all accommodation found in the regional sections.

★★★★
GUEST ACCOMMODATION

B&B PER ROOM PER NIGHT
D £61.00–£64.00

Palm Court

17 Huntington Road, York YO31 8RB t +44 (0) 1904 639387 e helencoll_2000@hotmail.com

thepalmcourt.org.uk

A very warm welcome awaits you at our elegant Victorian family-run guest accommodation, offering excellent value. Overlooking River Foss and five-minute walk to city. En suite rooms, free private parking.

open All year except Christmas and New Year
bedrooms 2 double, 2 twin, 4 family
bathrooms All en suite
payment Cash, cheques

Room 📺 👜 🍵 General 🛏 🏛 ⚲ P ⟨⟩ 🍴 ✿

★★★★
GUEST ACCOMMODATION

B&B PER ROOM PER NIGHT
S £28.00–£33.00
D £58.00–£68.00

Four-poster rooms
£34.00–£39.00
pppn.

York House

62 Heworth Green, York YO31 7TQ t +44 (0) 1904 427070 e yorkhouse.bandb@tiscali.co.uk

yorkhouseyork.co.uk

open All year except Christmas and New Year
bedrooms 5 double, 1 twin, 1 single, 1 family
bathrooms 7 en suite, 1 private
payment Credit/debit cards, cash, cheques

Located a short stroll from the heart of one of Europe's most historic cities. York House is the perfect base for a visit to beautiful York or the surrounding area. A Georgian house with later additions, rooms feature all the modern conveniences you could possibly need for a relaxing, enjoyable stay.

SAT NAV YO31 7TQ

Room 🛗 🖨 📺 👜 🍵 General 🛏 🏛 ⚲ P ⟨⟩ ♨ 🍴 ✿

★★★★★
SELF CATERING

Units **1**
Sleeps **1–6**

LOW SEASON PER WK
£1,230.00

HIGH SEASON PER WK
£1,230.00

10 George Street, York

contact Mrs Heather Robinson, 3 Old Bank, Slaithwaite, Huddersfield HD7 5AR
t +44 (0) 1484 841330 & +44 (0) 7753 958686 e info@10georgestreet.co.uk

10georgestreet.co.uk REAL-TIME BOOKING

open All year
payment Credit/debit cards
nearest pub less than 0.5 miles
nearest shop less than 0.5 miles

Luxury boutique-style accommodation in a three-storey Georgian town house within the city walls, featuring highly unusual, eclectic decor. Antiques, oak panelling and floors, chandeliers and roll-top baths. Charming courtyard garden, parking for one vehicle, short breaks available, minimum two nights' stay. Top quality fittings, and goodies on arrival.

SAT NAV YO1 9QB **ONLINE MAP**

Unit 📺 🆂🅲 📀 📺 🗄🗄 🍵 🗑 🍽 📋 ✿ 🔥 General 🛏 P ⟨⟩ 🆂

It's all quality-assessed accommodation

Our commitment to quality involves wide-ranging accommodation assessment. Ratings and awards were correct at the time of going to press but may change following a new assessment. Please check at time of booking.

YORK, North Yorkshire Map ref 4C1

★★★★–★★★★★★
SELF CATERING

Units **5**
Sleeps **1–4**

LOW SEASON PER WK
£700.00–£1,400.00

HIGH SEASON PER WK
£700.00–£1,400.00

The Blue Rooms, York

contact Miss Kirsty Reid, The Blue Bicycle York Ltd, 34 Fossgate, York YO1 9TA
t +44 (0) 1904 673990 **e** blue-rooms@thebluebicycle.com

thebluebicycle.com

open All year
payment Credit/debit cards, cash, cheques
nearest pub less than 0.5 miles
nearest shop less than 0.5 miles

Overlooking the River Foss, The Blue Rooms occupy a secluded mews position and are equipped to the very highest standards. They offer luxury, convenience, privacy and comfort for that short romantic break or business trip. You will be welcomed on arrival with a bottle of champagne and fresh fruit basket, with our compliments.

Unit 📺 🎧🔌 💻 🖥 🍽 🔽 ⚙ 🔲 General 🐾 P ⑤ Leisure ∪ ♪ ⏃ ⚲

YORK, North Yorkshire Map ref 4C1

★★★
SELF CATERING

Units **1**
Sleeps **2–5**

LOW SEASON PER WK
£302.00–£450.00

HIGH SEASON PER WK
£402.00–£600.00

Garnet House, York

contact Mr Gordon Robinson, Garnet House, Garnet Terrace, York YO26 4XX **t** +44 (0) 1904 412975
& +44 (0) 7973 409381 **e** herbie831@talktalk.net

Victorian three-bedroomed terrace family house, many original features, open aspects to conservation area. Twenty minutes' walk by the river into city, Free parking. Satellite TV, internet access, welcome hamper.

open All year
payment Credit/debit cards
nearest pub less than 0.5 miles
nearest shop less than 0.5 miles

Unit 📺 SC 🎧🔌 DVD 📷 🖥 🍽 🔽 ⚙ 🔲 ❄ General 🐾1 🎱♨ P ⑤ 🐕
Leisure ♪

YORK, North Yorkshire Map ref 4C1

★★★
SELF CATERING

Units **1**
Sleeps **4–10**

LOW SEASON PER WK
Min £400.00

HIGH SEASON PER WK
Max £800.00

Pavilion Cottage, York

contact Mrs Heidi Whitaker, Pavilion Cottage, Shipton Road, York YO30 5RE **t** +44 (0) 1904 639258
& +44 (0) 7974 853876 **e** pavcottage@yahoo.co.uk

pavilioncottage-holidayinyork.co.uk GUEST REVIEWS

A warm welcome awaits you. Pavilion Cottage sleeps eight to ten comfortably, has wonderful views over neighbouring cricket pitches and open countryside, yet lies close to York city centre.

open All year
payment Cash, cheques, euros
nearest pub 0.5 miles
nearest shop 0.5 miles

Unit 📺 📷 🖥 🍽 🔽 ⚙ 🔲 ❄ ♨ General 🐾 🎱♨ P ⑤ 🐕
Leisure ∪ ♪ ⚲

visit**Britain**.com

Get in the know – log on for a wealth of information and inspiration. All the latest news on places to visit, events and quality-assessed accommodation is literally at your fingertips. Explore all that Britain has to offer.

★★★
SELF CATERING

Units **2**
Sleeps **1–6**

LOW SEASON PER WK
£250.00–£550.00

HIGH SEASON PER WK
£450.00–£650.00

Part-weeks available. We offer livery for up to 2 horses or ponies.

Skipwith Station Holidays, Selby

contact Mrs Lizanne Southworth, Skipwith Station, North Duffield YO8 5DE **t** +44 (0) 1757 282288
e info@skipwithstation.com

skipwithstation.com REAL-TIME BOOKING

open All year
payment Cash, cheques
nearest pub 1 mile
nearest shop 1 mile

We offer elegant, stylish accommodation in two railway carriages in the grounds of the restored station. Both carriages offer contemporary and beautifully furnished interiors. Each carriage has a double bedroom, bunk room, shower room, kitchen and lounge. Views from the platform and from the lounges are across the open countryside.

ONLINE MAP

Unit 📺 ▣ ▢ ▦ ⬚ ⬚ ⬚ 🌣 🔥 General 🐴 🏕 P ▢ Ⓢ Leisure ∪ ⊿ ▸

★★★★★
TOURING &
CAMPING PARK

🚐 (102) £14.90–£28.30
🚐 (102) £14.90–£28.30
⛺   on application
102 touring pitches

Rowntree Park Caravan Club Site

Terry Avenue, York YO23 1JQ **t** +44 (0) 1904 658997

caravanclub.co.uk

open All year
payment Credit/debit cards, cash, cheques

On the banks of the river Ouse in the heart of York, this popular site is just a few minutes' walk from the city centre. York is a feast, there's so much to see and do – visit the lovely Minster with its dazzling stained glass windows and walk the city walls.

SAT NAV YO23 1JQ

Special member rates mean you can save your membership subscription in less than a week. Visit our website to find out more.

THE CARAVAN CLUB

General 🔲 🔌 🚽 🚿 💧 🔥 🛁 ☀ 📶 Leisure ⊿ ▸

★★★★★
TOURING PARK

🚐 (20) £14.00–£19.00
🚐 (20) £14.00–£19.00
⛺ (20) £14.00–£19.00
20 touring pitches

YCP York Caravan Park and Storage

Stockton Lane, York YO32 9UB **t** +44 (0) 1904 424222 **e** mail@yorkcaravanpark.com

yorkcaravanpark.com GUEST REVIEWS · SPECIAL OFFERS

A beautiful caravan park two miles from York, surrounded by countryside. All pitches have electricity, water, TV and drains, and are much larger than average. Hardstanding available. Bus stop outside.

open 15 March to 6 November
payment Credit/debit cards, cash, cheques, euros

General 🔲 🚽 🔌 🚿 💧 🔥 🛁 🐎 ☀ 📶 ♿ Leisure ⛰ ∪ ⊿ ▸

Remember to check when booking

Please remember that all information in this guide has been supplied by the proprietors well in advance of publication. Since changes do sometimes occur it's a good idea to check details at the time of booking.

Central England

Bedfordshire, Cambridgeshire, Derbyshire, Essex, Herefordshire, Hertfordshire, Leicestershire, Lincolnshire, Norfolk, Northamptonshire, Nottinghamshire, Rutland, Shropshire, Staffordshire, Suffolk, Warwickshire, West Midlands, Worcestershire

Clockwise: Holkham Hall, Norfolk; Royal Worcester, Worcestershire; Lincoln Cathedral, Lincolnshire

Great days out

Active pursuits, lazy days and family fun – find them all in Central England. Pull on your walking boots and challenge the Pennines, drift along the canals that criss-cross the region, follow the trail to the Major Oak in Sherwood Forest. And do come for the world-class – sometimes uniquely quirky – culture.

It's child's play

Game for anything? Then plunge in – there's such a wide choice of fun family days out. Start with a Thrill Hopper ticket giving great value access to four hair-raising theme park attractions: **Alton Towers** (try the exciting new Battle Galleons interactive water ride), **Drayton Manor Theme Park** (now with Europe's first Thomas Land for engine fiends), Tamworth **SnowDome** and **Waterworld**.

Bewilderwood, Norfolk

Next up, how about the **National Space Centre**, Leicester, where you can see if you cut it as an astronaut. Check your pulse and hit the assault course at **Conkers**, Swadlincote, in the heart of the National Forest, or tackle the zip wires and crocklebogs of **Bewilderwood**, Wroxham. Encounter lions, tigers and elephants at **Woburn Safari Park**, and get to **Dudley Zoological Gardens** for feeding time.

Good sport!

Discover natural sporting arenas to suit every pace and purpose. Walking, cycling, climbing, potholing: it's all here. Saunter along **Offa's Dyke Path**, stride part of the **Heart of England Way**, or dip into stretches of the **Pennine Way**. In the west of the region, the vistas that embrace the **Malverns** are superb. Cyclists of all ages love the flat terrain in the East of England, and you can hire bikes to explore the woodland trails at **Clumber Park**, Worksop. Mountain bikers (especially keen youngsters) can enjoy a challenge on traffic-free circular rides in **Bacton Woods**, Norfolk.

Then up the ante because action and adventure are bywords for the **Peak District and Derbyshire**. Climbers of all abilities come to grapple with limestone and gritstone crags. Potholers relish some of the most challenging caves in Britain. And if you're really more of a spectator, book your place trackside for sensational, high-octane Formula 1 racing at **Silverstone**, or have a flutter at **Newmarket**, the historical home of British horseracing.

Take the waters

Pack buckets, spades and binoculars then head for mile upon mile of sandy and shingle beaches from Essex to Lincolnshire. Hunker down in a hide along the coast at **RSPB Minsmere** to spy wading birds and waterfowl. Share the bustling delights of seaside resorts like Felixstowe, Southend-on-Sea and Great Yarmouth. For something quieter, seek out the havens of Frinton-on-Sea, Covehithe and Anderby Creek plus numerous quaint fishing villages.

Left to right: The Roaches, Staffordshire;
RSPB Minsmere Nature Reserve, Suffolk

did you know... Derbyshire's Dovedale was formed from ancient coral reefs? Enjoy the ultimate ramble!

Inland, explore rivers and dykes in the **Fens**, a magical water world extending over Cambridgeshire, Lincolnshire, Norfolk and Rutland. At **Fenscape** interactive discovery centre in Spalding, learn all about the unique landscape and heritage. For lazy days with friends and family, what could be more calming than the reed-fringed waterways of the **Norfolk Broads**? When energy levels rise again, cast off for some sailing at **Rutland Water & Nature Reserve** and exhilarating watersports at **Carsington Water**.

Creative culture

With such a rich mix of history and raw natural beauty it's not surprising Central England inspires creativity. Visit the haunts of famous local lads: the **Stour Valley** of John Constable immortalised in *The Hay Wain* and **Stratford-upon-Avon** where young William Shakespeare lived – look around his birthplace then catch a performance by the **Royal Shakespeare Company**, there's nothing like Shakespeare enacted in his home town. Tour Gothic **Newstead Abbey**, full of Lord Byron's possessions and manuscripts, and gain insights into the life and music of Sir Edward Elgar at **The Elgar Birthplace Museum**, Lower Broadheath.

Today the region thrives with festivals and events ranging from classical to contemporary culture. On a musical note, Benjamin Britten's **Aldeburgh Festival** at Snape Maltings, Suffolk, is the place for classical concerts in a rural setting.

Royal Shakespeare Company, Warwickshire

The annual **DH Lawrence Festival** helps to attract thousands to the author's home town of Eastwood. Unique and quirky happenings are also to the fore, at **Whittlesea Straw Bear Festival** and **Shrewsbury's Cartoon Festival**.

Historic highlights

Linger in **Shrewsbury** to savour the historic atmosphere, or browse the streets of **Worcester** – places noted for their charming Tudor half-timbered architecture. Reach for your camera as you pass through **Much Wenlock**, one of the beautiful black and white villages of Shropshire. Castles and grand homes dot the landscape – **Warwick Castle, Hatfield House** and **Chatsworth** are favourites. For Elizabethan architecture at its most impressive, **Hardwick Hall** is hard to beat. Gothic **Lincoln Cathedral** on its lofty hill and **Lincoln Castle**, where one of only four surviving copies of Magna Carta is held, are must-visit heritage showpieces.

did you know... Lincoln Cathedral doubled as Westminster Abbey in The Da Vinci Code film?

Also step back into the area's proud industrial past, at the **Ironbridge Gorge Museums** – kids soon switch on their imaginations to design and technology at **Enginuity**. Have a chat with working craftsmen at **The Black Country Living Museum**. Trace the history of fighter planes at the **Imperial War Museum Duxford**, Europe's premier aviation museum. At the **Wedgwood Visitor Centre**, Stoke-on-Trent, you can tour the factory and throw a pot or two under the helpful eye of an expert.

Plumbread, pies and shopping

Central England serves up a mouthwatering range of distinctive foods: succulent Melton Mowbray pork pies, Red Leicester and Stilton, Lincolnshire plumbread and Bakewell pudding – often imitated, never matched. Head for Britain's food capital, pretty **Ludlow** on the Welsh borders, to discover what lures so many top chefs to the **Ludlow Marches Food and Drink Festival**. And then there's retail therapy at its most irresistible. Remember the **Bullring** in **Birmingham**? A space the size of more than 26 football pitches – all dedicated to shopping and entertainment. Soak up the colourful atmosphere of multicultural **Leicester** and try on a sari or two.

Clockwise: Imperial War Museum Duxford, Cambridgeshire; Wedgwood Visitor Centre, Staffordshire; Henry Moore Foundation, Hertfordshire

Destinations

Birmingham

A dynamic city combining a fascinating history with a world-class cultural scene. Lose yourself in shopping heaven in the stunningly remodelled Bullring, wander through the historic Jewellery Quarter then sit back and enjoy the Symphony Orchestra in the magnificent Symphony Hall. Indulge your sweet tooth at Cadbury World, or take in a major event at the NEC or NIA. You'll also find yourself at the heart of a region full of history and heritage, beautiful quaint villages and access to lush rolling countryside – Birmingham really is a gateway to the heart of England!

Cambridge

Cambridge

The name Cambridge instantly summons breathtaking images – the Backs carpeted with spring flowers, King's College Chapel, punting on the river Cam and, of course, the calm of the historic college buildings. Cambridge still has the atmosphere of a bustling market town, notwithstanding its international reputation. Explore its winding streets and splendid architecture, and choose from a range of attractions, museums, hotels, restaurants and pubs. Situated in the heart of East Anglia but less than an hour from London by high-speed rail link.

Colchester

Find internationally important treasures located in award-winning museums or visit cutting-edge contemporary galleries. It's a shopper's heaven with specialist shops and big name stores, and the range of cuisine makes Colchester a magnet for food lovers – don't miss the annual Colchester Oyster Feast.

Great Yarmouth

One of the UK's most popular seaside resorts, with an enviable mix of sandy beaches, attractions, entertainment and heritage. Beyond the seaside fun is a charming town that is steeped in history. Visit the medieval town walls, stroll the historic South Quay and discover Nelson's 'other' column. When the sun goes down colourful illuminations light up the night sky.

Hereford

In this ancient city on the banks of the River Wye, you'll find historic buildings housing modern shops and modern buildings holding historic treasures. Don't miss Hereford Cathedral with its priceless Mappa Mundi and Chained Library. Wander through the spacious High Town and the new Left Bank Village. Visit the Cider Museum to learn about Hereford's claim to be 'The Apple of England's Eye'.

Lincoln

Possessing magnificent architectural heritage, centred on its world famous Cathedral and Castle, Lincoln is a vivacious City – mixing 2,000 years of heritage with excellent shopping and lively arts and events. The Brayford Waterfront quarter is home to some of the newest places to eat and drink. Events include the famous Christmas Market and the Brayford Waterfront Festival.

Left to right: Chatsworth, Derbyshire;
Alton Towers, Staffordshire

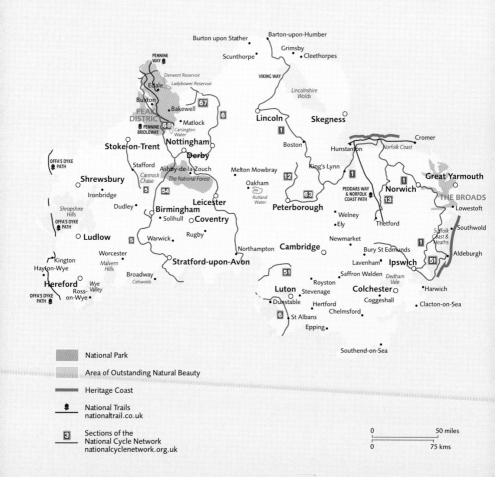

National Park

Area of Outstanding Natural Beauty

Heritage Coast

National Trails
nationaltrail.co.uk

3 Sections of the
National Cycle Network
nationalcyclenetwork.org.uk

0   50 miles

0   75 kms

     Where to Stay in Britain

Ludlow

Ludlow

Discover the place Betjemen described as 'the loveliest town in England.' Britain's first 'slow' town is also a gastronomic capital and host to the renowned Ludlow Marches Food & Drink Festival. You'll find a host of speciality food shops, and more restaurants and inns than you can shake a cocktail stick at. To walk off lunch, stroll in the enchanting Angel Gardens, or take in a performance at the open-air theatre in the stunning medieval ruin of Ludlow Castle.

Norwich

Norwich, county town of Norfolk, is an enchanting cathedral city and a thriving modern metropolis. See some of the finest medieval architecture in Britain in the cathedral and castle, and wander an intricate network of winding streets. The city's newest centrepiece, The Forum, represents contemporary architecture at its best. You'll find excellent shopping as well as a vibrant mix of theatres, cinemas, arts festivals, exhibitions, museums, and a vast array of restaurants.

Nottingham

Nottingham is the undisputed capital of the East Midlands, boasting a sophisticated urban environment with an enviable reputation for clubs, theatres, cinemas and galleries, not to mention a deserved reputation as one of the top retail centres in the country. History is never far away, though, with reminders of Nottingham's legendary hero Robin Hood and his adversary the Sheriff of Nottingham. Explore the Castle Museum and Art Gallery, and Wollaton Hall, one of the most ornate Tudor buildings in Britain, complete with 500-acre deer park.

Peak District

The Peak District is Britain's first and most popular National Park. Roam on open moorland to the north and take in the magnificent views over the Derwent Dams. Further south, stroll alongside sparkling rivers in wildlife-rich valleys far from the hustle and bustle of town. The Peak Park Rangers lead regular guided walks – choose from long hikes to village tours. Take in the grandeur of Chatsworth House or Haddon Hall, and sample the local oatcakes with Hartington Stilton, followed by a delicious Bakewell pudding.

Stratford-upon-Avon

Unearth a magical blend of heritage and drama in and around Shakespeare's home town. Explore five houses with Shakespeare connections including Anne Hathaway's Cottage and Shakespeare's Birthplace. Visit one of England's most beautiful parish churches at Holy Trinity to see Shakespeare's grave and enjoy some of his great works performed by the world's largest classical theatre company, the RSC. Take a boat out on the River Avon, wander the boutiques, specialist stores and gift shops, and discover some of Britain's finest historic houses and gardens.

Clockwise: Brayford Waterfront, Lincoln, Colchester Castle; Birmingham

For lots more great ideas visit visitbritain.com/destinations

Visitor attractions

Family and Fun

Adventure Island Southend

Southend-on-Sea, Essex
+44 (0) 1702 443400
adventureisland.co.uk
Great rides and attractions for all ages.

Alton Towers Theme Park
Alton, Staffordshire
+44 (0) 870 520 4060
altontowers.com
High-adrenalin adventure and family fun.

Banham Zoo
Banham, Norfolk
+44 (0) 1953 887771
banhamzoo.co.uk
Wildlife spectacular featuring rare and endangered animals.

Bewilderwood
Wroxham, Norfolk
+44 (0) 1603 783900
bewilderwood.co.uk
Treehouses, zip wires and jungle bridges.

Black Country Living Museum
Dudley, West Midlands
+44 (0) 121 557 9643
bclm.co.uk
Twenty-six acres of fascinating living history.

Cadbury World
Birmingham
+44 (0) 845 450 3599
cadburyworld.co.uk
Chocolate-making demonstrations and free samples.

Colchester Zoo
Stanway, Essex
+44 (0) 1206 331292
colchester-zoo.com
Featuring superb cat and primate collections.

Conkers
Swadlincote, Leicestershire
+44 (0) 1283 216633
visitconkers.com
Interactive adventure in the National Forest.

Coventry Transport Museum
Coventry, West Midlands
+44 (0) 24 7623 4270
transport-museum.com
World-renowned exhibition of British road transport.

Drayton Manor Theme Park
Tamworth, Staffordshire
+44 (0) 844 472 1950
draytonmanor.co.uk
The biggest, wettest and scariest rides around.

Dudley Zoological Gardens
Dudley, West Midlands
+44 (0) 1384 215313
dudleyzoo.org.uk
Lions and tigers, snakes and spiders!

Imperial War Museum Duxford
Large Visitor Attraction of the Year – Gold
near Cambridge
+44 (0) 1223 835000
duxford.iwm.org.uk
The sights, sounds and power of aircraft.

Ironbridge Gorge Museums
Ironbridge, Shropshire
+44 (0) 1952 884391
ironbridge.org.uk
World Heritage Site featuring ten superb museums.

National Sea Life Centre
Birmingham
+44 (0) 121 643 6777
sealifeeurope.com
Marvel at over 3,000 sea creatures.

National Space Centre
Leicester
+44 (0) 870 607 7223
spacecentre.co.uk
Test your abilities as an astronaut.

Nene Valley Railway
Peterborough, Cambridgeshire
+44 (0) 1780 784444
nvr.org.uk
The golden age of steam comes alive.

The Poppy Line – North Norfolk Railway
Sheringham, Norfolk
+44 (0) 1263 820800
nnr.co.uk
5.5 mile heritage railway through delightful countryside.

Pleasurewood Hills Leisure Park
Lowestoft, Suffolk
+44 (0) 1502 586000
pleasurewoodhills.co.uk
Adrenaline-fuelled thrills and spills.

Severn Valley Railway
Bewdley, Worcestershire
+44 (0) 1299 403816
svr.co.uk
Journey through 16 miles of beautiful countryside.

Twycross Zoo
Twycross, Leicestershire
+44 (0) 1827 880250
twycrosszoo.com
Meet the famous gorillas, orang-utans and chimpanzees.

Warwick Castle
Warwick, Warwickshire
+44 (0) 1926 406611
warwick-castle.co.uk
Enthralling medieval castle in 60-acre grounds.

Woburn Safari Park
Woburn, Bedfordshire
+44 (0) 1525 290407
woburnsafari.co.uk
Wild animals just a windscreen's width away.

Heritage

Alford Manor House
Alford, Lincolnshire
+44 (0) 1507 463073
alfordmanorhouse.co.uk
Britain's largest thatched manor house.

Althorp
Althorp, Northamptonshire
+44 (0) 1604 770107
althorp.com
Historic Spencer family seat containing Diana exhibition.

Belton House, Park and Gardens
Belton, Lincolnshire
+44 (0) 1476 566116
nationaltrust.org.uk
Fine example of Restoration country-house architecture.

Belvoir Castle
Belvoir, Leicestershire
+44 (0) 1476 871002
belvoircastle.com
Fine stately home in stunning setting.

Burghley House
Stamford, Lincolnshire
+44 (0) 1780 752451
burghley.co.uk
The grandest house of the Elizabethan age.

Canons Ashby House
Canons Ashby, Northamptonshire
+44 (0) 1327 861900
nationaltrust.org.uk
Tranquil Elizabethan home of the Dryden family.

Chatsworth House
Bakewell, Derbyshire
+44 (0) 1246 565300
chatsworth.org
One of Britain's truly great historic houses.

Doddington Hall & Gardens
Lincoln
+44 (0) 1522 694308
doddingtonhall.com
Superb Elizabethan mansion set in romantic gardens.

Ely Cathedral
Ely, Cambridgeshire
+44 (0) 1353 667735
cathedral.ely.anglican.org
Tour one of England's finest cathedrals.

Gainsborough Old Hall
Gainsborough, Lincolnshire
+44 (0) 1427 612669
lincolnshire.gov.uk
Medieval manor house with original interiors.

Haddon Hall
Bakewell, Derbyshire
+44 (0) 1629 812855
haddonhall.co.uk
Medieval and Tudor manor house with gardens.

Hardwick Hall
Chesterfield, Derbyshire
+44 (0) 1246 850430
nationaltrust.org.uk
Elizabethan country house, gardens and parkland.

Hatfield House
Hatfield, Hertfordshire
+44 (0) 1707 287010
hatfield-house.co.uk
Magnificent childhood home of Elizabeth I.

Hedingham Castle
Castle Hedingham, Essex
+44 (0) 1787 460261
hedinghamcastle.co.uk
The finest Norman keep in England.

Hereford Cathedral
Hereford, Herefordshire
+44 (0) 1432 374200
herefordcathedral.org
Magnificent cathedral housing the precious Mappa Mundi.

Holkham Hall
Wells-next-the-Sea, Norfolk
+44 (0) 1328 713103
holkham.co.uk
Classic 18thC Palladian-style mansion.

Kirby Hall
Corby, Northamptonshire
+44 (0) 1536 203230
Elizabethan house with superb carved decoration.

Knebworth House
Knebworth, Hertfordshire
+44 (0) 1438 812661
knebworthhouse.com
Re-fashioned Tudor house in 250-acre grounds.

Lincoln Cathedral
Lincoln
+44 (0) 1522 561600
lincolncathedral.com
One of Europe's finest gothic buildings.

Newstead Abbey
near Nottingham
+44 (0) 1623 455900
newsteadabbey.org.uk
The ancestral home of Lord Byron.

Norwich Cathedral
Norwich, Norfolk
+44 (0) 1603 218300
cathedral.org.uk
Majestic Norman cathedral with 14thC roof bosses.

Nottingham Castle
Nottingham
+44 (0) 115 915 3700
nottinghamcity.gov.uk/museums
17thC mansion on a medieval-castle site.

Rockingham Castle
Small Visitor Attraction of the Year – Silver
Rockingham, Northamptonshire
+44 (0) 1536 770240
rockinghamcastle.com
Elizabethan house with splendid artworks and gardens.

Sandringham
Sandringham, Norfolk
+44 (0) 1553 612908
sandringham-estate.co.uk
The country retreat of HM The Queen.

Shugborough – The Complete Working Historic Estate
Shugborough, Staffordshire
+44 (0) 1889 881388
shugborough.org.uk
Fine mansion set in rare, surviving estate.

Sulgrave Manor
Sulgrave, Northamptonshire
+44 (0) 1295 760205
sulgravemanor.org.uk
The home of George Washington's ancestors.

Weston Park
near Shifnal, Shropshire
+44 (0) 1952 852100
weston-park.com
Charming stately home with beautiful gardens.

Woburn Abbey
Woburn, Bedfordshire
+44 (0) 1525 290333
woburnabbey.co.uk
Palladian mansion set in 3,000-acre deer park.

Indoors

78 Derngate
Northampton
+44 (0) 1604 603407
78derngate.org.uk
Terraced house transformed by Charles Rennie Mackintosh.

Birmingham Museum & Art Gallery
Birmingham
+44 (0) 121 303 2834
bmag.org.uk
Fine and applied arts featuring Pre-Raphaelites.

Compton Verney
Compton Verney, Warwickshire
+44 (0) 1926 645500
comptonverney.org.uk
Art gallery housed in Robert Adam mansion.

The Elgar Birthplace Museum
Lower Broadheath, Worcestershire
+44 (0) 1905 333224
elgarmuseum.org
Fascinating insight into the great composer's life.

Fitzwilliam Museum
Cambridge
+44 (0) 1223 332900
fitzmuseum.cam.ac.uk
Internationally renowned collection of antiques and art.

Newark Castle
Newark, Nottinghamshire
+44 (0) 1636 655765
newark-sherwooddc.gov.uk
Discover an exciting Civil War history.

Red House Glass Cone
Stourbridge, West Midlands
+44 (0) 1384 812750
dudley.gov.uk/redhousecone
Live glassmaking, craft studios, tunnels and furnaces.

Royal Air Force Museum, Cosford
Cosford, Shropshire
+44 (0) 1902 376200
rafmuseum.org
Warplanes, missiles, aero-engines and flight simulator.

Royal Shakespeare Company
Stratford-upon-Avon, Warwickshire
+44 (0) 1789 403444
rsc.org.uk
Year-round performances of the great works.

Shakespeare's Birthplace
Stratford-upon-Avon, Warwickshire
+44 (0) 1789 204016
shakespeare.org.uk
Acclaimed exhibition housed in Shakespeare's childhood home.

Shuttleworth Collection
Biggleswade, Bedfordshire
+44 (0) 1767 627927
shuttleworth.org
Unique collection of historic aircraft.

Time and Tide – Museum of Great Yarmouth Life
Great Yarmouth, Norfolk
+44 (0) 1493 743930
museums.norfolk.gov.uk
Discover a rich maritime and fishing heritage.

The Wedgwood Visitor Centre
Stoke-on-Trent, Staffordshire
+44 (0) 1782 282986
thewedgwoodvisitorcentre.com
Famous pottery set in glorious Staffordshire countryside.

Outdoors

Castle Ashby Gardens
Castle Ashby, Northamptonshire
+44 (0) 1604 696187
castleashby.co.uk
Capability Brown landscaped gardens and parkland.

Foxton Locks
Foxton, Leicestershire
+44 (0) 1908 302500
foxtonlocks.com
Fascinating ten-lock 'staircase' climbing a 75ft hill.

Go Ape! High Wire Forest Adventure – Sherwood
Mansfield, Nottinghamshire
+44 (0) 845 643 9215
goape.co.uk
Rope bridges, swings and zip slides.

Peveril Castle

Castleton, Derbyshire
+44 (0) 1433 620613
english-heritage.org.uk
Ruined Norman castle with impressive curtain wall.

RHS Garden Hyde Hall
Chelmsford, Essex
+44 (0) 1245 400256
rhs.org.uk
28-acre hill-top garden with year-round interest.

RSPB Minsmere Nature Reserve
Saxmundham, Suffolk
+44 (0) 1728 648281
rspb.org.uk
One of the RSPB's finest reserves.

Rutland Water & Nature Reserve
Oakham, Rutland
+44 (0) 1572 770651
rutlandwater.org.uk
Important wildfowl sanctuary with leisure centre.

Sherwood Forest Country Park
Edwinstowe, Nottinghamshire
+44 (0) 1623 823202
sherwoodforest.org.uk
Native woodland packed with adventure.

Silverstone Circuit
Silverstone, Northamptonshire
+44 (0) 870 458 8200
silverstone.co.uk
The home of British motor racing.

Sutton Hoo Burial Site
Woodbridge, Suffolk
+44 (0) 1394 389700
nationaltrust.org.uk
Anglo-Saxon royal burial site.

The Trentham Estate

Stoke-on-Trent, Staffordshire
+44 (0) 1782 646646
trentham.co.uk
One of Britain's most important historic gardens.

Welney Wetland Centre

Welney, Norfolk
+44 (0) 1353 860711
wwt.org.uk
1,000-acre wetland reserve attracting wild swans.

Wrest Park

Silsoe, Bedfordshire
+44 (0) 1525 860152
english-heritage.org.uk
Magnificent 18thC formal gardens with orangery.

ASSURANCE OF A GREAT DAY OUT
Attractions with this sign participate in the Visitor Attraction Quality Assurance Scheme which recognises high standards in all aspects of the visitor experience.

Events 2009

Crufts
Birmingham
the-kennel-club.org.uk
5 - 8 Mar

St George's Day Festival, Wrest Park Gardens
Silsoe
english-heritage.org.uk
Apr

Luton Carnival
Luton
luton.gov.uk
May

Southend Airshow
Southend-on-Sea
southendairshow.com
May

University of the Great Outdoors - Activity event
Ledbury
visitherefordshire.co.uk
3 - 4 May

Aldeburgh Festival of Music and the Arts
Snape
aldeburgh.co.uk
Jun

Althorp Literary Festival
Northampton
althorp.com
Jun

Stamford Shakespeare Festival
Rutland
stamfordshakespeare.co.uk
Jun - Aug

Robin Hood Festival
Nottingham
nottinghamshire.gov.uk/robinhoodfestival
Jul - Aug

Flavours of Herefordshire Food Festival
Holmer
visitherefordshire.co.uk
24 - 25 Oct

Lincoln Christmas Market
Lincoln
Dec

Regional contacts and information

For more information on accommodation, attractions, activities, events and holidays in Central England, contact one of the following regional or local tourism organisations. Their websites have a wealth of information and many produce free publications to help you get the most out of your visit.

Heart of England

Further information is available from the following organisations:

Marketing Birmingham
t +44 (0) 121 202 5115
w visitbirmingham.com

Black Country Tourism
w blackcountrytourism.co.uk

Visit Coventry & Warwickshire
t +44 (0) 24 7622 7264
w visitcoventryandwarwickshire.co.uk

Visit Herefordshire
t +44 (0) 1432 260621
w visitherefordshire.co.uk

Shakespeare Country
t +44 (0) 870 160 7930
w shakespeare-country.co.uk

Shropshire Tourism
t +44 (0) 1743 462462
w shropshiretourism.info

Destination Staffordshire
t +44 (0) 870 500 4444
w enjoystaffordshire.com

Stoke-on-Trent
t +44 (0) 1782 236000
w visitstoke.co.uk

Destination Worcestershire
t +44 (0) 1905 728787
w visitworcestershire.org

Help before you go
To search for attractions and Tourist Information Centres on the move just text INFO to 62233, and a web link will be sent to your mobile phone.

Clockwise: Warwick Castle, Warwickshire;
Rutland Water, Rutland; The Broads, Norfolk

East of England

East of England Tourism
t +44 (0) 1284 727470
e info@eet.org.uk
w visiteastofengland.com

The comprehensive website is updated daily.
Online brochures and information sheets can
be downloaded including What's New; Major
Events; Lights, Camera, Action! (film and
television locations); Stars and Stripes
(connections with the USA) and a range of
Discovery Tours around the region.

East Midlands

The publications listed are available from the
following organisations:

East Midlands Tourism
w discovereastmidlands.com
• **Discover East Midlands**

Experience Nottinghamshire
t +44 (0) 844 477 5678
w visitnotts.com
• **Nottinghamshire Essential Guide,
  Where to Stay Guide, Stay Somewhere
  Different, City Breaks, Family Days Out**
• **Robin Hood Breaks**
• **Pilgrim Fathers**

Peak District and Derbyshire
t +44 (0) 870 444 7275
w visitpeakdistrict.com
• **Peak District and Derbyshire
  Visitor Guide**
• **Peak District and Derbyshire
  Short Break Ideas**
• **Camping and Caravanning Guide**
• **Bess of Hardwick 400th Anniversary**

Lincolnshire
t +44 (0) 1522 873800
w visitlincolnshire.com
• **Visit Lincolnshire – Destination Guide,
  Great days out, Gardens & Nurseries,
  Aviation Heritage, Good Taste**
• **Keep up with the flow**

Explore Northamptonshire
t +44 (0) 1604 838800
w explorenorthamptonshire.co.uk
• **Explore Northamptonshire Visitor
  Guide, County Map**

Leicestershire
t +44 (0) 844 888 5181
w goleicestershire.com
• **Inspiring short breaks and holidays
  in Leicestershire**
• **Stay, Play, Explore**
• **Great Days Out in Leicestershire**

Discover Rutland
t +44 (0) 1572 653026
w discover-rutland.co.uk
• **Discover Rutland**

Tourist Information Centres

When you arrive at your destination, visit an Official Partner Tourist Information Centre for quality assured help with accommodation and information about local attractions and events, or email your request before you go. To search for attractions and Tourist Information Centres on the move just text INFO to 62233, and a web link will be sent to your mobile phone. To find a Tourist Information Centre by region visit enjoyEngland.com/find-tic.

Aldeburgh	152 High Street	+44 (0) 01728 453637	atic@suffolkcoastal.gov.uk
Ashbourne	13 Market Place	+44 (0) 1335 343666	ashbourneinfo@derbyshiredales.gov.uk
Ashby-de-la-Zouch	North Street	+44 (0) 1530 411767	ashby.tic@nwleices.gov.uk
Bakewell	Bridge Street	+44 (0) 1629 813227	bakewell@peakdistrict-npa.gov.uk
Bewdley	Load Street	+44 (0) 1299 404740	bewdleytic@wyreforestdc.gov.uk
Birmingham Rotunda	150 New Street	+44 (0) 844 888 3883	callcentre@marketingbirmingham.com
Bishop's Stortford	The Old Monastery	+44 (0) 1279 655831	tic@bishopsstortford.org
Brackley	2 Bridge Street	+44 (0) 1280 700111	tic@southnorthants.gov.uk
Braintree	Market Square	+44 (0) 1376 550066	tic@braintree.gov.uk
Bridgnorth	Listley Street	+44 (0) 1746 763257	bridgnorth.tourism@shropshire.gov.uk
Burton upon Trent	Horninglow Street	+44 (0) 1283 508111	tic@eaststaffsbc.gov.uk
Bury St Edmunds	6 Angel Hill	+44 (0) 1284 764667	tic@stedsbc.gov.uk
Buxton	The Crescent	+44 (0) 1298 25106	tourism@highpeak.gov.uk
Castleton	Buxton Road	+44 (0) 1433 620679	castleton@peakdistrict-npa.gov.uk
Chesterfield	Rykneld Square	+44 (0) 1246 345777	tourism@chesterfield.gov.uk
Church Stretton	Church Street	+44 (0) 1694 723133	churchstretton.scf@shropshire.gov.uk
Colchester	Trinity Street	+44 (0) 1206 282920	vic@colchester.gov.uk
Coventry Cathedral	Cathedral Ruins, 1 Hill Top	+44 (0) 24 7623 4297	tic@cvone.co.uk
Coventry Ricoh	Phoenix Way	+44 (0) 844 873 6397	richoh@cvone.co.uk
Coventry Transport Museum	Hales Street	+44 (0) 24 7622 7264	tic@cvone.co.uk
Derby	Market Place	+44 (0) 1332 255802	tourism@derby.gov.uk
Felixstowe	91 Undercliff Road West	+44 (0) 1394 276770	ftic@suffolkcoastal.gov.uk
Flatford	Flatford Lane	+44 (0) 1206 299460	flatfordvic@babergh.gov.uk
Harwich	Iconfield Park	+44 (0) 1255 506139	harwichtic@btconnect.com
Hereford	1 King Street	+44 (0) 1432 268430	tic-hereford@herefordshire.gov.uk
Hunstanton	The Green	+44 (0) 1485 532610	hunstanton.tic@west-norfolk.gov.uk
Ipswich	St Stephens Lane	+44 (0) 1473 258070	tourist@ipswich.gov.uk
Ironbridge	Coalbrookdale	+44 (0) 1952 884391	tic@ironbridge.org.uk
King's Lynn	Purfleet Quay	+44 (0) 1553 763044	kings-lynn.tic@west-norfolk.gov.uk

Lavenham	Lady Street	+44 (0) 1787 248207	lavenhamtic@babergh.gov.uk
Leamington Spa	The Parade	+44 (0) 1926 742762	leamington@shakespeare-country.co.uk
Leek	Stockwell Street	+44 (0) 1538 483741	tourism.services@ staffsmoorlands.gov.uk
Leicester	7/9 Every Street	0906 294 1113**	info@goleicestershire.com
Lichfield	Castle Dyke	+44 (0) 1543 412112	info@visitlichfield.com
Lincoln	9 Castle Hill	+44 (0) 1522 873213	tourism@lincoln.gov.uk
Lowestoft	Royal Plain	+44 (0) 1502 533600	touristinfo@waveney.gov.uk
Ludlow	Castle Street	+44 (0) 1584 875053	ludlow.tourism@shropshire.gov.uk
Maldon	Coach Lane	+44 (0) 1621 856503	tic@maldon.gov.uk
Malvern	21 Church Street	+44 (0) 1684 892289	malvern.tic@malvernhills.gov.uk
Matlock	Crown Square	+44 (0) 1629 583388	matlockinfo@derbyshiredales.gov.uk
Matlock Bath	The Pavillion	+44 (0) 1629 55082	matlockbathinfo@ derbyshiredales.gov.uk
Newmarket	Palace Street	+44 (0) 1638 667200	tic.newmarket@forest-heath.gov.uk
Northampton	The Royal & Dernage Theatre	+44 (0) 1604 838800	northampton.tic@northamptonshire enterprise.ltd.uk
Oswestry	Mile End	+44 (0) 1691 662488	tic@oswestry-bc.gov.uk
Oundle	14 West Street	+44 (0) 1832 274333	oundletic@east-northamptonshire.gov.uk
Peterborough	3-5 Minster Precincts	+44 (0) 1733 452336	tic@peterborough.gov.uk
Ripley	Market Place	+44 (0) 1773 841488	touristinformation@ambervalley.gov.uk
Ross-on-Wye	Edde Cross Street	+44 (0) 1989 562768	tic-ross@herefordshire.gov.uk
Rugby	Rugby Art Gallery Museum & Library	+44 (0) 1788 533217	visitor.centre@rugby.gov.uk
Saffron Walden	Market Square	+44 (0) 1799 510444	tourism@uttleford.gov.uk
Shrewsbury	The Square	+44 (0) 1743 281200	visitorinfo@shrewsbury.gov.uk
Sleaford	Carre Street	+44 (0) 1529 414294	tic@n-kesteven.gov.uk
Solihull	Homer Road	+44 (0) 121 704 6130	artscomplex@solihull.gov.uk
Southwold	69 High Street	+44 (0) 1502 724729	southwold.tic@waveney.gov.uk
Stafford	Market Street	+44 (0) 1785 619619	tic@staffordbc.gov.uk
Stoke-on-Trent	Victoria Hall, Bagnall Street	+44 (0) 1782 236000	stoke.tic@stoke.gov.uk
Stowmarket	The Museum of East Anglian Life	+44 (0) 1449 676800	tic@midsuffolk.gov.uk
Stratford-upon-Avon	Bridgefoot	+44 (0) 870 160 7930	stratfordtic@shakespeare-country.co.uk
Sudbury	Market Hill	+44 (0) 1787 881320	sudburytic@babergh.gov.uk
Swadlincote	West Street	+44 (0) 1283 222848	Jo@sharpespotterymuseum.org.uk
Tamworth	29 Market Street	+44 (0) 1827 709581	tic@tamworth.gov.uk
Warwick	Jury Street	+44 (0) 1926 492212	touristinfo@warwick-uk.co.uk
Witham	61 Newland Street	+44 (0) 1376 502674	ticwitham@braintree.gov.uk
Woodbridge	Station Buildings	+44 (0) 1394 382240	wtic@suffolkcoastal.gov.uk
Worcester	High Street	+44 (0) 1905 728787	touristinfo@cityofworcester.gov.uk

*seasonal opening

**UK number only, charged at premium rate

where to stay in
Central England

All place names in the blue bands are shown on the maps at the front of this guide.

Accommodation symbols

Symbols give useful information about services and facilities. On pages 16 to 17 you can find a key to these symbols.

ABBERLEY, Worcestershire Map ref 4A3   SELF CATERING

★★★
SELF CATERING

Units **4**
Sleeps **1–4**

LOW SEASON PER WK
£175.00–£235.00

HIGH SEASON PER WK
£300.00–£400.00

Old Yates Cottages, Worcester

contact Mr & Mrs Richard & Sarah Goodman, Old Yates Cottages, Stockton Road, Abberley, Worcester WR6 6AT **t** +44 (0) 1299 896500 **e** oldyates@aol.com

oldyatescottages.co.uk GUEST REVIEWS · SPECIAL OFFERS · REAL-TIME BOOKING

open All year
payment Credit/debit cards, cash, cheques
nearest pub 2 miles
nearest shop 1 mile

Cosy cottages in tranquil surroundings amidst beautiful countryside. A personal welcome awaits you. Convenient for exploring the Midlands and Welsh Borders. Contact us for colour brochure.

ONLINE MAP

Unit 📺 🖾 🖳 🖦 🖪 ⛁ 🍽 💷 ❄ ♨ 🔊 General 🕮 🏠 🖝 P 🔲 🐕
Leisure ♦ ∪ ♪ ⛷ 🚴

ALSOP-EN-LE-DALE, Derbyshire Map ref 4B2   CAMPING, CARAVAN & HOLIDAY PARK

★★★★
**HOLIDAY, TOURING
& CAMPING PARK**

🚐(81) £10.50–£21.70
🚍(81) £10.50–£21.70
🛖(30) £10.50–£21.70
111 touring pitches

Receive £15 discount for every 7-night stay (includes multiples of 7 night stays).

Rivendale Caravan and Leisure Park

Buxton Road, Alsop-en-le-Dale, Ashbourne DE6 1QU **t** +44 (0) 1335 310311
e enqs@rivendalecaravanpark.co.uk

rivendalecaravanpark.co.uk

payment Credit/debit cards, cash, cheques

Surrounded by spectacular Peak District scenery, convenient for Alton Towers, Chatsworth, Dove Dale and Carsington Water. Ideal for cyclists and ramblers with a network of footpaths and trails accessible directly from site. Choice of all-grass, hardstanding or 50/50 pitches. Closed 7 January to 1 February.

SAT NAV DE6 1QU

General 🚐 🚍 🔌 🕛 🚻 🆿 🛁 📷 🛒 ✕ 🐕 ☼ Leisure 🍽 ♦ ⛷ ∪ ♪ 🚴

ALVECHURCH, Worcestershire Map ref 4B3 — GUEST ACCOMMODATION

★★★★
BED & BREAKFAST

B&B PER ROOM PER NIGHT
S £45.00
D £75.00–£85.00

EVENING MEAL PER PERSON
£8.50–£10.00

Woodlands Bed and Breakfast

Coopers Hill, Alvechurch, Nr Bromsgrove B48 7BX **t** +44 (0) 121 445 6772 **e** john.impey@gmail.com

woodlandsbedandbreakfast.com

open All year except Christmas and New Year
bedrooms 4 double
bathrooms All en suite
payment Credit/debit cards, cash, cheques, euros

Set in delightful countryside with extensive gardens and heated swimming pool. A warm welcome is offered by John and Amanda. Bedrooms are en suite, spacious and comfortable. A substantial breakfast is served in the elegant dining room. Close to Birmingham and the NEC and a short drive from Stratford and Warwick.

SAT NAV *B48 7BX* **ONLINE MAP**

Room 📺 💧 🍳 General 🛋 🎱 ⚷ P ⓦ ⚖ ✕ 🎮 💻 ✿ 🐾 Leisure ⚓ ∪ ⟼ 🚲

ANSTEY, Hertfordshire Map ref 2D1 — GUEST ACCOMMODATION

★★★★
FARMHOUSE

B&B PER ROOM PER NIGHT
S £50.00–£60.00
D £80.00–£100.00

Anstey Grove Barn

The Grove, Buntingford SG9 0BJ **t** +44 (0) 1763 848828 **e** enquiries@ansteygrovebarn.co.uk

ansteygrovebarn.co.uk GUEST REVIEWS

open All year
bedrooms 3 double, 2 twin, 1 suite
bathrooms All en suite
payment Credit/debit cards, cash, cheques, euros

Beautiful timber barn set in walled garden, recently converted to offer high quality bed and breakfast accommodation. Set in the heart of the tranquil Hertfordshire countryside, there are a wealth of country walks to enjoy with many village pubs nearby. Within easy reach of Cambridge and London.

SAT NAV *SG9 0BJ* **ONLINE MAP**

Room ♿ 🖥 📺 🆂 💧 🍳 General 🛋 12 P ⚖ 🎮 💻 ✿ Leisure ∪ ⟼

ASHTON, Northamptonshire Map ref 2C1 — SELF CATERING

★★★★
SELF CATERING

Units   **1**
Sleeps **4–6**

LOW SEASON PER WK
Min **£350.00**

Vale Farm House, Northampton

contact Mrs Zanotto, Vale Farm House, Stoke Road, Northampton NN7 2JN **t** +44 (0) 1604 863697
e teresa@valefarmhouse.co.uk

valefarmhouse.co.uk

A comfortable self-catering guest annexe set in extensive farm grounds with riding stables, located in the village of Ashton between Northampton and Milton Keynes.

open All year
payment Cash, cheques, euros
nearest pub 0.5 miles
nearest shop 7 miles

Unit 📺 🖥 📺. 🖨 🎛 🍳 📻 🍽 💿 ✿ ✐ General 🛋 6 🎱 ⚷ P ◉ 🆂 Leisure ⚲ ∪ ⟼

Don't forget www.

Web addresses throughout this guide are shown without the prefix www. Please include www. in the address line of your browser.
If a web address does not follow this style it is shown in full.

AYLSHAM, Norfolk Map ref 3B1

★★★★★
GUEST ACCOMMODATION
GOLD AWARD

B&B PER ROOM PER NIGHT
S £60.00–£85.00
D £75.00–£95.00

Old Pump House

Holman Road, Aylsham NR11 6BY **t** +44 (0) 1263 733789 **e** theoldpumphouse@btconnect.com

theoldpumphouse.com

open All year except Christmas and New Year
bedrooms 1 double, 2 twin, 2 family
bathrooms All en suite
payment Credit/debit cards, cash, cheques

Creature comforts, home cooking. Rambling 1750s house beside the thatched pump, a minute from church and market place. Non-smoking.

SAT NAV NR11 6BY **ONLINE MAP**

Room 🖨 📺 🌡 ⛄ General 🛏 📖 🔥 P ⚘ 🔌 ✕ 🎮 ☀ 🐕 Leisure 🚲

BACTON-ON-SEA, Norfolk Map ref 3C1

★★★★★
HOLIDAY PARK
ROSE AWARD

🚐 (25) £116.00–£525.00

10% discount on selected weeks for 2 persons or 2 persons and a baby under 2 years.

Cable Gap Holiday Park

Coast Road, Bacton, Norwich NR12 0EW **t** +44 (0) 1692 650667 **e** holiday@cablegap.co.uk

cablegap.co.uk

open February to November
payment Credit/debit cards, cash, cheques

Cable Gap Holiday Park is a friendly family-run park. You will receive a warm welcome from both us and our staff. Our caravans are of a high standard with most double-glazed and centrally heated. We also have a brick built chalet suitable for the disabled.

SAT NAV NR12 0EW

General 📶 📱 🔲 🐕 🔌

BAKEWELL, Derbyshire Map ref 4B2

★★★
COUNTRY HOUSE HOTEL
SILVER AWARD

B&B PER ROOM PER NIGHT
S £85.00–£100.00
D £145.00–£225.00
HB PER PERSON PER NIGHT
£102.50–£150.00

The Peacock at Rowsley

Bakewell Road, Rowsley, Matlock DE4 2EB **t** +44 (0) 1629 733518
e reception@thepeacockatrowsley.com

thepeacockatrowsley.com SPECIAL OFFERS

open All year
bedrooms 12 double, 2 twin, 2 single
bathrooms All en suite
payment Credit/debit cards, cash, cheques

We are a small luxury hotel located in the famous Peak District in the heart of England, near Matlock and conveniently close to the major towns of Chesterfield, Sheffield and Derby. Our restaurant and bar serve delicious food and we have been awarded two AA rosettes. We have excellent fly-fishing.

SAT NAV DE4 2EB

Room 🖨 ☎ 📺 🆂🅲 🌡 ⛄ 🔌 General 📖 🔥 P ⚘ 🍷 🎮 🍽 🍴 ☀ 🐕 Leisure ∪ ⚓ ► 🚲

What if I need to cancel?

It's advisable to check the proprietor's cancellation policy at the time of booking in case you have to change your plans.

BAKEWELL, Derbyshire Map ref 4B2 SELF CATERING

★★★★
SELF CATERING

Units **1**
Sleeps **1–4**

LOW SEASON PER WK
£220.00–£294.00

HIGH SEASON PER WK
£422.00–£485.00

Cartwheels, Bakewell

contact Pat Heawood, 2 Leyfield Road, Dore S17 3EE **t** +44 (0) 7821 858640
e julianheawood@yahoo.co.uk

cottageguide.co.uk/cartwheels SPECIAL OFFERS

open All year
payment Cash, cheques, euros
nearest pub less than 0.5 miles
nearest shop less than 0.5 miles

Elegantly furnished, old stone-built cottage in heart of Derbyshire's Peak District. In beautiful Bakewell, a peaceful backwater overlooking the town, but only five minutes' walk to the centre. Two bedrooms, multi-fuel burner, big, exposed oak beam in lounge. Special parking permit provided.

Unit 📺 📀 💻 📱 🍳 🔲 🍽 🗄 ❄ ⛽ 🎿 General 🐴 🏠 🔥 ⊚ Ⓢ 🐕 Leisure 🎣 🏌 🚴

BAKEWELL, Derbyshire Map ref 4B2 SELF CATERING

★★★
SELF CATERING

Units **1**
Sleeps **1–2**

LOW SEASON PER WK
£180.00–£220.00

HIGH SEASON PER WK
£220.00–£300.00

The Garden Lodge, Youlgrave, Nr Bakewell

contact Mrs Irene Shimwell, The Garden Lodge, c/o Crimble House, Main Street, Youlgrave, Bakewell DE45 1UW **t** +44 (0) 1629 636568 **e** irene.shimwell@hotmail.co.uk

thegardenlodgeyoulgrave.co.uk

Recently refurbished one bedroom converted architect's studio set in a private garden with views over Bradford Dale. All mod cons. A perfect base for a couple to explore the Peak District.

open All year
payment Cash, cheques
nearest pub less than 0.5 miles
nearest shop less than 0.5 miles

Unit 📺 📀 💻 📱 🔲 🍽 ❄ General 🏠 🔥 P Ⓢ 🐕

BAYTON, Worcestershire Map ref 4A3 SELF CATERING

★★★★
SELF CATERING

Units **2**
Sleeps **2–3**

LOW SEASON PER WK
£180.00–£230.00

HIGH SEASON PER WK
£230.00–£280.00

Church House, Kidderminster

contact Ms Maggie Gregory, Bayton, Kidderminster DY14 9LP **t** +44 (0) 1299 832304
e churchhouse1@tiscali.co.uk

churchhousebayton.co.uk

Charming, period, spacious ground-floor one-bedroom accommodation. Glorious views on edge of quiet village. Ideal for walking, cycling and touring.

open All year except Christmas
payment Cash, cheques
nearest pub 1 mile
nearest shop 1.5 miles

Unit 📺 📀 💻 📱 🍳 🔲 🍽 ❄ 🎿 General 🐴4 P Ⓢ Leisure ∪ 🎣 🏌 🚴

What do the star ratings mean?

For a detailed explanation of the quality and facilities represented by the stars, please refer to the information pages at the back of this guide.

BEESTON, Nottinghamshire Map ref 4C2

★★★
GUEST HOUSE

B&B PER ROOM PER NIGHT
S £27.50–£50.00
D £60.00

EVENING MEAL PER PERSON
£7.95–£15.00

Discounts available for groups and stays of 4 nights or longer. Extra discounts during winter. Please contact for details.

Hylands

Queens Road, Beeston, Nottingham NG9 1JB t +44 (0) 115 925 5472 e hyland.hotel@btconnect.com

accommodation.uk.net/hylands.htm REAL-TIME BOOKING

open All year except Christmas
bedrooms 6 double, 7 twin, 17 single, 8 family
bathrooms 23 en suite
payment Credit/debit cards, cash

A family-run hotel offering comfortable, clean accommodation within a warm and friendly atmosphere. Situated close to Nottingham University, the city indoor tennis centre and Attenborough nature reserve. Within easy walking distance of an award-winning pub and several excellent restaurants, and with frequent transport links to the city centre.

SAT NAV NG9 1JB **ONLINE MAP**

Room 🛗📞📺⚙️☕️ General 🐾🛏️🚿P📶🔥🍽️✖️🎮❄️🐴 Leisure 🎣

BEWDLEY, Worcestershire Map ref 4A3

★★★
SELF CATERING

Units   1
Sleeps   1–4

LOW SEASON PER WK
£195.00–£245.00

HIGH SEASON PER WK
£290.00–£390.00

Manor Holding, Bewdley

contact Mr & Mrs Nigel & Penny Dobson-Smyth, 32 Church Street, Hagley, Stourbridge DY9 0NA
t +44 (0) 7970 260010 e nds@landscapeconsultancy.freeserve.co.uk

Secluded 17thC farmhouse in tranquil, ancient forest (National Nature Reserve) laced with traffic-free foot, cycle and bridle paths. Enchanting, rolling countryside sprinkled with historic market towns. Near Birmingham, Ironbridge and Ludlow. GPS reference given upon booking of farmhouse.

open All year
payment Cash, cheques
nearest pub 2 miles
nearest shop 2 miles

Unit 📺📻📠🖥️🍴📶🍳🍽️💷✖️❄️🚿 General 🐾🛏️P⑤🐴 Leisure ∪🧦🏊🚴

BIGGIN-BY-HARTINGTON, Derbyshire Map ref 4B2

★★★★
SELF CATERING

Units   3
Sleeps   2

LOW SEASON PER WK
£260.00–£280.00

HIGH SEASON PER WK
£420.00–£450.00

Biggin Grange, Biggin-by-Hartington, Buxton

contact Mrs Jane Henry, Biggin by Hartington, Buxton SK17 0DJ t +44 (0) 1298 687254
e henrys@bigginrange.co.uk

bigginrange.co.uk

open All year
payment Credit/debit cards, cash, cheques
nearest pub 0.5 miles
nearest shop 2 miles

Located in rural countryside in the grounds of the owners' 135-acre property, Biggin Grange offers complete peace and seclusion. The immaculate cottages have all been converted to a very high standard and are centrally located. All cottages have a private patio or garden with uninterrupted views of Biggin Dale.

SAT NAV SK17 0DJ

Unit 📺📻🖥️🍴📶🍳🍽️💷❄️♨️ General P◻️⑤ Leisure 🎾🚴

Fancy a cycling holiday?

CYCLISTS WELCOME
WELCOME CYCLISTS

For a fabulous freewheeling break, seek out accommodation participating in our Cyclists Welcome scheme. Look out for the symbol and plan your route online at nationalcyclenetwork.org.

BILLERICAY, Essex Map ref 3B3

★★★★★
SELF CATERING

Units **1**
Sleeps **1–6**

LOW SEASON PER WK
£500.00–£1,000.00

HIGH SEASON PER WK
£630.00–£1,100.00

5% discount for stays of 4 weeks/ 10% discount for stays of 8 weeks against 2-/ 3-bedroom options.

Pump House Apartment, Billericay

contact Mr John Bayliss, Pump House, Church Street, Billericay CM11 2TR **t** +44 (0) 1277 656579
e johnwbayliss@btinternet.com

thepumphouseapartment.co.uk GUEST REVIEWS · REAL-TIME BOOKING

open All year
payment Credit/debit cards, cash, cheques, euros
nearest pub 0.5 miles
nearest shop 0.75 miles

The apartment is on two floors and luxuriously furnished, with air-conditioning. The accommodation comprises two living rooms, fully fitted kitchen/diner and the option of one, two or three bedrooms with one, two or three bath/shower rooms. Guests have use of heated outdoor pool (May to September), hot tub, gazebo and gardens. Personal supervision.

ONLINE MAP

Unit 📺 📠 🖥 💻 📷 🛗 🍳 📻 🍽 🧺 ❄ ⛱   General 🛋 🏛 🅿 Ⓢ
Leisure ⚲ ♨ 🎣 ▶ 🚴

BISHOP'S CASTLE, Shropshire Map ref 4A3

★★★★
INN

B&B PER ROOM PER NIGHT
S Min £50.00
D Min £70.00

EVENING MEAL PER PERSON
£6.00–£20.00

Discounts for longer stays – 3 nights or more. Please ask.

Inn on the Green

Wentnor, Bishop's Castle SY9 5EF **t** +44 (0) 1588 650105 **e** sempleaj@aol.com

theinnonthegreen.net

open All year
bedrooms 3 double, 1 twin, 1 family
bathrooms All en suite
payment Credit/debit cards, cash, cheques, euros

Family-run country inn situated in the heart of the Shropshire Hills walking country. Local real ales, bar snacks, restaurant meals using local produce. Dishes of the day including vegetarian. Snacks start at £4.00, main dishes start at £10.00. Wheelchair access to all public rooms and disabled toilet.

SAT NAV *SY9 5EF* **ONLINE MAP**

Room 📺 ♨ 🍳   General 🛋 🏛 🅿 📶 🔥 🍽 ✗ 🍴 ◻ ❄   Leisure ♨ 🎣 ▶ 🚴

BISHOP'S CASTLE, Shropshire Map ref 4A3

★★★
GUEST HOUSE

B&B PER ROOM PER NIGHT
S £35.00–£45.00
D £60.00–£70.00

EVENING MEAL PER PERSON
£12.00–£18.00

Old Brick Guesthouse

7 Church Street, Bishop's Castle, Shropshire SY9 5AA **t** +44 (0) 1588 638471
e enquiries@oldbrick.co.uk

oldbrick.co.uk

open All year
bedrooms 1 double, 1 twin, 1 family, 1 suite
bathrooms All en suite
payment Credit/debit cards, cash, cheques, euros

The guesthouse is a fine old 18thC Grade II Listed building, situated in a designated Area of Outstanding Natural Beauty. There are four guest rooms, off-street parking, secure cycle storage and wireless internet. Bishop's Castle is known for beer (two breweries and six pubs), walking and cycling.

SAT NAV *SY9 5AA* **ONLINE MAP**

Room 📺 ♨ 🍳   General 🛋 🏛 🅿 📶 🔥 ✗ 🍴 ◻ ❄ 🐕   Leisure ♨ 🚴

BOSTON, Lincolnshire Map ref 3A1 — SELF CATERING

★★★★–★★★★★★
SELF CATERING

Units **8**
Sleeps **1–5**

LOW SEASON PER WK
£320.00–£350.00

HIGH SEASON PER WK
£440.00–£490.00

Tastes of Lincolnshire welcome pack on weekly stays.

Elms Farm Cottages, Boston

contact Carol Emerson, Elms Farm Cottages, The Elms, Hubberts Bridge, Boston PE20 3QP
t +44 (0) 1205 290840 & +44 (0) 7887 652021 **e** carol@elmsfarmcottages.co.uk

elmsfarmcottages.co.uk

open All year
payment Credit/debit cards, cash, cheques
nearest pub less than 0.5 miles
nearest shop 2 miles

Relax and enjoy the peaceful Lincolnshire countryside at Elms Farm Cottages with level access, woodburning stoves, en suite bedrooms and shower rooms suitable for wheelchairs. All cottages are fully equipped and furnished to a high standard. Winner of East Midlands Self Catering Holidays and Lincolnshire Tourism Accommodation of the Year 2007/8.

SAT NAV PE20 3QP

Unit 📺 ... General ... P S ... Leisure ...

BRIDGNORTH, Shropshire Map ref 4A3 — SELF CATERING

★★★★
SELF CATERING

Units **1**
Sleeps **4**

LOW SEASON PER WK
£300.00–£400.00

HIGH SEASON PER WK
£500.00–£600.00

Forge Cottage, Bridgnorth

contact Mr Dennis Price, Apley Forge, Bridgnorth WV16 4RZ **t** +44 (0) 1746 762110
e apleyest@btconnect.com

apleyestate.com SPECIAL OFFERS

open All year
payment Cash, cheques, euros
nearest pub 2 miles
nearest shop 7 miles

Forge Cottage is a two-bedroom period cottage in the Severn Gorge. The property has been totally refurbished and benefits from full oil-fired central heating, ensuring a warm welcome all year round. Please go to Holiday Letting link on website for further details.

ONLINE MAP

Unit 📺 ... General 🛏6 P S Leisure ✈

BRIGSLEY, North East Lincolnshire Map ref 4D1 — SELF CATERING

★★★★
SELF CATERING

Units **4**
Sleeps **3–4**

LOW SEASON PER WK
£350.00–£400.00

HIGH SEASON PER WK
£350.00–£400.00

Prospect Farm Country Cottages, Brigsley

contact Mrs Janet Speight, Waltham Road, Brigsley DN37 0RQ **t** +44 (0) 1472 826491
e prospectfarm@btconnect.com

prospectfarm.co.uk SPECIAL OFFERS

open All year
payment Credit/debit cards, cash, cheques
nearest pub 1 mile
nearest shop 1 mile

Prospect Farm is situated down a long, leafy lane which opens out onto an expanse of fields with horses grazing. A sense of peace and tranquillity surrounds the cottages. Humberside Airport 20 minutes. Ideally situated for the Lincolnshire Wolds and the seaside town of Cleethorpes.

SAT NAV DN37 0RQ

Unit 📺 ... General 🛏 ... P S Leisure ✈

BROADWAY, Worcestershire Map ref 2B1 — GUEST ACCOMMODATION

Lowerfield Farm

★★★★
FARMHOUSE

B&B PER ROOM PER NIGHT
S £52.00–£65.00
D £62.00–£80.00

EVENING MEAL PER PERSON
£20.00

Off-season discounts. Please see website.

Willersey Fields, Broadway WR11 7HF **t** +44 (0) 1386 858273 **e** info@lowerfieldfarm.com

lowerfieldfarm.com GUEST REVIEWS · SPECIAL OFFERS · REAL-TIME BOOKING

open All year
bedrooms 3 double, 2 twin, 1 single, 2 family
bathrooms All en suite
payment Credit/debit cards, cash, cheques

A largely 17thC farmhouse just outside Broadway, with wonderful views of the Cotswold escarpment. All rooms en suite, beautifully furnished and with digital TV and DVD players. Doubles have king-size beds. We offer a varied and high quality breakfast menu, and farmhouse dinner by request. Licensed premises; Wi-Fi internet available.

SAT NAV *WR11 7HF* **ONLINE MAP**

Room 🛏🖨📺♨🍵 General 🐕🍴☂P👜🛎🍷✕🎮🌳🐾🏇 Leisure ⛵🚣🎣🚴

BURNHAM DEEPDALE, Norfolk Map ref 3B1 — CAMPING, CARAVAN & HOLIDAY PARK

Deepdale Camping

★★★★
CAMPING PARK

🚐 (78) Min £9.00
🏕 (78) Min £9.00

See website for list of events and activities run throughout the year, including conservation weekends, environmental courses and special breaks.

Deepdale Farm, Burnham Deepdale PE31 8DD **t** +44 (0) 1485 210256 **e** info@deepdalefarm.co.uk

deepdalefarm.co.uk GUEST REVIEWS · SPECIAL OFFERS

open All year
payment Credit/debit cards, cash, cheques

Quiet, eco-friendly campsite for tents and small camper vans in the heart of Burnham Deepdale on the beautiful Norfolk Coast Area of Outstanding Natural Beauty. Tipis, sleeping up to six people, also available. Perfect for walking, birdwatching, cycling, watersports, kiting or just as a place to relax.

SAT NAV *PE31 8DD* **ONLINE MAP**

General 🏕🛒🍴🖥🛗✕🏇☀🔥 Leisure ⛳⛵🚣🎣🚴

BURY ST EDMUNDS, Suffolk Map ref 3B2 — SELF CATERING

The Old Dairy at West Lodge, Bury St Edmunds

★★★★
SELF CATERING

Units **1**
Sleeps **1–6**

LOW SEASON PER WK
£300.00

HIGH SEASON PER WK
£500.00

Short breaks available low season. 2-person discounts available.

contact Mrs Lynn Cardale, The Old Dairy at West Lodge, Bradfield St George, Bury St Edmunds IP30 0DL **t** +44 (0) 1284 386327 **e** info@westlodgedairy.co.uk

westlodgedairy.co.uk

open All year
payment Cash, cheques
nearest pub 1.5 miles
nearest shop 2 miles

Sensitively restored, well equipped former dairy wing of Victorian house in parkland near historic market towns. Ground-floor double bedroom with adjacent bathroom. Upstairs double/twin and twin bedrooms, bathroom. Newly refurbished kitchen leads to enclosed courtyard. Sitting room with dining area and view of lake. Tennis court available.

SAT NAV *IP30 0DL* **ONLINE MAP**

Unit 📺🖥📺📼🔥🖥🍽🧺❄ General 🐕7 P🅂 Leisure ⛳🚣

Where can I get live travel information?

For the latest travel update – call the RAC on 1740 from your mobile phone.

BUXTON, Derbyshire Map ref 4B2 — SELF CATERING

★★★★
SELF CATERING

Units **8**
Sleeps **2–5**

LOW SEASON PER WK
£340.00–£467.00

HIGH SEASON PER WK
£488.00–£651.00

Contact us for special deals on late availability. 5% discount if you arrive by public transport.

Wheeldon Trees Farm, Earl Sterndale, Buxton

contact Deborah & Martin Hofman, Earl Sterndale, Buxton SK17 0AA t +44 (0) 1298 83219
e stay@wheeldontreesfarm.co.uk

wheeldontreesfarm.co.uk GUEST REVIEWS · SPECIAL OFFERS · REAL-TIME BOOKING

open All year
payment Credit/debit cards, cash, cheques
nearest pub 1 mile
nearest shop 2.5 miles

Relax and explore unspoilt landscapes, picturesque villages and lively market towns. 18thC dairy barn conversion, in quiet and secluded valley with fabulous views. Seven self-catering holiday cottage sleeping up to 28 (4 singles, 8 twins, 4 doubles). Newly refurbished with consideration to the environment. Communal dining and leisure facilities

SAT NAV SK17 0AA **ONLINE MAP**

Unit 📺 ▯ ▭ ▯▯ ▯ ⛄ ▯ ▯ ⁄⁄ ❋ General ▯ ▥ ▯ ▯ S ▯ Leisure ● ☂

CAMBRIDGE, Cambridgeshire Map ref 2D1 — GUEST ACCOMMODATION

★★★
GUEST HOUSE

B&B PER ROOM PER NIGHT
S £45.00–£60.00
D £65.00–£75.00

Bridge Guest House

151 Hills Road, Cambridge CB2 2RJ t +44 (0) 1223 247942 e bghouse@gmail.com

bridgeguesthouse.co.uk

Family-run business. Close to Addenbrooks Hospital, Cambridge Leisure Park, Botanic Gardens and city centre. M11 (Stansted) two miles. Easy access to buses and railway.

open All year except Christmas and New Year
bedrooms 2 double, 2 twin, 2 single, 1 family
bathrooms All en suite
payment Credit/debit cards, cash, cheques, euros

Room ▯ ☎ 📺 ▯ General ▯ P ▯ ▥ ▯ ❋

CAMBRIDGE, Cambridgeshire Map ref 2D1 — GUEST ACCOMMODATION

★★★★
GUEST HOUSE
SILVER AWARD

B&B PER ROOM PER NIGHT
S £40.00–£65.00
D £60.00–£85.00

Worth House

152 Chesterton Road, Cambridge CB4 1DA t +44 (0) 1223 316074 e enquiry@worth-house.co.uk

worth-house.co.uk GUEST REVIEWS · SPECIAL OFFERS

Worth House offers quiet, comfortable and spacious accommodation in this Victorian home. Within easy reach of the city centre. 'Which?' recommended.

open All year
bedrooms 4 suites
bathrooms All en suite
payment Credit/debit cards, cash, cheques, euros

Room ▯ 📺 ▯ ▯ ▯ General ▯ ▥ ▯ P ▯ ▯ ▥ ❋ Leisure ▯ ☂

CAMBRIDGE, Cambridgeshire Map ref 2D1 — SELF CATERING

★★★★
SELF CATERING

Units **2**
Sleeps **2–8**

LOW SEASON PER WK
£385.00–£550.00

HIGH SEASON PER WK
£490.00–£695.00

Cambridge Midsummer Apartments, Cambridge

contact Mrs Maria Fasano, Cambridge Midsummer Apartments, 4 Poynters Lodge, Chesterton Road, Cambridge CB4 1JB t +44 (0) 1223 316074 e enquiry@worth-house.co.uk

cambridgemidsummerapartments.com GUEST REVIEWS · SPECIAL OFFERS

Luxurious ground-floor apartments sleeping up to four people. Fully equipped and with parking available. Ten minutes' walk to city.

open All year
payment Credit/debit cards, cash, cheques, euros
nearest pub 0.3 miles
nearest shop less than 0.5 miles

Unit 📺 ▯ ▯ ▯ ▭ ▯ ▯ ⛄ ▯ ▯ ▯ ⁄⁄ ❋ General ▯ ▥ ▯ P S Leisure ▯ ☂

Looking for a wide range of facilities?

More stars means higher quality accommodation plus a greater range of facilities and services.

CAMBRIDGE, Cambridgeshire Map ref 2D1 CAMPING, CARAVAN & HOLIDAY PARK

★★★★★
TOURING &
CAMPING PARK

🚐 (60) £12.50–£15.00
🚐 (60) £12.50–£15.00
▲ (60) £9.75–£15.00
120 touring pitches

Low-season rate for
Senior Citizens –
10% discount for
stay of 3 nights or
longer.

Highfield Farm Touring Park

Long Road, Comberton, Cambridge CB23 7DG t +44 (0) 1223 262308
e enquiries@highfieldfarmtouringpark.co.uk

highfieldfarmtouringpark.co.uk

open April to October
payment Cash, cheques, euros

A popular, family-run park with excellent facilities
close to the university city of Cambridge and Imperial
War Museum, Duxford. Ideally situated for touring
East Anglia. Please view our website for further
information.

SAT NAV *CB23 7DG*

General 🖳 🚐 🔌 🗇 🔍 🅦 🍴 📻 🔋 🐾 ☼ Leisure ⚲ ∪ 🎵 🚴

CASTLE ACRE, Norfolk Map ref 3B1 SELF CATERING

★★★
SELF CATERING

Units 1
Sleeps 6

LOW SEASON PER WK
£300.00

HIGH SEASON PER WK
£350.00

Peddars Cottage, Castle Acre

contact Mrs Angela Swindell, St Saviour's Rectory, St Saviour JE2 7NP t +44 (0) 1534 736679
e angelaswindell@googlemail.com

castleacre.org.uk

Delightful cottage-style house in centre of village
facing green. Close to castle, priory, church, river,
pubs and shops.

open All year
payment Cash, cheques
nearest pub less than 0.5 miles
nearest shop less than 0.5 miles

Unit 📺 📷 🖥 📻 🍳 🎛 ❄ ⌀ General ⏚ ♣ P 🐾

CHAPEL-EN-LE-FRITH, Derbyshire Map ref 4B2 SELF CATERING

★★★★
SELF CATERING

Units 1
Sleeps 9

LOW SEASON PER WK
£400.00–£600.00

HIGH SEASON PER WK
£800.00–£1,250.00

Saffi House, High Peak

contact Ms Carole Coe, Carole Coe Leisure, 3 Cherry Tree Court, Chapel-en-le-Frith SK23 9HF
t +44 (0) 870 755 9700 e carole@saffihouse.co.uk

saffihouse.co.uk

Three-storey, four-bedroom property. All modern
amenities, sleeps up to nine persons plus cot.
Friday change-over except July and August.

open All year
payment Cash, cheques
nearest pub less than 0.5 miles
nearest shop less than 0.5 miles

Unit 📺 📷 🖥 🍳 📻 🎛 ❄ General ⏚ 🍴 ♣ P 🅾 🆂 Leisure 🎵 ▶

Like exploring
England's cities?

Let VisitBritain's Explorer series guide you through the streets
of some of England's great cities. All you need for the perfect
day out is in this handy pack – featuring an easy-to-use fold
out map and illustrated guide.

You can purchase the Explorer series from good bookshops
and online at visitbritaindirect.com for just £5.99.

CHESTERFIELD, Derbyshire Map ref 4B2 — SELF CATERING

★★★★★
SELF CATERING

Units **1**
Sleeps **2–4**

LOW SEASON PER WK
£260.00–£390.00

HIGH SEASON PER WK
£360.00–£580.00

Special offers Nov, Dec, Jan and Feb (excl Christmas and New Year). Short breaks all year. Early booking discounts.

Pear Tree Farm Barn, Rowthorne Village, Chesterfield

contact Mel Copley, Rowthorne Village, Glapwell, Chesterfield S44 5QQ **t** +44 (0) 1623 811694
e enquiries@peartreefarmbarn.co.uk

peartreefarmbarn.co.uk GUEST REVIEWS · SPECIAL OFFERS · REAL-TIME BOOKING

open All year
payment Cash, cheques
nearest pub 0.5 miles
nearest shop 0.5 miles

Luxury barn conversion in quiet conservation village. One double en suite, and one twin en suite, lounge, diner and kitchen. Full central heating and wood-burning stove. Ten minutes' walk to Hardwick Hall (National Trust). Ideally situated for visiting Peak District (Chatsworth 40 minutes). Pub and shop within walking distance.

ONLINE MAP

Unit 📺 ▫ ▪ ▪ ▫ ▫ ▫ ▫ ✿ ∅ General ⮑ P S Leisure ∪ ⟍ ⚲

CLUN, Shropshire Map ref 4A3 — GUEST ACCOMMODATION

★★★
INN

B&B PER ROOM PER NIGHT
S Min £32.50
D Min £55.00

EVENING MEAL PER PERSON
£5.25–£12.00

The White Horse Inn

The Square, Clun SY7 8JA **t** +44 (0) 1588 640305 **e** jack@whi-clun.co.uk

whi-clun.co.uk

Small, friendly, Good Beer Guide-listed public house with well-appointed, en suite family bedrooms in traditional style. Wide-ranging menu available in dining room. Shrewsbury and SW Shropshire Pub of the Year 2007.

open All year except Christmas
bedrooms 1 double, 3 family
bathrooms All en suite
payment Credit/debit cards, cash, cheques

Room 📺 ♨ ⚲ General ⮑ ▥ ♿ 🌐 ✆ ⟍ ✕ ▨ ▪ ✿ 🐾 Leisure ⟍

COLCHESTER, Essex Map ref 3B2 — HOTEL

★★★
HOTEL

B&B PER ROOM PER NIGHT
S Max £113.00
D Max £126.00

Treat yourself to the VIP suite for £195 per night: full English or continental breakfast, champagne, fresh flowers and chocolates.

Wivenhoe House

Wivenhoe Park, Colchester CO4 3SQ **t** +44 (0) 1206 863666 **e** wivrecep@essex.ac.uk

wivenhoehousehotel.co.uk SPECIAL OFFERS

open All year except Christmas and New Year
bedrooms 14 double, 25 twin, 5 single, 1 family, 1 suite
bathrooms All en suite
payment Credit/debit cards, cash, cheques

Set in beautiful parkland, Wivenhoe House is on the outskirts of historic Colchester. Book today to benefit from: a quiet location close to famous attractions such as Beth Chatto Gardens and Colchester Zoo; forty-six en suite bedrooms including our recently refurbished VIP suite and dining in our elegant Garden Room.

SAT NAV CO4 3SQ **ONLINE MAP**

Room ♿ ✆ 📺 SC ♨ ⚲ General ⮑ ▥ ♿ P 🌐 ⟍ ▨ ◑ ▪ ⟍ ✿ Leisure ⚲ ⟍

Do you like walking?

Walkers feel at home in accommodation participating in our Walkers Welcome scheme. Look out for the symbol. Consider walking all or part of a long-distance route – go online at nationaltrail.co.uk.

COLTISHALL, Norfolk Map ref 3C1 — GUEST ACCOMMODATION

★★★★★
**BED & BREAKFAST
SILVER AWARD**

B&B PER ROOM PER NIGHT
S £55.00
D £68.00–£78.00

10% reduction for 3 or more nights' stay.

Seven Acres House
Great Hautbois, Coltishall NR12 7JZ t +44 (0) 1603 736737 e william@hautbois.plus.com

norfolkbroadsbandb.com

open All year except Christmas and New Year
bedrooms 1 double, 1 twin
bathrooms All en suite
payment Credit/debit cards, cash, cheques, euros

Edwardian Seven Acres House is surrounded by extensive grounds in a peaceful rural location, yet close to village amenities. Easy access to the Broads, Norwich, National Trust properties and coast. Two spacious well-equipped, beautifully furnished south-facing bedrooms. A delicious cooked breakfast is served in the bright morning room leading onto the terrace.

SAT NAV NR12 7JZ

Room TV 🍴 General P 🍽 ✳ Leisure 🚲

COMBS, Derbyshire Map ref 4B2 — SELF CATERING

★★★★★
SELF CATERING

Units 1
Sleeps 1–2

LOW SEASON PER WK
£300.00–£330.00

HIGH SEASON PER WK
£350.00–£415.00

Pyegreave Cottage, High Peak
contact Mr & Mrs Noel & Rita Pollard, Pyegreave Cottage, High Peak SK23 9UX
t +44 (0) 1298 813444 e n.pollard@allenpollard.co.uk

holidayapartments.org

open All year
payment Credit/debit cards, cash, cheques, euros
nearest pub 0.5 miles
nearest shop 3 miles

Situated within the Peak District National Park and enjoying spectacular views, this cottage is finished and furnished to a very high standard whilst retaining original oak beams and many other interesting features. Ideal location for walking, golfing, the theatre (Buxton) or simply as an idyllic hideaway.

Unit TV 🍴 General P S Leisure U 🎣 ⚑ 🚲

CORBY, Northamptonshire Map ref 3A1 — GUEST ACCOMMODATION

★★★
BED & BREAKFAST

B&B PER ROOM PER NIGHT
S Min £35.00
D £60.00

Discount for full occupancy.

Home Farm
Main Street, Sudborough, Kettering NN14 3BX t +44 (0) 1832 730488
e bandbhomefarmsud@aol.com

homefarmsudborough.co.uk

open All year
bedrooms 1 double, 1 twin
bathrooms 2 private
payment Cash, cheques, euros

Just three miles from the A14, a restored barn to yourself in the picturesque village of Sudborough. The barn has a breakfast room, double bedroom, shower room, lounge with sofa bed and single bed, lockable storage room, private parking, and seating area in the garden, and includes a self-service continental breakfast.

SAT NAV NN14 3BX

Room TV 🍴 General P 🍴 ✳ Leisure U 🎣

CORPUSTY, Norfolk Map ref 3B1 — SELF CATERING

Carr's Barn, Norwich

★★★★★
SELF CATERING

Units **1**
Sleeps **13**

LOW SEASON PER WK
£950.00–£1,000.00

HIGH SEASON PER WK
£1,280.00–£1,700.00

contact Mrs Marion Anthony, Pound Corner, Elms Lane, Wangford NR34 8RS
t +44 (0) 1502 578278 **e** info@heritagehideaways.com

carrsbarn.co.uk

open All year
payment Credit/debit cards, cash, cheques
nearest pub less than 0.5 miles
nearest shop less than 0.5 miles

A sensitively converted barn in the heart of the North Norfolk countryside between Norwich and the sea at Sheringham. Six bedrooms, four bathrooms including studio bedroom with mezzanine sleeping two-plus-two. Secluded courtyard with garden. Very near Elizabethan Blickling Hall.

Unit 📺 ▨▨ ▣ ▨▨ ▨ ▨ ▨ ▨ ▨ ✻ ▨ ⊘ General ⛲ ▥ ♿ P ▢ S Leisure ✦ ♿

COTSWOLDS

See under Broadway, Long Compton
See also Cotswolds in South East and South West England sections

COTTESMORE, Rutland Map ref 3A1 — GUEST ACCOMMODATION

Tithe Barn

★★★★
GUEST ACCOMMODATION

B&B PER ROOM PER NIGHT
S £35.00–£40.00
D £55.00–£70.00

Discounts on stays of 5 or more days.

Clatterpot Lane, Cottesmore, Oakham LE15 7DW **t** +44 (0) 1572 813591 **e** jp@thetithebarn.co.uk

tithebarn-rutland.co.uk

open All year
bedrooms 3 double, 2 twin, 2 family
bathrooms 5 en suite, 2 private
payment Credit/debit cards, cash, cheques

An attractive 17thC converted tithe barn. Spacious, comfortable, en suite rooms. Two superior rooms have power showers and king-size beds. Five minutes from Rutland Water, Barnsdale Gardens and A1. A warm and friendly home with a panelled dining room, striking hall and a wealth of original features. All rooms have tea/coffee facilities.

SAT NAV *LE15 7DW*

Room ♿ 📺 ♿ ♿ General ⛲ ♿ P ✻ ☂ Leisure ∪ ✦ ♿

DUNWICH, Suffolk Map ref 3C2 — CAMPING, CARAVAN & HOLIDAY PARK

Cliff House Holiday Park

★★★★
HOLIDAY PARK

⊞ (30) £15.00–£26.00
⊞ (20) £15.00–£26.00
△ (20) £15.00–£26.00
110 touring pitches

Minsmere Road, Dunwich, Saxmundham IP17 3DQ **t** +44 (0) 1728 648282
e info@cliffhouseholidays.co.uk

cliffhouseholidays.co.uk

Secluded woodland park offering privacy with access to the beach. Last year's winner of East of England Holiday Park of the Year. Gold David Bellamy Conservation Award.

open All year except Christmas and New Year
payment Credit/debit cards, cash, cheques

General ▨ ♿ ♿ ☐ ♿ ⊞ ♿ ▨▨ ♿ ✕ ☂ ☼ Leisure ♟ ♫ ♦ ⚲ ♫ ▸ ♿

Where is my pet welcome?

PETS! WELCOME PETS! WELCOME

Want to take your cherished companion with you on holiday? Proprietors participating in our Welcome Pets! scheme go out of their way to make special provision for you and your pet. Look out for the symbol.

ELY, Cambridgeshire Map ref 3A2

★★★★
BED & BREAKFAST

B&B PER ROOM PER NIGHT
S £35.00
D £56.00

The Old School B & B

The Old School, School Lane, Coveney, Ely CB6 2DB t +44 (0) 1353 777087
e info@theoldschoolbandb.co.uk

theoldschoolbandb.co.uk

Quality accommodation in former village school, quiet location three miles from Ely. Set in gardens with views onto Ely Cathedral. Ground-floor bedrooms. Dogs welcome. Euros accepted. Wir sprechen Deutsch.

open All year except Christmas and New Year
bedrooms 1 double, 2 twin
bathrooms 1 en suite, 2 private
payment Cash, cheques, euros

Room ♿ ☕ 🕭   General P 🔥 ⛲ ▣ ❀ 🐴   Leisure ∪ 🚴

ELY, Cambridgeshire Map ref 3A2

★★★★
FARMHOUSE

B&B PER ROOM PER NIGHT
D £65.00

Spinney Abbey

Stretham Road, Wicken CB7 5XQ t +44 (0) 1353 720971 e spinney.abbey@tesco.net

spinneyabbey.co.uk

open All year except Christmas
bedrooms 1 double, 1 twin, 1 family
bathrooms 2 en suite, 1 private
payment Cash, cheques, euros

This attractive Georgian Grade II Listed farmhouse, surrounded by pasture fields, stands next to our livestock farm which borders the National Trust Nature Reserve, 'Wicken Fen', on the southern edge of the Fens. Guests are welcome to make full use of the spacious garden and all-weather tennis court. All rooms have en suite or private facilities.

SAT NAV CB7 5XQ

Room 📺 ☕ 🕭   General 🐂5 P ❀   Leisure ☋

ELY, Cambridgeshire Map ref 3A2

★★★
SELF CATERING

Units **2**
Sleeps **4–6**

LOW SEASON PER WK
£380.00–£420.00

HIGH SEASON PER WK
£380.00–£420.00

7 & 9 Lisle Lane, Ely

contact Ken Davis, Forty Farmhouse, Hurdle Drove, West Row, Bury St Edmunds IP28 8RG
t +44 (0) 1353 675249 & +44 (0) 7858 762721 e fortyfarmhouse@btinternet.com

Ideally placed, modern but traditional, two- and three-bedroom terrace town houses with enclosed patio garden and garage. Close to river, cathedral and market square. Private parking and walking distance to railway station.

open All year
payment Cash, cheques
nearest pub less than 0.5 miles
nearest shop less than 0.5 miles

Unit 📺 📀 📼 🖥 🕭 🔟 🍽 🗄 ❀   General 🐂 ⛲ 🚶 P Ⓢ 🐴   Leisure ⚓ ▶ 🚴

Touring made easy

Two to four-day circular routes with over 200 places to discover

- Lakes and Dales
- The West Country
- The Cotswolds and Shakespeare Country

Available in good bookshops and online at visitbritain.com for just £6.99 each.

★★★★
FARMHOUSE

B&B PER ROOM PER NIGHT
S £44.00–£49.00
D £78.00–£88.00

Crockwell Farm

Eydon, Daventry NN11 3QA t +44 (0) 1327 361358 e info@crockwellfarm.co.uk

crockwellfarm.co.uk GUEST REVIEWS

open All year
bedrooms 3 twin, 4 family
bathrooms All en suite
payment Credit/debit cards, cash, cheques

Beautiful 18thC ironstone farmhouse and cottages in an idyllic rural setting. Delicious breakfasts, featuring local and home-made specialities, served in the farmhouse. The cottages are self-contained. Evening meals and lunches are available in a good local pub approximately one mile away. Ideal location for walking and visiting local attractions.

SAT NAV NN11 3QA **ONLINE MAP**

Room   General   Leisure

★★★★
SELF CATERING

Units   **1**
Sleeps   **1–8**

LOW SEASON PER WK
£340.00–£590.00

HIGH SEASON PER WK
£510.00–£890.00

Small-party reductions and short breaks available – minimum 2 nights – during non-peak times.

Pollywiggle Cottage, West Raynham, Fakenham

contact Mrs Marilyn Farnham-Smith, 79 Earlham Road, Norwich NR2 3RE t +44 (0) 1603 471990
e marilyn@pollywigglecottage.co.uk

pollywigglecottage.co.uk GUEST REVIEWS · SPECIAL OFFERS · REAL-TIME BOOKING

open All year
payment Cash, cheques
nearest pub 3 miles
nearest shop 4 miles

Brimming with character, this pretty, well-equipped home wraps you in its cosy, comfortable interior. Nestled in secluded, rambling flower gardens, Pollywiggle lies on the fringe of a tranquil village 12 miles from the North Norfolk coast. A wealth of amenities and attractions are within an easy drive. Ramblers/cyclists are welcome.

SAT NAV NR21 7EX **ONLINE MAP**

Unit   General

★★★★
BED & BREAKFAST

B&B PER ROOM PER NIGHT
S £27.00–£35.00
D £54.00–£65.00

EVENING MEAL PER PERSON
£10.00–£15.00

The Cedars

Low Road, Barrowby, Grantham NG32 1DL t +44 (0) 1476 563400 e pbcbennett@mac.com

open All year
bedrooms 1 double, 1 twin
bathrooms 2 private
payment Cash, cheques, euros

Enjoy the relaxed atmosphere of this Grade II Listed farmhouse and its gardens. Delicious breakfasts, and evening meals if required, using our own, and local fresh produce. Italian cuisine a speciality. A five-minute drive from A1 motorway, and two miles from Grantham mainline station. French and Italian spoken. Horse and pony stabling available.

SAT NAV NG32 1DL

Room   General

What shall we do today?
For ideas on places to visit, see the beginning of this regional section or go online at enjoyengland.com.

GREAT DODDINGTON, Northamptonshire Map ref 3A2

SELF CATERING

★★★★★
SELF CATERING

Units **1**
Sleeps **2–4**

LOW SEASON PER WK
£275.00–£590.00

HIGH SEASON PER WK
£350.00–£725.00

Short breaks available all year. Special Christmas and New Year breaks.

The Old Watermill, Great Doddington, Wellingborough

contact Anne Lowe, The Old Watermill, Hardwater Mill, Hardwater Road, Great Doddington NN29 7TD **t** +44 (0) 1933 276870 **e** anne@watermillholidays.co.uk

watermillholidays.co.uk GUEST REVIEWS

open All year
payment Cash, cheques
nearest pub 1 mile
nearest shop 1 mile

A charming and historic former watermill, Grade II Listed. The well-equipped self-catering accommodation is on three floors. One four-poster double and one twin bedroom. Centrally heated. Double glazed. Plenty of old elm beams and oak floors. Pets welcome. Car park, garden, riverside walks.

SAT NAV NN29 7TD **ONLINE MAP**

Unit 📺 🖥 🖦 🗄 🔌 🍲 🖨 🕹 💷 ✳ 🖊 General **P** 🅿 **S** 🐴 Leisure 🎵 ►

HEREFORD, Herefordshire Map ref 2A1

HOTEL

★★★
HOTEL

B&B PER ROOM PER NIGHT
S £65.00–£85.00
D £80.00–£100.00
HB PER PERSON PER NIGHT
£50.00–£90.00

Three Counties Hotel

Belmont, Hereford HR2 7BP **t** +44 (0) 1432 299955 **e** enquiries@threecountieshotel.co.uk

threecountieshotel.co.uk

open All year
bedrooms 17 double, 43 twin
bathrooms All en suite
payment Credit/debit cards, cash, cheques

Excellently appointed hotel set in 3.5 acres. Emphasis on traditional, friendly service. Tasteful bedrooms, restaurant and bar offer today's guests all modern comforts. Town centre one mile.

SAT NAV HR2 7BP

Room 🛏 📞 📺 🖥 🚿 🍲 ♿ General 🛋 🏛 ⛪ **P** 🍽 🏵 ◐ 🍴 ✳ 🐴 Leisure ►

HEREFORD, Herefordshire Map ref 2A1

SELF CATERING

★★★★
SELF CATERING

Units **1**
Sleeps **6**

LOW SEASON PER WK
£400.00–£550.00

HIGH SEASON PER WK
£600.00–£850.00

Short breaks available all year. Claim a 10% discount by mentioning 'Where to Stay' or VisitBritain.

Castle Cliffe East, Hereford

contact Mr Mark Hubbard & Mr Phil Wilson, Castle Cliffe West, 14 Quay Street, Hereford HR1 2NH **t** +44 (0) 1432 272096 **e** mail@castlecliffe.net

castlecliffe.net GUEST REVIEWS · SPECIAL OFFERS

open All year
payment Cash, cheques
nearest pub 0.5 miles
nearest shop 0.5 miles

Originally a medieval watergate, Castle Cliffe provides luxury accommodation which is both tranquil and convenient. Set in parkland, it has period furniture, open fires and a south facing riverside garden. And with shops, restaurants and the cathedral within a few minutes' walk, it is the ideal place to relax and unwind.

ONLINE MAP

Unit 📺 🖥 🖦 🖥 🗄 🔌 🍲 🖨 🕹 💷 ✳ ♨ ✎ General 🛋 🏛 ⛪ **P** **S**
Leisure ∪ 🎵 ► 🚲

HILTON, Derbyshire Map ref 4B2 GUEST ACCOMMODATION

★★★★
GUEST ACCOMMODATION

B&B PER ROOM PER NIGHT
S £40.00–£43.99
D £60.00–£63.99

EVENING MEAL PER PERSON
£5.99–£9.99

Tudor Rose

Main Street, Derby DE65 5FF **t** +44 (0) 1283 734564 **e** hilton-tudor-rose@tiscali.co.uk

hilton-tudor-rose.co.uk

Small friendly family-run B&B. Home from home in heart of Derbyshire village. Use of garden and patio. On edge of National Forest, close to Derby, Burton, A50 and A38.

open All year except Christmas and New Year
bedrooms 1 double, 1 twin, 2 single
bathrooms All en suite
payment Credit/debit cards, cash, cheques

Room ⒯ 🔥 ▯ General 🐾 ▯ 🔥 ✕ ❊

HUNSTANTON, Norfolk Map ref 3B1 SELF CATERING

★★★★
SELF CATERING

Units **1**
Sleeps **1–4**

LOW SEASON PER WK
£265.00–£290.00

HIGH SEASON PER WK
£305.00–£475.00

Forget Me Not Cottage, Old Hunstanton, Hunstanton

contact Mr Gary Gibson, 11 Heron Close, Sawbridgeworth CM21 0BB **t** +44 (0) 7957 351250 & +44 (0) 7957 366745 **e** streetsaheadlettings@hotmail.com

holidayhomesnorfolk.co.uk

open All year
payment Cash, cheques
nearest pub less than 0.5 miles
nearest shop less than 0.5 miles

Beautiful two-bedroom cottage to let. Only five minutes' walk to the wide sandy beaches, and close to the extensive championship golf course behind the sand dunes. A charming property with private off-road parking at the rear for one vehicle. A small, enclosed, pretty patio garden is at the rear with patio heaters.

SAT NAV PE36 6HX

Unit ⒯ ⓈⒸ 🎦 🖥 📀 🔥 🔥 🔥 ❊ General 🐾 P ⊙ 🐕 Leisure ✎ ▶ 🚲

IRONBRIDGE, Shropshire Map ref 4A3 SELF CATERING

★★★★
SELF CATERING

Units **2**
Sleeps **4–5**

LOW SEASON PER WK
£275.00–£385.00

HIGH SEASON PER WK
£440.00–£655.00

5% discount for payment in full when making your booking.

Ironbridge Holiday Cottages, Ironbridge

contact Mr Mark Shelton, 29-30 The Wharfage, Ironbridge TF8 7NH **t** +44 (0) 800 633 5181 & +44 (0) 7977 598740 **e** info@ironbridgeholidaycottages.co.uk

ironbridgeholidaycottages.co.uk GUEST REVIEWS · SPECIAL OFFERS

open All year
payment Credit/debit cards
nearest pub less than 0.5 miles
nearest shop less than 0.5 miles

River Cottages are a pair of beautifully restored, self-catering cottages dating back to 1650, the time of the English Civil War, and are among the oldest buildings in the historic Ironbridge Gorge, right in the heart of Shropshire.

SAT NAV TF8 7NR

Unit ⒯ ⓈⒸ 🖥 🔥 🔥 🔥 ❊ ♨ General 🐾 P Ⓢ Leisure ∪ ✎ ▶ 🚲

Looking for an ideal family break?

For accommodation offering additional facilities and services for a range of ages and family units, look out for the Families Welcome symbol. Owners of these properties will go out of their way to welcome families.

KELLING, Norfolk Map ref 3B1

★★★★★
SELF CATERING

Units **1**
Sleeps **8**

LOW SEASON PER WK
£750.00–£1,150.00

HIGH SEASON PER WK
£1,400.00–£1,600.00

3-night midweek and weekend breaks available, out of season. Other seasonal promotions can be seen on our website.

Owl Place, Holt

contact Victoria Hamey, Kelling Estate Office, Kelling Hall Farms, Kelling, Holt NR25 7EW
t +44 (0) 1263 712201 **e** stay@kelling-estate.co.uk

kelling-estate.co.uk SPECIAL OFFERS

open All year
payment Cash, cheques
nearest pub 2 miles
nearest shop 2 miles

Situated in an Area of Outstanding Natural Beauty. Luxury barn conversion, sleeps eight, three twin and one king with two en suite and a family bathroom. Large open plan kitchen/living room with private decked terrace. Access to indoor swimming pool, two all-weather tennis courts and children's play area.

ONLINE MAP

Unit 📺 🆂🅲 🖼 🍳 🖥 📠 🗄 🍴 🍽 🗑 🧺 ✳ 🔥 General 🛴 🏛 🚶 P 🅿 🆂 🐕
Leisure 🎣 🔍 ∪ 🎵 🚲

KNIPTON, Leicestershire Map ref 4C2

★★★★
RESTAURANT WITH ROOMS

B&B PER ROOM PER NIGHT
S £56.00–£70.00
D £90.00–£130.00

EVENING MEAL PER PERSON
£10.00–£27.95

Manners Arms

Croxton Road, Knipton, Grantham NG32 1RH **t** +44 (0) 1476 879222 **e** info@mannersarms.com

mannersarms.com SPECIAL OFFERS

open All year
bedrooms 6 double, 2 twin, 2 single
bathrooms All en suite
payment Credit/debit cards, cash, cheques

Nestled in the charming village of Knipton, close to Belvoir Castle, this delightful country inn has ten bedrooms, a bar and restaurant, serving fresh, local seasonal food seven days a week.

SAT NAV NG32 1RH

Room 🛏 📞 📺 🚿 🍳 General 🛴 🏛 🚶 P 🛜 🍷 ✕ 🎱 ✳ 🔥 Leisure ∪ 🎵

LANGAR, Nottinghamshire Map ref 4C2

★★★
**COUNTRY HOUSE HOTEL
SILVER AWARD**

B&B PER ROOM PER NIGHT
S £80.00–£125.00
D £95.00–£210.00

For 1-night stay on Sun, double occupancy at single rate. Weekend discounts available on standard rooms only.

Langar Hall

Langar, Nottingham NG13 9HG **t** +44 (0) 1949 860559

langarhall.com

open All year
bedrooms 9 double, 1 twin, 1 single, 1 suite
bathrooms All en suite
payment Credit/debit cards, cash, cheques

This charming hotel near Nottingham offers a haven of tranquillity away from city life. It stands in quiet seclusion overlooking carp ponds and ancient trees in the park. Langar enjoys the reputation for exceptional hospitality, efficient, friendly service, comfortable bedrooms, award-winning food and an interesting wine list.

SAT NAV NG13 9HG

Room 🔒 🛏 📞 📺 🚿 🍳 ♿ General 🛴 🚶 P 🛜 🍷 🎱 🌙 ⚫ 🍴 ✳ 🔥 Leisure ∪ 🎵 ▶

LEAMINGTON SPA, Warwickshire Map ref 4B3 — GUEST ACCOMMODATION

★★★★
GUEST HOUSE

B&B PER ROOM PER NIGHT
S £52.00
D £70.00–£75.00

Victoria Park Lodge

12 Adelaide Road, Leamington Spa CV31 3PW t +44 (0) 1926 424195
e info@victoriaparkhotelleamingtonspa.co.uk

victoriaparkhotelleamingtonspa.co.uk REAL-TIME BOOKING

open All year except Christmas and New Year
bedrooms 10 double, 2 twin, 8 single, 9 family
bathrooms All en suite
payment Credit/debit cards, cash, cheques

Twenty-nine well-appointed bedrooms, all with en suite facilities and Wi-Fi. We pride ourselves on cleanliness and comfort, offering a home away from home in an excellent location. Four minutes' walk from the town centre and five minutes' drive from Warwick Castle. We also provide free off-street parking.

SAT NAV CV31 3PW

Room 🚿 📞 📺 🛏 🍳   General 🛋 🗄 🏊 P 🌐 ⚡🍽 🎮 ❄   Leisure ∪ 🚣 🚴

LEDBURY, Herefordshire Map ref 2B1 — SELF CATERING

★★★★★
SELF CATERING

Units **3**
Sleeps **2–9**

LOW SEASON PER WK
£310.00–£950.00

HIGH SEASON PER WK
£495.00–£1,700.00

Romantic breaks. 3- and 4-night breaks available.

The Woodhouse Farm Cottages, Ledbury

contact Mrs Susan Furnival, The Woodhouse, Staplow, Ledbury HR8 1NP t +44 (0) 1531 640030
e sue@thewoodhousefarm.co.uk

thewoodhousefarm.co.uk

open All year
payment Credit/debit cards, cash, cheques
nearest pub less than 0.5 miles
nearest shop 2 miles

Tranquil retreats close to Malvern Hills. Barn Croft and The Wainhouse share 15 acres of grounds with The Woodhouse, a medieval, Grade II* Listed, semi-moated hall house. Comfortably furnished to very high standards with antiques and prints. Each cottage has a private garden. Choice of dining solutions and food hampers.

Unit 📺 📀 🖥 🖨 🛏 🍽 🍲 🍳 🍴 ❄ 🔥 🧺   General 🛋 🗄 🏊 P Ⓢ   Leisure 🚣 🚴

LEICESTER, Leicestershire Map ref 4C3 — GUEST ACCOMMODATION

★★★
BED & BREAKFAST

B&B PER ROOM PER NIGHT
S £35.00
D £50.00

Weekend breaks £45 per room based on 2 people sharing, 2 nights minimum, off-peak.

Wondai B&B

47-49 Main Street, Newtown Linford, Leicester LE6 0AE t +44 (0) 1530 242728

open All year except Christmas
bedrooms 1 twin, 1 family
bathrooms All en suite
payment Credit/debit cards, cash, cheques

Our bed and breakfast is located in the village just a short walk from Bradgate Deer Park which was home to Lady Jane Grey, Queen of England for nine days in 1553. Great Central Railway, the only twin-track mainline steam train in England, is a short drive away.

SAT NAV LE6 0AE

Room 🛏   General 🛋 🗄 🏊 P 🍽 🎮 🐾   Leisure 🚣 ⚑

Do you have access needs?

Look for the National Accessible Scheme symbols if you have special hearing, visual or mobility needs.

LINCOLN, Lincolnshire Map ref 4C2 — HOTEL

★★
HOTEL

B&B PER ROOM PER NIGHT
S £70.00–£92.00
D £94.00–£115.00
HB PER PERSON PER NIGHT
£20.00–£25.00

The Castle Hotel

Westgate, Lincoln LN1 3AS **t** +44 (0) 1522 538801 **e** info@castlehotel.net

castlehotel.net

Located amid Lincoln's historic heart, a very comfortable traditional English hotel offering hospitality at its best. Also featuring Knights, an award-winning restaurant offering the best in modern English cuisine.

open All year
bedrooms 14 double, 4 twin, 1 single, 1 suite
bathrooms All en suite
payment Credit/debit cards, cash

Room ♨ 🖥 📞 📺 🌀 🍵 ⚸ General 8 P 🛜 🍽 🔌 ▣ 🍴 🐴 Leisure ∪

LONG COMPTON, Warwickshire Map ref 2B1 — GUEST ACCOMMODATION

★★★
FARMHOUSE

B&B PER ROOM PER NIGHT
S £35.00
D £50.00

Butlers Road Farm

Long Compton, Shipston-on-Stour CV36 5JZ **t** +44 (0) 1608 684262 **e** eileen@butlersroad.com

butlersroadfarm.co.uk

120-acre stock farm. Listed Cotswold-stone farmhouse adjacent to A3400 between Oxford and Stratford-upon-Avon. Home comforts. Local pub nearby. Rooms also function as family rooms.

open All year
bedrooms 1 double, 1 twin
payment Cash, cheques

Room 📺 🍵 General 🐎 ▥ ⚐ P 🎱 ▣ ❀ 🐴 Leisure ∪ ✦ ▶ ⚴

LOUTH, Lincolnshire Map ref 4D2 — SELF CATERING

★★★★–★★★★★★
SELF CATERING

Units   **3**
Sleeps **1–24**

LOW SEASON PER WK
£265.00–£655.00

HIGH SEASON PER WK
£325.00–£1,045.00

Short breaks always available. Any start day, length of stay.

Brackenborough Hall Coach House Holidays,
Brackenborough, Louth

contact Mr & Mrs Paul and Flora Bennett, Brackenborough Hall, Brackenborough, Louth LN11 0NS
t +44 (0) 1507 603193 & +44 (0) 7974 687779 **e** paulandflora@brackenboroughhall.com

brackenboroughhall.com GUEST REVIEWS · SPECIAL OFFERS

open All year
payment Credit/debit cards, cash, cheques
nearest pub 2 miles
nearest shop 2 miles

Three luxury apartments in listed 18thC coach house beside moated manor house. All original features retained. In ancient parkland on 800-acre farm. Beautiful, peaceful setting for walking, cycling, fishing, nature watching and relaxing/playing in extensive gardens. Between the Lincolnshire Wolds, coast and attractive market town of Louth. Children welcome.

SAT NAV *LN11 0NS* **ONLINE MAP**

Unit 📺 ▤ 🖥 🖵 🎛 🖴 🍵 🗄 🧺 ❀ 🍳 General 🐎 ▥ ⚐ P Ⓢ 🐴
Leisure ● ⚲ ∪ ✦ ▶ ⚴

LUDLOW, Shropshire Map ref 4A3 — GUEST ACCOMMODATION

★★★★
BED & BREAKFAST

B&B PER ROOM PER NIGHT
S £75.00–£110.00
D £110.00–£115.00

Bromley Court

18-20 Lower Broad Street, Ludlow SY8 1PQ **t** +44 (0) 1584 876996 & +44 (0) 7809 699665
e phil@ludlowhotels.com

ludlowhotels.com SPECIAL OFFERS

Tudor cottages of great charm, in Ludlow town. Each cottage forms a delightful, individually furnished suite – for total privacy and relaxation. Within walking distance of everything in Ludlow.

open All year
bedrooms 3 suites
bathrooms All en suite
payment Credit/debit cards, cash, cheques

Room 📞 📺 🌀 🍵 General 🐎 ▥ ❀ 🐴 Leisure ∪ ✦ ▶ ⚴

What do the star ratings mean?
Detailed information about star ratings can be found at the back of this guide.

LUDLOW, Shropshire Map ref 4A3

★★★★–★★★★★★
SELF CATERING

Units **3**
Sleeps **4–5**

LOW SEASON PER WK
£700.00–£750.00

HIGH SEASON PER WK
£1,050.00–£1,100.00

Ludlow Castle Lodgings, Ludlow

contact Helen Duce, Ludlow Castle Lodgings, Ludlow Castle, Castle Square, Ludlow SY8 1AX
t +44 (0) 1584 874465 **e** hduce@ludlowcastle.com

ludlowcastle.com GUEST REVIEWS

open All year
payment Credit/debit cards, cash, cheques
nearest pub less than 0.5 miles
nearest shop less than 0.5 miles

Castle House Lodgings comprise three newly renovated apartments, full of character features an finished to the highest of standards, set within the walls of Ludlow Castle. Each apartment provides sitting room/dining room, fully equipped kitchen, two twin bedrooms and two bathrooms and a car parking space.

Unit 📺 ▯🖥 ▯. ▯▯ ▯ ▯ ▯ ▯ 🗂 General 🎠 ▥ ▯ P S 🐾 Leisure ∪ ⚓ ♻

MABLETHORPE, Lincolnshire Map ref 4D2

★★★
GUEST HOUSE

B&B PER ROOM PER NIGHT
S Min £20.00
D £50.00–£55.00

EVENING MEAL PER PERSON
£5.00–£7.00

The Cannon Guest House

7 Waterloo Road, Mablethorpe LN12 1JR **t** +44 (0) 1507 473148 **e** info@cannon-guesthouse.co.u

cannon-guesthouse.co.uk

Open all year round for a warm and friendly welcome and good food. This delightful, small guesthouse comprises four comfortable letting bedrooms. You can even choose from a four-poster bed with en suite or a 7ft 7in bed with en suite.

open All year except Christmas and New Year
bedrooms 2 double, 1 twin, 1 family
bathrooms All en suite
payment Cash, cheques, euros

Room 🛏 🖵 📺 SC ▯ ▯ General 🎠 ▥ ▯ P ✕ 🍽 Leisure ⚓

MALVERN, Worcestershire Map ref 2B1

★★★
SELF CATERING

Units **1**
Sleeps **9**

LOW SEASON PER WK
£566.00–£927.00

HIGH SEASON PER WK
£927.00–£1,279.00

Short breaks available Mar-Oct. Sat-Mon, 2 or 3-night stay.

Wayfarers Cottage, Malvern

contact Mr & Mrs John & Caroline Roslington, Wayfarers, Park Road, Malvern WR14 4BJ
t +44 (0) 1684 575758 **e** info@wayfarerscottage.co.uk

wayfarerscottage.co.uk GUEST REVIEWS

open February to November and New Year
payment Cash, cheques
nearest pub less than 0.5 miles
nearest shop 1 mile

A real treat for family and friends, in attractive area rich in history and leisure activities. Spacious, extended cottage on Malvern Hills, superb views towards Wales. Parking for three cars. Library with over 1000 books. One single, two double and two twin bedrooms, bathroom, shower room, three toilets. Digital TV and computer with Wi-Fi internet Quiet pub with good food.

SAT NAV *WR14 4BJ* **ONLINE MAP**

Unit 📺 🖵 ▯. ▯▯ ▯ ▯ ▯ ❄ 🏕 ⌀ General 🎠 P ▯ S 🐾 Leisure ∪ ⚓ ▸ ♻

Using map references

The map references refer to the colour maps at the front of this guide. The first figure is the map number, the letter and figure that follow indicate the grid reference on the map.

MANNINGTREE, Essex Map ref 3B2   **GUEST ACCOMMODATION**

★★★★
**BED & BREAKFAST
SILVER AWARD**

B&B PER ROOM PER NIGHT
S £50.00–£60.00
D £60.00–£75.00

The perfect place to stay for walkers and birdwatchers. Single-let discounts on twin rooms.

Curlews
Station Road, Bradfield, Manningtree CO11 2UP   t +44 (0) 1255 870890
e margherita@curlewsaccommodation.co.uk

curlewsacccommodation.co.uk

open All year
bedrooms 3 double, 5 twin, 1 family, 1 suite
bathrooms All en suite
payment Credit/debit cards, cash, cheques

Curlews is a superb property situated on the outskirts of Bradfield village offering luxury bed and breakfast and self-catering accommodation including facilities for the disabled. Located approximately 30m above sea level, all bedrooms provide stunning elevated panoramic views over farmland and the Stour Estuary.

SAT NAV *CO11 2UP* **ONLINE MAP**

Room ♿ 📺 ⓦ ☏   General ❤8 P 🍴❄   Leisure ♪▶

MANNINGTREE, Essex Map ref 3B2   **GUEST ACCOMMODATION**

★★★★
BED & BREAKFAST

B&B PER ROOM PER NIGHT
S £40.00–£55.00
D £55.00–£65.00

Emsworth House
Station Road, Ship Hill, Bradfield, Manningtree CO11 2UP   t +44 (0) 1255 870860
e emsworthhouse@hotmail.com

emsworthhouse.co.uk

open All year
bedrooms 1 double, 1 twin, 1 single, 1 family
bathrooms 2 en suite
payment Cash, cheques

Formerly the vicarage. Spacious rooms with stunning views of the countryside and River Stour. Near Colchester and Harwich. On holiday, business or en route to the continent, it's perfect!

SAT NAV *CO11 2UP* **ONLINE MAP**

Room 📺 ⓦ ☏   General ❤ 🍴♨ P ⓦ 🍴❄   Leisure ∪♪▶ 🚲

MANSFIELD, Nottinghamshire Map ref 4C2   **HOTEL**

★★
SMALL HOTEL

B&B PER ROOM PER NIGHT
S £35.00–£60.00
D £55.00–£70.00
HB PER PERSON PER NIGHT
£44.50–£77.00

Pine Lodge Hotel
281-283 Nottingham Road, Mansfield NG18 4SE   t +44 (0) 1623 622308
e enquiries@pinelodge-hotel.co.uk

pinelodge-hotel.co.uk

Friendly and informal. Good food, good value, excellent service. Ideally situated close to many of Nottinghamshire's tourist and leisure attractions.

open All year except Christmas
bedrooms 4 double, 8 twin, 6 single, 1 family, 1 suite
bathrooms All en suite
payment Credit/debit cards, cash, cheques, euros

Room 📞 📺 SC ⓦ ☏ 🚿   General ❤ 🍴♨ P ⓦ ❗ 🍴◐ 🍷❄

What if I need to cancel?
It is advisable to check the proprietor's cancellation policy in case you have to change your plans at a later date.

MATLOCK, Derbyshire Map ref 4B2 SELF CATERING

★★★
SELF CATERING

Units **1**
Sleeps **1–5**

LOW SEASON PER WK
£245.00–£295.00

HIGH SEASON PER WK
£499.00–£549.00

Mansion Cottage, Crich, Matlock

contact Mrs Sally Parkin, Orchard House, Coasthill, Crich DE4 5DS **t** +44 (0) 1773 857883
e info@mansioncottage.co.uk

mansioncottage.co.uk SPECIAL OFFERS · REAL-TIME BOOKING

Newly renovated, this beautiful 19thC Derbyshire stone cottage is spacious, immaculately presented and homely, retaining main original features. Totally refurbished throughout, the three bedrooms sleep four/five guests comfortably.

open All year
payment Credit/debit cards, cash, cheques
nearest pub less than 0.5 miles
nearest shop less than 0.5 miles

Unit [TV] [icons] General [icons] P [icons] S Leisure [icons]

NAYLAND, Suffolk Map ref 3B2 SELF CATERING

★★★★–★★★★★★
SELF CATERING

Units **9**
Sleeps **2–8**

LOW SEASON PER WK
£260.00–£875.00

HIGH SEASON PER WK
£570.00–£1,800.00

Short breaks Oct-Easter. 3-night weekends or 4-night midweek breaks at 70% full-week rate.

Gladwins Farm, Nayland

contact Mr R Dossor, Gladwins Farm, Harpers Hill, Colchester CO6 4NU **t** +44 (0) 1206 262261
e gladwinsfarm@aol.com

gladwinsfarm.co.uk SPECIAL OFFERS

open All year
payment Credit/debit cards, cash, cheques
nearest pub less than 0.5 miles
nearest shop 0.5 miles

Extensive wooded grounds in Suffolk's rolling Constable Country with marvellous views make our a wonderful location. Charming villages and gardens to explore – not far from the sea. Heated indoor pool, sauna, hot tub, tennis, fishing, animals and playground. Pets welcome. Chelsworth and Melford cottages have private hot tubs.

ONLINE MAP

Unit [TV] [icons] General [icons] P [icons] S [icons]
Leisure [icons]

NETHERSEAL, Derbyshire Map ref 4B3 SELF CATERING

★★★★
SELF CATERING

Units **2**
Sleeps **2–8**

LOW SEASON PER WK
£280.00–£800.00

HIGH SEASON PER WK
£320.00–£900.00

Sealbrook Farm, Swadlincote

contact Rob & Jane Kirkland, Grangewood, Swadlincote DE12 8BG **t** +44 (0) 1827 373236
e info@sealbrookfarmcottages.co.uk

sealbrookfarmcottages.co.uk

Properties are in a quiet hamlet. Shops, pubs, restaurants, attractions are local, also in the heart of the National Forest. Within easy reach of motorway networks. Private off-road parking. Wi-Fi internet available.

open All year
payment Cash, cheques
nearest pub 1.5 miles
nearest shop 2 miles

Unit [TV] [icons] General [icons] P [icons] S Leisure [icons]

Country Code always follow the Country Code

- Be safe – plan ahead and follow any signs
- Leave gates and property as you find them
- Protect plants and animals, and take your litter home
- Keep dogs under close control
- Consider other people

NEWMARKET, Suffolk Map ref 3B2 — GUEST ACCOMMODATION

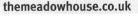

★★★★
GUEST ACCOMMODATION

B&B PER ROOM PER NIGHT
S £30.00–£35.00
D £60.00

Meadow House

2a High Street, Burwell, Cambridge CB25 0HB t +44 (0) 1638 741926
e hilary@themeadowhouse.co.uk

themeadowhouse.co.uk

open All year
bedrooms 1 double, 1 twin, 3 family, 1 suite
bathrooms 4 en suite
payment Cash, cheques, euros

Large, well-equipped, modern house set in grounds of two acres, close to Newmarket Racecourse, Cambridge and Ely. King-size beds. Family suites available, also coach house available in grounds. Large car park. Generous breakfasts. Two rooms suitable for moderately disabled people. More colour pictures available on our website.

SAT NAV CB25 0HB

Room 🖤 📺 🍴 🥤   General 🐴 🏛 ⚡ P ❄ 🐕

NEWPORT, Shropshire Map ref 4A3 — GUEST ACCOMMODATION

★★★★
BED & BREAKFAST
SILVER AWARD

B&B PER ROOM PER NIGHT
D £60.00–£70.00

Red Gables Country B&B

Longford, Newport TF10 8LN t +44 (0) 1952 811118 e sandracorbett@red-gables.com

red-gables.com

Red Cables Country B&B is a beautiful country house offering newly converted three bedroomed, en suite accommodation in coach house set in five acres of private grounds.

open All year
bedrooms 2 double, 1 twin
bathrooms All en suite
payment Cash, cheques

Room 📺 🆂🅲 🍴 🥤   General 🐴 P 📶 ♿ 🖥 ❄

NORFOLK BROADS

See under Aylsham, Coltishall, Norwich, Oulton Broad, South Walsham

NORWICH, Norfolk Map ref 3C1 — GUEST ACCOMMODATION

★★★
GUEST ACCOMMODATION

B&B PER ROOM PER NIGHT
S £38.00–£43.00
D £43.00–£48.00

Edmar Lodge

64 Earlham Road, Norwich NR2 3DF t +44 (0) 1603 615599 e mail@edmarlodge.co.uk

edmarlodge.co.uk GUEST REVIEWS

open All year
bedrooms 3 double, 1 twin, 1 family
bathrooms All en suite
payment Credit/debit cards, cash, cheques, euros

Edmar Lodge is a family-run guesthouse where you will receive a warm welcome from Ray and Sue. We are situated only ten minutes' walk from the city centre. All rooms have en suite facilities and digital TV. We are well known for our excellent breakfasts that set you up for the day.

SAT NAV NR2 3DF **ONLINE MAP**

Room 🖤 📺 🍴 🥤   General 🐴 🏛 ⚡ P ♿ 🍳 ❄ 🐕

Place index

If you know where you want to stay, the index by place name at the back of the guide will give you the page number listing accommodation in your chosen town, city or village. Check out the other useful indexes too.

OAKHAM, Rutland Map ref 4C3 — HOTE

★★★
HOTEL

B&B PER ROOM PER NIGHT
S £49.00–£67.00
D £69.00–£92.00

Weekend breaks from £53 per person per night DB&B.

Whitwell Hotel & Conference Centre

Main Road, Witwell, Oakham LE15 8BW **t** +44 (0) 1780 460334 **e** enquiries@whitwellhotel.co.uk

whitwellhotel.co.uk SPECIAL OFFERS

open All year
bedrooms 7 double, 9 twin, 6 single, 4 family
bathrooms All en suite
payment Credit/debit cards, cash, cheques

A 16thC converted leisure, conference and training venue on the shores of Rutland Water. Guests experience traditional style and professional service. Perfect for conferences, meetings, weddings and events. A perfect base to explore Rutland, England smallest county.

SAT NAV *LE15 8BW*

Room General Leisure

OAKHAM, Rutland Map ref 4C3 — GUEST ACCOMMODATION

★★★★
BED & BREAKFAST

B&B PER ROOM PER NIGHT
S £45.00–£55.00
D £75.00–£85.00

Discounts are available for stays of 3 or more nights.

17 Northgate

Oakham LE15 6QR **t** +44 (0) 1572 759271 **e** dane@danegould.wanadoo.co.uk

17northgate.co.uk

open All year except Christmas and New Year
bedrooms 1 double, 1 twin
bathrooms All en suite
payment Credit/debit cards, cash, cheques, euros

A recently renovated, 300-year-old thatched farmhouse in the centre of Oakham close to Rutland Water, the church, railway station and the excellent pubs and restaurants. The two en suite rooms are newly built, with their own patios and private entrance from the drive, where off-road parking is available.

SAT NAV *LE15 6QR*

Room General Leisure

OSWESTRY, Shropshire Map ref 4A3 — SELF CATERING

★★★★
SELF CATERING

Units **1**
Sleeps **4**

LOW SEASON PER WK
Max £350.00

HIGH SEASON PER WK
Max £550.00

Free Sunday lunch for 4 at The Walls for weekly bookings.

Courtyard, Oswestry

contact Katherine Bottoms, Underhill House, Racecourse Road, Oswestry SY10 7PN
t +44 (0) 1691 670066 **e** gohughes@aol.com

the-walls.co.uk

open All year
payment Credit/debit cards, cash, cheques
nearest pub 1.1 miles
nearest shop 1.1 miles

Characterful well-appointed cottage sleeping four. Both rooms double or twin and en suite. Lawn games, bikes available, large DVD/video library. Safe and peaceful but close to town. Lots of local attractions and activities, great restaurants.

ONLINE MAP

Unit General Leisure

Using map references

Map references refer to the colour maps at the front of this guide.

OULTON BROAD, Suffolk Map ref 3C1

★★★★
SELF CATERING

Units **4**
Sleeps **2–18**

LOW SEASON PER WK
Min £182.00

HIGH SEASON PER WK
Max £2,500.00

Camps Heath Barn, Oulton, Lowestoft

contact Mr J R Overy, Camps Heath Barn, Camps Heath, Lowestoft NR32 5DW
t +44 (0) 1502 562981 & +44 (0) 7917 147776 e campsheathbarn@hotmail.co.uk

campsheathbarn.co.uk

open All year
payment Cash, cheques
nearest pub 0.5 miles
nearest shop 0.5 miles

This recently converted barn on the edge of a nature reserve provides a charming mix of traditional and modern, with spacious accommodation in the main barn and three self-contained annexes sleeping two to eighteen people. These are all furnished and equipped to please the most discerning visitor.

SAT NAV NR32 5DW

Unit 📺 ▢▢ ▣ 🗄️ ▢▢ 🍳 🍴 💷 ✳ ⛺ ✎ General 🛞 P ▢ S 🐎 Leisure ♨ ♪ ▶

PEAK DISTRICT

See under Alsop-en-le-Dale, Bakewell, Biggin-by-Hartington, Buxton, Chapel-en-le-Frith, Tideswell

PETERBOROUGH, Cambridgeshire Map ref 3A1

★★★★★
HOLIDAY PARK
🚐 (252) £12.20–£25.10
🚏 (252) £12.20–£25.10
252 touring pitches

Ferry Meadows Caravan Club Site

Ham Lane, Peterborough PE2 5UU t +44 (0) 1733 233526

caravanclub.co.uk

open All year
payment Credit/debit cards, cash, cheques

Set in 500-acre Nene Country Park. Plenty of activities including canoeing, windsurfing and sailing. Also nature trails, two golf courses, pitch and putt and bird sanctuary.

SAT NAV PE2 5UU

Special member rates mean you can save your membership subscription in less than a week. Visit our website to find out more.

THE
**CARAVAN
CLUB**

General ▣ 🔌 🚿 🚽 💧 📶 📞 🐎 ☀ 📶 Leisure ⛰ ♪ ▶

PULHAM MARKET, Norfolk Map ref 3B2

★★★★★
GUEST ACCOMMODATION
GOLD AWARD

B&B PER ROOM PER NIGHT
S £45.00–£65.00
D £65.00–£80.00

Old Bakery

The Old Bakery, Church Walk, Pulham Market IP21 4SL t +44 (0) 1379 676492
e info@theoldbakery.net

theoldbakery.net GUEST REVIEWS · SPECIAL OFFERS

Oak-beamed former bakery in Waveney Valley conservation village with two inns. Beautifully appointed spacious en suite bedrooms, garden and delicious locally produced breakfasts. Ideally located for Broads, coast and countryside.

open All year
bedrooms 1 double, 1 twin, 1 family
bathrooms All en suite
payment Credit/debit cards, cash, cheques

Room 📺 ♨ 🍳 General 🛞10 P 📶 🔥 🍷 🍴▢ ✳ Leisure ♨ ♪ ▶

Do you have access needs?

Look for the National Accessible Scheme symbols if you have special hearing, visual or mobility needs. An index of accommodation participating in the scheme can be found at the back of this guide.

REEDHAM, Norfolk Map ref 3C1 — SELF CATERING

★★★★
SELF CATERING

Units **3**
Sleeps **2–6**

LOW SEASON PER WK
£200.00–£400.00

HIGH SEASON PER WK
£400.00–£600.00

Riverside Properties, Reedham

contact Mrs Heather Willies, Riverside Properties, Coombe Cottage, Grayswood Road, Haslemere GU27 2BU **t** +44 (0) 1428 658289 **e** rivitt@aol.com

tiscover.co.uk

One two-person and two six-person cottages in tranquil riverside location. Newly refurbished. River frontage and mooring. Swallow Cottage: one double bed. Yar Cottage and Water's Edge: two doubles, one twin.

open All year
payment Cash, cheques
nearest pub less than 0.5 miles
nearest shop less than 0.5 miles

Unit 📺 🆂 🛋 📠 🖥️ 🍽️ 🔥 🗑️ ♨️ 🛁 General 🛏️ 🚭 P 🅂
Leisure ∪ ♪ ► 🚲

RETFORD, Nottinghamshire Map ref 4C2 — SELF CATERING

★★★
SELF CATERING

Units **1**
Sleeps **1–4**

LOW SEASON PER WK
£300.00–£360.00

HIGH SEASON PER WK
£370.00–£400.00

Spruce Cottage, Ranby, Retford

t +44 (0) 131 447 6886

countrycottagesonline.net

open All year
payment Cash, cheques
nearest pub 3 miles
nearest shop 3 miles

Cottage lying in a beautiful setting surrounded by private woodland and grazing paddocks with 20 acres of private parkland for walking. One double and two single bedrooms. Warm and cosy in winter from wood-burning stove and log fire. Easy access to Sherwood Forest, Rufford Abbey and Lincoln Cathedral.

Unit 📺 🖥️ 🍽️ 🔥 🗑️ ♨️ 🛁 General 🛏️4 P

ROSS-ON-WYE, Herefordshire Map ref 2A1 — HOTEL

★★★
HOTEL

B&B PER ROOM PER NIGHT
S £90.00–£175.00
D £110.00–£195.00
HB PER PERSON PER NIGHT
£74.50–£117.50

> Check website for regular special offers.

Chase Classic Hotel

Gloucester Road, Ross-on-Wye HR9 5LH **t** +44 (0) 1989 763161 **e** res@chasehotel.co.uk

chasehotel.co.uk SPECIAL OFFERS · REAL-TIME BOOKING

open All year except Christmas
bedrooms 27 double, 9 twin
bathrooms All en suite
payment Credit/debit cards, cash, cheques, euros

With extensive grounds and gardens, the Chase Hotel is the perfect rural location for relaxation and comfort, whether on business or pleasure. Concessionary golf arrangements are available. Award-winning cuisine within our fine-dining restaurant and conference and events facility, catering for up to 300 guests, provide good quality of service and product within a country-house venue.

SAT NAV HR9 5LH **ONLINE MAP**

Room 🛏️ ☎ 📺 🆂 ♨️ 🔥 ♿ General 🛏️ 🚭 🅟 ♿ P (📶) 🍷 🍴 ◐ 🍽️ 🍵 ✳
Leisure ∪ ♪ ► 🚲

Check the maps for accommodation locations

Colour maps at the front pinpoint all the places where accommodation is featured within the regional sections of this guide. Pick your location and then refer to the place index at the back to find the page number.

ROSS-ON-WYE, Herefordshire Map ref 2A1 GUEST ACCOMMODATION

★★★★
BED & BREAKFAST

B&B PER ROOM PER NIGHT
S £25.00–£45.00
D £40.00–£60.00

EVENING MEAL PER PERSON
Max £18.50

Pay a maximum of £18.50 for an a la carte dinner, regardless of the menu price, if you are a resident.

Broome Farm

Peterstow, Ross-on-Wye HR9 6QG t +44 (0) 1989 562824 e broomefarm@tesco.net

broomefarmhouse.co.uk

open All year
bedrooms 2 double, 1 family
bathrooms All en suite
payment Credit/debit cards, cash, cheques

Working cider farm, providing en suite accommodation. Licensed dining room with a la carte menu featuring local produce. Set in tranquil countryside, looking over rural Herefordshire. Only two miles from the town of Ross-on-Wye. Orchard walks, cream teas and cider tasting available.

SAT NAV *HR9 6QG* **ONLINE MAP**

Room 📺 SC ♨ ⛾ General 🐴10 P ⟨ᴘ⟩ ♥ ✕ 🏕 ✱ 🐴 Leisure ∪ 🚣 ► 🚲

RUTLAND WATER

See under Oakham

ST IVES, Cambridgeshire Map ref 3A2 GUEST ACCOMMODATION

★★★★★
**GUEST ACCOMMODATION
SILVER AWARD**

B&B PER ROOM PER NIGHT
S £65.00–£72.00
D £75.00–£85.00

Close to Huntingdon and Newmarket races. Ask too about our walking, cycling and birdwatching breaks including maps and packed lunches.

Cheriton House

Mill Street, Houghton PE28 2AZ t +44 (0) 1480 464004 e sales@cheritonhousecambs.co.uk

cheritonhousecambs.co.uk

open All year
bedrooms 4 double, 1 twin
bathrooms All en suite
payment Credit/debit cards, cash, cheques

Award-winning B&B 150yds from the river and the mill in picturesque village of Houghton. Two miles from Huntingdon, just 20-25 minutes from Cambridge and Ely. Great breakfasts, home-made breads, jams, marmalade, cakes. Large garden, riverside walks to several good pubs with attractive gardens in summer and roaring log fires in winter.

SAT NAV *PE28 2AZ* **ONLINE MAP**

Room ♨ 📺 ♨ ⛾ General P ⟨ᴘ⟩ ♿ 🏕 🎮 ✱ Leisure ∪ 🚣 ► 🚲

ST NEOTS, Cambridgeshire Map ref 2D1 SELF CATERING

★★★★★
SELF CATERING

Units   1
Sleeps   6

LOW SEASON PER WK
£480.00–£512.00

HIGH SEASON PER WK
£554.00–£796.00

Take a short break and play golf at 3 of Cambridgeshire's top golf courses at a special discounted rate.

Abbotsley Country Homes, Eynesbury Hardwicke, St Neots

contact Mr Michael Wilton-Cox, Abbotsley Country Homes, Drewels Lane, Eynesbury Hardwicke, St Neots PE19 6EF t +44 (0) 1480 476312 e abbotsleyhomes@btconnect.com

abbotsleycountryhomes.co.uk REAL-TIME BOOKING

open All year
payment Cash, cheques, euros
nearest pub 0.5 miles
nearest shop 3 miles

These luxury, self-catering Norwegian log cabins overlook the stunning Cambridgeshire countryside. They are perfect for a family break, with three double bedrooms (one en suite). The lodges have classic Scandinavian styling and offer comfortable, spacious open-plan living. Adjacent to two golf courses, close to local amenities.

SAT NAV *PE19 6EF* **ONLINE MAP**

Unit 📺 🖥 💻 ▫ 🍽 🗄 ⛾ 🔥 🍽 🍴 ✱ ⛱ General 🐴 🏕 ♿ P S Leisure ►

★★★★
SELF CATERING

Units **1**
Sleeps **4**

LOW SEASON PER WK
£290.00–£490.00

HIGH SEASON PER WK
£390.00–£490.00

*Short breaks:
4 nights for the price
of 3 (4 nights
midweek for the
price of 3 at
weekends).
Telephone for
current offers/
promotions. Wine-
tastings, arts/music
events locally.*

Corner Cottage, Saxmundham

contact Dawn Ribnell, 35 North Road, Brentwood CM14 4UZ **t** +44 (0) 1277 210551 &
+44 (0) 7860 887653 **e** info@cornercottageholiday.com

cornercottageholiday.com GUEST REVIEWS · SPECIAL OFFERS

open All year
payment Cash, cheques
nearest pub less than 0.5 miles
nearest shop less than 0.5 miles

Quaint, single-storey period cottage in a quiet,
friendly market town location, four miles Snape,
eight miles Aldeburgh, on Suffolk Heritage Coast.
Light and airy, with pleasant views from each
window. Lovely feature fireplace for cosy log fires i
winter. Two comfortable bedrooms. One can be
arranged as either king-size double or two single
beds.

SAT NAV *IP17 1BJ* **ONLINE MAP**

Unit 📺 📷 💻 🖨 🔌 🔟 🍴 💟 🍳 ⊿ 🌿 General 🛋 🛏 ⚐ P ⬜ Ⓢ 🐾
Leisure ∪ ♪ ⚐ 🚲

★★★★
SELF CATERING

Units **1**
Sleeps **4**

LOW SEASON PER WK
£350.00–£400.00

HIGH SEASON PER WK
£450.00–£475.00

Rookery Park, Saxmundham

contact Mrs Eden McDonald, Rookery Park, Yoxford IP17 3HQ **t** +44 (0) 1728 668740

tiscover.co.uk

payment Cash, cheques
nearest pub 0.5 miles
nearest shop 0.5 miles

Convenient Heritage Coast (Southwold, Dunwich,
Minsmere, Snape, Aldeburgh) and rural Suffolk.
Attractively furnished. Clean, spacious lounge/diner,
kitchen (dishwasher, washing machine, dryer,
microwave etc). One double, one twin. Large patio
Panoramic parkland views. Own grounds on
120-acre country estate. Linen, heating and lighting
included. Parking. Closed 14 January to 1 March.

Unit 📺 📷 💻 🖨 🔌 🔟 🍴 💟 ❄ 🎮 General 🛋 P

★★★★
GUEST ACCOMMODATION
SILVER AWARD

B&B PER ROOM PER NIGHT
S £45.00–£50.00
D £70.00–£76.00

EVENING MEAL PER PERSON
£15.00–£20.00

*Anniversary stays,
alone or with friends
and family. Packages
include celebratory
meal (2-8 covers
dinner, 6-20 covers
buffet). Price on
application.*

Viburnham House B&B

Augusta Street, Sheringham NR26 8LB **t** +44 (0) 1263 822528 **e** viburnhamhouse@aol.com

viburnhamhouse.co.uk

open All year
bedrooms 2 double, 1 twin
bathrooms All en suite
payment Credit/debit cards, cash, cheques

Relax, unwind, and refresh in real comfort at
Viburnham House. Great hospitality, personal
friendly service in period surroundings. An easy stroll
to the sea and the town centre. All rooms en suite.
Visit us by car or train. Children over six and well-
behaved dogs welcome too.

SAT NAV *NR26 8LB*

Room 📺 💧 🔌 General 🛋6 ✕ 🍴 🖥 ❄ 🐾 Leisure ∪ ♪ ⚐ 🚲

SHERWOOD FOREST

See under Mansfield, Retford

SHREWSBURY, Shropshire Map ref 4A3 GUEST ACCOMMODATION

★★★★
GUEST HOUSE

B&B PER ROOM PER NIGHT
S £40.00–£45.00
D £60.00–£70.00

Discounted rates available for longer stays.

Abbey Court House

134 Abbey Foregate, Shrewsbury SY2 6AU **t** +44 (0) 1743 364416 **e** info@abbeycourt.biz

abbeycourt.biz

open All year
bedrooms 3 double, 4 twin, 2 single, 1 family
bathrooms All en suite
payment Credit/debit cards, cash, cheques, euros

Abbey Court offers quality accommodation in a Grade II Listed building. Refurbished to a high standard. Comfortable en suite guest rooms each with hospitality tray, TV and telephone. Convenient for the town centre. Off-road parking and some ground-floor rooms. Superb breakfasts include vegetarian options. A warm welcome is guaranteed.

SAT NAV *SY2 6AU* **ONLINE MAP**

Room ♿ 📞 📺 ⭐ General ♨ ▦ ♿ P ⛏

SHREWSBURY, Shropshire Map ref 4A3 GUEST ACCOMMODATION

★★★★
FARMHOUSE

B&B PER ROOM PER NIGHT
S £45.00–£60.00
D £55.00–£70.00

Midweek discounts for 2 nights or more.

Brimford House

Criggion, Shrewsbury SY5 9AU **t** +44 (0) 1938 570235 **e** info@brimford.co.uk

brimford.co.uk

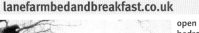

open All year
bedrooms 2 double, 1 twin
bathrooms All en suite
payment Cash, cheques

Comfortable Georgian farmhouse set in tranquil, Shropshire/Welsh countryside between Shrewsbury and Welshpool. Enjoy breathtaking views, wonderful walks and log fires, romantic weekends and stylish, spacious bedrooms (all en suite). Farmhouse breakfasts served with home made preserves and free-range eggs. Country pub three minutes' walk. Midweek discounts available.

SAT NAV *SY5 9AU*

Room 📺 ⭐ General ♨ ▦ ♿ P ⛏ 🐕

SHREWSBURY, Shropshire Map ref 4A3 GUEST ACCOMMODATION

★★★
FARMHOUSE

B&B PER ROOM PER NIGHT
S £30.00–£35.00
D £50.00–£54.00

2 nights or more @ £25.00pppn based on 2 sharing a room.

Lane Farm

Criggion, Nr Shrewsbury SY5 9BG **t** +44 (0) 1743 884288 **e** lane.farm@ukgateway.net

lanefarmbedandbreakfast.co.uk

open All year except Christmas and New Year
bedrooms 2 double, 2 twin
bathrooms All en suite
payment Cash, cheques

Warm welcome assured on our working organic farm situated between Welshpool and Shrewsbury. Nestling beneath the tranquil Bredden Hills in the picturesque Severn Valley, ideally placed to explore the stunning scenery of the Marches, Shropshire Hills and mid Wales. Four spacious, en suite bedrooms, hearty farmhouse breakfasts. Relax and stay awhile.

SAT NAV *SY5 9BG*

Room ♿ 📺 ⭐ General ♨ P ⛏ Leisure ∪ ♪ ▶

GUEST ACCOMMODATIO

★★★★
INN

B&B PER ROOM PER NIGHT
S £50.00–£60.00
D £75.00–£85.00

EVENING MEAL PER PERSON
£20.00–£30.00

Discounts on 4 or more nights. Special winter deals often available. Telephone or see website for further details.

Sibton White Horse Inn

Halesworth Road, Sibton, Saxmundham IP17 2JJ t +44 (0) 1728 660337
e info@sibtonwhitehorseinn.co.uk

sibtonwhitehorseinn.co.uk GUEST REVIEWS · SPECIAL OFFERS

open All year
bedrooms 3 double, 1 twin, 2 single, 1 family
bathrooms All en suite
payment Credit/debit cards, cash, cheques

You probably couldn't find a more quintessential country inn. Grade II Listed, wonderful features and timber frame dating back to 1580. Quiet village 15 minutes from coast. Peaceful attractive en suite bedrooms in separate building within spacious gardens. Good food, all freshly prepared, enchanting dining areas. Special in both summer and winter.

SAT NAV IP17 2JJ ONLINE MAP

Room ♿ 📺 🆂 ● 🍵 General 🛏 ♨ ⚓ P 📶 ♿ ♥ ✕ 🎱 ❄ Leisure 🚣 🚴

SELF CATERING

★★★★
SELF CATERING

Units **2**
Sleeps **4–5**

LOW SEASON PER WK
£275.00–£325.00

HIGH SEASON PER WK
£325.00–£460.00

Grasswells Farm Holiday Cottages, Louth

contact Ms Janice Foster, Grasswells Holiday Cottages (Saddleback Leisure Ltd), Saddleback Road, Howdales, South Cockerington, Louth LN11 7DJ t +44 (0) 1507 338508
e thefosters2002@talk-email.com

Single barn conversions, spacious, comfortable and well equipped. Set in three acres of grounds with private fishing lake.

open All year
payment Cash, cheques
nearest pub 3 miles
nearest shop 3 miles

Unit 📺 🆂 🖥 🍵 🍳 ❄ ⛺ General 🛏 ♨ ⚓ P 🔲 🆂 🐕 Leisure 🚣

GUEST ACCOMMODATION

★★★★
GUEST ACCOMMODATION

B&B PER ROOM PER NIGHT
S Min £35.00
D £50.00–£55.00

Old Hall Farm

Newport Road, South Walsham, Norwich NR13 6DS t +44 (0) 1603 270271
e veronica@oldhallfarm.co.uk

oldhallfarm.co.uk

open April to October
bedrooms 2 double, 1 twin
bathrooms All en suite
payment Cash, cheques

17thC thatched farmhouse with large garden on the edge of Broadland village. Within walking distance of Fairhaven Gardens, Ranworth and St Lawrence Arts Centre, South Walsham. Wide range of cooked breakfasts using our own free-range eggs. Business guests welcome. Wireless broadband available. Non smoking.

SAT NAV NR13 6DS

Room 📺 ● 🍵 General 🛏 ♨ ⚓ P 📶 ♿ 🎱 ● ❄ Leisure 🚴

Need some ideas?

Big city buzz or peaceful panoramas? Take a fresh look at England and you may be surprised at what's right on your doorstep. Explore the diversity online at enjoyengland.com

SOUTHEND-ON-SEA, Essex Map ref 3B3 **SELF CATERING**

★★★
SELF CATERING

Units **1**
Sleeps **1–5**

LOW SEASON PER WK
£350.00–£450.00

HIGH SEASON PER WK
£420.00–£450.00

Everhome Apartments, Southend-on-Sea

contact Mr Malcolm Taylor, 26 Drake Road, Westcliff-on-Sea SS0 8LP **t** +44 (0) 1702 434320
e malcolm-t@btconnect.com

everhome.co.uk

Lovely self-catering (two-bedroom) apartment situated in conservation area ten to fifteen minutes' walk from the sea, pier, high street, railway station (London 45 minutes), Cliffs Pavilion Theatre, restaurants and bars.

open All year
payment Credit/debit cards, cash, cheques, euros
nearest pub less than 0.5 miles
nearest shop less than 0.5 miles

Unit TV SC DVD ■ ⬚ ⬚ ⬚ ⬚ General ⏃ P ⽥

SOUTHWOLD, Suffolk Map ref 3C2 **GUEST ACCOMMODATION**

★★★★
BED & BREAKFAST

B&B PER ROOM PER NIGHT
S Min £45.00
D £75.00–£85.00

> *7 nights for the price of 6 (weekly).*

Poplar Hall

Frostenden Corner, Frostenden, Southwold NR34 7JA **t** +44 (0) 1502 578549
e poplarhall@tiscali.co.uk

southwold.ws/poplar-hall

open All year except Christmas and New Year
bedrooms 1 double, 1 single, 1 suite
bathrooms 1 en suite, 2 private
payment Cash, cheques

Peaceful and quiet, yet only minutes from the lovely seaside town of Southwold, Poplar Hall is a 16thC thatched house in a 1.5-acre garden. Luxury accommodation with TV, tea/coffee facilities and vanity units in all rooms. Enjoy our famed breakfasts of fresh fruit, local fish, sausage, bacon and home-made preserves.

SAT NAV NR34 7JA

Room ⬚ TV ⬚ ⬚ General ⏃9 P 🍴✳ Leisure ✦ ⚲

SPILSBY, Lincolnshire Map ref 4D2 **GUEST ACCOMMODATION**

★★★★
BED & BREAKFAST
SILVER AWARD

B&B PER ROOM PER NIGHT
S £30.00
D £60.00

Spye House

Main Road, West Keal, Spilsby PE23 4BE **t** +44 (0) 1790 752102 **e** spye.house@btinternet.com

open All year
bedrooms 2 double
bathrooms 1 en suite, 1 private
payment Cash, cheques

Spye House is a large, detached, comfortable family home with quality en suite accommodation, standing in large attractive grounds. Home baking and local produce are specialities. Parking is on the house drive.

SAT NAV PE23 4BE

Room TV ⬚ ⬚ General ⏃ P 🍴✳

Where can I get help and advice?

Tourist Information Centres offer friendly help with accommodation and holiday ideas as well as suggestions of places to visit and things to do. You'll find contact details at the beginning of each regional section.

STANSTED, Essex Map ref 2D1   GUEST ACCOMMODATION

★★★★
GUEST ACCOMMODATION
SILVER AWARD

B&B PER ROOM PER NIGHT
S £50.00–£60.00
D £75.00–£90.00

The Cottage

71 Birchanger Lane, Birchanger, Bishop's Stortford CM23 5QA **t** +44 (0) 1279 812349
e bookings@thecottagebirchanger.co.uk

thecottagebirchanger.co.uk

open All year except Christmas and New Year
bedrooms 7 double, 5 twin, 2 single
bathrooms 13 en suite, 1 private
payment Credit/debit cards, cash, cheques

17thC Listed house with panelled rooms and woodburning stove. Conservatory-style breakfast room overlooks mature garden. Quiet, peaceful village setting yet near M11 junction 8, Stansted Airport and Bishop's Stortford. Ample off-road parking. Guest rooms furnished in traditional cottage style, with colour TV, tea/coffee facilities and free Wi-Fi Internet. Award-winning pub in village.

SAT NAV *CM23 5QA* **ONLINE MAP**

Room   General   Leisure

STANSTED, Essex Map ref 2D1   GUEST ACCOMMODATION

★★★★
GUEST ACCOMMODATION

B&B PER ROOM PER NIGHT
S £60.00
D £65.00

EVENING MEAL PER PERSON
£7.50–£20.00

The White House

Smiths Green, Takeley CM22 6NR **t** +44 (0) 1279 870257 **e** enquiries@whitehousestansted.co.uk

whitehousestansted.co.uk GUEST REVIEWS · SPECIAL OFFERS · REAL-TIME BOOKING

open All year except Christmas and New Year
bedrooms 1 double, 1 twin, 1 single
bathrooms 2 en suite, 1 private
payment Credit/debit cards, cash, cheques, euros

A 15thC manor house set in one acre with ample parking. Two miles from Stansted Airport (but not on flight path). Recently renovated. Modern, en suite facilities in a traditional family environment. Evening meal available at nearby Lion and Lamb pub/restaurant, which is also owned by Mike and Linda

SAT NAV *CM22 6NR* **ONLINE MAP**

Room   General   Leisure

STOKE-ON-TRENT, Staffordshire Map ref 4B2   GUEST ACCOMMODATION

★★
GUEST HOUSE

B&B PER ROOM PER NIGHT
S Min £24.00
D £40.00–£44.00

Verdon Guest House

44 Charles Street, Stoke-on-Trent ST1 3JY **t** +44 (0) 1782 264244

verdonguesthouse.co.uk

Newly renovated, large, friendly guesthouse in Hanley town centre. Alton Towers 20 minutes. All rooms have large flat-screen televisions with HD Freeview channels and DVD. Exceptionally comfortable beds. Excellent value.

open All year
bedrooms 4 double, 3 twin, 1 single, 5 family
bathrooms 5 en suite
payment Credit/debit cards, cash, cheques

Room   General

It's all quality-assessed accommodation

Our commitment to quality involves wide-ranging accommodation assessment.
Ratings and awards were correct at the time of going to press but may change
following a new assessment. Please check at time of booking.

STOKE-ON-TRENT, Staffordshire Map ref 4B2 — CAMPING, CARAVAN & HOLIDAY PARK

★★★★★
**HOLIDAY, TOURING
& CAMPING PARK**
ROSE AWARD

🚐(60) £15.00–£18.00
🚎(10) £10.00–£20.00
⛺(50) £10.00–£12.00
🚍(7) £270.00–£420.00
120 touring pitches

Early-season discounts on caravan holiday homes. Free 2nd-day admission to Alton Towers for 2 persons (ring for information).

Star Caravan & Camping Park

Star Road, Cotton, Alton Towers Area ST10 3BZ **t** +44 (0) 1538 702219

starcaravanpark.co.uk GUEST REVIEWS

open All year except Christmas and New Year
payment Credit/debit cards, cash, cheques

The closest touring park to Alton Towers. Strict 11pm-all-quiet rule on site. No single-sex groups allowed. Families and mixed couples always welcomed. Set in stunning countryside surrounded by mature trees and hedgerows. Ten miles from four market towns, and only four miles from the Peak District National Park.

SAT NAV *ST10 3BZ* **ONLINE MAP**

General 🚐🚿🅿️🚻🔌🛒📶📷📱☎️🐕☀️ Leisure ⛺ ♨ 🎣 🚴

STOWMARKET, Suffolk Map ref 3B2 — GUEST ACCOMMODATION

★★★★★
**GUEST ACCOMMODATION
GOLD AWARD**

B&B PER ROOM PER NIGHT
S Min £60.00
D Min £70.00

Bays Farm

Forward Green, Stowmarket IP14 5HU **t** +44 (0) 1449 711286 **e** info@baysfarmsuffolk.co.uk

baysfarmsuffolk.co.uk

open All year
bedrooms 3 double
bathrooms All en suite
payment Credit/debit cards, cash, cheques, euros

A 17thC beamed farmhouse in the heart of the Suffolk countryside stands ready to welcome you. Four acres of formal garden and grassland with a wealth of wildlife, including bats, owls and bird life.

SAT NAV *IP14 5HU*

Room 📺👩‍🦽🍵 General 🅿️📶❄️🐕

STRATFORD-UPON-AVON, Warwickshire Map ref 2B1 — GUEST ACCOMMODATION

★★★★
GUEST ACCOMMODATION

B&B PER ROOM PER NIGHT
S £45.00–£59.00
D £69.00–£89.00

Discounts available Oct-May (excl Sat and locally important dates).

Melita

37 Shipston Road, Stratford-upon-Avon CV37 7LN **t** +44 (0) 1789 292432
e info@melitaguesthouse.co.uk

melitaguesthouse.co.uk SPECIAL OFFERS

open All year except Christmas and New Year
bedrooms 5 double, 2 twin, 3 single, 2 family
bathrooms 10 en suite, 2 private
payment Credit/debit cards, cash, cheques

Once a Victorian home, the Melita is now a warm, friendly establishment managed by caring proprietors. Accommodation and service are of a high standard. Breakfasts are individually prepared to suit guests' requirements. The Melita is only 400m from the theatres and town centre and has free, private, on-site car parking.

SAT NAV *CV37 7LN*

Room 🦽📞📺👩‍🦽🍵 General 👨‍🦽🖥️🛗🅿️📶📷❄️🐕 Leisure 🎣🏇🚴

STRATFORD-UPON-AVON, Warwickshire Map ref 2B1 — SELF CATERING

★★★
SELF CATERING

Units **1**
Sleeps **1–2**

LOW SEASON PER WK
£260.00–£300.00

HIGH SEASON PER WK
£395.00

Flexible start days. Short breaks (3-night weekend, 4-night midweek). 10% discount for returning guests.

4 Bancroft Place, Stratford-upon-Avon

contact Mr & Mrs D Barnett, 43 Orchard Close, Stanstead Abbotts SG12 8AH **t** +44 (0) 1920 871849
e carolannbarnett@yahoo.co.uk

4bancroftplace.com

open All year
payment Cash, cheques
nearest pub less than 0.5 miles
nearest shop less than 0.5 miles

Town centre, canalside, light and airy, first-floor studio apartment for two adults. Living area cleverly converts into a bedroom with fully sprung 4' 6' sofa bed. Very well equipped kitchen, shower room and hallway/dressing area. Within walking distance of everything Stratford offers. Off-road, dedicated parking for one vehicle.

Unit 📺 🔲 🍽 ⬛ 🧺 ✳ General P S Leisure 🚶 ► 🚲

STRATFORD-UPON-AVON, Warwickshire Map ref 2B1 — SELF CATERING

★★★★
SELF CATERING

Units **2**
Sleeps **1–6**

LOW SEASON PER WK
Max £595.00

HIGH SEASON PER WK
Max £750.00

Riverview Lodge & River Haven Lodge, Stratford-upon-Avon

t +44 (0) 7802 640372 **e** info@luxurylifestylelodges.co.uk

luxurylifestylelodges.co.uk

open All year
payment Cash, cheques
nearest pub less than 0.5 miles
nearest shop less than 0.5 miles

Luxury holiday retreats with decked areas overlooking the River Avon, only 0.75 miles from Stratford-upon-Avon town. A perfect base for exploring the many beautiful and historic sites of Warwickshire and the Cotswolds. Designed and decorated with style and comfort in mind.

ONLINE MAP

Unit 📺 SC 🔲 🍽 ⬛ 🧺 ✳ ⛰ General 🛷 🏚 🛗 P ◌ S
Leisure 🚶 ► 🚲

TELFORD, Shropshire Map ref 4A3 — GUEST ACCOMMODATION

★★★★★
INN
SILVER AWARD

B&B PER ROOM PER NIGHT
S £65.00–£98.00
D £75.00–£128.00

EVENING MEAL PER PERSON
£12.00–£35.00

Stay & Eat offer (DBB for £125 per couple) or the Wrekin Weekend (3 nights DBB plus extras £299). These prices may vary.

The Old Orleton

Holyhead Road, Wellington TF1 2HA **t** +44 (0) 1952 255011 **e** info@theoldorleton.com

theoldorleton.com GUEST REVIEWS · SPECIAL OFFERS · REAL-TIME BOOKING

open Closed for two weeks in January
bedrooms 6 double, 2 twin, 2 single
bathrooms All en suite
payment Credit/debit cards, cash, cheques

Contemporary-styled 17thC coaching inn facing the famous Wrekin Hill. The Old Orleton Inn, Wellington, Shropshire is a charming retreat for both work and pleasure. With ten boutique-style bedrooms, each one unique in design and character. A comprehensive selection of carefully prepared vegetarian, fish and meat dishes are served using fresh, quality, local produce.

SAT NAV TF1 2HA **ONLINE MAP**

Room 🛏 ☎ 📺 SC 🍵 General P 🛜 ☕ ♨ ✕ 🛗 ✳ Leisure ∪ 🚶 ► 🚲

TENBURY WELLS, Worcestershire Map ref 4A3

★★★★
SELF CATERING

Units **1**

LOW SEASON PER WK
£500.00

HIGH SEASON PER WK
£500.00

Long Cover Cottage, Tenbury Wells

contact Mrs Eleanor Van Straaten, Holiday Cottage, Fishpool Cottage, Kyre, Tenbury Wells WR15 8RL **t** +44 (0) 1885 410208 **e** ellie_vanstraaten@yahoo.co.uk

a-country-break.co.uk

open All year
payment Cash, cheques
nearest pub 3 miles
nearest shop 3 miles

A retreat from the outside world with magnificent views in all directions over the Teme and Kyre Valleys. The cottage has two double rooms and one twin. Exposed beams, oak/elm staircase, leaded light windows, Aga, woodburning stove. A network of paths and bridleways leads directly from the cottage. Badgers, woodpeckers and buzzards are regular visitors.

Unit 📺 🆂 📀 🖵 🍽🗄 ⚲ 🍴 ♨ ☀ 🧺 ⬤ General 🐾 ⛩ ♿ 🆂 🐕
Leisure ∪ ⚓ ▶ 🚲

THORNHAM MAGNA, Suffolk Map ref 3B2

★★★★★
GUEST ACCOMMODATION
SILVER AWARD

B&B PER ROOM PER NIGHT
S £55.00–£100.00
D £100.00

EVENING MEAL PER PERSON
£18.00–£25.00

Thornham Hall

Thornham Magna, Eye IP23 8HA **t** +44 (0) 1379 783314 **e** thornhamhall@aol.com

thornhamhall.com

open All year
bedrooms 2 double, 1 suite
bathrooms All en suite
payment Credit/debit cards, cash, cheques

Thornham Hall offers exclusive accommodation and function facilities, and is an idyllic wedding reception venue. The Hall is situated in its own private park at the centre of the Thornham estate, the baronial home of the Henniker family since 1750.

SAT NAV IP23 8HA **ONLINE MAP**

Room 🖵 🛁 🍴 General 🐾 P 🅿 ☕ 🍷 ✕ 🍴 ☀ 🐕 Leisure ♨ ⚓ ▶

THURLEIGH, Bedfordshire Map ref 2D1

★★★★
BED & BREAKFAST

B&B PER ROOM PER NIGHT
S £40.00–£45.00
D £60.00–£80.00

The Windmill

Milton Road, Thurleigh, Bedford MK44 2DF **t** +44 (0) 1234 771016 **e** wendy.armitage1@talk21.com

thewindmill.uk.com

A recently converted windmill which offers unique views over the surrounding countryside. Comfortable, spacious accommodation. Large gardens and ample parking space.

open All year except Christmas and New Year
bedrooms 1 double, 1 family, 1 suite
bathrooms 1 en suite, 1 private
payment Cash, cheques, euros

Room 📺 🛁 🍴 General 🐾8 P 🍴 ☀ Leisure ∪ ⚓ ▶ 🚲

Remember to check when booking

Please remember that all information in this guide has been supplied by the proprietors well in advance of publication. Since changes do sometimes occur it's a good idea to check details at the time of booking.

TIDESWELL, Derbyshire Map ref 4B2

★★★
SELF CATERING

Units **1**
Sleeps **4**

LOW SEASON PER WK
£205.00–£215.00

HIGH SEASON PER WK
£230.00

Geil Torrs, Buxton

contact Mr Harry Buttle, Geil Torrs, Buxton Road, Buxton SK17 8QJ **t** +44 (0) 1298 871302

Situated in Tideswell Dale, about 0.5 miles from the village of Tideswell, a village at the heart of the Peak District National Park.

open All year
payment Cash, cheques
nearest pub 0.5 miles
nearest shop 0.5 miles

Unit 📺 🆂 ■ 🖵 🎛 ✳ ⌀ General 🛋 🏠 P 🆂 🐴

TIDESWELL, Derbyshire Map ref 4B2

★★★★
SELF CATERING

Units **1**
Sleeps **2–4**

LOW SEASON PER WK
Min £250.00

HIGH SEASON PER WK
Max £450.00

Lavender Cottage, Tideswell, Buxton

contact Ruth Wilson, 100 Graham Road, Sheffield S10 3GQ **t** +44 (0) 114 230 7857
e ruth@thewilsons100.fsnet.co.uk

lavendercottagetideswell.co.uk GUEST REVIEWS · SPECIAL OFFERS · REAL-TIME BOOKING

Recently renovated cottage with woodburning stove, flatscreen TV, walk-in power shower and bath. New soft furnishings and carpets and several pieces of antique furniture. Well equipped kitchen, dishwasher, freezer and washing machine.

open All year
payment Cash, cheques
nearest pub less than 0.5 miles
nearest shop less than 0.5 miles

Unit 📺 🖥 ■ 💻 🖨 ☕ 🍳 🖵 🔌 ✳ ⌀ General 🛋 🏠 🕯 🆂

WATERHOUSES, Staffordshire Map ref 4B2

★★★★
BED & BREAKFAST
SILVER AWARD

B&B PER ROOM PER NIGHT
S £30.00–£35.00
D £50.00–£60.00

Leehouse Farm

Leek Road, Waterhouses, Leek ST10 3HW **t** +44 (0) 1538 308439

Charming, 18thC house in centre of a Staffordshire Moorlands village in Peak District National Park. Ideal for Derbyshire Dales, the Potteries and Alton Towers.

open All year except Christmas
bedrooms 2 double, 1 twin
bathrooms All en suite
payment Cash, cheques

Room 📺 ☕ 🍵 General 🛋 8 P 🍴 ✳ Leisure 🚴

WELLS-NEXT-THE-SEA, Norfolk Map ref 3B1

★★★★
GUEST HOUSE

B&B PER ROOM PER NIGHT
S Min £40.00
D Min £80.00

The Cobblers

Standard Road, Wells-next-the-Sea NR23 1JU **t** +44 (0) 1328 710155 **e** info@cobblers.co.uk

cobblers.co.uk

The Cobblers is situated in the centre of town, close to the harbour and restaurants, in Wells-next-the-Sea. An ideal base for exploring north Norfolk. Pets by arrangement. Midwinter midweek specials. Off-street parking.

open All year except Christmas and New Year
bedrooms 4 double, 1 twin, 3 single
bathrooms 7 en suite, 1 private
payment Credit/debit cards, cash, cheques

Room 🍳 📺 ☕ General 🛋 P 🔥 ✳ 🐴 Leisure 🚴

Do you like camping?

Love the great outdoors? Britain's Camping, Caravan & Holiday Parks 2009 is packed with information on quality sites in some spectacular locations. You can purchase the guide from good bookshops and online at visitbritaindirect.com.

WINGFIELD, Suffolk Map ref 3B2
GUEST ACCOMMODATION

★★★★
BED & BREAKFAST
SILVER AWARD

B&B PER ROOM PER NIGHT
S £40.00–£50.00
D £62.00–£65.00

Gables Farm

Earsham Street, Wingfield, Diss IP21 5RH t +44 (0) 1379 586355 & +44 (0) 7824 445464
e enquiries@gablesfarm.co.uk

gablesfarm.co.uk GUEST REVIEWS

open All year except Christmas and New Year
bedrooms 2 double, 1 twin
bathrooms All en suite
payment Cash, cheques

A 16thC timbered farmhouse in moated gardens. Wingfield is a quiet village in the centre of East Anglia, central to everywhere and in the middle of nowhere!

SAT NAV IP21 5RH **ONLINE MAP**

Room 📺 ⚿ 🍽 General 🐴 🏛 🛏 P 🛜 🔥 ❄ 🐎 Leisure ∪ 🥢

WOODHALL SPA, Lincolnshire Map ref 4D2
GUEST ACCOMMODATION

★★★★
GUEST ACCOMMODATION
SILVER AWARD

B&B PER ROOM PER NIGHT
S £30.00–£60.00
D £60.00–£80.00

Kirkstead Old Mill Cottage

Tattershall Road, Woodhall Spa LN10 6UQ t +44 (0) 1526 353637 e barbara@woodhallspa.com

woodhallspa.com GUEST REVIEWS · SPECIAL OFFERS

open All year except Christmas
bedrooms 1 double, 2 twin
bathrooms All en suite
payment Cash, cheques, euros

Barbara and Tony Hodgkinson would like to offer you a warm welcome to their detached home near the river Witham. They hope you will treasure the peace and tranquillity if you choose to sleep in one of their three en suite guest bedrooms, before enjoying a Gold Award breakfast. Pets only welcome in one bedroom.

SAT NAV LN10 6UQ **ONLINE MAP**

Room ♿ 📺 ⚿ 🍽 General P 🛜 🔥 🍳 ❄ 🐎 Leisure 🥢 ⛳ 🚴

WOODHALL SPA, Lincolnshire Map ref 4D2
GUEST ACCOMMODATION

★★★★
GUEST ACCOMMODATION

B&B PER ROOM PER NIGHT
S £42.00–£50.00
D £65.00–£75.00

10% discount for
4 nights or more.

Village Limits Motel

Stixwould Road, Woodhall Spa LN10 6UJ t +44 (0) 1526 353312 e info@villagelimits.co.uk

villagelimits.co.uk

open All year
bedrooms 8 twin
bathrooms All en suite
payment Credit/debit cards, cash, cheques

Award-winning Tastes of Lincolnshire Best Accommodation 2007. Village Limits Country Pub and Restaurant has a friendly, relaxing welcome. The comfortable ground-floor bedrooms all have en suite bathrooms, one with full facilities for the disabled. Food daily 1200-1400 and 1900-2100. Closed Sunday evening and Mondays. B&B seven days.

SAT NAV LN10 6UJ **ONLINE MAP**

Room ♿ 📺 ⚿ General 🐴 🏛 🛏 P 🍽 ✗ 🍳 ❄

WYE VALLEY

See under Hereford, Ross-on-Wye

South East England

Berkshire, Buckinghamshire, East Sussex,
Hampshire, Isle of Wight, Kent, Oxfordshire,
Surrey, West Sussex

Clockwise: Portsmouth Historic Dockyard, Hampshire; Deal, Kent; Oxford

Great days out

The South East is your quintessential slice of England. Explore iconic chalk cliffs and 400 miles of glorious coastline, fairytale castles, colourful gardens and historic cities. Whilst singles and couples will find plenty to enjoy, this region is bursting with great family days out that the kids will treasure forever.

Enjoy the ride!

Get set, **Go Ape!** on a high-wire forest adventure course, now at Bedgebury Pinetum and Wendover Woods as well as other exciting locations across the South East. White-knuckle rides like **Thorpe Park's** Inferno and Slammer keep the thrills coming and there's always something new to try: take a dizzying spin on **Legoland Windsor's** Longboat Invader, twirl and tilt on the amazing

Paultons Park, Hampshire

Sky Swinger at **Paultons Park**, or hop aboard the spooky ghost train Horror Hotel at **Brighton Pier**. At Winchester's **Intech Science Centre and Planetarium** you can even fly through the solar system and visit a black hole. Enjoy the rides of your life!

Who killed Harold?

Explore a region that has witnessed some of the most momentous events in British history, from the Battle of Hastings in 1066 to the air raids of the Second World War. At **Battle Abbey** stand on the exact spot where

tradition says King Harold fell and take the interactive audio tour of the battlefield to find out what really happened on that fateful day. Clamber aboard the world-famous HMS Victory at **Portsmouth Historic Dockyard**, then experience the challenges of the modern Navy in Action Stations.

Formidable **Dover Castle** on the Kent coast puts you right on the frontline of history: tour the **Secret Wartime Tunnels** deep beneath the gleaming White Cliffs, where the evacuation of Dunkirk was masterminded. Another of the country's dazzling landmarks, **Canterbury Cathedral**, opens the door on the infamous murder of Thomas Becket. And just for fun, why not follow in the footsteps of Morse and Lewis beneath the dreaming spires of **Oxford** to solve a fictional mystery or two?

Shore pleasures

South coast beaches keep alive all the best traditions of the seaside, with a zesty twist of watersport action. **Eastbourne**, **Bournemouth**, **Brighton** and **Margate** were popular playgrounds for the Victorians – Queen Victoria loved to escape to her Isle of Wight home, **Osborne House**. Save your small change for the slot machines on the pier where it's hot doughnuts or fish and chips all round. If you're looking for something a bit more peaceful, there are still many gems to uncover. Scamper about the sand dunes at **West Wittering**, just down the Sussex coast from **Bognor Regis**, and watch the zigzagging kitesurfers at **Pevensey Bay**. Get your own adrenalin fix at the **Calshot Activities Centre** where you can try all sorts of watersports, including sailing on the Solent.

Left to right: Hever Castle, Kent;
Royal Pavilion, Brighton, East Sussex

did you know... you're walking on 80 million years of geological history along the White Cliffs of Dover?

Castles, castles everywhere

Become king, queen, lord or lady for a day visiting the South East's magnificent castles. **Bodiam** is a picture-perfect medieval moated fortress and **Arundel** is full of priceless collections. Dreamy **Leeds** in Kent was restored by Henry VIII for his first queen, Catherine of Aragon. It might have been the ultimate romantic gesture, except that he abandoned her for his second wife, Anne Boleyn – visit Anne's beautiful childhood home, **Hever Castle**, too. **Windsor Castle** has been a royal residence for nine centuries and reflects changing royal tastes through the ages. But nothing quite prepares you for the **Royal Pavilion** at Brighton, George IV's eccentric Indian-style palace!

Follow nature's way

Kent is rightly famed as the Garden of England, so sample some real horticultural treats like **Sissinghurst Castle Garden**, lovingly created by Vita Sackville-West. Discover Kew's country garden and the Millennium Seed Bank at **Wakehurst Place**, near Haywards Heath. Follow the ancient tracks of the **South Downs Way** for an exhilarating breath of fresh air, or hop over to the **Isle of Wight** where you can cycle Round the Island in eight hours. Phew! Play hide and seek along the paths and bridleways of the **New Forest** and watch out for wild ponies as they gently graze. You'll encounter elephants and other exotic creatures at **Howletts Wild Animal Park**.

New Forest ponies

Have a Dickens of a time

Catch the buzz of a festival or event, whatever the time of year. From rock 'n' pop to hops, from rowing to sailing, from Dickens to dancing round a maypole – the rich tapestry of life. **The Brighton Festival** comes to the funky seaside town every May and is an exuberant celebration of world-class art and entertainment. If you're looking for the epitome of elegance, dress up for **Glyndebourne's** season of opera, **Royal Ascot**, **Henley Royal Regatta** or **Cowes Week** – four internationally famous spectacles.

Or join Mr Pickwick and other jolly characters in Victorian costume on the streets of Broadstairs during the **Dickens Festival**. The town was the author's favourite 'English watering place'. There's rock, pop and hip hop mixed with liberal helpings of mud at August's **Reading Festival**. And kids can always find something fantabulous to fill the school

holidays at **The Roald Dahl Museum and Story Centre**, Great Missenden: from whizzpopping, hands-on science workshops to delumptious cookery classes.

Time to indulge

Had your fill of sightseeing? Then it's time to indulge! Shopaholics: head for the charming world of The Lanes, **Brighton**, to hunt out stylish gifts and antiques. Browse for hours in the country's largest second-hand bookshop, Baggins at **Rochester**. Pop into **Oxford Castle** where boutique stalls, outdoor music performances, wining and dining are set against an unusual prison backdrop. If you need to boost your energy levels, you're in just the right region, too: embark on an epicurean journey through lots of orchards, breweries and vineyards, including England's largest vineyard at **Denbies Wine Estate**. Then savour more of the genuine flavours of South East England in the oyster houses and fine restaurants.

why not... visit the world's oldest and largest occupied castle – Windsor Castle?

Clockwise: The Roald Dahl Museum and Story Centre, Buckinghamshire; Cowes, Isle of Wight; Denbies Wine Estate, Surrey

Destinations

Brighton

England's favourite seaside city, Brighton is historic, elegant and offbeat. Wander a beachfront packed with cafés and bars, then step into town for fine antiques and designer boutiques. Don't miss the Royal Pavilion, surely the most extravagant royal palace in Europe, and come in springtime for an arts festival second to none. Find the world's cuisine in over 400 restaurants, and then relax with dance, comedy or music in the thriving pub and club culture. Brighton has it all – and just 50 minutes by train from central London.

Brighton

Canterbury

Marvel with fellow 'pilgrims' from the four corners of the world as Canterbury Cathedral dominates your approach to this World Heritage Site. Let Canterbury Tales 'Medieval Misadventures' take you on a journey back to Chaucer's England. Wander traffic-free daytime streets to enjoy historic buildings and modern attractions, and then head further afield to explore the valleys, woods and coastline of this beautiful region of Kent.

Dover

Discover the rich history of Dover – 'the lock and key of England'. Tour Dover Castle and relive the epic sieges of 1216-17. Delve into the secrets contained in the Wartime Tunnels, nerve centre for the evacuation of Dunkirk. Enjoy the pier and stroll the stylish marina before heading out of town to tour the scenic beaches of White Cliffs Country.

Isle of Wight

Sixty miles of spectacular coastline, picturesque coves and safe bathing in bays of golden sand. Explore the maritime history of Cowes, the beautiful and historic town of Newport and take the family to the welcoming resorts of Shanklin and Ventnor. Follow the trail of dinosaurs, ancient tribes, Romans and monarchs.

New Forest

Roam a landscape little changed since William the Conqueror gave it his special protection over 900 years ago. Discover wild heath and dappled woodland, roaming ponies, thatched hamlets, bustling market towns, and tiny streams meandering to the sparkling expanse of the Solent. Explore great attractions too, from Buckler's Hard to the National Motor Museum Beaulieu.

Oxford

This ancient university city is both timeless and modern. Wander among its 'dreaming spires' and tranquil college quadrangles. Find national and international treasures displayed in a family of museums. Hire a punt and spend the afternoon drifting along the River Cherwell or seek out bustling shops and fashionable restaurants. Experience candlelit evensong in college chapels or Shakespeare in the park, and after dark enjoy the cosmopolitan buzz.

Left to right: Great Dixter, East Sussex; Thorpe Park, Surrey

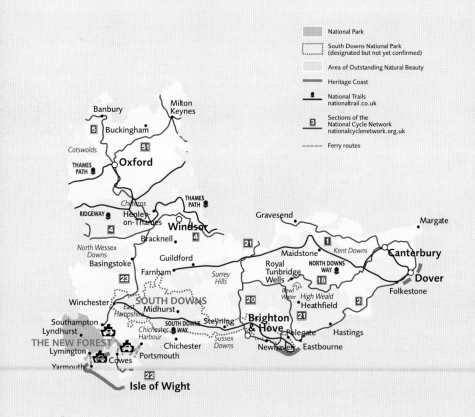

National Park

South Downs National Park
(designated but not yet confirmed)

Area of Outstanding Natural Beauty

Heritage Coast

National Trails
nationaltrail.co.uk

3 Sections of the
National Cycle Network
nationalcyclenetwork.org.uk

Ferry routes

Banbury
Milton Keynes
5 Buckingham
Cotswolds
51
THAMES PATH
Oxford
Chilterns
THAMES PATH
RIDGEWAY
Henley-on-Thames
Windsor
Bracknell
4
Gravesend
Margate
North Wessex Downs
Guildford
21
1
Maidstone
Kent Downs
Canterbury
Basingstoke
Farnham
Royal Tunbridge Wells
NORTH DOWNS WAY
Dover
23
Surrey Hills
18
Folkestone
Winchester
East Hampshire
SOUTH DOWNS
Midhurst
Bewl Water
High Weald
2
20
Heathfield
Southampton
Steyning
21
Lyndhurst
Chichester
SOUTH DOWNS WAY
Brighton & Hove
Hastings
THE NEW FOREST
Chichester Harbour
Chichester
Sussex Downs
Polegate
Lymington
Newhaven
Eastbourne
Yarmouth
Portsmouth
Cowes
22
Isle of Wight

0   50 miles
0   75 kms

Royal Tunbridge Wells

Portsmouth

At the heart of the city is Portsmouth Historic Dockyard where there is so much naval heritage to explore. Climb the new striking Spinnaker Tower or take a harbour tour to see naval ships. If you're after retail therapy, head for Gunwharf Quays. Portsmouth also has its own resort area, Southsea, with four miles of beach and promenade.

Royal Tunbridge Wells

Ever since the discovery of the Chalybeate Spring 400 years ago, visitors have been coming here. The health-giving waters still flow and the Pantiles, the famous colonnaded walkway, is now home to a wonderful selection of boutiques, antiques shops, bars and cafés. The village atmosphere of the old high street and Chapel Place, adds to the town's reputation as one of the most desirable destinations in the South East. Surrounded by beautiful countryside, and a wealth of castles, stately homes and gardens, there's so much to explore.

Winchester

Winchester is best known for its 11thC cathedral and the Great Hall, which for over 600 years has housed the mysterious Arthurian round table. Wander through the city's popular shopping streets, admire the architecture and enjoy quirky open air events. Home of good food, birthplace of cricket, resting place of author Jane Austen and inspiration to the many craft-makers and artists who live here, Winchester is a destination for all seasons.

Winchester Cathedral

Windsor

Explore Windsor and the Royal Borough to the west of London. Gaze at the priceless treasures in the Royal Collection at Windsor Castle, royal home and fortress for over 900 years. Henry VI founded Eton College in 1440. Lose yourself in the history of the cloisters and the chapel. Sail the rapids at Legoland's incredible Vikings' River Splash, and find peace and quiet in the rural landscape of Royal Berkshire, traversed by the timeless flow of the Thames.

Clockwise: Portsmouth; Windsor Castle; Dover Castle

For lots more great ideas visit visitbritain.com/destinations

Visitor attractions

Family and Fun

Blue Reef Aquarium
Hastings, East Sussex
+44 (0) 1424 718776
discoverhastings.co.uk
Meet tropical sharks and giant crabs.

The Canterbury Tales
Canterbury, Kent
+44 (0) 1227 479227
canterburytales.org.uk
Audiovisual recreation of life in medieval England.

Didcot Railway Centre
Didcot, Oxfordshire
+44 (0) 1235 817200
didcotrailwaycentre.org.uk
Living museum of the Great Western Railway.

Dinosaur Isle
Sandown, Isle of Wight
+44 (0) 1983 404344
dinosaurisle.com
Britain's first purpose-built dinosaur attraction.

Farming World
Boughton, Kent
+44 (0) 1227 751144
farming-world.com
Working farm packed with family fun.

Guildford Spectrum
Guildford, Surrey
+44 (0) 1483 443322
guildfordspectrum.co.uk
Olympic-sized ice rink and tenpin bowling.

Gulliver's Land
Milton Keynes, Buckinghamshire
+44 (0) 1925 444888
gulliversfun.co.uk
Family magic for children aged 2-13 years.

Harbour Park
Littlehampton, West Sussex
+44 (0) 1903 721200
harbourpark.com
All-weather theme park with dodgems.

The Historic Dockyard Chatham
Chatham, Kent
+44 (0) 1634 823800
chdt.org.uk
Maritime heritage site with stunning architecture.

The Hop Farm Country Park
Paddock Wood, Kent
+44 (0) 1622 872068
thehopfarm.co.uk
Once-working hop farm in 400 unspoilt acres.

Howletts Wild Animal Park
Canterbury, Kent
+44 (0) 1227 721286
totallywild.net
Gorillas and tigers in 90-acre parkland.

Isle of Wight Zoo
Sandown, Isle of Wight
+44 (0) 1983 403883
isleofwightzoo.com
Zoo specialising in big cats and primates.

LEGOLAND Windsor
Windsor, Berkshire
+44 (0) 870 504 0404
legoland.co.uk
More Lego bricks than you dreamed possible.

The Look Out Discovery Centre
Bracknell, Berkshire
+44 (0) 1344 354400
bracknell-forest.gov.uk/lookout
Interactive science park with over 70 exhibits.

Marwell Zoological Park
Winchester, Hampshire
+44 (0) 1962 777407
marwell.org.uk
Relaxing and fascinating zoological park.

Mid-Hants Railway Watercress Line
Alresford, Hampshire
+44 (0) 1962 733810
watercressline.co.uk
Ten-mile steam railway through beautiful countryside.

National Motor Museum Beaulieu
Beaulieu, Hampshire
+44 (0) 1590 612345
beaulieu.co.uk
Vintage cars in glorious New Forest setting.

Paultons Park
Romsey, Hampshire
+44 (0) 23 8081 4442
paultonspark.co.uk
Over 50 rides for all the family.

Port Lympne Wild Animal Park, Mansion and Gardens
Lympne, Kent
+44 (0) 1303 264647
totallywild.net
Rare and endangered species in 600-acre park.

Portsmouth Historic Dockyard
Portsmouth, Hampshire
+44 (0) 23 9283 9766
historicdockyard.co.uk
Home to the Mary Rose and HMS Victory.

River & Rowing Museum
Henley-on-Thames,
Oxfordshire
+44 (0) 1491 415600
rrm.co.uk
Award-wining museum with
year-round exhibitions.

The Roald Dahl
Museum and
Story Centre
Small Visitor Attraction
of the Year - Gold
Great Missenden,
Buckinghamshire
+44 (0) 1494 892192
roalddahlmuseum.org
The life behind so many
well-loved books.

Romney, Hythe
and Dymchurch
Railway
Littlestone-on-Sea, Kent
+44 (0) 1797 362353
rhdr.org.uk
The world's only main line
in miniature.

Thorpe Park
Chertsey, Surrey
+44 (0) 870 444 4466
thorpepark.com
Thrills and spills for all
the family.

Weald & Downland
Open Air Museum
Chichester, West Sussex
+44 (0) 1243 811348
wealddown.co.uk
Rescued historic buildings in
beautiful 50-acre setting.

Heritage

1066 Battle Abbey
and Battlefield
Battle, East Sussex
+44 (0) 1424 775705
english-heritage.org.uk
William the Conqueror's
abbey commemorates the
fallen.

Arundel Castle
Arundel, West Sussex
+44 (0) 1903 883136
arundelcastle.org
Castle and stately home
with priceless collections.

Bateman's
Burwash, East Sussex
+44 (0) 1435 882302
nationaltrust.org.uk
Jacobean house, the home
of Rudyard Kipling.

Blenheim Palace
Woodstock, Oxfordshire
+44 (0) 1993 811091
blenheimpalace.com
Baroque palace and beautiful
Capability Brown parkland.

Bodiam Castle
Bodiam, East Sussex
+44 (0) 1580 830196
nationaltrust.org.uk
Magical late-medieval
moated castle.

Canterbury Cathedral
Canterbury, Kent
+44 (0) 1227 762862
canterbury-cathedral.org
Seat of the Archbishop of
Canterbury.

Chichester Cathedral
Chichester, West Sussex
+44 (0) 1243 782595
chichestercathedral.org.uk
Splendid medieval cathedral
with art treasures.

Dapdune Wharf
Guildford, Surrey
+44 (0) 1483 561389
nationaltrust.org.uk
Interactive exhibitions and a
restored Wey barge.

Dover Castle and
Secret Wartime Tunnels
Dover, Kent
+44 (0) 1304 211067
english-heritage.org.uk
Historic nerve centre for
Battle of Britain.

Farnham Castle
Farnham, Surrey
+44 (0) 1252 721194
farnhamcastle.com
Historic home of the Bishops
of Winchester.

Fishbourne Roman
Palace
Chichester, West Sussex
+44 (0) 1243 785859
sussexpast.co.uk/fishbourne
Remains of Roman residence
with beautiful mosaics.

Goodwood House
Chichester, West Sussex
+44 (0) 1243 755048
goodwood.co.uk
Stately home with superb art
and furniture.

Guildford Castle
Guildford, Surrey
+44 (0) 1483 444750
guildford.gov.uk
Imposing ruins and restored
12thC stone keep.

Hever Castle and
Gardens
near Edenbridge, Kent
+44 (0) 1732 865224
hevercastle.co.uk
Moated castle, the childhood
home of Anne Boleyn.

Leeds Castle and Gardens
near Maidstone, Kent
+44 (0) 1622 765400
leeds-castle.com
Medieval castle set on two
islands.

Mottisfont Abbey Garden,
House and Estate
Mottisfont, Hampshire
+44 (0) 1794 340757
nationaltrust.org.uk
Glorious grounds of 13thC
former priory.

Osborne House
East Cowes, Isle of Wight
+44 (0) 1983 200022
english-heritage.org.uk
*Queen Victoria's opulent
seaside retreat.*

**Penshurst Place
and Gardens**
Penshurst, Kent
+44 (0) 1892 870307
penshurstplace.com
*Medieval manor house
with Tudor gardens.*

**Petworth House
& Park**
Petworth, West Sussex
+44 (0) 1798 342207
nationaltrust.org.uk
*Magnificent house and
internationally important
art collection.*

Polesden Lacey
near Dorking, Surrey
+44 (0) 1372 452048
nationaltrust.org.uk
*Opulent Edwardian interiors
in downland setting.*

Royal Pavilion
Brighton, East Sussex
+44 (0) 1273 290900
royalpavilion.org.uk
*King George IV's extravagant
seaside palace.*

Waverley Abbey
Farnham, Surrey
+44 (0) 1483 252000
english-heritage.org.uk
*Ruins of England's first
Cistercian abbey.*

Winchester Cathedral
Winchester, Hampshire
+44 (0) 1962 857200
winchester-cathedral.org.uk
*Magnificent medieval cathedral
with soaring Gothic nave.*

Windsor Castle
Windsor, Berkshire
+44 (0) 20 7766 7304
royalcollection.org.uk
*Official residence of HM The
Queen.*

**Indoors**

Ashford Designer Outlet
Ashford, Kent
+44 (0) 1233 895900
ashforddesigneroutlet.com
*One of Europe's most spectacular
shopping destinations.*

Bletchley Park
Bletchley, Buckinghamshire
+44 (0) 1908 640404
bletchleypark.org.uk
*Wartime code-breaking with
the famous Enigma machines.*

De La Warr Pavilion
Bexhill-on-Sea, East Sussex
+44 (0) 1424 229111
dlwp.com
*Superb Modernist pavilion
housing theatre and gallery.*

Denbies Wine Estate
Dorking, Surrey
+44 (0) 1306 876616
denbiesvineyard.co.uk
*Englands largest vineyard,
set in 265 acres.*

Dickens World
Chatham, Kent
+44 (0) 1634 890421
dickensworld.co.uk
*Fascinating journey through
Dickens' life and times.*

Gunwharf Quays
Portsmouth, Hampshire
+44 (0) 23 9283 6700
gunwharf-quays.com
*Innovative retail, restaurant
and leisure destination.*

Mercedes-Benz World
Weybridge, Surrey
+44 (0) 870 400 4000
mercedes-benzworld.co.uk
*Thrilling driving experiences
and fascinating attractions.*

Pallant House Gallery
Chichester, West Sussex
+44 (0) 1243 774557
pallant.org.uk
*Queen Anne house holding
renowned art collection.*

**Outdoors**

Ascot Racecourse
Ascot, Berkshire
+44 (0) 870 727 1234
ascot.co.uk
*Flat and jump racing
throughout the year.*

**Bedgebury National
Pinetum**
Goudhurst, Kent
+44 (0) 1580 879820
forestry.gov.uk/bedgebury
*The world's finest collection
of conifers.*

Borde Hill Garden
Haywards Heath, West Sussex
+44 (0) 1444 450326
bordehill.co.uk
*Beautiful and botanically rich
heritage garden.*

Claremont Landscape Garden
Esher, Surrey
+44 (0) 1372 467806
nationaltrust.org.uk
*One of the finest English
landscape gardens.*

**Exbury Gardens and
Steam Railway**
Exbury, Hampshire
+44 (0) 23 8089 1203
exbury.co.uk
*Vast woodland garden with
circular railway.*

**Gardens and Grounds of
Herstmonceux Castle**
Herstmonceux, East Sussex
+44 (0) 1323 833816
herstmonceux-castle.com
*Magnificent moated castle with
Elizabethan gardens.*

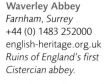

Go Ape!
Choose from three
South East locations

Bracknell, Berkshire

Leeds Castle,
near Maidstone, Kent

Wendover Woods,
Buckinghamshire

+44 (0) 845 643 9215
goape.co.uk
Rope bridges, swings and
zip slides.

High Beeches Gardens
Handcross, West Sussex
+44 (0) 1444 400589
highbeeches.com
Peaceful, landscaped woodland
and water gardens.

Leonardslee Lakes
and Gardens
Lower Beeding,
West Sussex
+44 (0) 1403 891212
leonardslee.com
Glorious rhododendrons and
azaleas in 240-acre valley.

Loseley Park
Guildford, Surrey
+44 (0) 1483 304440
loseley-park.com
Beautiful Elizabethan mansion
and gardens.

Nymans Garden
Handcross, West Sussex
+44 (0) 1444 405250
nationaltrust.org.uk
Romantic garden with outstanding
rare tree collection.

Painshill Park
Cobham, Surrey
+44 (0) 1932 868113
painshill.co.uk
Beatifully restored and renovated
park with follies.

RHS Garden Wisley
Woking, Surrey
+44 (0) 1483 224234
rhs.org.uk
A working encyclopedia of
British gardening.

Sissinghurst Castle Garden
Sissinghurst, Kent
+44 (0) 1580 710700
nationaltrust.org.uk
Celebrated gardens of enclosed
compartments around mansion.

Spinnaker Tower
Portsmouth, Hampshire
+44 (0) 23 9285 7520
spinnakertower.co.uk
Breathtaking views from
170m landmark.

Wakehurst Place
Gardens
near Haywards Heath,
West Sussex
+44 (0) 1444 894066
kew.org
Kew's beautiful country garden.

ASSURANCE OF
A GREAT DAY OUT
Attractions with this
sign participate in the
Visitor Attraction Quality
Assurance Scheme which
recognises high standards in all
aspects of the visitor experience.

Events 2009

Sea your history
Portsmouth
seayourhistory.org.uk
Until Apr 2009

A Study in Sherlock
Portsmouth
portsmouthmuseums.co.uk
All year

New Year Steam Day
Didcot
didcotrailwaycentre.org.uk
1 Jan

Sandown Park's Golden
Cup Final
Esher
sandown.co.uk
Apr

Brighton Festival
Brighton
brightonfestival.org
2 - 24 May

Derby Day at Epsom
Downs Racecourse
Epsom
epsomderby.co.uk
Jun

Royal Ascot
Ascot
royalascot.co.uk
16 - 20 Jun

Henley Royal Regatta
Henley-on-Thames
hrr.co.uk
1 Jul - 5 Jul

Skandia Cowes Week
Cowes
skandiacowesweek.co.uk
1 - 8 Aug

Ringwood Carnival
at Market Place and
The Bickerley
Ringwood
ringwoodcarnival.org
19 Sep*

* provisional date at time of going to press

Regional contacts and information

For more information on accommodation, attractions, activities, events and holidays in South East England, contact the regional tourism organisation below. The website has a wealth of information and you can order or download publications.

South East England

The following publications are available from Tourism South East by logging on to **visitsoutheastengland.com** or calling **+44 (0) 23 8062 5400**:

Publications

- **Escape into the Countryside**
- **Distinctive Country Inns**
- **We Know Just the Place**

E-Brochures

- **Family Fun**
- **Timeless Treasures**
- **Just the Two of Us**

Clockwise: Freshwater Bay, Isle of Wight; Savill Garden, Surrey; Bewl Water, Kent; Canterbury Cathedral, Kent

Tourist Information Centres

When you arrive at your destination, visit an Official Partner Tourist Information Centre for quality assured help with accommodation and information about local attractions and events, or email your request before you go. To search for attractions and Tourist Information Centres on the move just text INFO to 62233, and a web link will be sent to your mobile phone. To find a Tourist Information Centre by region visit enjoyEngland.com/find-tic.

Bicester	Unit 86a, Bicester Village	+44 (0) 1869 369055	bicester.vc@cherwell-dc.gov.uk
Brighton	Pavilion Buildings	0906 711 2255**	brighton-tourism@brighton-hove.gov.uk
Canterbury	12/13 Sun Street	+44 (0) 1227 378100	canterburyinformation@canterbury.gov.uk
Chichester	29a South Street	+44 (0) 1243 775888	chitic@chichester.gov.uk
Cowes	9 The Arcade	+44 (0) 1983 813818	info@islandbreaks.co.uk
Dover	The Old Town Gaol	+44 (0) 1304 205108	tic@doveruk.com
Hastings	Queens Square	+44 (0) 1424 781111	hic@hastings.gov.uk
Newport	High Street	+44 (0) 1983 813818	info@islandbreaks.co.uk
Oxford	15/16 Broad Street	+44 (0) 1865 726871	tic@oxford.gov.uk
Portsmouth	Clarence Esplanade	+44 (0) 23 9282 6722	vis@portsmouthcc.gov.uk
Portsmouth	The Hard	+44 (0) 23 9282 6722	vis@portsmouthcc.gov.uk
Rochester	95 High Street	+44 (0) 1634 843666	visitor.centre@medway.gov.uk
Royal Tunbridge Wells	The Pantiles	+44 (0) 1892 515675	touristinformationcentre @tunbridgewells.gov.uk
Ryde	81-83 Union Street	+44 (0) 1983 813818	info@islandbreaks.co.uk
Sandown	8 High Street	+44 (0) 1983 813818	info@islandbreaks.co.uk
Shanklin	67 High Street	+44 (0) 1983 813818	info@islandbreaks.co.uk
Southampton	9 Civic Centre Road	+44 (0) 23 8083 3333	tourist.information@southampton.gov.uk
Winchester	High Street	+44 (0) 1962 840500	tourism@winchester.gov.uk
Windsor	Royal Windsor Central Station	+44 (0) 1753 743900	windsor.tic@rbwm.gov.uk
Yarmouth	The Quay	+44 (0) 1983 813818	info@islandbreaks.co.uk

**UK number only, charged at premium rate

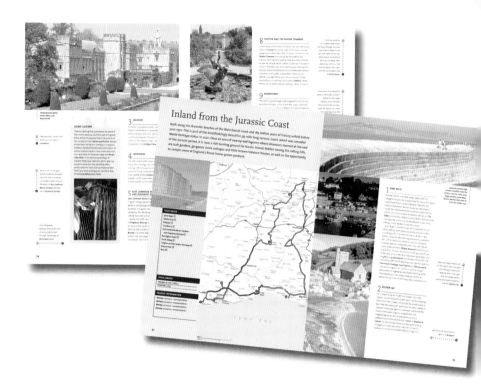

Take a tour of England

VisitBritain presents a series of **three** inspirational touring guides to the regions of England: South and South West, Northern England and Central England.

Each guide takes you on a fascinating journey through stunning countryside and coastlines, picturesque villages and lively market towns, historic houses and gardens.

- Easy-to-use maps
- Clear directions to follow the route
- Lively descriptions of all the places for you to discover
- Stunning photographs bring each area to life

Touring Central England – £14.99
Touring Northern England – £14.99
Touring South and South West England – £14.99
plus postage and handling

where to stay in
South East England

All place names in the blue bands are shown on the maps at the front of this guide.

Accommodation symbols

Symbols give useful information about services and facilities. On pages 16 to 17 you can find a key to these symbols.

ALRESFORD, Hampshire Map ref 2C2   **HOTEL**

★★
HOTEL

B&B PER ROOM PER NIGHT
S £45.00–£55.00
D £75.00–£85.00
HB PER PERSON PER NIGHT
£60.00–£120.00

The Swan Hotel

West Street, Alresford SO24 9AD t +44 (0) 1962 732302 e swanhotel@btinternet.com

swanhotelalresford.com

Delightful Grade II Listed former coaching inn. A free house serving real ales. Excellent food and wine, open daily. Close to Watercress Line. 15 minutes from Winchester.

open All year
bedrooms 14 double, 6 twin, 2 family
bathrooms All en suite
payment Credit/debit cards, cash, cheques, euros

Room ♿ 🛏 📞 📺 ⚑ ☕ General 🐕 🏛 ♿ P ♥ 🍴 ✗ ❄ 🐴 Leisure ∪ ⚓ ►

AMBERLEY, West Sussex Map ref 2D3   **SELF CATERING**

★★★
SELF CATERING

Units   **1**
Sleeps   **4**

LOW SEASON PER WK
£400.00–£500.00

HIGH SEASON PER WK
£600.00

Minimum stay three nights.

Culver Cottage, Amberley, Arundel

contact Mrs Stella Kemp, Swallow Barn, The Sqaure, Amberley BN18 9SR t +44 (0) 1798 831302 & +33 (0) 5659 96950 e stellainamberley@yahoo.co.uk

visitbritain.com

open All year
payment Cash, cheques, euros
nearest pub less than 0.5 miles
nearest shop less than 0.5 miles

Culver Cottage, a charming farm cottage with pretty garden and patios, in the heart of the picturesque village of Amberley which nestles at the foot of the South Downs. There are wonderful views, thatched houses, flowering stone walls, a Norman church, Amberley Castle Hotel, pubs, restaurants and shop within walking distance.

Unit 📺 📟 ▣ 🗚 🖨 ⚑ 🍲 ▯ 🗷 ❄ ♨ ∿ General 🐕 S Leisure ⚓ ►

CYCLISTS WELCOME WELCOME CYCLISTS

Fancy a cycling holiday?

For a fabulous freewheeling break, seek out accommodation participating in our Cyclists Welcome scheme. Look out for the symbol and plan your route online at nationalcyclenetwork.org.

ARUNDEL, West Sussex Map ref 2D3 — GUEST ACCOMMODATION

★★★★★
RESTAURANT WITH ROOMS
GOLD AWARD

B&B PER ROOM PER NIGHT
D £100.00–£180.00

EVENING MEAL PER PERSON
£16.00–£30.00

Enjoy a three-course dinner with coffee for £20 per person from Mon-Thu, saving £10 per person.

Arundel House Restaurant & Rooms

11 High Street, Arundel BN18 9AD t +44 (0) 1903 882136 & +44 (0) 1903 882136
e mail@arundelhouseonline.co.uk

arundelhouseonline.co.uk SPECIAL OFFERS

open All year except Christmas
bedrooms 5 double
bathrooms All en suite
payment Credit/debit cards, cash

Relax in one of our five contemporary yet cosseting bedrooms. Revive yourself under the deluge of hot water delivered from eight-inch shower roses, and revitalise in our intimate and welcoming restaurant serving modern British-led cuisine, with an occasional French or Mediterranean twist. Reward yourself with a stay at Arundel House.

SAT NAV BN18 9AD **ONLINE MAP**

Room 📞 📺 SC ⚙ ☕ General ⛱16 (i) 🔥 ♟ ✕ 🎱 Leisure ∪ ♪ ▶

ASHFORD, Kent Map ref 3B4 — SELF CATERING

★★★★★
SELF CATERING

Units **1**
Sleeps **4**

LOW SEASON PER WK
£350.00–£400.00

HIGH SEASON PER WK
£450.00–£600.00

Hazelhope Barn, Stalisfield, Nr Ashford

contact Mandy Southern, Hazelhope Barn, Hazelhope, Stalisfield Green, Faversham ME13 0HY
t +44 (0) 1233 713806 e mandy@hazelhopebarn.co.uk

hazelhopebarn.co.uk

open All year
payment Cash, cheques, euros
nearest pub 0.5 miles
nearest shop 2 miles

Excellent location. Luxury, first-floor apartment with stunning views. Built over stables in a Kent barn. Double with large, en suite shower and broadband Internet access. Large twin with adjacent bathroom. Fully fitted kitchen and separate utility room with washer/dryer. Very comfortable living/dining areas. Secure parking. Private garden with barbecue.

Unit 📺 SC 📀 🖥 📼🎚 ⏏🔲 📋 ❄ ♨ General ⛱ 🏠 🅿 ▢

ASHFORD, Kent Map ref 3B4 — CAMPING, CARAVAN & HOLIDAY PARK

★★★★★
HOLIDAY, TOURING
& CAMPING PARK

🚐 £14.00–£21.00
🚏 £14.00–£21.00
⛺ £12.00–£18.00
🏠(5) £220.00–£450.00
70 touring pitches

Broadhembury Holiday Park

Steeds Lane, Kingsnorth, Ashford TN26 1NQ t +44 (0) 1233 620859
e holidaypark@broadhembury.co.uk

broadhembury.co.uk GUEST REVIEWS · SPECIAL OFFERS · REAL-TIME BOOKING

For walking, cycling, visiting castles and gardens or just relaxing, Broadhembury, in quiet Kentish countryside, is a park for all seasons. Convenient for Channel crossings and Canterbury.

open All year
payment Credit/debit cards, cash, cheques, euros

General 🎮 🚿 🔌 🛁 ☎ 📶 🛒 🚿 🐕 ☀ (i) 🔥 Leisure 🎣 ⛰ ∪ ♪ ▶

WALKERS WELCOME · WELCOME WALKERS

Do you like walking?

Walkers feel at home in accommodation participating in our Walkers Welcome scheme. Look out for the symbol. Consider walking all or part of a long-distance route – go online at nationaltrail.co.uk.

BATTLE, East Sussex Map ref 3B4 — SELF CATERING

★★★★
SELF CATERING

Units **2**
Sleeps **2–5**

LOW SEASON PER WK
£250.00–£360.00

HIGH SEASON PER WK
£420.00–£470.00

Ninfield Holiday Cottages, Ninfield, Battle

contact Mr & Mrs D Godden, Moor Hall Farm, Moor Hall Drive, Ninfield, Battle TN33 9JT
t +44 (0) 1424 892686 **e** jill.godden@tiscali.co.uk

ninfieldholidaycottages.co.uk SPECIAL OFFERS

Two cosy, comfortable well-equipped cottages converted from farm buildings, peacefully situated off a private drive in a picturesque location. Interesting area to explore with many varied attractions.

open All year
payment Cash, cheques
nearest pub 0.5 miles
nearest shop 0.75 miles

Unit 📺 🖥️ 💻 🍳 🔌 🧺 🧷 ✳️ ⛺ General 🐴 🏬 🏠 P 🅾 Ⓢ Leisure 🚣 🚴

BEXHILL-ON-SEA, East Sussex Map ref 3B4 — HOTEL

★★
HOTEL

B&B PER ROOM PER NIGHT
S £43.00–£53.00
D £79.00–£99.00
HB PER PERSON PER NIGHT
£56.00–£66.00

3-/4-day Christmas breaks.

The Northern Hotel

72-82 Sea Road, Bexhill-on-Sea TN40 1JL **t** +44 (0) 1424 212836 **e** reception@northernhotel.co.uk

northernhotel.co.uk

open All year
bedrooms 8 double, 3 twin, 9 single
bathrooms All en suite
payment Credit/debit cards, cash, cheques

Family-managed for over 50 years and furnished with antique and reproduction furniture, creating a warm, friendly and homely atmosphere in elegant surroundings. Adjacent to seafront and close to town centre. All rooms en suite. Restaurants and bar open to non-residents. Short breaks, holiday and residential accommodation. Functions for up to 50 people.

SAT NAV TN40 1JL

Room 📞 📺 🍵 ♿ 🖥️ General 🐴 🏬 🏠 🍷 🍽️ 🎱 🐟 🐕

BIRDHAM, West Sussex Map ref 2C3 — SELF CATERING

★★★★★
SELF CATERING

Units **2**
Sleeps **4**

LOW SEASON PER WK
£400.00–£600.00

HIGH SEASON PER WK
£800.00–£850.00

Short breaks available throughout the year.

Martins Cottages, Chichester

contact Mrs Gillian Farquhar-Thomson, Martins Lane, Birdham, Chichester PO20 7AU
t +44 (0) 1243 512222 **e** gillift@martinscottages.plus.com

martinscottages.co.uk SPECIAL OFFERS

open All year
payment Cash, cheques, euros
nearest pub 2 miles
nearest shop 1 mile

Two new luxury cottages situated in a three-acre meadow in the Chichester Harbour Area of Outstanding Natural Beauty. From the doorstep there are gorgeous harbour walks. Each cottage is full of sunshine and has two double bedrooms and two bathrooms. They can be linked and used as one unit.

Unit 📺 🖥️ 💻 🧺 🍳 🔌 🧷 ✳️ ⛺ General 🐴 🏬 🏠 P 🅾 Ⓢ
Leisure ♨️ 🚣 🏌️ 🚴

Where is my pet welcome?

Want to take your cherished companion with you on holiday? Proprietors participating in our Welcome Pets! scheme go out of their way to make special provision for you and your pet. Look out for the symbol.

BOSHAM, West Sussex Map ref 2C3 — SELF CATERING

★★★★
SELF CATERING

Units **3**
Sleeps **2–4**

LOW SEASON PER WK
£300.00–£450.00

HIGH SEASON PER WK
£450.00–£650.00

Laneside, Chichester

contact Mr Antony Wallace, Bosham Lane, Bosham, Chichester PO18 8HL t +44 (0) 1243 573234
e info@millstream-hotel.co.uk

millstream-hotel.co.uk

open All year
payment Credit/debit cards, cash, cheques
nearest pub less than 0.5 miles
nearest shop 1 mile

Three newly-built cottages located just 200m from the shores of Chichester Harbour. Laneside is owne and managed by the Millstream Hotel in whose AA Rosette restaurant dinner can be taken. The cottage are superbly appointed and have a landscaped garden in which to relax.

Unit [TV] ▦ ▣ ▤ ▨ ▧ ▦ ▨ ❋ ▲ General ⟟ ▥ ⚐ P ▢ S Leisure U ♪ ⚑ ⚲

BRIGHTON & HOVE, East Sussex Map ref 2D3 — GUEST ACCOMMODATION

★★★★
GUEST ACCOMMODATION

B&B PER ROOM PER NIGHT
S £45.00–£55.00
D £70.00–£140.00

Adelaide House

51 Regency Square, Brighton BN1 2FF t +44 (0) 1273 205286 e info@adelaidehotel.co.uk

adelaidehotel.co.uk

Elegant Regency town-house hotel, centrally situated in Brighton's premier seafront square convenient for all amenities, NCP parking and conference venues. No lift.

open All year
bedrooms 7 double, 1 twin, 3 single, 1 family
bathrooms 9 en suite, 3 private
payment Credit/debit cards, cash

Room ▦ ▨ ☎ [TV] ⚲ ▨ General ⟟ ▥ ⚐ (?) ▥

BRIGHTON & HOVE, East Sussex Map ref 2D3 — GUEST ACCOMMODATION

★★★★
GUEST ACCOMMODATION

B&B PER ROOM PER NIGHT
S £55.00–£70.00
D £110.00–£170.00

The Neo

19 Oriental Place, Brighton BN1 2LL t +44 (0) 1273 711104 e info@neohotel.com

neohotel.com SPECIAL OFFERS

open All year except Christmas
bedrooms 8 double, 1 single
bathrooms All en suite
payment Credit/debit cards, cash, cheques

The Neo is a chic, stylish hotel with nine uniquely designed rooms, a cool cocktail bar, elegant dining room and massage/treatment room. Neo's friendly, professional staff place great emphasis on attention to detail and really care about your experience. Perfect for weddings/small conferences. This hotel is an absolute gem. Free Wi-Fi and ten minutes from The Brighton Centre, shopping and nightlife.

SAT NAV BN1 2LL

Room ☎ [TV] ⚲ ▨ General ⟟ (?) ✿ ▟ ▥ ☖ Leisure ⚑

FAMILIES WELCOME

Looking for an ideal family break?

For accommodation offering additional facilities and services for a range of ages and family units, look out for the Families Welcome symbol. Owners of these properties will go out of their way to welcome families.

BRIGHTON & HOVE, East Sussex Map ref 2D3 — SELF CATERING

★★★★
SELF CATERING

Units **3**
Sleeps **2–4**

LOW SEASON PER WK
Max £450.00

HIGH SEASON PER WK
Max £650.00

Brighton Marina Holiday Apartments, Brighton

contact Mrs A Wills, 5 Marlborough Road, Richmond TW10 6JT **t** +44 (0) 20 8940 6945
e averil.wills@london.com

brightonmarinaholidayapartments.co.uk

open All year
payment Cash, cheques, euros
nearest pub less than 0.5 miles
nearest shop less than 0.5 miles

Overlooking inner harbour with private waterside terrace or balcony. Luxury two-bedroom apartments. One twin, one double with en suite shower, bathroom, lounge/dining room, kitchen. Satellite TV, DVD, telephone, Wi-Fi broadband, private parking. Situated a mile east of Brighton, the marina boasts an extensive range of restaurants, leisure and dining facilities.

Unit 📺 🔣 📠 📀 💻 📷 🛋 🔌 📻 🍽 📱 💠 ✳ General ⛺ P 🐕

BRIGHTON & HOVE, East Sussex Map ref 2D3 — CAMPING, CARAVAN & HOLIDAY PARK

★★★★★
TOURING &
CAMPING PARK

🚐(169) £14.90–£28.30
🚐(169) £14.90–£28.30
⛺ on application
169 touring pitches

THE
CARAVAN
CLUB

Sheepcote Valley Caravan Club Site

East Brighton Park, Brighton BN2 5TS **t** +44 (0) 1273 626546

caravanclub.co.uk

open All year
payment Credit/debit cards, cash, cheques

Located on the South Downs, just two miles from Brighton. Visit the Marina, with its shops, pubs, restaurants and cinema, and take a tour of the exotic Royal Pavilion.

SAT NAV *BN2 5TS*

> *Special member rates mean you can save your membership subscription in less than a week. Visit our website to find out more.*

General 🅿 🔌 🚿 🚻 📶 📷 📠 🐕 ☀ 📶 Leisure 🎮 🚩

BROADSTAIRS, Kent Map ref 3C3 — SELF CATERING

★★★–★★★★★
SELF CATERING

Units **2**
Sleeps **1–6**

LOW SEASON PER WK
£250.00–£500.00

HIGH SEASON PER WK
£450.00–£650.00

Broadstairs Holiday Lets, Broadstairs

contact Linda & Harry Sear, Broadstairs Holiday Lets, Charity Farm, Eggington LU7 9PB
t +44 (0) 1525 210550 **e** lindaandharrysear@yahoo.co.uk

broadstairsholidaylets.co.uk

One- and two-bedroom ground-floor apartments in conservation area of Chandos Square near seafront, Victoria Gardens, shops, restaurants. Sunny patio. Sea view from one-bedroom apartment. Short breaks out of season.

open All year
payment Cash, cheques, euros
nearest pub less than 0.5 miles
nearest shop less than 0.5 miles

Unit 📺 🖥 💻 📷 🔌 📱 💠 General ⛺ 🚶 🅢

Using map references

The map references refer to the colour maps at the front of this guide. The first figure is the map number, the letter and figure that follow indicate the grid reference on the map.

★★★★
SELF CATERING

Units **1**
Sleeps **6**

LOW SEASON PER WK
Min £375.00

HIGH SEASON PER WK
Max £750.00

Chandos Square, Broadstairs

contact Matthew Dove
t +44 (0) 7940 650023 e enquiries@selfcateringbroadstairs.co.uk

selfcateringbroadstairs.co.uk GUEST REVIEWS · SPECIAL OFFERS · REAL-TIME BOOKING

Comfortable, bright three-bedroom, three-bathroom apartment. Perfect position opposite wonderful sandy beach. Less that two minutes' walk to town. Very well equipped. Ideal choice for a memorable seaside holiday.

open All year
payment Cash, cheques
nearest pub less than 0.5 miles
nearest shop less than 0.5 miles

Unit 📺🖥️💽🗄️🍴🔌🗑️📠 General 🛏️🍳🔥🆂 Leisure 🎣►

★★★★
BED & BREAKFAST

B&B PER ROOM PER NIGHT
S **£40.00**
D **£60.00**

Rate reduced for stays of more than one night.

Huntsmill Farm B&B

Shalstone, Nr Buckingham MK18 5ND t +44 (0) 1280 704852 & +44 (0) 7970 871104
e fiona@huntsmill.com

huntsmill.com

open All year except Christmas
bedrooms 2 double, 1 twin
bathrooms All en suite
payment Credit/debit cards, cash, cheques, euros

Home-made bread and preserves welcome you at Huntsmill Farm. Accommodation is in comfortable, en suite rooms adjacent to farmhouse, set in stone courtyard. Set in quiet location with views over ope countryside. Close to many National Trust propertie and Silverstone.

SAT NAV MK18 5ND

Room 🔌📺🐾🍴 General 🛏️5🔥🅿️◻️❄ Leisure ∪🎣►

★★★★
SELF CATERING

Units **6**
Sleeps **1–9**

LOW SEASON PER WK
£225.00–£450.00

HIGH SEASON PER WK
£300.00–£575.00

Additional rooms may be added from B&B on special room-only rate.

Huntsmill Farm Holidays, Buckingham

t +44 (0) 1280 704852 & +44 (0) 7970 871104 e fiona@huntsmill.com

huntsmill.com

open All year
payment Credit/debit cards, cash, cheques, euros
nearest pub 2 miles
nearest shop 2 miles

Courtyard of traditional stone, timber and slate barns, imaginatively converted from former calf sheds and pig sties, offering a high standard of accommodation. Set on a working farm in a quiet location with views of open countryside. Large gardens with easy access to footpaths. Close to Silverstone and many National Trust properties.

SAT NAV MK18 5ND

Unit 📺🖥️💽🗄️🍴🔌🗑️📠❄ General 🛏️🔥🅿️◻️🆂 Leisure ●∪🎣

What if I need to cancel?

It is advisable to check the proprietor's cancellation policy in case you have to change your plans at a later date.

BURFORD, Oxfordshire Map ref 2B1 — GUEST ACCOMMODATION

Cotland House B&B

★★★★
GUEST ACCOMMODATION

B&B PER ROOM PER NIGHT
S £35.00–£45.00
D £60.00–£80.00

Midweek special offers available on two nights or more. Discount given on Sunday night when staying the weekend.

Fulbrook Hill, Burford OX18 4BH t +44 (0) 1993 822382 e info@cotlandhouse.com

cotlandhouse.com GUEST REVIEWS · SPECIAL OFFERS

open All year except Christmas and New Year
bedrooms 1 double, 1 twin, 1 single, 1 family
bathrooms All en suite
payment Cash, cheques

Cotland House B&B is a charming Cotswold-stone home restored to an exceptional standard with stylish, luxurious en suite rooms. A fabulous breakfast, made from organic/local produce, is served in front of a wood-burning stove or on the sunny terrace depending on the season. A perfect Cotswold base.

SAT NAV *OX18 4BH* **ONLINE MAP**

Room 📺 🐾 🍽 General 🐎 🏛 🅿 📶 🛁 🍽 🎮 📷 💺 ❄ Leisure ♾ ⚓ ► 🚴

BURFORD, Oxfordshire Map ref 2B1 — SELF CATERING

Caswell House, Brize Norton

★★★★–★★★★★★★
SELF CATERING

Units 2
Sleeps 8

LOW SEASON PER WK
£456.00–£545.00

HIGH SEASON PER WK
£756.00–£901.00

contact Mrs Amanda Matthews, Caswell Lane, Brize Norton OX18 3NJ t +44 (0) 1993 701064 & +44 (0) 7718 390867 e stay@caswell-house.co.uk

caswell-house.co.uk

open All year
payment Credit/debit cards, cash, cheques
nearest pub 3 miles
nearest shop 5 miles

With rural views, walled gardens, orchard, moat and extensive lawns, Caswell House provides luxurious, spacious accommodation for up to 12 guests. It has been refurbished to an excellent standard, retaining all the original rural, historic charm. An ideal relaxing retreat, with that special feeling of warmth, comfort and country-house living.

ONLINE MAP

Unit 📺 📀 💻 🔊 🖨 🍽 🗄 🧺 ❄ ♨ General 🐎 🏛 🅿 🔲 Ⓢ
Leisure ♾ ⚓ ► 🚴

BURFORD, Oxfordshire Map ref 2B1 — CAMPING, CARAVAN & HOLIDAY PARK

Burford Caravan Club Site

★★★★★
TOURING PARK

🚐 (120) £12.20–£25.10
🚏 (120) £12.20–£25.10
120 touring pitches

Bradwell Grove, Burford OX18 4JJ t +44 (0) 1993 823080

caravanclub.co.uk

open March to November
payment Credit/debit cards, cash, cheques

Attractive, spacious site opposite Cotswold Wildlife Park. Burford has superb Tudor houses, a museum and historic inns. A great base from which to explore the Cotswolds.

SAT NAV *OX18 4JJ*

Special member rates mean you can save your membership subscription in less than a week. Visit our website to find out more.

THE
CARAVAN
CLUB

General 🔲 🔌 🚿 🚽 📶 🚰 💺 🐕 ☼ Leisure ⛺ ⚓ ►

BURLEY, Hampshire Map ref 2B3 — GUEST ACCOMMODATION

★★★★
BED & BREAKFAST

B&B PER ROOM PER NIGHT
S £35.00–£75.00
D £60.00–£75.00

EVENING MEAL PER PERSON
£18.00–£25.00

Wayside Cottage

27 Garden Road, Burley, Ringwood BH24 4EA t +44 (0) 1425 403414 e jwest@wayside-cottage.co.u

wayside-cottage.co.uk

open All year
bedrooms 3 double, 2 twin, 1 family
bathrooms 5 en suite, 1 private
payment Cash, cheques

Enchanting wisteria-covered Edwardian cottage in peaceful location in the heart of the New Forest. A haven of tranquillity, full of antique furniture and china, ideal for walking, cycling or exploring the forest and coast, or just relax in our delightful cottag gardens. Local produce cooked by ex-professional chef. Dinners by arrangement.

SAT NAV BH24 4EA

Room 🛏🗄 📺 ♨ ℞ General ☊🎖♿ P ⊕ ⚡ ✗ ℡ ❄ ☗ Leisure ∪ ⤵ ► ♻

CADNAM, Hampshire Map ref 2C3 — GUEST ACCOMMODATION

★★★★
**GUEST HOUSE
SILVER AWARD**

B&B PER ROOM PER NIGHT
S £35.00–£50.00
D £75.00–£80.00

Twin Oaks Guest House

Southampton Road, Cadnam, New Forest SO40 2NQ t +44 (0) 23 8081 2305
e enquiries@twinoaks-guesthouse.co.uk

Victorian guesthouse in beautiful village location. All en suite, off-road parking, close to restaurants, open forest and much more.

open All year except Christmas and New Year
bedrooms 3 double, 1 twin, 2 single
bathrooms All en suite
payment Cash, cheques, euros

Room 🛏 📺 ♨ ℞ General P ⚡ ℡

CANTERBURY, Kent Map ref 3B3 — GUEST ACCOMMODATION

★★★★★
**GUEST ACCOMMODATION
GOLD AWARD**

B&B PER ROOM PER NIGHT
S £55.00–£65.00
D £95.00–£125.00

EVENING MEAL PER PERSON
£30.00–£35.00

Magnolia House

36 St Dunstans Terrace, Canterbury CT2 8AX t +44 (0) 1227 765121
e info@magnoliahousecanterbury.co.uk

magnoliahousecanterbury.co.uk REAL-TIME BOOKING

Charming, late-Georgian house in quiet residential street, a ten-minute stroll from the city centre. Bedrooms have every facility for an enjoyable stay. Varied breakfasts are served overlooking the attractive walled garden.

open All year except Christmas
bedrooms 5 double, 1 twin, 1 single
bathrooms All en suite
payment Credit/debit cards, cash, cheques

Room 🛏🗄 📺 🆂🅲 ♨ ℞ General ☊12 P ⊕ ✗ ℡ ❄

CANTERBURY, Kent Map ref 3B3 — GUEST ACCOMMODATION

★★★★★
GUEST ACCOMMODATION

B&B PER ROOM PER NIGHT
S £50.00–£60.00
D £90.00–£115.00

Special low season deals. See website or ring for details.

Yorke Lodge

50 London Road, Canterbury CT2 8LF t +44 (0) 1227 451243 e info@yorkelodge.com

yorkelodge.com

open All year
bedrooms 5 double, 1 twin, 1 single, 1 family
bathrooms All en suite
payment Credit/debit cards, cash, cheques

Yorke Lodge is the ideal retreat after a long day sightseeing or a busy day at the office. Built in 1887 and fully refurbished over the last two years, this quintessential Victorian town house offers a warm home-from-home atmosphere, with all the modern conveniences now expected by the discerning traveller.

SAT NAV CT2 8LF

Room 🗄 📺 ♨ ℞ General ☊ ♿ P ⊕ ⚡ ℡ ❄ ☗ Leisure ∪ ⤵ ► ♻

CANTERBURY, Kent Map ref 3B3

★★★
SELF CATERING

Units	1
Sleeps	5

LOW SEASON PER WK
Min £350.00

HIGH SEASON PER WK
Max £450.00

Jubilee Lodge, Canterbury

contact Mrs S P Underwood, Dicksons Bourne, Aldington TN25 7AH t +44 (0) 1233 720370
e juck1@aol.com

A Victorian terraced house within the city walls, with enclosed sunny garden. Only 100m walk to St Peter's Street and shops. Double, twin and single rooms. Ground-floor bathroom and bed settee.

open All year
payment Cash, cheques, euros
nearest pub less than 0.5 miles
nearest shop less than 0.5 miles

Unit TV 🖥 ■. 🍽🗄 ✎🗄 🖵 🕯 ☼ ⛏ General ☕5 S Leisure 🚴

CANTERBURY, Kent Map ref 3B3

★★★
SELF CATERING

Units	5
Sleeps	2–4

LOW SEASON PER WK
£160.00–£300.00

HIGH SEASON PER WK
£300.00–£510.00

Special rates for parties requiring all the units (up to 18 people).

The Old Sawmill, Hastingleigh, Ashford

contact Mrs Caroline Gilson, The Old Sawmill, Hastingleigh, Ashford TN25 5HN
t +44 (0) 1233 750056 & +44 (0) 7765 963215 e carolinepilgrim@aol.com

hastingleighholidaylets.com

open All year
payment Credit/debit cards, cash, cheques
nearest pub 0.5 miles
nearest shop 3 miles

Five attractively converted cottages set in an Area of Outstanding Natural Beauty. Canterbury, London and France are all within easy reach. Every property is fully equipped with modern furnishings and appliances. A games room and children's play area are also on site and barbecues are available.

SAT NAV TN25 5HN

Unit TV 🖥 ■. 🍽✎ 🖵🕯 ☼ ⛏ General ☕ 🏛 🐾 P ◻ S 🐕 Leisure ♦ ∪ 🎣

CHICHESTER, West Sussex Map ref 2C3

★★★★★
SELF CATERING

Units	1
Sleeps	4

LOW SEASON PER WK
£350.00–£500.00

HIGH SEASON PER WK
£500.00–£700.00

Apple Barn, Runcton, Chichester

contact Mrs R Kendall, Saltham House, Saltham Lane, Runcton, Chichester PO20 1XJ
t +44 (0) 1243 775997 e applebarn@salthamhouse.co.uk

salthamhouse.co.uk

open All year
payment Credit/debit cards, cash, cheques
nearest pub 1 mile
nearest shop less than 0.5 miles

Apple Barn is an old single-storey barn which has been converted into a luxury two-bedroom/two-bathroom holiday cottage. It is open-plan and very spacious throughout. Set in a pretty, quiet location surrounded by farmland, it is well situated for Chichester and the surrounding area.

Unit TV 🖥 ■. 🍽✎ 🗄 🖵🕯 ☼ General ☕ 🏛 🐾 P Leisure ♦ ∪ ►

Place index

If you know where you want to stay, the index by place name at the back of the guide will give you the page number listing accommodation in your chosen town, city or village. Check out the other useful indexes too.

CHICHESTER, West Sussex Map ref 2C3

SELF CATERING

★★★★
SELF CATERING

| Units | 1 |
| Sleeps | 1–6 |

LOW SEASON PER WK
£425.00–£595.00

HIGH SEASON PER WK
£595.00–£695.00

Short breaks available Oct-May. Reduced rates for couples Oct-May.

Cornerstones, Chichester

contact Mrs Higgins, Greenacre, Goodwood Gardens, Chichester PO20 1SP **t** +44 (0) 1243 83909(
e v.r.higgins@dsl.pipex.com

cornercottages.com

open All year
payment Cash, cheques
nearest pub less than 0.5 miles
nearest shop 2 miles

Sussex-style house. Two bedrooms upstairs, one downstairs. Bathroom. Separate shower room. Equipped to high standard. Double garage. Enclose(gardens. Village between Chichester and coast. Eas: walks to pub/restaurant, post office/shop, church and Pagham nature reserve. Five-minute drive to Chichester. Ten minutes to Goodwood Racecourse.

Unit 📺 🆂🅲 📠📀 💻 📠📠 📠📠 General 🐎 ▥ ♿ P

CHICHESTER, West Sussex Map ref 2C3

SELF CATERING

★★★★
SELF CATERING

| Units | 1 |
| Sleeps | 1–2 |

LOW SEASON PER WK
£235.00–£315.00

HIGH SEASON PER WK
£315.00–£350.00

Short breaks available Oct-Apr. Minimum 3 nights.

Cygnet Cottage, Chichester

contact Mrs Higgins, Greenacre, Goodwood Gardens, Chichester PO20 1SP **t** +44 (0) 1243 839096
e v.r.higgins@dsl.pipex.com

cornercottages.com

open All year
payment Cash, cheques
nearest pub less than 0.5 miles
nearest shop 2 miles

Cosy one-bedroom detached cottage in village between Chichester and coast. Easy country walks t(pub/restaurant, post office/shop, church and Pagham nature reserve. Fully equipped to high standard. Suntrap patio. Off-road parking. Canalsid(walk or five minutes' drive to historic Chichester. Te(minutes' drive to Goodwood racecourse.

Unit 📺 🆂🅲 📠📀 💻 📠📠 📠📠 General 🐎 ▥ ♿ P 🆂

COTSWOLDS

See under Burford, Kingham, Standlake, Woodstock
See also Cotswolds in Central and South West England sections

DOVER, Kent Map ref 3C4

★★★★
HOTEL

B&B PER ROOM PER NIGHT
S £109.00–£139.00
D £129.00–£169.00
HB PER PERSON PER NIGHT
£104.50–£124.50

2-night/3-day spa break: £279pp – includes 2 nights' DB&B and 90-minute massage or beauty treatment.

Walletts Court Country House Hotel, Restaurant and Spa

Westcliffe, St Margaret's at Cliffe, Dover CT15 6EW t +44 (0) 1304 852424 e wc@wallettscourt.com

wallettscourt.com GUEST REVIEWS · SPECIAL OFFERS · REAL-TIME BOOKING

open All year except Christmas
bedrooms 11 double, 3 twin, 1 family, 2 suites
bathrooms All en suite
payment Credit/debit cards, cash, cheques, euros

Think rolling green hills a stone's throw from the sea, your own sumptuous four-poster bed. Roll-top baths, candles, fluffy towels, luxury bath goodies. Delicious canapes and cocktails, watching the sunset in landscaped gardens. A wonderful dinner made with super-fresh produce. A superb spa, pool, jacuzzi, sauna and gorgeous hot-stone massage …

SAT NAV CT15 6EW ONLINE MAP

Room 🛏🖨📞📺SC🔌🍵🕭 General 🛋🛗🛢P📶🍽🍴📠💺♨ Leisure 🏊♨🏌⊗🔍U🎿🏌🚲

EASTBOURNE, East Sussex Map ref 3B4

★★★★★
HOTEL
GOLD AWARD

B&B PER ROOM PER NIGHT
S £160.00–£405.00
D £190.00–£435.00
HB PER PERSON PER NIGHT
£126.00–£255.00

Promotions during 2009 include gourmet evenings, musical events and seasonal promotions. Visit our website for more information.

The Grand Hotel

King Edwards Parade, Eastbourne BN21 4EQ t +44 (0) 1323 412345
e reservations@grandeastbourne.com

grandeastbourne.com SPECIAL OFFERS · REAL-TIME BOOKING

open All year
bedrooms 46 double, 60 twin, 32 family, 14 suites
bathrooms All en suite
payment Credit/debit cards, cash, cheques, euros

Built in 1875 and recently restored to its former glory, The Grand Hotel is a stunning example of the highest levels of service. Facilities include health club, two restaurants, Junior Crew Club and two swimming pools. Only five minutes from magnificent Sussex countryside, 55 minutes from Gatwick.

SAT NAV BN21 4EQ ONLINE MAP

Room 🛏🖨📞📺SC🔌🍵🕭 General 🛋🛗🛢P📶🍽🍴🌙💺♨🐎 Leisure 🏊🔥♨🏌⊗U🎿🏌🚲

EASTBOURNE, East Sussex Map ref 3B4

★★★
GUEST ACCOMMODATION

B&B PER ROOM PER NIGHT
S £35.00–£65.00
D £60.00–£80.00

EVENING MEAL PER PERSON
£8.00–£19.00

3 nights for the price of 2, Oct-Mar (excl Bank Holidays, Christmas and New Year). Pre-booked only.

The Birling Gap

Birling Gap, Seven Sisters Cliffs, Eastbourne BN20 0AB t +44 (0) 1323 423197
e reception@birlinggaphotel.co.uk

birlinggaphotel.co.uk

open All year
bedrooms 5 double, 2 twin, 1 single, 1 family
bathrooms All en suite
payment Credit/debit cards, cash, cheques, euros

Magnificent cliff-top position on Seven Sisters cliffs with views of country, sea and beach. Superb downland and beach walks. Old-world Thatched Bar and Oak Room Restaurant. Coffee shop and games room, function and conference suite. Off A259 coast road at East Dean, 1.5 miles west of Beachy Head.

SAT NAV BN20 0AB

Room 🛏📞📺🕭 General 🛋🛗🛢P🍽✕🌙♨ Leisure 🎿🚲

★★★
GUEST ACCOMMODATION

B&B PER ROOM PER NIGHT
S £55.00–£75.00
D £65.00–£90.00

Travelrest Solent Gateway

22 The Avenue, Fareham PO14 1NS   t +44 (0) 1329 232175   e solentreservations@travelrest.co.uk

travelrest.co.uk/fareham

Recently refurbished, comfortable accommodation, in landscaped gardens. Free car park and within walking distance of town-centre bars, restaurants and railway station. Ideal location on A27 between Southampton and Portsmouth.

open All year
bedrooms 11 double, 5 twin, 1 single, 2 family
bathrooms All en suite
payment Credit/debit cards, cash, euros

Room 🛏 ☎ TV SC ☕   General 🗄 ▦ 🏃 P 📶 ⚡ ☍ ❀ ⌑

★★★★
SELF CATERING

Units   **2**
Sleeps   **4–6**

LOW SEASON PER WK
£400.00–£525.00

HIGH SEASON PER WK
£500.00–£750.00

Goodlake Barns, Faringdon

contact Mr Andrew Gantlett, Goodlake Barns, Church Farm, Church Street, Faringdon SN7 7QA
t +44 (0) 1367 710112   e info@goodlakebarns.co.uk

goodlakebarns.co.uk

Light and spacious cottages in a picturesque village setting on an organic farm. This is a relaxing place to stay and an ideal base for exploring Oxford and the Cotswolds.

open All year
payment Credit/debit cards, cash, cheques
nearest pub 2 miles
nearest shop 2 miles

Unit TV 📺 ▣ 🖥 📠 ⤢ 🗑 🍽 💷 ❀   General 🗄 ▦ 🏃 P ⏹ S   Leisure ✦

★★★
GUEST HOUSE

B&B PER ROOM PER NIGHT
S £29.00–£39.00
D £43.00–£57.00

Weekend and midweek breaks from £84–£122pp, min 2 nights. Also free child off-peak offers.

The Rob Roy Guest House

227 Dover Road, Folkestone CT19 6NH   t +44 (0) 1303 253341   e robroy.folkestone@ntlworld.com

therobroyguesthouse.co.uk GUEST REVIEWS · SPECIAL OFFERS · REAL-TIME BOOKING

open All year except Christmas
bedrooms 3 double, 3 twin, 1 family
bathrooms 3 en suite
payment Credit/debit cards, cash, cheques, euros

The Rob Roy: friendly service, comfortable accommodation and tasty breakfasts. Ideally situated ten minutes from M20 and Channel Tunnel and 20 minutes from Dover ferries and Eurostar Ashford. Only minutes from Folkestone's famous Leas, cliffs beaches and promenade and the lovely Folkestone Downs and North Downs Way.

SAT NAV *CT19 6NH* **ONLINE MAP**

Room 🛏 TV ☕   General 🗄 ▦ 🏃 P 📶 ⚡ 🎫 ⌑   Leisure ♪ ▸ 🚲

FOLKESTONE, Kent Map ref 3B4 **CAMPING, CARAVAN & HOLIDAY PARK**

★★★★★
TOURING & CAMPING PARK

(140) £12.20–£25.10
(140) £12.20–£25.10
140 touring pitches

Black Horse Farm Caravan Club Site

385 Canterbury Road, Densole, Folkestone CT18 7BG **t** +44 (0) 1303 892665

caravanclub.co.uk

open All year
payment Credit/debit cards, cash, cheques

Set in the heart of farming country in the Kentish village of Densole on the Downs. This is a quiet and relaxed country site, ideally suited for families wishing to visit the many interesting local attractions including the historic city of Canterbury. For nature lovers there are many walks.

SAT NAV *CT18 7BG*

Special member rates mean you can save your membership subscription in less than a week. Visit our website to find out more.

THE CARAVAN CLUB

General Leisure

FORDINGBRIDGE, Hampshire Map ref 2B3 **GUEST ACCOMMODATION**

★★★★
RESTAURANT WITH ROOMS

B&B PER ROOM PER NIGHT
S £69.00–£79.00
D £80.00–£125.00

EVENING MEAL PER PERSON
£29.00–£38.00

The Three Lions

Stuckton, Fordingbridge SP6 2HF **t** +44 (0) 1425 652489 **e** the3lions@btinternet.com

thethreelionsrestaurant.co.uk

open All year
bedrooms 2 double, 1 twin, 1 family, 3 suites
bathrooms All en suite
payment Credit/debit cards, cash, cheques

Welcome to the Three Lions, a restaurant with rooms in the New Forest National Park set in two acres of beautiful gardens. Enjoy Mike's rustic though refined cooking in front of our open log fire. Wheelchair access, whirlpool jacuzzi and sauna. Hampshire Restaurant of the Year 2006, Good Food Guide.

SAT NAV *SP6 2HF*

Room General P Leisure

FOREST ROW, East Sussex Map ref 2D2 **HOTEL**

★★★★
HOTEL
GOLD AWARD

B&B PER ROOM PER NIGHT
S £160.00–£390.00
D £190.00–£420.00
HB PER PERSON PER NIGHT
£260.00–£480.00

Ashdown Park Hotel

Wych Cross, Forest Row RH18 5JR **t** +44 (0) 1342 824988 **e** sales@ashdownpark.com

ashdownpark.com SPECIAL OFFERS · REAL-TIME BOOKING

Built in 1860s and sympathetically restored for modern-day luxury. Set in 186 acres in heart of the Ashdown Forest. Splendid rooms and suites. Award-winning restaurant, golf course and country club. Close Gatwick and M25.

open All year
bedrooms 33 double, 31 twin, 5 single, 36 suites
bathrooms All en suite
payment Credit/debit cards, cash, cheques, euros

Room General P Leisure

Do you have access needs?

Look for the National Accessible Scheme symbols if you have special hearing, visual or mobility needs. An index of accommodation participating in the scheme can be found at the back of this guide.

FORTON, Hampshire Map ref 2C2 GUEST ACCOMMODATION

★★★★★
**BED & BREAKFAST
SILVER AWARD**

B&B PER ROOM PER NIGHT
S £60.00–£75.00
D £80.00–£105.00

*Discounts on stays
of 4 or more days
(excl Sat). See
website for details.*

The Barn House B&B

Andover SP11 6NU **t** +44 (0) 1264 720544 **e** hello@thebarnhousebandb.co.uk

thebarnhousebandb.co.uk

open All year except Christmas and New Year
bedrooms 1 double, 1 twin
bathrooms All en suite
payment Credit/debit cards, cash, cheques

A luxury B&B in a quiet, pretty village situated in Hampshire's picturesque Test Valley. There are many places of interest nearby, as well as local pub and a variety of interesting walks. We provide the highest standards of accommodation, food and hospitality. For more information please visit our website.

SAT NAV *SP11 6NU* **ONLINE MAP**

Room TV ☕ ♨ General P ⌂

GATWICK, West Sussex Map ref 2D2 GUEST ACCOMMODATION

★★★★
**GUEST HOUSE
SILVER AWARD**

B&B PER ROOM PER NIGHT
S £45.00–£50.00
D £60.00–£65.00

The Lawn Guest House

30 Massetts Road, Horley RH6 7DF **t** +44 (0) 1293 775751 **e** info@lawnguesthouse.co.uk

lawnguesthouse.co.uk GUEST REVIEWS

open All year
bedrooms 3 double, 3 twin, 6 family
bathrooms All en suite
payment Credit/debit cards, cash, cheques, euros

Imposing Victorian house in pretty gardens. Five minutes Gatwick. Two minutes' walk Horley. Station 300yds. London 40 minutes. Bedrooms all en suite. Full English breakfast and continental for early departures. Guests' ice machine. On-line residents' computer for emails. Overnight/long-term parking. Airport transfers by arrangement.

SAT NAV *RH6 7DF* **ONLINE MAP**

Room ☎ TV ☕ ♨ General ⤢ ▥ ♿ P ⊕ ✿ ❋ ☇ Leisure ▸

GATWICK, West Sussex Map ref 2D2 GUEST ACCOMMODATION

★★★★
GUEST HOUSE

B&B PER ROOM PER NIGHT
S £47.00–£53.00
D £63.00–£68.00

Southbourne Guest House Gatwick

34 Massetts Road, Horley RH6 7DS **t** +44 (0) 1293 771991 **e** reservations@southbournegatwick.com

southbournegatwick.com

open All year
bedrooms 3 double, 3 twin, 2 single, 4 family
bathrooms All en suite
payment Credit/debit cards, cash, cheques

A warm welcome awaits you in our family-run guesthouse. Ideally located for Gatwick Airport, and exploring Surrey, Sussex and London. Five minutes' walk from Horley train station, restaurants, shops and pubs and 30 minutes by train from London. Five minutes' drive from Gatwick with free courtesy transport from 0930-2130.

SAT NAV *RH6 7DS*

Room ♿ ▦ TV ☕ General ⤢ ▥ ♿ P ⊕ ✿

GATWICK AIRPORT

See under Horsham, Redhill

GILLINGHAM, Kent Map ref 3B3 — HOTEL

★★
HOTEL

B&B PER ROOM PER NIGHT
S £45.00
D £56.00

King Charles Hotel

Brompton Road, Gillingham ME7 5QT **t** +44 (0) 1634 830303 **e** enquiries@kingcharleshotel.co.uk

kingcharleshotel.co.uk GUEST REVIEWS · SPECIAL OFFERS · REAL-TIME BOOKING

open All year
bedrooms 30 double, 30 twin, 10 single, 26 family, 2 suites
bathrooms All en suite
payment Credit/debit cards, cash, cheques, euros

A privately owned, modern hotel with a cosy restaurant and first-class conference and banqueting facilities. All bedrooms have en suite bathroom, tea-/coffee-making facilities, hairdryer, telephone and TV. We are ideal as a base for exploring South East England and London, and we offer extremely competitive group rates.

SAT NAV ME7 5QT **ONLINE MAP**

Room 🛁🛏🕻📺🆂🛎🧺 General 🕙🏬🏃P👁🍽🍴🌙🌞🎁🛎🔪✂🐕
Leisure 🏊🏃🚴

GOSPORT, Hampshire Map ref 2C3 — SELF CATERING

★★★
SELF CATERING

Units   1
Sleeps   5

LOW SEASON PER WK
Max £305.00

HIGH SEASON PER WK
Max £588.00

Eight The Mews, Gosport

contact Richard Jeal, 13 Sondes Farm, Glebe Road, Dorking RH4 3EF **t** +44 (0) 7771 990425
e info@eightthemews.co.uk

eightthemews.co.uk

open All year
payment Credit/debit cards, cash, cheques, euros
nearest pub 0.5 miles
nearest shop 0.5 miles

A three-bedroom self-catering town house offering accommodation for up to five people. The property is arranged over three floors, has a courtyard garden and parking for two cars. Our position in the centre of Gosport close to the ferry terminal, bus and train station makes a great spot to explore both Portsmouth and the surrounding area.

ONLINE MAP

Unit 📺🆂📀📼🖥🍴🍳🌞 General 🕙4 P🅂 Leisure 🏊🏃

GOUDHURST, Kent Map ref 3B4 — SELF CATERING

★★★★
SELF CATERING

Units   3
Sleeps   2–7

LOW SEASON PER WK
£285.00–£650.00

HIGH SEASON PER WK
£320.00–£795.00

Three Chimneys Farm, Cranbrook

contact Mrs Marion Fuller, Three Chimneys Farm, Bedgebury Road, Goudhurst, Cranbrook TN17 2RA **t** +44 (0) 1580 212175 & +44 (0) 7785 734639
e marionfuller@threechimneysfarm.co.uk

threechimneysfarm.co.uk

open All year
payment Credit/debit cards, cash, cheques
nearest pub 2 miles
nearest shop 2 miles

Mixed farm. Spacious cottages in a beautiful location, very quiet but not isolated. Wi-Fi internet connection.

Unit 📺🆂📀🖥🍴🍳🌞🖥 General 🕙🏃P🐕
Leisure 🎣⛳🏊🚴

HASTINGLEIGH, Kent Map ref 3B4

★★★★
SELF CATERING

Units **1**
Sleeps **1–2**

LOW SEASON PER WK
£300.00

HIGH SEASON PER WK
£300.00

Staple Farm, Hastingleigh, Ashford

contact Mr & Mrs Cliff & Betty Martindale, Staple Farm, Hastingleigh, Ashford TN25 5HF
t +44 (0) 1233 750248

payment Cash, cheques
nearest pub 1 mile
nearest shop 2.8 miles

Stable conversion displaying beams and original features, yet offering all modern amenities. Situated in Area of Outstanding Natural Beauty with excellent walks from front door, including the North Downs Way. Within easy reach of Canterbury, Eurostar terminals, Channel ports of Dover and Folkestone, plus many places of historic interest.

Unit 📺 ▣ ⚲ 🔲 🍽 🕯❄ General **P**

HASTINGS, East Sussex Map ref 3B4

★★★
HOTEL

B&B PER ROOM PER NIGHT
S £65.00–£95.00
D £79.00–£130.00
HB PER PERSON PER NIGHT
£59.00–£110.00

Special country-house breaks from £79pppn DB&B based on 2 people sharing a twin/ double room for 2 nights.

Beauport Park Hotel and Health Club

Battle Road, Battle TN38 8EA **t** +44 (0) 1424 851222 **e** reservations@beauportparkhotel.co.uk

bannatyne.co.uk SPECIAL OFFERS · REAL-TIME BOOKING

open All year
bedrooms 15 double, 4 twin, 3 single, 2 family, 2 suites
bathrooms All en suite
payment Credit/debit cards, cash, cheques

Set in 38 acres of woodland and gardens, three miles from the historic towns of Hastings and Battle, the hotel is an ideal base to explore 1066 Country. Built in 1719, this Georgian country house has been successfully transformed into a luxury hotel. All guests enjoy free access to Bannatyne's Health Club & Spa.

SAT NAV TN38 8EA

Room ♿ 🛋 ☎ 📺 🆂🅲 ⚲ ⚲ 🌀 ⟶ General 🐴 🏛 ♿ **P** 📶 ♿ 🍴 ● 🅱 ▪♿ ❄ 🐴
Leisure 🎣 ⚲ 🎿 ⊗ ⚲ ∪ ♪ ⟶

HASTINGS, East Sussex Map ref 3B4

★★★★
GUEST ACCOMMODATION
SILVER AWARD

B&B PER ROOM PER NIGHT
S £30.00–£35.00
D £60.00–£75.00

Discounts for 3 or more nights booked. Complimentary wine and gift with all honeymoon and anniversary stays.

Seaspray

54 Eversfield Place, St Leonards-on-Sea, Hastings TN37 6DB **t** +44 (0) 1424 436583
e jo@seaspraybb.co.uk

seaspraybb.co.uk GUEST REVIEWS · SPECIAL OFFERS · REAL-TIME BOOKING

open All year
bedrooms 3 double, 3 twin, 3 single, 1 family
bathrooms 8 en suite
payment Cash, cheques

Victorian seafront B&B on Hastings promenade. Your home from home with a bit extra. Refurbished to very high standard. Quiet location five minutes to town and all amenities. Rooms are modern and clean: superking beds, Wi-Fi, plasma TV, Freeview, fridge. Parking permits. Extensive breakfast menu, all diets catered for.

SAT NAV TN37 6DB **ONLINE MAP**

Room ♿ 📺 🆂🅲 ⚲ ⚲ General 🐴 🏛 ♿ 📶 ♿ 🍽 ▪ Leisure ♪ 🚲

HERNE BAY, Kent Map ref 3B3

★★★★
BED & BREAKFAST

B&B PER ROOM PER NIGHT
S £40.00–£45.00
D £55.00–£65.00

Bayview

Central Parade, Herne Bay CT6 5JJ t +44 (0) 1227 741458 e info@the-bayview-guesthouse.co.uk

the-bayview-guesthouse.co.uk GUEST REVIEWS

Centrally located in this popular seaside resort, Bayview offers eleven individually designed double bedrooms, each enjoying views of the beautiful Herne Bay coastline.

open All year
bedrooms 7 double, 2 twin, 1 family, 1 suite
bathrooms 5 en suite, 2 private
payment Credit/debit cards

Room 🚿📶 TV SC 🛁🍵 General 🛎️📶🔥🍴📮🖥️ Leisure ♾️⚓▶🚴

HEVER, Kent Map ref 2D2

★★★★
BED & BREAKFAST
SILVER AWARD

B&B PER ROOM PER NIGHT
S £48.00–£65.00
D £70.00–£85.00

Discount for stays of 4 days or more.

Becketts

Pylegate Farm, Hartfield Road, Cowden, Edenbridge TN8 7HE t +44 (0) 1342 850514
e jacqui@becketts-bandb.co.uk

becketts-bandb.co.uk SPECIAL OFFERS · REAL-TIME BOOKING

open All year except Christmas
bedrooms 1 double, 2 twin
bathrooms All en suite
payment Credit/debit cards, cash, cheques, euros

Beautiful, character 300-year-old barn with vaulted dining room and beams throughout, set in glorious countryside. Antique four-poster bed. All rooms en suite. Hever Castle, Penshurst and Chartwell all within four miles. Many other NT properties. Great walking and cycling. Cosy pubs with good food nearby. Wireless broadband. Online booking.

SAT NAV *TN8 7HE* **ONLINE MAP**

Room 🚿📶 TV 🛁🍵 General 🛎️🏠P 📶🔥🍴❄ Leisure ▶

HIGH WYCOMBE, Buckinghamshire Map ref 2C2

★★★★
BED & BREAKFAST
SILVER AWARD

B&B PER ROOM PER NIGHT
S £40.00–£50.00
D £55.00–£65.00

9 Green Road

High Wycombe HP13 5BD t +44 (0) 1494 437022

lovetostayat9.co.uk

Quiet family home with ample off-street parking. Rooms furnished to a high standard with power showers in all bathrooms. Full English breakfast. Easy access to M40 and M25. Family occupancy from £75.00 per night.

open All year except Christmas and New Year
bedrooms 2 double
bathrooms 1 en suite, 1 private
payment Credit/debit cards, cash, cheques

Room TV 🛁🍵 General 🛎️🏠🚶P 📶🔥❄

HOOK, Hampshire Map ref 2C2

★★★★
HOTEL
GOLD AWARD

B&B PER ROOM PER NIGHT
S £155.00–£450.00
D £205.00–£500.00
HB PER PERSON PER NIGHT
£185.00 £180.00

Promotions during 2009 include musical events, seasonal packages and gourmet evenings. Please visit our website for more information.

Tylney Hall Hotel

Tylney Hall, Rotherwick, Hook RG27 9AZ t +44 (0) 1256 764881 e sales@tylneyhall.com

tylneyhall.com SPECIAL OFFERS · REAL-TIME BOOKING

open All year
bedrooms 59 double, 23 twin, 1 family, 29 suites
bathrooms All en suite
payment Credit/debit cards, cash, cheques, euros

Set in 66 acres of historic gardens and parkland, Tylney Hall is in an idyllic location. With elegant lounges, exquisite bedrooms, breathtaking views, leisure and beauty facilities, Tylney Hall truly is a country-house hotel of distinction. Perfect for romantic getaways to seasonal breaks.

SAT NAV *RG27 9AZ* **ONLINE MAP**

Room 🚿📶📞 TV SC 🛁🍵🔥 General 🛎️🏠🚶P🍽️🍴◐🖥️🍴❄
Leisure 🎣🏓🎱🎯🎾♾️⚓▶🚴

HORSHAM, West Sussex Map ref 2D2 — SELF CATERING

★★★★
SELF CATERING

Units **1**
Sleeps **2–4**

LOW SEASON PER WK
£325.00–£400.00

HIGH SEASON PER WK
£550.00–£600.00

The Lodge, Two Mile Ash Road, Horsham

contact Mrs S Young, Ash Place Cottage, Two Mile Ash Road, Horsham RH13 0PG
t +44 (0) 1403 731329 e richard.young6@btinternet.com

thelodgecottage.co.uk GUEST REVIEWS

open All year
payment Cash, cheques, euros
nearest pub less than 0.5 miles
nearest shop 1 mile

The Lodge is a charming self-catering holiday cottage full of character with a splash of contemporary living. Exposed oak timber a feature throughout. Set in the heart of West Sussex countryside overlooking a small lake. Close to the Downs Link, walks and cycle routes. Horsham three miles.

SAT NAV RH13 0PG **ONLINE MAP**

Unit TV 🖭 🖵 🖳 🖰 🔌 🗇 🍽 🗓 ❄ General ☎12 P S Leisure U ➘ ⚲

HOVE

See under Brighton & Hove

HYTHE, Hampshire Map ref 2C3 — SELF CATERING

★★★★
SELF CATERING

Units **1**
Sleeps **10**

LOW SEASON PER WK
£600.00–£800.00

HIGH SEASON PER WK
£1,000.00–£1,500.00

Weekend and short breaks available low season; also high season subject to availability. Reductions for 2-person occupancy.

Mullins, Hythe, New Forest

contact Ms Alison Percy, 9 Upper Mullins Lane, Hythe SO45 5AG t +44 (0) 23 8084 5556
e alison@the-percys.co.uk

holiday-newforest.co.uk GUEST REVIEWS · SPECIAL OFFERS

open All year
payment Cash, cheques
nearest pub 0.5 miles
nearest shop 0.5 miles

Sunny house, sleeps eight to ten, private heated pool, countryside views, ample parking, four large bedrooms, three bath/shower rooms, sitting room with log fire, piano, modern and antique furniture. Nearby attractions: Beaulieu, Exbury Gardens, Lepe Beach, farmers' markets, woodland and heath walks.

Unit TV 🖭 🖵 🖳 🖰 🔌 🗇 🍽 🍳 🗓 ❄ 🏠 ✎ General ☎ 🛏 P ⊙ S Leisure ⟴ ⚑

ISLE OF WIGHT

See under Sandown, Shanklin, Ventnor, Wroxall

Don't forget www.

Web addresses throughout this guide are shown without the prefix www. Please include www. in the address line of your browser.
If a web address does not follow this style it is shown in full.

KINGHAM, Oxfordshire Map ref 2B1 — CAMPING, CARAVAN & HOLIDAY PARK

★★★★★
HOLIDAY PARK
ROSE AWARD

🏕 (30) £420.00–£1,125.00

> Prices from £61 per night.

Bluewood Park

Kingham, Chipping Norton OX7 6UJ t +44 (0) 1608 659946 e rachel@bluewoodpark.com

bluewoodpark.com GUEST REVIEWS · SPECIAL OFFERS · REAL-TIME BOOKING

open All year
payment Credit/debit cards, cash, cheques

Escape to Bluewood Park. Nestled in a bluebell wood in an Area of Outstanding Natural Beauty, the park is a superb base for exploring the Cotswolds. This exclusive development of luxury and contemporary accommodation, each with its own hot tub, is the perfect place to relax and unwind.

SAT NAV OX7 6UJ

General 🏚🐕 ⑨ Leisure ∪ ♪ ⚑ ⚙

KINGSDOWN, Kent Map ref 3C4 — CAMPING, CARAVAN & HOLIDAY PARK

★★★★★
HOLIDAY PARK

🏠 (50) £219.00–£677.00

Kingsdown Park Holiday Village

Upper Street, Kingsdown, Deal CT14 8AU t +44 (0) 1304 361205 e info@kingsdownpark.net

kingsdownpark.net SPECIAL OFFERS

This picturesque park provides the perfect base for exploring Kent. Comfortable lodges and excellent leisure facilities ensure you are not disappointed.

open March to October and 20 December to 3 January
payment Credit/debit cards, cash, cheques

General 🏚🖥 ✕ ☼ ⑨ Leisure ⚛ ♉ ⚫ ⚗ ⚘ ∪ ♪ ⚑ ⚙

LOWER ARNCOTT, Oxfordshire Map ref 2C1 — HOTEL

★★★
HOTEL

B&B PER ROOM PER NIGHT
S £74.00–£89.00
D £87.00–£98.00

> Stay for 2 nights – mention this advert and get a further 10% off our weekend rate.

Tally Ho Hotel Bar Restaurant

Ploughley Road, Bicester OX25 1NY t +44 (0) 1869 247170 e reception@tallyhotel.com

tallyhotel.com

open All year
bedrooms 11 double, 10 twin, 4 single, 1 family
bathrooms All en suite
payment Credit/debit cards, cash, cheques

This former farmhouse, situated 14 miles from Blenheim Palace and five miles from Bicester's famous designer shopping village, offers a friendly, welcoming atmosphere. Accommodation is spacious, yet cosy, comprehensively equipped and disabled-friendly. Enjoy a pre-dinner drink in our licensed residents' lounge. The food is prepared using the best local produce.

SAT NAV OX25 1NY

Room 🖥 ☎ 📺 💧 🍽 ♿ General 🛋 🎱 🅿 ♉ 🎮 ⬚ 🅟 ❄ 🐕 Leisure ∪ ⚑

MAIDENHEAD, Berkshire Map ref 2C2 — HOTEL

★★
HOTEL

B&B PER ROOM PER NIGHT
S £55.00–£95.00
D £70.00–£108.00

Elva Lodge Hotel

Castle Hill, Maidenhead SL6 4AD t +44 (0) 1628 622948 e reservations@elvalodgehotel.co.uk

elvalodgehotel.co.uk GUEST REVIEWS · REAL-TIME BOOKING

Well-appointed rooms. Ideally located for motorway network access and tourist attractions of Legoland, Windsor Castle, Ascot and Henley. Professional service in a relaxed family atmosphere.

open All year except Christmas
bedrooms 12 double, 13 single, 1 family
bathrooms 23 en suite, 3 private
payment Credit/debit cards, cash, cheques

Room 🖥 ☎ 📺 💧 🍽 ♿ General 🛋 🎱 🅿 ♉ 🎮 ⬚ 🅟 ❄ 🐕 Leisure ⚑

MAIDSTONE, Kent Map ref 3B3

★★★★
**BED & BREAKFAST
SILVER AWARD**

B&B PER ROOM PER NIGHT
S £35.00–£40.00
D £60.00–£65.00

Grove House

Grove Green Road, Maidstone ME14 5JT t +44 (0) 1622 738441

open All year except Christmas and New Year
bedrooms 1 double, 1 twin
bathrooms 1 en suite, 1 private
payment Credit/debit cards, cash, cheques

Attractive comfortable detached house in quiet road.
Off-street parking. Close to Leeds Castle, pubs,
restaurants, M20 and M2 motorways.

SAT NAV ME14 5JT

Room 📺 ♿ 🥤 General **P** Leisure ▶

MARDEN, Kent Map ref 3B4

★★★★
FARMHOUSE

B&B PER ROOM PER NIGHT
S Min £45.00
D £55.00–£60.00

Tanner House

Tanner Farm, Goudhurst Road, Tonbridge TN12 9ND t +44 (0) 1622 831214
e enquiries@tannerfarmpark.co.uk

tannerfarmpark.co.uk

Tudor farmhouse in centre of family farm. Good
access in secluded, rural position. Shire horses
kept on farm. Also, award-winning caravan and
camping park.

open All year except Christmas
bedrooms 1 double, 2 twin
bathrooms All en suite
payment Credit/debit cards, cash, cheques,
euros

Room 🖥 📺 ♿ 🥤 General 🕭12 **P** 📶 🔥 🍴 🖥 ❄ Leisure ♪

MARLOW, Buckinghamshire Map ref 2C2

★★★★★
INN

B&B PER ROOM PER NIGHT
D £140.00–£190.00

EVENING MEAL PER PERSON
£27.50–£35.50

The Hand and Flowers

West Street, Marlow SL7 2BP t +44 (0) 1628 482277

thehandandflowers.co.uk

open All year except Christmas
bedrooms 4 double
bathrooms All en suite
payment Credit/debit cards, cash, cheques

Cottages are described as quirky and luxurious,
perfect for a romantic weekend or as an escape from
the city. Enjoy a short walk to the river or relax in the
spa. Have breakfast in bed or full English in our pub.

SAT NAV SL7 2BP **ONLINE MAP**

Room 🔥 🖥 📞 📺 🆂🅲 🥤 General ⚡ **P** 📶 ✕ 🍴 🐕

MILTON KEYNES, Buckinghamshire Map ref 2C1   **GUEST ACCOMMODATION**

★★★
FARMHOUSE

B&B PER ROOM PER NIGHT
S £30.00–£40.00
D £60.00–£70.00

Chantry Farm

Pindon End, Hanslope, Milton Keynes MK19 7HL t +44 (0) 1908 510269 e chuff.wake@tiscali.co.uk

chantryfarmbandb.com GUEST REVIEWS

A 600-acre friendly working farm. Old stone farmhouse (1650) with inglenook fireplace, in beautiful countryside overlooking lake. Near Milton Keynes, London train 40 minutes. Convenient for Northampton, Silverstone, Woburn Abbey.

open All year except Christmas and New Year
bedrooms 1 double, 2 twin
bathrooms 1 en suite
payment Cash, cheques, euros

Room 📺 ☕ 🍷 General 🛏 ▥ ♿ P ⊛ ❄ 🐾 Leisure ⟁ ⚓ ►

NEW FOREST

See under Burley, Cadnam, Fordingbridge, Hythe, New Milton, Ringwood, Sway

---

NEW MILTON, Hampshire Map ref 2B3   **GUEST ACCOMMODATION**

★★★★
**BED & BREAKFAST
SILVER AWARD**

B&B PER ROOM PER NIGHT
S £34.00–£45.00
D £58.00–£66.00

Winter discounts (excl Bank Holidays). Discount for more than 7 days.

Taverners Cottage

Bashley Cross Road, Bashley, New Milton BH25 5SZ t +44 (0) 1425 615403
e judith@tavernerscottage.co.uk

tavernerscottage.co.uk

open All year except Christmas and New Year
bedrooms 1 double, 1 family
bathrooms All en suite
payment Cash, cheques, euros

Attractive 300-year-old cob cottage overlooking open farmland. Warm welcome guaranteed. Great breakfasts. Care and attention to detail a priority. Ideal for touring, golf, cycling, walking and riding.

SAT NAV *BH25 5SZ* **ONLINE MAP**

Room ♿ 📺 ☕ 🍷 General 🛏 ▥ ♿ P ⊛ 🛏 🐾 Leisure ∪ ⚓ 🚴

NEWBURY, Berkshire Map ref 2C2   **GUEST ACCOMMODATION**

★★★★
GUEST ACCOMMODATION

B&B PER ROOM PER NIGHT
S £40.00–£45.00
D £68.00–£80.00

Packages available for riders, walkers and cyclists, including stabling/ grazing, meals and luggage drop-off service.

East End Farm

East End, Newbury RG20 0AB t +44 (0) 1635 254895 e mp@eastendfarm.co.uk

eastendfarm.co.uk

open All year
bedrooms 1 double, 1 twin
bathrooms All en suite
payment Cash, cheques, euros

Five miles south of Newbury, in an Area of Outstanding Natural Beauty, this small working farm will give you a warm welcome. Accommodation is in a beautifully converted barn. Choice of breakfasts with home-made and local produce. Ideal base for country lovers or stopover for business or travel.

SAT NAV *RG20 0AB*

Room ♿ 📺 ☕ 🍷 General 🛏 ▥ ♿ P ⊛ ✕ 🛏 ❄ 🐾 Leisure ⟁ ↻ ∪ ⚓ ►

Check the maps for accommodation locations

Colour maps at the front pinpoint all the places where accommodation is featured within the regional sections of this guide. Pick your location and then refer to the place index at the back to find the page number.

NEWHAVEN, East Sussex Map ref 2D3 — GUEST ACCOMMODATION

★★★
GUEST HOUSE

B&B PER ROOM PER NIGHT
S £29.00–£35.00
D £54.00–£64.00

Newhaven Lodge Guest House

12 Brighton Road, Newhaven BN9 9NB t +44 (0) 1273 513736 e newhavenlodge@aol.com

newhavenlodge.co.uk GUEST REVIEWS

A comfortable, bright, family-run establishment located close to the Newhaven/Dieppe ferry terminal. Brighton, Lewes and South Downs nearby. The establishment motto is 'Arrive as a guest and leave as a friend'.

open All year
bedrooms 1 double, 2 single, 3 family
bathrooms 4 en suite
payment Credit/debit cards, cash, cheques, euros

Room ♿ TV 🛇 ⬚ General ⌂ ⊞ ♿ P ❉ 🐾 Leisure ∪ ♪ ⚐ ⚲

OXFORD, Oxfordshire Map ref 2C1 — HOTEL

★★
METRO HOTEL

B&B PER ROOM PER NIGHT
S £70.00–£75.00
D £80.00–£90.00

River Hotel

17 Botley Road, Oxford OX2 0AA t +44 (0) 1865 243475 e reception@riverhotel.co.uk

riverhotel.co.uk

open All year except Christmas and New Year
bedrooms 9 double, 2 twin, 4 single, 5 family
bathrooms 18 en suite, 2 private
payment Credit/debit cards, cash, cheques

Picturesque location beside Osney Bridge on the Thames Path. Originally a master builder's home built c1870s, later run as a small, independent hotel. The property is owned by an Oxford college. Well equipped rooms. Family rooms also let as double or twin occupancy. Car park on site. Easy walk to city, attractions and many restaurants.

SAT NAV OX2 0AA

Room ☎ TV 🛇 ⬚ ✉ General ⌂ 5 ♿ P ♟ ⚐ ❉ Leisure ⚐ ⚲

OXFORD, Oxfordshire Map ref 2C1 — GUEST ACCOMMODATION

★★★★
GUEST HOUSE

B&B PER ROOM PER NIGHT
S £65.00–£85.00
D £95.00–£130.00

The Buttery

11-12 Broad Street, Oxford OX1 3AP t +44 (0) 1865 811950 e enquiries@thebutteryhotel.co.uk

thebutteryhotel.co.uk

Set on Broad Street, surrounded by historic Oxford colleges and museums, The Buttery welcomes you to explore the wonders of Oxford from its central location. Spacious well-furnished en suite rooms.

open All year
bedrooms 10 double, 2 twin, 1 single, 3 family
bathrooms All en suite
payment Credit/debit cards, cash, cheques, euros

Room ☎ TV 🛇 ⬚ General ⌂ ⊞ ♿ ✉ Leisure ⚲

OXFORD, Oxfordshire Map ref 2C1 — GUEST ACCOMMODATION

★★★★
GUEST HOUSE

B&B PER ROOM PER NIGHT
S £30.00–£55.00
D £70.00–£90.00

Pickwick's Guest House

15-17 London Road, Headington, Oxford OX3 7SP t +44 (0) 1865 750487 e pickwicks@tiscali.co.uk

pickwicksguesthouse.co.uk

open All year except Christmas and New Year
bedrooms 4 double, 3 twin, 4 single, 4 family
bathrooms 13 en suite
payment Credit/debit cards, cash, cheques

Comfortable guesthouse within easy reach of Oxford's universities and hospitals. Nearby coach stop for 24-hour service to central London, Heathrow, Gatwick and Stansted Airports. Free car parking and Wi-Fi internet. Please contact us for family room rates.

SAT NAV OX3 7SP **ONLINE MAP**

Room ♿ ☎ TV 🛇 ⬚ General ⌂ ⊞ ♿ P 📶 ✉ ♟ ❉ 🐾

PLAXTOL, Kent Map ref 2D2

★★★
SELF CATERING

Units **1**
Sleeps **1–6**

LOW SEASON PER WK
£250.00–£340.00

HIGH SEASON PER WK
£280.00–£430.00

Golding Hop Farm Cottage, Sevenoaks

contact Mrs Jacqueline Vincent, Golding Hop Farm, Bewley Lane, Plaxtol, Sevenoaks TN15 0PS
t +44 (0) 1732 885432 e info@goldinghopfarm.com

goldinghopfarm.com

South-facing cottage on 12-acre cobnut farm. Quiet position but not isolated. Three bedrooms (two twin, one single), garden, all modern conveniences.

open All year
payment Cash, cheques
nearest pub less than 0.5 miles
nearest shop 1.5 miles

Unit 📺 🎮 💻 📀 🍳 🔲 ✳️ General ♨️ ♨️ P 🐕 Leisure U

PLUCKLEY, Kent Map ref 3B4

★★★★
GUEST ACCOMMODATION

B&B PER ROOM PER NIGHT
S £64.00–£84.00
D £80.00–£140.00

EVENING MEAL PER PERSON
£19.95–£23.95

Elvey Farm

Elvey Lane, Ashford TN27 0SU t +44 (0) 1233 840442 e bookings@elveyfarm.co.uk

elveyfarm.co.uk GUEST REVIEWS · SPECIAL OFFERS · REAL-TIME BOOKING

open All year
bedrooms 1 double, 2 family, 4 suites
bathrooms All en suite
payment Credit/debit cards, cash, cheques

Medieval farmstead set in 75 acres in the heart of Darling Buds of May country. Suites in stable block and 16thC barn, packed with period features and stylish, contemporary en suites. Private entrances and living rooms. Stunning Kentish restaurant.

SAT NAV TN27 0SU ONLINE MAP

Room 🛗 📺 SC ☕ 🍳 General ♨️ P 🐾 🍽️ ✳️ 🐕 Leisure U

PORTSMOUTH, Hampshire Map ref 2C3

★★★★
SELF CATERING

Units **1**
Sleeps **5**

LOW SEASON PER WK
£290.00–£400.00

HIGH SEASON PER WK
£400.00–£690.00

3-day breaks considered. 2 weeks+ bookings receive a discount. Christmas tree at Christmas and Easter eggs for Easter.

Cowes View, Coastguard Cottages, Hill Head

contact Mrs Melanie Vennis
t +44 (0) 1329 664236 e enquiries@cowesview.co.uk

cowesview.co.uk

open All year
payment Cash, cheques, euros
nearest pub less than 0.5 miles
nearest shop 1.5 miles

Cowes View is a delightful seaside cottage in a slightly elevated position overlooking the beach, with private access and enjoying fantastic panoramic views across the Solent to the Isle of Wight. Ideally located to visit historic Portsmouth, Southampton, New Forest and all of the heritage, countryside and culture of Hampshire.

SAT NAV PO14 3JJ ONLINE MAP

Unit 📺 SC 💻 🍳 🔲 ✳️ General ♨️ ♨️ S Leisure ♪ ⚓

Need some ideas?

Big city buzz or peaceful panoramas? Take a fresh look at England and you may be surprised at what's right on your doorstep. Explore the diversity online at enjoyengland.com

RAMSGATE, Kent Map ref 3C3 — SELF CATERING

★★★★
SELF CATERING

Units	1
Sleeps	6

LOW SEASON PER WK
£350.00–£450.00

HIGH SEASON PER WK
£450.00–£650.00

Short breaks available from 2 nights upwards at discounted rates.

Harbour Cottage, Ramsgate

The Property Management Company, 8 Military Road, Ramsgate CT11 9LG t +44 (0) 1843 596663
e enquiries@ramsgatecottage.co.uk

ramsgatecottage.co.uk SPECIAL OFFERS

open All year
payment Credit/debit cards, cash, cheques
nearest pub less than 0.5 miles
nearest shop less than 0.5 miles

Elegant, whitewashed period cottage, refurbished t the highest standards, set in Ramsgate's picturesqu conservation area. Only two minutes' walk to the beach, harbour, shops and restaurants. One twin an two double bedrooms, two bathrooms, fully equipped kitchen/breakfast room, separate living and dining rooms. Two gardens and private off-street parking.

ONLINE MAP

Unit 📺 🄪 🄬 🖥 🗄 🗃 ⛁ 🍳 🍽 🕯 ✻ ⌀ General 🛏4 🏃 P 🄿 🄢
Leisure ∪ ♪ ► 🚲

READING, Berkshire Map ref 2C2 — CAMPING, CARAVAN & HOLIDAY PARK

★★★★
TOURING & CAMPING PARK

🚐 (58)	£15.00–£22.00
🚍 (58)	£15.00–£22.00
⛺ (14)	£13.00–£18.00
58 touring pitches	

Wellington Country Park

Odiham Road, Riseley, Reading RG7 1SP t +44 (0) 118 932 6444
e info@wellington-country-park.co.uk

wellington-country-park.co.uk REAL-TIME BOOKING

A wealth of enjoyment. Nature trails, children's play areas, miniature railway, crazy golf. Special events throughout the season.

open February to November
payment Credit/debit cards

General 🖥 🚲 🔌 👶 🚻 🚿 📷 ⚖ ✕ 🐕 ☼ Leisure ⚖ ∪

REDHILL, Surrey Map ref 2D2 — CAMPING, CARAVAN & HOLIDAY PARK

★★★★
TOURING PARK

🚐 (150)	£12.20–£25.10
🚍 (150)	£12.20–£25.10
150 touring pitches	

THE
CARAVAN
CLUB

Alderstead Heath Caravan Club Site

Dean Lane, Redhill RH1 3AH t +44 (0) 1737 644629

caravanclub.co.uk

open All year
payment Credit/debit cards, cash, cheques

Quiet site with views over rolling, wooded North Downs. Denbies Wine Estate nearby. For day trips try Chessington and Thorpe Park and the lively city of Brighton. Non-members welcome.

SAT NAV RH1 3AH

Special member rates mean you can save your membership subscription in less than a week. Visit our website to find out more.

General 🖥 🔌 🚰 👶 🔌 📷 📷 🐕 ☼ 📶 Leisure ⚖ ►

Where can I get help and advice?

Tourist Information Centres offer friendly help with accommodation and holiday ideas as well as suggestions of places to visit and things to do. You'll find contact details at the beginning of each regional section.

RINGWOOD, Hampshire Map ref 2B3
CAMPING, CARAVAN & HOLIDAY PARK

★★★★
**TOURING &
CAMPING PARK**

🚐(150) £16.50–£27.00
🚐(150) £16.50–£27.00
⛺(150) £16.50–£27.00
150 touring pitches

Shamba Holidays
230 Ringwood Road, St Leonards, Ringwood BH24 2SB t +44 (0) 1202 873302
e enquiries@shambaholidays.co.uk

shambaholidays.co.uk

Family-run touring and camping park close to the New Forest and Bournemouth with its fine beaches. Modern toilet/shower facilities, heated indoor/outdoor pool, licensed clubhouse, games room, takeaway, shop.

open March to October
payment Credit/debit cards, cash, cheques

General 🚬🚗🆑♿🖥🛗🏧🛢🐕☀ Leisure 🎣🏹♟🔍⛰∪♪▶

ROCHESTER, Kent Map ref 3B3
SELF CATERING

★★★★
SELF CATERING

Units   **6**
Sleeps   **5–8**

LOW SEASON PER WK
£300.00–£500.00

HIGH SEASON PER WK
£550.00–£800.00

*Short breaks and
split weeks available.*

Stable Cottages, Rochester
contact Mrs Debbie Symonds, Stable Cottages, Fenn Croft, Newland Farm Road, St Mary Hoo, Rochester ME3 8QS t +44 (0) 1634 272439 & +44 (0) 7802 662702 e stablecottages@btinternet.com

stable-cottages.com

open All year
payment Cash, cheques
nearest pub 1 mile
nearest shop 3 miles

These luxury, oak-beamed cottages are set in 20 acres of secluded farmland close to RSPB reserve with panoramic views of the Thames. Access to motorways and ports. London/Canterbury 45 minutes. Perfect base for walking, bird-watching, sightseeing or just getting away from it all. Warm welcome. Family run. Indoor pool.

Unit 📺📷📀🎚🎮🍴🧺✳ General 🛋🛏♿P🅿🆂🐕 Leisure 🎣🔍

ROYAL TUNBRIDGE WELLS, Kent Map ref 2D2
HOTEL

★★★★
**HOTEL
SILVER AWARD**

B&B PER ROOM PER NIGHT
S £99.00–£125.00
D £145.00–£185.00
HB PER PERSON PER NIGHT
£120.50–£155.00

*See website or call
hotel for latest
promotional offers.*

The Spa Hotel
Mount Ephraim, Royal Tunbridge Wells TN4 8XJ t +44 (0) 1892 520331
e reservations@spahotel.co.uk

spahotel.co.uk SPECIAL OFFERS · REAL-TIME BOOKING

open All year
bedrooms 34 double, 22 twin, 5 single, 3 family, 5 suites
bathrooms All en suite
payment Credit/debit cards, cash, cheques, euros

Elegant mansion set in 14 acres of grounds. Classical Chandelier Restaurant, new Zagatos Champagne Bar, relaxing lounge, leisure club and pool with Spa Spa treatment rooms and comfortable well-appointed bedrooms. Superb ballroom and meeting facilities. The hotel is ideally located, only a short walk to the town centre.

SAT NAV *TN4 8XJ* **ONLINE MAP**

Room 🛏🖥📞📺🍴🎚✎ General 🛋🛏♿P📶♟🍴🎱🍷✉📶⬚🛢✱
Leisure 🎣🏊🎾⊗🎾♪▶🚴

It's all quality-assessed accommodation
Our commitment to quality involves wide-ranging accommodation assessment.
Ratings and awards were correct at the time of going to press but may change
following a new assessment. Please check at time of booking.

★★★★
GUEST ACCOMMODATION

B&B PER ROOM PER NIGHT
S Max £68.50
D Max £97.00

EVENING MEAL PER PERSON
£10.00–£28.00

The Beacon

Tea Garden Lane, Tunbridge Wells TN3 9JH t +44 (0) 1892 524252
e beaconhotel@btopenworld.com

the-beacon.co.uk

open All year
bedrooms 2 double, 1 single
bathrooms All en suite
payment Credit/debit cards, cash, cheques

Situated 1.5 miles from Tunbridge Wells, The Beacon, with its magnificent views and reputation for excellent cuisine and friendly, welcoming atmosphere, offers delightfully unique bedrooms – the Colonial (double), the Georgian (double) and the Contemporary (single) – each one attractively designed to make your stay a memorable one.

SAT NAV TN3 9JH

Room 📞 📺 🍵   General ♿ ♯ P ♇ ✕ 🛏 ❄   Leisure ♪ ►

★★★★★
BED & BREAKFAST

B&B PER ROOM PER NIGHT
S £55.00–£65.00
D £80.00–£100.00

EVENING MEAL PER PERSON
£20.00–£30.00

Discounts on stays of 3 days or more (excluding Saturdays).

Hayden's

108 High Street, Rye TN31 7JE t +44 (0) 1797 224501 e richard.hayden@mac.com

cheynehouse.co.uk

open All year except Christmas
bedrooms 2 double
bathrooms All en suite
payment Credit/debit cards, cash, cheques

Hayden's is a small, family-run, eco-friendly B&B and restaurant in the heart of the ancient town of Rye, set in a beautiful 18thC town house. Visitors can enjoy home cooking using organic local produce while gazing out at panoramic views across the Romney Marsh.

SAT NAV TN31 7JE

Room 📺 🍵 ☕   General ♯ ♇ 🛏 ❄   Leisure ∪ ♪ ► ♺

★★★★
GUEST ACCOMMODATION
SILVER AWARD

B&B PER ROOM PER NIGHT
D £65.00–£120.00

EVENING MEAL PER PERSON
Min £27.50

Christmas and New Year house party. Dinner, bed and breakfast special offers. Licensed for weddings and civil partnerships.

Strand House

Strand House, Tanyards Lane, The Strand, Winchelsea TN36 4JT t +44 (0) 1797 226276
e info@thestrandhouse.co.uk

thestrandhouse.co.uk GUEST REVIEWS · SPECIAL OFFERS · REAL-TIME BOOKING

open All year
bedrooms 7 double, 1 twin, 2 family
bathrooms 9 en suite, 1 private
payment Credit/debit cards, cash, cheques, euros

A Tudor house with rooms full of character with an inglenook fireplace in the lounge. Food is the heart of the house with Sussex breakfast, tea on the lawn and evening dinner. Explore the many houses and gardens in the area. A house of calm to while away the hours.

SAT NAV TN36 4JT **ONLINE MAP**

Room ♿ 📠 📺 🍵 ☕   General ♿5 🛏 P 📶 ♫ ♇ ✕ 🛏 ❄ 🐴   Leisure ∪ ♪ ► ♺

What if I need to cancel?

It's advisable to check the proprietor's cancellation policy at the time of booking in case you have to change your plans.

SANDHURST, Kent Map ref 3B4

★★★★
SELF CATERING

Units **1**
Sleeps **1–4**

LOW SEASON PER WK
£295.00–£395.00

HIGH SEASON PER WK
£395.00–£495.00

Short breaks subject to availability.

Granary Cottage, Sandhurst, Cranbrook

contact Mary Le Pla, Court Lodge Farm, Bodiam, Robertsbridge TN32 5UJ **t** +44 (0) 1580 830710 & +44 (0) 7733 340358 **e** office@sterlingquarterhorses.com

open All year
payment Credit/debit cards, cash, cheques, euros
nearest pub 1.2 miles
nearest shop 1.2 miles

Delightful two-bedroom single-storey cottage in idyllic farm location on a working arable and stud farm on the Kent/Sussex border. The property enjoys far-reaching views across the Rother Valley. Ideal base for walkers and families with children. Convenient for many National Trust properties and the coast.

SAT NAV *TN18 5NX*

Unit 📺 🖥 📠 🍳🔥 🥘 🔆 General ⛵🛏🚶P🅂

SANDOWN, Isle of Wight Map ref 2C3

★★★
GUEST ACCOMMODATION

B&B PER ROOM PER NIGHT
S £23.00–£29.00
D £46.00–£58.00

The Montpelier

Pier Street, Sandown PO36 8JR **t** +44 (0) 1983 403964 **e** enquiries@themontpelier.co.uk

themontpelier.co.uk

The Montpelier is situated opposite the pier and beaches with the high street just around the corner. We offer B&B, room-only and ferry-inclusive packages. Sea views available.

open All year
bedrooms 3 double, 2 twin, 1 single, 2 family
bathrooms All en suite
payment Credit/debit cards, cash, cheques

Room 📺 ♿ General ⛵🛏🔆

SHANKLIN, Isle of Wight Map ref 2C3

★★
HOTEL

B&B PER ROOM PER NIGHT
S £30.00–£50.00
D £60.00–£100.00
HB PER PERSON PER NIGHT
£40.00–£60.00

Excellent-value, ferry-inclusive breaks available Oct-May. Christmas and New Year packages. Discounts on ferry prices all year.

Orchardcroft Hotel

Victoria Avenue, Shanklin PO37 6LT **t** +44 (0) 1983 862133

open All year
bedrooms 7 double, 3 twin, 2 single, 4 family
bathrooms All en suite
payment Credit/debit cards, cash, cheques, euros

This elegant but friendly hotel has a private leisure complex, secluded gardens, and a reputation for good food and service. 'A very family-friendly hotel who do all they can to ensure a pleasant stay. Friendly staff, good food and wonderful pool and games facilities' – Hazel and Darren, London.

SAT NAV *PO37 6LT*

Room 🖥📺♿🍳 General ⛵🛏🚶P🅿♨🍷🍽🎱🎱🔆🐾
Leisure 🎣🏊U🎵🏃🚴

SHANKLIN, Isle of Wight Map ref 2C3

★★★
GUEST ACCOMMODATION

B&B PER ROOM PER NIGHT
S £25.00–£35.00
D £50.00–£70.00

The Palmerston

16 Palmerston Road, Shanklin PO37 6AS **t** +44 (0) 1983 865547 **e** info@palmerston-hotel.co.uk

palmerston-hotel.co.uk

Located in an ideal position in Shanklin just a few minutes' walk to the beach, town centre and Old Village. A family-run hotel offering a friendly and attentive service.

open All year
bedrooms 3 double, 1 twin, 1 single, 2 family, 1 suite
bathrooms All en suite
payment Credit/debit cards, cash, cheques

Room 📺♿🍳 General ⛵🛏🚶P🅿🍷✕🍽🔆🐾 Leisure U🎵🏃🚴

★★★
SELF CATERING

Units **7**
Sleeps **1–6**

LOW SEASON PER WK
£220.00–£480.00

HIGH SEASON PER WK
£400.00–£810.00

Luccombe Villa, Shanklin

contact Mrs Fiona Seymour, Luccombe Villa, 9 Popham Road, Shanklin PO37 6RF
t +44 (0) 1983 862825 e info@luccombevilla.co.uk

luccombevilla.co.uk SPECIAL OFFERS

open All year
payment Cash, cheques
nearest pub less than 0.5 miles
nearest shop less than 0.5 miles

Seven self-contained holiday apartments in Shanklin
Old Village. One to three bedrooms many with en
suite facilities. Comfortably furnished with digital TV
and DVD players. Well-equipped kitchens and
separate laundry room. Plenty of parking.

SAT NAV PO37 6RF

Unit ▣▣▣▣▣▣▣▣▣▣ General ▣▣▣P▣ Leisure ▣U▣▣

See under Portsmouth

★★★★★
TOURING &
CAMPING PARK

▣ (37) £15.90–£25.90
▣ (37) £15.90–£25.90
▲ (16) £14.90–£21.90
90 touring pitches

Lincoln Farm Park

High Street, Standlake OX29 7RH t +44 (0) 1865 300239 e info@lincolnfarm.co.uk

lincolnfarmpark.co.uk GUEST REVIEWS · REAL-TIME BOOKING

open All year except Christmas and New Year
payment Credit/debit cards, cash, cheques, euros

Award-winning park situated in the village of
Standlake with two village pubs, each serving food.
Our immaculate facilities comprise two indoor heated
pools, spas, saunas, steam room, children's pool,
launderette, campers' kitchen, family bathroom,
central heating. A bus stops at the park entrance for
those wishing to visit historic Oxford.

SAT NAV OX29 7RH ONLINE MAP

General ▣▣▣▣▣▣▣▣▣▣▣▣▣ Leisure ▣▣U▣

★★★★
FARMHOUSE
SILVER AWARD

B&B PER ROOM PER NIGHT
S £35.00–£65.00
D £50.00–£80.00

Great Field Farm

Misling Lane, Stelling Minnis, Canterbury CT4 6DE t +44 (0) 1227 709223 e Greatfieldfarm@aol.com

great-field-farm.co.uk GUEST REVIEWS

Delightful farmhouse set amidst lovely gardens
and countryside. Spacious, private suites; B&B or
self-catering. Hearty breakfasts with home-grown
fruits and eggs. Ten minutes to Canterbury/
Channel Tunnel.

open All year
bedrooms 2 double, 1 twin
bathrooms All en suite
payment Credit/debit cards, cash, cheques,
euros

Room ▣▣▣▣ General ▣▣▣P▣▣ Leisure U

Remember to check when booking

Please remember that all information in this guide has been supplied by the
proprietors well in advance of publication. Since changes do sometimes occur it's a
good idea to check details at the time of booking.

SWANLEY, Kent Map ref 2D2 GUEST ACCOMMODATION

★★★★
BED & BREAKFAST

B&B PER ROOM PER NIGHT
S Max £40.00
D Max £80.00

Greenacres

15 Greenacre Close, Swanley BR8 8HT t +44 (0) 1322 613656 e pauline.snow1@btinternet.com

greenacrebandb.co.uk

open All year except Christmas and New Year
bedrooms 1 double, 1 twin
bathrooms 2 private
payment Cash, cheques

Quality ground-floor annexe, double and twin rooms with private bathroom and private garden, kitchen with fridge and microwave, private conservatory. Four miles Brands Hatch, close Bluewater shopping centre.

SAT NAV BR8 8HT

Room ♿ TV SC ♨ ⚲ General ⌸ P ⟨⟩ ❋

SWAY, Hampshire Map ref 2C3 HOTEL

★★★
HOTEL

B&B PER ROOM PER NIGHT
S £66.50–£69.50
D £115.00–£121.00
HB PER PERSON PER NIGHT
£89.50–£92.50

3 nights for the price of 2, or 5 nights for the price of 3, Oct–Apr (excl Christmas).

Sway Manor Restaurant & Hotel

Station Road, Sway, Lymington SO41 6BA t +44 (0) 1590 682754 e info@swaymanor.com

swaymanor.com

open All year
bedrooms 7 double, 3 twin, 3 single, 2 family
bathrooms All en suite
payment Credit/debit cards, cash, cheques

Family-run Edwardian country house in the New Forest National Park. In the centre of Sway village, with five acres of grounds and large accessible car park, it is a good base for exploring the Forest or coast. Comfortable, with a relaxed and friendly atmosphere, Sway Manor provides full restaurant facilities.

SAT NAV SO41 6BA **ONLINE MAP**

Room ☎ TV ♨ ⚲ General ⟿ ⌸ ♨ P ♟ ⟨⟩ ▣ ❋ ♘ Leisure ⚲ ∪ ♪ ⟩ ⚲

THAME, Oxfordshire Map ref 2C1 SELF CATERING

★★★★
SELF CATERING

Units **1**
Sleeps **6**

LOW SEASON PER WK
£380.00–£430.00

HIGH SEASON PER WK
£480.00

The Hollies, Thame

contact Ms Julia Tanner, Little Acre, 4 High Street, Tetsworth, Thame OX9 7AT
t +44 (0) 1844 281423 e info@theholliesthame.co.uk

theholliesthame.co.uk

Beautifully appointed four-bedroomed dorma bungalow with peaceful gardens, situated in a secluded backwater near the oldest part of Thame, five minutes' walk from the centre of our historic market town.

open All year
payment Cash, cheques
nearest pub less than 0.5 miles
nearest shop less than 0.5 miles

Unit TV ⟨⟩ DVD ▦ . ⊟ ⟨⟩ ⟨⟩ ⟐ ❋ General ⟿ P ♘ Leisure ∪ ♪ ⟩ ⚲

TUNBRIDGE WELLS

See under Royal Tunbridge Wells

CYCLISTS
WELCOME
WELCOME
CYCLISTS

Fancy a cycling holiday?

For a fabulous freewheeling break, seek out accommodation participating in our Cyclists Welcome scheme. Look out for the symbol and plan your route online at nationalcyclenetwork.org.

For **key to symbols** see pages 16 and 17

215

VENTNOR, Isle of Wight Map ref 2C3 — GUEST ACCOMMODATION

★★★★
GUEST HOUSE

B&B PER ROOM PER NIGHT
S £36.00–£41.00
D £72.00

Family suite £150.00. Rates are discounted for people staying 3 nights or more. All special promotions can be seen via our website.

Brunswick House

Victoria Street, Ventnor PO38 1ET **t** +44 (0) 1983 852656 **e** brunswick@unicombox.co.uk

brunswickhouse-web.co.uk SPECIAL OFFERS

open All year
bedrooms 2 double, 2 twin, 2 single, 1 family
bathrooms All en suite
payment Credit/debit cards, cash, cheques, euros

A family-run guesthouse, over 150 years old, but retaining its spacious Victorian character and, with it recent refurbishment, offering warm, comfortable and welcoming accommodation. Located in the hea of Ventnor, ideally situated for walking, cycling and the many places of interest locally and around the island. Additional en suite family room available.

SAT NAV *PO38 1ET* **ONLINE MAP**

Room 📺 ⛤ 🗊 General 🐾 🎫 👘 🍴 💺 ❄ 🐕

WINCHESTER, Hampshire Map ref 2C3 — GUEST ACCOMMODATION

★★★★★
**GUEST ACCOMMODATION
GOLD AWARD**

B&B PER ROOM PER NIGHT
S £69.00–£109.00
D £87.00–£115.00

Giffard House

50 Christchurch Road, Winchester SO23 9SU **t** +44 (0) 1962 852628 **e** giffardhotel@aol.com

giffardhotel.co.uk

open All year
bedrooms 6 double, 2 twin, 4 single, 1 suite
bathrooms All en suite
payment Credit/debit cards, cash, cheques, euros

A warm welcome awaits those who visit this stunning Victorian house, recently refurbished to the highest standard. Relax in crisp, white bed linen and in luxurious, en suite bathrooms. Start the day with a traditional breakfast in our elegant dining room. Ten minutes' walk to town centre.

SAT NAV *SO23 9SU* **ONLINE MAP**

Room 🛁 📞 📺 ⛤ 🗊 General 🐾 🎫 👘 P 📶 🎫 🍴 👘 💺 ❄ Leisure ∪ ⤵ ⟡ 🚲

WINCHESTER, Hampshire Map ref 2C3 — SELF CATERING

★★★★
SELF CATERING

Units **1**
Sleeps **3**

LOW SEASON PER WK
£425.00

HIGH SEASON PER WK
£595.00

Cathedral View, Winchester

contact Mrs Sue Wustefeld, Heron Cottage, Water Lane, Bishops Sutton SO24 0AL
t +44 (0) 1962 732422 & +44 (0) 7708 331132 **e** help@justasksue.co.uk

cathedral-view.co.uk

In the heart of medieval Winchester, close to shops, this house provides exceptionally comfortable accommodation for two in light rooms, traditionally furnished. Roof terrace affords stunning views over cathedral. Internet access.

open All year except Christmas and New Year
payment Cash, cheques, euros
nearest pub less than 0.5 miles
nearest shop less than 0.5 miles

Unit 📺 📼 🖥 📠 🗄 🗊 💿 🍽 🧺 ❄ General P ⊙ S Leisure ∪ ⤵ ⟡ 🚲

WALKERS WELCOME
WELCOME WALKERS

Do you like walking?

Walkers feel at home in accommodation participating in our Walkers Welcome scheme. Look out for the symbol. Consider walking all or part of a long-distance route – go online at nationaltrail.co.uk.

★★★★
SELF CATERING

| Units | 1 |
| Sleeps | 1–6 |

LOW SEASON PER WK
Min £300.00

HIGH SEASON PER WK
Max £700.00

3-night stay: Fri-Mon. 4-night stay: Mon-Fri.

The Old Dairy, Winchester

t +44 (0) 1962 868214 e joy_ann_waldron@hotmail.com

beechcroftfarmholiday.co.uk

open All year
payment Credit/debit cards, cash, cheques
nearest pub 1.5 miles
nearest shop 1.5 miles

Located on a working farm in a stunning setting with extensive views, this delightful former dairy offers one en suite double bedroom (5ft bed), one twin, and one room with bunk beds. Lounge/dining/kitchen and shower room. Winchester is ten minutes away. Nearby walks in Farley Mount Country Park and on the Clarendon Way.

SAT NAV SO22 5QS **ONLINE MAP**

Unit 📺 📀 💻 📻 🔌 🍽 ♨ General 🎠 🛏 🐾 P 🅂

★★★
GUEST HOUSE

B&B PER ROOM PER NIGHT
S £45.00–£71.00
D £55.00–£82.00

The Clarence

9 Clarence Road, Windsor SL4 5AE t +44 (0) 1753 864436 e clarence.hotel@btconnect.com

clarence-hotel.co.uk

open All year except Christmas
bedrooms 4 double, 6 twin, 4 single, 6 family
bathrooms All en suite
payment Credit/debit cards, cash, cheques

Comfortable hotel with licensed bar and steam-sauna. Located near town centre and short walk from Windsor Castle, Eton College and River Thames. All rooms with en suite bathroom, TV, tea-/coffee-making facilities, hairdryer and radio-alarm. Free Wi-Fi Internet. Convenient for Legoland and Heathrow Airport.

SAT NAV SL4 5AE

Room 📺 💷 🔌 General 🎠 P 🛜 ♨ 🐴

★★★
SELF CATERING

| Units | 1 |
| Sleeps | 1–4 |

LOW SEASON PER WK
Min £495.00

HIGH SEASON PER WK
£500.00–£575.00

Flat 6 The Courtyard, Windsor

contact Mr Gavin Gordon, 5 Temple Mill Island, Marlow SL7 1SG t +44 (0) 1628 824267
e gavingordon@totalise.co.uk

windsor-selfcatering.co.uk

open All year
payment Cash, cheques

An elegant, well-equipped, first-floor apartment (with lift) centrally situated in a quiet courtyard almost opposite Windsor Castle. One double and one twin bedroom. With direct access to Windsor High Street, the many restaurants, excellent shops, Theatre Royal and castle are only minutes away. London approximately 30 minutes. Exclusive parking.

Unit 📺 💷 📀 💻 🔌 General 🎠 🛏 P

Where are the maps?

Colour maps can be found at the front of the guide. They pinpoint the location of all accommodation found in the regional sections.

WINDSOR, Berkshire Map ref 2D2 — SELF CATERING

★★★
SELF CATERING

Units **1**
Sleeps **4**

LOW SEASON PER WK
£450.00

HIGH SEASON PER WK
£550.00

Springfield Corner, Windsor

contact Mrs Anna Foxell, Springfield Corner, 78a Alma Road, Windsor SL4 3ET
t +44 (0) 1753 860900 e annafoxell@tiscali.co.uk

springfieldcorner.co.uk

Two-bedroom self-catering cottage. Well equipped and cosy. One double, one twin. All mod cons. Patio area, designated off-street parking. Town centre.

open All year
payment Cash, cheques, euros
nearest pub 0.5 miles
nearest shop 0.5 miles

Unit TV SC □■. ▯▤▯ ▯ ▯▯❊ General ☎ ▥ ♣ P

WOKING, Surrey Map ref 2D2 — GUEST ACCOMMODATION

★★
GUEST ACCOMMODATION

B&B PER ROOM PER NIGHT
S Max £47.00
D Max £69.00

EVENING MEAL PER PERSON
Max £25.00

Enquire about our exclusive-use rates.

St Columba's House

Maybury Hill, Woking GU22 8AB t +44 (0) 1483 766498 e retreats@stcolumbas.org.uk

stcolumbashouse.org.uk SPECIAL OFFERS

open All year except Easter, Christmas and New Year
bedrooms 4 twin, 23 single
bathrooms All en suite
payment Cash, cheques

A quiet retreat house and conference centre with 21stC facilities for business, leisure, and spiritual renewal. We welcome individuals and groups from all over the world and provide a range of meeting and catering facilities for groups of up to 50, whether for business or leisure.

SAT NAV *GU22 8AB* ONLINE MAP

Room ♿ ☎ TV ♠ General P ♿ ♈ ✗ ▦ ❊

Country ways

The Countryside Rights of Way Act gives people new rights to walk on areas of open countryside and registered common land.

To find out where you can go and what you can do, as well as information about taking your dog to the countryside, go online at countrysideaccess.gov.uk.

And when you're out and about…

Always follow the Country Code

- Be safe – plan ahead and follow any signs
- Leave gates and property as you find them
- Protect plants and animals, and take your litter home
- Keep dogs under close control
- Consider other people

WOODSTOCK, Oxfordshire Map ref 2C1

HOTEL

★ ★ ★

SMALL HOTEL

B&B PER ROOM PER NIGHT
S £75.00–£100.00
D £140.00–£150.00

Please enquire about seasonal offers on the website.

The Kings Arms Hotel

19 Market Street, Woodstock OX20 1SU t +44 (0) 1993 813636 e stay@kingshotelwoodstock.co.uk

kingshotelwoodstock.co.uk SPECIAL OFFERS

open All year
bedrooms 14 double, 1 twin
bathrooms All en suite
payment Credit/debit cards, cash, cheques

A late Georgian hotel in the centre of historic Woodstock. Airy, open-plan interiors, marble bar with stripped floors. Uncluttered bedrooms in cool colours, many with high ceilings. Head chef Brian Arnold runs a busy restaurant offering modern English food. Easily reached from London via M40. Nearest train station Oxford, eight miles.

SAT NAV OX20 1SU **ONLINE MAP**

Room 📞 📺 🛁 🍵 ♨ General 🛏12 📶 🍷 🍽

WROXALL, Isle of Wight Map ref 2C3

GUEST ACCOMMODATION

★ ★ ★

FARMHOUSE

B&B PER ROOM PER NIGHT
S £25.00–£50.00
D £50.00–£54.00

Little Span Farm B&B

Rew Lane, Ventnor PO38 3AU t +44 (0) 1983 852419 e info@spanfarm.co.uk

spanfarm.co.uk

open All year
bedrooms 2 double, 1 twin, 1 family
bathrooms All en suite
payment Cash, cheques

17thC stone farmhouse on working sheep farm in Area of Outstanding Natural Beauty. Short drive to sandy beaches of Shanklin, Sandown and Ventnor. Close to footpaths, cycle route, golf course and tourist attractions. Ideal for family holidays. Kennels available for dogs. English or vegetarian breakfast.

SAT NAV PO38 3AU

Room 📺 🛁 🍵 General 🛏 🎠 🅿 ♨ 🍽 ❀ 🐴

Help before you go

When it comes to your next break, the first stage of your journey could be closer than you think.

You've probably got a Tourist Information Centre nearby which is there to serve the local community – as well as visitors. Knowledgeable staff will be happy to help you, wherever you're heading.

Many Tourist Information Centres can provide you with maps and guides, and it's often possible to book accommodation and travel tickets too.

You'll find the address of your nearest centre in your local phone book, or look in the regional sections in this guide for a list of Tourist Information Centres.

London

Clockwise: Buckingham Palace; Shakespeare's Globe; Tower Bridge

Great days out

So you think you know London? Take another look because there's always another secret to discover or something new to try, as well as inspirational itineraries to follow for weekends and days out. Just remember to leave yourself with enough time for everything (a year or more should do).

Culture vulture

Does Turner turn you on? The Impressionists impress? Then London is your place. With some 70 large museums and over 30 major art galleries, it's a top culture capital. The **Museum of London** is a good start for insights into local life. Experience the Great Fire of London 1666 through the eyes of survivors – what really happened? New galleries opening 2010 include the city's 21stC story.

The National Gallery

At the **National Gallery** see famous works of art by Van Gogh, Monet and da Vinci amongst an outstanding collection of Western European paintings. Nearby, **Somerset House** is bursting with Old Master and Impressionist paintings, decorative arts and treasures from the Hermitage Museum, St Petersburg. Its Admiralty Restaurant serves delicious lunches, too. And **Tate Britain**, just along the Thames, explores over 500 years of British art.

Take a boat trip to **Greenwich** for an adventure through Britain's seafaring history at the **National Maritime Museum**. And do leave time for lesser-known gems like the **Ben Uri Gallery**, **The London Jewish Museum of Art**. Or the **Royal London Hospital Archives and Museum** telling the fascinating story of the hospital and featuring people like the unfortunate 'Elephant Man'.

Greenfingered London

Fabulous **Chelsea Flower Show** in May is a horticultural highspot of everyone's year. But at any time there are plenty of green (and every other floral colour) delights to dig into. **Kew Gardens** are the ultimate destination: over 300 acres growing more than 30,000 types of plants.

For an unusual surprise, take the train from Victoria Station to **Eltham Palace**, where 19-acre gardens combine medieval and 20thC elements. The trip to Charles Darwin's **Down House**, Orpington, also gets creative juices flowing: follow the path he paced in the beautiful gardens as he contemplated his revolutionary theories. And if you want a fragrant souvenir to take home, browse **Columbia Road Flower Market** on Sunday mornings, an absolute blaze of colour.

why not... climb the Monument (311 steps) in the City for superb views?

Left to right: South Bank; Westminster

did you know... dozens of museums and galleries are free to visit, including Tate Britain?

Ladies who lunch

London does shopping, eating and pampering so well! And, ladies, you deserve a girls' outing. Check what's chic in **Knightsbridge** and the top designer stores on the **Kings Road**. Or perfect the quirky and vintage look shopping around **Notting Hill** and **Portobello Road**. Then enjoy a leisurely lunch with **Bateaux London Restaurant Cruisers**, watching the sights drift by, or tea at **The Ritz** or **Browns**. Dinner at **The Ivy** or **Le Caprice** sounds tempting, too.

Sports galore

There's plenty of sport, too. London's great venues like **Wimbledon** – the **Lawn Tennis Museum** gives great insights into the world-famous championship. There's no need to wait for match days to enjoy a trip to **Chelsea Football Club**, the **Emirates Stadium** or **Lord's**. Behind-the-scenes tours bring to life soccer and cricket dreams. Take the kids, they love sport in the capital as well.

Luvvies London

Nearly 150 theatres raise the curtain on drama, opera, dance and more. Kick off in style with a **West End** show – ask about good deals at the tkts booth in **Leicester Square**, London's official reduced theatre ticket operation. Sip pre-performance drinks at the luvvie-friendly **French House**, **Toucan** or **Dog & Duck** pub, and digest the night's entertainment at **Joe Allen**, where you might spot a thesp or two. Next day, join a back-stage tour – the **Theatre Royal**, Drury Lane is just one venue that opens its doors. And stroll along the **South Bank**, the heart of cultural cool, to see what's on at the **Southbank Centre**. Round off with a tour of the magnificent **Shakespeare's Globe**.

Tea at Harrods

Big kids

For some family-friendly fun hop aboard the **London Eye**, rising slowly to view 55 famous landmarks across the city. Keep spirits high with a visit to the **Tower of London**, possibly the country's most haunted building – was that the scream of a ghostly nobleman being led to the executioner's block? **Hampton Court Palace** also has a host of spooks, including Henry VIII's fifth wife Catherine Howard. Who ever said history was dull?

Don't get lost in the palace's famous maze. Explore all nine decks of **HMS Belfast**, from the Captain's Bridge to the boiler and engine rooms, well below the ship's waterline. See the sick bay and operations room and imagine life on board during World War II. Who would guess you could be in a vast landscape of lagoons, lakes and ponds within 25 minutes of central London? The **London Wetland Centre** in Barnes is Europe's best urban site for watching wildlife, including hundreds of bird species. Come nose to nose with sharks and deadly stone fish at the **London Aquarium**. If you've energy to spare, let off steam in one of London's many parks. Picnic and play footie in **St James's Park** or go boating on the Serpentine in **Hyde Park**.

The main event

London living can be pretty high octane, no more so than for event-goers. From **Chinese New Year** Celebrations to **The Proms** to lights-on for Christmas, the calendar is packed. Gather beside the Thames for spring's **Oxford and Cambridge Boat Race**, everyone likes tradition. And a summer's evening at **Kenwood House**, Hampstead, passes perfectly at a picnic concert. Hit the streets around Ladbroke Grove for the steelbands and exuberant costumes that make **Notting Hill Carnival** swing. Admire the Golden State Coach at the **Lord Mayor's Show**, processing to the Royal Courts of Justice. And there are always those impromptu smile-breakers, like street performers around **Covent Garden**. Samuel Pepys watched a Punch and Judy show here in 1662 and open-air entertainment has flourished ever since.

why not... explore Regent's Canal from Little Venice to the Docklands?

Left to right: Covent Garden; Hampton Court Palace

Destinations

Covent Garden

Designer shops such as Paul Smith and Nicole Farhi, mid range shops like Karen Millen, Monsoon and Oasis and the downright quirky such as Lush, the cosmetic maker, all have a presence here. Sample the impressive array of organic cheeses at Neal's Yard or grab a table at Carluccio's Delicatessen. Settle down for some entertainment in the Piazza: music, comedy, pavement artists and jugglers. If it's culture your after, step into the magnificently refurbished Royal Opera House for a performance or a backstage tour.

Covent Garden

Greenwich

Stand with one foot in the East and one foot in the West astride the Greenwich Meridian, and set your watch by the red 'Time Ball' that drops each day at 1300hrs precisely and has done so for 170 years. There's a laid-back feel to Greenwich. Take time to browse the market stalls – crafts, antiques, records, bric-a-brac and, most famously, vintage clothing. Then pop into a riverside pub for lunch and some mellow jazz.

Kew

Stroll the finest botanic gardens in the country – 400 acres and 40,000 plant varieties. The Palm House hosts a tropical jungle of plants including bananas, pawpaws and mangoes. Marvel at the giant Amazonian water lily, aloe vera and several carnivorous plants in the Princess of Wales Conservatory where ten climatic zones are recreated. You'll find activities for children and a full calendar of special events.

Notting Hill

A colourful district filled with clubs, bars and dance venues, and now trendier than ever. Wander the celebrated Portobello Road market where over 1,500 traders compete for your custom at the Saturday antiques market. Find jewellery, silverware, paintings and more. Summertime is carnival time and the Caribbean influence has ensured the phenomenal growth of the world-famous, multi-cultural Notting Hill Carnival. Join the throng of millions – exotic costume recommended. On a quieter day, visit beautiful Holland Park, a haven of greenery with its own theatre.

Richmond

The River Thames runs through the heart of the beautiful borough of Richmond. Arrive by summer riverboat from Westminster Pier and explore the delightful village with its riverside pubs, specialist boutiques, galleries and museums. Glimpse herds of deer in the Royal parks and step into history in Henry VIII's magnificent Hampton Court Palace, the oldest Tudor palace in England. Round off your visit with a world-class rugby match at Twickenham Stadium.

Clockwise: Kenwood House;
Hyde Park; Chinese New Year

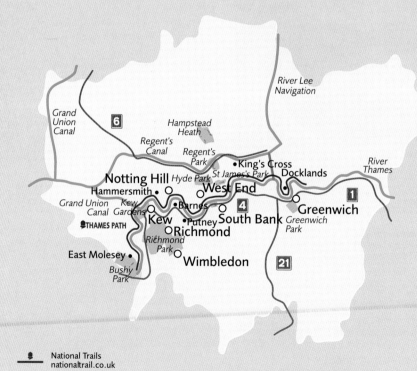

River Lee
Navigation

Grand
Union
Canal

6

Hampstead
Heath

Regent's
Canal

Regent's
Park

River
Thames

King's Cross
Notting Hill *Hyde Park* *St James's Park* Docklands
Hammersmith • **West End**
Grand Union *Kew* **1**
Canal *Gardens* •Barnes **4** • **Greenwich**
≗THAMES PATH **Kew** •Putney **South Bank** *Greenwich*
• *Park*
• **Richmond**
Richmond
Park **21**
East Molesey •
Bushy **Wimbledon**
Park

⚲ National Trails
    nationaltrail.co.uk

3 Sections of the National
    Cycle Network
    nationalcyclenetwork.org.uk

Kew Gardens

The West End

Shop in the best department stores and international designer boutiques in Oxford Street, Regent Street and Bond Street. Take lunch in a stylish eatery, and then see a major exhibition at the Royal Academy of Arts. At the heart of the West End are the landmarks of Trafalgar Square and Piccadilly Circus, and just a few minutes' stroll will take you into legendary Soho, the entertainment heart of the city, crammed with bars, pubs, clubs and restaurants.

Wimbledon

Wimbledon village is only ten miles from the centre of London but you could be in the heart of the countryside. Enjoy the open spaces of Wimbledon Common then wander along the charming high street with its unique medieval buildings, boutiques and pavement cafés. Visit the legendary All England Club where the Lawn Tennis Museum is a must-see for fans of the sport, not to mention the chance to tour the legendary Centre Court.

South Bank

One of London's coolest quarters, the South Bank positively teems with must-see attractions and cultural highlights. Tate Modern has gained a reputation as one of the greatest modern art galleries in the world boasting works by Moore, Picasso, Dali, Warhol and Hepworth. Take in a play at the National Theatre or Shakespeare's magnificently restored Globe, and hit the heights on British Airways London Eye, the world's highest observation wheel.

For lots more great ideas visit visitbritain.com/destinations

Clockwise: Greenwich; Notting Hill; Richmond Park

Visitor attractions

 Family and Fun

**Chelsea Football Club
Stadium Tours**
Fulham, SW6
+44 (0) 871 984 1955
chelseafc.com
*Get behind the scenes at
Stamford Bridge.*

**Emirates Stadium Tour
and Museum**
Highbury, N5
+44 (0) 20 7704 4504
arsenal.com
*Get to know Arsenal's
stunning stadium.*

HMS Belfast
Southwark, SE1
+44 (0) 20 7940 6300
iwm.org.uk
*A fascinating piece of British
naval history.*

London Aquarium
South Bank, SE1
+44 (0) 20 7967 8000
londonaquarium.co.uk
*Come face-to-face with
two-metre long sharks.*

The London Dungeon
Southwark, SE1
+44 (0) 20 7403 7221
thedungeons.com
So much fun it's frightening!

London Eye
South Bank, SE1
+44 (0) 870 5000 600
ba-londoneye.com
*The world's largest observation
wheel.*

**London Eye River
Cruise Experience**
Westminster, SE1
+44 (0) 870 500 0600
londoneye.com
*Circular cruise with fascinating
live commentary.*

**London Wetland
Centre**
Barnes, SW16
+44 (0) 20 8409 4400
wwt.org.uk
*Europe's best urban site for
watching wildlife.*

**Madame Tussauds and the
London Planetarium**
Marylebone, NW1
+44 (0) 870 999 0046
madame-tussauds.com/london
*Meet the stars then enter the
Chamber of Horrors.*

**National Maritime
Museum**
Greenwich, SE10
+44 (0) 20 8858 4422
nmm.ac.uk
*Over two million exhibits of
seafaring history.*

Royal Mews
St James Park, SW1
+44 (0) 20 7766 7302
royalcollection.org.uk
*One of the world's finest
working stables.*

Heritage

Apsley House
Piccadilly, W1
+44 (0) 20 7499 5676
english-heritage.org.uk
*Wellington's military
memorabilia and dazzling
art collection.*

Buckingham Palace
SW1
+44 (0) 20 7766 7300
royal.gov.uk
*HM The Queen's official
London residence.*

Chiswick House
W4
+44 (0) 20 8995 0508
english-heritage.org.uk
*Glorious example of 18thC
British architecture.*

Eltham Palace
SE9
+44 (0) 20 8294 2548
english-heritage.org.uk
*Spectacular Art Deco villa and
medieval hall.*

**Hampton Court
Palace**
East Molesey, KT8
+44 (0) 844 482 7777
hrp.org.uk
*Outstanding Tudor palace
with famous maze.*

**Kensington Palace
State Apartments**
W8
+44 (0) 844 482 7777
hrp.org.uk
*Home to the Royal Ceremonial
Dress Collection.*

Kenwood House
Hampstead, NW3
+44 (0) 20 8348 1286
english-heritage.org.uk
*Beautiful 18thC villa with fine
interiors.*

Where to Stay in Britain

Tower Bridge Exhibition
SE1
+44 (0) 20 7403 3761
towerbridge.org.uk
*Learn all about the world's
most famous bridge.*

Tower of London
EC3
+44 (0) 870 756 6060
hrp.org.uk
*Crown Jewels and 900 years
of history.*

Indoors

**Bateaux London
Restaurant Cruisers**
Embankment, WC2
+44 (0) 20 7695 1800
bateauxlondon.com
*Luxury dining and world-class
live entertainment.*

**BBC Television
Centre Tours**
Shepherd's Bush, W12
+44 (0) 870 603 0304
bbc.co.uk/tours
*Behind the scenes of world-
famous television studios.*

**Ben Uri Art Gallery,
London Jewish
Museum of Art**
St John's Wood, NW8
+44 (0) 20 7604 3991
benuri.org.uk
*Europe's only dedicated
Jewish museum of art.*

BFI London IMAX Cinema
Waterloo, SE1
+44 (0) 870 787 2525
bfi.org.uk
*The ultimate big-screen
experience.*

British Museum
WC1
+44 (0) 20 7323 8299
britishmuseum.org
*One of the great museums of
the world*

**Churchill Museum and
Cabinet War Rooms**
Westminster, SW1
+44 (0) 20 7930 6961
iwm.org.uk
*Churchill's wartime headquarters
untouched since 1945.*

**Down House – Home
of Charles Darwin**
Orpington, BR6
+44 (0) 1689 859119
english-heritage.org.uk
*The great naturalist's home
and workplace.*

Hayward Gallery
South Bank, SE1
+44 (0) 870 380 0400
hayward.org.uk
*Famous international gallery
showing major exhibitions.*

Imperial War Museum
Lambeth, SE1
+44 (0) 20 7416 5320
iwm.org.uk
*History of Britain at war
since 1914.*

Events 2009

New Year's Day Parade
London
londonparade.co.uk
1 Jan

Ideal Home Show
London
idealhomeshow.co.uk
20 Mar - 13 Apr

**Oxford and Cambridge
Boat Race**
London
theboatrace.org
29 Mar

Flora London Marathon
London
london-marathon.co.uk
26 Apr

Chelsea Flower Show
London
rhs.org.uk
19 - 23 May

**Wimbledon Lawn Tennis
Championships**
London
wimbledon.org/en_GB/index.
html
Jun - Jul

The Proms
London
bbc.co.uk/proms
Jul - Sep

Notting Hill Carnival
London
rbkc.gov.uk
30 - 31 Aug

**The Mayor's Thames
Festival**
London
thamesfestival.org
Sep

State Opening of Parliament
London
parliament.uk
Oct - Nov

Lord Mayor's Show
London
lordmayorsshow.org
Nov

Lord's Tour (MCC)
St John's Wood, NW8
+44 (0) 20 7616 8595
lords.org
Guided tour of the home of cricket.

Museum of London
EC2
+44 (0) 870 444 3852
museumoflondon.org.uk
The world's largest urban-history museum.

National Army Museum
Chelsea, SW3
+44 (0) 20 7730 0717
national-army-museum.ac.uk
The story of the British soldier.

National Portrait Gallery
WC2
+44 (0) 20 7306 0055
npg.org.uk
The world's largest collection of portraits.

Natural History Museum
Kensington, SW7
+44 (0) 20 7942 5000
nhm.ac.uk
World-class collections bringing the natural world to life.

Royal Air Force Museum Hendon
NW9
+44 (0) 20 8205 2266
rafmuseum.org
Historic aircraft from around the world.

Royal London Hospital Archives and Museum
Whitechapel, E1
+44 (0) 20 7377 7608
medicalmuseums.org
Fascinating history of Britain's largest voluntary hospital.

Royal Observatory Greenwich
SE10
+44 (0) 20 8858 4422
nmm.ac.uk
Explore the history of time and astronomy.

Science Museum
Kensington, SW7
+44 (0) 870 870 4868
sciencemuseum.org.uk
State-of-the-art simulators, IMAX cinema and more.

Somerset House
Strand, WC2
+44 (0) 20 7845 4600
somerset-house.org.uk
Arts and learning in magnificent 18thC house.

Southbank Centre
SE1
+44 (0) 871 663 2501
southbankcentre.co.uk
Year-round programme encompassing all the arts.

Southwark Cathedral
SE1
+44 (0) 20 7367 6700
southwark.anglican.org/cathedral
London's oldest Gothic church building.

Tate Britain
Millbank, SW1
+44 (0) 20 7887 8888
tate.org.uk/britain
The greatest single collection of British art.

Tate Modern
Bankside, SE1
+44 (0) 20 7887 8888
tate.org.uk/modern
Britain's flagship museum of modern art.

Victoria and Albert Museum
Large Visitor Attraction of Year - Gold
Kensington, SW7
+44 (0) 20 7942 2000
vam.ac.uk
World-reknowned museum, 3,000 years of art and design.

Wimbledon Lawn Tennis Museum
SW19
+44 (0) 20 8946 6131
wimbledon.org/museum
Superb memorabilia and history of the game.

Outdoors

Kew Gardens (Royal Botanic Gardens)
Richmond, TW9
+44 (0) 20 8332 5655
kew.org
Stunning plant collections and magnificent glasshouses.

ZSL London Zoo
Regent's Park, NW1
+44 (0) 20 7722 3333
zsl.org
The hairiest and scariest animals on the planet.

ASSURANCE OF A GREAT DAY OUT
Attractions with this sign participate in the Visitor Attraction Quality Assurance Scheme which recognises high standards in all aspects of the visitor experience.

Regional contacts and information

For more information on accommodation, attractions, activities, events and holidays in London, contact Visit London. When you arrive at your destination, visit an Official Partner Tourist Information Centre for quality assured help, or email your request before you go. To search for attractions and Tourist Information Centres on the move just text INFO to 62233, and a web link will be sent to your mobile phone.

London

Go to **visitlondon.com** for all you need to know about London. Look for inspirational itineraries with great ideas for weekends and short breaks.

Or call +44 (0) 870 1 LONDON (+44 (0) 870 1 566 366) for:

- **A London visitor information pack**

- **Visitor information on London**
  Speak to an expert for information and advice on museums, galleries, attractions, riverboat trips, sightseeing tours, theatre, shopping, eating out and much more! Or simply go to visitlondon.com.

- **Accommodation reservations**

Chelsea Flower Show

Tourist Information Centres

Britain & London Visitor Centre	1 Regent Street	+44 (0) 870 156636	blvcenquiries@visitlondon.com
Croydon	Katharine Street	+44 (0) 20 8253 1009	tic@croydon.gov.uk
Greenwich	2 Cutty Sark Gardens	+44 (0) 870 608 2000	tic@greenwich.gov.uk
Lewisham	199-201 Lewisham High Street	+44 (0) 20 8297 8317	tic@lewisham.gov.uk
Swanley	London Road	+44 (0) 1322 614660	touristinfo@swanley.org.uk

Quality
visitor attractions

VisitBritain operates a Visitor Attraction Quality Assurance Service.

Participating attractions are visited annually by trained, impartial assessors who look at all aspects of the visit, from initial telephone enquiries to departure, customer service to catering, as well as all facilities and activities.

Only those attractions which have been assessed by Enjoy England and meet the standard receive the quality marque, your sign of a Quality Assured Visitor Attraction.

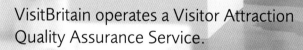

Look out for the quality marque and visit with confidence.

where to stay in
London

For maps of inner and outer London, see the front of this guide.

Accommodation symbols

Symbols give useful information about services and facilities. On pages 16 to 17 you can find a key to these symbols.

INNER LONDON
LONDON E1   SELF CATERING

★★★
SELF CATERING

Units **4**
Sleeps **4–6**

LOW SEASON PER WK
£580.00–£775.00

HIGH SEASON PER WK
£645.00–£835.00

Discounted last-minute and long-term lets.

Hamlet UK, St Katharine Docks, Tower Hill, London

contact Ms Renata Naufal, Hamlet UK, 47 Willian Way, Letchworth SG6 2HJ t +44 (0) 1462 678037
e hamlet_uk@globalnet.co.uk

hamletuk.com GUEST REVIEWS

open All year
payment Credit/debit cards, cash, cheques, euros
nearest pub less than 0.5 miles
nearest shop less than 0.5 miles

Friendly and personal service. Very attractive surroundings. Comfortable and clean accommodation close to public transport, supermarket, the Tower of London, Tower Bridge, the ExCeL exhibition centre and the O₂ Arena. Fully fitted kitchen, bathroom, linen and towels provided, TV, direct-dial phone, wireless broadband connection, washer/dryer, off-street parking. See guests' feedback on our website.

SAT NAV E1W 1ND

Unit 📺 📠 🖥 🍴 🍳 🔌 🧺 ✂ General ⛵ 🏭 🚶 P ⬜ S

LONDON N10   GUEST ACCOMMODATION

★★★
GUEST HOUSE

B&B PER ROOM PER NIGHT
S £48.00–£50.00
D £62.00–£65.00

The Muswell Hill

73 Muswell Hill Road, London N10 3HT t +44 (0) 20 8883 6447 e reception@muswellhillhotel.co.uk

muswellhillhotel.co.uk

A comfortable, three-storey, Edwardian corner property, close to Muswell Hill and Alexandra Palace, offering a warm, friendly service.

open All year except Christmas
bedrooms 4 double, 3 twin, 4 single, 3 family
bathrooms 10 en suite
payment Credit/debit cards, cash, cheques

Room 🛗 📺 ☕ General ⛵ 🏭 🚶 P ✂

PETS! WELCOME / WELCOME PETS!

Where is my pet welcome?

Want to take your cherished companion with you on holiday? Proprietors participating in our Welcome Pets! scheme go out of their way to make special provision for you and your pet. Look out for the symbol.

LONDON NW1

★★★★
GUEST ACCOMMODATION

B&B PER ROOM PER NIGHT
S £130.00–£175.00
D £130.00–£175.00

EVENING MEAL PER PERSON
£14.00–£20.00

MIC Conferences and Accommodation
81-103 Euston Street, London NW1 2EZ t +44 (0) 20 7380 0001 e sales@micentre.com

micentre.com GUEST REVIEWS · SPECIAL OFFERS · REAL-TIME BOOKING

open All year
bedrooms 17 double, 11 twin
bathrooms All en suite
payment Credit/debit cards, cash, cheques

Our hotel floor was completely rebuilt in 2004 and offers the highest standards and value. Contemporary, en suite double rooms feature air-conditioning, LCD TVs, desk with internet access, room safe. Twenty-four hour reception, concierge service and security for peace of mind. Full English breakfast included.

SAT NAV NW1 2EZ **ONLINE MAP**

Room ☎ 📺 ♨ ☜   General ☎ ▥ ♨ 🅿 ✿ ♟ ✕ 🍴 🖥   Leisure 🚲

LONDON SE2

★★★★★
TOURING &
CAMPING PARK

🚐 (202) £14.90–£28.30
🚏 (202) £14.90–£28.30
202 touring pitches

Abbey Wood Caravan Club Site
Federation Road, Abbey Wood, London SE2 0LS t +44 (0) 20 8311 7708

caravanclub.co.uk

open All year
payment Credit/debit cards, cash, cheques

Redeveloped to the highest standards, this site is the ideal base for exploring the capital. A green, gently sloping site with mature trees screening its spacious grounds.

SAT NAV SE2 0LS

Special member rates mean you can save your membership subscription in less than a week. Visit our website to find out more.

THE
CARAVAN
CLUB

General 🖼 📞 🅿 🚻 💧 ⛺ 🛗 🐴 ☀ ⚒   Leisure ⛰ ⚑

LONDON SE6

★★★
BED & BREAKFAST

B&B PER ROOM PER NIGHT
S £35.00–£40.00
D £50.00–£55.00

The Heathers
71 Verdant Lane, London SE6 1JD t +44 (0) 20 8698 8340 e berylheath@yahoo.co.uk

theheathersbb.com

A clean and comfortable, family-run, home from home. Beryl and Ron will do their best to ensure you really enjoy your visit. Nothing too much trouble.

open All year
bedrooms 2 twin
payment Cash, cheques

Room 📺 ♨ ☜   General ☎5 🍴✿

Don't forget www.

Web addresses throughout this guide are shown without the prefix www. Please include www. in the address line of your browser.
If a web address does not follow this style it is shown in full.

LONDON SE10

★★★
SELF CATERING

Units **1**
Sleeps **1–7**

LOW SEASON PER WK
£750.00–£1,200.00

HIGH SEASON PER WK
£850.00–£1,200.00

12 Burgos Grove, West Greenwich, London

contact Ms Dawn Harverson, 1 Egerton Drive, West Greenwich, London SE10 8JS
t +44 (0) 7894 661402   **e** info@greenwichholidaylets.co.uk

greenwichholidaylets.co.uk GUEST REVIEWS · SPECIAL OFFERS · REAL-TIME BOOKING

open All year
payment Cash, cheques
nearest pub less than 0.5 miles
nearest shop less than 0.5 miles

Quality, serviced, family self-catering accommodation in West Greenwich, in the heart of Maritime Greenwich, World Heritage Site. 12 Burgos Grove has been decorated and furnished by artist and stylist Dawn Harverson to a high standard using The White Company linen and Designer Guild fabrics and accessories.

SAT NAV SE10 8LL **ONLINE MAP**

Unit 📺 🆂 📼 💿 💻 🗄 🔌 🎙 🔄 💡 📷 ✏ ❄ ⚒ ⊘   General 🐕 🛏 🏃 P ◎ Ⓢ 🐕
Leisure 🎣 ∪ ▶ 🚲

LONDON SE19

★★★★★
TOURING & CAMPING PARK

🚐 (126)   £14.90–£28.30
🚚 (126)   £14.90–£28.30
126 touring pitches

Crystal Palace Caravan Club Site

Crystal Palace Parade, London SE19 1UF   **t** +44 (0) 20 8778 7155

caravanclub.co.uk

open All year
payment Credit/debit cards, cash, cheques

Popular with European families in the summer, a friendly site on the edge of a pleasant park, in close proximity to all of London's attractions.

SAT NAV SE19 1UF

> *Special member rates mean you can save your membership subscription in less than a week. Visit our website to find out more.*

THE CARAVAN CLUB

General 🖥 🚐 🚿 🍴 💧 🏔 💿 🐕 ☀ 📶   Leisure 🎱 ▶

LONDON SE20

★★★★
GUEST ACCOMMODATION

B&B PER ROOM PER NIGHT
S **£40.00–£45.00**
D **£60.00–£65.00**

EVENING MEAL PER PERSON
£14.50

Melrose House

89 Lennard Road, London SE20 7LY   **t** +44 (0) 20 8776 8884   **e** melrosehouse@supanet.com

uk-bedandbreakfast.com GUEST REVIEWS

open All year except Christmas and New Year
bedrooms 4 double, 3 twin, 1 single, 1 family
bathrooms 8 en suite, 1 private
payment Credit/debit cards, cash, euros

Superb accommodation in Victorian house with spacious, en suite bedrooms. Easy access to West End. Quiet, respectable, friendly and welcoming. Ground-floor rooms opening onto the lovely garden.

SAT NAV SE20 7LY

Room 🛗 🖥 ☎ 📺 🍵 🎙   General 🐕 8 P 📶 🔥 ❄

★★★

GUEST ACCOMMODATION

B&B PER ROOM PER NIGHT
S £50.00–£75.00
D £70.00–£110.00

Melita House

35 Charlwood Street, London SW1V 2DU t +44 (0) 20 7828 0471 e reserve@melitahotel.com

melitahotel.com GUEST REVIEWS · REAL-TIME BOOKING

Elegant, family-run hotel in excellent location close to Victoria station. Rooms have extensive modern facilities. Warm, friendly welcome, full English breakfast included.

open All year
bedrooms 10 double, 3 twin, 4 single, 2 family
bathrooms All en suite
payment Credit/debit cards, cash, cheques, euros

Room 🛏 ☎ 📺 🆂🅲 🍽 General 🛋 🏠 📶 Leisure 🚲

★★★★–★★★★★★

SELF CATERING

Units **19**
Sleeps **2–6**

LOW SEASON PER WK
£781.00–£1,875.00

HIGH SEASON PER WK
£781.00–£1,875.00

The Apartments, London

t +44 (0) 20 7589 3271 e sales@theapartments.co.uk

theapartments.co.uk

open All year
payment Credit/debit cards, cash, cheques
nearest pub less than 0.5 miles
nearest shop less than 0.5 miles

A selection of elegant, serviced studios and one- to two-bedroom apartments housed in prestigious Victorian buildings. Individually designed with a full range of modern amenities including broadband internet access, for the discerning, independent traveller. The apartments offer you a unique, luxurious environment combining privacy, independence and the relaxed atmosphere of home.

ONLINE MAP

Unit 📺 🖨 💻 🍽 🍴 ✏ General 🛋 🏠 🚶 📷 🅂

★★★

HOTEL

B&B PER ROOM PER NIGHT
S £99.00–£119.00
D £119.00–£139.00
HB PER PERSON PER NIGHT
£89.50–£99.50

Special offer – 20% discount available on food in the restaurant, for lunch or dinner.

Enterprise Hotel

15-25 Hogarth Road, London SW5 0QJ t +44 (0) 20 7373 4502 e info@enterprisehotel.co.uk

enterprisehotel.co.uk GUEST REVIEWS · SPECIAL OFFERS · REAL-TIME BOOKING

open All year
bedrooms 43 double, 32 twin, 10 single, 15 family
bathrooms All en suite
payment Credit/debit cards, cash, cheques, euros

Situated in Kensington close to Earls Court exhibition centres. Ideal for West End theatres. Shops and museums are within easy reach. Earls Court station is within walking distance and has direct links to London's Heathrow and Gatwick airports (via Victoria).

SAT NAV *SW5 0QJ* **ONLINE MAP**

Room 🛏 🚪 ☎ 📺 🍽 🍴 General 🛋 🏠 🚶 📶 🍷 ● 🛗 📷 🍽

Like exploring England's cities?

Let VisitBritain's Explorer series guide you through the streets of some of England's great cities. All you need for the perfect day out is in this handy pack – featuring an easy-to-use fold out map and illustrated guide. You can purchase the Explorer series from good bookshops and online at visitbritaindirect.com for just £5.99.

LONDON SW18 — SELF CATERING

★★★★
SELF CATERING

Units **2**
Sleeps **1–8**

LOW SEASON PER WK
£570.00–£850.00

HIGH SEASON PER WK
£620.00–£890.00

Beaumont Apartments, London

contact Mr & Mrs Alan & Monica Afriat, Beaumont Apartments, 24 Combemartin Road, London SW18 5PR **t** +44 (0) 20 8789 2663 **e** alan@beaumont-london-apartments.co.uk

beaumont-london-apartments.co.uk GUEST REVIEWS

Well-appointed flats in leafiest suburb within 25 minutes of West End. Close to Zone 3 Underground, Wimbledon tennis and convenient for A3, M4, M41, M25, Heathrow and Gatwick. Wi-Fi Internet.

open All year
payment Credit/debit cards, cash, cheques, euros
nearest pub less than 0.5 miles
nearest shop less than 0.5 miles

Unit 📺 SC 🚪 🔲 📀 🔌 🔒 General 🦽 🏠 ♿ P ⊡ Leisure ♨ 🎵 🚩 🚲

LONDON SW20 — SELF CATERING

★★★★
SELF CATERING

Units **2**
Sleeps **5–6**

HIGH SEASON PER WK
£682.50–£798.00

Thalia & Hebe Holiday Homes, Wimbledon, London

contact Mr & Mrs Peter & Ann Briscoe-Smith, 150 Westway, Wimbledon, London SW20 9LS **t** +44 (0) 20 8542 0505 **e** peter@briscoe-smith.org.uk

briscoe-smith.org.uk

Thalia and Hebe are both three-bedroomed houses in the residential suburban area of West Wimbledon. Home from home, with easy access to central London. Wi-Fi/LAN broadband.

open All year
payment Cash, cheques
nearest pub 0.5 miles
nearest shop 0.5 miles

Unit 📺 🚪 🔲 📀 🔌 🔒 General 🦽 🏠 ♿ P S

LONDON W2 — GUEST ACCOMMODATION

★★★
GUEST ACCOMMODATION

B&B PER ROOM PER NIGHT
S £48.00–£68.00
D £68.00–£85.00

10% discount on weekly bookings.

Kingsway Park Hotel Hyde Park

139 Sussex Gardens, London W2 2RX **t** +44 (0) 20 7723 5677 **e** info@kingswaypark-hotel.com

kingswaypark-hotel.com REAL-TIME BOOKING

open All year
bedrooms 6 double, 7 twin, 4 single, 5 family
bathrooms All en suite
payment Credit/debit cards, cash, cheques

Elegant, Victorian, Grade II Listed building refurbished to a high standard. Situated three minutes' walk from Paddington Station and Heathrow Express and five minutes from Hyde Park. Ten minutes to Oxford Street and Marble Arch.

SAT NAV *W2 2RX* **ONLINE MAP**

Room 🛏 ☎ 📺 ☕ 🍵 General 🦽 🏠 ♿ 🪑 🍷 ✕

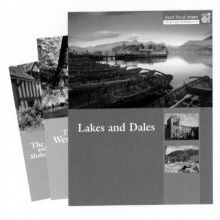

Touring made easy

Two to four-day circular routes with over 200 places to discover

- Lakes and Dales
- The West Country
- The Cotswolds and Shakespeare Country

Available in good bookshops and online at visitbritain.com for just £6.99 each.

LONDON W14

SELF CATERING

★★★★
SELF CATERING

Units **1**
Sleeps **2–4**

LOW SEASON PER WK
£630.00

HIGH SEASON PER WK
£630.00

For bookings of more than 14 days we offer a 10% discount.

Castletown House, London

contact Mr Richard Poppleton, Castletown House, 11 Castletown Road, London W14 9HE
t +44 (0) 20 7386 9423 **e** info@castletownhouse.co.uk

castletownhouse.co.uk GUEST REVIEWS · SPECIAL OFFERS · REAL-TIME BOOKING

open All year
payment Credit/debit cards, cash
nearest pub less than 0.5 miles
nearest shop less than 0.5 miles

Private apartment set in Victorian building, recently refurbished. Bedroom with balcony, lounge, kitchen, bathroom. One double bed and sofa bed in lounge. Located in West Kensington, convenient for London's main attractions. Earls Court and Olympia exhibition centres are nearby. West Kensington Underground is just a two-minute walk.

SAT NAV W14 9HE **ONLINE MAP**

Unit TV 🖥 💻 📠 🎧 📻 🍳 🍴 🧺 General 🛋 🛏 🚿 P S 🐾 Leisure ▶

OUTER LONDON
BECKENHAM

SELF CATERING

★★–★★★
SELF CATERING

Units **10**
Sleeps **2–6**

LOW SEASON PER WK
£250.00–£625.00

HIGH SEASON PER WK
£250.00–£625.00

Oakfield Apartments, Beckenham

t +44 (0) 20 8658 4441 **e** enquiry@oakfield.co.uk

oakfield.co.uk SPECIAL OFFERS

open All year
payment Credit/debit cards, cash, cheques, euros
nearest pub less than 0.5 miles
nearest shop less than 0.5 miles

Victorian mansion with a large garden in a semi-rural setting, three minutes' walk to Eden Park rail station, 25 minutes by rail or nine miles by road to central London. Mr and Mrs Deane live on the premises and welcome children but not pets.

ONLINE MAP

Unit TV SC 🖥 💻 📠 🎧 📻 🍳 🧺 🍴✏ ❄ General 🛋 🛏 🚿 P ○ S Leisure ▶ 🚲

HARROW **HOTEL**

★★★
HOTEL

B&B PER ROOM PER NIGHT
S £60.00–£105.00
D £70.00–£130.00
HB PER PERSON PER NIGHT
£87.00–£150.00

Best Western Cumberland Hotel

1-3 St Johns Road, Harrow HA1 2EF **t** +44 (0) 20 8863 4111 **e** reception@cumberlandhotel.co.uk

cumberlandhotel.co.uk GUEST REVIEWS · SPECIAL OFFERS · REAL-TIME BOOKING

Located in Harrow town centre; doorstep to London, gateway to Hertfordshire, and neighbouring Wembley. Best Western Cumberland offers the best of all worlds – catering for business, leisure and group travellers.

open All year
bedrooms 32 double, 12 twin, 32 single, 8 family
bathrooms All en suite
payment Credit/debit cards, cash, cheques

Room General Leisure

HARROW **HOTEL**

★
METRO HOTEL

B&B PER ROOM PER NIGHT
S £50.00–£55.00
D £65.00–£75.00
HB PER PERSON PER NIGHT
£30.00–£45.00

Crescent Hotel

58-60 Welldon Crescent, Harrow HA1 1QR **t** +44 (0) 20 8863 5491 **e** info@crescenthotels.co.uk

crescenthotels.co.uk GUEST REVIEWS · REAL-TIME BOOKING

open All year except Christmas and New Year
bedrooms 4 double, 4 twin, 11 single, 2 family
bathrooms 18 en suite
payment Cheques

We aim to give high quality service to all our guests to guarantee your stay with us is not only stress-free but enjoyable. Most bedrooms are en suite. Facilities include Sky TV, internet. Wi-Fi connections in most rooms.

SAT NAV *HA1 1QR* **ONLINE MAP**

Room General

Families Welcome

If you are looking for a great family break in quality-assessed accommodation, look out for the Families Welcome sign.

Participants in this scheme offer additional facilities and services catering for a range of ages and family units. For families with young children, they'll have facilities such as cots and highchairs, storage for push-chairs and somewhere to heat baby food or milk. Where meals are provided, children's choices will be clearly indicated, with healthy options available. They'll also have information on local walks, attractions, activities or events suitable for children, as well as local child-friendly pubs and restaurants.

Of course, not all accommodation is able to cater for all ages or combinations of family units, so do check when you book.

Wherever you're travelling in England, the Families Welcome scheme will help you find just the right place to stay to ensure everyone has a great time.

South West England

Bristol, Cornwall, Devon, Dorset, Gloucestershire,
Isles of Scilly, Somerset, Wiltshire

Clockwise: Porlock Bay, Somerset; Forest of
Dean, Gloucestershire; Stonehenge, Wiltshire

Great days out

Go rock pooling in sandy coves. Indulge your love of cream teas and clotted cream fudge. Ramble along the South West Coast Path. Brave the waves surfing in Newquay. Wonder at the Cerne Abbas Giant and the stunning landscaped gardens at Stourhead. What will you do in South West England?

Refreshing rambles

The South West is truly a walker's paradise, from the gentle **Cotswold Hills** to the wilder beauty of **Exmoor** and **Dartmoor** National Parks. Spend a day or two rambling parts of the 101-mile **Cotswold Way** through quintessential English countryside and golden-stone villages. **The Two Moors Way** over Dartmoor and Exmoor takes you through moorland, wooded valleys, farmland and coastal towns. Gee up the pace pony trekking or mountain biking – the National Parks have plenty of space for both. Then feel the sea-salted breezes along the **South West Coast Path**. It stretches for 630 miles from Somerset to Dorset, opening up dramatic views of a shoreline organically sculpted by waves. Children just love stomping 185 million years of earth history underfoot along the **Jurassic Coast**, a World Heritage Site. They could even find a dinosaur print. Who's got the biggest feet?

Sea, surf and fun

How's this for the perfect antidote to hectic modern life? Genuine bucket-and-spade fun with the family, pure and simple. With more Blue Flag beaches than anywhere else in England, the region's sandy bays and sheltered coves are perfect getaways. Some stretches make thrilling waves for watersports: hit the hip centres of **Newquay**, **Bude**, **Croyde** and **Woolacombe**, great places to learn to surf or kitesurf. Try sailing and windsurfing in **Poole**. Devon's English Riviera – the bustling seaside towns of **Torquay**, **Paignton** and **Brixham** – is ideal for families and you can meet friendly coastal creatures like penguins and fur seals at

Living Coasts in Torquay. Away from the beach quaint fishing villages, such as **Clovelly**, **Port Isaac** and **Beer**, are a picturesque maze of narrow streets and steep roads. And how's this for an unforgettable experience? Catch a play or musical at the open-air cliffside **Minack Theatre** at Porthcurno. The backdrop of sea vistas is breathtaking.

Torquay, Devon

Glorious gardens

The South West's balmy subtropical climate means exotic flora flourish, creating extraordinary gardens. Delight in the **Lost Gardens of Heligan** at Pentewan, neglected for years and now brought back to life complete with magical Jungle Garden. Take a helicopter ride to **Tresco**, one of the Scilly Isles, to browse some 20,000 luxuriant plants in the **Abbey Garden**. Explore the remarkable **Eden Project**, near St Austell, which features thousands of world plants in enormous glass biomes – and children become enthralled on the interactive trails. Then enjoy the pyrotechnic seasonal displays of trees and flowers at **Westonbirt Arboretum**,

Left to right: Eden Project, Cornwall;
Salisbury Cathedral, Wiltshire

why not... cycle along Devon's 180-mile Tarka Trail, named after Henry Williamson's Tarka the Otter?

Gloucestershire; the clipped yews and cascades at **Forde Abbey and Gardens**, Dorset; and the eye-catching tableaux of lakeside temples at **Stourhead**, Wiltshire.

Yum yum!

Indulge yourself in the region's delicious specialities. Cornish pasties taste good washed down with a pint of sweet cider. Look out for Mendip Oggies, too: pasties made with pork, apple and cheese pastry. Devour mouthwatering scones straight from the oven and topped with rich clotted cream. And sample a different cheese every day: world-famous Cheddar, Double Gloucester, Somerset Brie, Dorset Blue Vinny and nettle wrapped Cornish Yarg. Relish the best catches at **Rick Stein's Seafood Restaurant**, Padstow. Then finish your gourmet odyssey relaxing over a wine from **Three Choirs Vineyard**, Gloucestershire.

Mysterious and madcap

You're in just the right area for quirky customs and intriguing places. If you look hard enough you may spot the Witch of Wookey deep in **Wookey Hole Caves** where pagan and Christian legends intermingle. Ponder the mysteries of the ancient stone circles of **Stonehenge** and **Avebury** – just how were such enormous stones transported and arranged, and why? **Chipping Campden** in Gloucestershire is the location of the Cotswolds' unique version of the Olimpick Games: contests include shin-kicking, ouch! Meanwhile **Blackawton** in Devon hosts the annual International Worm Charming Festival. Seeing is believing!

Exmoor, Somerset

Splendid city highlights

Fill your days visiting attractions in Bristol and Bath, city neighbours yet so different. **Bristol's** maritime heritage has been channelled into the infectious vitality of the rejuvenated Harbourside of bars, eateries and sights. Clamber aboard Isambard Kingdom Brunel's **ss Great Britain**, the world's first great ocean liner. Treat the kids to an interactive science adventure at **Explore-at-Bristol** – freeze your shadow, fire a neuron, and get starry-eyed in the planetarium. Then revel in the Georgian elegance of **Bath** and tour the best-preserved Roman religious spa from the ancient world, beneath the watchful gaze of **Bath Abbey**. Dip your own toes – and more – into the natural thermal waters of the recently opened **Thermae Bath Spa**. Bliss!

why not... look for the Fossil Forest revealed at low tide near Little Bindon, Dorset?

Continue your journey with a trip to some of the West's other great cathedral cities. Stroll **Exeter's** historic Quayside; survey the medieval carvings of **Wells Cathedral's** majestic west front; wander the revitalised waterside of **Gloucester**; or take a guided tour of **Salisbury Cathedral**, its soaring spire the tallest in Britain.

More great days out

If you're looking for even more inspiration for great days out, add these to your love-to list. Have a fun time uncovering the history, sights and sounds of the railway at **Steam – Museum of the Great Western Railway** in Swindon, or take the kids on a wild animal safari at **Longleat**. Take a picnic to **Corfe Castle** whose evocative hilltop ruins recall a bold past. Or potter about on a driving tour – the scenic **Royal Forest Route** through the Forest of Dean and the **Romantic Road** via **Cheltenham** and **Cirencester** spring to mind. Floating skywards in a hot-air balloon over the countryside and llama-trekking also make memorable adventures!

Clockwise: Dartmoor, Devon; St Michael's Mount, Cornwall; ss Great Britain, Bristol

Destinations

Bath

Set in rolling countryside, less than two hours from London, this exquisite Georgian spa city was founded by the Romans and is now a World Heritage Site. Explore the compact city centre on foot and discover a series of architectural gems including the Roman baths and Pump Room, the 15thC Abbey, and stunning Royal Crescent. Follow in the footsteps of Romans and Celts and bathe in the naturally warm waters of the Thermae Bath Spa.

Bath

Bournemouth

Bournemouth is the perfect holiday and short-break destination, renowned for its seven miles of family-friendly, golden beaches, beautiful parks and gardens and cosmopolitan ambience. Enjoy the buzz of the town then head out and savour the beauty of the New Forest, the splendour of Dorset's spectacular World Heritage Jurassic Coastline, and the rolling countryside immortalised by Thomas Hardy.

Bristol

In bygone times, explorers and merchants set off on epic journeys from its harbour. Nowadays, Bristol's spirit of boldness and creativity expresses itself in art, architecture and an enviable quality of life. Take in Georgian terraces, waterfront arts centres, green spaces, great shopping and top-class restaurants. The city's heritage glitters with the work of historic figures such as Isambard Kingdom Brunel, and all set against a truly classic view – the River Avon and its dramatic gorge reaching almost into the heart of the city.

The Cotswolds

Escape to the rolling hills of the Cotswolds scattered with picturesque towns and villages built of distinctive honey-coloured limestone. Criss-cross the little bridges over the River Windrush in Bourton-on-the-Water; hunt for antiques in Stow-on-the-Wold; wander through the open-air street market of Moreton-in-Marsh and appreciate the beautifully preserved buildings in Chipping Campden and Tetbury.

Isles of Scilly

Just 20 minutes from Cornwall you'll find over 100 islands waiting to be explored– five of them inhabited: St Mary's, Tresco, St Martin's, St Agnes and Bryher. Discover fascinating prehistoric remains, rare species of birds and plant life, historic shipwrecks and some of the best beaches in Britain. Watersports, boat trips, wonderful gardens, including Tresco Abbey Gardens, keep everyone entertained.

Left to right: Corfe Castle, Dorset
Wells Cathedral, Somerset

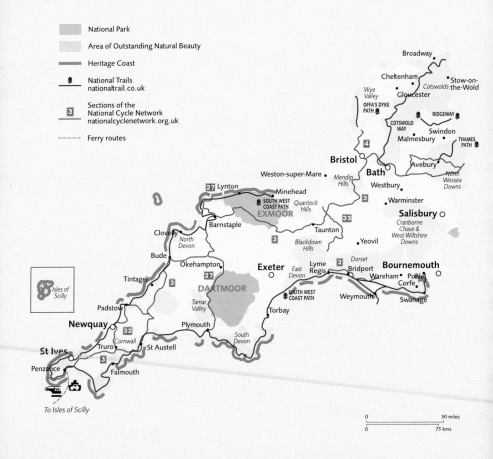

National Park

Area of Outstanding Natural Beauty

Heritage Coast

National Trails
nationaltrail.co.uk

3 Sections of the
National Cycle Network
nationalcyclenetwork.org.uk

Ferry routes

Broadway

Cheltenham · Stow-on-
Cotswolds the-Wold
Wye Gloucester
Valley
OFFA'S DYKE
PATH **♦** RIDGEWAY **♦**
COTSWOLD
WAY Swindon
4 Malmesbury THAMES
PATH **♦**
Bristol Avebury
Bath *North*
Wessex
Weston-super-Mare · Westbury *Downs*
Mendip
Hills **3** · Warminster
27 Lynton
Minehead **Salisbury** ○
SOUTH WEST *Cranborne*
COAST PATH *Quantock* **33** *Chase &*
Hills *West Wiltshire*
EXMOOR *Downs*
Barnstaple Taunton
Clovelly **3** · Yeovil
North *Blackdown*
Devon *Hills*
Bude *Dorset* **2**
Okehampton **Exeter** Lyme Bridport **Bournemouth**
Regis
Tintagel *East* Wareham · Poole ○
27 *Devon* Corfe
3 **DARTMOOR** SOUTH WEST Weymouth Swanage
Padstow *Tamar* COAST PATH **♦**
Valley Torbay
Newquay ○ Plymouth
32 *South*
Cornwall *Devon*
St Ives Truro St Austell
Penzance **3**
Falmouth

Isles of
Scilly

To Isles of Scilly

0 ———— 50 miles
0 ———— 75 kms

Bristol

Exeter

Devon's regional capital for culture, leisure and shopping is a vibrant city, steeped in ancient history. Don't miss the superb Decorated Gothic cathedral. Stroll along the historic Quayside, once the setting for a thriving wool trade and now a bustling riverside resort. Choose from over 700 shops, join a free Red Coat-guided city tour and dine in any one of numerous acclaimed restaurants. It's also the perfect base from which to explore the sweeping National Parks of Dartmoor and Exmoor.

Newquay

A beach paradise, stretching for seven miles, makes this one of Cornwall's premier resorts. Soaring cliffs alternate with sheltered coves, and thundering surf with secluded rock pools, smugglers' caves and soft golden sands. Whatever the weather, make a splash at Waterworld, or visit Newquay Zoo, one of the best wildlife parks in the country. Newquay offers an unforgettable holiday experience.

Clockwise: Exeter; Bournemouth; The Cotswolds

Poole

Poole is fast becoming known as the St Tropez of the south coast with its award-winning beaches, beautiful harbour, exhilarating watersports and famous pottery. Follow the Cockle Trail around the old town to discover its seafaring and trading history. Take the ferry to Brownsea Island between March and October for wonderful walks and wildlife spotting. Or relax and enjoy alfresco dining overlooking the harbour.

St Ives

What was once a small, thriving fishing village is now an internationally renowned haven for artists, attracted by the unique light. Explore the narrow streets and passageways and come upon countless galleries, studios and craft shops. Don't miss Tate St Ives and the Barbara Hepworth Museum. Enjoy the natural beauty of the harbour and explore Blue Flag beaches and coastal walks. Perfectly placed for all of West Cornwall's stunning scenery and famous attractions.

Tate, St Ives

Salisbury

Nestling in the heart of southern England, Salisbury is every bit the classic English city. The majestic cathedral boasts the tallest spire in England and rises elegantly above sweeping lawns. Wander through this medieval city and you'll find first-class visitor attractions, theatre and shopping. And, of course, no trip to Salisbury would be complete without the eight-mile pilgrimage to one of the greatest prehistoric sites in the world – Stonehenge.

For lots more great ideas visit visitbritain.com/destinations

Visitor attractions

Family and Fun

Babbacombe Model Village
Torquay, Devon
+44 (0) 1803 315315
babbacombemodelvillage.co.uk
England in miniature in four-acre gardens.

The Big Sheep
Bideford, Devon
+44 (0) 1237 472366
thebigsheep.co.uk
Family fun at the sheep races.

Blue Reef Aquarium
Newquay, Cornwall
+44 (0) 1637 878134
bluereefaquarium.co.uk
Close encounters with tropical sharks and rays.

Bristol Zoo Gardens
Bristol
+44 (0) 117 974 7399
bristolzoo.org.uk
Over 400 exotic and endangered species.

Cheddar Caves & Gorge
Cheddar, Somerset
+44 (0) 1934 742343
cheddarcaves.com
Britain's finest caves and deepest gorge.

Combe Martin Wildlife and Dinosaur Park
Combe Martin, Devon
+44 (0) 1271 882486
dinosaur-park.com
A subtropical bird, animal and dinosaur paradise.

Dairyland Farm World
Summercourt, Cornwall
+44 (0) 1872 510246
dairylandfarmworld.com
Country-life park, museum and adventure playground.

Devon's Crealy Great Adventure Park
near Exeter, Devon
+44 (0) 1395 233200
crealy.co.uk
All-weather attractions and friendly animals.

Farmer Palmer's Farm Park
Poole, Dorset
+44 (0) 1202 622022
farmerpalmers.co.uk
Farm activities for families with young children.

Kents Cavern Prehistoric Caves
Torquay, Devon
+44 (0) 1803 215136
kents-cavern.co.uk
Britain's most important Stone Age caves.

Living Coasts
Torquay, Devon
+44 (0) 1803 202470
livingcoasts.org.uk
Fascinating coastal creatures in a stunning location.

Longleat
Warminster, Wiltshire
+44 (0) 1985 844400
longleat.co.uk
Lions, tigers and a stately home.

The Monkey Sanctuary Trust
Looe, Cornwall
+44 (0) 1503 262532
monkeysanctuary.org
Colony of woolly monkeys.

National Marine Aquarium
Plymouth, Devon
+44 (0) 1752 600301
national-aquarium.co.uk
Sharks and seahorses at Britain's biggest aquarium.

Newquay Zoo
Newquay, Cornwall
+44 (0) 1637 873342
newquayzoo.org.uk
Exotic animals in subtropical lakeside gardens.

Noah's Ark Zoo Farm
Wraxall, Somerset
+44 (0) 1275 852606
noahsarkzoofarm.co.uk
Hands-on animal experiences for all ages.

Paignton Zoo Environmental Park
Paignton, Devon
+44 (0) 1803 697500
paigntonzoo.org.uk
Gorillas and crocodiles in 75-acre botanical gardens.

Pennywell - Devon's Farm and Wildlife Centre
Lower Dean, Devon
+44 (0) 1364 642023
pennywellfarm.co.uk
The South West's biggest farm-activity park.

Woodlands Leisure Park
Blackawton, Devon
+44 (0) 1803 712598
woodlandspark.com
Unique combination of indoor and outdoor attractions.

Wookey Hole Caves and Papermill
near Wells, Somerset
+44 (0) 1749 672243
wookey.co.uk
Spectacular caves and working Victorian papermill.

Heritage

The Bishop's Palace & Gardens
Wells, Somerset
+44 (0) 1749 678691
bishopspalacewells.co.uk
Splendid medieval palace and tranquil landscaped gardens.

Bowood House and Gardens
Chippenham, Wiltshire
+44 (0) 1249 812102
bowood.org
Wonderful 18thC Robert Adam house.

Corfe Castle
Corfe Castle, Dorset
+44 (0) 1929 477063
nationaltrust.org.uk
Majestic ruins of a former royal castle.

Cothay Manor & Gardens
near Wellington, Somerset
+44 (0) 1823 672283
cothaymanor.co.uk
Unspoilt medieval manor and romantic gardens.

Dunster Castle
Dunster, Somerset
+44 (0) 1643 821314
nationaltrust.org.uk
Romantic castle and subtropical gardens.

The Fashion Museum and Assembly Rooms
Bath, Somerset
+44 (0) 1225 477789
fashionmuseum.co.uk
Fine Georgian building with world-class dress collection.

Forde Abbey and Gardens
Small Visitor Attraction of the Year – Silver
Forde Abbey, Dorset
+44 (0) 1460 220231
fordeabbey.co.uk
Elegant former Cistercian monastery with gardens.

Lacock Abbey
Lacock, Wiltshire
+44 (0) 1249 730459
nationaltrust.org.uk
Fine country house with medieval cloisters.

Lanhydrock
Lanhydrock, Cornwall
+44 (0) 1208 265950
nationaltrust.org.uk
Re-built 17thC house with magnificent illustrated ceiling.

Lulworth Castle & Park
Wareham, Dorset
+44 (0) 845 450 1054
lulworth.com
Idyllic castle set in extensive park.

Montacute House
Montacute, Somerset
+44 (0) 1935 823289
nationaltrust.org.uk
Renaissance manor house filled with historic treasures.

Old Wardour Castle
Tisbury, Wiltshire
+44 (0) 1747 870487
english-heritage.org.uk
Unusual hexagonal ruins of a 14thC castle.

Pittville Pump Room
Cheltenham, Gloucestershire
+44 (0) 1242 523852
Beautiful, imposing example of Regency architecture.

Powderham Castle
Powderham, Devon
+44 (0) 1626 890243
powderham.co.uk
Restored medieval castle in beautiful deer park.

Roman Baths
Bath, Somerset
+44 (0) 1225 477785
romanbaths.co.uk
Magnificent Roman temple and hot-spring baths.

St Michael's Mount
Marazion, Cornwall
+44 (0) 1736 710507
stmichaelsmount.co.uk
Rocky island filled with astonishing history.

Salisbury Cathedral
Salisbury, Wiltshire
+44 (0) 1722 555120
salisburycathedral.org.uk
Britain's finest 13thC gothic cathedral.

Sherborne Castle
Sherborne, Dorset
+44 (0) 1935 813182
sherbornecastle.com
Tudor mansion built by Sir Walter Raleigh.

Sudeley Castle, Gardens and Exhibition
Winchcombe, Gloucestershire
+44 (0) 1242 602308
sudeleycastle.co.uk
Romantic castle and restored gardens.

Tintagel Castle
Tintagel, Cornwall
+44 (0) 1840 770328
english-heritage.org.uk
Evocative ruined castle on wind-swept coast.

Wells Cathedral
Wells, Somerset
+44 (0) 1749 674483
wellscathedral.org.uk
Superb 12thC cathedral in Early English style.

Wilton House
Wilton, Wiltshire
+44 (0) 1722 746714
wiltonhouse.com
Stunning 17thC state rooms and landscaped parkland.

Indoors

British Empire & Commonwealth Museum
Bristol
+44 (0) 117 925 4980
empiremuseum.co.uk
Explore a dramatic history and heritage.

Brunel's ss Great Britain
Bristol
+44 (0) 117 926 0680
ssgreatbritain.org
Experience life aboard Brunel's famous steam ship.

Cheltenham Art Gallery and Museum
Cheltenham, Gloucestershire
+44 (0) 1242 237431
cheltenham.artgallery.museum
World-renowned Arts and Crafts Movement collection.

The China Clay Museum
Carthew, Cornwall
+44 (0) 1726 850362
wheal-martyn.com
Restored clayworks in World Heritage mining landscape.

The Dinosaur Museum
Dorchester, Dorset
+44 (0) 1305 269880
thedinosaurmuseum.com
Life-sized reconstructions and hands-on displays.

Dorset County Museum
Dorchester, Dorset
+44 (0) 1305 262735
dorsetcountymuseum.org
The archeology and geology of Dorset.

The Dorset Teddy Bear Museum
Dorchester, Dorset
+44 (0) 1305 266040
teddybearmuseum.co.uk
Featuring a family of people-sized bears.

The Edward Jenner Museum
Berkeley, Gloucestershire
+44 (0) 1453 810631
jennermuseum.com
Life-story of the smallpox vaccine pioneer.

Explore-At-Bristol
Bristol
+44 (0) 845 345 1235
at-bristol.org.uk
An exciting hands-on science adventure.

Fleet Air Arm Museum
Yeovilton, Somerset
+44 (0) 1935 840565
fleetairarm.com
See Europe's largest collection of naval aircraft.

Geevor Tin Mine
Pendeen, Cornwall
+44 (0) 1736 788662
geevor.com
The largest preserved mining site in Britain.

The Museum of East Asian Art
Bath, Somerset
+44 (0) 1225 464640
meaa.org.uk
Jades, bronzes and ceramics from the East.

National Maritime Museum Cornwall
Falmouth, Cornwall
+44 (0) 1326 313388
nmmc.co.uk
Enthralling exhibits for landlubbers and sailors alike.

STEAM – Museum of the Great Western Railway
Swindon, Wiltshire
+44 (0) 1793 466646
swindon.gov.uk/steam
Interactive story of pioneering rail company.

Tate St Ives
St Ives, Cornwall
+44 (0) 1736 796226
tate.org.uk/stives
International art in striking beach-front gallery.

The Tutankhamun Exhibition
Dorchester, Dorset
+44 (0) 1305 269571
tutankhamun-exhibition.co.uk
Internationally-acclaimed exhibition with perfect reconstructions.

Outdoors

Abbey House Gardens
Malmesbury, Wiltshire
+44 (0) 1666 822212
abbeyhousegardens.co.uk
Wonderful displays featuring over 10,000 plants.

Eden Project
St Austell, Cornwall
+44 (0) 1726 811911
edenproject.com
A global garden for the 21st century.

Hidcote Manor Garden
near Chipping Campden, Gloucestershire
+44 (0) 1386 438333
nationaltrust.org.uk
Widely celebrated Arts and Crafts garden.

Land's End
Sennen, Cornwall
+44 (0) 871 720 0055
landsend-landmark.co.uk
Spectacular cliffs, breathtaking vistas and multi-sensory show.

The Lost Gardens of Heligan
near St Austell, Cornwall
+44 (0) 1726 845100
heligan.com
Glorious 200-acre restored garden and pleasure grounds.

The Minack Theatre and Visitor Centre
Porthcurno, Cornwall
+44 (0) 1736 810181
minack.com
Open-air cliff-side theatre with breathtaking views.

Painswick Rococo Garden
Painswick, Gloucestershire
+44 (0) 1452 813204
rococogarden.org.uk
A flamboyant piece of English garden design.

Pecorama
Beer, Devon
+44 (0) 1297 21542
peco-uk.com
Passenger-carrying miniature railway in spectacular gardens.

RHS Garden Rosemoor
Torrington, Devon
+44 (0) 1805 624067
rhs.org.uk/rosemoor
*Enchanting 65-acre year-round
garden.*

**Stonehenge and
Avebury World
Heritage Site**
near Salisbury, Wiltshire
+44 (0) 870 333 1181
english-heritage.org.uk
*World-famous prehistoric
monument.*

**Stourhead House
and Garden**
Stourton, Wiltshire
+44 (0) 1747 841152
nationaltrust.org.uk
*Palladian mansion with world-
renowned landscape gardens.*

Thermae Bath Spa
Bath, Somerset
+44 (0) 844 888 0848
thermaebathspa.com
*Enjoy Britain's only natural
thermal waters.*

Trelissick Garden
near Truro, Cornwall
+44 (0) 1872 862090
nationaltrust.org.uk
*Tender and exotic plants in
tranquil garden.*

Tresco Abbey Gardens
Isles of Scilly
+44 (0) 1720 424108
tresco.co.uk
*Tropical garden with species
from 80 countries.*

**Westonbirt, The
National Arboretum**
*Westonbirt,
Gloucestershire*
+44 (0) 1666 880220
forestry.gov.uk/westonbirt
*One of the world's finest tree
collections.*

**Wildfowl & Wetlands
Trust Slimbridge**
Slimbridge, Gloucestershire
+44 (0) 1453 891900
wwt.org.uk
*Home to an astounding array
of wildlife.*

**Willows & Wetlands
Visitor Centre**
Taunton, Somerset
+44 (0) 1823 490249
englishwillowbaskets.co.uk
*The art of willow growing and
basketmaking.*

**ASSURANCE OF
A GREAT DAY OUT**
Attractions with this
sign participate in the
Visitor Attraction Quality
Assurance Scheme which
recognises high standards in all
aspects of the visitor experience.

Events 2009

Walk Scilly
Isle of Scilly
walkscilly.co.uk
Mar

**Exeter Festival of South
West Food & Drink**
Exeter
visitsouthwest.co.uk/
exeterfoodfestival
Apr

Cheese Rolling
Brockworth
cheese-rolling.co.uk
25 May

Chippenham Folk Festival
Chippenham
chippfolk.co.uk
22 - 25 May

**Annual Nettle Eating
Contest**
Bridport
thebottleinn.co.uk
Jun

**Bristol International
Festival of Kites**
Bristol
kite-festival.org.uk
Aug

Spirit of the Sea
Weymouth
spiritofthesea.org.uk
Aug

Falmouth Oyster Festival
Falmouth
falmouthoysterfestival.co.uk
Oct

Bath Christmas Market
Bath
bathchristmasmarket.co.uk
Nov - Dec

Tar Barrels
Ottery St Mary
otterytourism.org.uk
5 Nov

**Bridgwater Guy Fawkes
Carnival**
Bridgwater
bridgwatercarnival.org.uk
6 Nov

Regional contacts and information

For more information on accommodation, attractions, activities, events and holidays in South West England, contact one of the following regional or local tourism organisations. Their websites have a wealth of information and many produce free publications to help you get the most out of your visit.

South West England

Visit the following websites for further information on South West England or call **+44 (0) 1392 360050**:

- visitsouthwest.co.uk
- swcp.org.uk
- accessiblesouthwest.co.uk

Publications available from South West Tourism:

- **The Trencherman's Guide to Top Restaurants in South West England**
- **Adventure South West**
  Your ultimate activity and adventure guide.
- **World Heritage Map**
  Discover our World Heritage.

Clockwise: Pedn Vounder, Cornwall; Gloucester Cathedral, Gloucestershire; Lynton, Devon

Tourist Information Centres

When you arrive at your destination, visit an Official Partner Tourist Information Centre for quality assured help with accommodation and information about local attractions and events, or email your request before you go. To search for attractions and Tourist Information Centres on the move just text INFO to 62233, and a web link will be sent to your mobile phone. To find a Tourist Information Centre by region visit enjoyEngland.com/find-tic.

Avebury	Green Street	+44 (0) 1672 539425	all.tic's@kennet.gov.uk
Bath	Abbey Church Yard	0906 711 2000**	tourism@bathtourism.co.uk
Bodmin	Mount Folly Square	+44 (0) 1208 76616	bodmintic@visit.org.uk
Bourton-on-the-Water	Victoria Street	+44 (0) 1451 820211	bourtonvic@btconnect.com
Bridport	47 South Street	+44 (0) 1308 424901	bridport.tic@westdorset-dc.gov.uk
Bristol	Harbourside	0906 711 2191**	ticharbourside@destinationbristol.co.uk
Brixham	The Quay	+44 (0) 1803 211 211	holiday@torbay.gov.uk
Bude	The Crescent	+44 (0) 1288 354240	budetic@visitbude.info
Burnham-on-Sea	South Esplanade	+44 (0) 1278 787852	burnham.tic@sedgemoor.gov.uk
Camelford*	The Clease	+44 (0) 1840 212954	manager@camelfordtic.eclipse.co.uk
Cartgate	A303/A3088 Cartgate Picnic Site	+44 (0) 1935 829333	cartgate.tic@southsomerset.gov.uk
Cheddar	The Gorge	+44 (0) 1934 744071	cheddar.tic@sedgemoor.gov.uk
Chippenham	Market Place	+44 (0) 1249 665970	tourism@chippenham.gov.uk
Chipping Campden	High Street	+44 (0) 1386 841206	information@visitchippingcampden.com
Christchurch	49 High Street	+44 (0) 1202 471780	enquiries@christchurchtourism.info
Cirencester	Market Place	+44 (0) 1285 654180	cirencestervic@cotswold.gov.uk
Coleford	High Street	+44 (0) 1594 812388	tourism@fdean.gov.uk
Corsham	31 High Street	+44 (0) 1249 714660	enquiries@corshamheritage.org.uk
Devizes	Market Place	+44 (0) 1380 729408	all.tic's@kennet.gov.uk
Dorchester	11 Antelope Walk	+44 (0) 1305 267992	dorchester.tic@westdorset-dc.gov.uk
Falmouth	Prince of Wales Pier	+44 (0) 1326 312300	info@falmouthtic.co.uk
Frome	Justice Lane	+44 (0) 1373 467271	frome.tic@ukonline.co.uk
Glastonbury	9 High Street	+44 (0) 1458 832954	glastonbury.tic@ukonline.co.uk
Gloucester	28 Southgate Street	+44 (0) 1452 396572	tourism@gloucester.gov.uk
Looe*	Fore Street	+44 (0) 1503 262072	looetic@btconnect.com
Lyme Regis	Church Street	+44 (0) 1297 442138	lymeregis.tic@westdorset-dc.gov.uk
Malmesbury	Market Lane	+44 (0) 1666 823748	malmesburyip@northwilts.gov.uk
Moreton-in-Marsh	High Street	+44 (0) 1608 650881	moreton@cotswold.gov.uk
Padstow	North Quay	+44 (0) 1841 533449	padstowtic@btconnect.com

Paignton	The Esplanade	+44 (0) 1803 211 211	holiday@torbay.gov.uk
Penzance	Station Road	+44 (0) 1736 362207	pztic@penwith.gov.uk
Plymouth Mayflower	3-5 The Barbican	+44 (0) 1752 306330	barbicantic@plymouth.gov.uk
St Ives	The Guildhall	+44 (0) 1736 796297	ivtic@penwith.gov.uk
Salisbury	Fish Row	+44 (0) 1722 334956	visitorinfo@salisbury.gov.uk
Shelton Mallet	70 High Street	+44 (0) 1749 345258	sheptonmallet.tic@ukonline.co.uk
Sherborne	3 Tilton Court, Digby Road	+44 (0) 1935 815341	sherborne.tic@westdorset-dc.gov.uk
Somerset	Sedgemoor Services	+44 (0) 1934 750833	somersetvisitorcentre@somerset.gov.uk
Stow-on-the-Wold	The Square	+44 (0) 1451 831082	stowvic@cotswold.gov.uk
Street	Farm Road	+44 (0) 1458 447384	street.tic@ukonline.co.uk
Stroud	George Street	+44 (0) 1453 760960	tic@stroud.gov.uk
Swanage	Shore Road	+44 (0) 1929 422885	mail@swanage.gov.uk
Swindon	37 Regent Street	+44 (0) 1793 530328	infocentre@swindon.gov.uk
Taunton	Paul Street	+44 (0) 1823 336344	tauntontic@tauntondeane.gov.uk
Tewkesbury	100 Church Street	+44 (0) 1684 855043	tewkesburytic@tewkesburybc.gov.uk
Torquay	Vaughan Parade	+44 (0) 1803 211 211	holiday@torbay.gov.uk
Truro	Boscawen Street	+44 (0) 1872 274555	tic@truro.gov.uk
Wadebridge	Eddystone Road	+44 (0) 870 1223337	wadebridgetic@btconnect.com
Wareham	South Street	+44 (0) 1929 552740	tic@purbeck-dc.gov.uk
Warminster	off Station Rd	+44 (0) 1985 218548	visitwarminster@btconnect.com
Wells	Market Place	+44 (0) 1749 672552	touristinfo@wells.gov.uk
Weston-super-Mare	Beach Lawns	+44 (0) 1934 888800	westontouristinfo@n-somerset.gov.uk
Weymouth	The Esplanade	+44 (0) 1305 785747	tic@weymouth.gov.uk
Winchcombe	High Street	+44 (0) 1242 602925	winchcombetic@tewkesbury.gov.uk
Yeovil	Hendford	+44 (0) 1935 845946/7	yeoviltic@southsomerset.gov.uk

*seasonal opening

**UK number only, charged at premium rate

Left to right: Jurassic Coast, Dorset; Minack Theatre, Cornwall

Help before you go

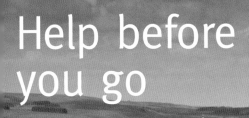

When it comes to your next break, the first stage of your journey could be closer than you think.

You've probably got a Tourist Information Centre nearby which is there to serve the local community – as well as visitors. Knowledgeable staff will be happy to help you, wherever you're heading.

Many Tourist Information Centres can provide you with maps and guides, and it's often possible to book accommodation and travel tickets too.

You'll find the address of your nearest centre in your local phone book, or look in the regional sections in this guide for a list of Tourist Information Centres.

where to stay in
South West England

All place names in the blue bands are shown on the maps at the front of this guide.

Accommodation symbols

Symbols give useful information about services and facilities. On pages 16 to 17 you can find a key to these symbols.

ALTARNUN, Cornwall Map ref 1C2 SELF CATERING

★★★
SELF CATERING

Units **1**
Sleeps **1–2**

LOW SEASON PER WK
£200.00–£240.00

HIGH SEASON PER WK
£250.00–£360.00

Trenarrett Cottage, Altarnun, Launceston

contact Mrs Anne Langley, Trenarrett Cottage, Little Trenarrett, Altarnun PL15 7SY
t +44 (0) 1566 86649 **e** anne@trenarrett.co.uk

trenarrett.co.uk

Comfortable, well-equipped, rural cottage with one double bedroom and en suite shower. Living room with moorland view. Baby equipment, pets welcome. Secluded, quiet location, easy access all of Cornwall. Good walking.

open All year
payment Cash, cheques, euros
nearest pub 1.6 miles
nearest shop 2 miles

Unit 📺 📀 💻 🖨 🍽 🔌 📻 🍴 💶 ✳ ⛺ General 🏢 ♿ P Ⓞ Ⓢ 🐕 Leisure ♪

ASHBURTON, Devon Map ref 1C2 CAMPING, CARAVAN & HOLIDAY PARK

Parkers Farm Cottages & Caravans

Mead Alston Cross, Ashburton, Devon TQ13 7LJ
Tel (01364) 653008
E-mail: parkerscottages@btconnect.com · Web: www.parkersfarm.co.uk

15 attractive holiday cottages set around a large courtyard with ample car parking areas. Each cottage is fully equipped with full size cooker, microwave, refrigerator, airing cupboard and colour TV. All bed linen is provided, with beds made up for your arrival. We also have 14 self-contained holiday caravans set in lovely open countryside, some with moorland views – see www.parkersfarm.co.uk

---

Check the maps for accommodation locations

Colour maps at the front pinpoint all the places where accommodation is featured within the regional sections of this guide. Pick your location and then refer to the place index at the back to find the page number.

BARNSTAPLE, Devon   Map ref 1C1 — GUEST ACCOMMODATION

★★★★
GUEST HOUSE
SILVER AWARD

B&B PER ROOM PER NIGHT
S £26.00–£29.00
D £52.00–£58.00

EVENING MEAL PER PERSON
Min £16.00

The Spinney

Shirwell, Barnstaple EX31 4JR   t +44 (0) 1271 850282   e thespinney@shirwell.fsnet.co.uk

thespinneyshirwell.co.uk

open All year
bedrooms 1 double, 1 twin, 1 single, 2 family
bathrooms 3 en suite, 2 private
payment Credit/debit cards, cash, cheques

A former rectory, set in over an acre of grounds with views towards Exmoor. Spacious accommodation, en suite available. Centrally heated. Delicious meals cooked by chef/proprietor, served during summer months in our restored Victorian conservatory under the ancient vine. Residential licence. The Spinney is non-smoking.

SAT NAV EX31 4JR

Room 📺 ⬥ ⌕   General ⛱ P ♟ ✕ ⛺ ✿ ♞

BATH, Somerset   Map ref 2B2 — GUEST ACCOMMODATION

★★★★★
GUEST HOUSE
GOLD AWARD

B&B PER ROOM PER NIGHT
S £55.00–£65.00
D £75.00–£88.00

3 nights for 2/50% off second night, Nov-Feb. 4 nights for 3/50% off third night, Mar-May and Sep-Oct.

Athole Guest House

33 Upper Oldfield Park, Bath BA2 3JX   t +44 (0) 1225 320000   e info@atholehouse.co.uk

atholehouse.co.uk GUEST REVIEWS · SPECIAL OFFERS · REAL-TIME BOOKING

open All year
bedrooms 4 double, 1 family
bathrooms All en suite
payment Credit/debit cards, cash, cheques, euros

Large Victorian home restored to give bright, inviting, quiet bedrooms, sleek furniture, sparkling bathrooms, digital TV, Wi-Fi internet in all bedrooms, safe. Hospitality is old style. Award-winning breakfasts. Relax in our gardens, or let us help you explore the area. Secure parking behind remote-control gates or in garage. Twelve minutes' walk from centre. Free transfer from/to station.

SAT NAV BA2 3JX **ONLINE MAP**

Room 📞 📺 SC ⬥ ⌕   General ⛱ ⛺ ♟ P ♫ ✿ ❋   Leisure 🚲

BATH, Somerset   Map ref 2B2 — GUEST ACCOMMODATION

★★★★★
GUEST ACCOMMODATION
GOLD AWARD

B&B PER ROOM PER NIGHT
D £80.00–£185.00

We offer short-break weekday packages during Dec-Feb winter season. Details available on request.

The Ayrlington

24-25 Pulteney Road, Bath BA2 4EZ   t +44 (0) 1225 425495   e mail@ayrlington.com

ayrlington.com SPECIAL OFFERS

open All year except Christmas and New Year
bedrooms 13 double, 1 twin
bathrooms All en suite
payment Credit/debit cards, cash, cheques

Located within an easy five-minute level walk of Bath city centre, The Ayrlington is a small, tranquil, non-smoking, luxury hotel. The Ayrlington has recently been extended and refurbished throughout – all fourteen bedrooms have an individual theme and are beautifully furnished, some with four poster beds.

SAT NAV BA2 4EZ

Room ⛲ 🖥 📞 📺 ⬥ ⌕   General ⛺ P ♫ ✿ ♟ ◻ ❋   Leisure ▶

Looking for a wide range of facilities?

More stars means higher quality accommodation plus a greater range of facilities and services.

★★★★
GUEST ACCOMMODATION

B&B PER ROOM PER NIGHT
S £80.00–£95.00
D £85.00–£140.00

£5 off each night for stays of 3 nights or more.

Marlborough House

1 Marlborough Lane, Bath BA1 2NQ   t +44 (0) 1225 318175   e mars@manque.dircon.co.uk

marlborough-house.net

open All year except Christmas
bedrooms 3 double, 2 twin, 1 single, 2 family
bathrooms All en suite
payment Credit/debit cards, cash, cheques, euros

Enchanting Victorian town house in Bath's Georgia centre, exquisitely furnished and run in an elegant and friendly style, with beautiful en suite rooms featuring four-poster or antique wood beds. Both vegetarian and organic, our amazing breakfast choices include freshly prepared fruit, organic yoghurts and juices. Also speciality omelettes and Marlborough House potatoes.

SAT NAV *BA1 2NQ*

Room 🛗🖼️📞📺☕🍷   General 🛏️🏛️🪑P 📶🍽️🥂🍴❄️🐾

★★★★
GUEST ACCOMMODATION

B&B PER ROOM PER NIGHT
S £35.00–£45.00
D £55.00–£65.00

Walton Villa

3 Newbridge Hill, Bath BA1 3PW   t +44 (0) 1225 482792   e walton.villa@virgin.net

walton.izest.com GUEST REVIEWS

Family-run bed and breakfast, offering pretty en suite/private facilities accommodation. One mile from city centre. Off-street parking and bus service nearby.

open All year except Christmas and New Year
bedrooms 2 double, 1 twin, 1 single
bathrooms 3 en suite, 1 private
payment Credit/debit cards, cash, cheques

Room 📺☕🍷   General 🛏️1 🪑P 📶🍴❄️   Leisure 🚲

★★★★
SELF CATERING

Units   **8**
Sleeps   **2–6**

LOW SEASON PER WK
£285.00–£645.00

HIGH SEASON PER WK
£465.00–£1,150.00

4-night midweek break (Mon-Thu) available at same price as 3-night weekend break (Fri-Sun), excl school holidays.

Church Farm Country Cottages, Bradford-on-Avon

contact Mrs Trish Bowles, Church Farm, Winsley, Bradford-on-Avon BA15 2JH
t +44 (0) 1225 722246   e stay@churchfarmcottages.com

churchfarmcottages.com GUEST REVIEWS · SPECIAL OFFERS

open All year
payment Credit/debit cards, cash, cheques, euros
nearest pub less than 0.5 miles
nearest shop less than 0.5 miles

Eight well equipped, tastefully converted single-storey cottages sleeping two, four or six. Working farm with sheep and horses. Luxurious, heated indoor swimming pool (12m x 5m), games room. Pub/shop 500m. Kennet & Avon Canal nearby for boating, cycling and walking. Welcome cream tea. Green Tourism Business Scheme Silver Award.

ONLINE MAP

Unit 📺🖼️📀📼🍳🍽️❄️🪑   General 🛏️🏛️🪑P◻️S🐾
Leisure 🎣🎾U🎿🏌️🚲

Need some ideas?

Big city buzz or peaceful panoramas? Take a fresh look at England and you may be surprised at what's right on your doorstep. Explore the diversity online at enjoyengland.com

BATH, Somerset Map ref 2B2

★★★★–★★★★★
SELF CATERING

Units **5**
Sleeps **2–4**

LOW SEASON PER WK
£231.00–£366.00

HIGH SEASON PER WK
£378.00–£549.00

Fully flexible bookings and short breaks available all year round. Availability calendar and full details available on our website.

Greyfield Farm Cottages, High Littleton

contact Mrs June Merry, Greyfield Farm Cottages, Greyfield Road, High Littleton, Bristol BS39 6YQ
t +44 (0) 1761 471132 **e** june@greyfieldfarm.com

greyfieldfarm.com SPECIAL OFFERS · REAL-TIME BOOKING

open All year
payment Cash, cheques, euros
nearest pub 0.5 miles
nearest shop 0.5 miles

Attractive stone cottages in peaceful, private, 3.5-acre setting overlooking the Mendips. The cottages are spacious, fully equipped, warm and very comfortable. Each enjoys its own garden/patio and adjacent safe parking. Free facilities include hot tub, sauna, fitness and barbecue centres plus video/DVD library.

ONLINE MAP

Unit TV 📺 🖥 ⬛ 🔲🔒 🍴🔥 🗄 📀 ❄ ☀ 🍖 🌡 General 🛏 🏠 🌳 P 🅾 Ⓢ 🐴
Leisure ↻ ♪ ►

BATH, Somerset Map ref 2B2

★★★★
TOURING &
CAMPING PARK

🚐 (90)   £19.50–£22.00
🚎 (90)   £19.50–£22.00
⛺ (105)   £7.00–£19.50
195 touring pitches

New Year party package.

Newton Mill Camping

Twaebrook Ltd, Newton Mill Camping Park, Newton Road, Bath BA2 9JF **t** +44 (0) 1225 333909
e newtonmill@hotmail.com

campinginbath.co.uk

open All year
payment Credit/debit cards, cash, cheques

Situated in an idyllic hidden valley close to the city centre with easy access by frequent, local buses or nearby level, traffic-free cycle path. Superb heated amenities (5-star Loo of the Year 2008) including showers, bathrooms and private facilities. Old Mill bar/restaurant open all year. David Bellamy Gold Award for Conservation. ADAC Campingplatz Auszeichnung 2008.

SAT NAV *BA2 9JF* **ONLINE MAP**

General 🖥 🚗 💷 🖐 ♨ 📶 📡 📇 🛒 ✗ 🐴 ☀ Leisure 🍴 🎣 ⛰ ↻ ♪ ► 🚲

BERRYNARBOR, Devon Map ref 1C1

Smythen Farm Coastal Holiday Cottages, Ilfracombe

★★★
SELF CATERING

Units **4**
Sleeps **2–7**

LOW SEASON PER WK
£95.00–£301.00

HIGH SEASON PER WK
£320.00–£994.00

contact Mr & Ms Thompson & Elstone, Smythen Farm Coastal Holiday Cottages, Symthen, Sterrid Valley, Berrynarbor, Ilfracombe EX34 9TB t +44 (0) 1271 882875
e jayne@smythenfarmholidaycottages.co.uk

smythenfarmholidaycottages.co.uk SPECIAL OFFERS

open March to January
payment Cash, cheques
nearest pub 1.5 miles
nearest shop 1.5 miles

Near golden sands with sea and coastal views. Heated, covered swimming pool in a suntrap enclosure, gardens and games room with pool tab table tennis, football machine. Tree-house on two levels. Free pony rides, ball pond and bouncy cast 14-acre recreation field and dog walk. For colour brochure phone Jayne.

ONLINE MAP

Unit 📺 📼 💻 🔲 🖥️ 🍽️ ♨️ ⛱️ General 🐴 🏛️ 🚶 P ⭕ Ⓢ 🐕
Leisure 🎿 ⛳ 🎣 ♨️ 🏊 🚲

BIDEFORD, Devon Map ref 1C1

Coachmans Cottage, Monkleigh, Bideford

★★★
SELF CATERING

Units **1**
Sleeps **2**

LOW SEASON PER WK
£150.00–£200.00

HIGH SEASON PER WK
£200.00–£275.00

contact Mr & Mrs Tom & Sue Downie, Cream Tea Cottages, Staddon House, Monkleigh, Bideford EX39 5JR t +44 (0) 1805 623670 e tom.downie@ukonline.co.uk

creamteacottages.co.uk GUEST REVIEWS · SPECIAL OFFERS

Charming character cottage set in traditional courtyard surroundings. Our price includes all linen, logs for the woodburner and a cream tea to help you settle in after your journey.

open All year
payment Credit/debit cards, cash, cheques
nearest pub less than 0.5 miles
nearest shop less than 0.5 miles

Unit 📺 📼 💻 🔲 🖥️ 🍽️ ♨️ ⛱️ General 🐴 🏛️ 🚶 P ⭕ Ⓢ 🐕 Leisure 🚲

BIDEFORD, Devon Map ref 1C1

Cream Tea Cottages, Little Torrington, Torrington

★★★★
SELF CATERING

Units **3**
Sleeps **4–14**

LOW SEASON PER WK
£180.00–£250.00

HIGH SEASON PER WK
£250.00–£575.00

Special prices for out-of-season 3-night or weekend breaks. Please ring for details.

contact Mr & Mrs Tom & Sue Downie, Staddon House, Monkleigh, Bideford EX39 5JR
t +44 (0) 1805 623670 e tom.downie@ukonline.co.uk

creamteacottages.co.uk GUEST REVIEWS · SPECIAL OFFERS

open All year
payment Credit/debit cards, cash, cheques
nearest pub 2 miles
nearest shop 2 miles

Set in a lovely location, these cottages are converte barns dating back to the 1700s. They retain many original features but are renovated to modern standards. The properties all have french windows opening onto their own patios. There is also a play and picnic area for children.

ONLINE MAP

Unit 📺 📼 💻 🔲 🖥️ 🍽️ ♨️ ⛱️ General 🐴 🏛️ 🚶 P ⭕ Ⓢ 🐕 Leisure 🚲

Where can I get help and advice?

Tourist Information Centres offer friendly help with accommodation and holiday ideas as well as suggestions of places to visit and things to do. You'll find contact details at the beginning of each regional section.

BIGBURY-ON-SEA, Devon Map ref 1C3 — SELF CATERING

★★★★★
SELF CATERING

Units **1**
Sleeps **1–4**

LOW SEASON PER WK
£451.00–£1,031.00

HIGH SEASON PER WK
£1,155.00–£1,621.00

Bargain weekend and short-stay breaks available in autumn and winter months.

Apartment 5, Burgh Island Causeway, Bigbury-on-Sea

Helpful Holidays, Mill Street, Chagford, Newton Abbot TQ13 8AW t +44 (0) 1647 433593
e help@helpfulholidays.com

helpfulholidays.com GUEST REVIEWS · SPECIAL OFFERS · REAL-TIME BOOKING

open All year
payment Credit/debit cards, cash, cheques
nearest pub less than 0.5 miles
nearest shop less than 0.5 miles

Luxury, modern, ground-floor apartment set into cliff with panoramic southerly views from large patio. Facilities include pool, gym, sauna, cafe/bar, grassy cliff-top grounds and direct access to beautiful large sandy beach and coastal path. Popular for surfing and near golf course and village shop/post office. View www.burghislandcauseway.com

SAT NAV TQ7 4AS **ONLINE MAP**

Unit TV SC ⊞ 🔌 DVD 🎮 ⬛ 📠 🔒 ⊑ 🔁 🍴 ❄ General 🛏 🏠 ♿ P S 🐕
Leisure ⚲ ♪ ▸

BINEGAR, Somerset Map ref 2B2 — SELF CATERING

★★★★
SELF CATERING

Units **1**
Sleeps **5**

LOW SEASON PER WK
£370.00–£450.00

HIGH SEASON PER WK
£495.00–£610.00

Short breaks available Oct-Mar, 2-/3-night stays.

Spindle Cottage, Binegar Green, Nr Bath

contact Mrs Angela Bunting, Spindle Cottage, Binegar Green, Binegar, Near Bath BA3 4UE
t +44 (0) 1749 840497 e angela@spindlecottage.co.uk

spindlecottage.co.uk SPECIAL OFFERS

open All year
payment Cash, cheques
nearest pub 0.5 miles
nearest shop 1 mile

Fairy-tale 17thC cottage, high on Mendip Hills. Garden has summerhouse, gazebo, conservatory. Cottage is a place of charm and delight. Lovely sitting room with low ceiling and oak beams. Wood-burning stove. Three bedrooms: one double, one twin, one single. Wells, Glastonbury, Bath, Cheddar, Wookey Hole within easy reach.

ONLINE MAP

Unit TV DVD ⬛ 📠 🔒 ⊑ 🔁 🍴 ❄ 🧺 ✏ General 🛏 🏠 ♿ P ◌ S Leisure ∪ ♪ ▸

BLANDFORD FORUM, Dorset Map ref 2B3 — GUEST ACCOMMODATION

★★★★
FARMHOUSE

B&B PER ROOM PER NIGHT
S £60.00
D £60.00–£65.00

B&B for your horse is available.

Lower Bryanston Farm B&B

Lower Bryanston, Blandford Forum DT11 0LS t +44 (0) 1258 452009 e andrea@bryanstonfarm.co.uk

brylow.co.uk

open All year except Christmas and New Year
bedrooms 3 double, 1 twin, 1 family
bathrooms 3 en suite, 2 private
payment Cash, cheques

Attractive Georgian farmhouse with spacious rooms and beautiful rural views. All rooms equipped with hospitality tray, TV and DVD player. Fantastic full English breakfast. Safe off-road parking. Superb central location to explore the interesting county of Dorset. Within walking distance of Blandford. Blandford Camp and Bryanston school nearby.

SAT NAV DT11 0LS

Room TV ☕ 🔒 General 🛏 🏠 ♿ P 📶 🔥 🧺 ❄ Leisure ∪

BOSCASTLE, Cornwall Map ref 1B2 — HOTE

★★
HOTEL
SILVER AWARD

Wellington Hotel

The Harbour, Boscastle PL35 0AQ t +44 (0) 1840 250202 e info@boscastle-wellington.com

boscastle-wellington.com SPECIAL OFFERS

B&B PER ROOM PER NIGHT
S £40.00–£45.00
D £80.00–£130.00
HB PER PERSON PER NIGHT
£60.00–£85.00

Special breaks
available throughout
the year. 10%
discount for 4 or
more nights; 15%
discount for 7 or
more nights.

open All year
bedrooms 8 double, 1 twin, 4 single, 2 family
bathrooms All en suite
payment Credit/debit cards, cash, cheques

Listed 16thC coaching inn in the Elizabethan harbou of Boscastle. Fantastic fine-dining restaurant. Traditional pub with Cornish ales, home-cooked foo and log fire. Ten acres of private woodland walks and close to coastal path. Ideal location for discovering Cornwall. Recently refurbished after th Boscastle floods.

SAT NAV *PL35 0AQ* ONLINE MAP

Room ☎ 📺 ♿ ⚑ ✎ ▭ General ☎ ▥ ♟ P ⚐ ▼ ⬛ ● ☂ ✳ Leisure ∪ ♦ ► ♣

BOSCASTLE, Cornwall Map ref 1B2 — SELF CATERING

★★★
SELF CATERING

Old Newham Farm, Camelford

contact Mr & Mrs Purdue, Old Newham Farm, Otterham, Camelford PL32 9SR
t +44 (0) 1840 230470 **e** tbg@old-newham.co.uk

old-newham.co.uk

Units   **3**
Sleeps   **1–4**

LOW SEASON PER WK
£200.00–£450.00

HIGH SEASON PER WK
£300.00–£600.00

Short breaks
available Oct-Mar.

open All year
payment Credit/debit cards, cash, cheques
nearest pub 2 miles
nearest shop 2 miles

Characterful stone cottages on peaceful 30-acre organic farm dating back to medieval times with cattle, sheep and other small animals for children. Well away from traffic down a quiet lane, the peac of the Cornish countryside only three miles from th most spectacular National Trust coastline/beaches. Internet access.

Unit 📺 📻 ▭ 🖥 🍴 ⚑ 🍽 ✎ ✳ ⛏ General ☎ ▥ ♟ ◻ 🐕 Leisure ∪ ♦ ♣

BOURNEMOUTH, Dorset Map ref 2B3 — GUEST ACCOMMODATION

★★★★
GUEST ACCOMMODATION

Cransley

11 Knyveton Road, East Cliff, Bournemouth BH1 3QG t +44 (0) 1202 290067 e info@cransley.com

cransley.com

B&B PER ROOM PER NIGHT
S £35.00–£40.00
D £70.00–£80.00

open All year except Christmas
bedrooms 6 double, 3 twin, 2 single
bathrooms 10 en suite, 1 private
payment Credit/debit cards, cash

A quiet, tree-lined road in the attractive East Cliff area of Bournemouth is the setting for this homely B&B for non-smokers. The hotel's sunny position means bedrooms are bright and welcoming. French windows lead from the sitting room and dining room to a secluded, south-facing, award-winning garden.

SAT NAV *BH1 3QG*

Room ♿ 📺 ♿ ⚑ General ☎ 14 P ⚐ ⚑ ✳

What shall we do today?

For ideas on places to visit, see the beginning of this regional section
or go online at enjoyengland.com.

BOURNEMOUTH, Dorset Map ref 2B3 — GUEST ACCOMMODATION

★★★
GUEST ACCOMMODATION

B&B PER ROOM PER NIGHT
S £25.00–£35.00
D £60.00–£80.00

Cremona

St Michaels Road, West Cliff, Bournemouth BH2 5DP t +44 (0) 1202 290035
e enquiries@cremona.co.uk

cremona.co.uk GUEST REVIEWS

Victorian terraced town house covering three floors. Clean and comfortable, European feel throughout. Good location for the beach, gardens, town centre and Bournemouth International Centre.

open All year
bedrooms 4 double, 2 twin, 1 single, 2 family
bathrooms All en suite
payment Credit/debit cards, cash, euros

Room 🛏 📺 🆂 🚻 🍴 General 🛅 🛏 🔥 ⓘ 🍽 ✲ 🐾 Leisure ∪ 🚣 🚲

BOURNEMOUTH, Dorset Map ref 2B3 — CAMPING, CARAVAN & HOLIDAY PARK

★★★★★
HOLIDAY &
TOURING PARK
ROSE AWARD

🚐 (41)   £8.00–£26.00
🚙 (41)   £8.00–£26.00
🏠 (75) £170.00–£895.00
41 touring pitches

Meadow Bank Holidays

Stour Way, Christchurch BH23 2PQ t +44 (0) 1202 483597 e enquiries@meadowbank-holidays.co.uk

meadowbank-holiday.co.uk SPECIAL OFFERS

open March to October
payment Credit/debit cards, cash, cheques

Meadowbank Holidays operate Bournemouth's closest holiday caravan and touring park. We are superbly located on the beautiful River Stour and provide a wonderful relaxing environment for a peaceful, carefree holiday or break visiting the superb local beaches, New Forest or the famous Jurassic Coast.

SAT NAV BH23 2PQ

General 🔌 🚻 🚿 🅦 📶 📷 🛒 ☀ Leisure 🎣 ⛰ ∪ 🚣 ▸

BOX, Wiltshire Map ref 2B2 — GUEST ACCOMMODATION

Rating Applied For
GUEST HOUSE

B&B PER ROOM PER NIGHT
S £40.00–£50.00
D £70.00–£80.00

Lorne House

London Road, Box, Corsham SN13 8NA t +44 (0) 1225 742597 e info@lornehouse.box.co.uk

lornehousebox.co.uk

open All year except Christmas and New Year
bedrooms 4 double/twin
bathrooms All en suite
payment Credit/debit cards, cash, cheques

Newly refurbished B&B close to Bath with charm and character. Childhood home of the Reverend Awdry of Thomas the Tank Engine fame. Lovingly restored, individually designed bedrooms, creature comforts including flat-screen TVs. A warm and friendly welcome.

SAT NAV SN13 8NA

Room 📺 🚻 🍴 General 🛅 🛏 🔥 P ⓘ 🔥 🍽 ✲ Leisure ∪ ▸ 🚲

It's all quality-assessed accommodation

Our commitment to quality involves wide-ranging accommodation assessment. Ratings and awards were correct at the time of going to press but may change following a new assessment. Please check at time of booking.

BRADFORD-ON-AVON, Wiltshire Map ref 2B2 | **SELF CATERING**

★★★★★
SELF CATERING

Units **3**
Sleeps **1-15**

LOW SEASON PER WK
£650.00-£750.00

HIGH SEASON PER WK
£900.00-£1,300.00

Short breaks available Sep-Jun.

Fairfield Barns, Atworth

contact Mr & Mrs Taff & Gilly Thomas, Bradford Road, Atworth, Melksham SN12 8HZ
t +44 (0) 1225 703585 **e** gilly@fairfieldbarns.com

fairfieldbarns.com GUEST REVIEWS · SPECIAL OFFERS

open All year
payment Credit/debit cards, cash, cheques
nearest pub 0.5 miles
nearest shop less than 0.5 miles

In a quiet village near Bath, two luxurious barn conversions with panoramic views of the Wiltshire countryside. En suite bedrooms. Also a cosy terrace cottage in the heart of the village. All superbly equipped. Use of indoor swimming pool, gym, tennis court, sauna, children's playhouse and adventure playground. Perfect for sightseeing and touring.

ONLINE MAP

Unit ⬛⬛⬛⬛⬛⬛⬛⬛⬛⬛⬛⬛ General ⬛⬛⬛P⬛
Leisure ⬛⬛⬛⬛⬛

BRIDGWATER, Somerset Map ref 1D1 | **GUEST ACCOMMODATION**

★★★★
RESTAURANT WITH ROOMS

B&B PER ROOM PER NIGHT
S £49.50-£55.00
D £65.00-£75.00

The Olive Mill

Chilton Polden Hill, Bridgwater TA7 9AH **t** +44 (0) 1278 722202 **e** enquiries@theolivemill.co.uk

theolivemill.co.uk GUEST REVIEWS · SPECIAL OFFERS · REAL-TIME BOOKING

Mediterranean cuisine prepared and served with excellence in the heart of the West Country. Rooms with outstanding views of the Mendips.

open All year
bedrooms 7 double
bathrooms All en suite
payment Credit/debit cards, cash, cheques

Room ⬛⬛⬛⬛ General ⬛P⬛⬛⬛X⬛⬛ Leisure ⬛⬛⬛

BRIDPORT, Dorset Map ref 2A3 | **HOTEL**

★★
HOTEL

B&B PER ROOM PER NIGHT
S £59.00-£78.00
D £89.00-£122.00

Bridge House Hotel

115 East Street, Bridport DT6 3LB **t** +44 (0) 1308 423371 **e** info@bridgehousebridport.co.uk

bridgehousebridport.co.uk

open All year
bedrooms 3 double, 1 twin, 3 single, 3 family
bathrooms All en suite
payment Credit/debit cards, cash, cheques

18thC Georgian character town house, next to the river and its gardens. Offers quiet elegance, traditional ambience and friendly service. Elegant lounge, ten en suite bedrooms and a fine, fully licensed restaurant using fresh, local, quality produce prepared individually for your enjoyment. Free parking near the town centre.

SAT NAV DT6 3LB

Room ⬛⬛⬛⬛⬛ General ⬛⬛⬛P⬛⬛⬛⬛⬛⬛ Leisure ⬛⬛⬛⬛

Remember to check when booking

Please remember that all information in this guide has been supplied by the proprietors well in advance of publication. Since changes do sometimes occur it's a good idea to check details at the time of booking.

BRIDPORT, Dorset Map ref 2A3

★★★
HOTEL

B&B PER ROOM PER NIGHT
S £60.00–£100.00
D £70.00–£180.00

Please check our website or call for current offers.

The Bull Hotel

34 East Street, Bridport DT6 3LF **t** +44 (0) 1308 422878 **e** info@thebullhotel.co.uk

thebullhotel.co.uk SPECIAL OFFERS

open All year
bedrooms 9 double, 1 twin, 1 single, 2 family, 1 suite
bathrooms All en suite
payment Credit/debit cards, cash, cheques

The Bull Hotel and Restaurant is set right in the heart of the bustling, historic, market town of Bridport and just a mile from the Jurassic Coast and spectacular walking. A Grade II Listed coaching inn with gorgeous rooms, delicious food, funky bar, Georgian ballroom. Family-run and child-friendly.

SAT NAV DT6 3LF **ONLINE MAP**

Room 🖼 📞 📺 ☕ 🍷 General 🛎 🏚 🔥 P 📶 🍴 🎱 🍽 ❄ Leisure ∪ 🚶 🏇 🚴

BRIDPORT, Dorset Map ref 2A3

★★★
INN

B&B PER ROOM PER NIGHT
S Min £50.00
D Min £60.00

EVENING MEAL PER PERSON
£6.95–£9.95

The Tiger Inn

14-16 Barrack Street, Bridport DT6 3LY **t** +44 (0) 1308 427543 **e** jacquie@tigerinnbridport.co.uk

tigerinnbridport.co.uk

Grade II Listed freehouse pub. Town-centre location. All rooms en suite. Superb food, skittles alley. Pretty courtyard garden.

open All year
bedrooms 1 double, 1 twin, 2 family
bathrooms All en suite
payment Credit/debit cards, cash, cheques

Room 📺 ☕ 🍷 General 🛎 🔥 🍴 ✕ ❄

BRIXHAM, Devon Map ref 1D2

★★★★
GUEST ACCOMMODATION

B&B PER ROOM PER NIGHT
S £36.00–£40.00
D £64.00–£80.00

3-day break B&B £108-£114 per person. 7-day break B&B £245-£259 per person.

Ranscombe House

Ranscombe Road, Brixham TQ5 9UP **t** +44 (0) 1803 882337 **e** ranscombe@lineone.net

ranscombehousehotel.co.uk

open All year except Christmas and New Year
bedrooms 5 double, 1 twin, 1 single, 2 family
bathrooms All en suite
payment Credit/debit cards, cash, cheques, euros

A picturesque turn-of-the-19thC house standing in its own grounds and with garden and ample car park, overlooking Brixham's outer harbour and Torbay. The walk to the harbour and marina is about 300yds. Whatever the time of year, there will be a warm welcome for you.

SAT NAV TQ5 9UP **ONLINE MAP**

Room 📺 ☕ 🍷 General 🛎 🏚 🔥 P 📶 🍴 ❄ Leisure 🚶

BRIXHAM, Devon Map ref 1D2

★★★
SELF CATERING

Units **2**
Sleeps **1–4**

LOW SEASON PER WK
Min £255.00

HIGH SEASON PER WK
Max £515.00

Galmpton Touring Park Cottages, Brixham

contact Mrs Pam Collins, Galmpton Touring Park Cottages, Greenway Road, Brixham TQ5 0EP **t** +44 (0) 1803 842066 **e** galmptontouringpark@hotmail.com

gtpcottages.co.uk

Two comfortable cottages in beautiful countryside on edge of village near Brixham. A quiet base from which to explore South Devon. Beaches and attractions nearby – lovely walks from your doorstep.

open All year
payment Credit/debit cards, cash, cheques
nearest pub 0.5 miles
nearest shop 0.5 miles

Unit 📺 📻 📺 🍴 ❄ General 🛎 🏚 🔥 P ◯ S Leisure 🚶

BRIXHAM, Devon Map ref 1D2 · SELF CATERING

★★★
SELF CATERING

Units **1**
Sleeps **2–6**

LOW SEASON PER WK
£350.00–£450.00

HIGH SEASON PER WK
£570.00–£700.00

Overquay Cottage, Brixham

contact Mrs Moira Withey, Ranscombe House, Ranscombe Road, Brixham TQ5 9UP
t +44 (0) 1803 882337   e info@ranscombehousehotel.co.uk

ranscombehousehotel.co.uk

open All year
payment Cash, cheques
nearest pub less than 0.5 miles
nearest shop less than 0.5 miles

Grade II Listed cottage on Brixham harbour. Sleeps six. Ground-floor: dining room, large well equipped kitchen and courtyard. First floor: sitting room with great views, double bedroom and bathroom. Second floor: two twin bedded rooms and shower room. Private off-street parking nearby. Bed linen and towels provided.

SAT NAV TQ5 9TH ONLINE MAP

Unit 📺🖥️📀📱📷🍴📻🛋️📼❄️ General 🎠🏬♿◎🐾 Leisure 🎣

BRIXHAM, Devon Map ref 1D2 · CAMPING, CARAVAN & HOLIDAY PARK

★★★★
**TOURING &
CAMPING PARK**

🚐 (60)   £9.60–£17.20
🚚 (10)   £9.60–£17.20
⛺ (60)   £9.60–£17.20
🏠 (4) £205.00–£515.00
120 touring pitches

Off-peak reductions.

Galmpton Touring Park

Greenway Road, Galmpton, Brixham TQ5 0EP t +44 (0) 1803 842066
e galmptontouringpark@hotmail.com

galmptontouringpark.co.uk

open Easter to September
payment Credit/debit cards, cash, cheques

Overlooking the River Dart with superb views from pitches. A quiet base for families and couples to explore Torbay and South Devon. Self-catering cottages available.

SAT NAV TQ5 0EP

General 🚐📶🍴🛋️📷📱📷🐕☀️ Leisure ⛰️🎣

BRIXTON, Devon Map ref 1C3 · GUEST ACCOMMODATION

★★★★
GUEST ACCOMMODATION

B&B PER ROOM PER NIGHT
s £40.00–£45.00
D £55.00–£60.00

Venn Farm

Brixton, Plymouth PL8 2AX t +44 (0) 1752 880378 e info@vennfarm.co.uk

vennfarm.co.uk

open All year
bedrooms 2 double, 2 twin, 1 single
bathrooms All en suite
payment Credit/debit cards, cash, cheques

A 300-year-old working farm. Enjoy traditional farmhouse bed and breakfast, relax in one of the beautiful new self-contained en suite rooms converted from the original stone barns. Central for coast and country. Off-road parking.

SAT NAV PL8 2AX ONLINE MAP

Room 📶📺🍴☕ General 🎠🏬♿P❄️

Do you have access needs?

Look for the National Accessible Scheme symbols if you have special hearing, visual or mobility needs.

BROAD CHALKE, Wiltshire Map ref 2B3 GUEST ACCOMMODATION

★★★★
BED & BREAKFAST

B&B PER ROOM PER NIGHT
S £25.00–£30.00
D £50.00–£60.00

Lodge Farmhouse Bed & Breakfast

Lodge Farmhouse, Broad Chalke, Salisbury SP5 5LU **t** +44 (0) 1725 519242 **e** mj.roe@virgin.net

lodge-farmhouse.co.uk GUEST REVIEWS

open All year except Christmas and New Year
bedrooms 1 double, 2 twin
bathrooms All en suite
payment Credit/debit cards, cash, cheques

Peaceful brick and flint farmhouse with Wiltshire's finest views overlooking 1,000 square miles of Southern England. Comfortable and welcoming, the perfect tour base for Wessex. Lying on the Ox Drove 'green lane', a paradise for walkers and byway cyclists. For neighbouring nature reserves and archaeological sites see website.

SAT NAV *SP5 5LU* **ONLINE MAP**

Room 📺 ♿ 🐾 General 🎠 12 P ✳ 🐎 Leisure ♪

BUCKLAND NEWTON, Dorset Map ref 2B3 SELF CATERING

★★★★
SELF CATERING

Units **3**
Sleeps **4**

LOW SEASON PER WK
£240.00–£350.00

HIGH SEASON PER WK
£375.00–£550.00

Domineys Cottages, Buckland Newton, Nr Dorchester

contact Mrs Jeanette Gueterbock, Domineys Cottages, Domineys Yard, Buckland Newton, Dorchester DT2 7BS **t** +44 (0) 1300 345295 **e** cottages@domineys.com

domineys.com

open All year
payment Cash, cheques, euros
nearest pub less than 0.5 miles
nearest shop 1 mile

Delightful, Victorian, two-bedroomed cottages, comfortably furnished and equipped and maintained to highest standards. Surrounded by beautiful gardens with patios. Heated summer swimming pool. Peaceful location on village edge in heart of Hardy's Dorset. Well situated for touring Wessex, walking and country pursuits. Regret no pets. Children 5+ and babies welcome.

Unit 📺 📻 📀 🖥 🍽 ✳ General 🎠 5 🏛 ♿ P Leisure ⚡ U ♪

BUDE, Cornwall Map ref 1C2 HOTEL

★★★
HOTEL
SILVER AWARD

B&B PER ROOM PER NIGHT
S £60.00–£65.00
D £120.00–£130.00

Special 3-day B&B breaks available all year. Special package for New Year's Eve party.

Falcon Hotel

Bude EX23 8SD **t** +44 (0) 1288 352005 **e** reception@falconhotel.com

falconhotel.com

open All year except Christmas Day
bedrooms 17 double, 4 single, 7 family, 1 suite
bathrooms All en suite
payment Credit/debit cards, cash, cheques

Overlooking the Bude Canal, with beautiful walled gardens and only minutes from the beaches and shops, this hotel is set in a most attractive location. The well-appointed bedrooms have flat-screen TVs and luxurious bathrooms. The hotel has an excellent reputation for food both in the bar and the restaurant.

SAT NAV *EX23 8SD*

Room 🛏 📞 📺 🆂 ♿ 🐾 ⚡ General 🎠 🏛 ♿ P 🕯 ☕ 🍴 ◐ 🔲 ⚓ ✳
Leisure U ♪ 🏇 🚲

BUDE, Cornwall Map ref 1C2
GUEST ACCOMMODATION

★★★
GUEST ACCOMMODATION

B&B PER ROOM PER NIGHT
D £56.00–£76.00

Discounts on bookings of 4 days or more.

Beach House

Marine Drive, Widemouth Bay, Bude EX23 0AW **t** +44 (0) 1288 361256
e beachhousebookings@tiscali.co.uk

beachhousewidemouth.co.uk

open Easter to end of October
bedrooms 8 double, 1 twin, 2 family
bathrooms All en suite
payment Credit/debit cards, cash, cheques

The Wilkins family welcome you to their unique site with private access onto Widemouth Beach. All bedrooms are en suite, the majority with sundeck balconies. Sun lounge, new bar lounge, on-site post office, shop, surf shop and hire. Restaurant serving traditional Cornish and seafood menus. Outside dining on decked patios.

SAT NAV *EX23 0AW*

Room 📺 ⚲ General 🛋 ♛ P ☕ ✕ ❄ Leisure ∪ 🏊 🚲

BUDE, Cornwall Map ref 1C2
SELF CATERING

★★★★–★★★★★★
SELF CATERING

Units **6**
Sleeps **2–8**

LOW SEASON PER WK
Min £240.00

HIGH SEASON PER WK
Max £1,550.00

Wooldown Farm Cottages, Marhamchurch, Bude

contact Mr & Mrs Susan Blewett, Wooldown Farm Cottages, Wooldown, Marhamchurch, Bude EX23 0HP **t** +44 (0) 1288 361216 **e** holidays@wooldown.com

wooldown.com GUEST REVIEWS · SPECIAL OFFERS · REAL-TIME BOOKING

open All year
payment Cash, cheques
nearest pub less than 0.5 miles
nearest shop less than 0.5 miles

Offering a choice of delightful self-catering cottages, romantic barns for couples and larger properties perfect for families, all of which have spectacular sea views across open countryside to Widemouth Bay and Bude. We are a few minutes' walk from the village of Marhamchurch, with post office/shop and pub/restaurant.

SAT NAV *EX23 0HP* **ONLINE MAP**

Unit 📺 🖥 📺 🎛 🍳 📻 🍽 ❄ 🍖 General 🛋 🛏 ♛ P 🅿 Ⓢ Leisure ∪ 🏊 🚲

CALLINGTON, Cornwall Map ref 1C2
GUEST ACCOMMODATION

★★★★
FARMHOUSE

B&B PER ROOM PER NIGHT
S £30.00–£38.00
D £56.00–£64.00

Higher Manaton

Callington PL17 8PX **t** +44 (0) 1579 370460 **e** dtrewin@manaton.fsnet.co.uk

cornwall-devon-bandb.co.uk

open All year except Christmas
bedrooms 1 double, 1 twin, 1 family
bathrooms 2 en suite, 1 private
payment Cash, cheques

Located on the edge of the rolling hills of Bodmin Moor, we offer our guests home-cooked British food on this traditional Cornish working farm. Within easy reach of Cornish beaches and attractions such as the Eden Project and Heligan Gardens. We offer you the opportunity to relax and enjoy Cornwall at its best.

SAT NAV *PL17 8PX*

Room 📺 ⚲ General 🛋2 P 🍽 ❄ Leisure ∪ 🏊 ▶

What do the star ratings mean?
Detailed information about star ratings can be found at the back of this guide.

CARBIS BAY, Cornwall Map ref 1B3 — GUEST ACCOMMODATION

★★★★
GUEST ACCOMMODATION

B&B PER ROOM PER NIGHT
D £56.00–£76.00

Beechwood House

St Ives Road, Carbis Bay, St Ives TR26 2SX t +44 (0) 1736 795170
e beechwood@carbisbay.wanadoo.co.uk

open All year
bedrooms 5 double, 1 twin, 2 family
bathrooms All en suite
payment Credit/debit cards, cash, cheques

Five minutes' walk to sandy beach. Looks out over St Ives Bay. All rooms are en suite. Guests' private lounge, garden and parking. We have golf, fishing, St Michael's Mount and trips to the Isles of Scilly all within easy reach. Courtesy lift from local train or bus stations, when available. Family rates from £75.00.

SAT NAV TR26 2SX

Room 🛏 📺 ♿ 🗒 General 🐾 🏢 🚳 P 📶 ❄ Leisure ∪ ⚓ ► ⚲

CHARD, Somerset Map ref 1D2 — GUEST ACCOMMODATION

★★★★
GUEST ACCOMMODATION

B&B PER ROOM PER NIGHT
S £35.00–£37.00
D £60.00–£65.00

Ammonite Lodge

43 High Street, Chard TA20 1QL t +44 (0) 1460 63839 e info@ammonitelodge.co.uk

ammonitelodge.co.uk REAL-TIME BOOKING

Grade II Listed character house in town centre on main A30. Warm welcome with every comfort, only 20 minutes from M5 motorway. Pretty garden and sumptuous breakfast. Parking at rear.

open All year except Christmas
bedrooms 3 double, 2 twin, 2 single
bathrooms 5 en suite, 2 private
payment Credit/debit cards, cash

Room 📺 ♿ 🗒 General 🐾 🏢 🚳 P 📶 🍴 📷 ❄ Leisure ⚓ ►

CHARMOUTH, Dorset Map ref 1D2 — GUEST ACCOMMODATION

★★★★
GUEST ACCOMMODATION

B&B PER ROOM PER NIGHT
D £60.00–£65.00

Cliffend

Higher Sea Lane, Charmouth, Bridport DT6 6BD t +44 (0) 1297 561047

cliffend.org.uk

open All year
bedrooms 2 double
bathrooms All en suite
payment Cash, cheques

Chalet bungalow situated in large garden with gate onto coastal path. Two minutes' stroll to beach. Newly refurbished rooms with sitting corner and attractive en suite facilities. Ideal for exploring this beautiful area of Dorset. A warm welcome is guaranteed. Higher price is for one night's stay only.

SAT NAV DT6 6BD

Room 📺 ♿ 🗒 General P

visit**Britain**.com

Get in the know – log on for a wealth of information and inspiration. All the latest news on places to visit, events and quality-assessed accommodation is literally at your fingertips. Explore all that Britain has to offer.

CHEDDAR, Somerset Map ref 1D1 — CAMPING, CARAVAN & HOLIDAY PARK

★★★★
HOLIDAY, TOURING
& CAMPING PARK
ROSE AWARD

🚐 (100)   £14.00–£27.00
🚛 (20)   £12.00–£20.00
⛺ (80)   £14.00–£27.00
🏠 (37)   £180.00–£600.00
200 touring pitches

Broadway House Holiday Touring Caravan and Camping Park

Axbridge Road, Cheddar BS27 3DB t +44 (0) 1934 742610 e info@broadwayhouse.uk.com

broadwayhouse.uk.com

open March to November
payment Credit/debit cards, cash, cheques, euros

Nestling at the foot of the Mendip Hills, this family run park is only one mile from England's Grand Canyon: Cheddar Gorge. Every facility your family could ever want: shop, bar, launderette, swimming pool, BMX track, skateboard park, nature trails, archery, caving and canoeing. Holiday caravans and lodges for hire.

SAT NAV BS27 3DB

General 🖥 🚐 🅿 🔌 🌐 🐾 🏧 🔁 ✕ 🐕 ☼ 📶 Leisure ⚓ 🍽 🎣 ⛰ ∪ 🎣 🏌 🚴

CHELTENHAM, Gloucestershire Map ref 2B1 — HOTEL

★★★
SMALL HOTEL

B&B PER ROOM PER NIGHT
S £65.00–£85.00
D £99.00–£125.00

2-night weekend break special DB&B from £60pppn sharing a double room. 3- and 5-night breaks also available.

Charlton Kings Hotel

London Road, Charlton Kings, Cheltenham GL52 6UU t +44 (0) 1242 231061
e enquiries@charltonkingshotel.co.uk

charltonkingshotel.co.uk

open All year
bedrooms 8 double, 2 twin, 2 single, 1 family
bathrooms All en suite
payment Credit/debit cards, cash, cheques

Surrounded by the Cotswold Hills, on the outskirts of Cheltenham. Quality, comfort and friendliness are hallmarks of this privately owned hotel. All rooms have satellite TV. Wi-Fi internet available. Very comfortable standard rooms. Superior rooms are larger, with many upgraded facilities. Excellent restaurant open seven days a week. Ample parking.

SAT NAV GL52 6UU

Room ♿ 📞 📺 🔤 🛁 ⛲ 🛎 General 🖼 ⫘ ♿ P 📶 🍽 🍴 ⊕ ✱ 🐕

CHIPPING CAMPDEN, Gloucestershire Map ref 2B1 — HOTEL

★★★
HOTEL
SILVER AWARD

B&B PER ROOM PER NIGHT
S £83.00–£109.00
D £140.00–£218.00
HB PER PERSON PER NIGHT
£98.00–£130.00

Pudding Club breaks, walking weekends, chocoholic breaks and gardens of Gloucestershire breaks available throughout the year.

Three Ways House

Chapel Lane, Mickleton, Chipping Campden GL55 6SB t +44 (0) 1386 438429
e reception@puddingclub.com

puddingclub.com

open All year
bedrooms 20 double, 20 twin, 3 single, 5 family
bathrooms All en suite
payment Credit/debit cards, cash, cheques

Cotswold-village hotel close to Chipping Campden, Broadway and Stratford-upon-Avon. Comfortable bedrooms, some with pudding themes, cosy bar, good food and attentive service. Seen many times on TV as 'Home of The Pudding Club' where meetings of pudding lovers occur regularly. Stylish, air-conditioned restaurant.

SAT NAV GL55 6SB

Room ♿ 📞 📺 🛁 ⛲ 🛎 General 🖼 ⫘ ♿ P 📶 🍽 🍴 ● ⊕ ⊕ 🍴 ✱ 🐕
Leisure ∪ 🎣 🏌 🚴

CHIPPING CAMPDEN, Gloucestershire Map ref 2B1 — SELF CATERING

★★★★
SELF CATERING

Units **1**
Sleeps **6**

LOW SEASON PER WK
Min **£550.00**

HIGH SEASON PER WK
Max **£920.00**

Short breaks out of season/close to date – min 3 nights. Other cottages available Chipping Campden/ Broadway area – sleeping 2-6, from £290.

Orchard Cottage, Saintbury

contact Ms Sheila Rolland, Campden Cottages, Folly Cottage, Paxford, Chipping Campden GL55 6XG t +44 (0) 1386 593315 e info@campdencottages.co.uk

campdencottages.co.uk

open All year
payment Credit/debit cards, cash, cheques
nearest pub 1 mile
nearest shop 1 mile

16thC Cotswold-stone cottage overlooking beautiful, peaceful countryside. Chipping Campden or Broadway three miles. Many original features including exposed beams, flagstone and wood floors, inglenook fireplace in sitting room (logs supplied), separate dining room, three bedrooms, two bathrooms. Garden, barbecue, parking. We regret no dogs. Prices excl Christmas and New Year. Wireless broadband.

ONLINE MAP

Unit 📺 🔌 📻 📀 💻 🍽 📷 ♨ 🔥 🧺 💡 ✳ ⚒ ✂ General 🛋 🏠 🏃 P Ⓢ Leisure ∪ ⚑ 🚲

CLEARWELL, Gloucestershire Map ref 2A1 — SELF CATERING

★★★★
SELF CATERING

Units **1**
Sleeps **6**

LOW SEASON PER WK
£400.00-£450.00

HIGH SEASON PER WK
£450.00-£600.00

Weekend breaks available.

Rosedean Cottage, Clearwell

contact Mrs Andrea Dombrowe
t +44 (0) 1483 538615 e clearwell@gmail.com

forestofdeancottage.co.uk GUEST REVIEWS · SPECIAL OFFERS · REAL-TIME BOOKING

open All year
payment Credit/debit cards, cash, cheques, euros
nearest pub less than 0.5 miles
nearest shop 2.5 miles

Beautifully presented three-bedroom detached cottage (master en suite) situated in Wye Valley. Full range of modern appliances. Off-road parking, child-friendly enclosed garden. Lockable garage. Linen and all utilities included. Forest of Dean on doorstep. Walking, cycling, riding, canoeing, Symonds Yat, Tintern, Chepstow, Monmouth, Hay-on-Wye.

ONLINE MAP

Unit 📺 SC 📻 📀 💻 🍽 📷 ♨ 🔥 🧺 💡 ✳ ⚒ General 🛋 🏠 🏃 P Ⓞ Ⓢ Leisure ∪ 🚲

COLD ASHTON, Gloucestershire Map ref 2B2 — SELF CATERING

★★★★
SELF CATERING

Units **1**
Sleeps **10**

LOW SEASON PER WK
£2,290.00-£3,230.00

HIGH SEASON PER WK
£3,465.00-£3,805.00

Sayres House, Nr Bath, Chippenham

contact Elaine Molyneux, Dunster Living, Halswell House, Goathurst, Somerset TA5 2DH
t +44 (0) 845 208 1066 e info@dunsterliving.co.uk

sayreshouse.co.uk SPECIAL OFFERS · REAL-TIME BOOKING

Elegant, period Cotswold-stone house with excellent facilities and one acre of beautiful gardens with terrace and barbecue. Three double bedrooms, two triple, Aga, indoor heated swimming pool.

open All year
payment Credit/debit cards, cash, cheques
nearest pub 2 miles
nearest shop 2 miles

Unit 📺 SC 📻 📀 💻 🍽 📷 ♨ 🔥 🧺 💡 ✳ ⚒ ✂ General 🛋 🏠 🏃 P Ⓞ Ⓢ 🐕 Leisure 🎣 ∪ ♪ ⚑ 🚲

Fancy a cycling holiday?

For a fabulous freewheeling break, seek out accommodation participating in our Cyclists Welcome scheme. Look out for the symbol and plan your route online at nationalcyclenetwork.org.

COLYTON, Devon   Map ref 1D2

GUEST ACCOMMODATION

★★★★
GUEST ACCOMMODATION
SILVER AWARD

B&B PER ROOM PER NIGHT
S £40.00–£45.00
D £60.00–£70.00

Short breaks or 'piggy' weekends and 'Introduction to Pig-Keeping' courses available.

Smallicombe Farm

Northleigh, Colyton EX24 6BU   t +44 (0) 1404 831310   e maggie_todd@yahoo.com

smallicombe.com SPECIAL OFFERS

open All year
bedrooms 1 double, 1 twin, 1 family
bathrooms All en suite
payment Credit/debit cards, cash, cheques

Relax in a really special place, an idyllic rural setting abounding with wildlife, yet close to the coast. Enjoy scrumptious farmhouse breakfasts including prize-winning Smallicombe sausages from our rare-breed pigs. All rooms en suite, overlooking an unspoilt valley landscape. The Garden Suite of sitting room, bedroom and bathroom is wheelchair-accessible.

SAT NAV *EX24 6BU* **ONLINE MAP**

Room ♿ 📺 ♨ ⚃   General ⌖ 🏢 ♿ P ⚏ ▣ ✳   Leisure ∪ ► ⚴

COLYTON, Devon   Map ref 1D2

SELF CATERING

★★★★
SELF CATERING

Units   **4**
Sleeps **2–8**

LOW SEASON PER WK
£155.00–£295.00

HIGH SEASON PER WK
£395.00–£725.00

Short breaks or 'Piggy Weekends'. 'Introduction to Pig-Keeping' courses. Monthly rates or longer lets Sep-Mar.

Smallicombe Farm, Colyton

contact Mrs Maggie Todd, Smallicombe Farm, Northleigh, Colyton EX24 6BU   t +44 (0) 1404 831310   e maggie_todd@yahoo.com

smallicombe.com SPECIAL OFFERS

open All year
payment Credit/debit cards, cash, cheques
nearest pub 2 miles
nearest shop less than 0.5 miles

Relax in cosy, well-equipped, award-winning converted barns enjoying idyllic rural views. Roam our ancient pastures and woodland, abounding in wildlife, with only the sights and sounds of the countryside. Close to the World Heritage Coastline. Meet our prize-winning Berkshire sows and piglets. Sample our succulent rare-breed pork.

ONLINE MAP

Unit 📺 ⌨ 📀 🖥 ▤ 🗄 ⚃ 🔲 🍽 ✳ ⛺   General ⌖ 🏢 ♿ P ▣ Ⓢ
Leisure ● ∪ ► ⚴

CONSTANTINE BAY, Cornwall   Map ref 1B2

HOTEL

★★★★
COUNTRY HOUSE HOTEL

B&B PER ROOM PER NIGHT
S £63.25–£92.00
D £126.50–£184.00
HB PER PERSON PER NIGHT
£80.00–£110.00

Treglos Hotel

Constantine Bay, Padstow PL28 8JH   t +44 (0) 1841 520727   e stay@tregloshotel.com

tregloshotel.com SPECIAL OFFERS

open February to January
bedrooms 23 twin, 3 single, 10 family, 6 suites
bathrooms All en suite
payment Credit/debit cards, cash, cheques, euros

This luxurious hotel is on the North Cornish coast has 42 rooms and suites, many with dramatic views over Constantine Bay. Facilities include indoor pool, jacuzzi, treatment rooms and award-winning restaurant. Treglos has its own golf course and self-catering apartments. Beaches and coastal paths are within a short stroll.

SAT NAV *PL28 8JH* **ONLINE MAP**

Room ♿ ☎ 📺 ♨ ⚃ ✎   General ⌖ 🏢 ♿ P ♕ ⚲ 🍽 ◐ ▤ ▣ ✳
Leisure ☄ ⊗ ∪ ► ⚴

COTSWOLDS

See under Cheltenham, Chipping Campden, Moreton-in-Marsh, Slimbridge, Stow-on-the-Wold, Stroud, Tetbury, Tewkesbury

See also Cotswolds in Central and South East England sections

COVERACK, Cornwall Map ref 1B3 — SELF CATERING

14 Coverack Headland, Helston

★★★★
SELF CATERING

Units **1**
Sleeps **1–2**

LOW SEASON PER WK
£190.00–£300.00

HIGH SEASON PER WK
£310.00–£400.00

contact Mrs Anne Bradley-Smith, Dorland Cottage, The Mint, Church Lane, Bletchingley, Redhill RH1 4LP **t** +44 (0) 1883 743442

coverack.org.uk

Beautiful two-person apartment. Panoramic sea views. Linen supplied. Digital flat-screen TV, VCR, DVD and tennis court. Gardens lead down to beach below.

open All year
payment Cash, cheques
nearest pub 0.5 miles
nearest shop 0.5 miles

Unit 📺 ▦▦ ▣ 🗂 ▯ ▯ ✱ General P ▣ S 🐕 Leisure ✎ ∪

DARTMEET, Devon Map ref 1C2 — SELF CATERING

Coachman's Cottage, Dartmeet

★★★
SELF CATERING

Units **1**
Sleeps **2–4**

LOW SEASON PER WK
£240.00–£315.00

HIGH SEASON PER WK
£330.00–£465.00

Short breaks available in low season.

contact Mrs Toni Evans, Hunter's Lodge, Dartmeet, Princetown PL20 6SG **t** +44 (0) 1364 631173
e huntlodge@pobox.com

dartmeet.com

open All year
payment Credit/debit cards, cash, cheques, euros
nearest pub 1 mile
nearest shop 4 miles

Granite cottage at the meeting of the East and West Darts in the heart of Dartmoor National Park. Fully equipped kitchen/dining room. Large, comfortable lounge and spacious double/twin bedroom. Breathtaking view of the Dart Valley and surrounding tors from bedroom and patio. Immediate access to riverbank, woodland and open moorland.

SAT NAV PL20 6SG

Unit 📺 ▣ 🗂 ▯ ▯ ✱ ♨ General ♨ ▥ ♠ P ▣ S 🐕 Leisure ∪ 🚣 🚲

DARTMOOR

See under Dartmeet, Okehampton, Tavistock, Yelverton

DARTMOUTH, Devon Map ref 1D3 — GUEST ACCOMMODATION

Valley House

★★★★
BED & BREAKFAST

B&B PER ROOM PER NIGHT
S £60.00–£65.00
D £60.00–£90.00

Discounts for stays of 4 days or more.

46 Victoria Road, Dartmouth TQ6 9DZ **t** +44 (0) 1803 834045
e enquiries@valleyhousedartmouth.com

valleyhousedartmouth.com GUEST REVIEWS

open All year except Christmas
bedrooms 2 double, 1 twin
bathrooms All en suite
payment Cash, cheques

Receive a warm welcome to Dartmouth from Angela and Martin Cairns-Sharp. Central location, five minutes' walk to River Dart and town centre. Off-road (on-site) parking – a particular advantage in Dartmouth. Well-equipped rooms, lovely breakfasts served in dining room. Britain in Bloom prize winner 2005, 2006 and 2007.

SAT NAV TQ6 9DZ **ONLINE MAP**

Room 📺 ♦ ▯ General ♨ 12 P ▥ Leisure ∪ 🚣 ▶

DARTMOUTH, Devon Map ref 1D3 — SELF CATERING

★★★
SELF CATERING

Units **4**
Sleeps **2–6**

LOW SEASON PER WK
£330.00–£400.00

HIGH SEASON PER WK
£420.00–£725.00

The Old Bakehouse, Dartmouth

contact Mrs Sylvia Ridalls, The Old Bakehouse, 7 Broadstone, Dartmouth TQ6 9NR
t +44 (0) 1803 834585 **e** gparker@pioneerps.co.uk

oldbakehousedartmouth.co.uk

Four character cottages, with beams and old stone fireplaces. In a conservation area, two minutes from historic town centre and river. Free parking. Beach 15 minutes' drive. Dogs free. Non-smoking.

open All year
payment Credit/debit cards, cash, cheques
nearest pub less than 0.5 miles
nearest shop less than 0.5 miles

Unit 📺 📀 ▣ 🍽 General 🐴 🏢 🛗 🆂 🐕 Leisure 🎵

DEERHURST, Gloucestershire Map ref 2B1 — SELF CATERING

★★★★
SELF CATERING

Units **2**
Sleeps **2–4**

LOW SEASON PER WK
Min £200.00

HIGH SEASON PER WK
Max £465.00

Short breaks available Nov-Mar (excl Christmas and New Year), min 3-night stay.

Deerhurst Cottages, Deerhurst, Tewkesbury

contact Mrs Nicole Samuel, Deerhurst Cottages, Abbots Court Farm, Deerhurst, Tewkesbury GL19 4BX **t** +44 (0) 1684 275845 **e** enquiries@deerhurstcottages.co.uk

deerhurstcottages.co.uk GUEST REVIEWS

open All year
payment Credit/debit cards, cash, cheques
nearest pub 1.5 miles
nearest shop 3 miles

Deerhurst Cottages are situated on our working dairy farm, on the banks of the River Severn in the quiet village of Deerhurst. Both cottages offer comfortable, spacious and well-equipped holiday accommodation. The perfect base for exploring the Cotswolds, the Forest of Dean and the Malvern Hills.

Unit 📺 📀 ▣ 🖥 🗄 🍽 🍳 ✳ General 🐴 🏢 🛗 P Leisure 🎵 ▶

DEVIZES, Wiltshire Map ref 2B2 — GUEST ACCOMMODATION

★★★★
GUEST ACCOMMODATION

B&B PER ROOM PER NIGHT
S Min £36.00
D Min £64.00

Double en suite at single occupancy rate. Discount for 4 or more consecutive nights.

Rosemundy Cottage

London Road, Devizes SN10 2DS **t** +44 (0) 1380 727122 **e** info@rosemundycottage.co.uk

rosemundycottage.co.uk GUEST REVIEWS · SPECIAL OFFERS · REAL-TIME BOOKING

open All year
bedrooms 2 double, 1 twin, 1 family
bathrooms All en suite
payment Credit/debit cards, cash, cheques

Canal-side cottage, short walk to Market Place. Fully equipped rooms, include a four-poster and a ground floor room. Sitting room with guides provided. Guest office, free Wi-Fi internet. Garden with barbecue and heated pool in summer. Wiltshire Breakfast, Kennet five-star Food Hygiene, Green Tourism Silver and Fairtrade awards. Off-road parking. Perfect for business or leisure.

SAT NAV SN10 2DS **ONLINE MAP**

Room 🛗 🛏 📺 🆂🅲 🚿 🍽 General ♿ P 📶 🔥 🍴 ✳ Leisure 🏊 ∪ 🎵 🚲

Do you like walking?

Walkers feel at home in accommodation participating in our Walkers Welcome scheme. Look out for the symbol. Consider walking all or part of a long-distance route – go online at nationaltrail.co.uk.

WALKERS WELCOME · WELCOME WALKERS

DINTON, Wiltshire Map ref 2B3

★★★★
BED & BREAKFAST

B&B PER ROOM PER NIGHT
S £40.00–£60.00
D £55.00–£65.00

Marshwood Farm B&B

Dinton, Salisbury SP3 5ET **t** +44 (0) 1722 716334 **e** marshwood1@btconnect.com

marshwoodfarm.co.uk

open All year
bedrooms 1 twin, 1 family
bathrooms All en suite
payment Credit/debit cards, cash, cheques, euros

Beautiful farmhouse dating from the 17thC on working farm, surrounded by fields and woodland. Ideal location for cycling, walking and exploring the Wiltshire countryside, Salisbury, Stonehenge, Bath and many places of interest. Guests are welcome to relax in our garden and use our tennis court.

SAT NAV SP3 5ET

Room 📺 ♿ 🍵 General 🛁 🏠 ⬆ P ❄ Leisure ⚲

DRYBROOK, Gloucestershire Map ref 2B1

★★★★
HOLIDAY, TOURING
& CAMPING PARK

🚐 (20)   £16.00
🚏 (20)   £16.00
⛺ (35)   £14.00
40 touring pitches

From 1 Apr to 30 Jun, 3 weekday nights for the price of 2.

Greenway Farm Caravan & Camping Park

Puddlebrook Road, Hawthorns, Drybrook GL17 9HW **t** +44 (0) 1594 543737
e greenwayfarm@aic.co.uk

greenwayfarm.org GUEST REVIEWS · SPECIAL OFFERS

open All year
payment Credit/debit cards, cash, cheques

David and Lorraine welcome you to Greenway Farm, an independently owned smallholding of five acres. Situated along a quiet country lane, the site enjoys beautiful views, and with woodland walks within 100yds, you can be assured of a relaxing break in the heart of the forest.

SAT NAV GL17 9HW **ONLINE MAP**

General 🏛 🔌 👕 ☎ 🆗 📷 🗑 ✖ 🐴 ☀ ♿ Leisure 🚲

DUNSTER, Somerset Map ref 1D1

★★★
SMALL HOTEL

B&B PER ROOM PER NIGHT
S £50.00–£70.00
D £80.00–£120.00
HB PER PERSON PER NIGHT
£60.00–£90.00

Discounted rates for longer stays and midweek bookings. Ring for newsletter with information on special events. Group bookings welcome.

Yarn Market Hotel (Exmoor)

25 High Street, Dunster, Minehead TA24 6SF **t** +44 (0) 1643 821425 **e** yarnmarket.hotel@virgin.net

yarnmarkethotel.co.uk SPECIAL OFFERS

open All year
bedrooms 10 double, 2 twin, 1 single, 2 family
bathrooms All en suite
payment Credit/debit cards, cash, cheques

Within Exmoor National Park, our hotel is ideal for walking, riding and fishing. Family-run with a friendly, relaxed atmosphere. All rooms en suite with colour TV. Four-poster and superior rooms available. Totally non-smoking. Home-cooked dishes to cater for all tastes. Group bookings welcomed. Conference facilities. Special Christmas and New Year breaks.

SAT NAV TA24 6SF

Room 🏠 ☎ 📺 ♿ 🍵 ♿ General 🛁 🏠 ⬆ 🍷 🍴 ▢ 🍴 🐴 Leisure ∪ ♪ ▶ 🚲

EXETER, Devon Map ref 1D2

★★★★★
SELF CATERING

Units **1**
Sleeps **4**

LOW SEASON PER WK
£200.00–£380.00

HIGH SEASON PER WK
£420.00–£540.00

Coach House Farm, Exeter

contact Mr & Miss John & Polly Bale, Coach House Farm, Moor Lane, Broadclyst, Exeter EX5 3JH
t +44 (0) 1392 461254 **e** selfcatering@mpprops.co.uk

open All year
payment Credit/debit cards, cash, cheques, euros
nearest pub 1 mile
nearest shop 1 mile

Surrounded by the National Trust Killerton estate, the converted stables of our Victorian coach house provide comfortable ground-floor accommodation (no steps) with private entrance and garden overlooking sheep meadows. Working arable and sheep farm. Spectacular East Devon coastline, Exmoor, Dartmoor and Exeter are easily reached. Internet access.

Unit 📺 📀 📼 ▦ 🍴 🍳 🔥 🍽 ⌨ ✿ ⚒ General ⌂ 🏛 ⚼ P 🐾

EXMOOR

See under Dunster, Lynton, Porlock, Simonsbath

FALMOUTH, Cornwall Map ref 1B3

★★★
HOTEL
SILVER AWARD

B&B PER ROOM PER NIGHT
S £60.00–£115.00
D £90.00–£190.00
HB PER PERSON PER NIGHT
£60.00–£140.00

Special terms on DB&B based on 2 people sharing a twin/double for 3/ 5/7 nights. Spring and autumn breaks.

Green Lawns Hotel

Western Terrace, Falmouth TR11 4QJ **t** +44 (0) 1326 312734 **e** info@greenlawnshotel.com

greenlawnshotel.com SPECIAL OFFERS

open All year except Christmas
bedrooms 13 double, 12 twin, 6 single, 8 family
bathrooms All en suite
payment Credit/debit cards, cash, cheques

Elegant, chateau-style hotel in prize-winning gardens with views across Falmouth Bay. Distinguished by its ivy exterior, the hotel is between the main beaches and town centre. The Green Lawns offers the perfect holiday setting or business retreat. It is privately owned and renowned for friendly hospitality and professional service.

SAT NAV TR11 4QJ

Room ♿ 🛏 📞 📺 ☕ 🍳 🔥 🗄 General ⌂ 🏛 ⚼ P 📶 🍽 🍴 ● 🔥 🐾
Leisure 🎱 🏊 ✽ ∪ ♪ ▶ 🚴

FERNDOWN, Dorset Map ref 2B3

★★★★
SELF CATERING

Units **1**
Sleeps **1–8**

LOW SEASON PER WK
£415.00–£540.00

HIGH SEASON PER WK
£570.00–£1,170.00

Weekend breaks available during low seasons. Special activity weekends for golfers, etc. Fully-catered group bookings.

Birchcroft, Ferndown

contact Miss Leanne Hemingway, Dorset Cottage Holidays, 11 Tyneham Close, Sandford, Wareham BH20 7BE **t** +44 (0) 1929 553443 **e** enq@dhcottages.co.uk

dhcottages.co.uk GUEST REVIEWS · SPECIAL OFFERS

open All year
payment Credit/debit cards, cash, cheques
nearest pub 0.5 miles
nearest shop 0.5 miles

A nature lover's secret hideaway, Birchcroft is surrounded by rhododendron bushes in over an acre of land. With accessible accommodation, it's large enough for two families. Terrace enjoys breathtaking local views. Deer, foxes, rabbits, and birds are often seen. Only five miles from Bournemouth beaches. Great for walkers and golfers.

SAT NAV BH22 ONLINE MAP

Unit 📺 📀 📼 ▦ 🍴 🍳 🔥 🍽 ⌨ ✿ ⚒ ✐ General ⌂ ⚼ P S Leisure ∪ ♪ ▶ 🚴

FOREST OF DEAN

See under Clearwell, Drybrook, Mitcheldean, Newnham

FOWEY, Cornwall Map ref 1B3 — SELF CATERING

★★★★★
SELF CATERING

Units **1**
Sleeps **4**

LOW SEASON PER WK
£515.00–£751.00

HIGH SEASON PER WK
£802.00–£1,254.00

See website for prices. Weekly lettings. Saturday change-over.

Dolphins at Penlee, Fowey

contact Mr Gittus, Dolphins at Penlee, 4 Snuff Mill Walk, Bewdley DY12 2HG t +44 (0) 1299 400447
e john.gittus@btopenworld.com

qualityholidaylets.com

open All year
payment Cash, cheques, euros
nearest pub 0.5 miles
nearest shop 0.5 miles

Exceptionally spacious first-floor apartment in a prime position. Stunning views, easy access to town, beach, cliff walks. Excellent standard of accommodation and the enviable benefit of a private parking space opposite. Readymoney Beach, which inspired Daphne Du Maurier to write Fisherman's Creek, 200yds. Pay phone provided.

Unit 📺 🆂🅲 🛗 📠 📀 🖥️🖊 🍳 🔲 🗄 💷❄ General 🐾5 **P** Leisure ♪▶

GILLINGHAM, Dorset Map ref 2B3 — SELF CATERING

★★★★
SELF CATERING

Units **1**
Sleeps **2**

LOW SEASON PER WK
£185.00–£195.00

HIGH SEASON PER WK
£230.00–£330.00

Woolfields Barn, Milton on Stour, Gillingham

contact Mr & Mrs Thomas, Woolfields Barn, Woolfields Farm, Milton on Stour, Gillingham SP8 5PX
t +44 (0) 1747 824729 e info@woolfieldsbarn.co.uk

woolfieldsbarn.co.uk

Extremely comfortable barn conversion (sleeps two), well equipped with all essentials for a peaceful and enjoyable stay in a lovely rural village. All quality linen provided. One dog welcome.

open All year except Christmas
payment Cash, cheques, euros
nearest pub 1 mile
nearest shop 0.5 miles

Unit 📺 📠 🖥️ 🍳 🔲 🗄 💷❄ General 🛏 **P** 🆂 🐕 Leisure ♠ ∪ ♪

GLASTONBURY, Somerset Map ref 2A2 — GUEST ACCOMMODATION

Rating Applied For
GUEST ACCOMMODATION

B&B PER ROOM PER NIGHT
S £45.00–£75.00
D £60.00–£90.00

Chindit House

23 Wells Road, Glastonbury BA6 9DN t +44 (0) 1458 830404 e peter@chindit-house.co.uk

chindit-house.co.uk GUEST REVIEWS

open All year except Christmas
bedrooms 2 double, 2 single
bathrooms All en suite
payment Credit/debit cards, cash, cheques, euros

Centrally located, stylish, Gothic stone mansion offering the highest standards of modern luxury, comfort and hospitality. Period furnishings complement new contemporary bathrooms. A spacious guest lounge opens onto a terrace overlooking the croquet lawn in secluded grounds. Romantic, grand doubles and two elegant adjoining singles – all en suite.

SAT NAV *BA6 9DN* **ONLINE MAP**

Room 🛏 📺 🆂🅲 ☕ 🍳 General 🦮 🍽 ❄

PETS!
WELCOME
WELCOME
PETS!

Where is my pet welcome?

Want to take your cherished companion with you on holiday? Proprietors participating in our Welcome Pets! scheme go out of their way to make special provision for you and your pet. Look out for the symbol.

GLASTONBURY, Somerset Map ref 2A2 GUEST ACCOMMODATION

★★★★
BED & BREAKFAST

B&B PER ROOM PER NIGHT
D £65.00–£85.00

B&B may also be available in some of our larger cottages – please call us with your requirements.

Mapleleaf Middlewick

Wick Lane, Nr Glastonbury BA6 8JW t +44 (0) 1458 832351 e middlewick@btconnect.com

middlewickholidaycottages.co.uk REAL-TIME BOOKING

open All year
bedrooms 1 double, 1 family
bathrooms All en suite
payment Credit/debit cards, cash, cheques

Enjoy the ease and flexibility of B&B with the comfort of a cottage to yourself. Add to that, Wendy's fabulous breakfasts, an indoor heated swimming pool, steam room, treatment room, Wi-Fi and stunning views to the Mendips. All this is set amongst gardens and paddocks, a walk from Glastonbury Tor.

SAT NAV BA6 8JW

Room 🛏 📺 🍵 🗮 General 🐴 P ⓦ 🍽 🖥 ☀ Leisure 🌊 ♆

GLASTONBURY, Somerset Map ref 2A2 SELF CATERING

★★★
SELF CATERING

Units   **8**
Sleeps   **2–6**

LOW SEASON PER WK
£240.00–£325.00

HIGH SEASON PER WK
£475.00–£830.00

Short breaks and B&B available.

MapleLeaf Middlewick Holiday Cottages, Wick, Glastonbury

contact Ms Amanda I'Ons, Middlewick Holiday Cottages, Wick Lane, Glastonbury BA6 8JW
t +44 (0) 1458 832351 e middlewick@btconnect.com

middlewickholidaycottages.co.uk REAL-TIME BOOKING

open All year
payment Credit/debit cards, cash, cheques
nearest pub 2 miles
nearest shop 1.6 miles

The cottages within this Grade II Listed farmstead have been restored to provide comfortable, well-equipped accommodation. Walk to Glastonbury Tor from the back door, explore the region, relax in the heated indoor swimming pool, try out the steam room or have a massage in our treatment room. Wi-Fi Internet access.

SAT NAV BA6 8JW

Unit 📺 🖥 ▣ 🗄 🍵 🖫 🗇 ☀ ⚒ General 🐴 🏢 🛱 🖥 Ⓢ Leisure 🌊 ♆ 🦆 🚲

GOONHAVERN, Cornwall Map ref 1B2 SELF CATERING

★★★
SELF CATERING

Units   **5**
Sleeps   **5–6**

LOW SEASON PER WK
£400.00–£650.00

HIGH SEASON PER WK
£650.00–£1,050.00

Greenmeadow, Perranporth

contact Mr Ian Bodie, Green Meadow Cottages, Bridge Road, Truro TR4 9NN t +44 (0) 1872 540483
e ianbodie@aol.com

Five cottages in a tree-lined meadow offering a quiet and relaxing environment with open beams and log fires in winter.

open All year
payment Cash, cheques, euros
nearest pub 0.5 miles
nearest shop 0.5 miles

Unit 📺 📀 ▣ 🗄 🍵 🖫 🗇 ✎ General 🐴 🏢 🛱 P 🖥 Ⓢ 🐕

Looking for an ideal family break?

For accommodation offering additional facilities and services for a range of ages and family units, look out for the Families Welcome symbol. Owners of these properties will go out of their way to welcome families.

HELSTONE, Cornwall   Map ref 1B2

SELF CATERING

★★★–★★★★★
SELF CATERING

Units **6**
Sleeps **1–6**

LOW SEASON PER WK
£250.00–£800.00

HIGH SEASON PER WK
£900.00–£1,300.00

Ideal for family reunions, group holidays etc. Catering help available. Short breaks available Oct–Mar.

Mayrose Farm, Camelford

contact Mrs Jane Maunder, Mayrose Farm, Camelford PL32 9RN **t** +44 (0) 1840 213509
e info@mayrosefarmcottages.co.uk

mayrosefarmcottages.co.uk GUEST REVIEWS · SPECIAL OFFERS · REAL-TIME BOOKING

open All year
payment Credit/debit cards, cash, cheques
nearest pub 2 miles
nearest shop 1 mile

Mayrose luxury holiday cottages are set in 17 acres of fields overlooking the picturesque Allen Valley in north Cornwall. The self-catering luxury accommodation is ideal for couples and families with children and toddlers. Heated swimming pool and farm animals. Relaxed, friendly and within easy reach of sandy beaches, gardens, great houses and Bodmin Moor.

ONLINE MAP

Unit 📺 🖂 🖥 🕮 🗇 🍳 🍽 🗲 ✳ ♨ ∅   General ⏰ 🏚 ♿ P 🅾 Ⓢ
Leisure ⟡ ♦ ∪ ▶ 🚲

HEMYOCK, Devon   Map ref 1D2

GUEST ACCOMMODATION

★★★★
FARMHOUSE

B&B PER ROOM PER NIGHT
D **£60.00–£80.00**

Discounts on stays of 2 or more days. Telephone or see website for details.

Pounds Farm

Hemyock EX15 3QS **t** +44 (0) 1823 680802 **e** shillingscottage@yahoo.co.uk

poundsfarm.co.uk GUEST REVIEWS · SPECIAL OFFERS · REAL-TIME BOOKING

open All year
bedrooms 1 double
bathrooms En suite
payment Cash, cheques

17thC stone farmhouse completely surrounded by large gardens, set in Blackdown Hills Area of Outstanding Natural Beauty. Heated outdoor pool. Open log fires. Elegant, spacious bedrooms, en suite with walk-in shower, far-reaching views. Delicious farmhouse breakfasts with free-range eggs, home-made bread, jam and marmalade. Half a mile to village pub. Easy reach of M5/A303.

SAT NAV *EX15 3QS* **ONLINE MAP**

Room 📺 🕯 🍳 ⬜   General ⏰ 🏚 ♿ P 🔥 🍽 🖳 ✳   Leisure ⟡ ∪ ⨶ ▶ 🚲

HEYTESBURY, Wiltshire   Map ref 2B2

GUEST ACCOMMODATION

★★★★
BED & BREAKFAST

B&B PER ROOM PER NIGHT
S **£55.00–£65.00**
D **£60.00–£70.00**

The Resting Post

High Street, Heytesbury, Warminster BA12 0ED **t** +44 (0) 1985 840204
e enquiries@therestingpost.co.uk

therestingpost.co.uk

Grade II Listed period house offering friendly, comfortable, en suite accommodation in the centre of a delightful village. There are two pubs in the village serving evening meals.

open All year except Christmas
bedrooms 2 double, 1 twin
bathrooms All en suite
payment Cash, cheques

Room 📺 🕯 🍳   General ⏰ 10 🍽   Leisure ∪ ⨶ ▶

Using map references

The map references refer to the colour maps at the front of this guide. The first figure is the map number, the letter and figure that follow indicate the grid reference on the map.

HOLSWORTHY, Devon Map ref 1C2 — CAMPING, CARAVAN & HOLIDAY PARK

★★
HOLIDAY, TOURING
& CAMPING PARK

🚐 (5)	£4.00–£6.00
🚏 (5)	£4.00–£6.00
⛺ (15)	£4.00–£6.00
🏕 (1)	£150.00–£400.00

Noteworthy Caravan & Camping Site

Bude Road, Holsworthy EX22 7JB **t** +44 (0) 1409 253731 & +44 (0) 7811 000071
e enquiries@noteworthy-devon.co.uk

noteworthy-devon.co.uk

Rural caravan and camping site, self-contained park on the Devon/Cornwall border. Four miles Holsworthy, six miles Bude.

open All year
payment Cash

General 🚲 📶 🍴 📷 📺 🐕 ☼ Leisure ⚑

HONITON, Devon Map ref 1D2 — HOTEL

★★★
COUNTRY HOUSE HOTEL
GOLD AWARD

B&B PER ROOM PER NIGHT
S £150.00–£170.00
D £170.00–£375.00
HB PER PERSON PER NIGHT
£122.00–£229.00

Midweek short breaks DB&B, see website for details. Perfect for special occasions.

Combe House

Gittisham, Honiton, Nr Exeter EX14 3AD **t** +44 (0) 1404 540400 **e** stay@thishotel.com

thishotel.com GUEST REVIEWS · SPECIAL OFFERS · REAL-TIME BOOKING

open All year
bedrooms 4 double, 9 twin, 3 suites
bathrooms 16 en suite
payment Credit/debit cards, cash, cheques

Winner of the South West, and silver Enjoy England 'Award for Excellence', Small Hotel of the Year 2008. A magical Grade I Listed, 15 bedroom Elizabethan manor and a thatched cottage for two in 3,500 acres of Devon estate where horses and pheasants roam freely. Open for coffee, lunch and dinner. A Michelin Rising Star. Visitors always made most welcome.

SAT NAV *EX14 3AD* **ONLINE MAP**

Room 🖥 📞 📺 🍷 ♿ General 🕭 🛏 🏃 P 🌐 🍴 🍽 🍵 🍸 ❀ 🐴 Leisure ∪ ⚓ ▶ 🚴

ILMINSTER, Somerset Map ref 1D2 — SELF CATERING

★★★
SELF CATERING

Units **1**
Sleeps **1–7**

LOW SEASON PER WK
£300.00–£420.00

HIGH SEASON PER WK
£500.00–£670.00

Myrtle House, Horton, Ilminster

contact Mr & Mrs Gordon & Marion Denman, 16 Challis Green, Barrington, Cambridge CB22 7RJ
t +44 (0) 1223 871294 **e** denman@myrtleonline.co.uk

myrtleonline.co.uk

Comfortable and spacious renovated farmhouse with some features dating back to 17thC. Log fire available. Adjoins fields in quiet village. Convenient for countryside and coast.

open All year
payment Credit/debit cards, cash, cheques
nearest pub less than 0.5 miles
nearest shop less than 0.5 miles

Unit 📺 📷 🖥 💻 🖨 🍷 🔲 🍽 ❀ 🧺 🍳 General 🕭 🛏 🏃 P S Leisure ∪ ⚓ ▶ 🚴

KILCOT, Gloucestershire Map ref 2B1 — SELF CATERING

★★★★
SELF CATERING

Units **1**
Sleeps **2–3**

LOW SEASON PER WK
£225.00–£350.00

HIGH SEASON PER WK
£375.00–£450.00

Short breaks off-season by arrangement with owners.

Coach House, Newent

contact Mrs Jane Merritt, Coach House, Orchard House, Aston Ingham Road, Newent GL18 1NP
t +44 (0) 1989 720417 **e** jane.merritt@btinternet.com

holidaycottage.uk.com

open All year
payment Cash, cheques, euros
nearest pub 0.5 miles
nearest shop 1 mile

Picturesque, quiet country cottage set in outstanding garden. Renovated autumn 2006. Accommodation comprises one twin bedroom plus large sofa bed in sitting room. Excellent base for exploring Gloucestershire, Forest of Dean, Herefordshire, Monmouthshire and Worcestershire. Small market town 1.5 miles away; good pubs close by.

Unit 📺 📷 🖥 🖨 🍷 🔲 🍳 📺 ❀ General 🕭 P Leisure ▶

LANREATH-BY-LOOE, Cornwall Map ref 1C2 — SELF CATERING

★★★
SELF CATERING

Units **6**
Sleeps **2–8**

LOW SEASON PER WK
£170.00–£370.00

HIGH SEASON PER WK
£415.00–£650.00

Weekend and midweek short breaks available (excl Jun-Sep). Please telephone for further information.

The Old Rectory, Lanreath, Looe

contact Mrs Julie Edge, The Old Rectory, Lanreath, Looe PL13 2NU **t** +44 (0) 1503 220247
e ask@oldrectory-lanreath.co.uk

oldrectory-lanreath.co.uk SPECIAL OFFERS

open All year
payment Credit/debit cards, cash, cheques
nearest pub less than 0.5 miles
nearest shop less than 0.5 miles

Georgian mansion converted into spacious, well-equipped apartments. Large, beautiful, secluded gardens with heated outdoor pool. Children's play area; table tennis. Picturesque, tranquil village with shop and pub in breathtaking countryside, minutes from pretty fishing villages and beaches. Visit stately homes and lovely gardens. Families and dogs welcome. On-site parking.

SAT NAV *PL13 2NU*

Unit 📺 ▣ ▣ ▣ ▢ ❖ ♨ ♨ General ⌇ ▥ ♁ ◎ ⑤ 🐕 ⛢ Leisure ⚲ ∪ ✈ ⛵ 🚴

LAUNCESTON, Cornwall Map ref 1C2 — GUEST ACCOMMODATION

★★★★
BED & BREAKFAST

B&B PER ROOM PER NIGHT
S £25.00–£27.50
D £50.00–£55.00

Oakside

South Petherwin, Launceston PL15 7JL **t** +44 (0) 1566 86733 **e** janet.crossman@tesco.net

open All year
bedrooms 2 double, 1 twin
bathrooms 2 en suite, 1 private
payment Cash, cheques

Panoramic views of Bodmin Moor from farm bungalow, nestling peacefully amongst delightful surroundings, conveniently situated one minute from A30. Ideal base for touring Devon and Cornwall. Twenty-five minutes from Eden Project. English breakfasts a speciality with home-made bread and preserves. Warm welcome awaits. Cosy, well-equipped rooms. Ideal place to relax.

SAT NAV *PL15 7JL*

Room ♿ 📺 ⚄ ♨ General ⌇ ▥ ♁ P ⚲ ❖ Leisure ▶

LAUNCESTON, Cornwall Map ref 1C2 — GUEST ACCOMMODATION

★★★★★
FARMHOUSE
SILVER AWARD

B&B PER ROOM PER NIGHT
D £30.00–£37.50

Trevadlock Farm

Congdon Shop, Launceston PL15 7PW **t** +44 (0) 1566 782239 **e** trevadlock@farming.co.uk

trevadlock.co.uk

Trevadlock Farm, just 1.5 miles off A30, a Grade II Listed 18thC farmhouse. Pretty en suite rooms, tea tray, hairdryer, TV. Ideal for touring Cornwall and Devon and both coasts.

open All year except Christmas and New Year
bedrooms 1 double, 1 twin
bathrooms All en suite
payment Credit/debit cards, cash, cheques

Room 📺 ⚄ ♨ General P ⚲ ❖

What do the star ratings mean?

For a detailed explanation of the quality and facilities represented by the stars, please refer to the information pages at the back of this guide.

LAUNCESTON, Cornwall Map ref 1C2 · SELF CATERING

★★★★
SELF CATERING

Units **8**
Sleeps **2-8**

LOW SEASON PER WK
£210.00-£385.00

HIGH SEASON PER WK
£545.00-£1,270.00

For special offers see our website.

Bamham Farm Cottages, Launceston

contact Mrs Jacki Chapman, Bamham Farm Cottages, Higher Bamham Farm, Launceston PL15 9LD
t +44 (0) 1566 772141 **e** jackie@bamhamfarm.co.uk

bamhamfarm.co.uk SPECIAL OFFERS

open All year
payment Credit/debit cards, cash, cheques
nearest pub 1 mile
nearest shop 1 mile

Individually designed cottages, ideally situated in beautiful countryside one mile from Launceston, the ancient capital of Cornwall, dominated by its Norman castle. The north and south coasts are easily accessible as are both Dartmoor and Bodmin Moor. Facilities include a heated indoor swimming pool, sauna, solarium, video recorders and DVD players.

Unit TV 📻🖥️💿📺. 🔌🗄️ ❄️ 🍷 🍴 ❄️ General 🎠🏛️🚶P○S Leisure 🎣🔦U♪🏃

LAUNCESTON, Cornwall Map ref 1C2 · SELF CATERING

★★★-★★★★★
SELF CATERING

Units **4**
Sleeps **2-4**

LOW SEASON PER WK
£140.00-£260.00

HIGH SEASON PER WK
£260.00-£480.00

Langdon Farm Holiday Cottages, Launceston

contact Mrs Fleur Rawlinson, Langdon Farm Holiday Cottages, Langdon Farm, Launceston PL15 8NW **t** +44 (0) 1566 785389 **e** g.f.rawlinson@btinternet.com

langdonholidays.com SPECIAL OFFERS · REAL-TIME BOOKING

One- and two-bedroom, well-equipped cottages, four-poster beds, countryside setting, near pub, ten miles from sea. Easy drive to Eden Project. Short breaks available.

open All year
payment Credit/debit cards, cash, cheques
nearest pub 1 mile
nearest shop 4 miles

Unit TV 💿📺. 🔌🍷🗄️❄️🍴 General 🎠🏛️🚶P○S🐾 Leisure U♪🏃🚲

LIFTON, Devon Map ref 1C2 · SELF CATERING

★★★★
SELF CATERING

Units **3**
Sleeps **2-4**

LOW SEASON PER WK
£425.00-£595.00

HIGH SEASON PER WK
£695.00-£1,125.00

Short breaks available. Telephone for details.

Barbary Ball House, Lifton

contact Mr Richard Street, Barbary Ball, Lifton PL16 0AU **t** +44 (0) 1566 780457
e info@devoncountrybarns.co.uk

devoncountrybarns.co.uk GUEST REVIEWS · SPECIAL OFFERS · REAL-TIME BOOKING

open All year
payment Credit/debit cards, cash, cheques
nearest pub 0.75 miles
nearest shop 1.5 miles

Exceptional barns, newly converted, set in a lush green valley. Superb views, private terraces, top-quality furnishings and equipment. Stone and slate floors, oak beams and doors, underfloor heating. Fantastic location, equidistant from the north and south coasts, twenty minutes from Dartmoor. Award-winning pubs and farm shops nearby.

SAT NAV PL16 0AU **ONLINE MAP**

Unit TV SC 💿📺. 🔌🗄️🍷🔆🍴🗄️🕯️❄️⛏️∅ General 🎠🏛️🚶PS🐾
Leisure U♪🚲

What if I need to cancel?

It is advisable to check the proprietor's cancellation policy in case you have to change your plans at a later date.

LONGDOWN, Devon Map ref 1D2

★★★★
SELF CATERING

Units **1**
Sleeps **1–2**

LOW SEASON PER WK
£225.00–£250.00

HIGH SEASON PER WK
£325.00–£385.00

Valley View, Exeter

contact Mrs Jane Steele, Valley View, Woodside, Longdown, Exeter EX6 7SR **t** +44 (0) 1392 811858
e janeeileensteele@talktalk.net

Spacious self-contained annexe in lovely setting three miles outside Exeter. Large lounge-diner, fully equipped kitchen and comfortable en suite double bedroom. Good access to Dartmoor and beaches, city and university.

open All year except Christmas and New Year
payment Cash, cheques, euros
nearest pub 1 mile
nearest shop 1.5 miles

Unit 📺 🖳 📼 🖥 🎛 🔲 🗑 ❄ General **P** Leisure ∪

LOOE, Cornwall Map ref 1C2

★★★★
GUEST HOUSE
SILVER AWARD

B&B PER ROOM PER NIGHT
S £50.00–£60.00
D £60.00–£75.00

Call, or visit our website for special promotions.

Dovers House

St Martins Road, St Martin, Looe PL13 1PB **t** +44 (0) 1503 265468 **e** twhyte@btconnect.com

dovershouse.co.uk

open All year except Christmas
bedrooms 2 double, 1 twin, 1 family
bathrooms All en suite
payment Credit/debit cards, cash, cheques

Just a few minutes' drive from Looe harbour, Dovers House is an ideal base for exploring or visiting Cornwall's many attractions and scenic views. Looe is an old fishing port with friendly people and good inns and restaurants. Our accommodation offers twin, double and large family rooms, all with en suite. Comfortably designed to make your stay pleasant and relaxing.

SAT NAV *PL13 1PB*

Room 📺 🍴 🍷 General 🎋8 **P** 🅿 🔥 🍽 ❄ Leisure ∪ 🎣 ►

LOOE, Cornwall Map ref 1C2

★★★★–★★★★★★
SELF CATERING

Units **8**
Sleeps **2–6**

LOW SEASON PER WK
£275.00–£775.00

HIGH SEASON PER WK
£855.00–£1,395.00

Special short breaks available – please call for details.

Barclay House Luxury Cottages, Looe

contact Mr Graham Brooks, Barclay House Luxury Cottages, St Martins Road, East Looe, Looe PL13 1LP **t** +44 (0) 1503 262929 **e** info@barclayhouse.co.uk

barclayhouse.co.uk GUEST REVIEWS · SPECIAL OFFERS · REAL-TIME BOOKING

open All year
payment Credit/debit cards, cash, cheques
nearest pub less than 0.5 miles
nearest shop less than 0.5 miles

Luxury, award-winning holiday cottages. Breathtaking views over the Looe River valley. Heated pool nestled in a natural sun trap. Five minutes' walk to harbour, town and beach. Superb award-winning restaurant and bar/lounge on site. Gymnasium. Come stay at Barclay House, you will be glad you did!

ONLINE MAP

Unit 📺 🆂🅲 📼 📼 🖳 🎛 🔲 🍷 🗑 🗑 🗑 ❄ General 🎋 🍽 🕯 3 🐕
Leisure 🌡 ∪ 🎣 ►

Place index

If you know where you want to stay, the index by place name at the back of the guide will give you the page number listing accommodation in your chosen town, city or village. Check out the other useful indexes too.

LOOE, Cornwall Map ref 1C2

SELF CATERING

★★★
SELF CATERING

Units **5**
Sleeps **2–5**

LOW SEASON PER WK
£173.00–£234.00

HIGH SEASON PER WK
£415.00–£722.00

Short breaks available Oct-Mar (excl Christmas and New Year), minimum 2 nights.

Talehay, Looe

contact Neil & Theresa Dennett, Talehay, Tremaine, Looe PL13 2LT t +44 (0) 1503 220252
e infobooking@talehay.co.uk

talehay.co.uk GUEST REVIEWS · SPECIAL OFFERS

open All year
payment Credit/debit cards, cash, cheques
nearest pub 1 mile
nearest shop 1 mile

Tastefully converted and very comfortable stone holiday cottages set around 17thC non-working farmstead. Set in unspoilt, peaceful countryside with breathtaking coastal walks and beaches nearby. Close to Eden Project, Lost Gardens of Heligan and many National Trust properties. An ideal base for exploring the many varied delights of Cornwall.

ONLINE MAP

Unit 📺 🆂🅲 ▣ 💻 🔌 🔟 🎛 ✳ ⛺   General 🎠 🏚 🏕 P 🐕 🐎   Leisure ∪ ⚓ ⛳ 🚲

LOSTWITHIEL, Cornwall Map ref 1B2

SELF CATERING

★★★–★★★★★
SELF CATERING

Units **7**
Sleeps **1–6**

LOW SEASON PER WK
£210.00–£330.00

HIGH SEASON PER WK
£330.00–£905.00

Short breaks out of season. Reduced green fees. Pets accepted in some cottages. Canoe trips available with safety boat.

Lanwithan Cottages, Lostwithiel

contact Mr V B Edward-Collins, Lanwithan Cottages, Lanwithan Road, Lostwithiel PL22 0LA
t +44 (0) 1208 872444 e info@lanwithancottages.co.uk

lanwithancottages.co.uk

open All year
payment Cash, cheques, euros
nearest pub 0.5 miles
nearest shop 0.5 miles

Charming selection of Georgian estate cottages nestling in the Fowey Valley with two delightful waterside properties. Cottages with leaded-light windows, crackling log fires, four-poster bed and glass-topped well. Parkland, river frontage and boat. Woodland and riverside walks from your garden gate. Come and relax and soak up the Cornish atmosphere.

Unit 📺 ▣ 💻 🔟 🎛 ✳ ⛺ 🐾   General 🎠 🏚 🏕 P 🔳 🐎
Leisure 🔍 ∪ ⚓ ⛳ 🚲

LOSTWITHIEL, Cornwall Map ref 1B2

SELF CATERING

★★★★
SELF CATERING

Units **1**
Sleeps **1–4**

LOW SEASON PER WK
£300.00–£450.00

HIGH SEASON PER WK
£450.00–£600.00

Short weekend and midweek breaks available during spring, autumn and winter.

Trevorry, Lostwithiel

contact Ms Helen Carlisle, Trevorry Farm, Lostwithiel PL22 0JH t +44 (0) 1208 872279
e trevorryfarm@hotmail.com

trevorry.com SPECIAL OFFERS

open All year
payment Cash, cheques
nearest pub 1 mile
nearest shop 2 miles

Trevorry Cottage, with stunning views overlooking lake and copse, offers high quality accommodation in the heart of Cornwall. Tourist attractions close by include Eden, Heligan, Lanhydrock, Fowey, Mevagissey, Looe, Polperro and Fowey. With a wealth of glorious beaches, historic towns and fishing villages on our doorstep, Trevorry is perfect for exploring Cornwall.

SAT NAV PL22 0JH **ONLINE MAP**

Unit 📺 📀 💻 🔟 🎛 📺 ✳   General P 🆂   Leisure ⚓ ⛳

★★★★★
SELF CATERING

Units **6**
Sleeps **2–12**

LOW SEASON PER WK
£336.00–£1,179.00

HIGH SEASON PER WK
£531.00–£2,298.00

Short breaks available Oct-May: 3 nights Fri-Mon, 4 nights Mon-Fri.

Champernhayes Cottages, Wootton Fitzpaine, Lyme Regis

contact Mr & Mrs T Dutton, Champernhayes Bookings, 22 Ringley Park Avenue, Reigate RH2 7ET
t +44 (0) 1297 560853 **e** champernhayes@btinternet.com

champernhayes.com SPECIAL OFFERS

open All year
payment Credit/debit cards, cash, cheques, euros
nearest pub 2 miles
nearest shop 2 miles

Luxury accommodation set in beautiful countryside near to Jurassic Coast and beaches at Charmouth and Lyme Regis. Designated an Area of Outstanding Natural Beauty. Cottages converted from original farmhouse buildings dating back to 1482. Each cottage has its own private garden with patio and hardwood garden furniture.

SAT NAV *DT6 6DF* **ONLINE MAP**

Unit 📺🗄🖥📠🏠🎛🔲🍳🔌🎨❄⛺✏ General 🐕🏛♿P⑤🐾 Leisure 🎣

★★★
SELF CATERING

Units **1**
Sleeps **4–9**

LOW SEASON PER WK
£350.00–£500.00

HIGH SEASON PER WK
£500.00–£950.00

Harbour House Flats, Lyme Regis

contact Mrs Alison Stait, Pound Cottage, Brampford Speke, Exeter EX5 5DU **t** +44 (0) 1392 841507
e info@bythecobb.co.uk

bythecobb.co.uk GUEST REVIEWS · SPECIAL OFFERS

Harbour House is immediately overlooking the beach and harbour. Seafront location. Second-floor penthouse flat. Superb views over the Cobb and Lyme Bay. Three bedrooms. Large rooftop patio. Parking. Dishwasher.

open All year
payment Cheques
nearest pub less than 0.5 miles
nearest shop less than 0.5 miles

Unit 📺🗄🖥📠🏠🎛🔲🍳🔌🎨❄ General 🐕🏛♿P⑤

★★★★
SELF CATERING

Units **2**
Sleeps **2–4**

LOW SEASON PER WK
£295.00–£420.00

HIGH SEASON PER WK
£465.00–£695.00

Short breaks available in the low season.

Sea Tree House, Lyme Regis

contact Mr David Parker, Sea Tree House, 18 Broad Street, Lyme Regis DT7 3QE
t +44 (0) 1297 442244 **e** seatree.house@ukonline.co.uk

lymeregis.com/seatreehouse

open All year
payment Cash, cheques
nearest pub 0.5 miles
nearest shop 0.5 miles

Romantic, elegant apartments overlooking the sea, three minutes from the beach. Spacious living room with dining area overlooking the sea. Central position giving easy access to restaurants, pubs and walks in Area of Outstanding Natural Beauty. Wi-Fi Internet. Warm, friendly welcome from owners.

Unit 📺🗄🖥📠🏠🎛🔲🍳🔌🎨❄ General 🐕🏛♿P◯⑤🐾 Leisure ∪♪▶

Do you have access needs?

Look for the National Accessible Scheme symbols if you have special hearing, visual or mobility needs. An index of accommodation participating in the scheme can be found at the back of this guide.

LYNTON, Devon Map ref 1C1 GUEST ACCOMMODATION

★★★★
**GUEST HOUSE
SILVER AWARD**

B&B PER ROOM PER NIGHT
D £50.00–£60.00

EVENING MEAL PER PERSON
£12.00–£15.00

Beaujolais Nouveau weekend. New Year specials. Gift vouchers. 3-night DB&B.

The Denes Guest House

15 Longmead, Lynton EX35 6DQ t +44 (0) 1598 753573 e j.e.mcgowan@btinternet.com

thedenes.com REAL-TIME BOOKING

open All year except Christmas
bedrooms 3 double, 2 family
bathrooms 4 en suite, 1 private
payment Credit/debit cards, cash, cheques

Peacefully located close to the Valley of Rocks, but a short walk to the heart of the village, The Denes is an ideal base to explore Exmoor, whether walking, cycling or driving. Our bedrooms are spacious, all with en suite or private facilities. Freshly cooked breakfasts and evening meals appeal to discerning appetites.

SAT NAV EX35 6DQ **ONLINE MAP**

Room 📺 ♿ 🕸 General 🛏 🏛 ♿ P ⚥ ✗ 🍴 ❄ Leisure ⚲ ∪ 🎵

LYNTON, Devon Map ref 1C1 GUEST ACCOMMODATION

★★★★
**GUEST ACCOMMODATION
SILVER AWARD**

B&B PER ROOM PER NIGHT
S £28.00–£35.00
D £54.00–£72.00

Longmead House

9 Longmead, Lynton EX35 6DQ t +44 (0) 1598 752523 e info@longmeadhouse.co.uk

longmeadhouse.co.uk

open All year except Christmas and New Year
bedrooms 4 double, 1 twin, 1 single, 1 family, 1 suite
bathrooms All en suite
payment Credit/debit cards, cash, cheques

One of Lynton's best-kept secrets! Delightful Victorian house with many original features, quietly situated towards the Valley of Rocks. Beautiful gardens and croquet lawn with ample parking. Comfortable, relaxed atmosphere with warm welcome, excellent hospitality and delicious home cooking. Not to be missed.

SAT NAV EX35 6DQ

Room 📺 ♿ 🕸 General 🛏 P 🎧 ⚥ ❄ Leisure ∪

LYNTON, Devon Map ref 1C1 SELF CATERING

★★★
SELF CATERING

Units **3**
Sleeps **2–8**

LOW SEASON PER WK
£230.00–£485.00

HIGH SEASON PER WK
£520.00–£985.00

Short breaks and weekend breaks available during off-peak seasons. Special rates for advanced and late bookings.

Cloud Farm, Lynton

contact Mrs Jill Harman, Oare, Lynton EX35 6NU t +44 (0) 1598 741234
e doonevalleyholidays@hotmail.com

doonevalleyholidays.co.uk SPECIAL OFFERS

open All year
payment Credit/debit cards, cash, cheques
nearest pub 3 miles
nearest shop less than 0.5 miles

Cloud Farm is a lovely riverside farmhouse in the heart of Exmoor's beautiful Doone Valley. The cottages, with tea room, shop, off-licence and gardens, provide an idyllic base for families and children, walkers and tourers seeking an 'away-from-it-all' break at any time of year. Riding for all ages and abilities.

ONLINE MAP

Unit 📺 📀 📽 🖥 🍳 🧺 🎮 ❄ General 🛏 🏛 ♿ P 🅾 Ⓢ 🐾 Leisure ∪ 🎵

Using map references

Map references refer to the colour maps at the front of this guide.

MAIDENCOMBE, Devon Map ref 1D2 SELF CATERING

★★★
SELF CATERING

Units **6**
Sleeps **2–4**

LOW SEASON PER WK
£230.00–£325.00

HIGH SEASON PER WK
£270.00–£570.00

Short breaks available. Low season: 20% discount for couples (except for 'Poppy' unit).

Bowden Close House, Maidencombe

contact Mrs Sarah Farquharson, Bowden Close House, Teignmouth Road, Maidencombe, Torquay TQ1 4TJ **t** +44 (0) 1803 328029 **e** enquiries@bowdenclose.co.uk

bowdenclose.co.uk SPECIAL OFFERS · REAL-TIME BOOKING

open All year
payment Cash, cheques, euros
nearest pub 0.5 miles
nearest shop 3 miles

Relax in very comfortable apartments or two-storey, self-contained wings of large Victorian house overlooking Lyme Bay, four miles from Torquay. Acre of gardens with stunning views. Minutes from sheltered Maidencombe Cove and the South West Coast Path. Easy access to Dartmoor and the lovely South Devon countryside.

ONLINE MAP

Unit 📺 📼 🍴 🗒 ✳ General 🛏 🏭 ⚹ ⊙ S Leisure ∪ ♪ ►

MAWGAN PORTH, Cornwall Map ref 1B2 SELF CATERING

★★★★
SELF CATERING

Units **1**
Sleeps **1–2**

LOW SEASON PER WK
£310.00–£410.00

HIGH SEASON PER WK
£600.00–£920.00

White Lodge, Mawgan Porth, Newquay

contact Reservations, Beach Retreats, On the Beach, Watergate Bay, Newquay TR8 4AA
t +44 (0) 1637 861005 & +44 (0) 1637 861241 **e** kelly@beachretreats.co.uk

beachretreats.co.uk SPECIAL OFFERS · REAL-TIME BOOKING

A luxury one-bedroom, ground-floor apartment with furnished patio overlooking the beach with designated car parking. Beach 150m, shops 400m. Closed 10-29 January and 22 November-18 December.

payment Credit/debit cards, cheques, euros
nearest pub less than 0.5 miles
nearest shop less than 0.5 miles

Unit 📺 🗄 📼 🗒 🍴 ⚲ 🗒 ✳ General P ⊙ S Leisure ∪ ♪ ►

MELCOMBE BINGHAM, Dorset Map ref 2B3 SELF CATERING

★★★★
SELF CATERING

Units **1**
Sleeps **1–7**

LOW SEASON PER WK
£450.00–£600.00

HIGH SEASON PER WK
£675.00–£850.00

Short breaks available outside summer peak, Christmas and Easter. Min 3-night stay. Linen, towels and heating included.

Greygles, Melcombe Bingham, Dorchester

contact Mr Paul Sommerfeld, 22 Tiverton Road, London NW10 3HL **t** +44 (0) 20 8969 4830
e enquiry@greygles.co.uk

greygles.co.uk

open All year
payment Cash, cheques, euros
nearest pub 0.5 miles
nearest shop 0.5 miles

Rural peace in spacious, well-equipped stone cottage with delightful views. Hardy Country, on edge of friendly village with well-known pub. Four bedrooms, one on ground floor. Log fire. Wendy house in garden. In an Area of Outstanding Natural Beauty, just off Wessex Ridgeway walkers' path. Coast, abbeys, castles, gardens, many attractions within 30 minutes' drive.

SAT NAV *DT2 7PE* **ONLINE MAP**

Unit 📺 🗄 📼 🗒 ⚲ 🗒 ✳ ♨ General 🛏 🏭 ⚹ P ⊙ 🐕

Has every property been assessed?

All accommodation in this guide has been rated for quality, or is awaiting assessment, by a professional national tourist board assessor.

MEVAGISSEY, Cornwall Map ref 1B3 · SELF CATERING

★★★★
SELF CATERING

Units **1**
Sleeps **1**

LOW SEASON PER WK
£375.00–£530.00

HIGH SEASON PER WK
£530.00–£680.00

Eden Cottage offers special midweek discounts and late availabilities end Sep-end Apr. Refer to website bookings.

Eden Cottage, Mevagissey, St Austell

contact Mrs Helen Whatty, Mevagissey Holiday Cottages, Mevagissey House, Vicarage Hill, Mevagissey PL26 6SZ **t** +44 (0) 1726 842525 **e** hwhatty@yahoo.co.uk

edencottage.co.uk SPECIAL OFFERS · REAL-TIME BOOKING

open All year
payment Credit/debit cards, cheques
nearest pub less than 0.5 miles
nearest shop less than 0.5 miles

A charming 300-year-old, cosy but very spacious, character cottage with a modern twist in the heart o Mevagissey. Equipped with everything you will need. Ideal location for couples, families or walkers A perfect central base, you can relax or have an energetic holiday, the choice is yours!

SAT NAV PL26 6SS **ONLINE MAP**

Unit 📺 📀 🖥️ 🗄️ 🍳 🔲 🖥️ General 🛏️ 🏛️ ♨️ Ⓞ Ⓢ Leisure ⚲ ∪ 🎵 ↑ 🚲

MEVAGISSEY, Cornwall Map ref 1B3 · SELF CATERING

★★★★★
SELF CATERING

Units **2**
Sleeps **5**

LOW SEASON PER WK
£450.00–£550.00

HIGH SEASON PER WK
£650.00–£1,099.00

Short breaks sometimes available during low season.

The Lookout and The Penthouse, Mevagissey

contact Mr Andrew Main Wilson, The Lookout and The Penthouse, The West Wing, 3 Tawsden Manor, Spout Lane, Brenchley TN2 7AS **t** +44 (0) 1892 722323 & +44 (0) 7725 562563 **e** amw@iod.com

penthouseholidays.com GUEST REVIEWS

open All year
payment Cash, cheques, euros
nearest pub less than 0.5 miles
nearest shop less than 0.5 miles

Two magnificent luxury cliff-top apartments. Private balconies overlooking breathtaking sea and coastline panoramas. Nare Court's most spectacular and stylish properties. Spa baths, ceiling-to-floor glass windows and doors, beautifully furnished. Romantic and private, yet just five minutes' walk to restaurants and shops in picturesque Mevagissey fishing village

Unit 📺 📀 🖥️ 🗄️ 🔲 🍴 ❄️ General 🛏️10 P Ⓞ Ⓢ Leisure ∪ ↑ 🚲

MILTON ABBAS, Dorset Map ref 2B3 · SELF CATERING

★★★★
SELF CATERING

Units **6**
Sleeps **2–6**

LOW SEASON PER WK
£320.00–£495.00

HIGH SEASON PER WK
£415.00–£1,250.00

Luccombe Farm, Blandford Forum

contact Mr & Mrs Murray & Amanda Kayll, Luccombe Farm, Milton Abbas, Blandford Forum DT11 0BE **t** +44 (0) 1258 880558 **e** mkayll@aol.com

luccombeholidays.co.uk

open All year
payment Credit/debit cards, cash, cheques
nearest pub 2 miles
nearest shop 2 miles

Comfortable converted cottages, with traditional character. Idyllic, peaceful setting in middle of proper working farm close to the historic village of Milton Abbas. Many facilities, including indoor pool.

Unit 📺 📠 📀 🖥️ 🗄️ 🍳 🔲 🍴 ❄️ 🔥 General 🛏️ 🏛️ ♨️ P Ⓞ Ⓢ 🐕
Leisure 📶 🎣 ⚲ ∪ 🎵 ↑ 🚲

MITCHELDEAN, Gloucestershire Map ref 2B1 — SELF CATERING

★★★★
SELF CATERING

Units **1**
Sleeps **2**

LOW SEASON PER WK
£290.00

HIGH SEASON PER WK
£325.00–£335.00

The Old Dairy, Mitcheldean

contact Lorraine Morgan, The White House, Trinity Road, Harrow Hill, Drybrook GL17 9LD
t +44 (0) 1594 543737 e theolddairy@aic.co.uk

olddairycottage.com GUEST REVIEWS · SPECIAL OFFERS

Situated along a quiet, rural lane, The Old Dairy is a luxury cottage featuring slate floors and beamed ceilings throughout. Private patio area and parking for two vehicles.

open All year
payment Cash, cheques
nearest pub 1.5 miles
nearest shop 1.5 miles

Unit 📺 🖥 💻 🛗 ♨ 🍳 🔌 🧺 ✻ General P 🅿 S 🐕

MORETON-IN-MARSH, Gloucestershire Map ref 2B1 — GUEST ACCOMMODATION

★★★
FARMHOUSE

B&B PER ROOM PER NIGHT
S £45.00–£65.00
D £65.00–£80.00

Discounts available for stays of 3 nights or more.

Old Farm

Dorn, Moreton-in-Marsh GL56 9NS t +44 (0) 1608 650394 e info@oldfarmdorn.co.uk

oldfarmdorn.co.uk REAL-TIME BOOKING

open All year except Christmas
bedrooms 2 double, 1 twin
bathrooms All en suite
payment Credit/debit cards, cash, cheques

'Comfortable beds, friendly hosts and great breakfasts'. A working farm, the house dates back to the 15th century with spacious en suite bedrooms (including four-poster), guest lounge and large gardens. Local breakfast served with home-produced eggs and Old Spot sausages and bacon. Peaceful, rural location but only one mile from Moreton-in-Marsh.

SAT NAV GL56 9NS

Room 🛏 📺 💆 ♨ General ⛱ 🏠 ⛵ P ♿ 🛅 ✻ Leisure ∪ ♩ 🚲

MORETON-IN-MARSH, Gloucestershire Map ref 2B1 — GUEST ACCOMMODATION

★★★★
GUEST HOUSE

B&B PER ROOM PER NIGHT
S £45.00
D £60.00–£65.00

Treetops

London Road, Moreton-in-Marsh GL56 0HE t +44 (0) 1608 651036 e treetops1@talk21.com

treetopscotswolds.co.uk

open All year except Christmas
bedrooms 4 double, 2 twin
bathrooms All en suite
payment Credit/debit cards, cash, cheques

Family guesthouse on the A44, set in 0.5 acres of secluded gardens. Five minutes' walk from the village centre.

SAT NAV GL56 0HE

Room 🛏 📺 💆 ♨ General ⛱ 🏠 ⛵ P ✻ Leisure ♩

Check the maps for accommodation locations

Colour maps at the front pinpoint all the places where accommodation is featured within the regional sections of this guide. Pick your location and then refer to the place index at the back to find the page number.

MULLION, Cornwall Map ref 1B3

★ ★ ★ ★
GUEST ACCOMMODATION

B&B PER ROOM PER NIGHT
S £34.00–£40.00
D £60.00–£68.00

5% discount for 3 nights.

Trenance Farmhouse

Mullion, Helston TR12 7HB t +44 (0) 1326 240639 e info@trenancefarmholidays.co.uk

trenancefarmholidays.co.uk GUEST REVIEWS · SPECIAL OFFERS

open March to October
bedrooms 3 double, 1 twin
bathrooms All en suite
payment Credit/debit cards, cash, cheques

Welcome to our Victorian farmhouse, set in matur
gardens on the outskirts of the village and only half
mile from picturesque Mullion Cove and beaches.
footpath crosses fields to the coast offering
magnificent views. Bedrooms are all en suite; relax
our guest lounge; enjoy breakfast in the garden
room.

SAT NAV *TR12 7HB*

Room 🛏 📺 🚽 ⚲ General P ♨ 🖥 ✿ 🐾 Leisure ⌇ ∪ ♪ ⇂

MULLION, Cornwall Map ref 1B3

★ ★ ★
SELF CATERING

Units **9**
Sleeps **2–6**

LOW SEASON PER WK
£220.00–£375.00

HIGH SEASON PER WK
£450.00–£725.00

10% discount for 2 sharing Apr-Jun (excl Easter and Spring break holiday weeks). Winter short breaks.

Trenance Farm Cottages, Helston

contact Mr & Mrs Richard, Jenny & Tamara Tyler-Street, Trenance Farm, Mullion, Helston TR12 7HE
t +44 (0) 1326 240639 e info@trenancefarmholidays.co.uk

trenancefarmholidays.co.uk GUEST REVIEWS · SPECIAL OFFERS

open All year
payment Credit/debit cards, cash, cheques
nearest pub 0.5 miles
nearest shop less than 0.5 miles

Quality cottages, each with their own garden,
converted from old farm buildings and set in
13 acres. Heated summer pool. Games rooms.
Barbecues. Five minutes' walk across fields to coas
and lovely walks. Swimming/surfing coves and
Mullion village 0.5 miles. A peaceful location in an
Area of Outstanding Natural Beauty.

Unit 📺 🖥 🗄 ⚲ 🍽 ✿ ⛱ General 🐎 ♨ ⚙ P 🖥 S 🐾 Leisure ⌇ ◖ ∪ ♪ ⇂

NEWNHAM, Gloucestershire Map ref 2B1

★ ★ ★
SELF CATERING

Units **1**
Sleeps **2–6**

LOW SEASON PER WK
£280.00–£400.00

HIGH SEASON PER WK
£350.00–£600.00

Short breaks welcome.

Stroods, Broadoak, Newnham

contact Miss Annabelle Gillman, Orchard Cottage, The Strood, Broadoak, Newnham GL14 1JL
t +44 (0) 1594 516976 & +44 (0) 7710 269563 e annabelle@annab.entadsl.com

forestofdeancottage.com REAL-TIME BOOKING

open All year except Christmas and New Year
payment Credit/debit cards, cash, cheques, euros
nearest pub less than 0.5 miles
nearest shop 0.5 miles

Charming cottage situated close to riverside town of
Newnham-on-Severn. Pleasant garden with patio
area and adequate parking for three vehicles. Fitted
kitchen with dishwasher and washing machine.
Logburner in lounge with TV and DVD
entertainment. Family bathroom and separate
shower room. Conservatory and private driveway.

SAT NAV *GL14 1JL* ONLINE MAP

Unit 📺 📀 🖥 🗄 🗄 ⚲ 🖥 ⚙ 📱 ✿ ⛱ ⊘ General 🐎 2 P 🖥 S Leisure ∪ ♪ 🚴

Chichester Interest Holidays

★★
GUEST ACCOMMODATION

B&B PER ROOM PER NIGHT
S Min £24.00
D Min £48.00

14 Bay View Terrace, Newquay TR7 2LR **t** +44 (0) 1637 874216 **e** sheila.harper@virgin.net

http://freespace.virgin.net/sheila.harper

Comfortable, licensed, convenient for shops, beaches and gardens. Showers in most bedrooms, many extras. Walking, mineral collecting, archaeology and Cornish Heritage holidays in spring and autumn.

open March to October
bedrooms 3 double, 2 twin, 1 single, 1 family
payment Cash, cheques

Room 🚿 General ☎2 P 🔔 ⅋ 🏧 🖨

Cornwall Coast Holidays, Newquay

★★★★
SELF CATERING

Units   **4**
Sleeps   **2–6**

HIGH SEASON PER WK
£475.00–£995.00

contact Mrs Deborah Spencer-Smith, Cornwall Coast Holidays **t** +44 (0) 20 8440 7518 & +44 (0) 7910 583050 **e** deborah@cornwallcoastholidays.com

cornwallcoastholidays.com

open All year
payment Cheques

Cornwall Coast Holidays offer apartments and cottages that are in the perfect location for wonderful beach holidays. The cottages are modern, and the apartments have stunning sea views. Both apartments and cottages have one en suite bathroom and are close to the town centre, golf course and other amenities.

Unit 📺 🖥 📀 💻 📠 🔥 🗄 🛏 🧺 ❄ ﹡ General ☎ 🏢 ⅋ P

Hendra Paul Cottages, Porth, Newquay

★★★–★★★★★
SELF CATERING

Units   **4**
Sleeps   **2–8**

LOW SEASON PER WK
£290.00–£520.00

HIGH SEASON PER WK
£575.00–£1,380.00

contact Mrs Julia Schofield, Hendra Paul Cottages - BE020, Porth, Newquay TR8 4JL **t** +44 (0) 1637 874695 **e** info@hendrapaul.co.uk

hendrapaul.co.uk SPECIAL OFFERS

Charming cluster of four detached, beamed cottages, equipped to highest standard. Quiet countryside location, two miles Porth beach. Sleep two to eight people. Short breaks from October to May welcome.

open All year
payment Credit/debit cards, cash, cheques
nearest pub 2 miles
nearest shop 2 miles

Unit 📺 🆂 📀 💻 📠 🔥 🗄 🧺 ❄ 🍴 General ☎ 🏢 ⅋ ⊙ 🆂 Leisure ∪ ♪ ⚓ 🚴

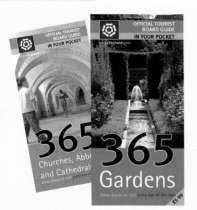

OKEHAMPTON, Devon Map ref 1C2

★★★★
SELF CATERING

Units **1**
Sleeps **2**

LOW SEASON PER WK
£215.00–£443.00

HIGH SEASON PER WK
£143.00–£317.00

Heather Cottage, Okehampton

contact Yvette Martin
t +44 (0) 1837 658820 & +44 (0) 7971 258040 **e** yvettemartin@btinternet.com

lastminute-cottages.co.uk/north-and-mid-devon/dem2028/ GUEST REVIEWS · SPECIAL OFFERS · REAL-TIME BOOKIN

open All year
payment Credit/debit cards, cash, cheques
nearest pub less than 0.5 miles
nearest shop less than 0.5 miles

A quiet and comfortable cottage/garden flat for tw
featuring a locally planted verdant garden and
located just five minutes' walk from Dartmoor
National Park and eight to Okehampton's bustling
town centre with all amenities including cinema, ar
gallery and Waitrose supermarket! Twin or double
beds. Wireless internet connection.

SAT NAV EX20 1EH

Unit 📺 🆂 📧 ♦ 🖥 🎮 ♦ General P 🅂 🐕 Leisure ⚲ ∪ ♪ ⚑ 🚲

PADSTOW, Cornwall Map ref 1B2

★★★★★
SELF CATERING

Units **9**
Sleeps **2–8**

LOW SEASON PER WK
£425.00–£900.00

HIGH SEASON PER WK
£700.00–£2,300.00

Retallack Resort and Spa, Nr Padstow

contact Miranda Waldron, Retallack Resort and Spa, Winnards Perch TR9 6DE
t +44 (0) 1637 881580 **e** miranda@retallackresort.com

retallackresort.com GUEST REVIEWS · SPECIAL OFFERS · REAL-TIME BOOKING

open All year
payment Credit/debit cards, cash, cheques
nearest pub 1 mile
nearest shop 1 mile

A selection of two- and four-bedroom lodges, set in
luxury resort. On-site spa facilities, golf, tennis and
much more for the whole family.

ONLINE MAP

Unit 📺 🆂 🖥 🎮 📧 🖨 🎮 🖥 🕹 🖥 🎮 ♦ 🍴 General 🛏 🏛 🧖 P 🅂 🐕
Leisure 🎣 ⚲ ∪ ♪ ⚑ 🚲

PADSTOW, Cornwall Map ref 1B2

★★★–★★★★★
SELF CATERING

Units **4**
Sleeps **1–8**

LOW SEASON PER WK
£210.00–£525.00

HIGH SEASON PER WK
£540.00–£1,295.00

*Special offers
available upon
request for low
season (Nov–May)
for couples and
long-weekend stays.*

Yellow Sands Apartments & House, Padstow

contact Mr Dakin, Yellow Sands Apartments & House, Harlyn Bay, Padstow PL28 8SE
t +44 (0) 1841 520376 **e** martin@yellowsands.fsnet.co.uk

yellowsands.net SPECIAL OFFERS

open All year
payment Cash, cheques
nearest pub less than 0.5 miles
nearest shop 1 mile

Resident proprietor provides spacious, quality
accommodation with stunning sea views! Just 200yds
from superb sandy beach and coastal footpath in a
designated Area of Outstanding Natural Beauty.
Landscaped gardens. Shops and golf one mile.
Historic Padstow 2.5 miles. For sightseeing daytrips,
all parts of Cornwall within one hour's drive.

Unit 📺 🖥 🎮 📧 🖨 🎮 🖥 🕹 🖥 🎮 ♦ General 🛏 🏛 🧖 P 🔘 🅂 🐕
Leisure ∪ ♪ ⚑ 🚲

PAIGNTON, Devon Map ref 1D2 — HOTEL

★★
HOTEL

Marine Hotel

Seafront, Paignton TQ4 6AP t +44 (0) 1803 559778 e stay@marinehotelpaignton.co.uk

marinehotelpaignton.co.uk SPECIAL OFFERS

B&B PER ROOM PER NIGHT
S £20.00–£40.00
D £40.00–£80.00
HB PER PERSON PER NIGHT
£30.00–£50.00

Great-value weekend breaks Oct–May.

open All year
bedrooms 12 double, 21 twin, 11 single, 8 family
bathrooms All en suite
payment Credit/debit cards, cash, cheques

A family-run hotel set in the middle of Paignton right on the seafront, commanding beautiful views across Torbay. Convenient level walk to all amenities. Here you will always find a smile and quality comfort and company within a lively, yet relaxed atmosphere. Simply, great value.

SAT NAV *TQ4 6AP* ONLINE MAP

Room General Leisure

PAIGNTON, Devon Map ref 1D2 — HOTEL

Rating Applied For
HOTEL

Redcliffe Lodge Hotel

Marine Drive, Paignton TQ3 2NJ t +44 (0) 1803 551394 e davies.valleyview@tiscali.co.uk

redcliffelodge.co.uk

B&B PER ROOM PER NIGHT
S £20.00–£30.00
D £40.00–£60.00
HB PER PERSON PER NIGHT
£32.00–£42.00

2-4 year olds half-price when sharing with adults. Winter 2-night breaks, B&B and evening meal from £30pp.

open All year
bedrooms 10 double, 3 twin, 2 single, 2 family
bathrooms All en suite
payment Credit/debit cards, cash, cheques, euros

Redcliffe Lodge occupies one of Paignton's finest seafront positions, in its own grounds with large free car park. All rooms are en suite and comfortably furnished with modern facilities. Licensed bar. Panoramic views from both our sun lounge and dining room. High standard of cuisine.

SAT NAV *TQ3 2NJ* ONLINE MAP

Room General Leisure

PAIGNTON, Devon Map ref 1D2 — SELF CATERING

★★★★
SELF CATERING

All Seasons Holiday Apartments, Paignton

contact Mr Colin Livesey, 18 Garfield Road, Paignton TQ4 6AX t +44 (0) 1803 552187
e enquiries@allseasonsholidayapartments.co.uk

allseasonsholidayapartments.co.uk SPECIAL OFFERS · REAL-TIME BOOKING

Units 5
Sleeps 2–6

LOW SEASON PER WK
£185.00–£265.00

HIGH SEASON PER WK
£290.00–£625.00

Short breaks available (4 nights) except Jul & Aug. Free Wi-Fi internet access for your laptop.

open April to October
payment Cash, cheques
nearest pub less than 0.5 miles
nearest shop less than 0.5 miles

'Ideal location, very clean, comfortable and home from home' as frequently quoted by our guests. Our high-quality apartments are all non-smoking and are situated on level ground close to the beach, shops, coach, rail and bus stations. Apartments have lounge, one or two double bedrooms, separate kitchen and full-size bathroom. Sorry no pets.

SAT NAV *TQ4 6AX* ONLINE MAP

Unit General

Where are the maps?

Colour maps can be found at the front of the guide. They pinpoint the location of all accommodation found in the regional sections.

★★★
**HOTEL
SILVER AWARD**

B&B PER ROOM PER NIGHT
S £75.00–£80.00
D £110.00–£170.00
HB PER PERSON PER NIGHT
£80.00–£105.00

Oct-Apr: dinner in
The Bay restaurant
included in room
rate.

Hotel Penzance
Britons Hill, Penzance TR18 3AE t +44 (0) 1736 363117 e enquiries@hotelpenzance.com

hotelpenzance.com GUEST REVIEWS · SPECIAL OFFERS · REAL-TIME BOOKING

open All year
bedrooms 12 double, 9 twin, 3 single
bathrooms All en suite
payment Credit/debit cards, cash, cheques

Be assured of consistently high levels of comfort an
friendly service at this Cornwall Tourism Awards
Hotel of the Year 2006 and also Restaurant of the
Year 2006 and 2007 for The Bay. Traditional or
contemporary-style rooms with sea views across
Penzance Harbour and towards St Michael's Moun

SAT NAV TR18 3AE

Room   General   Leisure

★★★
HOTEL

B&B PER ROOM PER NIGHT
S £58.00–£85.00
D £116.00–£175.00
HB PER PERSON PER NIGHT
£80.00–£100.00

Special offers
throughout the year.
Please call our
reception for further
details.

Queens Hotel
The Promenade, Penzance TR18 4HG t +44 (0) 1736 362371 e enquiries@queens-hotel.com

queens-hotel.com GUEST REVIEWS · SPECIAL OFFERS

open All year
bedrooms 18 double, 24 twin, 19 single, 9 family
bathrooms All en suite
payment Credit/debit cards, cash, cheques

Elegant, award-winning, independently owned
Victorian hotel with majestic views of Mounts Bay
and St Michael's Mount. Lovingly restored to
preserve the elegance of the era with sweeping
staircase and Victorian ballroom. Relaxed ambience
award-winning restaurant serving local meat and
fish. Centrally located for exploring West Cornwall.
Free parking.

SAT NAV TR18 4HG **ONLINE MAP**

Room   General   Leisure

★★★
GUEST ACCOMMODATION

B&B PER ROOM PER NIGHT
S £30.00
D £60.00

EVENING MEAL PER PERSON
Min £16.50

Cornerways Guest House
5 Leskinnick Street, Penzance TR18 2HA t +44 (0) 1736 364645
e enquiries@cornerways-penzance.co.uk

penzance.co.uk/cornerways

Cornerways is an attractively decorated
townhouse, four minutes from car parks, bus and
railway stations. We offer freshly cooked
breakfast to order, and evening meal is optional.
Ideal as a base for touring Cornwall.

open All year except Christmas
bedrooms 1 double, 1 twin, 2 single
bathrooms All en suite
payment Credit/debit cards, cash, cheques

Room   General   Leisure

Need some ideas?
Big city buzz or peaceful panoramas? Take a fresh look at England and you
may be surprised at what's right on your doorstep. Explore the diversity online
at enjoyengland.com

PENZANCE, Cornwall Map ref 1A3 — GUEST ACCOMMODATION

★★★
FARMHOUSE

B&B PER ROOM PER NIGHT
S Min £28.00
D Min £56.00

EVENING MEAL PER PERSON
Min £12.00

Menwidden Farm

Ludgvan, Penzance TR20 8BN **t** +44 (0) 1736 740415 **e** coramenwidden@tiscali.co.uk

open March to October
bedrooms 4 double, 1 twin
bathrooms 3 en suite
payment Cash, cheques

Quiet farmhouse set in countryside with views towards St Michael's Mount. Centrally situated in West Cornwall. Land's End, St Ives, Lizard Peninsula and Penzance Heliport all within easy reach. Good home-cooking.

SAT NAV TR20 8BN

Room ♿ General P ✗ ❄ 🐕 Leisure ∪ ♪

PENZANCE, Cornwall Map ref 1A3 — GUEST ACCOMMODATION

★★★★★
**GUEST ACCOMMODATION
GOLD AWARD**

B&B PER ROOM PER NIGHT
D £95.00–£125.00

EVENING MEAL PER PERSON
£25.00–£33.00

Special midweek breaks in early and late season.

The Summer House

Cornwall Terrace, Penzance TR18 4HL **t** +44 (0) 1736 363744
e reception@summerhouse.cornwall.com

summerhouse-cornwall.com SPECIAL OFFERS

open March to October
bedrooms 4 double, 1 twin
bathrooms All en suite
payment Credit/debit cards, cash

Boutique B&B and two-rosette restaurant by the sea. Set in a beautiful listed building, this individually designed hotel has frequently been featured in glossy magazines in the UK and Europe. With just five bedrooms, there is a friendly, intimate atmosphere where guests unwind in the lovely public rooms and tropical walled garden.

SAT NAV TR18 4HL ONLINE MAP

Room 📺 ♿ 🍴 General P 🛜 🔌 ♿ ✗ 🍴 ❄ Leisure ∪ ♪ ▶ 🚲

PENZANCE, Cornwall Map ref 1A3 — SELF CATERING

★★
SELF CATERING

Units   **1**
Sleeps   **1–5**

LOW SEASON PER WK
£130.00–£200.00

HIGH SEASON PER WK
£400.00–£650.00

Old Court 36, Kenegie Manor, Gulval, Penzance

contact Mrs Margaret Lewis, 6 Carter Avenue, Codsall WV8 1HQ **t** +44 (0) 1902 845139
e margellen@googlemail.com

kenegie.com

Holiday house, rural setting, within beautiful grounds of country manor house. Close to St Ives. Accommodation to high standard. Sleeps five. Indoor pool, bar, sauna and tennis during season.

open All year
payment Cash, cheques
nearest pub 1 mile
nearest shop 1 mile

Unit 📺 📻 📺 🍴 🔌 🍴 ❄ General 🛋 🏠 ⬚ Leisure 🎣 ⚲

Touring made easy

Two to four-day circular routes with over 200 places to discover

- Lakes and Dales
- The West Country
- The Cotswolds and Shakespeare Country

Available in good bookshops and online at visitbritain.com for just £6.99 each.

★★★★
GUEST ACCOMMODATION

B&B PER ROOM PER NIGHT
S £30.00–£42.00
D £44.00–£56.00

Athenaeum Lodge

4 Athenaeum Street, The Hoe, Plymouth PL1 2RQ t +44 (0) 1752 665005 & +44 (0) 1752 670090
e us@athenaeumlodge.com

athenaeumlodge.com SPECIAL OFFERS · REAL-TIME BOOKING

open All year except Christmas and New Year
bedrooms 3 double, 2 twin, 1 single, 3 family
bathrooms 7 en suite
payment Credit/debit cards, cash, cheques

Elegant, Grade II Listed guesthouse, ideally situated on The Hoe. Centrally located for the Barbican, Theatre Royal, Plymouth Pavilions, ferry port and the National Marine Aquarium. The city centre and university are a few minutes' walk. Divers' and sailors' paradise. Excellent, central location for touring Devon and Cornwall. Wi-Fi Internet and free use of computer if required.

SAT NAV PL1 2RQ **ONLINE MAP**

Room 🛏 📺 ⛟ ⌕ General 👜5 P ⊕ ⅍ 🍽 Leisure 🏊

★★★★
GUEST HOUSE

B&B PER ROOM PER NIGHT
S £30.00–£40.00
D £45.00–£55.00

Brittany Guest House

28 Athenaeum Street, The Hoe, Plymouth PL1 2RQ t +44 (0) 1752 262247
e enquiries@brittanyguesthouse.com

brittanyguesthouse.co.uk

open All year except Christmas and New Year
bedrooms 4 double, 2 twin, 2 single, 2 family
bathrooms All en suite
payment Credit/debit cards, cash, cheques, euros

Non-smoking, all rooms en suite, some 5ft beds, crisp white linen. Private car park, close to shops, bars, pavilions, seafront. Credit and debit cards taken. Run by resident proprietors.

SAT NAV PL1 2RQ **ONLINE MAP**

Room 🛏 📺 ⛟ ⌕ General 👜3 P ⊕ ⅍ 🍽

★★★★
HOLIDAY &
TOURING PARK

🚐 (58) £7.60–£18.80
🚛 (58) £7.60–£18.80
58 touring pitches

Plymouth Sound Caravan Club Site

Bovisand Lane, Down Thomas, Plymouth PL9 0AE t +44 (0) 1752 862325

caravanclub.co.uk

open March to October
payment Credit/debit cards, cash, cheques

Within easy reach of the historic port. Superb views over the Sound. Close to the South West Coast Path and lovely beaches.

SAT NAV PL9 0AE

> Special member rates mean you can save your
> membership subscription in less than a week.
> Visit our website to find out more.

THE
CARAVAN
CLUB

General 🚗 👆 WP 🐾 Leisure ▶

POOLE, Dorset Map ref 2B3 — SELF CATERING

★★★ SELF CATERING

| Units | 1 |
| Sleeps | 3–5 |

LOW SEASON PER WK
£220.00–£350.00

HIGH SEASON PER WK
£450.00–£1,000.00

Poole Harbour Holiday Homes, Poole

contact Miss Brown, Poole Harbour Holidays, The Esplanade, Poole BH15 2BA **t** +44 (0) 7778 586710 & +44 (0) 1202 743614 **e** stay@pooleharbourholidays.com

pooleharbourholidays.com SPECIAL OFFERS

A selection of executive accommodation around Poole Harbour, furnished to the highest standard. Double/single beds, harbour view/private courtyard, free broadband, TV/DVD/CD player, linen/towels, washing machine, microwave, parking, garden.

open All year
payment Credit/debit cards, cash, cheques, euros
nearest pub less than 0.5 miles
nearest shop less than 0.5 miles

Unit 📺 🆂 ⏰ 📷 ▣ ⊟ ⏰ 🗓 ❄ ⚒ General 🐎 🏚 🅿 🆂 Leisure ∪ 🚲

POOLE, Dorset Map ref 2B3 — SELF CATERING

★★★ SELF CATERING

| Units | 1 |
| Sleeps | 2 |

LOW SEASON PER WK
Min £125.00

HIGH SEASON PER WK
Max £300.00

Sunnydale, Poole

contact Mr Ian Hull, 94 Blandford Road North, Beacon Hill, Poole BH16 6AD **t** +44 (0) 7880 501940 **e** ianhpoole@btinternet.com

Ground-floor one-bedroom flat with lounge, kitchen, bathroom, patio area. Off-road parking.

open All year
payment Cash, cheques, euros
nearest pub 0.5 miles
nearest shop 0.75 miles

Unit 📺 ▣ ⊟ 🗓 ❄ ⚒ General 🐎 🆂 🐕 Leisure ∪ 🎵

PORLOCK, Somerset Map ref 1D1 — GUEST ACCOMMODATION

★★★★ GUEST ACCOMMODATION

B&B PER ROOM PER NIGHT
S £55.00
D £80.00

EVENING MEAL PER PERSON
£28.00

Glen Lodge

Hawkcombe, Minehead TA24 8LN **t** +44 (0) 1643 863371 **e** glenlodge@gmail.com

glenlodge.net

Historic Victorian house with welcoming rooms, scrumptious food and views of the sea, woods and Exmoor. Ideal for exploring, relaxing, activities and more.

open All year except Christmas and New Year
bedrooms 4 double, 1 twin
bathrooms 1 en suite, 2 private
payment Cash, cheques

Room 📺 🛎 🍵 General 🐎8 🅿 🛜 🔌 ✗ 🍴◉❄ Leisure ∪ 🎵 🏇 🚲

PORTHTOWAN, Cornwall Map ref 1B3 — SELF CATERING

★★★★★ SELF CATERING

| Units | 5 |
| Sleeps | 1–6 |

LOW SEASON PER WK
£300.00–£540.00

HIGH SEASON PER WK
£620.00–£1,490.00

Rosehill Lodges, Porthtowan

contact Mr John Barrow, Rosehill Lodges, Porthtowan TR4 8AR **t** +44 (0) 1209 891920 **e** reception@rosehilllodges.com

rosehilllodges.com GUEST REVIEWS · SPECIAL OFFERS · REAL-TIME BOOKING

open All year
payment Credit/debit cards, cash, cheques
nearest pub 0.5 miles
nearest shop 0.5 miles

Luxurious lodges, set within a wooded valley in a Cornish seaside village just five minutes' walk to Porthtowan's Blue Flag sandy beach, pubs and restaurants. Relax and unwind with king-size beds, log burners and your own personal hot tub. Grass roofs and glass-covered decking for those stargazing nights complete the package.

ONLINE MAP

Unit 📺 🆂 ⏰ 📷 ▣ ⊟ 🗓 ❄ ⚒ 🌐 General 🐎 🏚 🅿 🆂
Leisure ∪ 🎵 🏇 🚲

PORTLAND, Dorset Map ref 2B3 — GUEST ACCOMMODATION

★★
GUEST ACCOMMODATION

B&B PER ROOM PER NIGHT
S £25.00–£45.00
D £50.00–£70.00

Alessandria House
71 Wakeham Easton, Portland DT5 1HW t +44 (0) 1305 822270

open All year
bedrooms 6 double, 2 twin, 3 single, 4 family
bathrooms 11 en suite, 1 private
payment Credit/debit cards, cash, cheques, euros

Friendly, good old-fashioned personal service and good value. Under the same management for 19 years, highly commended by our guests. With 15 bedrooms, two on the ground floor, and four spacious en suite family rooms. Some rooms with sea view. Quiet, desirable location. Vegetarians catered for. Free parking.

SAT NAV DT5 1HW

Room General Leisure

PORTLOE, Cornwall Map ref 1B3 — SELF CATERING

★★★★
SELF CATERING

Units   1
Sleeps   1–5

LOW SEASON PER WK
£300.00–£450.00

HIGH SEASON PER WK
£450.00–£600.00

Trehaven View, Truro
contact Mr & Mrs Mlynski, Compass North, Veryan, Truro TR2 5QF t +44 (0) 1872 501824
e julie.mlynski@virgin.net

cottageguide.co.uk/trehaven

Luxury apartment with balcony and sea views in a picturesque fishing village, Portloe, on the Roseland Peninsula.

open All year
payment Cash, cheques
nearest pub less than 0.5 miles
nearest shop 1.5 miles

Unit General

PORTREATH, Cornwall Map ref 1B3 — HOTEL

★★
COUNTRY HOUSE HOTEL
SILVER AWARD

B&B PER ROOM PER NIGHT
S £53.00
D £83.00–£89.00
HB PER PERSON PER NIGHT
£63.00–£68.00

Aviary Court Hotel
Marys Well, Redruth TR16 4QZ t +44 (0) 1209 842256 e info@aviarycourthotel.co.uk

aviarycourthotel.co.uk

open All year
bedrooms 4 double, 1 twin, 1 family
bathrooms All en suite
payment Credit/debit cards, cash, cheques

Charming country house in two acres of secluded, well-kept gardens with tennis court. Family run, personal service, good food. Superior en suite bedrooms with TV, telephone, tea/coffee, fresh fruit. Ideal touring location (coast five minutes). St Ives, Tate, Heligan and Eden Project all within easy reach. Half-board prices are based on two people sharing.

SAT NAV TR16 4QZ **ONLINE MAP**

Room General 3 Leisure

Country Code always follow the Country Code

- Be safe – plan ahead and follow any signs
- Leave gates and property as you find them
- Protect plants and animals, and take your litter home
- Keep dogs under close control
- Consider other people

PORTREATH, Cornwall Map ref 1B3 — SELF CATERING

★★★–★★★★★
SELF CATERING

Units **7**
Sleeps **2–6**

LOW SEASON PER WK
£225.00–£450.00

HIGH SEASON PER WK
£350.00–£780.00

Short breaks available from Nov to Mar.

Trengove Farm Cottages, Redruth
contact Mrs Richards, Trengove Farm, Cot Road, Illogan, Redruth TR16 4PU **t** +44 (0) 1209 843008
e richards@farming.co.uk

trengovefarm.co.uk

open All year
payment Credit/debit cards, cash, cheques, euros
nearest pub 1 mile
nearest shop 1 mile

Traditional, well-equipped cottages and farmhouse on a 140-acre arable farm. Close to beautiful beaches, cliffs and countryside park, yet within easy reach of the main towns. Centrally heated, free wireless broadband available. A superb location for walking, swimming, touring or just relaxing.

SAT NAV *TR16 4PU* **ONLINE MAP**

Unit 📺 General Leisure

PRAA SANDS, Cornwall Map ref 1B3 — SELF CATERING

★★★
SELF CATERING

Units **6**
Sleeps **2–8**

LOW SEASON PER WK
£295.00–£500.00

HIGH SEASON PER WK
£500.00–£1,300.00

Discounts available for smaller parties and for late availability throughout the year.

Sea Meads Holiday Homes, Penzance
contact Ms Pierpoint, Best Leisure, Old House Farm, Fulmer Road, Fulmer, Slough SL3 6HU
t +44 (0) 1753 664336 **e** enquiries@bestleisure.co.uk

bestleisure.co.uk SPECIAL OFFERS · REAL-TIME BOOKING

open All year
payment Cash, cheques
nearest pub 0.5 miles
nearest shop 0.5 miles

Well-equipped detached houses, each with private garden, situated in superb subtropical position on a private estate. Spacious lounge with large patio windows. Balcony to the first floor from which to enjoy the view of the glorious mile-long Praa Sands beach, only five minutes' walk away. All houses have Wi-Fi broadband access.

SAT NAV *TR20 9TA* **ONLINE MAP**

Unit 📺 General Leisure

REDRUTH, Cornwall Map ref 1B3 — GUEST ACCOMMODATION

★★★★
GUEST HOUSE

B&B PER ROOM PER NIGHT
S Min £38.00
D Min £56.00

EVENING MEAL PER PERSON
£12.50–£15.00

Goonearl Cottage
Wheal Rose, Scorrier, Redruth TR16 5DF **t** +44 (0) 1209 891571 **e** goonearl@onetel.com

goonearlcottage.com REAL-TIME BOOKING

open All year
bedrooms 4 double, 1 twin, 1 family, 1 suite
bathrooms 5 en suite, 2 private
payment Credit/debit cards, cash, cheques, euros

Family-run guesthouse; beaches close by; easy access to the whole of Cornwall; superb English breakfast.

SAT NAV *TR16 5DF* **ONLINE MAP**

Room General Leisure

REDRUTH, Cornwall Map ref 1B3 **SELF CATERING**

★★★
SELF CATERING

Units **1**
Sleeps **2–6**

LOW SEASON PER WK
£230.00–£300.00

HIGH SEASON PER WK
£330.00–£535.00

The Barn at Little Trefula, St Day, Redruth

contact Mr & Mrs Bill & Ann Higgins, The Barn at Little Trefula, Little Trefula Farm, Trefula, Redruth TR16 5ET t +44 (0) 1209 820572 & +44 (0) 7789 044602 e barn@trefula.com

trefula.com SPECIAL OFFERS · REAL-TIME BOOKING

The Barn at Little Trefula, in Cornwall's historic mining country yet surrounded by fields, is a recent architect-designed conversion offering panoramic views and the perfect base for a peaceful, comfortable family holiday.

open All year
payment Credit/debit cards, cash, cheques, euros
nearest pub less than 0.5 miles
nearest shop 0.5 miles

Unit 📺 🖥 💻 🎛 🔲 💡 ✳ ⛺ General 🛋 🏛 🔥 P 🅾 Ⓢ 🐾 Leisure ∪ 🎣 🏇 🚴

ROSUDGEON, Cornwall Map ref 1B3 **CAMPING, CARAVAN & HOLIDAY PARK**

★★★★
HOLIDAY, TOURING & CAMPING PARK
ROSE AWARD

🚐 (25) £14.50–£22.00
🚐 (25) £14.50–£22.00
⛺ (50) £10.00–£22.00
🏠 (9) £220.00–£515.00
50 touring pitches

No single-sex groups or large parties.

Kenneggy Cove Holiday Park

Higher Kenneggy, Rosudgeon, Penzance TR20 9AU t +44 (0) 1736 763453 e enquiries@kenneggycove.co.uk

kenneggycove.co.uk

open 17 May to 4 October
payment Cash, cheques, euros

Flat, lawned pitches in a beautiful garden setting with panoramic sea views. Twelve minutes' walk to South West Coast Path and secluded, sandy beach. Home-made breakfasts available. Please note: this is a quiet site, operating a policy of no noise between 2200 and 0800. German and French spoken.

SAT NAV TR20 9AU

General 🚲 🐕 👐 🎁 📷 🕹 🖥 🐾 ☀ Leisure ⛰ ∪ 🎣 🏇 🚴

RUAN HIGH LANES, Cornwall Map ref 1B3 **GUEST ACCOMMODATION**

★★★
FARMHOUSE

B&B PER ROOM PER NIGHT
S £28.00–£40.00
D £56.00–£60.00

Discounts for stays of 4 or more nights for children and for family rooms.

Trenona Farm Holidays

Ruan High Lanes, Truro TR2 5JS t +44 (0) 1872 501339 e info@trenonafarmholidays.co.uk

trenonafarmholidays.co.uk REAL-TIME BOOKING

open March to November
bedrooms 1 double, 3 family
bathrooms 3 en suite, 1 private
payment Credit/debit cards, cash, cheques

Enjoy a warm welcome in our Victorian farmhouse on a working farm on the beautiful Roseland Peninsula. Our guest bedrooms have en suite or private bathrooms, and we welcome children and pets. Public footpaths lead to Veryan and the south coast (three miles).

SAT NAV TR2 5JS **ONLINE MAP**

Room 📺 🛁 🎛 General 🛋 🏛 🔥 P 🌐 🍽 ✳ 🐾 Leisure ∪

Where can I get help and advice?

Tourist Information Centres offer friendly help with accommodation and holiday ideas as well as suggestions of places to visit and things to do. You'll find contact details at the beginning of each regional section.

RUDFORD, Gloucestershire Map ref 2B1
GUEST ACCOMMODATION

The Dark Barn Lodge

★★★★
GUEST ACCOMMODATION

Barbers Bridge, Rudford, Gloucester GL2 8DX t +44 (0) 1452 790412 e info@barbersbridge.co.uk

barbersbridge.co.uk GUEST REVIEWS · SPECIAL OFFERS · REAL-TIME BOOKING

B&B PER ROOM PER NIGHT
S Min £42.00
D Min £60.00

EVENING MEAL PER PERSON
£12.50–£15.00

open All year
bedrooms 15 double, 2 family, 1 suite
bathrooms All en suite
payment Credit/debit cards, cash, cheques

Family-run establishment, new accommodation, in quiet, rural setting. Ample floodlit parking. Internet access, complimentary use of gym and swimming pool during stay.

SAT NAV GL2 8DX **ONLINE MAP**

Room 🛁 📺 ♿ 🍽 General 🐕 🍳 ♨ P 🌐 🎮 🍷 ✗ 🎱 ❄ 🐴 Leisure 🎣 ∪ ⚓ ►

ST AUSTELL, Cornwall Map ref 1B3
HOTEL

Cliff Head Hotel

★★★
HOTEL

Sea Road, Carlyon Bay, St Austell PL25 3RB t +44 (0) 1726 812345 e info@cliffheadhotel.com

cliffheadhotel.com

B&B PER ROOM PER NIGHT
S £60.00–£70.00
D £120.00–£190.00
HB PER PERSON PER NIGHT
£80.00–£115.00

Please check website or telephone hotel for seasonal specials.

open All year
bedrooms 19 double, 17 twin, 14 single, 8 family
bathrooms All en suite
payment Credit/debit cards, cash, cheques

South-facing hotel, close to the beach with fine sea views and cliff walks, and standing in its own grounds. Situated in the centre of the Cornish Riviera, it is ideally positioned for exploring Cornwall and visiting the Eden Project.

SAT NAV PL25 3RB

Room 🛁 🚗 📞 📺 ♿ 🍽 General 🐕 🍳 ♨ P 🌐 🍷 🎱 ◐ ☰ ♨ ❄ Leisure 🎣 ⚽ ►

ST IVES, Cornwall Map ref 1B3
SELF CATERING

Chylowen & Bluewater, St Ives

★★★★
SELF CATERING

contact Miss Linda Higgins, 4 Vine Close, Bournemouth BH7 7JX t +44 (0) 1202 258743
e lindahiggins@stivesdownalong.com

stivesdownalong.com

Units   2
Sleeps   6

LOW SEASON PER WK
£325.00–£975.00

HIGH SEASON PER WK
£975.00–£1,350.00

Our new property Bluewater is a three-bedroom fisherman's cottage with fantastic views over the harbour area of St Ives.

open All year
payment Cash, cheques

Unit 📺 🆂🅲 📻 🖥 🍽 🗄 🎛 🍳 🔌 📂 General 🐕 🍳 ♨

ST IVES, Cornwall Map ref 1B3
SELF CATERING

Happy Days, St Ives

★★★★★
SELF CATERING

contact Miss Amanda Dumbleton
e info@happydaysstives.co.uk

happydaysstives.co.uk GUEST REVIEWS

Units   1
Sleeps   1–6

LOW SEASON PER WK
Min £450.00

HIGH SEASON PER WK
Max £1,150.00

Happy Days is a luxury, three-bedroom, split-level penthouse apartment that sleeps up to six and overlooks the beautiful Porthminster beach in picturesque St Ives, Cornwall.

open All year
payment Cheques
nearest pub less than 0.5 miles
nearest shop less than 0.5 miles

Unit 📺 🆂🅲 📻 🎮 🖥 🍽 🗄 🎛 🍳 🔌 📂 General 🐕4 P 🅾 🆂 Leisure ∪ ⚓ ►

ST JUST IN ROSELAND, Cornwall Map ref 1B3 **GUEST ACCOMMODATION**

★★★★
BED & BREAKFAST

B&B PER ROOM PER NIGHT
D £80.00–£85.00

Roundhouse Barns

Truro TR2 5JJ t +44 (0) 1872 580038 e info@roundhousebarnholidays.co.uk

roundhousebarnholidays.co.uk

open All year except Christmas and New Year
bedrooms 2 double
bathrooms All en suite
payment Credit/debit cards, cash, cheques

Beautifully converted 17thC barn in peaceful surroundings on the Roseland Peninsula. Instant access to walks by Fal river. St Just in Roseland church with its subtropical gardens and the picturesque harbour of St Mawes are both nearby. Delightful rooms with luxury bedding. Locally sourced breakfasts. All guests welcomed with complimentary home-made Cornish cream tea.

SAT NAV TR2 5JJ

Room 🛏 📺 🕯 🍵 General 🐎16 P 🔥 ⛺ ☀ Leisure ∪ ♪ ► 🚴

ST NEOT, Cornwall Map ref 1C2 **SELF CATERING**

★★★★
SELF CATERING

Units **3**
Sleeps **2–4**

LOW SEASON PER WK
£160.00–£360.00

HIGH SEASON PER WK
£320.00–£610.00

Up to 20% discount on short breaks, excl school holidays.

Badgers Holiday Cottages, St Neot, Liskeard

contact Phil & Allison Harris, Badgers Holiday Cottages, Badgers Sett, West Draynes, St Neot, Liskeard PL14 6RY t +44 (0) 1579 320741 & +44 (0) 7855 807183 e phil.harris@btinternet.com

badgersholidaycottages.co.uk SPECIAL OFFERS

open All year
payment Cash, cheques
nearest pub 2 miles
nearest shop 2 miles

Relax in one of our three recently converted, beautiful cottages, in this tranquil and stunning area of Cornwall. All cottages have character, are comfortable, well equipped and centrally heated with own south-facing garden, set within two acres. Ideally situated for touring the South West, walking, visiting gardens and coastlines.

SAT NAV PL14 6RY

Unit 📺 📀 📼 🖥 🍳 🔌 📶 ☀ ♨ 🍳 General 🐎 🛏 🔥 P 🅿 S Leisure ∪ ♪ 🚴

SALCOMBE, Devon Map ref 1C3 **HOTEL**

★★★
HOTEL
GOLD AWARD

HB PER PERSON PER NIGHT
£65.00–£160.00

Winter, Spring and Autumn Bargain Breaks.

Tides Reach Hotel

Cliff Road, Salcombe TQ8 8LJ t +44 (0) 1548 843466 e enquire@tidesreach.com

tidesreach.com SPECIAL OFFERS · REAL-TIME BOOKING

bedrooms 14 double, 14 twin, 2 single, 3 family, 2 suites
bathrooms All en suite
payment Credit/debit cards, cash, cheques

Elegant and well-appointed hotel in an unrivalled position of outstanding natural beauty on edge of a secluded tree-fringed sandy cove. Well-equipped indoor pool and leisure complex with tropical atmosphere. Award-winning cuisine and friendly, caring staff. All this combines to produce an ideal location for a short break or holiday. Closed December to January.

SAT NAV TQ8 8LJ **ONLINE MAP**

Room ☎ 📺 📺 🕯 🍵 🔥 General 🐎8 P ⓦ ♟ ⛺ ● ▣ ☀ 🐕
Leisure 🎣 ♨ ☀ ⊗ ∪ ♪ ►

SALCOMBE, Devon Map ref 1C3

★★★
HOLIDAY, TOURING
& CAMPING PARK

🚐 (20) £10.00–£19.00
🚎 (20) £10.00–£19.00
⛺ (50) £8.00–£19.00
🚕 (10) £110.00–£530.00
70 touring pitches

*Special rates, low
season only for
couples over 50 –
from £60 per week
(incl electric).*

Bolberry House Farm Caravan & Camping Park

Bolberry, Malborough TQ7 3DY t +44 (0) 1548 561251 e bolberry.house@virgin.net

bolberryparks.co.uk

open April to October
payment Cash, cheques

Beautiful coastal area, our friendly family-run park is
situated between the sailing paradise of Salcombe
and the old fishing village of Hope Cove. It is
peaceful and mostly level with good facilities.
Children's play area. Good access to coastal
footpaths. Sandy beaches nearby. Small shop (high
season only).

SAT NAV *TQ7 3DY*

General 🖥 🚗 🍴 🚻 📶 📺 🐕 ☀ Leisure 🎣

SALISBURY, Wiltshire Map ref 2B3

★★★★
BED & BREAKFAST

B&B PER ROOM PER NIGHT
S £40.00–£55.00
D £55.00–£80.00

The Old Rectory Bed & Breakfast

75 Belle Vue Road, Salisbury SP1 3YE t +44 (0) 1722 502702 e stay@theoldrectory-bb.co.uk

theoldrectory-bb.co.uk

Victorian rectory in quiet street, a short walk from
the heart of Salisbury and convenient for all
attractions. Warm, welcoming atmosphere and
well-appointed rooms. A relaxing bolthole. Wi-Fi
internet.

open All year except Christmas and New Year
bedrooms 1 double, 1 twin, 1 single
bathrooms 2 en suite, 1 private
payment Cash, cheques

Room 📺 🚿 🍵 General 🛏10 P 📶 ♨ 🍽 ❄ Leisure 🚴

SALISBURY, Wiltshire Map ref 2B3

★★★★
SELF CATERING

Units   **1**
Sleeps   **5**

LOW SEASON PER WK
£320.00–£385.00

HIGH SEASON PER WK
£425.00–£530.00

*Special rates for last
minute bookings,
short breaks and
extended stays in
off-peak periods.
See website or
telephone for
details.*

Rustic Cottage, Salisbury

contact Mrs Cheryl Beeney, 75 Church Rd, Laverstock SP1 1QS t +44 (0) 1722 337870
e cheribeen@aol.com

rustic-cottage-salisbury.co.uk GUEST REVIEWS · SPECIAL OFFERS · REAL-TIME BOOKING

open All year
payment Credit/debit cards, cash, cheques, euros
nearest pub less than 0.5 miles
nearest shop less than 0.5 miles

Cosy, newly renovated character cottage (1810)
close to historic centre of the cathedral city of
Salisbury and tourist attractions of Stonehenge, the
New Forest and south coast. Delightful country
walks start from doorstep. Furnished and equipped
throughout to high standard. Broadband connection,
terraced garden, pond, large decking area with
barbecue.

ONLINE MAP

Unit 📺 🎮 💿 📻 🎙 🍵 🔥 🍽 ❄ 🔨 🧺 General 🛏5 P 🅂 Leisure ∪ 🏊 🏹 🚴

It's all quality-assessed accommodation

Our commitment to quality involves wide-ranging accommodation assessment.
Ratings and awards were correct at the time of going to press but may change
following a new assessment. Please check at time of booking.

SALISBURY, Wiltshire Map ref 2B3
SELF CATERING

★★★★
SELF CATERING

Units **3**
Sleeps **1–2**

LOW SEASON PER WK
Max £395.00

HIGH SEASON PER WK
Max £455.00

Salisbury Apartments, Salisbury

contact Mrs Mary Webb, 50 Upper Street, West Harnham, Salisbury SP2 8LY t +44 (0) 1722 340892
& +44 (0) 7759 474115 e enquiries@salisbury-apartments.co.uk

salisbury-apartments.co.uk GUEST REVIEWS · SPECIAL OFFERS · REAL-TIME BOOKING

Off street parking: yes. Broadband connection:
yes. Welcome pack: yes. Convenient for city: yes.
Best for business: yes. Lovely for leisure: yes.
Salisbury Apartments say YES to all your needs.

open All year
payment Credit/debit cards, cash, cheques
nearest pub less than 0.5 miles
nearest shop less than 0.5 miles

Unit 📺 [SC] [symbols] General ⬧ P [S] Leisure ♪ ▶ ☙

SAMPFORD BRETT, Somerset Map ref 1D1
SELF CATERING

★★★
SELF CATERING

Units **2**
Sleeps **4**

LOW SEASON PER WK
£220.00

HIGH SEASON PER WK
£350.00–£450.00

*Short breaks and
weekend stays from
£120 (excl Jul, Aug).*

Old Rectory Coach House, Sampford Brett

contact Jan Swan, The Old Rectory, Sampford Brett, Taunton TA4 4LA t +44 (0) 1984 633787
e enquiries@oldrectorycoachhouse.co.uk

oldrectorycoachhouse.co.uk SPECIAL OFFERS · REAL-TIME BOOKING

open All year
payment Cash, cheques, euros
nearest pub 1 mile
nearest shop 1 mile

Cosy and comfortable accommodation within a
beautifully restored coach house. Farm View has one
double bedroom and a twin room with bunks; The
Elms has two double bedrooms. Ideally situated in
the heart of a tranquil and pretty village, nestling
between Exmoor, the Quantocks and the Somerset
coast.

SAT NAV TA4 4LA **ONLINE MAP**

Unit 📺 [symbols] General ⬧ 🏠 P ◯ [S] 🐾 Leisure ⌛ ∪ ♪ ▶ ☙

SEATON, Devon Map ref 1D2
GUEST ACCOMMODATION

★★★★
GUEST HOUSE

B&B PER ROOM PER NIGHT
S **£45.00–£55.00**
D **£60.00–£75.00**

Beaumont

Castle Hill, Seaton EX12 2QW t +44 (0) 1297 20832 e jane@lymebay.demon.co.uk

smoothhound.co.uk/hotels/beaumon1.html

open All year except Christmas and New Year
bedrooms 2 double, 2 twin, 1 family
bathrooms All en suite
payment Cash, cheques

Select, Victorian, seafront, family guesthouse on
World Heritage Coast. Two minutes' walk from
town. Excellent walks, country parks, attractions and
sporting facilities. Unrivalled views over Lyme Bay.
Limited parking.

SAT NAV EX12 2QW

Room 🛏 📺 🕯 🍵 General ⬧ P 🕸 🐾 🐾 Leisure ♪ ▶

Remember to check when booking

Please remember that all information in this guide has been supplied by the
proprietors well in advance of publication. Since changes do sometimes occur it's a
good idea to check details at the time of booking.

SEATON, Devon Map ref 1D2 — SELF CATERING

★★★
SELF CATERING

Units **1**
Sleeps **1–4**

LOW SEASON PER WK
£225.00–£325.00

HIGH SEASON PER WK
£385.00–£525.00

10% reduction for 2 persons only, throughout booking period.

West Ridge Bungalow, Seaton

contact Mrs Hildegard Fox, West Ridge Bungalow, Harepath Hill, Seaton EX12 2TA
t +44 (0) 1297 22398 **e** fox@foxwestridge.co.uk

cottageguide.co.uk/westridge

open March to October
payment Cash, cheques
nearest pub 1 mile
nearest shop 0.5 miles

Comfortably furnished bungalow on elevated ground in 1.5 acres of gardens. Beautiful, panoramic views of Axe Estuary and sea. Close by are Beer and Branscombe. Lyme Regis seven miles, Sidmouth ten miles. Excellent centre for touring, walking, sailing, fishing, golf. Full gas central heating, double glazing throughout.

SAT NAV *EX12 2TA*

Unit 📺 🆂🅲 🖥 📀 🍴 🧺 ❄ General 🐾 🏛 ♿ P 🐕 Leisure ⛳

SHERBORNE, Dorset Map ref 2B3 — HOTEL

★★★
HOTEL

B&B PER ROOM PER NIGHT
S £90.00
D £109.00–£150.00
HB PER PERSON PER NIGHT
£81.50–£112.00

The Grange at Oborne

Oborne, Sherborne DT9 4LA **t** +44 (0) 1935 813463 **e** reception@thegrange.co.uk

thegrangeatoborne.co.uk

Situated just one mile from Sherborne, The Grange is a splendid mellow-stone country-house hotel in a peaceful location.

open All year
bedrooms 15 double, 3 twin
bathrooms All en suite
payment Credit/debit cards, cash, cheques

Room ♿ 🖂 ☎ 📺 ✎ 🧺 General 🐾 🏛 ♿ P 📶 ♟ 🍴 ❄ Leisure ⛳

SIDMOUTH, Devon Map ref 1D2 — HOTEL

★★★★
HOTEL
GOLD AWARD

B&B PER ROOM PER NIGHT
S £99.00–£155.00
D £198.00–£288.00
HB PER PERSON PER NIGHT
£114.00–£184.00

Luxury 3-day breaks and carefree weekend breaks at certain times of year. Christmas and New Year programme also available.

Hotel Riviera

The Esplanade, Sidmouth EX10 8AY **t** +44 (0) 1395 515201 **e** enquiries@hotelriviera.co.uk

hotelriviera.co.uk

open All year
bedrooms 11 double, 7 twin, 6 single, 2 suites
bathrooms All en suite
payment Credit/debit cards, cash, cheques

The hotel has a long tradition of hospitality and is perfect for unforgettable holidays, long weekends, unwinding breaks and all the spirit of the glorious festive season...you will be treated to the kind of friendly, personal attention that can only be found in a private hotel of this quality.

SAT NAV *EX10 8AY*

Room ☎ 📺 ✎ 🧺 General 🐾 🏛 ♿ P 🍴 ♟ 🍷 ❄ 🐕 Leisure ⟳ ♨ ⛳ 🚴

SIMONSBATH, Somerset Map ref 1C1 — SELF CATERING

★★★★
SELF CATERING

Units **5**
Sleeps **1–6**

LOW SEASON PER WK
£275.00–£380.00

HIGH SEASON PER WK
£375.00–£780.00

Wintershead Farm, Simonsbath, Exmoor

contact Mrs Jane Styles, Wintershead Farm, Simonsbath, Exmoor TA24 7LF **t** +44 (0) 1643 831222
e wintershead@yahoo.co.uk

wintershead.co.uk SPECIAL OFFERS

Five converted stone cottages, perfect for exploring the moor. Where a lot of the traffic has four legs, and the only street lighting is the stars above. Colour brochure.

open 14 March to 21 November
payment Cash, cheques
nearest pub 3 miles
nearest shop 7 miles

Unit 📺 🆂🅲 📀 🖥 🍴 🧺 ❄ General 🐾 🏛 ♿ P 🐕 Leisure 🎣 ⟳ ♨

SLIMBRIDGE, Gloucestershire Map ref 2B1 — SELF CATERING

★★★★★
SELF CATERING

Units **1**
Sleeps **13**

LOW SEASON PER WK
£2,075.00–£2,825.00

HIGH SEASON PER WK
£3,075.00–£3,625.00

Rectory Park, Gloucester

contact Elaine Molyneux, Dunster Living, Halswell House, Goathurst TA5 2DH
t +44 (0) 845 208 1066 **e** info@dunsterliving.co.uk

rectorypark.co.uk SPECIAL OFFERS · REAL-TIME BOOKING

Elegant Regency rectory with excellent facilities. Six double bedrooms, one single. Extensive grounds, hot tub, croquet lawn, swings and barbecue. Home cinema, snooker table and table tennis.

open All year
payment Credit/debit cards, cash, cheques
nearest pub 1 mile
nearest shop 3 miles

Unit 📺 SC ▦▦ ▦ ▦▦▦▦▦ ✿ ♨ ✎ General ⛺ ▦▦P ◻ S ⊢
Leisure ● ∪ ♪ ▸ ◉

SOMERTON, Somerset Map ref 2A3 — GUEST ACCOMMODATION

★★★
GUEST ACCOMMODATION

B&B PER ROOM PER NIGHT
S £40.00–£45.00
D £50.00–£60.00

EVENING MEAL PER PERSON
£9.50–£18.00

The White Hart Inn

Market Place, Somerton TA11 7LX **t** +44 (0) 1458 272314 **e** white.hart@virgin.net

whitehartsomerton.co.uk

Historic town-centre coaching inn offering fine dining and newly appointed en suite accommodation. Courtyard, garden and real fires.

open All year
bedrooms 3 double, 1 twin
bathrooms All en suite
payment Credit/debit cards, cash, cheques

Room 📺 ♨ ⊿ General ⛺ ▦▦ ⊕ ⊻ ✕ ▦✿⊢ Leisure ♪

STOGUMBER, Somerset Map ref 1D1 — GUEST ACCOMMODATION

★★★★
GUEST HOUSE

B&B PER ROOM PER NIGHT
S £30.00–£44.00
D £60.00–£68.00

EVENING MEAL PER PERSON
£9.00–£30.00

Home-cooked meals in our licensed restaurant. Special rates for full-week and midweek breaks. Residential upholstery courses.

Wick House

2 Brook Street, Stogumber, Taunton TA4 3SZ **t** +44 (0) 1984 656422 **e** sheila@wickhouse.co.uk

wickhouse.co.uk

open All year
bedrooms 2 double, 3 twin
bathrooms All en suite
payment Credit/debit cards, cash, cheques

Listed family home in the picturesque village of Stogumber, situated in a designated Area of Outstanding Natural Beauty. The village nestles between the Quantock and Brendon Hills of Exmoor National Park. Offering a friendly, informal atmosphere and high standard of accommodation – perfect for escaping the stresses of the modern world.

SAT NAV TA4 3SZ

Room ♿ 📺 ♨ ⊿ General ⛺ ▦▦P ⊕ ⊻ ✕ ▦✿ Leisure ∪ ♪ ▸

Where is my pet welcome?

Some proprietors welcome well-behaved pets. Look for the ⊢ symbol in the accommodation listings.

You can also buy a copy of our popular guide – Pets Come Too! – available from good bookshops and online at visitbritaindirect.com.

★★★★★
SELF CATERING

Broad Oak Cottages, Stow-on-the-Wold, Cheltenham

contact Mrs Wilson, Broad Oak Cottages, The Counting House, Oddington Road, Stow on the Wold, Cheltenham GL54 1AL t +44 (0) 1451 830794 e mary@broadoakcottages.co.uk

broadoakcottages.co.uk

Units **1**
Sleeps **1–4**

LOW SEASON PER WK
Min **£325.00**

HIGH SEASON PER WK
Min **£595.00**

Short breaks available (except in high season).

open All year
payment Cash, cheques, euros
nearest pub less than 0.5 miles
nearest shop less than 0.5 miles

May Cottage is a delightful two-bedroomed cottage all on one level and within a few minutes' walk of Stow Square. It has recently been completely renovated and extended to include a master suite with luxury bathroom, a conservatory and enlarged sitting room opening onto a patio. Parking and private garden.

SAT NAV GL54 1AL

Unit TV SC ⊞ ⟲ DVD ▦ ⬚ 🗗 🖳 🖩 🗳 🗓 ❆ ⌘ ∅ General ➴ ⛺ ⚲ P ⬚ S 🐾
Leisure ✦ ▸ ⚲

★★★★
BED & BREAKFAST

1 Woodchester Lodge

Southfield Road, North Woodchester, Stroud GL5 5PA t +44 (0) 1453 872586
e anne@woodchesterlodge.co.uk

woodchesterlodge.co.uk

B&B PER ROOM PER NIGHT
S £35.00–£40.00
D £55.00–£65.00

EVENING MEAL PER PERSON
£12.50

Weekly rates on request.

open All year except Christmas and New Year
bedrooms 1 double, 1 twin
bathrooms 1 en suite, 1 private
payment Credit/debit cards, cash, cheques

Historic, Victorian timber merchant's property; peaceful village setting near Cotswold Way. Attractive gardens, parking, spacious and comfortable rooms, separate TV lounge/dining room. Meals cooked by qualified chef using our own produce and eggs. Outdoor activities, scenic villages, local attractions, links to main cities: Bristol, Bath, Gloucester, Cheltenham and London.

SAT NAV GL5 5PA

Room TV ♦ 🖳 General ➴ P 🔥 ✕ 🍴 🖳 ❆ Leisure ∪ ▸

★★★★
BED & BREAKFAST
SILVER AWARD

Pretoria Villa

Wells Road, Eastcombe, Stroud GL6 7EE t +44 (0) 1452 770435 e pretoriavilla@btinternet.com

bedandbreakfast-cotswold.co.uk

B&B PER ROOM PER NIGHT
S Min £35.00
D £56.00–£70.00

Discounted rates for 4 or more nights.

open All year except Christmas
bedrooms 1 double, 2 twin
bathrooms All en suite
payment Cash, cheques

Enjoy luxurious bed and breakfast in a relaxed family country house, set in peaceful secluded gardens. Spacious bedrooms with many home comforts. Guest lounge with TV. Superb breakfast served at your leisure. An excellent base from which to explore the Cotswolds. Personal service and your comfort guaranteed.

SAT NAV GL6 7EE

Room ♦ 🖳 General ➴ P 🍴 ❆ Leisure ▸

SWANAGE, Dorset Map ref 2B3 — GUEST ACCOMMODATION

★★★★
GUEST ACCOMMODATION

B&B PER ROOM PER NIGHT
S £30.00–£50.00
D £60.00–£100.00

The Castleton

1 Highcliffe Road, Swanage BH19 1LW t +44 (0) 1929 423972 e stay@thecastleton.co.uk

thecastleton.co.uk GUEST REVIEWS

open All year except Christmas
bedrooms 5 double, 1 twin, 1 single, 2 family
bathrooms All en suite
payment Credit/debit cards, cash, cheques

Welcome to The Castleton, truly a 'once discovered, never forgotten' place to stay. A delightful escape from everyday life, where the welcoming nature and friendliness of your hosts add to your pleasure. The Castleton is ideally situated 100 metres from Swanage's beautiful sandy beach and a short level stroll along the seafront to the town centre with its many shops, restaurants and bars.

SAT NAV BH19 1LW **ONLINE MAP**

Room 🛗 📺 🌡 🍵   General 🛏4 P 🔌 🎱❄   Leisure 🎣🏇🚲

SWANAGE, Dorset Map ref 2B3 — CAMPING, CARAVAN & HOLIDAY PARK

★★★★
HOLIDAY, TOURING
& CAMPING PARK

🚐 £17.50–£38.00
🚚 £17.50–£38.00
⛺ £5.50–£10.00
🏚 (140) £181.00–£723.00
77 touring pitches

Ulwell Cottage Caravan Park

Ulwell BH19 3DG t +44 (0) 1929 422823 e enq@ulwellcottagepark.co.uk

ulwellcottagepark.co.uk

open 1 March to 7 January
payment Credit/debit cards, cash, cheques

Quiet site in picturesque setting adjoining Purbeck Hills. One and a half miles from Swanage and two miles from Studland, the entrance is on the Swanage to Studland road.

SAT NAV BH19 3DG

General 🖥🚿🌡🚽🚾🔌🚰🖥🛋✗🏇☀🔌   Leisure 🎣🍽⛰∪🎣🏇🚲

TAUNTON, Somerset Map ref 1D1 — GUEST ACCOMMODATION

★★★★
BED & BREAKFAST

B&B PER ROOM PER NIGHT
S £45.00–£48.00
D £68.00–£70.00

EVENING MEAL PER PERSON
£20.00–£24.00

Causeway Cottage

Barbers Lane, West Buckland, Nr Taunton TA21 9JZ t +44 (0) 1823 663458 e causewaybb@aol.com

causewaycottage.co.uk

open All year except Christmas and New Year
bedrooms 1 double, 2 twin
bathrooms All en suite
payment Cash, cheques, euros

A 200-year-old stone and beamed Somerset cottage privately tucked away with views across fields to Lofty Church. Easy access to M5, junction 26. Spacious, restful sitting room. Lesley is renowned for her cooking. Home-baked bread, free-range eggs, farm sausages for breakfast. Supper by arrangement. An informal, relaxed family home.

SAT NAV TA21 9JZ

Room 🌡🍵   General 🛏10 ✗❄   Leisure 🏇

What if I need to cancel?

It's advisable to check the proprietor's cancellation policy at the time of booking in case you have to change your plans.

TAVISTOCK, Devon Map ref 1C2 — GUEST ACCOMMODATION

★★★★★
**GUEST ACCOMMODATION
GOLD AWARD**

B&B PER ROOM PER NIGHT
S £94.00
D £140.00–£150.00

Autumn/spring breaks: 3 nights for price of 2. Special Valentine breaks. Gourmet tray suppers to order. 10% discount on 7-night stay.

Tor Cottage
Chillaton, Lifton PL16 0JE **t** +44 (0) 1822 860248 **e** info@torcottage.co.uk

torcottage.co.uk REAL-TIME BOOKING

open All year except Christmas and New Year
bedrooms 3 double, 1 twin, 1 suite
bathrooms All en suite
payment Credit/debit cards, cash

Enjoy complete peace and privacy in beautiful en suite bed-sitting rooms, each with own log fire and private garden, terrace or conservatory. Streamside setting in hidden valley, 28 acres of wildlife hillsides, beautiful gardens, heated outdoor pool. Adjacent Dartmoor. Visit Devon/Cornwall coastlines, National Trust properties or the Eden Project (45-minute drive).

SAT NAV *PL16 0JE* **ONLINE MAP**

Room 🛁 📺 🍵 🍷 General 🛋14 P 🚲 🎱 ✳ Leisure 🎣 ∪ ⚓ ⛳ 🚴

TAVISTOCK, Devon Map ref 1C2 — CAMPING, CARAVAN & HOLIDAY PARK

★★★★
**HOLIDAY, TOURING
& CAMPING PARK**
ROSE AWARD

🚐 (40) £11.25–£16.75
🚚 (40) £11.25–£16.75
⛺ (40) £11.25–£16.75
🏠 (12) £240.00–£485.00
120 touring pitches

Holiday let: £15 off 2-week booking. £10 Senior Citizen discount.

Harford Bridge Holiday Park
Peter Tavy, Tavistock PL19 9LS **t** +44 (0) 1822 810349 **e** enquiry@harfordbridge.co.uk

harfordbridge.co.uk

open All year
payment Credit/debit cards, cash, cheques

Beautiful, level, sheltered park set in Dartmoor with delightful views of Cox Tor. The River Tavy forms a boundary, offering riverside and other spacious, level camping pitches. Luxury, self-catering caravan holiday homes. Ideal for exploring Devon and Cornwall, walking the moor or just relaxing on this beautiful park.

SAT NAV *PL19 9LS*

General 🚐 🍳 🛒 🎁 ⚡ 🚿 ♿ 📷 🐕 ☀ 🚲 Leisure 🎣 🎢 🔍 ∪ ⚓ ⛳ 🚴

TAVISTOCK, Devon Map ref 1C2 — CAMPING, CARAVAN & HOLIDAY PARK

★★★★
**HOLIDAY, TOURING
& CAMPING PARK**
ROSE AWARD

🚐 (40) £13.00–£15.00
🚚 (40) £13.00–£15.00
⛺ (40) £13.00–£15.00
🏠 (7) £170.00–£465.00
40 touring pitches

£25 discount for 2-week booking in holiday homes. 20% discount for 2 sharing on weekly bookings in holiday accommodation (off-peak).

Langstone Manor Caravan and Camping Park
Moortown, Tavistock PL19 9JZ **t** +44 (0) 1822 613371 **e** jane@langstone-manor.co.uk

langstone-manor.co.uk

payment Credit/debit cards, cash, cheques

Fantastic location with direct access onto moor. Peace and quiet, with secluded pitches. Bar and restaurant. Excellent base for South Devon and Cornwall. Discover Dartmoor's secret!

SAT NAV *PL19 9JZ*

General 🚐 🍳 🛒 🎁 📷 📦 ✕ 🐕 ☀ Leisure 🍴 🔍 🎢 ∪ ⚓ ⛳ 🚴

TETBURY, Gloucestershire Map ref 2B2 — HOTEL

★★★★
**HOTEL
GOLD AWARD**

B&B PER ROOM PER NIGHT
S £198.00–£247.50
D £220.00–£275.00
HB PER PERSON PER NIGHT
£140.00–£178.00

Calcot Manor Hotel & Spa
Calcot, Tetbury GL8 8YJ t +44 (0) 1666 890391 e reception@calcotmanor.co.uk

calcotmanor.co.uk SPECIAL OFFERS · REAL-TIME BOOKING

A charming English farmhouse, elegantly converted into a stylish hotel. Beautifully furnished bedrooms, a choice of two restaurants and a luxurious spa, including outdoor hot tub and beauty-treatment rooms.

open All year
bedrooms 7 double, 15 twin, 12 family, 1 suite
bathrooms All en suite
payment Credit/debit cards, cash, cheques

Room 🛗🖭📞📺🆂 💧🍵 🔥 🔌 General 🏬🍴P🛜🍷🎱🍺🌙🎮🎯🖥🌂 ❄🐎
Leisure 🏑🎣🎿🏹🚫🎯U🏊🏌🦯🚴

TEWKESBURY, Gloucestershire Map ref 2B1 — GUEST ACCOMMODATION

**Rating Applied For
BED & BREAKFAST**

B&B PER ROOM PER NIGHT
S £45.00–£50.00
D £75.00–£80.00

EVENING MEAL PER PERSON
£20.00–£22.00

*Discounts on stays
of 3 nights or more.*

Green Orchard
Deerhurst Walton, Tewkesbury GL19 4BS t +44 (0) 1242 680362 e wendy@green-orchard.co.uk

green-orchard.co.uk GUEST REVIEWS · SPECIAL OFFERS · REAL-TIME BOOKING

open All year
bedrooms 1 double, 1 suite
bathrooms All en suite
payment Cash, cheques

Recently refurbished 17thC cottage in quiet countryside. Our luxury double room en suite is on the ground floor, annexed from the main dwelling with its own entrance. The rooms are spacious with LCD TV and DVD library. The fridge contains complimentary milk, fruit juice, wine and mineral water.

SAT NAV GL19 4BS **ONLINE MAP**

Room 🛗📺🆂💧🍵 General P🛜🔥✕🍺🖥❄ Leisure U🏌🦯🚴

TINCLETON, Dorset Map ref 2B3 — SELF CATERING

★★★★
SELF CATERING

Units   **1**
Sleeps   **4**

LOW SEASON PER WK
£350.00–£450.00

HIGH SEASON PER WK
£600.00–£950.00

*Short breaks
available within six
weeks of arrival
date. Please
telephone for
further information.*

The Courtyard At Clyffe, Dorchester
contact Dr Ian Mew, The Courtyard At Clyffe, Brock Cottage, Clyffe House, Dorchester DT2 8QR
t +44 (0) 7748 417974 e info@tincleton.co.uk

tincleton.co.uk SPECIAL OFFERS · REAL-TIME BOOKING

open All year
payment Cash, cheques

Built in the 1840s, this cosy cottage cleverly combines period features with modern-day living, ensuring your holiday is both one of relaxation and comfort. Woodland walks are two minutes from the front door. Remarkable historic locations such as Thomas Hardy's cottage lie within a few miles of this cottage.

SAT NAV DT2 8QR

Unit 📺🆂📻🖥📀📼🖨📷🍵📶📹📋💻❄🛏📳 General 🍳🏬🔥P🆂

Fancy a cycling holiday?
For a fabulous freewheeling break, seek out accommodation participating in our Cyclists Welcome scheme. Look out for the symbol and plan your route online at nationalcyclenetwork.org.

CYCLISTS WELCOME
WELCOME CYCLISTS

TINTAGEL, Cornwall Map ref 1B2

★★★★★
GUEST HOUSE

B&B PER ROOM PER NIGHT
S £40.00–£52.00
D £60.00–£84.00

The Avalon

Atlantic Road, Tintagel PL34 0DD **t** +44 (0) 1840 770116 **e** avalontintagel@googlemail.com

avalon-tintagel.co.uk GUEST REVIEWS

Perfect Tintagel village location. Recent total renovation and refurbishment. Stunning panoramic views of Tintagel Island and the sea. Car parking. Wi-Fi. Licensed. Breakfast produce local, free-range and organic whenever possible.

open February to November
bedrooms 5 double, 2 twin
bathrooms All en suite
payment Credit/debit cards, cash, cheques

Room 📺 ⓓ 🕮   General 🛳 🍽 🛪 P 🌐 🍷 🎱 🎮 ⬛ ✳   Leisure ♪ ►

TINTINHULL, Somerset Map ref 2A3

★★★★
INN

B&B PER ROOM PER NIGHT
S £65.00–£75.00
D £80.00–£90.00

EVENING MEAL PER PERSON
£18.00–£35.00

Enjoy fine wines and local real ales in summer in our beautiful gardens or by our roaring log fire in winter.

The Crown and Victoria Inn

14 Farm Street, Nr Yeovil BA22 8PZ **t** +44 (0) 1935 823341 **e** info@thecrownandvictoria.co.uk

thecrownandvictoria.co.uk

open All year
bedrooms 4 double, 1 single
bathrooms All en suite
payment Credit/debit cards, cash, cheques

Our award-winning inn is situated in the beautiful village of Tintinhull. Open all day, seven days a week, we have an inviting lunch menu (1200-1430), or our a la carte menu is available (1830-2130). We offer a traditional Sunday roast and our delicious home-made desserts are a must.

SAT NAV BA22 8PZ

Room 📺 ⓓ 🕮   General 🛳 🛪 P 🌐 🍷 ✗ 🍽 ✳

TORQUAY, Devon Map ref 1D2

★★★
HOTEL
SILVER AWARD

B&B PER ROOM PER NIGHT
S £45.00–£150.00
D Min £70.00
HB PER PERSON PER NIGHT
£35.00–£160.00

Please enquire about special promotions. Stay 7 nights for the price of 6.

Corbyn Head Hotel

Torbay Road, Torquay TQ2 6RH **t** +44 (0) 1803 213611 **e** info@corbynhead.com

corbynhead.com GUEST REVIEWS · SPECIAL OFFERS · REAL-TIME BOOKING

open All year
bedrooms 29 double, 10 twin, 3 single, 3 family
bathrooms All en suite
payment Credit/debit cards, cash, cheques, euros

The Corbyn Head Hotel is one of Torquay's leading hotels with its seafront location. Many of the bedrooms boast sea views and have private balconies. With two award-winning restaurants to choose from, and with its outstanding service, you can expect an enjoyable stay.

SAT NAV TQ2 6RH **ONLINE MAP**

Room ♿ 📞 📺 ⓓ 🕮 ♿   General 🛳 🍽 🛪 P 🌐 🍷 🍽 🌑 ⬛ ♟ ✳ 🐎
Leisure 🏹 ♨ ✝ ∪ ♪ ► 🚲

Do you like walking?

Walkers feel at home in accommodation participating in our Walkers Welcome scheme. Look out for the symbol. Consider walking all or part of a long-distance route – go online at nationaltrail.co.uk.

TORQUAY, Devon Map ref 1D2 — GUEST ACCOMMODATION

★★★★
GUEST ACCOMMODATION

B&B PER ROOM PER NIGHT
S £34.00–£36.00
D £68.00–£72.00

EVENING MEAL PER PERSON
£12.00–£14.00

Coombe Court

67 Babbacombe Downs Road, Torquay TQ1 3LP t +44 (0) 1803 327097
e enquiries@coombecourthotel.co.uk

coombecourthotel.co.uk

open All year except Christmas and New Year
bedrooms 10 double, 3 twin, 1 single, 1 family
bathrooms All en suite
payment Credit/debit cards, cash, cheques

Family-run hotel. Traditional cooking, 50yds from Babbacombe Downs. Non-smoking, no pets. Car parking for all guests.

SAT NAV TQ1 3LP

Room 🛏 📺 🍵 🍳 General 🦮10 P♟ ✕ 🍽 ❄ Leisure ♪ ▶

TORQUAY, Devon Map ref 1D2 — SELF CATERING

★★★★★
SELF CATERING

Units   6
Sleeps   4–8

LOW SEASON PER WK
£900.00–£1,850.00

HIGH SEASON PER WK
£1,500.00–£2,400.00

Corbyn Lodge Apartments, Torquay

contact Reservations, c/o OJ Developments Ltd, Ilsham House, Ilsham Marine Drive,
Torquay TQ1 2HT t +44 (0) 1803 295744 e reservations@corbyn-lodge.co.uk

corbyn-lodge.co.uk

open All year
payment Credit/debit cards, cheques
nearest pub less than 0.5 miles
nearest shop 0.5 miles

Luxury holiday apartments in Torquay. The perfect choice for top-quality self catering accommodation in Torbay, enjoying panoramic views across the Riviera.

SAT NAV TQ2 6QH

Unit 📺 📀 🖥 🗄🗐 🍳🍲 🍽 🧺 ❄ 🍳 General 🦮 🛏 ♿ P

TRURO, Cornwall Map ref 1B3 — SELF CATERING

★★★★★
SELF CATERING

Units   46
Sleeps   1–7

LOW SEASON PER WK
£490.00–£870.00

HIGH SEASON PER WK
£755.00–£1,580.00

Call for short-break special offers and out-of-season discounts at Cornwall's chic country retreat.

The Valley, Carnon Downs, Truro

The Valley, Bissoe Road, Carnon Downs, Truro TR3 6LQ t +44 (0) 1872 862194
e info@the-valley.co.uk

the-valley.co.uk REAL-TIME BOOKING

open All year
payment Credit/debit cards, cash, cheques, euros
nearest pub 0.5 miles
nearest shop 0.5 miles

When it's time for your next well earned break why not escape to a hidden valley and combine the service of a luxury hotel with the intimacy of your own contemporary cottage. Relax in architect-designed luxury with exclusive leisure facilities and enjoy exquisite cuisine and a superb selection of wines in the stylish Cafe Azur.

ONLINE MAP

Unit 📺 SC 📀 🖥 🗄🗐 🍳🍲 🍽 🧺 ✏❄ General 🦮 🛏 ♿ P ⬤ S 🐕
Leisure 🎣 ⟶ ⚓ 🏊 ♪ ▶ 🚲

TRURO, Cornwall Map ref 1B3   CAMPING, CARAVAN & HOLIDAY PARK

★★★★
TOURING PARK
⊞ (40) £10.50–£13.50
⊞ (5) £10.50–£13.50
⚑ (15) £10.50–£13.50
60 touring pitches

Summer Valley Touring Park

Shortlanesend, Truro TR4 9DW t +44 (0) 1872 277878 e res@summervalley.co.uk

summervalley.co.uk

Situated in a sheltered valley surrounded by woods and farmland, we have been awarded for our peaceful, rural environment. We have the ideal site for visiting the gardens in spring.

open April to October
payment Credit/debit cards, cash, cheques

General 🏕🔌🚿🚽 WP 🅿 📶📺🍴🐕☀ Leisure 🏔🎣

VERYAN, Cornwall Map ref 1B3   SELF CATERING

★★★★
SELF CATERING

Units 2
Sleeps 6

LOW SEASON PER WK
£275.00–£470.00

HIGH SEASON PER WK
£470.00–£790.00

Short breaks available Oct-Mar.

Trenona Farm Holidays, Veryan

contact Mrs Pamela Carbis, Trenona Farm, Ruan High Lanes, Truro TR2 5JS t +44 (0) 1872 501339
e pam@trenonafarmholidays.co.uk

trenonafarmholidays.co.uk REAL-TIME BOOKING

open All year
payment Credit/debit cards, cash, cheques
nearest pub 2 miles
nearest shop 1 mile

The former farmhouse, and old stone workshop, have been tastefully converted to provide quality accommodation with modern furnishings and appliances for relaxing holidays on a mixed working farm on the beautiful Roseland Peninsula. Private gardens and patios. Many public gardens and attractions nearby. Children/pets welcome. Disabled access.

SAT NAV TR2 5JS ONLINE MAP

Unit 📺 📶📠📀 🖥 🍳🔥🍽🗄🧺🧼 General 🛏🚽🅿🐕 Leisure ∪

WAREHAM, Dorset Map ref 2B3   CAMPING, CARAVAN & HOLIDAY PARK

★
HOLIDAY, TOURING
& CAMPING PARK
⊞ (40) £8.00–£28.00
⊞ (40) £8.00–£28.00
⚑ (40) £8.00–£28.00
40 touring pitches

Luckford Wood Farm Caravan & Camping Park

Luckford Wood House, East Stoke, Wareham BH20 6AW t +44 (0) 1929 463098 &
+44 (0) 7888 719002 e luckfordleisure@hotmail.co.uk

luckfordleisure.co.uk REAL-TIME BOOKING

open March to November
payment Credit/debit cards, cash, cheques, euros

Old-fashioned camping around a camp fire with a relaxed, traditional feel. Central position makes Luckford Wood an ideal location for you to enjoy the Jurassic Coastline, wonderful beaches and bays, coastal and inland walks, many exciting places to explore. Country-house accommodation available. Telephone for details.

SAT NAV BH20 6AW ONLINE MAP

General 📺🏕🔌🚽 WP 🅿🐕☀📶♿ Leisure 🎣🏹🚲

PETS!
WELCOME
WELCOME
PETS!

Where is my pet welcome?

Want to take your cherished companion with you on holiday? Proprietors participating in our Welcome Pets! scheme go out of their way to make special provision for you and your pet. Look out for the symbol.

WATERGATE BAY, Cornwall Map ref 1B2

CAMPING, CARAVAN & HOLIDAY PARK

★★★★
HOLIDAY, TOURING
& CAMPING PARK

(171) £10.00–£17.50
(171) £10.00–£17.50
(171) £10.00–£17.50
(2) £175.00–£500.00
171 touring pitches

Watergate Bay Touring Park

Watergate Bay TR8 4AD t +44 (0) 1637 860387 e email@watergatebaytouringpark.co.uk

watergatebaytouringpark.co.uk GUEST REVIEWS

Half a mile from Watergate Bay's sand, surf and cliff walks. Rural location in an Area of Outstanding Natural Beauty. Personally supervised by resident owners.

open March to October
payment Credit/debit cards, cash, cheques

General

Leisure

WELLS, Somerset Map ref 2A2

SELF CATERING

★★★★
SELF CATERING

Units **1**
Sleeps **1–5**

LOW SEASON PER WK
£300.00–£450.00

HIGH SEASON PER WK
£475.00–£575.00

Short stays available.

Honeysuckle Cottage, Wells

contact Mrs Luana Law, Honeysuckle Cottage, Worth, Wookey, Wells BA5 1LW
t +44 (0) 1749 678971 e honeycroft2@aol.com

open All year
payment Cash, cheques
nearest pub less than 0.5 miles
nearest shop 2 miles

Barn conversion on working farm in beautiful countryside. One double en suite and one double with adjoining single bedrooms. Large bathroom upstairs, shower room downstairs. Spacious kitchen/diner/lounge leading to large patio and garden overlooking stunning Mendip Hills. All modern equipment from dishwasher to DVD.

Unit   General   Leisure

WEMBURY, Devon Map ref 1C3

CAMPING, CARAVAN & HOLIDAY PARK

★★★★
HOLIDAY PARK

(56) £255.00–£865.00

Promotions include Midsummer Bargain Weekend and Midweek Breaks, Senior Citizens and second week discounts.

Churchwood Valley Holiday Cabins

Churchwood Valley, Wembury Bay, Plymouth PL9 0DZ t +44 (0) 1752 862382
e churchwoodvalley@btconnect.com

churchwoodvalley.com SPECIAL OFFERS

open April to mid-January
payment Credit/debit cards, cash, cheques

Churchwood Valley is a haven of peace! Set in a beautiful wooded valley, close to beaches, coastal walks and glorious countryside. Comfortable timber cabins, each with its own secluded patio. Wildlife abounds and the walks are stunning. Pets welcome.

SAT NAV *PL9 0DZ* **ONLINE MAP**

General   Leisure

FAMILIES WELCOME

Looking for an ideal family break?

For accommodation offering additional facilities and services for a range of ages and family units, look out for the Families Welcome symbol. Owners of these properties will go out of their way to welcome families.

WESTWARD HO!, Devon Map ref 1C1 — GUEST ACCOMMODATION

★★★★
BED & BREAKFAST

B&B PER ROOM PER NIGHT
S £35.00–£45.00
D £60.00–£70.00

Brockenhurst

11 Atlantic Way, Westward Ho!, Bideford EX39 1HX t +44 (0) 1237 423346
e info@brockenhurstindevon.co.uk

brockenhurstindevon.co.uk SPECIAL OFFERS · REAL-TIME BOOKING

Comfortable detached house adjoining the village centre (shops, restaurants, pubs). Within sight and sound of the sea. Good walking, cycling and bus service. Vast beach.

open All year except Christmas and New Year
bedrooms 2 double, 1 twin
bathrooms All en suite
payment Credit/debit cards, cash, cheques, euros

Room ⊤⊻ 💧 ⌇ General P 🍴 🐴 Leisure ∪ ♪ ► ♻

YELVERTON, Devon Map ref 1C2 — GUEST ACCOMMODATION

★★★★
GUEST ACCOMMODATION

B&B PER ROOM PER NIGHT
S £39.50–£45.00
D £70.00–£80.00

Overcombe House

Old Station Road, Yelverton PL20 7RA t +44 (0) 1822 853501 e enquiries@overcombehotel.co.uk

overcombehotel.co.uk REAL-TIME BOOKING

open All year except Christmas
bedrooms 4 double, 3 twin, 1 single
bathrooms All en suite
payment Credit/debit cards, cash

Offering a warm, friendly welcome in relaxed, comfortable surroundings with a substantial breakfast using local and home-made produce. Enjoying beautiful views over the village and Dartmoor. Conveniently located for exploring the varied attractions of both Devon and Cornwall, in particular Dartmoor National Park and the adjacent Tamar Valley.

SAT NAV PL20 7RA **ONLINE MAP**

Room ♿ ⊤⊻ 💧 ⌇ General ☏5 P ⓦ 🍴 🍴 ✻ Leisure ∪ ♪ ► ♻

YEOVIL, Somerset Map ref 2A3 — CAMPING, CARAVAN & HOLIDAY PARK

★★★★
HOLIDAY, TOURING & CAMPING PARK

🚐 (30)   £17.00
🚎 (30)   £17.00
▲ (20)   £17.00
🏠 (2) £375.00–£800.00
50 touring pitches

Long Hazel Park

High Street, Sparkford, Yeovil BA22 7JH t +44 (0) 1963 440002 e longhazelpark@hotmail.com

sparkford.f9.co.uk/lhi.htm

Adult-only park in a village location just off A303T. Level, landscaped grounds. Hardstandings, full disabled facilities. Two lodges for hire. Pub/restaurant, shop, post office, services and bus stop 200m.

open All year
payment Cash, cheques, euros

General 🚿 🔌 🍴 📶 🛝 🛒 🐴 ☀ ⓦ ♨ Leisure ∪ ♪ ► ♻

Do you like camping?

Love the great outdoors? Britain's Camping, Caravan & Holiday Parks 2009 is packed with information on quality sites in some spectacular locations.

You can purchase the guide from good bookshops and online at visitbritaindirect.com.

Scotland

Clockwise: Cairngorms, Highlands;
St Andrews, Fife; Loch Laich, Argyll and Bute

Great days out

Relax, recharge and rediscover yourself! Scotland's natural paradise of dramatic mountains, lochs and glens is the ideal escape from too-busy living. Climb mighty Munros and dawdle around romantic castles. Then soak up Scotland's world-class culture in its historic cities or at festival time.

Mountains and eagles

As the sun sinks, streaking the sky with flame, you spot the red deer stags in silhouette. An unforgettable experience, and just one reason to escape to Scotland. The country's ancient geology has created the most amazingly diverse landscapes, of mountain, loch and coast. Wildlife thrives and so will you. Start with the magical corner of **Dumfries and Galloway**, meandering along deserted beaches. Follow the **Fife Coastal Walk** to spot seabirds and grey seals, stopping off at quaint fishing villages like Pittenweem.

Glencoe, Highlands

Scenery and fauna are at their most spectacular in Scotland's two National Parks: **Loch Lomond & The Trossachs**, and the Arctic plateau of the **Cairngorms**. Journey through heather-clad peaks on The Trossachs Trail. Then look out for red squirrels, deer, golden eagles and ospreys in the **Highlands**, where land and sea collide to create stunning perspectives.

Adventures before tee-time

Opportunities for outdoor adventure are breathtaking, literally! If you're up for it, tackle a Munro – Scottish mountains over 3,000ft. **Ben Nevis**, Britain's highest mountain at 4,408ft, throws down the gauntlet to climbers, and the Nevis Range is a blast for mountain biking and winter skiing. Or, for something gentler, pedal the **Great Glen Cycle Route** along canal towpaths, forestry roads and quiet lanes.

Take to the waters sailing – **Argyll's** west coast is good for novices and old seadogs alike. Atlantic and North Sea swells all around the coast provide great breakers for surfing, and inland rivers give canoeists and white-water rafters a brilliant adrenalin rush. Find a peaceful stretch for fishing: the **River Tweed** is a classic. And there's no place like the home of golf for a round or two. Scotland has over 550 courses, including world-famous **St Andrews**, where you can also browse the **British Golf Museum**.

Keys to the castles

Scotland's tumultuous past is vividly etched on its landscapes in the shape of immense castles. View the ancient crowning site of Scottish kings at **Scone Palace** and hear tales of the Atholl Highlanders private army at **Blair Castle**. Follow in the steps of ill-fated Mary Queen of Scots to grand old **Stirling Castle**, or relax at **Balmoral** as Queen Victoria did. Words simply can't capture **Eilean Donan Castle**, you just have to see for yourself the striking ruin amid mountains mirrored in the waters of the loch. And at **Urquhart Castle** keep one eye out for the Loch Ness monster!

Left to right: Edinburgh Festival;
Eilean Donan Castle, Highlands

why not... cruise the Caledonian Canal and lochs linking Scotland's east and west coasts?

Tales of two cities

Scotland's great cities beckon. Get 'three in one' in **Edinburgh**, whose World Heritage Site embraces the medieval Old Town, the Georgian New Town and award-winning modern architecture. Follow the cobbled **Royal Mile** to magnificent **Edinburgh Castle** – check out those Crown Jewels for sparkle! Then take your pick of top museums and galleries, and share the kids' excitement in **Our Dynamic Earth**: flying over glaciers, encountering a tropical rainstorm and discovering the new Earthscape Scotland gallery. Come for August's celebrated arts and fringe festivals or the **Edinburgh Military Tattoo** – there's always something happening in the 'Festival City'.

Change scene, change mood and hit **Glasgow**: Scotland's largest city has reinvented itself as a buzzing cultural hotspot. Charles Rennie Mackintosh led the way with his streamlined building designs – visit the refurbished **Kelvingrove Art Gallery and Museum** to learn more about him and the Glasgow Style. Among 30-plus galleries and museums, Clydebuilt **Scottish Maritime Museum** reveals the city's shipping heritage. For R&R you can't beat the **Merchant City** quarter, an irresistible mix of sublime shopping and eateries. Do you fancy Scottish, Italian, or noodles in a Pop Art-decorated café?

Kelvingrove Art Gallery and Museum, Glasgow

Flings and drams

Brush up on national poet Robert Burns, recalled at venues throughout the **Scottish Borders** in May each year. Watch caber tossing, dancing and games at Highland Gatherings from Cowal to Tomintoul and all points in between. If bagpipes and fiddles are less your thing, there's also plenty of rock 'n' pop, or gigs at **Murrayfield** stadium. Keep energy levels up by tucking into a food festival, or toast some colourful occasions with a dram of 'uisge beatha', the 'water of life'. **Aberdeen** is a fine place from which to tour distilleries on the world's only **Malt Whisky Trail**.

why not... enjoy Sir Walter Scott's favourite picnic spot, Scott's View onto the Eildon Hills?

Island life

And just when you think you've 'done' Scotland, think again: you've countless islands to experience. Conveniently reached by air or ferry, they nevertheless remain worlds apart, each with its own unique character, crafts and traditions. Find dreamy beaches and a warm Gaelic welcome in the **Outer Hebrides**. Follow romantic tales of Bonnie Prince Charlie to **Skye**. Off Scotland's northeast tip, the archipelago of **Orkney** offers a scattering of 70 or so islands and skerries (small, rocky isles). Step back 5,000 years on mainland Orkney to **Skara Brae** Neolithic village complete with homes featuring stone beds. Then catch the ferry and ramble the **Eday Heritage Walk** past standing stones and ancient cairns. Puffins by the million await birdwatchers in **Shetland**, where Viking influences live on through the fire festival of Up Helly Aa and the famous Shetland knitwear.

Clockwise: Skara Brae, Orkney; Highland Games; Shetland

Destinations

Duthie Park, Aberdeen

Aberdeen

Prosperous and cosmopolitan, the 'Granite City' can hold its own as a cultural and academic centre. You'll find spectacular architecture, captivating museums, a wealth of art and culture and a lively social scene. The famous 'Granite Mile', Union Street, is the gateway to over 800 shops, restaurants and bars. Wander the cobbled lanes of Old Aberdeen and soak up the life and colour of the historic harbour. Find flower-filled parks and even a two-mile sweep of golden, sandy beach.

Dundee

The 'City of Discovery' is Scotland's sunniest city. You'll find superb shopping and a lively pub and club scene. Step into a bygone age on Captain Scott's famous polar exploration ship Discovery or check out the hip and exciting Dundee Contemporary Arts, a stunning complex on Nethergate. Enjoy panoramic views from Dundee Law – the plug of an extinct volcano – and nearby Broughty Ferry has one of the cleanest beaches in the UK.

Edinburgh

One of the most visited cities in Europe, the capital of Scotland is historic, cosmopolitan and cultured. Its magnificent castle dominates the city-centre skyline. The Old and New Towns are a World Heritage Site: explore the winding alleys of the medieval Old Town and the neoclassical buildings and broad, straight streets of the New Town. Edinburgh is not called the Festival City lightly, as its incredible calendar of annual events clearly shows.

Glasgow

Glasgow, Scotland's capital of style, is positively oozing with things to see and do. From superb shopping and a vibrant nightlife, to some of the best free museums and galleries in the country. At The Lighthouse, a Charles Rennie Mackintosh conversion, you'll find dynamic art and architecture exhibitions and a stunning, uninterrupted view over the city. Or take a stroll through the city's West End, a bohemian district of cafés, bars, clubs and boutiques.

Inverness

Visit Inverness for the perfect cocktail of city life and adventure sports enjoyed in the great outdoors. Crowned by a Gothic red sandstone castle, the compact city centre is lavishly decorated with flowers. You'll find great shopping, food and drink and plenty of places to relax. See the tropical gardens at the Floral Hall, head out to Culloden, site of the famous battle, or go monster-spotting on nearby Loch Ness.

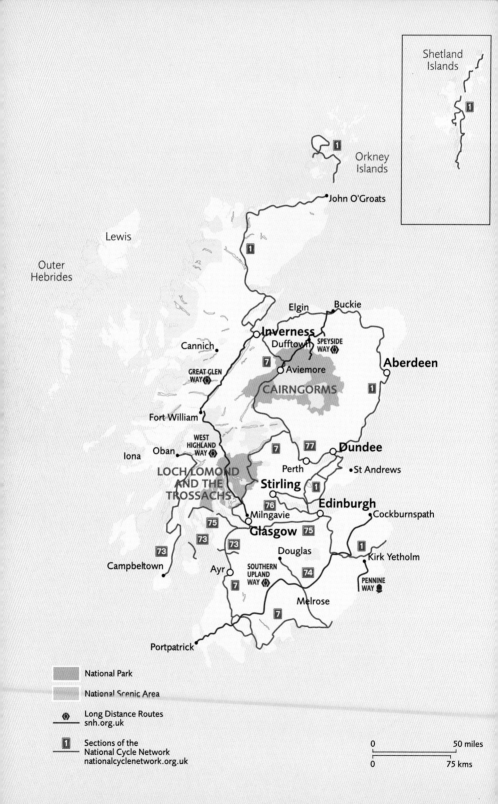

Shetland
Islands

Orkney
Islands

John O'Groats

Lewis

Outer
Hebrides

Elgin • Buckie
Inverness
Cannich • Dufftown SPEYSIDE
WAY

GREAT GLEN
WAY
Aviemore
CAIRNGORMS
Aberdeen

Fort William

WEST
HIGHLAND
WAY

Iona Oban

LOCH LOMOND
AND THE
TROSSACHS

Dundee

Perth • St Andrews

Stirling

Edinburgh

Milngavie
Glasgow Cockburnspath

Douglas

Campbeltown Ayr
SOUTHERN
UPLAND
WAY

Kirk Yetholm

PENNINE
WAY

Melrose

Portpatrick

National Park

National Scenic Area

Long Distance Routes
snh.org.uk

Sections of the
National Cycle Network
nationalcyclenetwork.org.uk

0   50 miles

0   75 kms

Lewis

Orkney

The island's history goes back more than 4,500 years to Neolithic times – discover it for yourself at stunning Skara Brae. Spectacular wildlife abounds: listen to the sea cliffs resounding with the calls of auks and kittiwakes and see rare birds of prey on the moorlands. Learn about the Viking invasions and see the magnificent St Magnus Cathedral in Kirkwall, the islands' capital. Follow the Orkney Craft Trail which includes the world-renowned Orcadian jewellery or sample whisky from Highland Park, the most northerly of whisky distilleries.

Lewis

Lewis forms part of a chain of islands with spectacular silver beaches, culture and wildlife. Fish in freshwater and sea lochs, take a boat trip to spot whales, dolphins, seals and puffins, or a guided walk to see otters, buzzards and deer. In the main town of Stornoway, visit Lewis Castle for great views of the port, and the Nan Eilean museum for the history of the Outer Hebrides. Gain a fascinating insight into the traditional island dwellings at the cottage museum of Arnol Blackhouse and experience the atmosphere surrounding the Calanais Standing Stones that are older than Stonehenge.

Stirling Castle

Clockwise: Glasgow; Edinburgh; Inverness

Stirling

Stirling may be Scotland's youngest city, but, as the centre of Braveheart country, you can touch and feel the sense of history that marks it out as unique. Take in the magnificent view from the ramparts of the cliff-top castle, or meander along the compact heritage mile of the Old Town, boasting the finest concentration of historic buildings in Scotland. Modern Stirling has a bustling centre with a cosmopolitan edge, quality local attractions and a café culture.

For lots more great ideas go to visitbritain.com/destinations and visitscotland.com

Visitor attractions

Family and Fun

Edinburgh Dungeon
Edinburgh
+44 (0) 131 240 1001
thedungeons.com
*From local legends to
world-famous vampires.*

Historic Paddle Steamer 'Maid of the Loch'
*Balloch,
West Dunbartonshire*
+44 (0) 1389 711865
maidoftheloch.com
*The ongoing restoration of a
historic craft.*

Our Dynamic Earth
Edinburgh
+44 (0) 131 550 7800
dynamicearth.co.uk
*Discover our planet's past,
present and future.*

The Royal Yacht Britannia
Leith Docks, Edinburgh
+44 (0) 131 555 5566
*Award-winning tour of a unique
royal residence.*

Scottish Sea Life Sanctuary
*Barcaldine, Argyll
and Bute*
+44 (0) 1631 720386
sealsanctuary.co.uk
*Marine marvels from around our
shores.*

Heritage

Balmoral Castle
Balmoral, Aberdeenshire
+44 (0) 1339 742534
balmoralcastle.com
*Scottish holiday home of the
Royal Family.*

Blair Castle
Blair Atholl, Perth and Kinross
+44 (0) 1796 481207
blair-castle.co.uk
*Ancient seat of the Dukes of
Atholl.*

Edinburgh Castle
Edinburgh
+44 (0) 131 225 9846
edinburghcastle.gov.uk
*Magnificent fortress dominating
the capital's skyline.*

National Wallace Monument
Causewayhead, Stirling
+44 (0) 1786 472140
nationalwallacemonument.com
*Spectacular tower
commemorating Scotland's
'Braveheart'.*

Palace of Holyroodhouse
Edinburgh
+44 (0) 131 556 5100
royalcollection.org.uk
*HM The Queen's official
residence in Scotland.*

Robert Burns Centre
*Dumfries, Dumfries &
Galloway*
+44 (0) 1387 264808
dumgal.gov.uk/museums
*Compelling exhibition featuring
original manuscripts and
memorabilia.*

Scone Palace
Scone, Perth and Kinross
+44 (0) 1738 552300
scone-palace.co.uk
*The ancient crowning place of
Scottish kings.*

Stirling Castle
Stirling
+44 (0) 1786 450000
historic-scotland.gov.uk
*Historic fortress perched on
dramatic volcanic crag.*

Urquhart Castle
*near Drumnadrochit,
Highland*
+44 (0) 1456 450551
historic-scotland.gov.uk
*Magnificent ruins on banks
of Loch Ness.*

Indoors

Auld Reekie Tours
Edinburgh
+44 (0) 131 557 4700
auldreekietours.co.uk
*The scariest ghost tours in
the world.*

British Golf Museum
St Andrews, Fife
+44 (0) 1334 460046
britishgolfmuseum.co.uk
*Unsurpassed collection of
golfing memorabilia.*

Clydebuilt Scottish Maritime Museum
Glasgow
+44 (0) 141 886 1013
scottishmaritimemuseum.org
*Interactive history of Glasgow's
emblematic river.*

Glasgow Cathedral
Glasgow
+44 (0) 141 552 6891
glasgowcathedral.org.uk
*Splendid Gothic building founded
by St Mungo.*

Hunterian Art Gallery
Glasgow
+44 (0) 141 330 4221
hunterian.gla.ac.uk
Distinguished gallery housing the Mackintosh Collection.

Hunterian Museum
Glasgow
+44 (0) 141 330 4221
hunterian.gla.ac.uk
A million items from meteorites to mummies.

John Paul Jones Cottage
Kirkbean, Dumfries & Galloway
+44 (0) 1387 880613
jpj.demon.co.uk
Traditional cottage home of naval hero.

The National Gallery Complex
Edinburgh
+44 (0) 131 624 6200
nationalgalleries.org
Interconnected galleries housing outstanding art collections.

Scottish Maritime Museum
Irvine, North Ayrshire
+44 (0) 1294 278283
scottishmaritimemuseum.org
Harbourside museum featuring historic vessels and tools.

Scottish National Portrait Gallery
Edinburgh
+44 (0) 131 624 6200
natgalscot.ac.uk
Portraits of those who shaped Scottish history.

World Famous Old Blacksmith's Shop Centre
Gretna Green, Dumfries & Galloway
+44 (0) 1461 338224
gretnagreen.com
World-famous marriage venue for eloping couples.

Outdoors

Glasgow Botanic Gardens
Glasgow
+44 (0) 141 276 1614
glasgow.gov.uk
Renowned collections of tropical plants.

ASSURANCE OF A GREAT DAY OUT

Attractions with this sign participate in the Visitor Attraction Quality Assurance Scheme which recognises high standards in all aspects of the visitor experience.

Go Ape!
Aberfoyle, Stirling
+44 (0) 845 643 9215
goape.co.uk
Rope bridges, swings and zip slides.

Mercat Walking Tours of Edinburgh
Edinburgh
+44 (0) 131 225 5445
mercattours.com
The dark, magical history of the city.

Royal Botanic Garden
Edinburgh
+44 (0) 131 552 7171
rbge.org.uk
Plant treasures from around the globe.

The Tall Ship at Glasgow Harbour
Glasgow
+44 (0) 141 222 2513
thetallship.com
Historic Clydebuilt ship restored to former glory.

Events 2009

Celtic Connections
Glasgow
celticconnections.com
14 Jan - 1 Feb

Up-Helly-Aa
Shetland Islands
visitshetland.com
27 Jan

Gourock Highland Games
Gourock
inverclyde.gov.uk
10 May

Edinburgh International Film Festival
Edinburgh
edfilmfest.org.uk
17 - 28 Jun*

The Open Golf Championships 2009
Turnberry
opengolf.com
16 - 19 Jul

The Gathering
Edinburgh
clangathering.org
25 Jul - 26 Sep

Langholm Common Riding
Langholm
langholm-online.co.uk
31 Jul

Edinburgh Military Tattoo
Edinburgh
edintattoo.co.uk
7 - 29 Aug

Piping Live!
Glasgow
pipingfestival.co.uk
10 - 16 Aug

Edinburgh International Festival
Edinburgh
eif.co.uk
14 Aug - 6 Sep

Scottish International Storytelling Festival
Edinburgh
scottishstorytellingcentre.co.uk
23 Oct - 1 Nov

* provisional date at time of going to press

Regional contacts and information

For more information on accommodation, attractions, activities, events and holidays in Scotland, contact the regional tourism organisation below. The website has a wealth of information and you can order or download publications.

Scotland

The following is a selection of publications available online from **VisitScotland.com** or by calling the information and booking service on **+44 (0) 845 22 55 121**:

Where to Stay Hotels & Guest Houses £8.99
Over 3,000 places to stay in Scotland – from luxury town houses and country hotels to budget-priced guesthouses. Details of prices and facilities, with location maps.

Where to Stay Bed & Breakfast £6.99
Over 2,000 Bed and Breakfast establishments throughout Scotland offering inexpensive accommodation – the perfect way to enjoy a budget trip and meet Scottish folk in their own homes. Details of prices and facilities, with location maps.

Where to Stay Caravan & Camping £4.99
Over 280 parks detailed with prices, available facilities and lots of other useful information. Also includes caravan homes for hire, with location maps.

Where to Stay Self Catering £5.99
Over 3,400 cottages, apartments and chalets to let – many in scenic areas. Details of prices and facilities, with location maps.

Touring Guide to Scotland £7.99
A fully revised edition of this popular guide which now lists over 1,700 things to do and places to visit in Scotland. Easy to use index and locator maps. Details of opening hours, admission charges, general description and information on disabled access.

Touring Map of Scotland £4.99
An up-to-date touring map of Scotland. Full colour with comprehensive motorway and road information, the map details over 20 categories of tourist information and names over 1,500 things to do and places to visit in Scotland.

Loch Lomond

Visitor Information Centres

When you arrive at your destination, visit a Visitor Information Centre for help with accommodation and information about local attractions and events. Alternatively call **+44 (0) 845 22 55 121** to receive information and book accommodation before you go.

Aberdeen	23 Union Street	Drumnadrochit	The Car Park
Aberfeldy	The Square	Dufftown*	The Square
Aberfoyle	Trossachs Discovery Centre	Dumbarton*	Milton, A82 Northbound
Abington	Junction 13, M74 Services	Dumfries	64 Whitesands
Alford*	Old Station Yard	Dunbar*	141 High Street
Alva	Sterling Mills Outlet Village	Dundee	21 Castle Street
Anstruther*	Scottish Fisheries Museum	Dunfermline	1 High Street
Arbroath	Fishmarket Quay	Dunkeld	The Cross
Ardgartan*	By Arrochar	Dunoon	7 Alexandra Parade
Aviemore	Grampian Road	Dunvegan	2 Lochside
Ayr	22 Sandgate	Durness*	Sangomore
Ballater	Station Square	Edinburgh	Princess Mall, 3 Princes Street
Balloch	The Old Station Building		
Banchory*	Bridge Street	Edinburgh Airport	Main Concourse
Banff*	Collie Lodge	Elgin	17 High Street
Biggar*	155 High Street	Eyemouth*	Auld Kirk, Manse Road
Blairgowrie	26 Wellmeadow	Falkirk	The Falkirk Wheel
Bo'ness*	Union Street	Fort William	15 High Street
Bowmore	The Square	Fraserburgh*	3 Saltoun Square
Braemar	Mar Road	Glasgow	11 George Square
Brechin	Pictavia Centre	Glasgow Airport	International Arrivals Hall
Brodick	The Pier	Grantown on Spey*	54 High Street
Callander	Rob Roy Centre	Gretna	Gretna Gateway Outlet Village
Campbeltown	The Pier		
Castlebay*	Main Street	Hawick	Tower Mill
Castle Douglas*	Market Hill Car Park	Helensburgh*	The Clock Tower
Craignure	The Pier	Huntly*	9a The Square
Crail*	Crail Museum, 62 Marketgate	Inveraray	Front Street
		Inverness	Castle Wynd
Crathie*	The Car Park	Inverurie*	18 High Street
Crieff	High Street	Jedburgh	Murrays Green
Daviot Wood*	Picnic Area, A9	Kelso	The Square

Killin	Breadalbane Folklore Centre	Rothesay	Winter Gardens
Kirkcaldy	339 High Street	St Andrews	70 Market Street
Kirkcudbright	Harbour Square	Selkirk*	Halliwells House
Kirkwall	6 Broad Street	Southwaite	M6 Service Area
Lanark	Horsemarket, Ladyacre Road	Stirling	41 Dumbarton Road
Largs*	Main Street	Stirling (Pirnhall)	Junction 9, M9 Services
Lerwick	The Market Cross	Stonehaven*	66 Allardice Street
Lochboisdale*	Pier Road	Stornoway	26 Cromwell Street
Lochgilphead	Lochnell Street	Stranraer	Burns House, 28 Harbour Street
Lochinver*	Kirk Lane		
Lochmaddy*	Pier Road	Stromness	Ferry Terminal Building
Melrose	Abbey Street	Strontian*	Acharacle
Moffat*	Churchgate	Sumburgh	Sumburgh Airport
Newtongrange*	Scottish Mining Museum	Tarbert (Harris)*	Pier Road
Newton Stewart*	Dashwood Square	Tarbert (Loch Fyne)*	Harbour Street
North Berwick	Quality Street	Tarbet (Loch Lomond)*	Main Street
Oban	Argyll Square		
Paisley	9A Gilmour Street	Thurso*	Riverside Road
Peebles	High Street	Tobermory*	The Pier
Perth	West Mill Street	Tomintoul*	The Square
Pitlochry	22 Atholl Road	Tyndrum	Main Street
Portree	Bayfield Road	Ullapool*	Argyle Street

* seasonal opening

Clockwise: Dunnottar Castle, Aberdeenshire; Italian Chapel, Orkney; The Falkirk Wheel

Country ways

The Countryside Rights of Way Act gives people new rights to walk on areas of open countryside and registered common land.

To find out where you can go and what you can do, as well as information about taking your dog to the countryside, go online at countrysideaccess.gov.uk.

And when you're out and about…

Always follow the Country Code
- Be safe – plan ahead and follow any signs
- Leave gates and property as you find them
- Protect plants and animals, and take your litter home
- Keep dogs under close control
- Consider other people

where to stay in
Scotland

All place names in the blue bands are shown on the maps at the front of this guide.

Accommodation symbols

Symbols give useful information about services and facilities. On pages 16 to 17 you can find a key to these symbols.

ABINGTON, South Lanarkshire Map ref 6C2 **CAMPING, CARAVAN & HOLIDAY PARK**

★★★★
HOLIDAY PARK
THISTLE AWARD

🚐	£11.00–£16.00
🚎	£11.00–£16.00
⛺ (8)	£6.00–£16.00
🚐 (3)	£160.00–£374.00

50 touring pitches

Mount View Caravan Park

Abington ML12 6RW t +44 (0) 1864 502808 e info@mountviewcaravanpark.co.uk

A developing park, surrounded by the Southern Uplands and handily located between Carlisle and Glasgow. It is an excellent stopover site for those travelling between Scotland and the South. The West Coast railway passes beside the park.

open March to October
payment Credit/debit cards, cash, cheques

General 🚐🚗🏠🐾🔥📷🐕 Leisure ☕

ACHARN, Perth and Kinross Map ref 6C1 **SELF CATERING**

★★★
SELF CATERING

Units **6**
Sleeps **2–8**

LOW SEASON PER WK
£250.00–£350.00

HIGH SEASON PER WK
£465.00–£580.00

Availability always updated on website. Reductions for 2 persons in house or one disabled person in 'Laggan'.

Loch Tay Lodges, Acharn, By Aberfeldy

contact A&J Duncan Millar, Loch Tay Lodges, Remony, By Aberfeldy PH15 2HR
t +44 (0) 1887 830209 **e** remony@btinternet.com

lochtaylodges.co.uk

open All year
payment Credit/debit cards, cash, cheques, euros
nearest pub 1.5 miles
nearest shop 1.5 miles

Six self-catering units in beautiful Highland Perthshire in the centre of Scotland. Lots to do on the farm, on the water or up the hill. Return to the warm welcome of log fires (in four only) after a tour of castles, gardens or distilleries.

ONLINE MAP

Unit 📺📻💻🔲🍴🧺♨️🌀 General 🛋️🏨🚶P🅿️🐕 Leisure ⚲∪☕▶🚲

Using map references

The map references refer to the colour maps at the front of this guide. The first figure is the map number, the letter and figure that follow indicate the grid reference on the map.

AVIEMORE, Highland Map ref 7C3 — SELF CATERING

★★★
SELF CATERING

| Units | 1 |
| Sleeps | 1–5 |

LOW SEASON PER WK
£300.00–£350.00

HIGH SEASON PER WK
£375.00–£425.00

Short breaks sometimes available (minimum 3 nights). Discounts for repeat bookings and long lets.

Lairig Vue, Aviemore

contact Mrs S McDonald, 5 Dalnabay, Aviemore PH22 1RE **t** +44 (0) 7746 608065
e lairigvuedalnabay@btinternet.com

lairigvue.co.uk GUEST REVIEWS · REAL-TIME BOOKING

open All year
payment Cash, cheques, euros
nearest pub 0.5 miles
nearest shop 0.5 miles

A well-equipped and very comfortable two-bedroom detached house with splendid views of the Cairngorm Mountains. Everything is provided to ensure that your stay is enjoyable. A perfect base for exploring the wonderful surrounding countryside. Numberous outdoor activities are on offer nearby including fishing, golf, cycling, climbing, skiing and sailing.

SAT NAV PH22 1RE **ONLINE MAP**

Unit 📺 🖥️ 🔌 ⚙️ 🍳 🔥 🧊 🍽️ 🧺 ☀️ ⛺ ✎ General 🐴 🏠 ☕ P ⭕ Ⓢ
Leisure ∪ 🧦 ► 🚴

BALLANTRAE, South Ayrshire Map ref 6B3 — SELF CATERING

★★★
SELF CATERING

| Units | 1 |
| Sleeps | 1–6 |

LOW SEASON PER WK
Min £200.00

HIGH SEASON PER WK
Max £500.00

Short breaks off season. Free-range eggs. Farm tours.

Downanhill Cottage, Ballantrae

contact Mrs Sheila Shankland, Langdale Farm, Ballantrae, Girvan **t** +44 (0) 1465 831368
e shankland_langdale@yahoo.co.uk

ailsacraigholidays.com GUEST REVIEWS · SPECIAL OFFERS · REAL-TIME BOOKING

open All year
payment Cash, cheques
nearest pub 1.5 miles
nearest shop 1.5 miles

Downanhill Cottage nestles at the end of a private lane, on a working dairy farm, approximately one mile from Ballantrae. Cottage has one family room and two single rooms, sleeping four to six. Spectacular, uninterrupted views of Mull of Kintyre, Arran and Ailsa Craig. View our website – you won't be disappointed.

SAT NAV KA26 0PB **ONLINE MAP**

Unit 📺 📠 🖥️ 🔌 ⚙️ 🍳 🔥 🧊 🍽️ 🧺 ☀️ ⛺ General 🐴 🏠 ☕ P ⭕ Ⓢ 🐕
Leisure ✦ 🧦 ►

BALLINTUIM, Perth and Kinross Map ref 6C1 — SELF CATERING

★★★★
SELF CATERING

| Units | 2 |
| Sleeps | 1–5 |

LOW SEASON PER WK
£275.00–£375.00

HIGH SEASON PER WK
£475.00

East & West Cromald Cottages, Blairgowrie

contact Mrs Kim Hodgson, Whitehouse Farm, Ballintuim, Blairgowrie PH10 7NG
t +44 (0) 1250 886391 **e** stay@cromaldcottages.co.uk

cromaldcottages.co.uk GUEST REVIEWS

open All year except Christmas and New Year
payment Cash, cheques
nearest pub 2 miles
nearest shop 2 miles

East & West Cromald cottages lie in an elevated position looking down onto trees and fields. The cottages have one double, one twin and one single room, sleeping a maximum of five. All electricity, heating oil, towels and bed linen are included. Four-poster bed in double-room cottage will not disappoint.

SAT NAV PH10 7NG **ONLINE MAP**

Unit 📺 📟 📠 🖥️ 🔌 ⚙️ 🍳 🔥 🧊 🍽️ 🧺 ☀️ ⛺ ✎ General 🐴 🏠 P 🐕

BALLOCH, West Dunbartonshire Map ref 6B2 — CAMPING, CARAVAN & HOLIDAY PARK

★★★★★
HOLIDAY PARK
THISTLE AWARD

£18.00–£22.00
£18.00–£22.00
(6) £195.00–£550.00
120 touring pitches

Lomond Woods Holiday Park

Tullichewan, Old Luss Road, Balloch, Loch Lomond G83 8QP **t** +44 (0) 1389 755000
e lomondwoods@holiday-parks.co.uk

holiday-parks.co.uk SPECIAL OFFERS · REAL-TIME BOOKING

Beside Loch Lomond and at the gateway to the National Park, this superbly appointed, family-run park offers pine lodges and caravans for holiday hire and sunny, secluded pitches for touring caravans and motor homes.

open All year
payment Credit/debit cards, cash, cheques

General 🔲🚐🔌🖐🅿🆆🅿🖼🖳🐄☀📶♨ Leisure ♣⛺∪♪▶🚲

BANCHORY, Aberdeenshire Map ref 7D3 — SELF CATERING

★★★★
SELF CATERING

Units **1**
Sleeps **1–10**

LOW SEASON PER WK
£450.00–£600.00

HIGH SEASON PER WK
£650.00–£1,200.00

Discounts available for returning guests, short stays or small groups.

Manse Croft, Strachan

contact Tricia Macphail
t +44 (0) 7702 269609 **e** mansecroft@gmail.com

mansecroft.com SPECIAL OFFERS

open All year
payment Credit/debit cards, cash, cheques
nearest pub 1.5 miles
nearest shop less than 0.5 miles

A well-appointed and very spacious five-bedroomed house with enclosed garden and stunning views over the Feugh Valley. Ideal for relaxed gatherings with family and friends. Excellent walking and mountain biking on the doorstep and the facilities and attractions of Royal Deeside and Aberdeen within easy reach.

SAT NAV AB31 6NN

Unit 📺 🆂🅲 📀 📶 🖥 🗄 🍳🅾 🔌 🖳 🛁❄🍳♨ General 🛋🛏🅿🅾🆂🐄
Leisure ∪♪▶🚲

BLAIRGOWRIE, Perth and Kinross Map ref 6C1 — GUEST ACCOMMODATION

★★
INN

B&B PER ROOM PER NIGHT
S £45.00
D £70.00

EVENING MEAL PER PERSON
£8.95–£20.00

Glenisla Hotel

Kirkton of Glenisla, Blairgowrie PH11 8PH **t** +44 (0) 1575 582223 **e** enquiries@glenisla-hotel.com

glenisla-hotel.com GUEST REVIEWS · REAL-TIME BOOKING

open All year
bedrooms 3 double, 2 twin, 1 single
bathrooms All en suite
payment Credit/debit cards, cash, cheques

Glenisla Hotel and Restaurant, near Blairgowrie, in the Angus glens – the heart of Scotland. The inn and restaurant are conveniently located for all country sports. Recently renovated and refurbished to the highest standard, retaining its 17thC charm.

SAT NAV PH11 8PH **ONLINE MAP**

Room 🚿 General 🛋🛏🔑🅿📶♨✕🍳❄🐄 Leisure ∪♪

What if I need to cancel?

It is advisable to check the proprietor's cancellation policy in case you have to change your plans at a later date.

BRAEMAR, Aberdeenshire Map ref 7C3 — CAMPING, CARAVAN & HOLIDAY PARK

★★★★
TOURING PARK
🚐 (97) £12.20–£25.10
🚐 (97) £12.20–£25.10
97 touring pitches

The Invercauld Caravan Club Site
Glenshee Road, Braemar, Ballater AB35 5YQ t +44 (0) 1342 326944

caravanclub.co.uk

open December 2008 to October 2009
payment Credit/debit cards, cash, cheques

Set on the edge of Braemar village, gateway to the Cairngorms. Ideal centre for mountain lovers. See red deer, capercaillie and golden eagles.

SAT NAV AB35 5YQ

Special member rates mean you can save your membership subscription in less than a week. Visit our website to find out more.

THE CARAVAN CLUB

General 🔲 🔌 🚻 ☎ WP 📷 📠 🛒 🐕 ☀️ Leisure ⛺ 🎵 🏹

CARBOST, Highland Map ref 7A3 — GUEST ACCOMMODATION

Rating Applied For
BED & BREAKFAST

B&B PER ROOM PER NIGHT
S £50.00–£55.00
D £68.00–£73.00

EVENING MEAL PER PERSON
£15.00–£20.00

Reduced rates for extended stays, please enquire.

Phoenix House
Carbost, Isle of Skye IV47 8SR t +44 (0) 1478 640775 e skyeman460@btinternet.com

phoenixhousebandb.co.uk

open All year
bedrooms 3 double
bathrooms All en suite
payment Cash, cheques

Formerly the old excise man's house owned by Talisker Distillery. Stay in a little piece of history. Newly renovated to offer luxurious accommodation for discerning guests. Chris and Elaine welcome you to our home. 'Fàilte'.

SAT NAV IV47 8SR

Room 📺 🆂 ♨ 🍵 General P 📶 🔥 ✕ 🍽 💻 ❄ Leisure 🎵 🏹

CRIEFF, Perth and Kinross Map ref 6C1 — SELF CATERING

★★★★
SELF CATERING

Units **1**
Sleeps **6**

LOW SEASON PER WK
£370.00–£420.00

HIGH SEASON PER WK
£520.00–£570.00

Short breaks of two or three nights available Oct-Mar.

Aberturret Cottage, Crieff
contact Judy Watt, Aberturret House, Crieff PH7 4HA t +44 (0) 1764 650064
e judywatt@aberturret.com

aberturret.com

open All year
payment Credit/debit cards, cash, cheques, euros
nearest pub 1 mile
nearest shop 1 mile

Aberturret is a beautiful and traditional old cottage in a rural location just outside the lovely town of Crieff. It has its own enormous garden complete with river running through. This immaculate and tasteful cottage has a well-equipped kitchen, comfortable sitting room, two bathrooms and three bedrooms.

WALKERS CYCLISTS WELCOME

Unit 📺 🆂 📶 📻 🖥 🎛 🍵 📷 🍵 🍽 ❄ ⛲ General 🛋 🏠 🅿 📷 🆂 🐕
Leisure ♻ 🎵 🏹 🚴

CRIEFF, Perth and Kinross Map ref 6C1 SELF CATERING

★★★★
SELF CATERING

Units **1**
Sleeps **4**

LOW SEASON PER WK
£270.00–£340.00

HIGH SEASON PER WK
£395.00–£435.00

*Short breaks
available Oct-Mar,
3-night stay.
Discounts for 3 or
more weeks.*

Avonlea, Crieff

contact Chris and Elaine Vermeulen, 23 Huntley Avenue, Giffnock, Glasgow G46 6LW
t +44 (0) 141 620 3734 e admin@avonlea-crieff.co.uk

avonlea-crieff.co.uk SPECIAL OFFERS

open All year
payment Cash, cheques, euros
nearest pub less than 0.5 miles
nearest shop less than 0.5 miles

Relax in the beautiful Perthshire town of Crieff. This luxury period cottage accommodates up to four people (double and twin bedrooms). Based in the town centre where there is a good selection of pubs, restaurants and interesting local shops to meander through. Ideal for relaxing, hill-walking, golfing and cycling.

SAT NAV PH7 3BU

Unit 📺 SC 💿 🖥 🔌🛁🗄 ❓🗑🍽📖 General 🦮 🛏 S Leisure ∪ ♪ 🏌 🚴

DALMALLY, Argyll and Bute Map ref 6B1 SELF CATERING

★★★★
SELF CATERING

Units **4**
Sleeps **2–6**

LOW SEASON PER WK
£185.00–£340.00

HIGH SEASON PER WK
£360.00–£720.00

*Short breaks
available Nov-end
Mar, minimum
3-night stay.*

Blarghour Farm Cottages, Loch Awe

Blarghour Farm Cottages, South Lochaweside by Dalmally PA33 1BW t +44 (0) 1866 833246
e blarghour@btconnect.com

self-catering-argyll.co.uk SPECIAL OFFERS · REAL-TIME BOOKING

open All year
payment Credit/debit cards, cash, cheques
nearest pub 6 miles
nearest shop 20 miles

On a hill farm of sheep and Highland cattle by lovely Loch Awe in the West Highlands of Scotland. We offer four quality cottages in a beautiful, quiet, rural location off the beaten track. Non-smoking. Loch Lomond, Oban and the islands, Ben Nevis and Kintyre all within two hours of Blarghour.

SAT NAV PA33 1BW **ONLINE MAP**

Unit 📺 📻 💿 🖥 🔌🛁🗄 ❓🗑📖 ❄ General 🦮 🛏 ♿ P 🅾 S Leisure ♪ 🏌

DRYMEN, Stirling Map ref 6B2 HOTEL

★★★
HOTEL

B&B PER ROOM PER NIGHT
S £49.00–£94.00
D £49.00–£124.00
HB PER PERSON PER NIGHT
£43.50–£81.00

*Murder Mystery
evenings from
£65pp incl overnight
stay. Spooky
packages from
£79pp incl overnight
stay.*

Winnock Hotel

The Square, Drymen, Loch Lomond G63 0BL t +44 (0) 1360 660245 e info@winnockhotel.com

winnockhotel.com GUEST REVIEWS · SPECIAL OFFERS · REAL-TIME BOOKING

open All year
bedrooms 26 double, 19 twin, 8 single, 20 family
bathrooms All en suite
payment Credit/debit cards, cash, cheques, euros

The Winnock Hotel is a 73-bedroom hotel and former 18thC coaching inn, centrally situated, minutes from Loch Lomond. This fine family-owned hotel has recently been carefully extended and refurbished, whilst retaining all its original character. It is full of historic charm, friendly service and great food, and is well known for its lively Scottish evenings, murder mystery weekends and walking holidays.

SAT NAV G63 0BL **ONLINE MAP**

Room 🛗 🚪 📞 📺 SC ♿ ❓ General 🦮 🛏 ♿ P 📶 🍽 🍴 ❄ Leisure ∪ ♪ 🏌 🚴

DUFFTOWN, Moray Map ref 7D3

★★★
BED & BREAKFAST

B&B PER ROOM PER NIGHT
S £35.00
D £50.00–£52.00

Braehead Villa

Braehead Terrace, Dufftown AB55 4AN **t** +44 (0) 1340 820461 **e** info@visit-dufftown-scotland.co.uk

visit-dufftown-scotland.co.uk

open All year except Christmas
bedrooms 1 double, 1 twin, 1 family
bathrooms All en suite
payment Cash, cheques

Personal attention from the owners, Liz and Adam, a local Scottish couple who will give you the benefit of their local knowledge. Follow the Malt Whisky Trail, Dufftown being the malt whisky capital. Visit the distilleries and see malt whisky being produced. Also nearby are golf and fishing.

SAT NAV AB55 4AN **ONLINE MAP**

Room 🛏 📺 💧 🍵 General 🐴12 P 🍽 🐕 Leisure ∪ 🎣 🏌 🚴

DUNDEE, Dundee Map ref 6C1

★★★★
BED & BREAKFAST

B&B PER ROOM PER NIGHT
S £45.00–£50.00
D £70.00–£90.00

EVENING MEAL PER PERSON
£20.00

Duntrune House

Main Wing, Duntrune House, Duntrune, Dundee DD4 0PJ **t** +44 (0) 1382 350239
e info@duntrunehouse.co.uk

duntrunehouse.co.uk

open March to October
bedrooms 1 double, 1 twin, 1 family
bathrooms All en suite
payment Credit/debit cards, cash, cheques

Superior accommodation in 1820s country house offering superb views and spacious, well-maintained grounds. Situated in a quiet, rural area close to the city and well located for touring the east of Scotland. Guests dine with the hosts, whose interests include family history, gardening and antiques. Wireless internet access available.

SAT NAV DD4 0PJ

Room 🛏 💧 🍵 General P 📶 🔥 ✗ 🔲 ❄ Leisure 🎣 🏌

DURNESS, Highland Map ref 7B1

Rating Applied For
GUEST HOUSE

B&B PER ROOM PER NIGHT
S £35.00–£50.00
D £54.00–£60.00

EVENING MEAL PER PERSON
£9.00–£15.00

Wild Orchid Guest House

Durness, Sutherland IV27 4PN **t** +44 (0) 1971 511280 **e** wildorchidguesthouse@hotmail.co.uk

wildorchidguesthouse.co.uk

open All year except Christmas and New Year
bedrooms 3 double, 5 twin
bathrooms All en suite
payment Cash, cheques

A warm welcome awaits you in our purpose-built guesthouse located in Durness. Our rooms are en suite, light, airy and tastefully decorated. In our guest lounge you can relax, read, watch TV or enjoy our selection of videos, DVDs and books. Breakfast is served in our recently added conservatory.

SAT NAV IV27 4PN

Room 🛏 💧 🍵 General P 🔥 ✗ 🍽 Leisure 🎣 🏌

Where can I get live travel information?
For the latest travel update – call the RAC on 1740 from your mobile phone.

EARLSTON, Scottish Borders Map ref 6D2 — SELF CATERING

★★★
SELF CATERING

Units **1**

LOW SEASON PER WK
£290.00–£350.00

HIGH SEASON PER WK
£400.00–£450.00

Sorrowlessfield Cottage, Earlston

contact Mrs Susan King, Sorrowlessfield Farm, Earlston TD4 6AG **t** +44 (0) 1896 849809
e susanking1@mac.com

sorrowlessfieldcottage.co.uk REAL-TIME BOOKING

A beautiful, traditional stone cottage in the middle of the Scottish Borders with woods and river. There are two bedrooms, bathroom, living room, kitchen/dining room, utility room and toilet. Central heating.

open All year
payment Credit/debit cards, cash, cheques, euros
nearest pub 1.5 miles
nearest shop 1.5 miles

Unit 📺 🖥 ⬛ 🗄 🍳 🗑 🧺 🖇 ✻ ♨ ∅ General ⌂ 🛏 P Ⓢ 🐕 Leisure ♒ 🎣 🏌 🚴

EDINBURGH, Edinburgh Map ref 6C2 — GUEST ACCOMMODATION

★★★★
GUEST HOUSE

B&B PER ROOM PER NIGHT
S £45.00–£80.00
D £60.00–£125.00

Quote 'VisitBritain' for a discount on off-peak time.

23 Mayfield

23 Mayfield Gardens, Newington, Edinburgh EH9 2BX **t** +44 (0) 131 667 5806
e info@23mayfield.co.uk

23mayfield.co.uk GUEST REVIEWS · SPECIAL OFFERS · REAL-TIME BOOKING

open All year
bedrooms 4 double, 3 twin, 2 family
bathrooms All en suite
payment Credit/debit cards, cash, cheques

23 Mayfield is a family-run Victorian detached house, situated one mile from Edinburgh city centre. Within the 19thC exterior, you will find many original features. The accommodation has everything you need for a comfortable and relaxing atmosphere. We have private parking. Free Wi-Fi, residents' lounge.

SAT NAV EH9 2BX **ONLINE MAP**

Room 🛗 🖨 📺 ♨ 🍵 General ⌂5 P 📶 ⚷ 🍴 🎮 ✻ Leisure 🏌 🚴

EDINBURGH, Edinburgh Map ref 6C2 — GUEST ACCOMMODATION

★★★★
BED & BREAKFAST

B&B PER ROOM PER NIGHT
S £35.00–£60.00
D £60.00–£120.00

During low season 3 nights for 2, excl rugby weekends, Easter, Christmas, New Year and Bank Holiday weekends.

No 45

45 Gilmour Road, Edinburgh EH16 5NS **t** +44 (0) 131 667 3536
e w.cheape@gilmourhouse.freeserve.co.uk

edinburghbedbreakfast.com

open All year
bedrooms 1 double, 1 twin, 1 single, 1 family
bathrooms 3 en suite, 1 private
payment Credit/debit cards, cash, cheques, euros

No 45 is a lovely, fully refurbished Victorian villa overlooking a grassy bowling green. Close to most tourist attractions and Edinburgh University, also on a main bus route. Free on-street parking.

SAT NAV EH16 5NS

Room 📺 SC ♨ 🍵 General ⌂ P 🍴 ✻ Leisure 🏌

Place index

If you know where you want to stay, the index by place name at the back of the guide will give you the page number listing accommodation in your chosen town, city or village. Check out the other useful indexes too.

EDINBURGH, Edinburgh Map ref 6C2

★★
SELF CATERING

Units **2**
Sleeps **1–6**

LOW SEASON PER WK
£350.00–£420.00

HIGH SEASON PER WK
£840.00–£1,155.00

10% last-minute discount when arriving within 7 days of booking.

AJEM Self Catering, Edinburgh

contact A Megaughin-Helder, 132 Easter Road, Edinburgh EH7 5RJ **t** +44 (0) 7828 122904
e info@selfcateringedinburgh.co.uk

selfcateringedinburgh.eu SPECIAL OFFERS · REAL-TIME BOOKING

open All year
payment Credit/debit cards, cash, cheques
nearest pub less than 0.5 miles
nearest shop less than 0.5 miles

Two nice second-floor apartments close to the city centre. Apartment 4 sleeps six, apartment 5 sleeps four. Internet and large-screen TV, fully equipped kitchen and bathroom with bath and shower. Linen/towels included. We are non-smoking and pet-friendly. Open all year, prices from £50 per night.

SAT NAV EH7 5RJ

Unit 📺 🔲 ▨ 🔳 🍳 🔩 🗄 🍴 🕹 🎛 General ⛵ 🏔 ⛳ Ⓢ 🐕 Leisure ∪ 🎿 🚴

EDINBURGH, Edinburgh Map ref 6C2

★★★
SELF CATERING

Units **1**
Sleeps **1–2**

LOW SEASON PER WK
£378.00–£420.00

HIGH SEASON PER WK
£420.00–£560.00

Short breaks available all year 1-3 nights' stay. 10% discount on longer breaks of more than 10 days booked. Nightly prices also available from £54.00.

Aurora Apartment, Edinburgh

contact Jane Groombridge, 23 Pitcairn Road, Dundee DD3 9EE **t** +44 (0) 1382 810526
e jane.groombridge@blueyonder.co.uk

open All year
payment Cash, cheques, euros
nearest pub less than 0.5 miles
nearest shop less than 0.5 miles

Excellent standard modern, third-floor self-catering apartment. Your ideal Edinburgh city home to relax and unwind. Double bedroom (queen-size bed/twin), bath and shower, lounge, dining area and kitchenette. Quiet location with roof-top views. Free parking. Good local services. Facilities all-inclusive except personal needs and food.

SAT NAV EH14 1PJ

Unit 📺 🔲 🗄 🍳 🔩 🗄 🍴 🎛 ✳ General ⛵ 🏔 Ⓟ Ⓢ Leisure 🚴

EDINBURGH, Edinburgh Map ref 6C2

★★★★
SELF CATERING

Units **2**
Sleeps **1–4**

LOW SEASON PER WK
£260.00–£370.00

HIGH SEASON PER WK
£390.00–£640.00

City Nights, Edinburgh

contact Eleanor Simpson, 97 Market Street, Musselburgh EH21 6PY **t** +44 (0) 131 665 7140
e simpson@edinburgh-nights.co.uk

edinburgh-nights.co.uk

Two lovely ground-floor apartments in Edinburgh city centre. Lady Wynd, right beside Edinburgh Castle, sleeps three people. Terrars Croft, beautifully located by Holyrood Park, with private parking, sleeps four.

open All year
payment Credit/debit cards, cash, cheques, euros
nearest pub less than 0.5 miles
nearest shop less than 0.5 miles

Unit 📺 🆑 📻 🔲 🗄 🍳 🔩 🗄 🎛 ✳ General ⛵ 🏔 ⛳ Ⓟ Ⓢ 🐕

Do you have access needs?

Look for the National Accessible Scheme symbols if you have special hearing, visual or mobility needs. An index of accommodation participating in the scheme can be found at the back of this guide.

EDINBURGH, Edinburgh Map ref 6C2 — **CAMPING, CARAVAN & HOLIDAY PARK**

★★★★★
TOURING PARK
(197) £14.00–£26.60
(197) £14.00–£26.60
197 touring pitches

Special member rates mean you can save your membership subscription in less than a week. Visit our website to find out more.

THE CARAVAN CLUB

Edinburgh Caravan Club Site

35-37 Marine Drive, Edinburgh EH4 5EN **t** +44 (0) 131 312 6874

open All year
payment Credit/debit cards, cash, cheques

Situated to the north of the city on the Firth of Forth the site provides easy access to Edinburgh. It's a historic setting – yet Edinburgh is a friendly, modern, cosmopolitan city with something for everyone.

SAT NAV *EH4 5EN*

General · Leisure

FORT AUGUSTUS, Highland Map ref 7B3 — **HOTEL**

★★★
HOTEL

B&B PER ROOM PER NIGHT
S £70.00–£125.00
D £90.00–£270.00
HB PER PERSON PER NIGHT
Min £35.00

Quote VisitBritain for 10% discount on bed & breakfast rates throughout 2009 – some conditions may apply.

Lovat Arms, Hotel Bar Restaurant

Loch Ness, Fort Augustus PH32 4DU **t** +44 (0) 845 450 1100 & +44 (0) 1456 459250
e info@lovatarms-hotel.com

lovatarms-hotel.com GUEST REVIEWS · SPECIAL OFFERS · REAL-TIME BOOKING

open All year
bedrooms 23 double, 5 twin, 1 single
bathrooms All en suite
payment Credit/debit cards, cash, cheques

Come home to the Lovat with delicately offered contemporary comfort amidst traditional Victorian charm. Rosette-awarded kitchen, modern facilities and genuine hospitality are all complemented by attentive service. In addition, a biomass woodchip-burner and an acute environmental policy make the hotel a unique venue to Loch Ness.

SAT NAV *PH32 4DU* **ONLINE MAP**

Room · General P
Leisure

FORT WILLIAM, Highland Map ref 6B1 — **HOTEL**

★★
HOTEL

B&B PER ROOM PER NIGHT
S £45.00–£100.00
D £79.00–£160.00
HB PER PERSON PER NIGHT
£59.50–£120.00

Free child places 0-4 years. Half-price 5-14 years. Christmas and New Year breaks available. Special last-minute offers see website. Group discounts available.

Alexandra Hotel

The Parade, Fort William PH33 6AZ **t** +44 (0) 1397 702241 **e** salesalexandra@strathmorehotels.com

strathmorehotels.com SPECIAL OFFERS · REAL-TIME BOOKING

open All year
bedrooms 26 double, 44 twin, 12 single, 11 family
bathrooms All en suite
payment Credit/debit cards, cash, cheques

The Alexandra Hotel has been part of the very fabric of Fort William since 1876. Ideally situated in the centre of town, come and sample some traditional warm Scottish hospitality. Take advantage of free Leisure Club facilities at the nearby Ben Nevis Hotel.

SAT NAV *PH33 6AZ* **ONLINE MAP**

Room · General P · Leisure

Looking for a wide range of facilities?

More stars means higher quality accommodation plus a greater range of facilities and services.

FORT WILLIAM, Highland Map ref 6B1 — HOTEL

★★
HOTEL

Ben Nevis Hotel & Leisure Club

North Road, Fort William PH33 6TG t +44 (0) 1397 702331 e salesbennevis@strathmorehotels.dom

strathmorehotels.com SPECIAL OFFERS · REAL-TIME BOOKING

B&B PER ROOM PER NIGHT
S £45.00–£100.00
D £79.00–£150.00
HB PER PERSON PER NIGHT
£59.50–£120.00

Free child places 0-4 years. Half-price 5-14 years. Christmas and New Year breaks available. Special last-minute offers – see website. Group discounts available.

open All year
bedrooms 46 double, 45 twin, 18 single, 9 family
bathrooms All en suite
payment Credit/debit cards, cash, cheques

You will find the Ben Nevis Hotel & Leisure Club a great place to stay and relax. Sitting at the foot of Ben Nevis, the hotel provides a superb base from which to explore the beautiful Lochaber area. Enjoy free Leisure Club membership for the duration of your stay.

SAT NAV PH33 6TG **ONLINE MAP**

Room 🛗🖨📞📺🍴🥤♿ General 🐕🏧♿P🛜🍽🍷🎱🌙🕐🐾
Leisure 🛜🏊🏋🚫♿🌙🎵

GLASGOW, Glasgow Map ref 6B2 — SELF CATERING

★★★★
SELF CATERING

My Place in Glasgow

contact Mrs Lorna Nimmo, My Place in Glasgow, Glasgow t +44 (0) 7858 381583
e info@myplaceinglasgow.co.uk

myplaceinglasgow.co.uk GUEST REVIEWS · SPECIAL OFFERS

Units   **3**
Sleeps   **2–3**

LOW SEASON PER WK
Min £450.00

HIGH SEASON PER WK
Max £510.00

Stay by the night from just £75! Other special offers are occasionally available, please check our website.

open All year
payment Credit/debit cards, cash, cheques

Our luxury apartments, within the impressive former Sheriff Court building, at the heart of the Merchant City, are ideally located to explore the city. Each apartment consists of a fully fitted kitchen, living and dining area, double bedroom with king-sized bed, shower room and cloakroom. Free Wi-Fi access is provided.

SAT NAV G1 1DW **ONLINE MAP**

Unit 📺🆑🚿🖥💻🖨🍴🔥🍳🧺🧼❄ General 🐕🏧P🆂

INVERARAY, Argyll and Bute Map ref 6B1 — GUEST ACCOMMODATION

★★★★
GUEST HOUSE

Rudha-Na-Craige

The Avenue, Inveraray PA32 8YX t +44 (0) 1499 302668 e enquiries@rudha-na-craige.com

rudha-na-craige.com

B&B PER ROOM PER NIGHT
S Min £65.00
D £90.00–£118.00

EVENING MEAL PER PERSON
Min £24.00

Unwind in winter (Nov-Feb) stay 4 nights and only pay for 3, excludes public holidays, Christmas and New Year.

open All year
bedrooms 3 double, 1 single, 2 suites
bathrooms All en suite
payment Credit/debit cards, cash, cheques

Susan & Howard Spicer welcome you to their beautiful and historic home where the Duke of Argyll's ancestors once lived. Exceptional accommodation, great food, stunning Loch Fyne views, Inveraray centre nearby. An individual experience with a high standard of hospitality and comfort. Excellent base for touring Argyll and the Highlands.

SAT NAV PA32 8YX

Room 📺🥤🍴 General P🛜✖🍽❄ Leisure 🌙🎵🐾🚴

★★★
GUEST HOUSE

B&B PER ROOM PER NIGHT
S £25.00–£50.00
D £37.00–£60.00

3 nights for the price of 2 from Nov-Mar (some dates excluded).

Dunhallin House

164 Culduthel Road, Inverness IV2 4BH t +44 (0) 1463 220824 e info@dunhallin.co.uk

dunhallin.co.uk GUEST REVIEWS · SPECIAL OFFERS

open All year
bedrooms 3 double, 1 twin, 1 family
bathrooms All en suite
payment Credit/debit cards, cash, cheques

Dunhallin is an extremely comfortable modern house within easy reach of Inverness city centre. All rooms are en suite and the lounge has a selection of books, games and DVDs. Free internet access is available from our computer or Wi-Fi. Vegetarian and other diets catered for.

SAT NAV IV2 4BH **ONLINE MAP**

Room 📺 👜 ▯ General ☎10 P 📶 ⚡ 🍴 🎮 Leisure ∪ ♪ ▸ 🚲

★★★–★★★★★
SELF CATERING

Units **3**
Sleeps **4–6**

LOW SEASON PER WK
£160.00–£215.00

HIGH SEASON PER WK
£380.00–£510.00

Easter Dalziel Farm Cottages, Inverness

contact Neil and Marcia Pottie, Easter Dalziel Farm, Dalcross, Inverness IV2 7JL
t +44 (0) 1667 462213 e bwsg@easterdalzielfarm.co.uk

easterdalzielfarm.co.uk

open All year
payment Credit/debit cards, cash, cheques
nearest pub 4 miles
nearest shop 4 miles

Set amidst farmland with its abundant wildlife and our hairy Highland cattle, these three traditional stone cottages provide a superb base. Panoramic views, central location for castle and whisky trails, golfing, touring, and family holidays. Mostly ground-floor accommodation. All linen included. Long or short breaks? You're welcome all year.

SAT NAV IV2 7JL

Unit 📺 📀 🖥️ ▯ 🍽️ 🐾 ❄ General ☎ 🏛 ♨ P Ⓢ 🐕

See under Portree

★★★★
SELF CATERING

Units **3**

LOW SEASON PER WK
£260.00–£300.00

HIGH SEASON PER WK
£355.00–£390.00

Short breaks available Nov-Apr. Gold award under the Green Tourism Business Scheme. Textile art workshops held on site.

Burnbrae Holidays, Nr Kelso

contact Sam and Pat Lewis, Burnbrae Mill, Nenthorn, Kelso TD5 7RY t +44 (0) 1573 225570
e vbr@burnbraehol.co.uk

burnbraehol.co.uk GUEST REVIEWS · SPECIAL OFFERS · REAL-TIME BOOKING

open All year
payment Credit/debit cards, cash, cheques, euros
nearest pub 3 miles
nearest shop 3 miles

Three light and airy cottages. Warm and comfortable all seasons. Breakfast in your south-facing conservatory, explore the glorious Borders coast and countryside, then relax in front of your log fire. Nearby are magnificent stately homes, including Floors Castle and Mellerstain, and the ancient abbey towns of Kelso, Jedburgh and Melrose.

Unit 📺 📀 🖥️ 🍽️ ▯ 🐾 ❄ 🔌 General ☎ 🏛 ♨ P ⚪ Ⓢ 🐕 Leisure ∪▸

KINLOCH RANNOCH, Perth and Kinross Map ref 6C1

★★★–★★★★★
SELF CATERING

Units **9**
Sleeps **2–8**

LOW SEASON PER WK
£305.00–£473.00

HIGH SEASON PER WK
£537.00–£880.00

Late-availability discount available.

Dunalastair Holiday Houses, Kinloch Rannoch

contact Mrs Melanie Macintyre, Dunalastair Holiday Houses, 2 The Walled Gardens, Donavourd, Pitlochry PH16 5JS t +44 (0) 1796 474179 e cottages@dunalastair.com

dunalastair.com GUEST REVIEWS · SPECIAL OFFERS · REAL-TIME BOOKING

open All year
payment Credit/debit cards, cheques
nearest pub 2.5 miles
nearest shop 2.5 miles

Hidden amidst magnificent Highland scenery, our nine secluded holiday homes are fully equipped with your comfort in mind, including cosy log fires. They make a great base for sightseeing, and there is a huge variety of activities in the area to suit everyone. Children and pets are most welcome.

SAT NAV PH16 5PD ONLINE MAP

Unit 📺 🖥 💻 🗄 🍳 🌀 🔥 ❄ General 🛒 🍴 ♿ P S 🐕 Leisure ✎ U ♪ ▶ 🚲

KINROSS, Perth and Kinross Map ref 6C2

★★
GUEST HOUSE

B&B PER ROOM PER NIGHT
D £50.00–£80.00

Roxburghe Guest House

126 High Street, Kinross KY13 8DA t +44 (0) 1577 862498 e guests@roxburgheguesthouse.co.uk

roxburgheguesthouse.co.uk

The Roxburghe has five bedrooms, from double, twin and family rooms. Although there are no en suite facilities, the rooms each have hospitality tray, television and hairdryer. Outstanding breakfast and award-winning garden.

open All year
bedrooms 1 double, 2 twin, 2 family
payment Credit/debit cards, cash, cheques

Room ♿ 📺 💈 🍳 General 🛒 P 🍴 🐕 Leisure ♪ ▶ 🚲

KIRKCALDY, Fife Map ref 6C2

★★★
BED & BREAKFAST

B&B PER ROOM PER NIGHT
S £35.00–£50.00
D £56.00–£64.00

Scotties B&B

15 Bennochy Road, Kirkcaldy KY2 5QU t +44 (0) 1592 268596 e bhscott43@msn.com

scottiesbandb.co.uk

open All year
bedrooms 3 twin
bathrooms All en suite
payment Credit/debit cards, cash, cheques

Recently refurbished to a high standard, a friendly, comfortable and clean non-smoking establishment. Near all amenities, town centre, bus and rail stations. Three twin rooms have flat screen TV/DVD players, hospitality trays, complimentary safes, internet access (for guests' own laptops), and radio/alarm clocks. Own keys and private parking.

SAT NAV KY2 5QU

Room ♿ 📺 SC 💈 🍳 General 🛒 🍴 ♿ P 🌀 🍴 Leisure U ♪

Check the maps for accommodation locations

Colour maps at the front pinpoint all the places where accommodation is featured within the regional sections of this guide. Pick your location and then refer to the place index at the back to find the page number.

KIRKWALL, Orkney Islands Map ref 7D1 — SELF CATERING

★★★★
SELF CATERING

Units **2**
Sleeps **2–4**

LOW SEASON PER WK
£250.00–£350.00

HIGH SEASON PER WK
£375.00–£475.00

During off-peak season you can book for short breaks or long weekends.

Scapa Flow Chalets, Kirkwall

contact Mrs Shona Drever, Verona, Holm Branch Road, Kirkwall KW15 1RY t +44 (0) 1856 874106
e info@scapaflow-chalets.co.uk

scapaflow-chalets.co.uk SPECIAL OFFERS · REAL-TIME BOOKING

open All year
payment Cash, cheques
nearest pub less than 0.5 miles
nearest shop 0.5 miles

Scapa Flow Chalets are newly built in 2007, situated in Kirkwall in a quiet peaceful residential location, ten minutes' walk from the town centre and all local amenities. The chalets comprise two bedrooms, kitchen, lounge and modern shower room.

SAT NAV KW15 1RL **ONLINE MAP**

Unit 📺 📀 🖥. 🗄🔥 🍴🔌🍽🧺💧❄ General 🐾 P Leisure ▶ 🚴

KIRRIEMUIR, Angus Map ref 6C1 — SELF CATERING

★★★★
SELF CATERING

Units **3**
Sleeps **2–8**

LOW SEASON PER WK
£250.00–£300.00

HIGH SEASON PER WK
£390.00–£580.00

Short breaks available Oct–Mar.

Crawford Cottages, Angus Glens

contact Mrs Kathleen J Smith, Crawford Park, Mid Road, Northmuir, Kirriemuir DD8 4PJ
t +44 (0) 1575 572655 e kathleen@crawfordcottages.co.uk

crawfordcottages.co.uk GUEST REVIEWS · SPECIAL OFFERS · REAL-TIME BOOKING

open All year
payment Credit/debit cards, cash, cheques, euros
nearest pub 3 miles
nearest shop 3 miles

Bonny glens, quaint castles, lochs and welcoming hospitality await you in this beautiful part of Scotland. Luxury holiday cottages with spacious accommodation enjoying breathtaking views of the Angus glens. Safe play area with trampoline and paddling pool. Wi-Fi. Close to local amenities and within easy reach of wonderful beaches, munros and many local attractions.

ONLINE MAP

Unit 📺 SC 📀 🖥. 🗄🔥 🍴🔌🍽🧺💧❄🔥🧹 General 🐾 🛏♿P ⭕ S 🐕
Leisure ✎ ♨ 🏊 ♪ ▶ 🚴

LOCHINVER, Highland Map ref 7B2 — GUEST ACCOMMODATION

★★★★★
BED & BREAKFAST

B&B PER ROOM PER NIGHT
S £100.00–£120.00
D £100.00–£180.00

EVENING MEAL PER PERSON
£25.00–£45.00

Honeymoon holidays. Exclusive Red Deer Stalking packages. Fabulous Fishing holidays. Wonderful Winter breaks. Special Spring short stays.

Ruddyglow Park Country House

Loch Assynt, By Lairg, Sutherland IV27 4HB t +44 (0) 1571 822216 e info@ruddyglowpark.com

ruddyglowpark.com GUEST REVIEWS · SPECIAL OFFERS

open All year
bedrooms 2 double, 1 twin, 1 suite
bathrooms 2 en suite, 2 private
payment Credit/debit cards, cash, cheques, euros

Ruddyglow Park is a small, boutique country house, nestled between the foothills of Quinag and the edge of Loch Assynt in the beautiful north-west Highlands of Scotland. We offer outstanding personal service and luxurious accommodation all set against a backdrop of lovely antique furniture, original paintings and individually designed rooms.

SAT NAV IV27 4HB **ONLINE MAP**

Room ♿ 📺 SC ☕ 🍵 General 🐾 14 P 🎱 ♨ ✕ 🛁 💧 🐕 Leisure ♪ ▶ 🚴

LONGHOPE, Orkney Islands Map ref 7C1   **SELF CATERING**

★★★★
SELF CATERING

Cantick Head Lighthouse Cottages, Longhope, Island of Hoy

Units **2**
Sleeps **1–4**

contact Ms C H Willers, Cantick Head Lighthouse, Longhope, Island of Hoy, Orkney KW16 3PQ
t +44 (0) 1856 701255 **e** cantick@gmail.com

orkneylighthouse.com GUEST REVIEWS · SPECIAL OFFERS

LOW SEASON PER WK
£325.00–£475.00

HIGH SEASON PER WK
£400.00–£575.00

3- or 4-night mini-breaks usually available Sep-May excl Christmas and New Year weeks.

open All year
payment Cash, cheques
nearest pub 2 miles
nearest shop 4 miles

Truly stunning panoramic sea and island views! Stevenson-designed lightkeeper's homes situated in one acre of walled grounds overlooking Cantick Sound and the southern entrance to Scapa Flow. Dramatic scenery, bird, marine and plant life in abundance. Two cottages sleeping one to four in two doubles and one to three in a double and single.

ONLINE MAP

Unit 📺 ⅏ 🖥️ 🔲 ⅏ ⅏ ⅏ ⅏ ⅏ ☀ 🜨 General ⅏ 12 P ⅏ S Leisure ⅏ ⅏

MELROSE, Scottish Borders Map ref 6C2   **CAMPING, CARAVAN & HOLIDAY PARK**

★★★★★
TOURING PARK

Gibson Park Caravan Club Site

🚐 (60) £14.00–£26.60
🚌 (60) £14.00–£26.60
Å on application
60 touring pitches

High Street, Melrose TD6 9RY **t** +44 (0) 1896 822969

caravanclub.co.uk

Special member rates mean that you can save your membership subscription in less than a week. Visit our website to find out more.

open All year
payment Credit/debit cards, cash, cheques

Peaceful, award-winning site on edge of town. Adjacent tennis courts and playing fields. Melrose Abbey, where Robert the Bruce's head is buried, is within walking distance. Non-members welcome.

SAT NAV TD6 9RY

THE
CARAVAN
CLUB

General ⅏ ⅏ ⅏ ⅏ WP ⅏ ⅏ 🐾 ☀ Leisure ⅏ ⅏ ▶

MONTROSE, Angus Map ref 6D1   **HOTEL**

★★★
HOTEL

Park Hotel

61 John Street, Montrose DD10 8RJ **t** +44 (0) 1674 663400 **e** reservations@parkmontrose.com

parkmontrose.com SPECIAL OFFERS · REAL-TIME BOOKING

B&B PER ROOM PER NIGHT
S £55.00–£90.00
D £70.00–£115.00
HB PER PERSON PER NIGHT
£50.00–£135.00

Weekend breaks from £60pp B&B, minimum 2 nights, or £95 DB&B.

open All year except Christmas
bedrooms 20 double, 29 twin, 7 single, 1 family
bathrooms All en suite
payment Credit/debit cards, cash, cheques

The hotel is situated in the quiet Mid-Links area of Montrose yet only a few minutes' walk from the town centre, two excellent golf courses and the beach. It is an excellent base for golfing, fishing, walking, exploring the Angus Glens and castle, and Montrose itself.

SAT NAV DD10 8RJ

Room ⅏ ⅏ 📺 ⅏ ⅏ ⅏ General ⅏ ⅏ ⅏ P ⅏ ⅏ ⅏ ⅏ ⅏ ⅏ ☀ 🜨 Leisure ⅏ ▶

What shall we do today?

For ideas on places to visit, see the beginning of this regional section or go online at enjoyengland.com.

NAIRN, Highland Map ref 7C3 — HOTEL

★★★★
SMALL HOTEL

B&B PER ROOM PER NIGHT
S £69.00–£99.00
D £80.00–£140.00
HB PER PERSON PER NIGHT
£65.00–£95.00

Discounted rates for stays of 2 nights or more on a dinner, bed and breakfast basis.

Sunny Brae Hotel

Marine Road, Nairn IV12 4EA t +44 (0) 1667 452309 e vb@sunnybraehotel.com

sunnybraehotel.com GUEST REVIEWS · SPECIAL OFFERS

open All year except Christmas and New Year
bedrooms 4 double, 3 twin, 1 single
bathrooms All en suite
payment Credit/debit cards, cash, cheques

Stunning uninterrupted sea view from family-run, non-smoking, small hotel offering the highest standards of comfort and personal service. Cuisine prepared from fresh, local produce available in our Taste of Scotland-recommended restaurant. Close to Loch Ness, Cawdor Castle, Fort George, Whisky Trail and Moray Firth dolphins.

SAT NAV IV12 4EA

Room 👤 📞 📺 ♿ 🚻   General P 🅿 ♿ 🍽 ⚙ 🖥 ❄

NETHY BRIDGE, Highland Map ref 7C3 — HOTEL

★★★
HOTEL

B&B PER ROOM PER NIGHT
S £40.00–£100.00
D £79.00–£150.00
HB PER PERSON PER NIGHT
£59.50–£120.00

Free child places 0-4 years. Half-price 5-14 years. Christmas and New Year breaks available. Special last-minute offers – see website. Group discounts available.

Nethybridge Hotel

Nethy Bridge PH25 3DP t +44 (0) 1479 821203 e salesnethybridge@strathmorehotels.com

strathmorehotels.com SPECIAL OFFERS · REAL-TIME BOOKING

open All year
bedrooms 18 double, 37 twin, 8 single, 3 family
bathrooms All en suite
payment Credit/debit cards, cash, cheques

The Nethybridge Hotel is well known to generations of travellers. An hotel of Victorian splendour, it is set amidst the breathtaking beauty of the wooded slopes of the Cairngorm mountains. Central to Royal Deeside, Loch Ness and much, much more.

SAT NAV PH25 3DP ONLINE MAP

Room 👤 🛏 📞 📺 ♿ 🚻   General 🛋 🍴 P 🍽 🍽 ◑ 🖥 🍷 ❄ 🐾   Leisure ∪ ♪

OBAN, Argyll and Bute Map ref 6B1 — HOTEL

★★★
HOTEL

B&B PER ROOM PER NIGHT
S £40.00–£100.00
D £70.00–£150.00
HB PER PERSON PER NIGHT
£55.00–£120.00

Free child places 0-4 years. Half-price 5-14 years. Christmas and New Year breaks available. Special last-minute offers – see website. Group discounts available.

Royal Hotel 0 1631 563 021

Argyll Square, Oban PA34 4BE t +44 (0) 1631 563201 e salesroyaloban@strathmorehotels.com

strathmorehotels.com SPECIAL OFFERS · REAL-TIME BOOKING

open All year
bedrooms 17 double, 47 twin, 21 single, 5 family, 1 suite
bathrooms All en suite
payment Credit/debit cards, cash, cheques

This Victorian hotel is situated in the centre of Oban and overlooks the town square, with the harbour and train station nearby. An ideal base to explore the surrounding West Coast and Isles! The hotel offers traditional Scottish hospitality within quality, modern surroundings.

SAT NAV PA34 4BE ONLINE MAP

Room 🛏 📞 📺 ♿ 🚻   General 🛋 🍴 P 🅿 🍽 🍽 ◑ 🖥 🍷 🐾   Leisure ♪

Do you have access needs?

Look for the National Accessible Scheme symbols if you have special hearing, visual or mobility needs.

OBAN, Argyll and Bute Map ref 6B1 — GUEST ACCOMMODATION

★★★★
BED & BREAKFAST

B&B PER ROOM PER NIGHT
S £45.00–£55.00
D £58.00–£68.00

Don Muir Guest House

Crannaig A Mhinister, Pulpit Hill, Oban PA34 4LX **t** +44 (0) 1631 564536 **e** dina.donmuir@tesco.net

donmuir.co.uk GUEST REVIEWS

open All year except Christmas and New Year
bedrooms 3 double, 1 twin
bathrooms 3 en suite, 1 private
payment Cash, cheques

Situated in a quiet residential area, only three minutes' walk from Pulpit Hill view point which overlooks Oban Bay and surrounding islands. Modern, comfortable home providing genuine Highland hospitality. All rooms well equipped and upgraded to a very high standard. Don Muir is a ten-minute walk into town and to the ferry terminals. Known as the Gateway to the Islands.

SAT NAV *PA34 4LX* **ONLINE MAP**

Room ♿ 📺 🛁 🍵   General 🐴 P 📶 📠 ♿ 🐾   Leisure ∪ ♪ ⚲ 🚴

OBAN, Argyll and Bute Map ref 6B1 — GUEST ACCOMMODATION

★★★
BED & BREAKFAST

B&B PER ROOM PER NIGHT
S £25.00–£30.00
D £52.00–£70.00

EVENING MEAL PER PERSON
Max £22.00

Strumhor

Connel, By Oban PA37 1PJ **t** +44 (0) 1631 710167 **e** info@strumhor.co.uk

strumhor.co.uk

open All year except Christmas
bedrooms 1 double, 2 single, 1 suite
bathrooms 2 en suite, 2 private
payment Cash, cheques

Lochside accommodation with views over sea and hills. Friendly welcome with tea/coffee and home baking served in conservatory on arrival. Contemporary decor. Wide choice of home-cooked breakfasts and buffet. Evening meal available. Library and DVD collection for use of guests.

SAT NAV *PA37 1PJ* **ONLINE MAP**

Room ♿ 📺 🛁 🍵   General 🐴8 P 📶 ✕ 🍽 ❄   Leisure ∪ ♪

PERTH, Perth and Kinross Map ref 6C1 — HOTEL

★★
HOTEL

B&B PER ROOM PER NIGHT
S £40.00–£100.00
D £60.00–£150.00
HB PER PERSON PER NIGHT
£50.00–£120.00

Free child places 0-4 years. Half-price 5-14 years. Christmas and New Year breaks available. Special last-minute offers – see website. Group discounts available.

Salutation Hotel

34 South Street, Perth PH2 8PH **t** +44 (0) 1738 630066 **e** salessalutation@strathmorehotels.com

strathmorehotels.com SPECIAL OFFERS · REAL-TIME BOOKING

open All year
bedrooms 23 double, 41 twin, 16 single, 3 family, 1 suite
bathrooms All en suite
payment Credit/debit cards, cash, cheques

One of the oldest hotels in Scotland, the Salutation Hotel is situated in the very heart of the historic city of Perth, the Gateway to the Highlands. The welcome is warm and, through careful refurbishment, the hotel has retained its original charm and character.

SAT NAV *PH2 8PH* **ONLINE MAP**

Room 📶 📞 📺 🛁 🍵   General 🐴 🛗 📶 🍷 🍽 ◐ 🔲 ⎁ 🐾   Leisure ∪ ♪

What do the star ratings mean?

Detailed information about star ratings can be found at the back of this guide.

PITLOCHRY, Perth and Kinross Map ref 6C1

★★★
SELF CATERING

Units **1**
Sleeps **1–4**

LOW SEASON PER WK
£190.00–£260.00

HIGH SEASON PER WK
£290.00–£370.00

Tummel View, Pitlochry

contact Ross and Lynda Gardiner, 3 Knockard Avenue, Pitlochry PH16 5JE t +44 (0) 1796 472157
e tummelview@yahoo.co.uk

pitlochryselfcatering.co.uk

open All year
payment Cash, cheques
nearest pub less than 0.5 miles
nearest shop less than 0.5 miles

Comfortable modern semi-detached bungalow with excellent views over the Tummel Valley. In a quiet location about 500m from Pitlochry's main street. Owner-maintained with central heating, private parking and garden with garden furniture. Double bedroom and twin bedroom. Ideal for touring, walking, golfing and fishing, or just enjoying all the local attractions.

SAT NAV PH16 5HD

Unit TV 🖭 💻 🗪 🗇 🖳 🗓 ✱ General 🛋 🛏 ⚹ P Leisure ♪ ▸ 🚴

PITTENWEEM, Fife Map ref 6D2

★★★★★
SELF CATERING

Units **1**
Sleeps **4**

LOW SEASON PER WK
Min £595.00

HIGH SEASON PER WK
Min £950.00

Spindle Cottage, Pittenweem

contact Sue Foan, 18 Cecil Avenue, Queens Park, Bournemouth BH8 9EH t +44 (0) 1202 257914
e sue@spindlecottage.com

spindlecottage.com

open All year
payment Cash, cheques
nearest pub less than 0.5 miles
nearest shop less than 0.5 miles

Idyllic 18thC cottage in the centre of this charming, historic fishing village. The cottage has been completely and lovingly refurbished to the highest standards, incorporating beautiful soft furnishings, antiques and linens. The garden provides a delightful seating and dining area complete with barbecue. Sleeps four adults. St Andrews ten miles.

SAT NAV KY10 2QB **ONLINE MAP**

Unit TV SC 🖭 🗪 💻 🖳 🗓 🗇 🖳 🗓 ✱ 🚿 ∅ General P Leisure ♪ ▸ 🚴

PORTREE, Highland Map ref 7B3

★★★
BED & BREAKFAST

B&B PER ROOM PER NIGHT
S £25.00–£30.00
D £46.00–£55.00

Carnbeag

Earlish, By Portree, Isle of Skye IV51 9XL t +44 (0) 1470 542398 e carnbeag@btinternet.com

carnbeag.co.uk

Modern house located half a mile from Uig. Ideal for the Western Isles ferry and only a 20-minute drive from Portree. An ideal base for touring Skye.

open All year except Christmas and New Year
bedrooms 1 double, 1 twin, 1 single
bathrooms 2 en suite, 1 private
payment Cash, cheques

Room 🛋 TV SC 🛉 🗪 General 🛏 P

Need some ideas?

Big city buzz or peaceful panoramas? Take a fresh look at England and you may be surprised at what's right on your doorstep. Explore the diversity online at enjoyengland.com

★★★★
SELF CATERING

Units **1**
Sleeps **2–6**

LOW SEASON PER WK
£280.00–£425.00

HIGH SEASON PER WK
£475.00–£625.00

Short breaks available Nov-Mar, 3 nights minimum.

Gleniffer House, Portree

contact Mrs C Rohwer, Cedar Mount, 5 Waterend, Brompton, Northallerton DL6 2RN
t +44 (0) 1478 612048 e rohwersafaris@hotmail.com

selfcatering-isleofskye-scotland.com

open All year
payment Cash, cheques
nearest pub less than 0.5 miles
nearest shop less than 0.5 miles

Magnificent seafront location, spectacular views over to Isle of Raasay and the bay. Spacious three-storey stone-fronted Georgian house, beautifully furnished and fully equipped. Large lounge, kitchen, study and utility room. Three bedrooms, two baths, one en suite. Walking distance to shops, bars, restaurants, swimming pool and gym. Seafront garden and parking.

SAT NAV DL6 2RN

Unit 📺 ▦ ▣ ▪ 🛏 🍽 🔘 🖥 📶 🛁✿⌀ General 🛋 ♨ P 🐾 Leisure 🎣 ∪ ⤵ 🚶 🚴

★★★★
SELF CATERING

Units **4**
Sleeps **2–5**

LOW SEASON PER WK
£250.00–£375.00

HIGH SEASON PER WK
£375.00–£600.00

Longer lets considered Oct to end Mar, prices on application. Short breaks available, minimum 3 days Fri to Mon, Mon to Fri.

Stirling Flexible Lettings, Stirling

contact Mrs Fiona Graham, c/o Mackeanston House, Doune FK16 6AX t +44 (0) 1786 850213
e info@stirling-flexible-lettings.co.uk

stirling-flexible-lettings.co.uk SPECIAL OFFERS

open All year
payment Credit/debit cards, cash, cheques
nearest pub 1 mile
nearest shop 1 mile

Outstanding selection of town-centre and rural accommodation for holiday or business rentals. Close to Loch Lomond National Park, Stirling Castle, Wallace Monument and Falkirk Wheel. Golf courses, hill walking, Sustrans cycle network. Edinburgh, Glasgow, Perth within one hour. Wireless broadband in all properties. Sleep two to five.

Unit 📺 🆂 ▦ ▣ ▪ 🛏 🍳 🔘 🖥 📶☀♨⌀ General 🛋 ♨ 🅿 P 🅾 🆂 🐾
Leisure 🎣 ⚲ ∪ ⤵ 🚶 🚴

★★★★
SELF CATERING

Units **1**
Sleeps **1–6**

LOW SEASON PER WK
£350.00–£455.00

HIGH SEASON PER WK
£455.00–£550.00

Short breaks available Oct-Apr, 3-night stay.

Springfield Cottage, Stromness

contact Mrs Sandra Deans, Byvagen, Garson Drive, Stromness, Orkney KW16 3JG
t +44 (0) 1856 850776 & +44 (0) 7917 196906 e enquiries@orkneyholidayhomes.co.uk

orkneyholidayhomes.co.uk GUEST REVIEWS · SPECIAL OFFERS

open All year
payment Cash, cheques
nearest pub 1.5 miles
nearest shop 1.5 miles

Beautifully renovated three-bedroom former croft house set in a delightful rural setting. Elevated position offers panoramic views over marshland teeming with wildlife. Stunning scenic trails and fishing available on your doorstep. Peaceful location, yet within two miles of the amenities offered by the picturesque harbour town of Stromness.

SAT NAV KW16 3HT ONLINE MAP

Unit 📺 🆂 ▦ ▣ ▪ 🛏 🍳 🔘 🖥 📶✿⌀ General 🛋 ♨ 🅿 P 🅾 🆂 Leisure ⤵ 🚴

THURSO, Highland Map ref 7C1 — HOTEL

★★★
SMALL HOTEL

B&B PER ROOM PER NIGHT
S Min £48.00
D £40.00–£88.00

Come off-season weekends for bargain rates.

Park Hotel

Thurso KW14 8RE **t** +44 (0) 1847 893251 **e** reception@parkhotelthurso.co.uk

parkhotelthurso.co.uk SPECIAL OFFERS · REAL-TIME BOOKING

open All year
bedrooms 10 double, 8 twin, 1 single, 2 family
bathrooms All en suite
payment Credit/debit cards, cash, cheques

Family-run 21-bedroomed hotel in small town of Thurso. Ideal base to tour north of Scotland and Orkney Isles. See Castle of Mey, John o' Groats, Cape Wrath or any of the many distilleries and castles. Green Tourism Gold Award. Disabled facilities.

SAT NAV *KW14 8RE* **ONLINE MAP**

Room 🛁 📞 📺 SC ♨ 🍴 🦽 🔌 General 🛏 🚪 ⬆ P 📶 ▮ 🍽 ◗ ⬤ ⬤ ✝ Leisure ⏏ ▶ 🚲

THURSO, Highland Map ref 7C1 — CAMPING, CARAVAN & HOLIDAY PARK

★★★★★
TOURING PARK

🚐 (57)   £12.20–£25.10
🚌 (57)   £12.20–£25.10
57 touring pitches

Dunnet Bay Caravan Club Site

Dunnet, Thurso KW14 8XD **t** +44 (0) 1847 821319

caravanclub.co.uk

open April to October
payment Credit/debit cards, cash, cheques

A good place for those who like to be solitary. Views to Dunnet Head, northernmost point of mainland Britain. Good for bird-watching and fishing.

SAT NAV *KW14 8XD*

Special member rates mean you can save your membership subscription in less than a week. Visit our website to find out more.

THE **CARAVAN CLUB**

General 🔌 📤 WP 📻 ◻ ✝ Leisure ⏏

Where can I find accessible accommodation?

If you have special hearing, visual or mobility needs, there's an index of National Accessible Scheme participants featured in this guide.

For more accessible accommodation buy a copy of Easy Access Britain available online at visitbritaindirect.com, and from Tourism for All on 0845 124 997 or visit tourismforall.org.uk.

TYNRON, Dumfries & Galloway Map ref 6C3 — SELF CATERING

Rating Applied For
SELF CATERING

| Units | 1 |
| Sleeps | 4 |

LOW SEASON PER WK
£255.00–£350.00

HIGH SEASON PER WK
£475.00–£575.00

Short breaks available Oct-Mar, 3-night stay.

Millhouse Cottage, Tynron
contact Mr M Zetland, PO Box 10799, London N10 2BA t +44 (0) 7765 252760
e mzetland@hotmail.com

millhousecottage.net

open All year
payment Credit/debit cards, cash, cheques, euros
nearest pub 2 miles
nearest shop 2 miles

The Millhouse is set in the picturesque hamlet of Tynron, which lies between the villages of Moniaive and Penpont. Relatively untouched by modern progress, Tynron has a peaceful, green and natural environment. There are many walks and cycle trails to explore, much wildlife to see and fantastic, clean, country air to breathe.

Unit 📺 🆂🅲 ⧉ 🖥 🕹 ▣ 🗄 🍳 🔲 🍽 🎮 📷 ❄ ⚲ 🌀 General 🐕1 🏠 🔥 P 🄾 🆂 🐴
Leisure 🎣 🏖 🚲

WIGTOWN, Dumfries & Galloway Map ref 6B3 — GUEST ACCOMMODATION

★★★
GUEST HOUSE

B&B PER ROOM PER NIGHT
S £35.00–£40.00
D £60.00–£75.00

EVENING MEAL PER PERSON
Max £20.00

Free under-12 sharing with 2 adults during school holidays. 10% discount on 3+ nights throughout the year.

Hillcrest House
Maidland Place, Wigtown DG8 9EU t +44 (0) 1988 402018 e info@hillcrest-wigtown.co.uk

hillcrest-wigtown.co.uk GUEST REVIEWS · REAL-TIME BOOKING

open All year
bedrooms 3 double, 2 twin, 1 family
bathrooms All en suite
payment Credit/debit cards, cash, cheques

Lovely Victorian villa set on the southerly edge of Scotland's National Book Town. Bright, airy rooms with open views over Wigtown Bay and beyond. Six en suite rooms, lounge and licensed dining room. Excellent B&B accommodation, and winner of Scottish Hotel of the Year – Local Flavours Food Award 2008. Secure storage and kennels available.

SAT NAV *DG8 9EU* **ONLINE MAP**

Room 🛗 📺 ♿ 🍵 General 🐕 🏠 🔥 P 🍷 ✕ 🍴 ❄ 🐴 Leisure 🎣

Do you like visiting gardens?

Discover Britain's green heart with this easy-to-use guide. Featuring a selection of the most stunning gardens in the country, The Gardens Explorer is complete with a handy fold-out map and illustrated guide.

You can purchase the Explorer series from good bookshops and online at visitbritaindirect.com.

Wales

Clockwise: Whitesands Bay, Pembrokeshire; Brecon Beacons, Powys; Caernarfon Castle, Gwynedd

Great days out

For a small country Wales is big on things to see and do. We're not just talking about mountains, valleys and beaches – culture, exercise, adventure and tranquillity are here too. Land of legend, land of song, it's rich with heritage, and it looks forward with exciting city living and attractions.

Breathing spaces

Fill your lungs with fresh air and feast your eyes on the exhilarating scenery! A quarter of Wales is covered by **National Parks** and **Areas of Outstanding Natural Beauty**. And that's a lot of space to explore, as well as stretches of **Heritage Coast** and hundreds of nature and wildlife reserves. Savour the contrasts in the three National Parks: conquer Snowdonia's **Mount Snowdon** by foot, or

Snowdon Mountain Railway, Snowdonia

railway, it'll certainly put you in high spirits. Ramble the famous Welsh 'green, green grass' in the **Brecon Beacons** – there are plenty of ups and downs for mountain bikers, too, or take a leap paragliding. What a buzz! Mosey along to **Pembrokeshire Coast's** big beaches and little coves, ideal for family fun and wildlife watching.

Take a dip

Did you know: Wales has lots of water! To swim, paddle, surf, sail, coasteer, white-water raft and fish – 750 miles of coast, nearly 500 lakes and reservoirs, and around 15,000 miles of rivers and canals. Saddle up and gallop over the beach on **Carmarthen Bay**, spot bottlenose dolphins along the coast of **Cardigan Bay**. And don't forget seaside treats like cockles and laverbread. Another day, simply relax on a canal boat, or ambling the river meadows, woods and villages of the **Wye Valley**. In many places you can even play a round of golf beside the sea – Llyn's amazing clifftop Nefyn & District course, Gwynedd, is unforgettable.

Iron ring or fairytale?

Throughout Wales you'll encounter prehistoric, Roman and Norman sites, but nothing tells the story of the land's turbulent and thrilling past like its castles. There were around 641 at the last count ranging from war-torn ruins to whimsical fancies. Seek out King Edward I's 13thC 'iron ring' of fortresses in the north, including the World Heritage Sites of **Caernarfon** and **Beaumaris**. You simply have to admire the ingenious 'walls within walls' design of Beaumaris – state of the defensive art at the time. Castles like **Chirk** near Wrexham, transformed from a 14thC fortress into an elegant mansion home, reveal how life has changed. And turreted **Castell Coch**, hidden in woodlands overlooking a gorge in the Taff Valley, is the ultimate fairytale castle: a flamboyant Victorian vision of the Middle Ages replete with dazzling interiors and fantastic furnishings.

Left to right: National Botanic Garden of Wales, Carmarthenshire; Powis Castle, Powys

did you know... the unique Snowdon Lily has survived on Mount Snowdon for 10,000 years?

Inspiring gardens

Wales' gardens dazzle, too, showcasing a breathtaking diversity. Include on your must-see list the world-famous Italianate terraces with enormous clipped yews and statuary beneath medieval **Powis Castle**. Stroll the enchanting cloister, pool and walled gardens at **Aberglasney**, tucked away in the lovely Tywi Valley and an inspiration to poets since 1477. The woods and lakes at exotic **Portmeirion Village and Gardens** are wonderfully relaxing. And there's something for everyone at the **National Botanic Garden of Wales**, Llanarthne – from Bog and Japanese gardens to an Apothecaries' Garden. Travel through continents in a few steps in the Great Glasshouse, past thousands of Mediterranean-climate plants.

Capital attractions

Join the cafe culture and enjoy shopping in one of the many attractive arcades in Cardiff. Check out sporting fixtures or concerts at the iconic **Millennium Stadium**, too. Wales' capital is a sassy place, no more so than along the revitalised waterfront of **Cardiff Bay** – take a look at superb landmarks like the **Millennium Centre** for arts and performance plus the Senedd, Wales' National Assembly. Drop into historic **Cardiff Castle** or the treasure-filled **National Museum and Gallery**, and do browse the speciality shops of the glass-canopied Victorian and Edwardian arcades. Welsh kilt, anyone?

Millennium Centre, Cardiff

Iechyd da!

It means 'cheers' or 'good health' (say, 'yekkee-da') – you'll hear it in friendly pubs up and down. Welsh is a Celtic language and a lyrical, living part of the country's heritage, making the principality just that bit different. For a colourful celebration of Welsh culture visit the **National Eisteddfod**, on the outskirts of Bala in 2009. Or head for **Swansea**, sandy city by the sea, and share the life of its world-famous son at the Dylan Thomas Centre.

Music, of course, resounds countrywide – join the cosmopolitan gathering at **Llangollen International Musical Eisteddfod** in July, or tap your foot to the super-cool sounds of **Brecon Jazz** in August. And make time to discover a land of legends. Begin at **St Davids**, Britain's smallest city, where the relics of Wales' patron saint are said to rest in the 12thC cathedral. Then get on the trail of King Arthur, wizards and dragons...

Family favourites

Wherever you go, there's plenty to enthral children (and fascinate parents, too). Wander around more than 40 authentic buildings from different eras at the **Museum of Welsh Life**, St Fagans, and see how people in the past worked and played. Tour underground at **Big Pit**, Blaenavon, to get a taste of mining, or take a scenic ride on the narrow-gauge **Ffestiniog Railway** – one of the charming Great Little Trains of Wales.

At the **Centre for Alternative Technology**, Machynlleth, you'll find the village of the future with lots of child-friendly exhibits and events throughout the year. Try the Carbon Gym to assess how 'green' your lifestyle is! For the wackiest day out, watch the extraordinary **World Bog Snorkelling Championships** near Llanwrtyd Wells on August Bank Holiday Monday. Muddee!

why not... enjoy some of Britain's best sunsets, at Whitesands Bay, Pembrokeshire?

Clockwise: St Davids Cathedral, Pembrokeshire; Ffestiniog Railway, Gwynedd; World Bog Snorkelling Championship, Powys

Destinations

Aberystwyth

This established and cosmopolitan holiday resort is home to many of Wales' cultural institutions – start by tracing your Welsh ancestors in Wales' literary treasure, the National Library of Wales. Situated on spectacular coastline, it's an ideal base for exploring hidden coves, sandy beaches and the striking and unspoilt countryside on its doorstep. Enjoy secluded walks along the Rheidiol and Ystwyth valleys or take a steam train from Aberystwyth up to the mysteriously named Devils Bridge, passing through some of the most rugged terrain of any railway in the United Kingdom.

Bangor

This university and cathedral city is located in a breathtaking landscape, with Snowdonia National Park to the south and the Isle of Anglesey to the north. The city centre combines historic atmosphere with the best of modern amenities. Visit the cathedral, founded on one of the earliest Christian settlements in Britain, or the restored Victorian pier, extending out into the Menai Straits and surrounded by traditional pubs and restaurants, or head further afield to explore local villages.

Caernarfon

This market town has a long and fascinating history: make its striking castle, built by Edward I, your first port of call. It's undoubtedly one of the most architecturally impressive castles in the country. Discover other evidence of the town's historical past including prehistoric remains and the ruins of Segontium, a Roman military fort. Take a ride on the scenic Welsh Highland Railway and explore the magnificent Snowdonia National Park.

Cardiff

The capital city of Wales has plenty to keep you entertained. One of the UK's top shopping destinations, it's a true shoppers' paradise – from pedestrian Queen Street to the city's network of Victorian and Edwardian arcades. You can find great gifts including handmade Welsh textiles, love spoons and rugby shirts in the arcades, as well as plenty of places to enjoy a drink and a bite to eat. Stroll through the regenerated Cardiff Bay and catch a performance at the spectacular Wales Millennium Centre. Cardiff Castle and the National Museum Wales are just two of the great attractions to visit in and around the city.

Cardiff Castle

Carmarthen

Legend suggests this is the birthplace of the wizard Merlin. Explore the remains of the Norman Castle, sample local delicacies such as Carmarthenshire Ham and Penclawdd Cockles in the indoor market, or visit on a Wednesday to experience the lively Farmers Market. The nearby National Botanic Garden of Wales is a must-see, where the largest single-span glasshouse in the world houses many endangered plant species. Aberglasney Gardens is also worthy of a visit – the secret past of this historic garden is only now being rediscovered.

National Park

Area of Outstanding Natural Beauty

Heritage Coast

National Trails
nationaltrail.co.uk

⑤ Sections of the National
Cycle Network
nationalcyclenetwork.org.uk

Holyhead

Anglesey ⑤

Bangor Conwy Prestatyn

Caernarfon ⑧ *Clwydian Range* OFFA'S DYKE PATH

⑧ SNOWDONIA **Llangollen**

Llŷn Peninsula Portmeirion

⑧ Welshpool
Machynlleth GLYNDWR'S WAY

⑧¹ ⑧¹
Aberystwyth Knighton

Rhayader
⑧

PEMBROKESHIRE COAST ⑧²
St Dogmaels Cardigan Llanwrtyd Wells
Whitesands Bay Fishguard ④⁷
④ PEMBROKESHIRE COAST PATH **BRECON BEACONS** ④²
St Davids ④ ④⁷ OFFA'S DYKE PATH
Milford Haven ④ Amroth Blaenafon ④² *Wye Valley*
Pembroke **Tenby** ④ ⑧ ④⁷ ④⁶ Sedbury
Swansea ④⁷ **Newport** ④
Gower ④
Cardiff

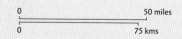

0   50 miles

0   75 kms

**For lots more great ideas visit
visitbritain.com/destinations
and visitwales.com**

Clockwise: Gower Peninsular; Swansea;
Celtic Manor Resort, Newport

Newport

Newport is a city of contrasts – where medieval cathedral and castle rub shoulders with exuberant Victorian architecture, and Roman walls and amphitheatre contrast with high-tech developments. Visit one of the last working transporter bridges in the world, tour the fascinating Roman site at Caerleon, or take in a show at the impressive new Riverfront Arts Centre. For golf lovers, there's the world-class Celtic Manor Resort, venue for the 2010 Ryder Cup.

St Davids

Britain's smallest city, located in the Pembrokeshire Coast National Park, has been a favourite destination for pilgrims, travellers and artists through the ages. Visit the starkly beautiful cathedral, reputedly founded on the site of St Davids 6th-century monastery and enjoy fresh local food in the highly-rated refectory. Walk coastal paths amid some of the finest natural scenery in Europe, relax on unspoilt beaches or take a boat trip to spot dolphins and whales.

Swansea

Wales' 'City by the Sea' is the only place in the UK where you can shop, eat out and enjoy a vibrant arts, entertainment and club scene yet be so close to an Area of Outstanding Natural Beauty. Visit the stunning new National Waterfront Museum or sample local delicacies such as cockles and laverbread at the largest indoor market in Wales. If you're looking for sun, sand and watersports, the beaches stretch from Swansea Bay to the rugged beauty of the Gower Peninsula.

Tenby

Tenby is a town steeped in ancient history, with a medieval heart, yet is a thoroughly modern holiday destination. With its miles of European Blue Flag-winning beaches, picturesque working harbour and rich heritage, Tenby mixes cosmopolitan style with traditional seaside fun. Take time out from the beach to wander the town walls, dating back as far as 1260, and to explore a wealth of historic buildings. What's more you are only minutes away from some of Pembrokeshire's finest attractions and the sweeping landscapes of the Pembrokeshire Coast National Park.

Tenby

Visitor attractions

Family and Fun

Anglesey Sea Zoo
Brynsiencyn, Isle of Anglesey
+44 (0) 1248 430411
angleseyseazoo.co.uk
Wales' largest marine aquarium.

Big Pit National Mining Museum of Wales
Blaenavon, Torfaen
+44 (0) 1495 790311
museumwales.ac.uk/en/bigpit
Travel 300ft underground guided
by an ex-miner.

Ffestiniog Railway
Porthmadog, Gwynedd
+44 (0) 1766 516000
festrail.co.uk
Heritage rail journey from coast
to mountains.

Gower Heritage Centre
Parkmill, Swansea
+44 (0) 1792 371206
gowerheritagecentre.co.uk
Family attraction on the beautiful
Gower peninsula.

King Arthur's Labyrinth
Corris, Gwynedd
+44 (0) 1654 761584
kingarthurslabyrinth.com
An underground boat trip through
spectacular caverns.

National Showcaves for Wales
near Abercraf, Powys
+44 (0) 1639 730284
showcaves.co.uk
Spectacular caves and children's
dinosaur park.

Welsh Highland Railway
Porthmadog, Gwynedd
+44 (0) 1766 51600
25miles of scenic 2ft steam rail
travel from Caernarfon to
Porthmadog.

Heritage

Abergavenny Museum & Castle
Abergavenny, Monmouthshire
+44 (0) 1873 854282
abergavennymuseum.co.uk
Local museum in grounds of
ruined fortress.

Beaumaris Castle
Beaumaris, Isle of Anglesey
+44 (0) 1443 336000
cadw.wales.gov.uk
Awesome, unfinished masterpiece
begun in 1295.

Caernarfon Castle and Town Walls
Caernarfon, Gwynedd
+44 (0) 1286 677617
cadw.wales.gov.uk
Medieval fortress, now a
World Heritage Site.

Carew Castle & Tidal Mill
Carew, near Tenby,
Pembrokeshire
+44 (0) 1646 651782
carewcastle.com
From Norman fortification to
Elizabethan country house.

Castell Coch
Cardiff
+44 (0) 29 2050 0200
cadw.wales.gov.uk
The ultimate fairytale castle.

Chirk Castle and Gardens
Chirk, Wrexham
+44 (0) 1691 777701
nationaltrust.org
Magnificent medieval fortress
of the Welsh Marches.

Powis Castle and Garden
Welshpool, Powys
+44 (0) 1938 551929
nationaltrust.org.uk
Wander the world-famous
terraced garden.

St Davids Cathedral
St Davids, Pembrokeshire
+44 (0) 1437 720199
stdavidscathedral.org.uk
Majestic 12thC cathedral with
6thC roots.

Indoors

Cardiff Bay Visitor Centre
Cardiff
+44 (0) 29 2046 3833
cardiffharbour.com
Interactive attraction housed in
stunning 'Tube' building.

Ceredigion Museum
Aberystwyth, Ceredigion
+44 (0) 1970 633088
museum.ceredigion.gov.uk
A fascinating chronicle of
local life.

Dylan Thomas Centre
Swansea
+44 (0) 1792 463980
dylanthomas.com
The life of Swansea's
world-famous son.

Inigo Jones Slate Works
Caernarfon, Gwynedd
+44 (0) 1286 830242
inigojones.co.uk
Engrave your own piece of slate.

The Museum of Modern Art, Wales
Machynlleth, Powys
+44 (0) 1654 703355
momawales.org.uk
Beautiful galleries set in historic
market town.

National Museum Wales

Cardiff
+44 (0) 29 2039 7951
museumwales.ac.uk
Dazzling displays of art and natural history.

National Waterfront Museum

Swansea
+44 (0) 1792 638950
waterfrontmuseum.co.uk
Inspirational museum of industrial and maritime history.

Swansea Museum

Swansea
+44 (0) 1792 653763
swansea.gov.uk/swanseamuseum
Treasure house of the ordinary and extraordinary.

Tenby Museum & Art Gallery

Tenby, Pembrokeshire
+44 (0) 1834 842809
tenbymuseum.org.uk
Discover the culture and heritage of Pembrokeshire.

Outdoors

Aberdulais Falls

Aberdulais, Neath Port Talbot
+44 (0) 1639 636674
nationaltrust.org.uk
Famous waterfalls and fascinating industrial site.

Aberglasney Gardens

Llangathen, Carmarthenshire
+44 (0) 1558 668998
aberglasney.org
Spectacular gardens set in beautiful Tywi valley.

Hafod Eryri

Snowdon Summit, Gwynedd
+44 (0) 871 720 0033
The new £8.3m visitor centre on the summit of Snowdon, Wales' highest mountain.

Museum of Welsh Life

St Fagans, Cardiff
+44 (0) 29 2057 3500
nmgw.ac.uk
One of Europe's foremost open-air museums.

National Botanic Garden of Wales

Llanarthney, Carmarthenshire
+44 (0) 1558 668768
gardenofwales.org.uk
Beautiful 500-acre gardens with Foster's Great Glasshouse.

Portmeirion Village and Gardens

Portmeirion, Gwynedd
+44 (0) 1766 770000
portmeirion-village.com
Italianate resort village built by Clough Williams-Ellis.

ASSURANCE OF A GREAT DAY OUT
Attractions with this sign participate in a quality assurance scheme.

Events 2009

St David's Day (Dydd Gwyl Dewi Sant)
1 Mar

Hay Festival of Literature
Hay-on-Wye
hayfestival.com
21 - 31 May

Celtic Manor Resort Wales Open
Newport
walesopen.com
4 - 7 Jun

Ryder Cup Wales Seniors Open
Royal Porthcawl Golf Club
rydercupwales2010.com
19 - 21 Jun

Llangollen International Musical Eisteddfod
Llangollen
international-eisteddfod.co.uk
7 - 12 Jul

The Ashes 2009 Series England v Australia
Swalec Stadium, Cardiff
glamorgancricket.com
8 - 12 Jul

Royal Welsh Show
Builth Wells
rwas.co.uk
20 - 23 Jul

National Eisteddfod of Wales
Bala
eisteddfod.org.uk
1 - 8 Aug

Brecon Jazz Festival
Brecon
breconjazz.co.uk
7 - 9 Aug

Bryn Terfel's Faenol Festival
Faenol Estate, Near Bangor
brynfest.com
28 - 31 Aug

Abergavenny Food Festival
Abergavenny
abergavennyfoodfestival.com
19 - 20 Sep

Dylan Thomas Festival
Swansea
dylanthomas.com
27 Oct - 9 Nov

Wales Rally GB
Cardiff, South & Mid Wales
walesrallygb.com
End of October

Regional contacts and information

For more information on accommodation, attractions, activities, events and holidays in Wales, contact the regional tourism organisation below. The website has a wealth of information and you can order or download publications.

Wales

For any further information contact:

Visit Wales
Brunel House, 2 Fitzalan Road,
Cardiff CF24 0UY
t +44 (0) 870 121 1251
   +44 (0) 870 121 1255 (minicom)
w visitwales.com

Clockwise: Ogmore Castle, Glamorgan; Plas Newydd, Denbighshire; Snowdonia; Mumbles, Swansea

Tourist Information Centres

When you arrive at your destination, visit a Tourist Information Centre for help with accommodation and information about local attractions and events, or email your request before you go.

Aberaeron	The Quay	+44 (0) 1545 570602	aberaerontic@ceredigion.gov.uk
Aberdulais Falls	The National Trust	+44 (0) 1639 636674	aberdulaistic@nationaltrust.org.uk
Aberdyfi*	The Wharf Gardens	+44 (0) 1654 767321	tic.aberdyfi@eryri-npa.gov.uk
Abergavenny	Monmouth Road	+44 (0) 1873 853254	abergavennyic@breconbeacons.org
Aberystwyth	Terrace Road	+44 (0) 1970 612125	aberystwythtic@ceredigion.gov.uk
Bala*	Pensarn Road	+44 (0) 1678 521021	bala.tic@gwynedd.gov.uk
Bangor*	Deiniol Road	+44 (0) 1248 352786	bangor.tic@gwynedd.gov.uk
Barmouth	Station Road	+44 (0) 1341 280787	barmouth.tic@gwynedd.gov.uk
Barry Island*	The Promenade	+44 (0) 1446 747171	barrytic@valeofglamorgan.gov.uk
Beddgelert*	Canolfan Hebog	+44 (0) 1766 890615	tic.beddgelert@eryri-npa.gov.uk
Betws y Coed	Royal Oak Stables	+44 (0) 1690 710426	tic.byc@eryri-npa.gov.uk
Blaenau Ffestiniog*	Unit 3, High Street	+44 (0) 1766 830360	tic.blaenau@eryri-npa.gov.uk
Blaenavon*	Church Road	+44 (0) 1495 742333	blaenavon.tic@torfaen.gov.uk
Borth*	Cambrian Terrace	+44 (0) 1970 871174	borthtic@ceredigion.gov.uk
Brecon	Cattle Market Car park	+44 (0) 1874 622485	brectic@powys.gov.uk
Bridgend	Bridgend Designer Outlet	+44 (0) 1656 654906	bridgendtic@bridgend.gov.uk
Builth Wells	The Groe Car Park	+44 (0) 1982 553307	builtic@powys.gov.uk
Caerleon	5 High Street	+44 (0) 1633 422656	caerleon.tic@newport.gov.uk
Caernarfon	Castle Street	+44 (0) 1286 672232	caernarfon.tic@gwynedd.gov.uk
Caerphilly	The Twyn	+44 (0) 29 2088 0011	tourism@caerphilly.gov.uk
Cardiff	The Old Library	+44 (0) 870 121 1258	visitor@cardiff.gov.uk
Cardigan	Bath House Road	+44 (0) 1239 613230	cardigantic@ceredigion.gov.uk
Carmarthen	113 Lammas Street	+44 (0) 1267 231557	carmarthentic@carmarthenshire.gov.uk
Chepstow	Bridge Street	+44 (0) 1291 623772	chepstow.tic@monmouthshire.gov.uk
Conwy	Castle Buildings	+44 (0) 1492 592248	conwytic@conwy.gov.uk
Dolgellau	Eldon Square	+44 (0) 1341 422888	tic.dolgellau@eryri-npa.gov.uk
Fishguard Harbour	The Parrog	+44 (0) 1348 872037	fishguardharbour.tic@ pembrokeshire.gov.uk
Fishguard Town	Market Square	+44 (0) 1437 776636	fishguard.tic@pembrokeshire.gov.uk
Harlech*	High Street	+44 (0) 1766 780658	tic.harlech@eryri-npa.gov.uk
Haverfordwest	Old Bridge	+44 (0) 1437 763110	haverfordwest.tic@ pembrokeshire.gov.uk

Holyhead	Stena Line, Terminal 1	+44 (0) 1407 762622	holyhead@nwtic.com
Knighton	West Street	+44 (0) 1547 528753	oda@offasdyke.demon.co.uk
Llanberis*	41b High Street	+44 (0) 1286 870765	llanberis.tic@gwynedd.gov.uk
Llandovery	Kings Road	+44 (0) 1550 720693	llandovery.ic@breconbeacons.org
Llandudno	Mostyn Street	+44 (0) 1492 876413	llandudnotic@conwy.gov.uk
Llanelli	North Dock	+44 (0) 1554 777744	DiscoveryCentre@ carmarthenshire.gov.uk
Llanfairpwllgwyngyll	Station Site	+44 (0) 1248 713177	llanfairpwll@nwtic.com
Llangollen	Castle Street	+44 (0) 1978 860828	llangollen@nwtic.com
Machynlleth	Penrallt Street	+44 (0) 1654 702401	mactic@powys.gov.uk
Merthyr Tydfil	14a Glebeland Street	+44 (0) 1685 379884	tic@merthyr.gov.uk
Milford Haven*	94 Charles Street	+44 (0) 1646 690866	milford.tic@pembrokeshire.gov.uk
Mold	Earl Road	+44 (0) 1352 759331	mold@nwtic.com
Monmouth	Agincourt Square	+44 (0) 1600 713899	monmouth.tic@monmouthshire.gov.uk
Mumbles	Mumbles Road	+44 (0) 1792 361302	info@mumblestic.co.uk
New Quay*	Church Street	+44 (0) 1545 560865	newquaytic@ceredigion.gov.uk
Newport	John Frost Square	+44 (0) 1633 842962	newport.tic@newport.gov.uk
Newport (pembs)*	Long Street	+44 (0) 1239 820912	newportTIC@pembrokeshire coast.org.uk
Oswestry Mile End	Mile End Services	+44 (0) 1691 662488	tic@oswestry-bc.gov.uk
Oswestry Town	2 Church Terrace	+44 (0) 1691 662753	ot@oswestry-welshborders.org.uk
Pembroke*	Commons Road	+44 (0) 1646 622388	pembroke.tic@pembrokeshire.gov.uk
Penarth*	Penarth Pier	+44 (0) 29 2070 8849	penarthtic@valeofglamorgan.gov.uk
Porthcawl*	John Street	+44 (0) 1656 786639	porthcawltic@bridgend.gov.uk
Porthmadog	High Street	+44 (0) 1766 512981	porthmadog.tic@gwynedd.gov.uk
Presteigne*	Broad Street	+44 (0) 1544 260650	presteignetic@powys.gov.uk
Pwllheli	Station Square	+44 (0) 1758 613000	pwllheli.tic@gwynedd.gov.uk
Rhyl	West Parade	+44 (0) 1745 355068	rhyl.tic@denbighshire.gov.uk
St Davids	1 High Street	+44 (0) 1437 720392	enquiries@ stdavids.pembrokeshirecoast.org.uk
Saundersfoot*	Harbour Car Park	+44 (0) 1834 813672	saundersfoot.tic@pembrokeshire.gov.uk
Swansea	Plymouth Street	+44 (0) 1792 468321	tourism@swansea.gov.uk
Tenby	Unit 2, The Gateway Complex	+44 (0) 1834 842402	tenby.tic@pembrokeshire.gov.uk
Tywyn*	High Street	+44 (0) 1654 710070	tywyn.tic@gwynedd.gov.uk
Welshpool	Church Street	+44 (0) 1938 552043	weltic@powys.gov.uk
Wrexham	Lambpit Street	+44 (0) 1978 292015	tic@wrexham.gov.uk

* seasonal opening

Help before you go

When it comes to your next break, the first stage of your journey could be closer than you think.

You've probably got a Tourist Information Centre nearby which is there to serve the local community – as well as visitors. Knowledgeable staff will be happy to help you, wherever you're heading.

Many Tourist Information Centres can provide you with maps and guides, and it's often possible to book accommodation and travel tickets too.

You'll find the address of your nearest centre in your local phone book, or look in the regional sections in this guide for a list of Tourist Information Centres.

where to stay in
Wales

All place names in the blue bands are shown on the maps at the front of this guide.

Accommodation symbols

Symbols give useful information about services and facilities. On pages 16 to 17 you can find a key to these symbols.

ABERAERON, Ceredigion Map ref 8A2 **CAMPING, CARAVAN & HOLIDAY PARK**

★★★★
HOLIDAY, TOURING
& CAMPING PARK

⊟ £15.00–£24.00
⊞ £15.00–£24.00
▲ £15.00–£24.00
100 touring pitches

Aeron Coast Caravan Park
North Road, Aberaeron SA46 0JF **t** +44 (0) 1545 570349 **e** enquiries@aeroncoast.co.uk

aeroncoast.co.uk REAL-TIME BOOKING

open March to October
payment Credit/debit cards, cash, cheques

We are privileged to be part of Aberaeron with its picturesque harbour, shops and restaurants. River and coastal walks. Quiet out of high season but good leisure provision for families in school holidays including entertainment every evening. Apart from laundry, all facilities on-site including entertainment are free of charge.

SAT NAV *SA46 0JF* **ONLINE MAP**

General 🚐 🔌 ⬦ 🚿 📶 🏠 📠 🛒 🐴 ☀ Leisure ⟡ 🍽 🎱 ⛰ ⚲ ∪ ⚓ ➤

ABERGAVENNY, Monmouthshire Map ref 8B3 **SELF CATERING**

★★★★
SELF CATERING

Units   **2**
Sleeps   **2–5**

LOW SEASON PER WK
£180.00–£280.00

HIGH SEASON PER WK
£200.00–£410.00

Tyr Pwll Holiday Cottages, Abergavenny
contact Steve Mear, 2 Tyr Pwll, Hardwick, Abergavenny NP7 9AB **t** +44 (0) 1873 850457
e stevemear@talktalk.net

tyr-pwll.co.uk

Two well-furnished and equipped former farm buildings, one with kitchen, bedroom (double bed), living room on ground level, one with double bedroom downstairs and family room upstairs (double and single bed).

open All year
payment Credit/debit cards, cash, cheques
nearest pub 0.5 miles
nearest shop 2 miles

Unit 📺 🆂🅲 🆅 💿 ▪ 🗄 🖥 ♨ 📁 ♨ General 🐕 🏠 🚶 P 🆂 Leisure ∪ ⚓ ➤

Where can I get help and advice?

Tourist Information Centres offer friendly help with accommodation and holiday ideas as well as suggestions of places to visit and things to do. You'll find contact details at the beginning of each regional section.

AXTON, Flintshire Map ref 8B1 GUEST ACCOMMODATION

★★★★★
GUEST ACCOMMODATION

B&B PER ROOM PER NIGHT
S £40.00–£50.00
D £60.00–£80.00

EVENING MEAL PER PERSON
£10.00–£20.00

Meadowcroft Guest House

Llanasa Road, Axton CH8 9DH t +44 (0) 1745 570785 e helen.morgan14@btinternet.com

meadowcroftguesthouse.net

open All year
bedrooms 2 double, 1 twin
bathrooms All en suite
payment Credit/debit cards, cash, cheques

This luxury guesthouse is in a peaceful, rural setting, 0.75 miles from the picturesque village of Llanasa but just four miles from the A55, with spectacular views over the Dee and Mersey estuaries. It is ideally situated for outings to Chester, Llandudno, Snowdonia and Anglesey.

SAT NAV CH8 9DH

Room 📺 ♿ 🍵 General 🦮 P 📶 ✕ 🍴 ❄ 🐾 Leisure ▶

BALA, Gwynedd Map ref 8B1 GUEST ACCOMMODATION

★★★★
BED & BREAKFAST

B&B PER ROOM PER NIGHT
S £37.50
D £65.00

The Railway Cottage

Frongoch, Bala LL23 7NT t +44 (0) 1678 520945 e ros.rhodes@virgin.net

therailwaycottage.net SPECIAL OFFERS

Quiet and peaceful location set in one acre of riverside garden in Snowdonia National Park. Close to National Whitewater Centre. Conservatory for guests' sole use. Ideal for a relaxing break. Single occupancy available.

open All year
bedrooms 1 double/twin/single
bathrooms En suite
payment Cash, cheques

Room ♿ 📺 🆑 ♿ 🍵 General 🦮 🏠 🏃 P 📶 🍴 ❄ Leisure ⌥ ▶ 🚴

BETWS-Y-COED, Conwy Map ref 8B1 GUEST ACCOMMODATION

★★★
GUEST HOUSE

B&B PER ROOM PER NIGHT
S £25.00–£35.00
D £50.00–£65.00

Discounts on longer stays.

Garth Dderwen

Vicarage Road, Betws-y-coed LL24 0AD t +44 (0) 1690 710491 e eifionmorris@btconnect.com

garth-dderwen.co.uk SPECIAL OFFERS · REAL-TIME BOOKING

open All year except New Year
bedrooms 3 double, 2 twin, 1 single
bathrooms 3 en suite, 3 private
payment Credit/debit cards, cash, cheques

Ideally situated for touring Snowdonia National Park, this detached Victorian B&B is in a quiet position in the centre of the village, close to restaurants, walks, fishing, mountain bike hire, golf course, horse riding etc. We have a private car park and bike store. A drying room is available – just in case!

SAT NAV LL24 0AD **ONLINE MAP**

Room ♿ 📺 ♿ 🍵 General 🦮9 P 🍴 ❄ Leisure ∪ ⌥ ▶ 🚴

Don't forget www.

Web addresses throughout this guide are shown without the prefix www. Please include www. in the address line of your browser. If a web address does not follow this style it is shown in full.

BETWS-Y-COED, Conwy Map ref 8B1 — SELF CATERING

★★★★
SELF CATERING

Units **1**
Sleeps **12**

LOW SEASON PER WK
£900.00–£1,470.00

HIGH SEASON PER WK
£1,470.00–£2,000.00

Cae Du, Dolwyddelan

contact Mr T Carter, 180 The Broadway, Wimbledon SW19 1RX t +44 (0) 20 8542 3480
e tim@caedu-cottage.co.uk

caedu-cottage.co.uk

open All year
payment Cash, cheques
nearest pub 0.5 miles
nearest shop 1 mile

Standing in 14 acres of undulating grass and woodlands, bounded by the River Lleder in the Snowdonia National Park close to Betws-y-coed. Cae Du comfortably accommodates 11/12 adults. There are six bedrooms, three twins, two doubles, one single with a small double bed. Two bedrooms have riverside balconies.

SAT NAV LL25 0LZ ONLINE MAP

Unit 📺 🆂 ⬚ ⬚ 🖥 ⬚⬚ ⬚⬚ ⬚ ⬚ ⬚ ⬚ ⬚ ☀ ⬚ General ⬚ P ◻ 🐴
Leisure ∪ ♪ ► 🚴

BRECON, Powys Map ref 8B3 — GUEST ACCOMMODATION

★★★★
GUEST HOUSE

B&B PER ROOM PER NIGHT
S £50.00
D £65.00–£75.00

Cantre Selyf

5 Lion Street, Brecon LD3 7AU t +44 (0) 1874 622904 e enquiries@cantreselyf.co.uk

cantreselyf.co.uk

open All year except Christmas and New Year
bedrooms 2 double, 1 twin
bathrooms All en suite
payment Cash, cheques

One of the oldest town houses in Brecon. Built in the 17th century to a grand design, retaining lots of original features, oak beams, moulded ceilings and fireplaces. Although in a central location, with its own parking, it is very quiet. Beautiful walled garden. Good selection of restaurants and shops within walking distance.

SAT NAV LD3 7AU

Room ⬚ ⬚ General P ⬚ ⬚ ☀ Leisure ∪ ♪ ► 🚴

BRECON, Powys Map ref 8B3 — SELF CATERING

★★★★
SELF CATERING

Units **3**
Sleeps **4–5**

LOW SEASON PER WK
£300.00–£360.00

HIGH SEASON PER WK
£500.00–£580.00

Short breaks available Nov–Mar, 3-night stay.

Carno Farm Self Catering, Brecon

contact June and Bob Scarbrough, Carno Farm, Libanus, Brecon LD3 8NF t +44 (0) 1874 625630
e enquiries@carnofarmbrecon.co.uk

carnofarmbrecon.co.uk GUEST REVIEWS · SPECIAL OFFERS

open All year
payment Cash, cheques, euros
nearest pub 2 miles
nearest shop 5 miles

In the heart of the Brecon Beacons National Park, nestling under Pen y Fan, circled by mountains, hills and fields. We offer guests a warm welcome to our lovingly restored 17thC cottages. Ideal for people of all ages interested in walking, cycling, birdwatching, or just relaxing. Pets welcome.

SAT NAV LD3 8NF ONLINE MAP

Unit 📺 🆂 ⬚ 🖥 ⬚⬚ ⬚ ⬚ ⬚ ⬚ ☀ ⬚ ⬚ General ⬚ ⬚ ⬚ P ◻ 🆂 🐴
Leisure ⬚ ∪ ♪ ► 🚴

BROAD HAVEN, Pembrokeshire Map ref 8A3 — SELF CATERING

★★★★★
SELF CATERING

Units **1**
Sleeps **1–4**

Morawelon, Broad Haven

contact Sandra Rollins, Lyndhurst, Spurlands End Road, Great Kingshill, High Wycombe HP15 6PE
t +44 (0) 1494 714612 e morawelon@tesco.net

morawelon.co.uk SPECIAL OFFERS

LOW SEASON PER WK
£245.00–£280.00

HIGH SEASON PER WK
£410.00–£695.00

Luxury holiday apartment on the seafront at
Broad Haven overlooking the safe, sandy beach.
Stunning sea views! Sleeps four in one double
and one twin bedroom. Short breaks outside main
season.

open All year
payment Cash, cheques, euros
nearest pub less than 0.5 miles
nearest shop less than 0.5 miles

Unit 📺 🔌 📼 🖥 🎛 🍳 🧺 🗄 General 🛋 P 🖨 🛎 Leisure ∪ ⚓ 🚲

BROAD HAVEN, Pembrokeshire Map ref 8A3 — CAMPING, CARAVAN & HOLIDAY PARK

★★★★★
TOURING &
CAMPING PARK

🚐 (62) £14.00–£16.00
🚍 (10) £14.00–£16.00
⛺ (10) £14.00–£17.50
🏠 (1) £250.00–£420.00
72 touring pitches

Creampots Touring Caravan & Camping Park

Broadway, Broad Haven, Haverfordwest SA62 3TU t +44 (0) 1437 781776
e creampots@btconnect.com

creampots.co.uk GUEST REVIEWS

Peaceful, quiet, immaculate, friendly, family-run
park in countryside, close to the National Park and
only 1.5 miles from Broad Haven and Littlehaven's
safe sandy beaches. Ideal central location. Large
pitches.

open March to November
payment Credit/debit cards, cash, cheques

General 🚗 📞 🅿 🍴 🛒 📖 🐕 ☼ Leisure ∪ ⚓ ►

BUILTH WELLS, Powys Map ref 8B2 — GUEST ACCOMMODATION

★★★★
GUEST ACCOMMODATION

B&B PER ROOM PER NIGHT
S £39.00–£44.00
D £58.00–£68.00

EVENING MEAL PER PERSON
Max £18.00

*The longer you stay,
the less you pay!*

Trericket Mill Vegetarian Guesthouse

Erwood, Builth Wells LD2 3TQ t +44 (0) 1982 560312 e mail@trericket.co.uk

trericket.co.uk

open All year except Christmas
bedrooms 2 double, 1 twin
bathrooms All en suite
payment Cash, cheques, euros

Historic water cornmill in the picturesque Upper
Wye Valley. Friendly and informal, log fires, cycle
lock-up, drying room, wholesome food. Brilliant base
for mountain biking, canoeing, hiking, horse-riding,
exploring the second-hand book town of Hay-on-
Wye, birdwatching and exploring the natural beauty
of the area.

SAT NAV LD2 3TQ ONLINE MAP

Room 🛏 🍴 General P 🌐 ✗ 🍽 ❄ Leisure ∪ ⚓ ► 🚲

Where can I find accessible accommodation?

If you have special hearing, visual or mobility needs, there's
an index of National Accessible Scheme participants featured
in this guide.

For more accessible accommodation buy a copy of
Easy Access Britain available online at visitbritaindirect.com,
and from Tourism for All on 0845 124 997 or visit
tourismforall.org.uk.

★★★★
GUEST ACCOMMODATION

Plas Dinas Country House

Bontnewydd, Caernarfon, Gwynedd LL54 7YF t +44 (0) 1286 830214 e info@plasdinas.co.uk

plasdinas.co.uk SPECIAL OFFERS · REAL-TIME BOOKING

B&B PER ROOM PER NIGHT
S £79.00–£159.00
D £89.00–£169.00

EVENING MEAL PER PERSON
£28.95–£33.95

Please check our website for details of reduced dinner, bed and breakfast rates, special breaks and Murder Mystery events.

open All year
bedrooms 8 double, 2 twin
bathrooms All en suite
payment Credit/debit cards, cash, cheques

The 400-year-old ancestral home of the Armstrong-Jones family, most notably Lord Snowdon and HRH Princess Margaret. Still retaining the feeling of a family country residence with original portraits, furniture and memorabilia. Ten individually designed luxury bedrooms. Roaring fire in the drawing room. 15 acres with beautiful views.

SAT NAV LL54 7YF **ONLINE MAP**

Room 🛏 🖨 ☎ 📺 ♿ 🍴 General P 🌐 🔥 🍷 ✗ 🎱 ❄ 🐴 Leisure ∪ ♣ ►

★★★★–★★★★★
SELF CATERING

Bryn Bras Castle, Nr Caernarfon

contact Mrs Marita Gray-Parry, Bryn Bras Castle, Llanrug, Caernarfon LL55 4RE
t +44 (0) 1286 870210 e holidays@brynbrascastle.co.uk

brynbrascastle.co.uk

Units **7**
Sleeps **2–4**

LOW SEASON PER WK
Min £500.00

HIGH SEASON PER WK
Max £900.00

Special pricing for short breaks available all year.

open All year
payment Credit/debit cards, cash, cheques
nearest pub 0.5 miles
nearest shop 1 mile

Unique, graciously appointed apartments including antiques, within Grade II* Listed Regency castle. Sleep two to four persons. Extensive tranquil grounds with fine views. Centrally situated for beautiful north Wales. Excellent pubs/restaurants nearby. Flexible start/depart days. No children. Peaceful and relaxing, ideal for couples. Rents fully inclusive, including breakfast hamper.

SAT NAV LL55 4RE

Unit 📺 📼 🖥 🍷 🍴 📁 ❄ General Ⓢ Leisure ∪ ♣ ► 🚲

★★
GUEST HOUSE

Austins Guesthouse

11 Coldstream Terrace, Cardiff CF11 6LJ t +44 (0) 29 2037 7148 e austins@hotelcardiff.com

hotelcardiff.com

B&B PER ROOM PER NIGHT
S £30.00–£40.00
D £44.00–£65.00

open All year
bedrooms 1 double, 4 twin, 5 single, 1 family
bathrooms 4 en suite
payment Credit/debit cards, cash, cheques

Small, friendly B&B in the city centre 300m from the castle and overlooking the river. Cardiff central bus and train station is a ten-minute walk along the river bank. All the central attractions including the Millennium Stadium and International Arena are just a few minutes' walk. A warm welcome to all.

SAT NAV CF11 6LJ **ONLINE MAP**

Room 🛏 📺 ♿ 🍴 General 🪀 P 🌐 🔥 🐴

Using map references

Map references refer to the colour maps at the front of this guide.

CARDIGAN, Ceredigion Map ref 8A2 — SELF CATERING

★★★★
SELF CATERING

Units **5**
Sleeps **2–7**

LOW SEASON PER WK
£200.00–£420.00

HIGH SEASON PER WK
£210.00–£895.00

Short breaks available out of main holiday season and Bank Holidays, subject to availability.

Penwern Fach Cottages, Nr Cenarth Falls

contact Yvonne Davies, Penwern Fach Cottages, Ponthirwaun, Nr Cenarth Falls, Cardigan SA43 2RL
t +44 (0) 1239 710694   **e** info@penwernfach.co.uk

penwernfach.co.uk SPECIAL OFFERS

open All year
payment Credit/debit cards, cash, cheques
nearest pub 1 mile
nearest shop 1.5 miles

Penwern Fach is in the heart of beautiful countryside with glorious views overlooking the Teifi valley and Preseli mountains. Near sandy beaches and one mile from the picturesque fishing village of Cenarth. Accommodation varies from a pretty studio cottage for two, to a four-bedroomed cottage for the larger family.

SAT NAV SA43 2RL **ONLINE MAP**

Unit 📺 🎬 📀 · 🍳 🛁 🧺 ♨ 🧺 ❄ 📶 ⌀   General 🐴 🏛 🕴 P ◉ Ⓢ 🐕   Leisure ∪ 🎣 🚲

CARMARTHEN, Carmarthenshire Map ref 8A3 — GUEST ACCOMMODATION

★★★★
GUEST HOUSE

B&B PER ROOM PER NIGHT
S £30.00–£40.00
D £46.00–£60.00

EVENING MEAL PER PERSON
£9.95–£16.95

Weekend breaks from £92–£108. See our website for special promotions or call us for further assistance.

Ty Castell – Home of the Kingfisher

Station Road, Nantgaredig, Carmarthen SA32 7LQ **t** +44 (0) 1267 290034
e enquiries@ty-castell.co.uk

ty-castell.co.uk GUEST REVIEWS · SPECIAL OFFERS · REAL-TIME BOOKING

open All year except Christmas and New Year
bedrooms 2 double, 1 twin, 1 family
bathrooms 3 en suite, 1 private
payment Credit/debit cards, cash, cheques, euros

Once a farmhouse on the banks of the River Towy in the heart of the Carmarthenshire countryside, now a luxury guesthouse, with own licensed bar and restaurant, opening its doors to weekenders, rural explorers, nature and garden admirers, golfers and fishermen, offering high standard hotel-style comfort and facilities.

SAT NAV SA32 7LQ **ONLINE MAP**

Room 🖥 📺 ♨ 🍽   General 🐴 10 P 📶 🔥 🍷 ✕ 🎮 ◉ ❋   Leisure 🎣 ▶ 🚲

CONWY, Conwy Map ref 8B1 — GUEST ACCOMMODATION

★★★
GUEST HOUSE

B&B PER ROOM PER NIGHT
S £35.00–£37.00
D £50.00–£60.00

Bryn Derwen Guest House

Woodlands, Gyffin, Conwy LL32 8LT **t** +44 (0) 1492 596134 **e** info@conwybrynderwen.co.uk

conwybrynderwen.co.uk SPECIAL OFFERS

open All year except Christmas
bedrooms 3 double, 2 twin, 1 family
bathrooms All en suite
payment Cash, cheques

Spacious Victorian property set well back from roadway on rising ground in commanding position with good views. Comfortable, well-appointed accommodation complemented by excellent breakfast. 800m from town centre, local amenities/ transport services. Ideal location for access to Snowdonia's attractions.

SAT NAV LL32 8LT **ONLINE MAP**

Room 📺 ♨ 🍽   General 🐴 🏛 🕴 P 📶 ❋   Leisure ∪ 🎣

Has every property been assessed?

All accommodation in this guide has been rated for quality, or is awaiting assessment, by a professional national tourist board assessor.

CONWY, Conwy Map ref 8B1

★★★★★
GUEST ACCOMMODATION

B&B PER ROOM PER NIGHT
S £79.00–£119.00
D £99.00–£159.00

Oct–May, 3 nights
for 2. Quote
'VisitBritain'.

The Old Rectory Country House

Llansanffraid Glan Conwy, Nr Conwy LL28 5LF   t +44 (0) 1492 580611
e info@oldrectorycountryhouse.co.uk

oldrectorycountryhouse.co.uk

open All year except Christmas and New Year
bedrooms 3 double, 2 twin, 1 single
bathrooms All en suite
payment Credit/debit cards

Idyllically situated in beautiful gardens overlooking the grand sweep of the Conwy estuary, historic Conwy castle and Snowdonia. Enjoy a calm, relaxing atmosphere in this elegant Georgian house decorated with old paintings and antiques. Help with touring routes. Excellent restaurants and inns nearby. Championship golf three miles.

SAT NAV LL28 5LF

Room 🛏🖨📞📺🆂🕭🍴   General ♨5 P🔥❄🐎   Leisure ✦🚲

DEVIL'S BRIDGE, Ceredigion Map ref 8B2

★★★★
BED & BREAKFAST

B&B PER ROOM PER NIGHT
S £20.00–£30.00
D £40.00–£60.00

Ffynnon Cadno Guesthouse

Ponterwyd, Aberystwyth SY23 3AD   t +44 (0) 1970 890224   e ffynnoncadno@btinternet.com

ffynnoncadno.co.uk GUEST REVIEWS

open All year except Christmas and New Year
bedrooms 2 double, 1 twin
bathrooms 2 en suite, 1 private
payment Credit/debit cards, cash, cheques

Large family house with mature gardens, ponds and woods. Ideally situated for exploring mid Wales, Cambrian mountains, Devil's Bridge and Aberystwyth. Four-poster bedroom, red kites fly overhead. A warm welcome assured. Our motto: 'Arrive as a guest – leave as a friend'.

SAT NAV SY23 3AD ONLINE MAP

Room 🖨📺🆂🕭   General P📶🍴❄   Leisure ∪✦

FISHGUARD, Pembrokeshire Map ref 8A2

★★★★
BED & BREAKFAST

B&B PER ROOM PER NIGHT
S £45.00–£49.00
D £71.00–£89.00

EVENING MEAL PER PERSON
£18.00–£25.00

Short breaks
(2 nights B&B + 1
dinner) £91–£109pp.

Cefn-y-Dre Country House

Cefn-Y-Dre, Fishguard SA65 9QS   t +44 (0) 1348 875663   e welcome@cefnydre.co.uk

cefnydre.co.uk SPECIAL OFFERS

open All year
bedrooms 2 double, 1 twin
bathrooms 2 en suite, 1 private
payment Cash, cheques, euros

Enjoy a warm welcome in this friendly country house, one of Pembrokeshire's oldest historic homes. Elegantly proportioned rooms, a large woodland garden, home-grown food and amazing views to the Preseli Hills add to the peace and tranquillity. Only 2km from the breathtaking coastal path, secluded beaches and the ferry to Ireland.

SAT NAV SA65 9QS ONLINE MAP

Room 📺🆂🕭🍴   General ♨🏛🎅P🔥🍷✖🍴❄   Leisure ∪✦🏇🚲

Where are the maps?

Colour maps can be found at the front of the guide. They pinpoint the location of all accommodation found in the regional sections.

LLANBERIS, Gwynedd Map ref 8A1

★★★
SELF CATERING

| Units | 1 |
| Sleeps | 7 |

LOW SEASON PER WK
Max £300.00

HIGH SEASON PER WK
£375.00–£475.00

Short breaks available Oct-Mar, min 2 nights: £70 per night.

Ripon House, Llanberis

contact Ms Beryl Swift, Chantrey Cottage, 65 Chantrey Road, Sheffield S8 8QU
t +44 (0) 114 258 9358 **e** bswift27@yahoo.co.uk

riponhouse.co.uk

open All year
payment Cash, cheques
nearest pub less than 0.5 miles
nearest shop less than 0.5 miles

A character cottage in small village, close to lake and surrounded by mountains. Spacious, beamed lounge with comfortable sofas. Separate dining room with doors opening onto patio with outdoor furniture. Recently modernised kitchen and bathroom with shower. Large main bedroom with king-size bed. Cosy single bedroom. Twin attic room.

SAT NAV LL55 4HH

Unit 📺 General Leisure

LLANDOVERY, Carmarthenshire Map ref 8B3

★★★
GUEST HOUSE

B&B PER ROOM PER NIGHT
S £32.00–£38.00
D £64.00–£76.00

EVENING MEAL PER PERSON
£15.50–£16.50

Stay midweek: 3 nights' DB&B for £127.00pp.

Llanerchindda Farm Guest House

Cynghordy, Llandovery SA20 0NB **t** +44 (0) 1550 750274 **e** info@cambrianway.com

cambrianway.com

open All year
bedrooms 3 double, 4 twin, 1 single, 1 family
bathrooms All en suite
payment Credit/debit cards, cash, cheques

Family-run guesthouse with spectacular views of the Brecon Beacons. En suite bedrooms, comfortable lounge bar, excellent home-cooked food and log fires. Ideal for exploring mid and south Wales. Self-catering cottages also available. Activities available on-site including quad-bike trekking, clay-pigeon shooting and fly-fishing.

SAT NAV SA20 0NB

Room General Leisure

LLANDUDNO, Conwy Map ref 8B1

★★
METRO HOTEL

B&B PER ROOM PER NIGHT
S £27.00–£33.00
D £46.00–£60.00

Sherwood Hotel

Promenade, Llandudno LL30 1BG **t** +44 (0) 1492 875313 **e** info@sherwoodhotel.net

sherwoodhotel.net

open All year except Christmas and New Year
bedrooms 5 double, 3 family
bathrooms All en suite
payment Cash, cheques

A warm welcome awaits you at the Sherwood Hotel, personally run by the proprietors. The hotel is in a magnificent position on Llandudno's beautiful Promenade close to the theatre and conference centre, and offers a comfortable friendly environment in which to relax. Private car park, licensed lounge bar, all en suite bedrooms.

SAT NAV LL30 1BG

Room General Leisure

What if I need to cancel?

It's advisable to check the proprietor's cancellation policy at the time of booking in case you have to change your plans.

LLANDUDNO, Conwy Map ref 8B1 — SELF CATERING

★★★★★
SELF CATERING

Units **4**
Sleeps **2–4**

LOW SEASON PER WK
£199.00–£339.00

HIGH SEASON PER WK
£269.00–£499.00

Short breaks available Nov-Apr, 3-night stay.

Hamilton, Llandudno

contact Mrs L Sheppard, 40 Trinity Avenue, Llandudno LL30 2TQ t +44 (0) 1492 878177
e hamilton.luxury@virgin.net

hamiltonllandudno.co.uk SPECIAL OFFERS

open All year
payment Cash, cheques
nearest pub 0.5 miles
nearest shop 0.5 miles

Fully self-contained all-electric one- or three-bedroom apartments for two-four people. DVD player and recorder. Ideal for couples or up to four people. All spotlessly clean. A real home from home. On level, only minutes from promenade, shops, easy walk to all amenities. Children over ten welcome. Sorry no pets.

SAT NAV LL30 2TQ ONLINE MAP

Unit 📺 ⟨⟩ 🖥 🍽 ❄ General ⚲10 P ⊙ Leisure ▶

LLANFYLLIN, Powys Map ref 8B2 — GUEST ACCOMMODATION

★★★★★
FARMHOUSE

B&B PER ROOM PER NIGHT
S £80.00–£90.00
D £95.00–£110.00

EVENING MEAL PER PERSON
£27.50

Short breaks, (serviced and self-catering), available all year at special rates; evening meals available Wed-Sat. Good for your wellbeing!

Cyfie Farm

Llanfihangel, Llanfyllin SY22 5JE t +44 (0) 1691 648451 e info@cyfiefarm.co.uk

cyfiefarm.co.uk GUEST REVIEWS · SPECIAL OFFERS · REAL-TIME BOOKING

open All year except Christmas and New Year
bedrooms 4 suites
bathrooms All en suite
payment Credit/debit cards, cash, cheques, euros

17thC luxury farm guesthouse and two self-catering cottages, close to Lake Vyrnwy, in spectacular setting with views across Wales and Vyrnwy Valley. Three stunning suites (two double, one twin), with private sitting rooms and kitchenettes, in which to relax all day. Organic local food, cordon bleu cuisine, hot tub and sauna spa. Spectacular gardens.

SAT NAV SY22 5JE ONLINE MAP

Room ♿ 📺 💨 🍷 General ⚲10 P 🖶 ⚡ ✕ 🚾 ⬚ ❄ Leisure ∪ ♪ ▶ 🚵

LLANGORSE, Powys Map ref 8B3 — CAMPING, CARAVAN & HOLIDAY PARK

★★★
HOLIDAY, TOURING
& CAMPING PARK

🚐 (20) £11.00–£13.00
🚙 (20) £11.00–£13.00
⛺ (40) £11.00–£13.00
🏠 (10) £215.00–£395.00
20 touring pitches

Lakeside Caravan Park

Llangorse Lake, Llangorse LD3 7TR t +44 (0) 1874 658226 e holidays@llangorselake.co.uk

llangorselake.co.uk

Lakeside Caravan Park is surrounded by the Brecon Beacons National Park and is adjacent to Llangorse Common, which leads down to Llangorse Lake.

open All year except Christmas and New Year
payment Credit/debit cards, cash, cheques

General 🚿 🅿 🚰 🛒 🏠 📺 🧺 ✕ 🐾 ☼ Leisure 🍷 ♪ ⛰ ∪ ♪ 🚵

It's all quality-assessed accommodation

Our commitment to quality involves wide-ranging accommodation assessment. Ratings and awards were correct at the time of going to press but may change following a new assessment. Please check at time of booking.

NEW QUAY, Ceredigion Map ref 8A2

★★★★
SELF CATERING

Units **1**
Sleeps **2–20**

LOW SEASON PER WK
£1,620.00–£1,650.00

HIGH SEASON PER WK
£1,990.00–£2,820.00

Short breaks available Oct-Mar. 3-night breaks Fri-Mon. 4-night breaks Mon-Fri.

Park Hall, Cwmtydu

contact Roger & Carol Burgess, Park Hall, Cwmtydu, Llwyndafydd, Llandysul SA44 6LQ
t +44 (0) 1545 560996 **e** parkhall.office@btconnect.com

park-hall.co.uk SPECIAL OFFERS

open All year
payment Cash, cheques
nearest pub 1.8 miles
nearest shop 4.5 miles

Former Edwardian gentleman's residence set in 2.5 acres of lovely lawned garden. Outstanding views of the sea, 300m from Cwmtydu Cove on the Ceredigion Heritage Coast. Spacious, comfortable and relaxing with eight bedrooms (seven en suite). Perfect for family holidays/celebrations or special anniversaries. Snowdon, Tenby and the Gower within driving distance.

ONLINE MAP

Unit 📺 🎮 🖥 🗄 🎛 🗑 🍴 ❄ ♨ 🍃 General 🛋 🍴 🔥 P 🅿 Ⓢ 🐾
Leisure ⚓ ♪ 🏃

NEWCASTLE EMLYN, Ceredigion Map ref 8A2

★★★★★
BED & BREAKFAST

B&B PER ROOM PER NIGHT
S £45.00–£55.00
D £60.00–£75.00

EVENING MEAL PER PERSON
£15.00–£28.00

10% discount for stays of 5 nights or more.

Maes-y-Derw B&B

Maes-Y-Derw, Cardigan Road, Newcastle Emlyn SA38 9RD **t** +44 (0) 1239 710860
e info@maes-y-derw.co.uk

maes-y-derw.co.uk GUEST REVIEWS

open All year
bedrooms 2 double, 1 twin
bathrooms All en suite
payment Cash, cheques

Ten minutes' walk from the bustling town of Newcastle Emlyn, this imposing Edwardian house overlooks the River Tiefi Valley. It offers spacious en suite rooms containing original features and a plethora of antiques. A hearty Welsh breakfast awaits guests. Holiday cottage also available. Free Tiefi fishing permits available.

SAT NAV SA38 9RD **ONLINE MAP**

Room 📺 🍴 🍽 General 🛋12 P 📶 ♨ ✗ 🍴 🐾 Leisure ♪ 🏃 🚴

NEWPORT, Newport Map ref 8B3

★★
HOTEL

B&B PER ROOM PER NIGHT
S £65.00–£75.00
D £95.00–£140.00

Weekend deals: dinner, bed & breakfast – £70-£120. Dinner, bed, breakfast and lunch – £80-£150.

The Waterloo Hotel and Bistro

113 Alexandra Road, Pillgwenlly, Newport NP20 2JG **t** +44 (0) 1633 264266
e info@thewaterloohotel.co.uk

thewaterloohotel.co.uk GUEST REVIEWS

open All year except Christmas
bedrooms 12 double, 6 twin, 3 single
bathrooms All en suite
payment Credit/debit cards, cash, cheques

The Waterloo is a newly refurbished hotel and restaurant offering a choice of luxury en suite bedrooms, spacious and tastefully decorated. Displaying all the features of a traditional Victorian hotel with the modern amenities required by today's traveller. A superb bistro restaurant serving lunch and dinner to residents and non-residents.

SAT NAV NP20 2JG **ONLINE MAP**

Room 🛏 📞 📺 SC 🍴 🍽 ♨ General 🛋 🔥 P 📶 🍷 📧 🍴

NEWPORT, Newport Map ref 8B3

CAMPING, CARAVAN & HOLIDAY PARK

★★★★★
TOURING &
CAMPING PARK

🚐 (80) £12.20–£25.10
🚍 (80) £12.20–£25.10
80 touring pitches

Tredegar House & Park Caravan Club Site

Coedkernew, Newport NP10 8TW t +44 (0) 1342 326944 e natalie.tiller@caravanclub.co.uk

caravanclub.co.uk

open All year
payment Credit/debit cards, cash, cheques

High-standard site within the park, bordering one of the ornamental lakes. Just off the M4, seven miles from Cardiff. Non-members welcome.

SAT NAV NP10 8TW

Special member rates mean you can save your membership subscription in less than a week. Visit our website to find out more.

THE
CARAVAN
CLUB

General 🚐 🍴 📶 🐾 🗄 🐕 ☼ 📶 Leisure ⚠ 🎵 ▶

NEWPORT, Pembrokeshire Map ref 8A2

GUEST ACCOMMODATION

★★★★
BED & BREAKFAST

B&B PER ROOM PER NIGHT
S £40.00
D £65.00–£70.00

Soar Hill B&B

Soar Hill, Cilgwyn Road, Newport SA42 0QG t +44 (0) 1239 820506 e jean@soarhill.com

soarhill.com

A renovated 140-year-old house at the foot of the Preseli hills just a short distance outside Newport and the Pembrokeshire Coast National Trail. Great welcome and fantastic views.

open All year except Christmas and New Year
bedrooms 1 double, 1 twin
bathrooms 1 en suite, 1 private
payment Cash, cheques

Room 📺 🆂 ♨ 🍵 General 🛏 🍽 🅿 🎮 ☼ 🐕 Leisure ♨ ∪ 🎵 ▶ 🚲

PEMBREY, Carmarthenshire Map ref 8A3

SELF CATERING

★★★★
SELF CATERING

Units **1**
Sleeps **6**

LOW SEASON PER WK
£295.00–£350.00

HIGH SEASON PER WK
£395.00–£550.00

Short breaks available Oct-Mar (minimum 3 nights).

Tanyffynnon Cottage, Pembrey

contact Mrs G Leaf
t +44 (0) 29 2084 3069 e stay@tanyffynnon.co.uk

tanyffynnon.co.uk

open All year
payment Cash, cheques
nearest pub 0.5 miles
nearest shop 0.5 miles

Spacious, luxury cottage in the coastal village of Pembrey. Accommodation comprises two sitting rooms, large fully fitted kitchen/diner, three double bedrooms and two bathrooms. Large garden with play area. Ideally situated for Pembrey Country Park and Millennium Coastal Path.

SAT NAV SA16 0TP

Unit 📺 🆂 🍴 📷 🗄 🗄 🗄 🍵 📻 ☼ 🎮 General 🛏 🍽 🅿 Leisure ∪ 🎵 🚲

Do you like camping?

Love the great outdoors? Britain's Camping, Caravan & Holiday Parks 2009 is packed with information on quality sites in some spectacular locations. You can purchase the guide from good bookshops and online at visitbritaindirect.com.

PEMBROKE, Pembrokeshire Map ref 8A3 — GUEST ACCOMMODATION

★★★★
BED & BREAKFAST

B&B PER ROOM PER NIGHT
S £30.00–£35.00
D £50.00–£55.00

Off-peak weekend breaks. Please ring for availability and prices. Minimum 2 people.

Blickerage B&B

3 Martello Road, St Patricks Hill, Llanreath, Pembroke Dock SA72 6XW t +44 (0) 1646 689972
e theblickerage@yahoo.com

theblickerage.co.uk SPECIAL OFFERS

open All year except Christmas
bedrooms 2 double, 2 single
bathrooms All en suite
payment Cash, cheques

You are assured of a warm welcome and very clean accommodation at The Blickerage. Situated 200yds from the water, we are minutes from the Irish ferry terminal. Private off-road parking available. Freshly cooked breakfast with plenty of choice. Use of guest lounge, and patio which overlooks the water.

SAT NAV SA72 6XW

Room 🛗 📺 🍴 ｢ General P 🍴 🎱 ❄ 🐾 Leisure ∪ ♪ ▶ 🚲

PRESTEIGNE, Powys Map ref 8B2 — GUEST ACCOMMODATION

★★★★★
GUEST ACCOMMODATION

B&B PER ROOM PER NIGHT
D £95.00–£130.00

EVENING MEAL PER PERSON
£35.00–£40.00

We specialise in country house parties. Email or phone for details.

The Old Vicarage

Norton, Presteigne LD8 2EN t +44 (0) 1544 260038 e paul@nortonoldvic.co.uk

oldvicarage-nortonrads.co.uk

open All year
bedrooms 2 double, 1 twin
bathrooms All en suite
payment Credit/debit cards, cash, cheques

Winner National Tourism Awards for Wales 2007. 'The Old Vicarage is a treasure trove of Victorian fittings. The effect is impressive with warming colours, restful bedrooms and the gentle chiming of antique clocks. Calm prevails with a nightly dinner party to foster sparkling conversation'. The Times of London, December 6, 2007.

SAT NAV LD8 2EN **ONLINE MAP**

Room ｢ General P 🌀 🍷 ✕ 🍴 ❄ Leisure ∪ ▶ 🚲

PWLLHELI, Gwynedd Map ref 8A1 — GUEST ACCOMMODATION

★★★★★
BED & BREAKFAST

B&B PER ROOM PER NIGHT
S £65.00–£90.00
D £90.00

The Old Rectory

Boduan, Pwllheli LL53 6DT t +44 (0) 1758 721519 e thepollards@theoldrectory.net

theoldrectory.net GUEST REVIEWS · SPECIAL OFFERS

open All year except Christmas
bedrooms 2 double, 1 twin
bathrooms All en suite
payment Cash, cheques

Welcoming, beautiful Georgian home in three acres of grounds in the centre of the Llyn Peninsula. Stylish accommodation, friendly informality. Substantial traditional breakfasts with home-made jams, breads and compotes, scrambled eggs and smoked salmon, continental. Pretty, comfortable en suite bedrooms overlooking the gardens. Guest drawing room. Come and go as you please.

SAT NAV LL53 6DT **ONLINE MAP**

Room 📺 🍴 ｢ General 🐕 🛏 🚶 P 🍴 🎱 ❄ Leisure ∪ ♪ 🚲

Where can I get live travel information?

For the latest travel update – call the RAC on 1740 from your mobile phone.

REYNOLDSTON, Swansea Map ref 8A3 — GUEST ACCOMMODATION

★★★★★
RESTAURANT WITH ROOMS

B&B PER ROOM PER NIGHT
S £145.00–£250.00
D £165.00–£275.00

EVENING MEAL PER PERSON
£30.00–£40.00

Sun-Thu minimum 2-night break. Dinner bed and breakfast from £110.00 pppn.

Fairyhill
Reynoldston, Gower, Swansea SA13 1BS t +44 (0) 1792 390139 e postbox@fairyhill.net

fairyhill.net SPECIAL OFFERS

open Open all year except Christmas and January.
bedrooms 8 double
bathrooms All en suite
payment Credit/debit cards

Fairyhill is a charming 18thC house set in 24 acres in the heart of the Gower Peninsula. An award-winning restaurant serving seasonal local produce and the finest of wines. Eight intimate, individually designed luxury bedrooms. Serious and stylish without pretension – pure magic.

SAT NAV SA13 1BS **ONLINE MAP**

Room ✆ TV ℡ General ☌8 P ⽔ ⚡ ♈ ✗ ⽕ ❄ Leisure ∪

RHYL, Denbighshire Map ref 8B1 — HOTEL

★★
HOTEL

B&B PER ROOM PER NIGHT
S £35.00–£55.00
D £55.00–£90.00

Stay 3+ nights and breakfast is half-price. Free bedroom upgrades with stays of 5+ nights.

Westminster Hotel
11-12 East Parade, Rhyl, Denbighshire LL18 3AH t +44 (0) 1745 342241
e reservations@westminster24.freeserve.co.uk

open All year
bedrooms 21 double, 14 twin, 19 single, 24 family
bathrooms All en suite
payment Credit/debit cards, cash, cheques, euros

Rhyl's premier and largest seafront hotel, now family-owned and run, in a friendly home-from-home atmosphere. Sympathetically refurbished with modern refinements to include passenger lift and a visual open-plan kitchen. Spacious well-appointed en suite bedrooms. 'The large hotel with the personal touch'.

SAT NAV LL18 3AH

Room ▤ TV ⍾ ℡ ⍂ General ☌ ⽳ ♈ P ♈ ⽕ ● ▦ ❄ ⽥ Leisure ∪ ♫ ► ⚲

RUTHIN, Denbighshire Map ref 8B1 — GUEST ACCOMMODATION

★★★★
RESTAURANT WITH ROOMS

B&B PER ROOM PER NIGHT
S £45.00–£65.00
D £70.00–£105.00

EVENING MEAL PER PERSON
£9.50–£30.00

2 nights' DB&B from £99 per person Mon-Thu.

The Wynnstay Arms
Well Street, Ruthin LL15 1AN t +44 (0) 1824 703147 e reservations@wynnstayarms.com

wynnstayarms.com GUEST REVIEWS · SPECIAL OFFERS · REAL-TIME BOOKING

open All year
bedrooms 3 double, 2 twin, 1 family, 1 suite
bathrooms All en suite
payment Credit/debit cards, cash, cheques

This award-winning restaurant with rooms is a refurbished inn opened by two experienced hoteliers and their wives, one the head chef and one front of house, in 2005. It has become synonymous with good food, either gastro pub in the cafe-bar, or fine food in the brasserie, including bouillabaisse, sea bass, and weekly Italian specials.

SAT NAV LL15 1AN **ONLINE MAP**

Room TV SC ⍾ ℡ General ☌ ⽳ ♈ P ⽔ ♈ ✗

Looking for a wide range of facilities?
More stars means higher quality accommodation plus a greater range of facilities and services.

RUTHIN, Denbighshire Map ref 8B1 — SELF CATERING

★★★★★
SELF CATERING

Units **1**
Sleeps **2–5**

LOW SEASON PER WK
£350.00–£400.00

HIGH SEASON PER WK
£450.00–£525.00

Short breaks available Oct–Mar, 3-nights' stay from £180–£250.

The Gwalia, Nr Ruthin

contact Mrs D Warburton, Gwalia, Llangynhafal, Denbigh LL16 4LN t +44 (0) 1824 790489
e info@thegwalia.co.uk

thegwalia.co.uk

open All year
payment Cash, cheques, euros
nearest pub 0.5 miles
nearest shop 4 miles

Comfortable and relaxing with panoramic views of the Vale of Clwyd. Ideally situated for exploring this beautiful region. Sleeps up to five. Ground-floor bedroom with king-size bed and en suite shower room. First-floor bedroom with king-size bed and one single bed, en suite with roll-top bath.

Unit 📺 🖥 💻 🖲 🔲 🍳 🍽 🔌 ♨ 🎯 ⛰ General 🛏 🏠 🔥 P 🅾 S
Leisure ∪ 🎵 🏃 🚲

RUTHIN, Denbighshire Map ref 8B1 — SELF CATERING

★★★
SELF CATERING

Units **2**
Sleeps **2–5**

LOW SEASON PER WK
£170.00–£250.00

HIGH SEASON PER WK
£250.00–£380.00

Tyddyn Isaf, Ruthin

contact Mrs Nerys Jones, Tyddyn Isaf, Rhewl, Ruthin LL15 1UH t +44 (0) 1824 703367
e nerystyddynisaf@btinternet.com

tyddyn-isaf.co.uk

open All year
payment Cash, cheques
nearest pub 1 mile
nearest shop 3 miles

The self-contained part of the farmhouse is spacious and comfortable. With its own private entrance, modern comforts are combined with old-world charm. Rooms consist of two bedrooms; the first has a double bed, single bed and visitor's bed, the second has a double bed. We also have a converted granary sleeping two-four persons.

ONLINE MAP

Unit 📺 💻 🍳 🖲 🔌 ♨ General 🛏 🏠 🔥 P S Leisure ∪ 🎵

SAUNDERSFOOT, Pembrokeshire Map ref 8A3 — GUEST ACCOMMODATION

★★★★★
GUEST HOUSE

B&B PER ROOM PER NIGHT
S **£56.25–£68.75**
D **£90.00–£110.00**

Seasonal discounts for stays of two nights or more. Offers vary, contact for details.

Stoney Bridge

Moreton, Saundersfoot SA69 9DX t +44 (0) 1834 811470
e enquiries@stoneybridgeguesthouse.co.uk

stoneybridgeguesthouse.co.uk GUEST REVIEWS · SPECIAL OFFERS · REAL-TIME BOOKING

open All year
bedrooms 2 double, 1 twin
bathrooms All en suite
payment Credit/debit cards, cash, cheques, euros

Luxurious, relaxing spa accommodation perfect for holidays, honeymoons, short breaks and special celebrations. Adults only. Minibars, safes in room, spa baths en suite. Luxurious complementary therapies. Traditional Welsh recipes, local, seasonal and organic produce, special diets a speciality. Late breakfasts in lounge, room or garden. Events, restaurants, activities, transport arranged.

SAT NAV SA69 9DX **ONLINE MAP**

Room 📺 🆂🅲 🍸 🍳 General P 🔥 🍽 🛁 🖥 ♨ Leisure ∪ 🎵 🏃 🚲

TENBY, Pembrokeshire Map ref 8A3 HOTEL

★★
HOTEL

B&B PER ROOM PER NIGHT
S £40.00–£50.00
D £70.00–£85.00

Castle View Hotel

14 The Norton, Tenby SA70 8AA **t** +44 (0) 1834 842666 **e** info@castleviewhotel.co.uk

castleviewhotel.co.uk REAL-TIME BOOKING

open All year except Christmas and New Year
bedrooms 8 double, 1 twin, 3 single, 3 family
bathrooms All en suite
payment Credit/debit cards, cash, cheques

Private Grade II Listed hotel overlooking bay and old harbour. Residential licence in comfortable bar lounge and large, quiet first-floor lounge with spectacular views over Tenby Bay. All rooms en suite, TV, complimentary tea/coffee facilities. Limited parking by arrangement. Good Welsh breakfasts in bright dining room. Non-smoking hotel. Prices for family and sea-view rooms on request.

SAT NAV *SA70 8AA* **ONLINE MAP**

Room General 1 P Leisure

TINTERN, Monmouthshire Map ref 8B3 GUEST ACCOMMODATION

★★★★
GUEST HOUSE

B&B PER ROOM PER NIGHT
S £45.00–£60.00
D £65.00–£85.00

Parva Farmhouse Riverside Guesthouse & Restaurant

Monmouth Road, Tintern NP16 6SQ **t** +44 (0) 1291 689411 **e** parvahoteltintern@fsmail.net

parvafarmhouse.co.uk REAL-TIME BOOKING

open All year
bedrooms 4 double, 2 twin, 2 family
bathrooms All en suite
payment Credit/debit cards, cash, cheques

A 17thC former farmhouse, on the banks of the River Wye, in this Area of Outstanding Natural Beauty less than a mile from Tintern Abbey. Family-run, friendly, informal and comfortable, an ideal location to relax and de-stress. Plenty of walks and activities in the area for the more energetic. A la carte meals available.

SAT NAV *NP16 6SQ*

Room General 12 P Leisure

TYWYN, Gwynedd Map ref 8A2 GUEST ACCOMMODATION

★★★★
BED & BREAKFAST

B&B PER ROOM PER NIGHT
S £33.00–£35.00
D £28.00–£30.00

Reduction for two nights or more.

Coed Talon

Ffordd Y Crynwyr, Llwyngwril LL37 2JP **t** +44 (0) 1341 251025 **e** info@snowdonia-holiday.co.uk

snowdonia-holiday.co.uk GUEST REVIEWS · REAL-TIME BOOKING

open All year
bedrooms 2 double, 1 twin
bathrooms 2 en suite, 1 private
payment Cash, cheques

Coed Talon offers relaxation, or a base for exploring mid Wales and the Snowdonia National Park. Close to many beaches. Good walking and cycling area. Visit historic castles and narrow gauge railways. Explore Cardigan Bay on our coastal railway. Garaging for bikes and cars on request.

SAT NAV *LL37 2JP* **ONLINE MAP**

WALKERS WELCOME CYCLISTS WELCOME

Room General P Leisure

TYWYN, Gwynedd Map ref 8A2

★★★
SELF CATERING

Units   **1**
Sleeps   **7**

LOW SEASON PER WK
£130.00–£250.00

HIGH SEASON PER WK
£180.00–£500.00

Nantcaw Farm, Tywyn

contact Mrs Wendy Jones, Gesail Farm, Bryncrug, Tywyn LL36 9TL **t** +44 (0) 1654 782286
e wendy@jones5686.fsnet.co.uk

nantcaw.co.uk

open All year
payment Credit/debit cards, cash, cheques
nearest pub 3 miles
nearest shop 6 miles

Spend a week on a true working hill farm, nestling at the foothills of Cadair Idris. Traditional, well-equipped house, tastefully decorated, many extras. Four bedrooms, three double, inglenook fireplace. Breathtaking views, quietly surrounded by sheep and cattle. Excellent hill walks, great cycling routes. Children enjoy the freedom of the countryside.

SAT NAV LL36 9TR

Unit 📺 🆂🅲 📠 📀 📷 ♨ 🔆 🅿 ⬜ 🆂 General 🐴 🏛 ⚐ P ⬜ 🆂
Leisure ∪ ♪ ⚑ 🚲

Walkers and cyclists welcome

Look out for quality-assessed accommodation displaying the Walkers Welcome and Cyclists Welcome signs.

Participants in these schemes actively encourage and support walking and cycling. In addition to special meal arrangements and helpful information, they'll provide a water supply to wash off the mud, an area for drying wet clothing and footwear, maps and books to look up cycling and walking routes and even an emergency puncture-repair kit! Bikes can also be locked up securely undercover.

The standards for these schemes have been developed in partnership with the tourist boards in Northern Ireland, Scotland and Wales, so wherever you're travelling in the UK you'll receive the same welcome.

Northern Ireland

Clockwise: Giant's Causeway, County Antrim; Londonderry, County Londonderry; Sika deer

Great days out

How do you like to escape? Following wave-swept coastal drives, walking romantic mountains and lakelands, delving into Celtic mysteries or the rich heritage of cosmopolitan cities? You can do them all in Northern Ireland, be active or relax. Plus there's always plenty of time for a chat with the locals.

Living city history

Visit **Belfast** for a start, where Victorian streetscapes recall the city's great heydays of shipbuilding, engineering, rope works and linen. Now its industrial heritage is a major tourist attraction – come for the annual **Titanic Made in Belfast Festival Week** around Easter time, and tour the shipyard where the historic vessel was built. At the **Ulster Folk & Transport Museum** you can relive town and country life in the early 1900s. And in spring 2009 the **Ulster Museum** re-opens after major redevelopment: be among the first to view its newly presented art, history and sciences collections.

Ulster Folk and Transport Museum, Cultra

For a break from history, take the kids to **Belfast Zoo** – the rare red pandas and Barbary lions are sure-fire favourites. Then have a few peaceful hours wandering the glorious **Botanic Gardens and Queen's University**. Hungry yet? Tuck into local goodies like Champ and Irish stew, or have a gourmet treat in a top restaurant.

Drive of your life

Up the tempo now, fasten your seat belts and set off for the drive of your life. The 80-mile **Causeway Coastal Route** from Belfast to Londonderry, also known as the Walled City of Derry, is rated as one of the world's Top Five Road Trips. Just look at the kaleidoscope of landscapes to see why: dramatic cliffs, nine green glacier-cut glens and heather-covered mountains all cascading by. Head along the north east coast to pretty villages like Cushendun and step out at rocky **Torr Head** for exhilarating views to the Mull of Kintyre. Feel your heart pound again later when you walk the **Carrick-a-Rede Rope Bridge** swaying more than 78 feet above the foaming sea near Ballintoy. Do you think nature or the giant Finn McCool created the amazing geometric columns of the **Giant's Causeway**? What happened on the stormy night in 1639 when part of **Dunluce Castle** fell into the sea? You'll still be talking about it all when you're relaxing on the beautiful beach at **Downhill**.

Within these walls

Londonderry, also referred to as the **Walled City of Derry**, is one of the best-preserved walled cities in Europe. So where better to start exploring than with a stroll along the 400-year-old fortifications? Built to protect the new Plantation town from marauding Irish clans, they're 26 feet high in places and were never breached. Stop along the way to admire original cannons and sights like the Neo-Gothic Guildhall. Then drop into the old town to browse atmospheric streets, shops and pubs. Find more eye-openers into the past

Left to right: Sperrin Mountains, County Tyrone;
Ulster American Folk Park, County Tyrone

why not... visit Tyrone Crystal and let the designers create a unique piece for you?

at **The Workhouse Museum** where exhibitions on the Great Irish Famine 1840-49 reveal the harshness of Victorian life. Or blow away the cobwebs, stretching your legs on family-friendly routes through **Prehen Wood** on the River Foyle – look out for red squirrels and other colourful wildlife.

North West adventure

Want some more fresh air? Then the heather-coloured **Sperrin Mountains** straddling Counties Londonderry and Tyrone in the north west of the country are ideal. Ramble or cycle vast moors and spruce forests, and let the space and solitude revive your senses.
The **An Creagán Visitor Centre** at the mountain's foot tells the story behind the landscapes, Celtic culture and traditions. Find more outdoor fun at **Roe Valley Country Park** – will you go fishing, canoeing, rock climbing, or simply meander beside the River Roe? Take your time, let nature set the pace.

Step indoors for a while to peruse the treasures of **The Argory**, a 19th-century Irish gentry house at Moy. Climb aboard an emigrant ship at **Ulster American Folk Park**, Omagh, and learn about Northern Ireland's rich links to the USA – the **Annual Appalachian & Bluegrass Music Festival** will stir your soul, just as the north west's landscapes do.

Carrick-a-Rede Rope Bridge, County Antrim

Enchanted lakelands

Mystery and magnificence await you around the **Fermanagh** lakelands in the south west. Sense the spirits of the Celtic tribe that settled these shores as you view the enigmatic pagan stone idols of Boa Island. Wander the twin lakes of Lough Erne and catch the ferry from Trory to **Devenish Island** to be inspired by the monastic site originally founded by St Molaise in the sixth century. The waterways and islands are a paradise for fishing and boating, and there's even an underground river to travel at **Marble Arch Caves**, where stalagmites and stalactites provide a breathtaking natural architectural show. Compare the man-made magnificence of stately homes – 18th-century **Florence Court** and **Castle Coole** – that recall the county's influential Anglo-Irish families. Take your own treasures home, from **Belleek Pottery**.

> **did you know...** it's claimed the Mourne Mountains inspired CS Lewis's Kingdom of Narnia?

St Patrick's country

Now follow in the steps of Ireland's patron saint. Patrick took his mission throughout the land but he is most closely associated with the lovely countryside around **Armagh** and **Downpatrick** in the south east. He founded Armagh, Ireland's ecclesiastical capital – find out more about his life in the fascinating interactive *Armagh Story* at the **Saint Patrick's Trian Visitor Complex**. Trace his living heritage in the city's two cathedrals and, before you leave, visit **Armagh Planetarium** for a gaze into the heavens. Then make a pilgrimage to St Patrick's Grave at **Down Cathedral**. If you can, come in March and experience countrywide **St Patrick's Day Celebrations**.

Patrick seldom ventured into the **Mountains of Mourne**, but you should, to enjoy fantastic rollercoaster walks. **Mount Stewart House** is another must, with its famous gardens flourishing in the sub-tropical micro-climate around Strangford Lough. Complete your visit with luscious oysters fresh from the waters!

Clockwise: Devenish Island, County Fermanagh; Florence Court, County Fermanagh; Mournes area, County Down; Marble Arch Caves, County Fermanagh

Destinations

Belfast Castle

Downpatrick

One of Ireland's most ancient towns, Downpatrick's links with Ireland's patron saint give the visitor a vivid glimpse of Ireland's Celtic and Christian past. Saint Patrick visited the town many times and is laid to rest here. The cathedral site has been a place of pilgrimage for 1,500 years, and the nearby Saint Patrick Centre presents the saint's story in a thrilling, interactive exhibition. No visit to County Down would be complete without an excursion into the beautiful, rugged Mourne Mountains featuring the famous Mourne Wall, running 22 miles from peak to peak.

Belfast

Belfast is a vibrant capital city and the gateway to the rural retreat of Northern Ireland. Compact and easy to get around, by car or on foot, the city offers a multitude of stylish bars, gourmet restaurants and fashionable clubs, as well as some of the best shopping in the UK. Belfast's rich architectural and industrial heritage has shaped a city steeped in culture, portrayed at its best in a wonderful range of civic buildings, whilst the many parks and gardens offer a perfect haven in which to relax.

The Causeway Coast and Glens

A unique region where nature has perfected a landscape of unsurpassed beauty and man has woven a rich tapestry of history, heritage and myth. This is a place where rugged coastline merges into still, silent glens and unfolds into lush forest parks. You'll find beautiful beaches and rolling lowlands crossed by wandering rivers. Take the glorious Causeway Coastal Route, from the outskirts of Belfast to the World Heritage Site at the Giant's Causeway, and enjoy one of Europe's most scenic routes.

Enniskillen

Situated between the lakes of Upper and Lower Lough Erne, Enniskillen is County Fermanagh's largest town. The lakeland landscape confers a special, almost continental feel, as a well as offering unsurpassed watersports and fishing. Climb the 108 steps of Coles Monument for a wonderful panoramic view, then take advantage of its shopping centres which blend big names with traditional, family-run businesses. Discover the turbulent history of Enniskillen Castle, medieval seat of the Maguires, chieftains of Fermanagh, and don't miss magnificent Castle Coole, one of Ireland's greatest neo-classical houses.

Enniskillen Castle

Left to right: Derry Jazz Festival;
Mount Stewart; Lough MacNean

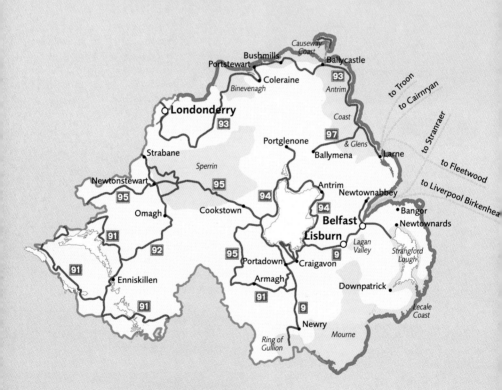

Area of Outstanding Natural Beauty

Coastal Landscape Character Areas

9 Sections of the National Cycle Network
nationalcyclenetwork.org.uk

Ferry route

0   40 miles
0   60 kms

**For lots more great ideas go to
visitbritain.com/destinations and
discovernorthernireland.com**

Fermanagh Lakelands

The lakeland paradise of Fermanagh offers the visitor an unforgettable experience of diversity and quality. The twin lakes of Lough Erne cover one third of the county, creating an enchanted landscape to explore. Enjoy the rich flora and fauna of the tranquil lakeland shores, then take a ferry to the remarkable monastic site at Devenish Island. Wander magnificent stately homes or head back to the water for cruises, watersports and fishing. You'll find world-famous, award-winning craftsmanship in the shops and no shortage of first-class cuisine. End your day relaxing to the sound of traditional Irish music.

Omagh and the Sperrins

Tyrone's county town, less than two hours from Belfast, nestles in the foothills of the Sperrin Mountains and makes an ideal central location to explore Northern Ireland. Classical and gothic architecture form the backdrop to a town whose rich culture is encapsulated in music, song and literary celebrations throughout the year. The rivers Drumragh and Camowen merge in the centre of town to form the River Strule, a pulsing artery that provides some of the finest salmon and sea trout fishing in the Northern Hemisphere.

Clockwise: Whiterocks, Portrush; Omagh; Downpatrick; Mussenden Temple, near Portstewart

Visitor attractions

Family and Fun

Belfast Zoo
Belfast
+44 (0) 28 9077 6277
belfastzoo.co.uk
White tigers, red pandas,
gorillas and Barbary lions.

**Ulster Folk and
Transport Museum**
Cultra
+44 (0) 28 9042 8428
uftm.org.uk
Vivid recreation of 20thC life
in Ulster.

Heritage

The Argory
Dungannon
+44 (0) 28 8778 4753
ntni.org.uk
Fine early-18thC country
house with wooded estate.

Castle Coole
Enniskillen
+44 (0) 28 6632 2690
ntni.org.uk
Elegant, opulent neoclassical
masterpiece in parkland.

**Down Cathedral and
Saint Patrick's Grave**
Downpatrick
+44 (0) 28 4461 4922
downcathedral.org
Ancient ecclesiastical site,
Saint Patrick's final resting
place.

Dunluce Castle
Bushmills
+44 (0) 28 2073 1938
ehsni.gov.uk
16thC castle ruins dramatically
perched on rocky cliffs.

Florence Court
Enniskillen
+44 (0) 28 6634 8249
ntni.org.uk
Quintessential 18thC house
with exquisite rococo
plasterwork.

**The Guildhall and Harbour
Museum**
Londonderry
+44 (0) 28 9127 5787
derrycity.gov.uk/museums
Neo-Gothic guildhall with
adjacent maritime museum.

**Saint Patrick's Trian and Saint
Patrick Cathedrals**
Armagh
+44 (0) 28 3752 1800
visitarmagh.com
Exciting visitor complex
incorporating three major
exhibitions.

Saint Patrick Centre
Downpatrick
+44 (0) 28 4461 9000
saintpatrickcentre.com
Compelling displays and
fabulous early Christian
artefacts.

Saint Patrick's Trian
Armagh
+44 (0) 28 3752 1801
visitarmagh.com
Fascinating interactive displays
tell Saint Patrick's story.

Springhill House
Moneymore
+44 (0) 28 8674 8210
ntni.org.uk
17thC Plantation home with
superb costume collection.

Workhouse Museum
Londonderry
+44 (0) 28 7131 8328
derrycity.gov.uk/museums
Museum on two floors of original
workhouse building.

Indoors

Belleek Pottery
Belleek
+44 (0) 28 6865 9300
belleek.ie
Witness the techniques that
create this famous porcelain.

**Linenhall Library and
Literary Tours**
Belfast
+44 (0) 28 9032 1707
linenhall.com
Renowned library featuring in
famous literary walking tours.

Tyrone Crystal
Dungannon
+44 (0) 28 8772 5335
tyronecrystal.com
Watch master craftsmen continue
200 years of tradition.

Outdoors

**Botanic Gardens and
Queen's University**
Belfast
+44 (0) 28 9097 5252
qub.ac.uk/vcentre
Glorious haven of lawn, trees
and historic buildings.

Carrick-a-Rede Rope Bridge
Ballintoy
+44 (0) 28 2076 9839
ntni.org.uk
Tackle a 24m bridge swaying
above the sea.

Cushendun and Torr Head
Cushendun
+44 (0) 28 2177 1180
moyle.council.org
Cornish-style village set on
beautiful, rugged coastline.

Derry City Walls
Londonderry
+44 (0) 28 7126 7284
derryvisitor.com
Completely intact for 400 years
with 24 original cannons.

Giant's Causeway
Bushmills
+44 (0) 28 2073 1855
ntni.org.uk
Northern Ireland's most
famous and spectacular
visitor attraction.

Janus Figures and
Boa Island
Enniskillen
+44 (0) 28 90543030
ehsni.gov.uk
Enigmatic pagan statues in
an ancient churchyard.

Marble Arch Caves
Enniskillen
+44 (0) 28 6634 8855
marblearchcaves.net
Ride an underground river
through these magnificent
caverns.

Mourne Mountains
Newcastle
+44 (0) 28 4372 2222
downdc.gov.uk
Ancient granite mountains
that inspired CS Lewis.

Mussenden Temple and
Downhill Demesne
Castlerock
+44 (0) 28 2073 1582
ntni.org.uk
Striking 18thC temple
overlooking golden sands.

Oxford Island National
Nature Reserve
Craigavon
+44 (0) 28 3832 2205
oxfordisland.com
Woodland and wildflower
meadows with events and
exhibitions.

Prehen Woods
Londonderry
+44 (0) 28 9127 5787
woodland-trust.org.uk
Ancient woodland with
abundant wildlife and
walking routes.

Roe Valley County Park
Limavady
+44 (0) 28 7772 2074
ehsni.gov.uk
Woodland walks, superb
watersports and rock climbing.

Sperrin Mountains and
An Creagán Centre
Omagh
+44 (0) 28 8076 1112
an-creagan.com
Wild, unspoilt landscape rich
in Celtic heritage.

Ulster American
Folk Park
Castletown, Omagh
+44 (0) 28 8224 3292
folkpark.com
Relive the drama of Irish
emigration to America.

Events 2009

Saint Patrick's Festival
in Armagh and
Downpatrick
Armagh and Downpatrick
armaghanddown.com
17 Mar

May Day Celebrations
and Fair
Holywood, County Down
northdowntourism.com
4 May

Balmoral Show
King's Hall, Belfast
balmoralshow.co.uk
15 - 17 May

Guinness Blues on the
Bay Festival
Warren Point, County Down
bluesonthebay.co.uk
21 - 25 May

Castle Ward Opera
Strangford, County Down
castlewardopera.com
Dates throughout June

Tall Ships Atlantic
Challenge 2009
Belfast
belfastcity.gov.uk
13 - 16 Aug

Auld Lammas Fair
Ballycastle, County Antrim
causewaycoastandglens.com
31 Aug - 1 Sep

Appalachian and Bluegrass
Music Festival
Ulster American Folk Park,
Omagh
folkpark.com
4 - 5 Sep

Belfast Festival at Queen's
Venues throughout Belfast
belfastfestival.com
16 Oct - 1 Nov

Christmas Market,
Belfast City Hall
Belfast
belfastcity.gov.uk
Nov-Dec

Regional contacts and information

For more information on accommodation, attractions, activities, events and holidays in Northern Ireland, contact one of the following regional or local tourism organisations. Their websites have a wealth of information and many produce free publications to help you get the most out of your visit.

Northern Ireland

Visit the Northern Ireland Tourist Board's website at **discovernorthernireland.com** for further information on accommodation, activities and destinations. A range of free guides are available to order online or by calling **+44 (0) 28 9024 6609**:

Publications

- **Northern Ireland Visitor Guide**
  Available in English, French, German, Italian and Spanish.
- **Uniquely Northern Ireland**

Belfast Visitor and Convention Bureau
t +44 (0) 28 9024 6609
e welcomecentre@belfastvisitor.com
w gotobelfast.com

**Causeway Coast and Glens
Tourism Partnership**
t +44 (0) 28 7032 7720
e mail@causewaycoastandglens.com
w causewaycoastandglens.com

Derry Visitor and Convention Bureau
t +44 (0) 28 7126 7284
e info@derryvisitor.com
w derryvisitor.com

Sperrin Tourism Limited
t +44 (0) 28 8674 7700
e info@sperrinstourism.com
w sperrinstourism.com

Fermanagh Lakelands Tourism
t +44 (0) 28 6632 3110
e info@fermanaghlakelands.com
w fermanaghlakelands.com

Armagh and Down Tourism Partnership
t +44 (0) 28 9182 2881
e info@armaghanddown.com
w armaghanddown.com

Left to right: St Patrick's Day; Dunluce Castle, County Antrim

Tourist Information Centres

Antrim	16 High Street	+44 (0) 28 9442 8331	info@antrim.gov.uk
Armagh	40 English Street	+44 (0) 28 3752 1800	tic@armagh.gov.uk
Ballycastle	7 Mary Street	+44 (0) 28 2076 2024	tourism@moyle-council.org
Ballymena	1-29 Bridge Street	+44 (0) 28 2563 5900	tourist.information@ballymena.gov.uk
Ballymoney	1 Townhead Street	+44 (0) 28 2766 0230	touristinfo@ballymoney.gov.uk
Banbridge	The Outlet, Bridgewater Park	+44 (0) 28 4062 3322/ +44 (0) 28 4062 9054	tic@banbridge.gov.uk
Bangor	Tower House, Quay St	+44 (0) 28 9127 0069	tic@northdown.gov.uk
Belfast Welcome Centre (Belfast and Northern Ireland)	47 Donegall Place	+44 (0) 28 9024 6609	welcomecentre@belfastvisitor.com
Belfast International Airport	Arrivals Hall	+44 (0) 28 9448 4677	welcomecentre@belfastvisitor.com
George Best Belfast City Airport	Sydenham Bypass	+44 (0) 28 9093 5372	welcomecentre@belfastvisitor.com
Carrickfergus	11 Antrim Street	+44 (0) 28 9335 8049	touristinfo@carrickfergus.org
Coleraine	Railway Road	+44 (0) 28 7034 4723	info@northcoastni.com
Cookstown	The Burnavon, Burn Rd	+44 (0) 28 8676 9949	tic@cookstown.gov.uk
Downpatrick	The Saint Patrick Centre	+44 (0) 28 4461 2233	downpatrick.tic@downdc.gov.uk
Enniskillen	Wellington Road	+44 (0) 28 6632 3110	tic@fermanagh.gov.uk
Giant's Causeway	44 Causeway Road	+44 (0) 28 2073 1855	info@giantscausewaycentre.com
Hillsborough	The Courthouse	+44 (0) 28 9268 9717	tic.hillsborough@lisburn.gov.uk
Kilkeel	The Nautilus Centre	+44 (0) 28 4176 2525	kdakilkeel@hotmail.com
Killymaddy	190 Ballygawley Road	+44 (0) 28 8776 7259	killymaddy.reception@dungannon.gov.uk
Larne	Narrow Gauge Road	+44 (0) 28 2826 0088	larnetourism@btconnect.com
Limavady	7 Connell Street	+44 (0) 28 7776 0307	tourism@limavady.gov.uk
Lisburn	15 Lisburn Square	+44 (0) 28 9266 0038	tic.lisburn@lisburn.gov.uk
Londonderry	44 Foyle Street	+44 (0) 28 7126 7284	info@derryvisitor.com
Magherafelt	The Bridewell	+44 (0) 28 7963 1510	thebridewell@magherafelt.gov.uk
Newcastle	10-14 Central Promenade	+44 (0) 28 4372 2222	newcastle.tic@downdc.gov.uk
Newry	Bagenal's Castle	+44 (0) 28 3031 3170	newrytic@newryandmourne.gov.uk
Newtownards	31 Regent Street	+44 (0) 28 9182 6846	tourism@ards-council.gov.uk
Omagh	Strule Arts Centre	+44 (0) 28 8224 7831	info@omagh.gov.uk
Portaferry*	The Stables, Castle Street	+44 (0) 28 4272 9882	tourism.portaferry@ards-council.gov.uk
Portrush*	Dunluce Centre, Sandhill Drive	+44 (0) 28 7082 3333	portrushtic@btconnect.com
Strabane	Alley Arts & Conference Centre	+44 (0) 28 7138 4444	tic@strabanedc.com

*seasonal opening

where to stay in
Northern Ireland

All place names in the blue bands are shown on the maps at the front of this guide.

Accommodation symbols

Symbols give useful information about services and facilities. On pages 16 to 17 you can find a key to these symbols.

BELFAST, County Antrim Map 9 **SELF CATERING**

★★★★★
SELF CATERING

Units **1**
Sleeps **4**

LOW SEASON PER WK
£995.00–£1,125.00

HIGH SEASON PER WK
£1,095.00–£1,695.00

Rates from £160 per night. No minimum stay.

New Life Apartments, Belfast

contact Christine McKay, Apartment 30, Clarendon Quay, Pilot Place, Belfast BT1 3AG
t +44 (0) 7943 425980 **e** info@newlifeapartments.co.uk

newlifeapartments.co.uk

open All year
payment Credit/debit cards
nearest pub less than 0.5 miles
nearest shop less than 0.5 miles

Luxury penthouse apartment. Located five minutes from Belfast city centre. Panoramic views across Belfast, Cavehill and North Down. Sleeps four (two king beds). Magnificent bathroom with freestanding bath and double shower enclosure. Secure parking. Wi-Fi internet.

ONLINE MAP

Unit 📺 🆂 ⬛ 🖥️ 📀 ▪️ 📱 🗄️ 🎛️ 🍳 🔌 🍽️ 🧺 ✏️ ✂️ General ♨️ 🏠 P ◻️ Ⓢ
Leisure ∪ ♪ ► 🚲

COLERAINE, County Londonderry Map 9 **GUEST ACCOMMODATION**

BED & BREAKFAST

B&B PER ROOM PER NIGHT
S Min £32.00
D Min £50.00

Ballinteer B&B

70 Ballinteer Road, Macosquin, Coleraine BT51 4LZ **t** +44 (0) 28 7032 0565 & +44 (0) 7724 082731
e lulu.kane@fsmail.net

ballinteerbandb.co.uk

Located three miles from Coleraine, this en suite room with digital TV has views of the garden and surrounding countryside. Close to all North Coast attractions, Londonderry and Donegal.

open All year
bedrooms 1 double
bathrooms En suite
payment Cash, cheques, euros

Room 📺 💆 🍳 General P ❄️ Leisure ∪ ♪ ►

Remember to check when booking

Please remember that all information in this guide has been supplied by the proprietors well in advance of publication. Since changes do sometimes occur it's a good idea to check details at the time of booking.

COLERAINE, County Londonderry Map 9

★★★★
SELF CATERING

| Units | 1 |
| Sleeps | 6 |

LOW SEASON PER WK
£250.00–£300.00

HIGH SEASON PER WK
£300.00–£375.00

Short breaks available Sep-June, complimentary bottle of wine provided. Special weekend breaks during Jan and Feb, see website for details.

Causeway Holiday Homes

contact Trevor Boyce, 36 Cloonavin Green, Coleraine **t** +44 (0) 28 9447 9806
e info@causewayholidayhomes.com

causewayholidayhomes.com

open All year
payment Cash, cheques
nearest pub 0.5 miles
nearest shop less than 0.5 miles

The Mallow is a modern town house set in scenic surroundings on the north coast of Northern Ireland. It has three bedrooms (sleeping six), one with en suite, bathroom with separate shower, living room which features a real fire, large kitchen and dining area opening onto an enclosed rear garden. Friendly welcome assured.

Unit 📺 🖭 ▣ 🖬 🖥 🗄 🗑 📷 ✳ ⚒ ⊘ General 🎠 🏚 🛇 P ⬚ S 🐾 Leisure ∪ ♪ ►

GLENARM, County Antrim Map 9

★★★★
SELF CATERING

| Units | 1 |
| Sleeps | 2 |

LOW SEASON PER WK
£406.00

HIGH SEASON PER WK
£476.00

Special offers available during low season Jan-May and Sep-Dec.

The Barbican Gatelodge, Glenarm

Irish Landmark Trust, 25 Eustace Street, Temple Bar Dublin 2 **t** +353 1 670 4733
e bookings@irishlandmarktrust.com

irishlandmark.com GUEST REVIEWS · SPECIAL OFFERS

open All year
payment Credit/debit cards, cash, cheques
nearest pub less than 0.5 miles
nearest shop less than 0.5 miles

The Barbican was built in 1825. The Gatelodge is approached by a bridge over the Glenarm River. A turret staircase leads to the flat roof of the main block which affords significant views of the surrounding countryside. Its setting makes it a romantic retreat for two people.

SAT NAV *BT44 0AP* **ONLINE MAP**

Unit 🗑 📷 ✳ ⊘ General 🎠 🏚 S Leisure ∪ ♪ ►

HILLSBOROUGH, County Down Map 9

BED & BREAKFAST

B&B PER ROOM PER NIGHT
S £35.00–£45.00
D £55.00–£65.00

EVENING MEAL PER PERSON
£10.00–£15.00

Off-peak discounts available. Contact Dunhill Cottage for further details.

Dunhill Cottage Farm B&B

47 Carnreagh, Hillsborough BT26 6LJ **t** +44 (0) 28 9268 3024 **e** dunhillcottage@btinternet.com

dunhillcottage.co.uk GUEST REVIEWS · SPECIAL OFFERS

open All year
bedrooms 2 double, 1 twin, 1 single, 1 family
bathrooms All en suite
payment Credit/debit cards, cash, cheques, euros

This newly-built bed and breakfast cottage offers the very best in luxury accommodation. Located adjoining the family dairy farm, this is a unique opportunity to stay on a working dairy farm just minutes from the city. Only five minutes' walk from the picturesque Georgian village of Hillsborough. Enjoy a tour around Hillsborough Castle, or a walk in Hillsborough Forest Park.

SAT NAV *BT26 6LJ* **ONLINE MAP**

Room 🔥 📺 🛏 ☕ General 🎠 🏚 🛇 P ⚲ ⅙ ✕ 🎱 ▣ ✳ 🐾 Leisure ∪ ♪ ► 🚲

IRVINESTOWN, County Fermanagh Map 9 — GUEST ACCOMMODATION

BED & BREAKFAST

B&B PER ROOM PER NIGHT
S Min £35.00
D £50.00–£60.00

Necarne Manor

Castle Irvine Road, Irvinestown BT94 1GG t +44 (0) 28 6862 8553 e haroldrankin@hotmail.co.uk

open All year except Christmas
bedrooms 2 double, 1 twin, 1 family
bathrooms All en suite
payment Cash, cheques, euros

This Georgian-style residence, surrounded by mature woodland, is located in Necarne Estate yet only a few minutes' walk from Irvinestown centre and Necarne Equestrian Centre, and is centrally located in Fermanagh Lakeland to attractions such as Marble Arch Caves, Florence Court House, Castle Coole and Belleek Pottery. Stabling also available on site.

SAT NAV BT94 1GG

Room 📺 🕭   General 🎠 🏛 🛠 P 🍴 ❄   Leisure ∪ 🎣 🏹 🚲

NEWCASTLE, County Down Map 9 — SELF CATERING

★★★
SELF CATERING

Units **9**
Sleeps **2–7**

LOW SEASON PER WK
£230.00–£410.00

HIGH SEASON PER WK
£330.00–£560.00

£100, two-night special price for couples, from 1600 on day of arrival to 1600 on day or departure.

Tory Bush Cottages, Newcastle

contact David Magin, 13 Spelga Avenue, Newcastle, Country Down BT33 0DR
t +44 (0) 28 4372 4348 e tory.bush@which.net

torybush.com GUEST REVIEWS · REAL-TIME BOOKING

open All year
payment Credit/debit cards, cash, cheques, euros
nearest pub 4 miles
nearest shop 1 mile

A group of traditional-style cottages in a rural location, with spectacular views of the Mourne Mountains, yet only four miles from the lively resort of Newcastle. Ideal base for hill-walking, cycling, golfing and general sightseeing. Sleeps two to seven in one- to four-bedroom cottages.

SAT NAV BT34 5LD **ONLINE MAP**

Unit 📺 🖥 💻 🔔 🕭 🔔 📷 🍳 ❄ 🎮 ✎   General 🎠 🏛 🛠 P 🅾 Ⓢ
Leisure ⚲ ∪ 🎣 🏹 🚲

PORTRUSH, County Antrim Map 9 — SELF CATERING

★★★
SELF CATERING

Units **3**
Sleeps **5–8**

LOW SEASON PER WK
£330.00–£360.00

HIGH SEASON PER WK
£375.00–£425.00

West Bay Apartments, Portrush

contact John Burrell, Cran Lodge, 19 Crievehill Road, Fivemiletown BT75 0ST
t +44 (0) 28 8952 1413 e burrellcranlodge@talk21.com

westbayportrush.com

Three large, self-contained apartments overlooking the beach, bay and resort. 80m from beach and 25m from rail halt. Golf, fishing, Ulster Way walk nearby. Private parking, front lawn, rear patio. Close to town.

open All year
payment Cash, cheques
nearest pub less than 0.5 miles
nearest shop less than 0.5 miles

Unit 📺 🖥 💻 📷 🔔 🕭 ❄   General 🎠 🏛 P 🅾 Ⓢ   Leisure 🎣 🏹

Fancy a cycling holiday?

For a fabulous freewheeling break, seek out accommodation participating in our Cyclists Welcome scheme. Look out for the symbol and plan your route online at nationalcyclenetwork.org.

SELF CATERING

Rating Applied For
SELF CATERING

Units **1**
Sleeps **5**

HIGH SEASON PER WK
£425.00–£475.00

100 Old Mill Grange, Portstewart

contact Ian Kennedy, 48 Kirkliston Park, Belfast BT5 6ED **t** +44 (0) 28 9065 7111
e i.k.golfer@ntlworld.com

High-quality four bedroom (one double and three single) semi-detached house featuring lounge with patio doors leading to secluded grassed garden. Kitchen has all mod cons. On Northern Ireland Tourist Board listings.

open June, July and August
payment Cash, cheques, euros
nearest pub 1 mile
nearest shop 1 mile

Unit TV 🖥 💻 📺 🔲 🍽 📺 ❄ General 🎠 P Leisure 🎣 🏹 🚲

SELF CATERING

★★★★
SELF CATERING

Units **2**
Sleeps **5–7**

LOW SEASON PER WK
£532.00–£665.00

HIGH SEASON PER WK
£756.00–£973.00

Special offers available during low season Jan-May and Sep-Dec.

Blackhead Light Keeper's Houses, Whitehead

Irish Landmark Trust, 25 Eustace Street, Temple Bar Dublin 2 **t** +353 1 670 4733
e bookings@irishlandmark.com

irishlandmark.com GUEST REVIEWS · SPECIAL OFFERS

open All year
payment Credit/debit cards, cash, cheques
nearest pub 1.8 miles
nearest shop 1.8 miles

Ideally situated near the small town of Whitehead, just beyond the entrance to Belfast Lough, making a stunning panoramic view. The houses, built in 1901, are a proud example of Ireland's maritime heritage. Climb down the cliff path and walk along the shore to the seaside village of Whitehead.

SAT NAV BT38 9PA **ONLINE MAP**

Unit 🖥 📺 🍽 📺 ✏ General 🎠 🏠 P S Leisure 🎣 🏹

Bank holiday dates

holiday	2009	2010
New Year's Day	1 January	1 January
January Bank Holiday (Scotland)	2 January	4 January
St Patrick's Day (Northern Ireland)	17 March	17 March
Good Friday	10 April	2 April
Easter Monday (not Scotland)	13 April	5 April
Early May Bank Holiday	4 May	3 May
Liberation Day (Channel Islands)	9 May	9 May
Spring Bank Holiday	25 May	31 May
Battle of the Boyne Orangemen's Day (Northern Ireland)	13 July	12 July
Summer Bank Holiday (Scotland)	3 August	2 August
Summer Bank Holiday (not Scotland)	31 August	30 August
St Andrews Day* (Scotland)	30 November	30 November
Christmas Day Holiday	25 December	27 December
Boxing Day Holiday	28 December	28 December

*(a voluntary public holiday)

The Channel Islands

Jersey, Guernsey, Herm, Sark and Alderney

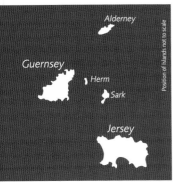

Alderney

Guernsey

Herm

Sark

Jersey

Position of Islands not to scale

Clockwise: St Ouens Bay, Jersey; Alderney;
St Peters Port, Guernsey

Great days out

The Channel Islands combine the spirit of Britain with the heart of Old Normandy in a rare fusion of English and French. Ancient customs blend with global commerce, beach and country living, the modern, the cosmopolitan and the homespun. Welcome to five distinct islands, two cultures and one memorable holiday.

Rock pools to rural treasures

Enjoy beautiful, safe sandy beaches, secret coves and rock pools, rugged harbours, stunning cliffs and fantastic flora and fauna. Inland, each island has a country character that follows the rhythm of the seasons. Sleepy lanes, private gardens, nature reserves and migrating birds are just some of the rural treasures waiting to surprise you. Take the charming Heritage Walk from **Samarès Manor** on Jersey, or spot the rare Aquatic Warbler on the wetland reserve at **La Claire Mare** on Guernsey. And with a temperate climate offering more warmth and sunshine than elsewhere in the British Isles, you'll find the islands in bloom all year round.

Bonne Nuit Bay, Jersey

Frontline history

Roll back the years to uncover Channel Island history, beginning with Neolithic Man and some of the oldest manmade structures in Europe: visit **La Hougue Bie** on Jersey, an extraordinary burial chamber and focal point for religious activity or Guernsey's Dehus

Dolmen to see mysterious carvings. Twentieth-century turmoil also left its mark when the islands became bulwarks in Europe's WWII Atlantic Wall. Get a taste of daily life under occupation in the superbly preserved **Jersey War Tunnels** built by forced labour and now home to a gripping exhibition. Train your sights with the very rangefinders used by German forces in Guernsey's **Pleinmont Observation Tower**, or wander through a skilfully recreated wartime street scene at the **German Occupation Museum**.

Five lives

Each of the five islands has a distinctive personality – explore and you'll be charmed by their open welcome.

Guernsey is a heady mix of dazzling scenery and the best of contemporary living. Take inspiring walks or spend lazy days on wonderful beaches. Then explore the bustling harbour town of **St Peter Port** and let its tapestry of architectural styles tell the story of the region's changing fortunes. Here bistros, restaurants and boutiques jostle for your attention while, in the harbour, ferries are readied to take you to the sister islands. Wander through the museums at **Castle Cornet** and witness the firing of the noon day gun.

In Jersey, culture vultures will discover history at every turn, walkers will be captivated by breathtaking natural beauty and families can relax without a care on pristine beaches. In St Helier, take the Castle Ferry to the rocky islet where Sir Walter Raleigh built **Elizabeth Castle** and witness the 12-noon 'call to arms'

Left to right: Dehus Dolmen, Guernsey; Creux, Guernsey

did you know... these low-duty islands are a shopper's paradise – treat yourself!

and the firing of the castle cannon. Learn bygone skills and catch up with gossip from the time of Charles II at **Hamptonne**, a country life museum, or explore local marine ecology and learn how tides work, at the **Discovery Pier**. Jersey is also the ideal place to clear your head – come and indulge in some exhilarating outdoor sports, or simply live the life.

Herm, a tranquil island idyll that's easily reached from Guernsey by ferry, is a favourite with visitors and locals alike. No wonder: as soon as you step off the boat, the stresses of the modern world evaporate. **Alderney**, the closest island to France, feels more remote, although quickly accessible by air. Now you're in a paradise for nature lovers, where varied and rare wildlife from blonde hedgehogs to gannets share the invigorating landscapes. Refresh in the restaurants and lively pubs of the capital, **St Anne's**. Another day, step back in time in traffic-free **Sark** whose superb coastal views and picturesque rural interior can be best experienced on foot, by hired bicycle or horse and trap.

Best of two cultures

Throughout history, the islands have taken the best of Gallic and British culture: taste it now in the delicious cuisine, whether a casual snack of a fresh crab sandwich in a country pub or luxury seafood in a Michelin-starred restaurant. Norman Law, street names, surnames and local patois – a form of ancient French – give a romantic air. English conversation, the main language, extends a contemporary welcome. Stamps and currency, distinct from mainland Britain, also add to the islands' special sense of place.

Herm

Small islands, big attractions

Jersey, just 45 square miles, is packed with things to do, from shopping in the colourful town of **St Helier** to visiting the internationally famed **Durrell Wildlife Conservation Trust** to see exotic and endangered species. Delve into the island's past and rich maritime heritage at award-winning museums, unlock the secrets of **Mont Orgueil Castle**, Gorey. And plenty of attractions provide fun-filled family days out, like **Jersey Pottery** and **The Living Legend** adventure and leisure village.

Guernsey, too, embraces a wide range of must-sees, from the tiny wildlife preserve and remains of a 12th-century priory on **Lihou Island**, to museums, family activity and craft centres, quaint tearooms and top quality restaurants. Take in the extraordinary decoration of **Victor Hugo House**, where the writer of Les Misérables spent 14 years in exile, or discover the fate of ships wrecked on the infamous Hanois reefs on the rocky west coast at **Fort Grey and Shipwreck Museum**. Find out what life was like 100 years ago at the **National Trust of Guernsey Folk and Costume Museum** and thrill to the momentous events that **Castle Cornet** has witnessed.

why not... island hop to see some of the most beautiful scenery in Europe?

Walks to water-skiing

Feeling active? The islands are made for walkers! How about a slow stroll across the sands, or an energetic hike along cliff-top paths and into rocky coves. And the perfect way of taking in all the sights, sounds and smells is from the seat of a bicycle. Rent one or bring your own, enjoy a leisurely scenic ride for a few miles or gear yourself up for a more challenging route. Anglers, of course, are spoilt for choice – there's never a bad time to fish in the Channel Islands because such a wide variety of species flourish in the waters: bass to ballan wrasse, grey mullet to good old reliable garfish; something for every season.

Check the calendar for year-round high-level events like motor sports, powerboating, athletics and bowling. Watch classic cars tackle a twisting, scenic route across the island at the **Jersey Festival of Motoring** in June, then set sail for Guernsey's **Rocquaine Regatta** in August and the **Jersey Regatta** in September. Don't forget to save some energy, though – you'll need it to complete the famous Around Island Walk during Jersey's **Autumn Walking Week**. If you are looking for something a little more unusual, Guernsey hosts an **Underwater Cycling Race** in September where you can marvel at cyclists in full diving kit taking to the local outdoor bathing pools on specially modified bikes! Raise your pulse in Jersey wakeboarding, water-skiing, on banana rides, speedboat trips and ocean kayaks, or in Guernsey take an exhilarating rib ride!

Left to right: Fort Grey, Guernsey; St Brelades Bay, Jersey

Destinations

Alderney

With its rich and varied wildlife Alderney remains almost totally unaffected by the outside world, and is a paradise for nature lovers. Pull on your boots and discover over 30 miles of walks over cliffs and golden bays, across exposed commons, past Victorian fortresses and World War II batteries and alongside a scenic and challenging golf course. St Anne, the capital town, is a pretty community of colour-washed houses, cobbled streets and shops. Its magnificent church, known as 'the cathedral of the Channel Islands' is a must-see, and there are plenty of welcoming pubs and restaurants in which to relax and soak up the atmosphere.

Guernsey

Just seventy miles by fast ferry, or a short flight from mainland England, you'll find a heady mix of stunning scenery and the best of contemporary living. From its capital of St Peter Port – often regarded as the prettiest harbour in Europe – its miles of golden beaches, clear blue sea and breathtaking cliff walks to its early spring, superb seafood and fascinating history, Guernsey is the perfect mix of Continental and natural beauty.

St Peter Port, the island's capital, is a bustling harbour town in which a tapestry of architectural styles tells the story of the region's changing fortunes.

Enjoy a wide choice of dining experiences, where unsurprisingly fresh fish is in abundance. Shopping in St Peter Port is an experience not to be missed: electronic and photographic equipment, jewellery and perfume are all good, low-duty buys, and, of course, the famous Guernsey jumper. Small boutiques offer exclusive clothes, shoes and leather goods, whilst the Old Quarter is the place to find antiques. For a memorable excursion, take a trip to one of Guernsey's sister islands (Alderney, Herm or Sark) – frequent ferries run from St Peter Port harbour. And planes fly to Alderney regularly.

Herm

Disover this unspoiled paradise of sand dunes, long golden beaches, hidden bays, cliffwalks and seabreeze-combed common, just twenty minutes by boat from Guernsey. Allow yourself time to spend at least a couple of hours on Shell Beach, where clear waters lap the white sand made from millions of tiny shell fragments. It's easy to visit Herm in a day, but to really appreciate the island's charm, consider an overnight stay.

Shell Beach, Herm

Left to right: St Peter Port, Guernsey;
Bluebell Valley, Guernsey; St Aubin, Jersey

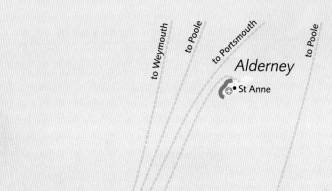

to Weymouth

to Poole

to Portsmouth

to Poole

Alderney

St Anne

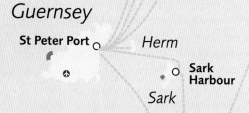

Guernsey

St Peter Port

Herm

Sark Harbour

Sark

Jersey

St Helier

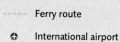

━━━ Ramsar sites

┄┄┄ Ferry route

◉ International airport

◉ Domestic airport

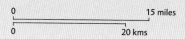

| 0 | | 15 miles |
| 0 | | 20 kms |

Sark

The picturesque island of Sark is the perfect escape. Traffic-free and overflowing with natural beauty, the island is easily reached by ferry from Guernsey. Take advantage of this walkers' paradise and follow one of the many coastal walks. Experience peace and tranquillity, admire wildflowers and seabirds, and feel like you have been transported to another world. If you wish to stay a little longer, there are a number of hotels and good restaurants to choose from.

Jersey

Clear water and beaches surround some 45 miles of coastline – the island's greatest natural treasure. Sweeping bays in the south give way to dramatic cliffs in the north offering spectacular scenery and stunning vistas. If food is your passion your taste buds are in for a real treat with over 170 eateries featuring Jersey's delicious local produce, top chefs and gourmet delights from around the world.

The streets of St Helier buzz with life. By day shop 'til you drop, dine al fresco whilst watching exciting street theatre or take a nautical jaunt with an appointed Blue Badge guide around the town's historic harbours. There are lots of attractions to explore, too. By night, linger in the warm evening sun in Royal Square, join theatre-goers at the Jersey Opera House or enjoy live music in one of the town's many pubs.

Hog's Back, Sark

For lots more great ideas go to visitbritain.com/destinations, visitguernsey.com and jersey.com

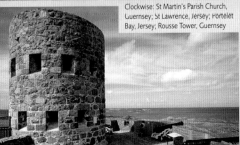

Clockwise: St Martin's Parish Church, Guernsey; St Lawrence, Jersey; Portelet Bay, Jersey; Rousse Tower, Guernsey

Visitor attractions

Family and Fun

aMaizin! Maze and Adventure Park
St Peter, Jersey
+44 (0) 1534 482116
jerseyleisure.com
Award-winning attraction featuring maize maze, activities and entertainment.

Discovery Pier
Gorey, Jersey
+44 (0) 1534 617704
gov.je
Interactive fun bringing Jersey's marine ecology to shore.

Guernsey Aquarium
St Peter Port, Guernsey
+44 (0) 1481 723301
visitguernsey.com
Local, European and tropical marine life.

Jersey Goldsmiths and Lion Park
St Lawrence, Jersey
+44 (0) 1534 482098
jerseygoldsmiths.com
Gold and gemstones set among beautiful lakes and gardens.

La Mare Wine Estate
St Mary, Jersey
+44 (0) 1534 481178
lamarewineestate.com
Vineyards, winery and visitor centre with children's activities.

The Living Legend
St Peter, Jersey
+44 (0) 1534 485496
jerseyslivinglegend.co.je
Adventure and leisure village packed with family fun.

Oatlands Village
St Sampson, Guernsey
+44 (0) 1481 244282
Watch craftspeople at work, plus shops and café.

Samarès Manor
St Clement, Jersey
+44 (0) 1534 870551
samaresmanor.com
Historic house, splendid gardens, crafts and children's activities.

Heritage

Castle Cornet
St Peter Port, Guernsey
+44 (0) 1481 721657
museums.gov.gg
Ancient harbour fortress containing maritime and military museums.

Elizabeth Castle
St Helier, Jersey
+44 (0) 1534 723971
jerseyheritage.com
16thC stronghold with daily call to arms.

German Occupation Museum
Forest, Guernsey
+44 (0) 1481 238205
visitguernsey.com
Life during the WWII featuring authentic occupation street.

Jersey Museum and Art Gallery
St Helier, Jersey
+44 (0) 1534 633300
jerseyheritage.com
Discover the history, traditions and culture of Jersey.

Jersey War Tunnels
St Lawrence, Jersey
+44 (0) 1534 860808
jerseywartunnels.com
Gripping glimpse of life on Jersey under occupation.

La Hougue Bie
St Saviour, Jersey
+44 (0) 1534 833823
jerseyheritage.com
One of the finest burial mounds in Europe.

La Vallette Underground Military Museum
St Peter Port, Guernsey
+44 (0) 1481 722300
visitguernsey.com
Military museum housed in air-conditioned German tunnel complex.

The Little Chapel
St Andrews, Guernsey
+44 (0) 1481 237200
thelittlechapel.org
Possibly the smallest chapel in the world.

Mont Orgueil Castle
Gorey, Jersey
+44 (0) 1534 853292
jerseyheritage.com
Superbly preserved castle, the jewel in Jersey's crown.

Pleinmont Observation Tower
Torteval, Guernsey
+44 (0) 1481 238205
visitguernsey.com
Naval observation tower used by the Germans 1942-45.

Victor Hugo House
St Peter Port, Guernsey
+44 (0) 1481 721911
visitguernsey.com
Where the famous writer spent 14 years in exile.

Indoors

Fort Grey & Shipwreck Museum
Rocquaine, Guernsey
+44 (0) 1481 265036
museums.gov.gg
Martello tower housing museum with many salvaged artefacts.

Guernsey Museum and Art Gallery
St Peter Port, Guernsey
+44 (0) 1481 726518
museums.gov.gg
The island's natural and human history plus exhibitions.

The Guernsey Tapestry
St Peter Port, Guernsey
+44 (0) 1481 727106
guernseytapestry.org.gg
Tells the 1,000-year story of Guernsey in a remarkable tapestry.

Jersey Pottery
Gorey, Jersey
+44 (0) 1534 850850
jerseypottery.com
Decorate your own pottery at this famous attraction.

Maritime Museum and Occupation Tapestry
St Helier, Jersey
+44 (0) 1534 811043
jerseyheritage.com
Interactive museum and famous tapestry commemorating wartime Jersey.

National Trust of Guernsey Folk and Costume Museum
Castel, Guernsey
+44 (0) 1481 255384
nationaltrust-gsy.org.gg
Exhibitions and displays of old Guernsey life.

Outdoors

Durrell Wildlife
Trinity, Jersey
+44 (0) 1534 860000
durrell.org
World-famous sanctuary for exotic and endangered species.

Hamptonne
St Lawrence, Jersey
+44 (0) 1534 863955
jerseyheritage.com
Superbly restored farm buildings recreate rural life.

La Claire Mare
St Pierre du Bois, Guernsey
+44 (0) 1481 725093
societe.org.gg
Nature reserve featuring wet grassland and reedbeds.

Le Vaux de Monel and La Varde Rock
Rocquaine, Guernsey
nationaltrust-gsy.org.gg
Naturalised garden with panoramic views over Rocquaine Bay.

Lihou Island
St Pierre du Bois, Guernsey
+44 (0) 1481 266294
lihouisland.com
Unspoilt bird sanctuary reached by tidal causeway.

Events 2009

Liberation Day
Various venues, Jersey
jersey.com/liberation
9 May 2009

World Jersey Cheese Festival
Trinity, Jersey
jerseycheese.com
23 - 25 May 2009

Seafood Festival
Various venues, Guernsey
goodfoodguernsey.gg
1 - 31 Jul 2009

Out of the Blue Maritime Festival
St Helier, Jersey
jersey.com
4 - 5 Jul 2009

Battle of Flowers Carnival
St Helier, Jersey
battleofflowers.com
13 - 14 Aug 2009

Battle of Britain Week
Various venues, Guernsey
visitguernsey.com
7 - 13 Sep 2009

International Chess Festival
Vale, Guernsey
visitguernsey.com
18 - 24 Oct 2009

Guernsey Jazz Festival
St Peter Port, Guernsey
dukeofrichmond.com
30 Oct - 1 Nov 2009

La Fête dé Noué
Various venues, Jersey
jersey.com
28 Nov - 14 Dec 2009

Regional contacts and information

For more information on accommodation, attractions, activities, events and holidays in the Channel Islands, contact one of the following tourism organisations. Their websites have a wealth of information and publications to help you get the most out of your visit.

Guernsey

Guernsey Information Centre
North Esplanade, St Peter Port
Guernsey GY1 3AN
t +44 (0) 1481 723552
t +44 (0) 800 028 5353 (information pack request)
e enquiries@visitguernsey.com
w visitguernsey.com

Alderney

States of Alderney
PO Box 1
Alderney
GY9 3AA
t +44 (0) 1481 822811

Jersey

Jersey Tourism
Liberation Place
St Helier
Jersey
JE1 1BB
t +44 (0) 1534 448800
e info@jersey.com
w jersey.com

Free publications available to order from Jersey Tourism include:

- **What's on**
- **Jersey Map**
- **Walking Guide**

Clockwise: Liberation Day, Guernsey; Regatta, Guernsey; La Fête dé Noué, Jersey

where to stay in
The Channel Islands

For the location of the accommodation listed, refer to the maps at the front of this guide.

Accommodation symbols

Symbols give useful information about services and facilities. On pages 16 to 17 you can find a key to these symbols.

ALDERNEY Map 10   **HOTEL**

Rating Applied For
HOTEL

B&B PER ROOM PER NIGHT
D £100.00–£160.00
HB PER PERSON PER NIGHT
Min £25.00

7 nights for the price of 6. Advantageous travel-inclusive packages and great-value short breaks available.

Braye Beach Hotel

Braye Street, Alderney GY9 3XT t +44 (0) 1481 824300 e reception@brayebeach.com

brayebeach.com GUEST REVIEWS · SPECIAL OFFERS · REAL-TIME BOOKING

open All year
bedrooms 21 double, 6 twin
bathrooms All en suite
payment Credit/debit cards, cash, cheques

The luxurious Braye Beach Hotel stands on the edge of Alderney's finest sandy beach, offering spectacular views across the bay. Delicious, fresh, local food is served in the restaurant and alfresco on the terrace and the whole hotel is furnished to an exceptional standard of decor. Facilities include a residents' private cinema.

SAT NAV GY9 3XT

Room 🖵 📞 📺 🆂 🚻 🍴 General 🛏 🏛 🛗 P ⓦ 🍷 🍽 ⊞ 🍽 🍴 ❄ Leisure ∪ 🎣 🏌 🚴

GUERNSEY Map 10   **HOTEL**

★★
HOTEL

B&B PER ROOM PER NIGHT
S £39.00–£62.00
D £58.00–£84.00
HB PER PERSON PER NIGHT
£39.00–£52.00

Free hire car, bus tickets or cycles (minimum 3-night stay).

Blue Horizon Hotel

Le Mont Durand, St Martin GY4 6DJ t +44 (0) 1481 238639 e info@bluehorizonguernsey.com

bluehorizonguernsey.com GUEST REVIEWS · REAL-TIME BOOKING

open April to October
bedrooms 13 double, 10 twin, 2 family
bathrooms All en suite
payment Credit/debit cards, cash, cheques

Blue Horizon Hotel is a warm, friendly hotel situated in a relaxed, cliff-top location. Ideal for walkers and those looking for an ideal base to explore our beautiful island.

SAT NAV GY4 6DJ ONLINE MAP

Room 🦽 📺 🚻 🍴 General 🛏 12 P ⓦ 🍷 🍽 ❄ Leisure 🎣 🚴

★★★
**HOTEL
SILVER AWARD**

B&B PER ROOM PER NIGHT
S £65.00–£230.00
D £65.00–£230.00
HB PER PERSON PER NIGHT
£54.00–£140.00

Hotel Bon Port

Moulin Huet Bay, St Martin GY4 6EW **t** +44 (0) 1481 239249 **e** mail@bonport.com

bonport.com SPECIAL OFFERS

Hotel Bon Port is situated in the midst of Guernsey's most beautiful coastal scenery. Renoir chose this location to paint some of his most famous works. With a heated pool, nine-hole golf course and award-winning bistro, Bon Port truly is a magnificent holiday venue.

open March to December
bedrooms 14 double, 6 twin, 2 family, 1 suite
bathrooms All en suite
payment Credit/debit cards, cash, cheques

Room ⛵ ☎ TV SC ⬇ ⬆ ♨ General 🛎 🏥 🅿 ⊕ 🍽 ⛶ ◉ 🍴 ❄ 🐾
Leisure ⌇ ∪ ⬳ ▶ 🚲

★★★★
HOTEL

B&B PER ROOM PER NIGHT
D £140.00–£230.00
HB PER PERSON PER NIGHT
Min £25.00

7 nights for the price of 6. Advantageous travel-inclusive packages and great-value short breaks available.

Fermain Valley Hotel

Fermain Lane, St Peter Port GY1 1ZZ **t** +44 (0) 1481 235666 **e** info@fermainvalley.com

fermainvalley.com GUEST REVIEWS · SPECIAL OFFERS · REAL-TIME BOOKING

open All year
bedrooms 37 double, 5 twin, 1 suite
bathrooms All en suite
payment Credit/debit cards, cash, cheques

A stunning hotel nestled amongst fabulous cliff walks in the island's prettiest valley, with individually designed bedrooms offering breathtaking views out to sea. Only five minutes from Guernsey's charming harbour capital, St Peter Port, this luxury hotel offers a choice of three restaurants, cosy lounges and a residents' private cinema.

SAT NAV GY1 1ZZ

Room ☎ TV SC ⬇ ♨ General 🛎 🏥 🅿 ⊕ 🍽 ◉ ⊞ ◉ 🍴 ❄
Leisure ⌇ ♨ ∪ ⬳ ▶ 🚲

★★★
SELF CATERING

Units **3**
Sleeps **1–6**

LOW SEASON PER WK
Min £500.00

HIGH SEASON PER WK
Max £975.00

Hotel Bon Port, St Martin

Moulin Huet Bay, St Martin GY4 6EW **t** +44 (0) 1481 239249 **e** mail@bonport.com

bonport.com SPECIAL OFFERS

Set in the grounds of Hotel Bon Port. Two-bedroom cottages and one-bedroom apartments. Enjoy all the facilities with the independence of self-catering.

open All year
payment Credit/debit cards, cash, cheques
nearest pub 1 mile
nearest shop 2 miles

Unit TV SC 🏠 🖥 ▪ ♨ 🍳 💧 ❄ ⛺ General 🛎 🏥 🅿 ◉ S 🐾
Leisure ⌇ ∪ ⬳ ▶ 🚲

★★★
SELF CATERING

Units **21**
Sleeps **2–5**

LOW SEASON PER WK
Min £255.00

HIGH SEASON PER WK
Max £865.00

Del Mar Court, St Martin

Booking Office, Del Mar Court, Le Varclin, St Martin GY4 6AL **t** +44 (0) 1481 237491
e reservations@selfcatering.co.gg

selfcatering.co.gg GUEST REVIEWS · SPECIAL OFFERS · REAL-TIME BOOKING

We are situated in a country lane above Fermain Bay yet only three minutes' drive from St Peter Port's shops and harbour. The apartments provide you with all you need for your family holiday.

open All year
payment Credit/debit cards, cash, cheques
nearest pub 0.5 miles
nearest shop 1 mile

Unit TV 🖥 ▪ 💧 🍳 ❄ General 🛎 🏥 🅿 ◉ S Leisure ⌇ ⬳ 🚲

GUERNSEY Map 10 | SELF CATERING

★★★–★★★★★
SELF CATERING

Units **4**
Sleeps **2–4**

LOW SEASON PER WK
Min £255.00

HIGH SEASON PER WK
Max £780.00

Le Douit Farm, St Martin

Del Mar Court, Le Varclin, St Martin GY4 6AL **t** +44 (0) 1481 237491
e reservations@selfcatering.co.gg

selfcatering.co.gg GUEST REVIEWS · SPECIAL OFFERS · REAL-TIME BOOKING

open March to November
payment Credit/debit cards, cash, cheques
nearest pub 0.5 miles
nearest shop 0.5 miles

We are situated in a country lane by St Martin's Church in the ancient hamlet of La Bellieuse. You will be able to relax and unwind in these peaceful surroundings. The famous scenic cliff walks are within a one and a half mile radius giving access to over 20 miles of pedestrian paths.

SAT NAV GY4 6RW **ONLINE MAP**

Unit 📺 🖥 🎞 🛋 📱 ✳ General 🐴 🏛 🛗 P ⊙ S Leisure 🎣 🚴

GUERNSEY Map 10 | SELF CATERING

★★★★–★★★★★★
SELF CATERING

Units **4**
Sleeps **2–6**

LOW SEASON PER WK
£400.00–£485.00

HIGH SEASON PER WK
£950.00–£1,700.00

Mille Fleurs, St Pierre Du Bois

Mille Fleurs, Rue Du Bordage, St Pierre Du Bois GY7 9DW **t** +44 (0) 1481 263911
e mfleurs@cwgsy.net

millefleurs.co.uk

open All year
payment Cash, cheques
nearest pub 1 mile
nearest shop 1 mile

Set in beautiful, award-winning gardens in peaceful, conservation valley in the south west of Guernsey, our luxury cottages are tastefully furnished and fully equipped to a very high standard. One, two or three bedrooms. Heated outdoor swimming pool. Close to unspoilt beaches. Ideal for garden lovers, birdwatchers and keen walkers.

Unit 📺 🆂🅲 📠 🖥 🎞 🛋 🍳 🛋 📱 ✳ 🎿 General 🐴 🏛 🛗 P ⊙ S
Leisure 🏊 ♨ 🎣 🚶 🚴

JERSEY Map 10 | HOTEL

★★
HOTEL

B&B PER ROOM PER NIGHT
S £39.50–£61.50
D £62.00–£106.00
HB PER PERSON PER NIGHT
£45.00–£75.50

Free car hire (excl insurance, petrol and taxes). Free bottle of wine each night (HB only). Offers based on 2 sharing for minimum 3 nights.

Les Charrieres Country Hotel

Les Charrieres, St Peter JE3 7ZQ **t** +44 (0) 1534 481480 **e** enquiries@lescharrieshotel.co.uk

lescharrieshotel.co.uk SPECIAL OFFERS

open All year
bedrooms 4 triple, 10 double, 2 twin, 25 family
bathrooms All en suite
payment Credit/debit cards, cash, cheques

Les Charrieres Country Hotel is situated in the beautiful countryside within the peaceful heart of St Peter. Convenient for many of the island's major attractions, golf courses and beaches and only 1.5 miles from St Helier. The hotel has many facilities including restaurants, bar, tennis court and indoor heated pool.

SAT NAV JE3 7ZQ **ONLINE MAP**

Room 🛏 📞 📺 🆂🅲 ♨ 🍵 General 🐴 🏛 🛗 P 📶 🍽 🎱 ⚹
Leisure ♨ 🏓 ☂ 🎯 🎾 ♨ 🎣 🚶 🚴

Country ways

The Countryside Rights of Way Act gives people new rights to walk on areas of open countryside and registered common land.

To find out where you can go and what you can do, as well as information about taking your dog to the countryside, go online at countrysideaccess.gov.uk.

And when you're out and about...

Always follow the Country Code

- Be safe – plan ahead and follow any signs
- Leave gates and property as you find them
- Protect plants and animals, and take your litter home
- Keep dogs under close control
- Consider other people

Further information

Clockwise from above: Big Ben, London; Eilean Donan Castle, Scotland; Caernarfon Castle, Wales

411

Quality assessment schemes

When you're looking for a place to stay, you need a rating system you can trust. Quality ratings are your clear guide to what to expect, in an easy-to-understand form.

Most national assessing bodies (VisitBritain, VisitScotland, Visit Wales, Jersey Tourism, VisitGuernsey and the AA) operate to a common set of standards. National tourist board professional assessors pay unannounced visits to establishments that are new to the rating scheme and stay overnight where appropriate. Once in the scheme establishments receive an annual pre-arranged day visit, with an overnight stay generally every other year for hotel and bed and breakfast accommodation. On these occasions the assessors book in anonymously, and test all the facilities and services.

Based on internationally recognised star ratings, the system puts great emphasis on quality, and reflects exactly what consumers are looking for. Ratings are awarded from one to five stars – the more stars, the higher the quality and the greater the range of facilities and services provided – and are the sign of quality assurance, giving you the confidence to book the accommodation that meets your expectations.

Northern Ireland has a separate classification scheme for hotels, guest accommodation, bed and breakfasts and self catering properties. All properties are inspected by the Northern Ireland Tourist Board but bed and breakfast accommodation and hostels are not awarded a star rating. To find out more visit discovernorthernireland.com/information.

Look out, too, for Enjoy England Gold and Silver Awards, which are awarded to hotels and bed and breakfast accommodation in England achieving the highest levels of quality within their star rating. While the overall rating is based on a combination of facilities and quality, the Gold and Silver Awards are based solely on quality.

Hotels

All hotels that are awarded a star rating will meet the minimum standards – so you can be confident that you will find the basic services, such as:

- All bedrooms with an en suite or private bathroom
- A designated reception facility and staff members who will be available during the day and evening (24hrs in case of an emergency)
- A licence to serve alcohol (unless a temperance hotel)
- Access to the hotel at all times for registered guests
- Dinner available at least five days a week (with the exception of a Town House Hotel or Metro Hotel)
- All statutory obligations will be met.

Hotels have to provide certain additional facilities and services at the higher star levels, some of which may be important to you:

TWO-STAR hotels must provide:
- Dinner seven nights a week.

THREE-STAR hotels must provide:
- All en suite bedrooms (ie no private bathrooms)
- Direct dial phones in all rooms
- Room service during core hours
- A permanently staffed reception.

FOUR-STAR hotels must provide:
- 24-hour room service
- 50% of all en suites with bath **and** shower.

FIVE-STAR hotels must provide:
- Some permanent suites
- Enhanced services, such as concierge.

Sometimes a hotel with a lower star rating has exceptional bedrooms and bathrooms and offers its guests a very special welcome, but cannot achieve a higher rating because, for example, it does not offer dinner every evening (two star), room service (three star) or does not have the minimum 50% of bathrooms with bath and shower (four star).

Bed and breakfast accommodation

All bed and breakfast accommodation that is awarded a star rating will meet the minimum standards – so you can be confident that you will find the basic services that you would expect, such as:

- A clear explanation of booking charges, services offered and cancellation terms
- A full cooked breakfast or substantial continental breakfast
- At least one bathroom or shower room for every six guests
- For a stay of more than one night, rooms cleaned and beds made daily
- Printed advice on how to summon emergency assistance at night
- All statutory obligations will be met.

Proprietors of bed and breakfast accommodation have to provide certain additional facilities and services at the higher star levels, some of which may be important to you:

THREE-STAR accommodation must provide:
- Private bathroom/shower room (cannot be shared with the owners)
- Bedrooms must have a washbasin if not en suite.

FOUR-STAR accommodation must provide:
- 50% of bedrooms en suite or with private bathroom.

FIVE-STAR accommodation must provide:
- All bedrooms with en suite or private bathroom.

Sometimes a bed and breakfast establishment has exceptional bedrooms and bathrooms and offers guests a very special welcome, but cannot achieve a higher star rating because, for example, there are no en suite bedrooms, or it is difficult to put washbasins in the bedrooms (three star). This is sometimes the case with period properties.

Quality in hotels and bed and breakfast accommodation
The availability of additional services and facilities alone is not enough for an establishment to achieve a higher star rating. Hotels and bed and breakfast accommodation have to meet exacting standards for quality in critical areas. Consumer research has shown the critical areas to be: cleanliness, bedrooms, bathrooms, hospitality and services, and food.

Self-catering accommodation

All self-catering accommodation that is awarded a star rating will meet the minimum standards – so you can be confident that you will find the basic services that you would expect, such as:

- Clear information prior to booking on all aspects of the accommodation including location, facilities, prices, deposit, policies on smoking, children etc
- No shared facilities, with the exception of a laundry room in multi-unit sites
- All appliances and furnishings will meet product safety standards for self-catering accommodation, particularly regarding fire safety
- At least one smoke alarm in the unit and a fire blanket in the kitchen
- Clear information on emergency procedures, including who to contact
- Contact details for the local doctor, dentist etc
- All statutory obligations will be met including an annual gas check and public liability insurance.

Certain additional facilities and services are required at the higher star levels, some of which may be important to you:

TWO-STAR accommodation must provide:
- Single beds which are a minimum of 3ft wide and double beds a minimum of 4ft 6in.

THREE-STAR accommodation must provide:
- Bed linen (with or without additional charge).

FOUR-STAR accommodation must provide:
- All advertised sleeping space in bedrooms (unless a studio)
- Bed linen included in the hire charge and beds are made up for arrival.

FIVE-STAR accommodation must provide:
- Full-size beds, including those for children
- At least two of the following items: tumble-dryer, telephone, Hi-Fi, video, DVD.

Some self-catering establishments offer a choice of units that may have different ratings. In this case, the entry shows the range available.

Quality in self-catering accommodation
The availability of additional facilities, such as a dishwasher or DVD, is not enough to achieve a higher star rating – the quality of the furnishings, equipment and decoration must be of a high standard. Self-catering accommodation with a lower star rating may offer some or all of the above, but to achieve the higher star ratings, the overall quality score has to be reached and exacting standards have to be met in critical areas. Consumer research has shown these to be: cleanliness, bedrooms, bathrooms, kitchens and public areas.

Holiday, touring and camping parks

Holiday, touring and camping parks are assessed under the British Graded Holiday Parks Scheme. Operated jointly by the national tourist boards for England, Scotland, Wales and Northern Ireland, it was devised in association with the British Holiday and Home Parks Association and the National Caravan Council. It gives you a clear guide of what to expect in an easy-to-understand form.

The process to arrive at a star rating is very thorough to ensure that when you make a booking you can be confident it will meet your expectations. Professional assessors visit parks annually and take into account over 50 separate aspects, from landscaping and layout to maintenance, customer care and, most importantly, cleanliness.

Strict guidelines are in place to ensure that every park is assessed to the same criteria. A random check is made of a sample of accommodation provided for hire (caravans, chalets etc) **but the quality of the accommodation itself is not included in the grading assessment**.

In addition to The British Graded Holiday Parks Scheme, VisitBritain operates a rating scheme for Holiday Villages. The assessor stays on the site overnight and grades the overall quality of the visitor experience, including accommodation, facilities, cleanliness, service and food.

Parks are required to meet progressively higher standards of quality as they move up the scale from one to five stars:

ONE STAR Acceptable
To achieve this grade, the park must be clean with good standards of maintenance and customer care.

TWO STAR Good
All the above points plus an improved level of landscaping, lighting, refuse disposal and maintenance. May be less expensive than more highly rated parks.

THREE STAR Very good
Most parks fall within this category; three stars represent the industry standard. The range of facilities provided may vary from park to park, but they will be of a very good standard and will be well maintained.

FOUR STAR Excellent
You can expect careful attention to detail in the provision of all services and facilities. Four star parks rank among the industry's best.

FIVE STAR Exceptional
Highest levels of customer care will be provided. All facilities will be maintained in pristine condition in attractive surroundings.

Holiday villages

Holiday Villages are assessed under a separate rating scheme and are awarded one to five stars based on both the quality of facilities and the range of services provided. The option to include breakfast and dinner is normally available. A variety of accommodation if offered, mostly in chalets.

★ Simple, practical, no frills

★★ Well presented and well run

★★★ Good level of quality and comfort

★★★★ Very good standard throughout

★★★★★ Excellent facilities and services

Quality signage

Signage for the quality ratings schemes in each of the countries differ but the ratings and classifications are the same (except in Northern Ireland). Here are some examples of the different signs you may see.

Accommodation advice and information

Making a booking

When enquiring about accommodation, make sure you check prices, the quality rating and other important details. You will also need to state your requirements clearly and precisely, for example:

* Arrival and departure dates, with acceptable alternatives if appropriate

* The type of accommodation you need – for example, room with twin beds, en suite bathroom

* The terms you want – for example, room only, bed and breakfast

* The age of any children with you, whether you want them to share your room or be next door, and any other special requirements, such as a cot

* Any particular requirements you may have, such as a special diet, ground-floor room.

Confirmation

Misunderstandings can easily happen over the telephone, so do request a written confirmation, together with details of any terms and conditions.

Deposits

If you make a hotel or bed and breakfast reservation weeks or months in advance, you will probably be asked for a deposit, which will then be deducted from the final bill when you leave. The amount will vary from establishment to establishment and could be payment in full at peak times.

Proprietors of self-catering accommodation will normally ask you to pay a deposit immediately, and then to pay the full balance before your holiday date. This safeguards the proprietor in case you decide to cancel at a late stage or simply do not turn up. He or she may have turned down other bookings on the strength of yours and may find it hard to re-let if you cancel.

In the case of caravan, camping and touring parks, and holiday villages the full charge often has to be paid in advance. This may be in two instalments – a deposit at the time of booking and the balance by, say, two weeks before the start of the booked period.

Payment on arrival

Some establishments, especially large hotels in big towns, ask you to pay for your room on arrival if you have not booked it in advance. This is especially likely to happen if you arrive late and have little or no luggage.

If you are asked to pay on arrival, it is a good idea to see your room first, to make sure it meets your requirements.

Cancellations

Legal contract

When you accept accommodation that is offered to you, by telephone or in writing, you enter a legally binding contract with the proprietor. This means that if you cancel your booking, fail to take up the accommodation or leave early, the proprietor may be entitled to compensation if he or she cannot re-let for all or a good part of the booked period. You will probably forfeit any deposit you have paid, and may well be asked for an additional payment.

At the time of booking you should be advised of what charges would be made in the event of cancelling the accommodation or leaving early. If this is not mentioned you should ask so that future disputes can be avoided. The proprietor cannot make a claim until after the booked period, and during that time he or she should make every effort to re-let the accommodation. If there is a dispute it is sensible for both sides to seek legal advice on the matter. If you do have to change your travel plans, it is in your own interests to let the proprietor know in writing as soon as possible, to give them a chance to re-let your accommodation.

And remember, if you book by telephone and are asked for your credit card number, you should check whether the proprietor intends charging your credit card account should you later cancel your reservation. A proprietor should not be able to charge your credit card account with a cancellation fee unless he or she has made this clear at the time of your booking and you have agreed. However, to avoid later disputes, we suggest you check whether this is the intention.

Insurance

A travel or holiday insurance policy will safeguard you if you have to cancel or change your holiday plans. You can arrange a policy quite cheaply through your insurance company or travel agent. Some hotels also offer their own insurance schemes and many self-catering agencies insist their customers take out a policy when they book their holidays.

Arrival time

If you know you will be arriving late in the evening, it is a good idea to say so when you book. If you are delayed on your way, a telephone call to say that you will be late would be appreciated.

It is particularly important to liaise with the owner of self-catering accommodation about key collection as he or she will not necessarily be on site.

Service charges and tipping

These days many places levy service charges automatically. If they do, they must clearly say so in their offer of accommodation, at the time of booking. The service charge then becomes part of the legal contract when you accept the offer of accommodation.

If a service charge is levied automatically, there is no need to tip the staff, unless they provide some exceptional service. The usual tip for meals is 10% of the total bill.

Telephone charges

Establishments can set their own charges for telephone calls made through their switchboard or from direct-dial telephones in bedrooms. These charges are often much higher than telephone companies' standard charges (to defray the cost of providing the service).

Comparing costs

It is a condition of the quality assessment schemes that an establishment's unit charges are on display by the telephones or with the room information. It is not always easy to compare these charges with standard rates, so before using a telephone for long-distance calls, you may decide to ask how the charges compare.

Security of valuables

You can deposit your valuables with the proprietor or manager during your stay, and we recommend you do this as a sensible precaution. Make sure you obtain a receipt for them. Some places do not accept articles for safe custody, and in that case it is wisest to keep your valuables with you.

Disclaimer

Some proprietors put up a notice that disclaims liability for property brought on to their premises by a guest. In fact, they can only restrict their liability. By law, a proprietor is liable for the value of the loss or damage to any property (except a car or its contents) of a guest who has engaged overnight accommodation, but if the proprietor has the notice on display, liability is limited to £50 for one article and a total of £100 for any one guest. The notice must be prominently displayed in the reception area or main entrance. These limits do not apply to valuables you have deposited with the proprietor for safekeeping, or to property lost through the default, neglect or wilful act of the proprietor or his staff.

Finding a camping or touring park

Tourist signs similar to the one shown here are designed to help visitors find their park. They clearly show whether the park is for tents or caravans or both.

Tourist information centres throughout Britain are able to give campers and caravanners information about parks in their areas. Some tourist information centres have camping and caravanning advisory services that provide details of park availability and often assist with park booking.

Electric hook-up points

Most parks now have electric hook-up points for caravans and tents. Voltage is generally 240v AC, 50 cycles. Parks may charge extra for this facility, and it is advisable to check rates when making a booking.

Travelling with pets

Dogs, cats, ferrets and some other pet mammals can be brought into the UK from certain countries without having to undertake six months' quarantine on arrival provided they meet all the rules of the Pet Travel Scheme (PETS).

For full details, visit the PETS website at
w defra.gov.uk/animalh/quarantine/index.htm or contact the PETS Helpline
t +44 (0) 870 241 1710
e quarantine@animalhealth.gsi.gov.uk
Ask for fact sheets which cover dogs and cats, ferrets or domestic rabbits and rodents.

What to expect

Hotels, guest and self-catering accommodation, holiday villages

The proprietor/management is required to undertake the following:

- To maintain standards of guest care, cleanliness and service appropriate to the type of establishment;

- To describe accurately in any advertisement, brochure or other printed or electronic media, the facilities and services provided;

- To make clear to visitors exactly what is included in all prices quoted for accommodation, including taxes, and any other surcharges. Details of charges for additional services/facilities should also be made clear;

- To give a clear statement of the policy on cancellations to guests at the time of booking ie by telephone, fax, email, as well as information given in a printed format;

- To adhere to and not to exceed prices quoted at the time of booking for accommodation and other services;

- To advise visitors at the time of booking, and subsequently if any change, if the accommodation offered is in an unconnected annexe or similar and to indicate the location of such accommodation and any difference in comfort and/or amenities from accommodation in the establishment;

- To register all guests on arrival (except self-catering accommodation);

- To give each visitor on request details of payments due and a receipt, if required;

- To deal promptly and courteously with all enquiries, requests, bookings and correspondence from visitors;

- To ensure complaint handling procedures are in place and that complaints received are investigated promptly and courteously and that the outcome is communicated to the visitor;

- To give due consideration to the requirements of visitors with disabilities and visitors with special needs, and to make suitable provision where applicable;

- To provide public liability insurance or comparable arrangements and to comply with all applicable planning, safety and other statutory requirements;

- To allow a quality ratings assessor reasonable access to the establishment on request, to confirm the Code of Conduct is being observed.

What to expect

Holiday, touring and camping parks

In addition to fulfilling its statutory obligations, including having applied for a certificate under the Fire Precautions Act 1971 (if applicable) and holding public liability insurance, and ensuring that all caravan holiday homes/chalets for hire and the park and all buildings and facilities thereon, the fixtures, furnishings, fittings and decor are maintained in sound and clean condition and are fit for the purposes intended, the management is required to undertake the following:

- To ensure high standards of courtesy, cleanliness, catering and service appropriate to the type of park;

- To describe to all visitors and prospective visitors the amenities, facilities and services provided by the park and/or caravan holiday homes/chalets whether by advertisement, brochure, word of mouth or other means;

- To allow visitors to see the park or caravan holiday homes/chalets for hire, if requested, before booking;

- To present grading awards and/or any other national tourist board awards unambiguously;

- To make clear to visitors exactly what is included in prices quoted for the park or caravan holiday homes/chalets, meals and refreshments, including service charge, taxes and other surcharges. Details of charges, if any, for heating or for additional services or facilities available should also be made clear;

- To adhere to, and not to exceed, prices current at time of occupation for caravan holiday homes/chalets or other services;

- To advise visitors at the time of booking, and subsequently if any change, if the caravan holiday home/chalet or pitch offered is in a different location or on another park, and to indicate the location of this and any difference in comfort and amenities;

- To give each visitor, on request, details of payments due and a receipt if required;

- To advise visitors at the time of booking of the charges that might be incurred if the booking is subsequently cancelled;

- To register all guests on arrival;

- To deal promptly and courteously with all visitors and prospective visitors, including enquiries, requests, reservations, correspondence and complaints;

- To allow a national tourist board representative reasonable access to the park and/or caravan holiday homes/chalet whether by prior appointment or on an unannounced assessment, to confirm that the VisitBritain Code of Conduct is being observed and that the appropriate quality standard is being maintained;

- The operator must comply with the provision of the caravan industry Codes of Practice.

Comments and complaints

The law
Places that offer accommodation have legal and statutory responsibilities to their customers, such as providing information about prices, providing adequate fire precautions and safeguarding valuables. They must also describe their accommodation and facilities accurately. All the places featured in this guide have declared that they do fulfil all applicable statutory obligations.

Information
The proprietors themselves supply the descriptions of their establishments and other information for the entries, (except Enjoy England ratings and awards). The publishers cannot guarantee the accuracy of information in this guide, and accept no responsibility for any error or misrepresentation. All liability for loss, disappointment, negligence or other damage caused by reliance on the information contained in this guide, or in the event of bankruptcy or liquidation or cessation of trade of any company, individual or firm mentioned, is hereby excluded. We strongly recommend that you carefully check prices and other details when you book your accommodation.

Quality signage
All establishments displaying a quality sign have to hold current membership of a quality assessment scheme. When an establishment is sold the new owner has to reapply and be reassessed. In some areas the rating may be carried forward in the interim.

Problems
Of course, we hope you will not have cause for complaint, but problems do occur from time to time. If you are dissatisfied with anything, make your complaint to the management immediately. Then the management can take action at once to investigate the matter and put things right. The longer you leave a complaint, the harder it is to deal with it effectively.

In certain circumstances, the national tourist boards may look into complaints. However they have no statutory control over establishments or their methods of operating and cannot become involved in legal or contractual matters, nor can they get involved in seeking financial recompense.

If you do have problems that have not been resolved by the proprietor and which you would like to bring to our attention, please write to:

England
Quality in Tourism, Farncombe House, Broadway, Worcestershire, United Kingdom WR12 7LJ

Scotland
Customer Feedback Department, VisitScotland, Cowan House, Inverness Retail and Business Park, Inverness, United Kingdom IV2 7GF

Wales
VisitWales, Tŷ Glyndŵr, Treowain Enterprise Park, Machynlleth, Powys, United Kingdom SY20 8WW

Northern Ireland
Visitor Information, Northern Ireland Tourist Board, 59 North Street, Belfast, United Kingdom BT1 1NB

Guernsey
Quality Development Manager, Commerce and Employment Department, PO Box 459, St Martin, Guernsey GY1 6AF

Jersey
Tourism Office, Liberation Place, St Helier, Jersey JE1 1BB

About the accommodation entries

Entries

All the accommodation featured in this guide has been assessed or has applied for assessment under a quality assessment scheme.

Proprietors have paid to have their establishment featured in either a standard entry (includes description, facilities and prices) or enhanced entry (photograph and extended details).

Locations

Places to stay are generally listed under the town, city or village where they are located. If a place is in a small village, you may find it listed under a nearby town (providing it is within a seven-mile radius).

Place names are listed alphabetically within each regional section of the guide, along with the name of the ceremonial county they are in and their map reference.

Complete addresses for self-catering properties are not given and the town(s) listed may be a distance from the actual establishment. Please check the precise location at the time of booking.

Map references

These refer to the colour location maps at the front of the guide. The first figure shown is the map number, the following letter and figure indicate the grid reference on the map. Some entries were included just before the guide went to press, so they do not appear on the maps.

Addresses

County names, which appear in the place headings, are not repeated in the entries. When you are writing, you should of course make sure you use the full address and postcode.

Telephone numbers

Telephone numbers, listed below the accommodation address for each entry, are shown with the international access code +44. If dialling from outside the UK, use +44 and omit the number in brackets. If dialling from within the UK, there is no need to dial +44 – simply start with the number in brackets.

Prices

The prices shown are only a general guide; they were supplied to us by proprietors in summer 2008. Remember, changes may occur after the guide goes to press, so we strongly advise you to check prices when you book your accommodation.

Prices are shown in pounds sterling and include VAT where applicable. Some places also include a service charge in their standard tariff, so check this when you book.

Bed and breakfast: the prices shown are per room for overnight accommodation with breakfast. The double room price is for two people. (If a double room is occupied by one person there is sometimes a reduction in price.)

Half board: the prices shown are per person per night for room, evening meal and breakfast. These prices are usually based on two people sharing a room.

Evening meal: the prices shown are per person per night.

Some places only provide a continental breakfast in the set price, and you may have to pay extra if you want a full cooked breakfast.

According to the law, establishments with at least four bedrooms or eight beds must display their overnight accommodation charges in the reception area or entrance. In your own interests, do make sure you check prices and what they include.

Self catering: prices shown are per unit per week and include VAT.

Touring pitches: prices are based on the minimum and maximum charges for one night for two persons, car and either caravan or tent. (Some parks may charge separately for car, caravan or tent, and for each person and there may be an extra charge for caravan awnings.)

Caravan holiday homes: minimum and maximum prices are given per week.

Children's rates

You will find that many places charge a reduced rate for children, especially if they share a room with their parents. Some places charge the full rate, however, when a child occupies a room which might otherwise have been let to an adult. The upper age limit for reductions for children varies from one establishment to another, so check this when you book.

Seasonal packages and special promotions

Prices often vary through the year and may be significantly lower outside peak holiday weeks. Many places offer special package rates – fully inclusive weekend breaks, for example – in the autumn, winter and spring. A number of establishments taking an enhanced entry have included any special offers, themed breaks etc that are available.

You can get details of other bargain packages that may be available from the establishments themselves, regional tourism organisations or your local Tourist Information Centre (TIC). Your local travel agent may also have information and can help you make reservations.

Bathrooms (hotels and bed and breakfast)

Each accommodation entry shows you the number of en suite and private bathrooms available. En suite bathroom means the bath or shower and wc are contained behind the main door of the bedroom. Private bathroom means a bath or shower and wc solely for the occupants of one bedroom, on the same floor, reasonably close and with a key provided. If the availability of a bath, rather than a shower, is important to you, remember to check when you book.

Meals (hotels and bed and breakfast)

It is advisable to check availability of meals and set times when making your reservation. Some smaller places may ask you at breakfast whether you want an evening meal. The prices shown in each entry are for bed and breakfast or half board, but many places also offer lunch.

Opening period

If an entry does not indicate an opening period, please check directly with the establishment.

Symbols

The at-a-glance symbols included at the end of each entry show many of the services and facilities available at each establishment. You will find the key to these symbols on pages 16 and 17.

Smoking

In the UK, it is illegal to smoke in enclosed public spaces and places of work. This means that smoking is banned in the public and communal areas of hotels, guesthouses and B&Bs, and in restaurants, bars and pubs.

Some hotels, guesthouses and B&Bs may choose to provide designated smoking bedrooms, and B&Bs and guest houses may allow smoking in private areas that are not used by any staff. Smoking may also be allowed in self-contained short-term rental accommodation, such as holiday cottages, flats or caravans, if the owner chooses to allow it.

If you wish to smoke, it is advisable to check whether it is allowed when you book.

Alcoholic drinks

All hotels (except temperance hotels) hold an alcohol licence. Some bed and breakfast accommodation may also be licensed, however, the licence may be restricted – to diners only, for example. If a bar is available this is shown by the ♥ symbol.

Pets

Many places accept guests with dogs, but we do advise that you check this when you book, and ask if there are any extra charges or rules about exactly where your pet is allowed. The acceptance of dogs is not always extended to cats and it is strongly advised that cat owners contact the establishment well in advance. Some establishments do not accept pets at all. Pets are welcome by arrangement where you see this symbol ♪.

The quarantine laws have changed, and dogs, cats and ferrets are able to come into the UK and the Channel Islands from certain countries. For details of the Pet Travel Scheme (PETS) please turn to page 416.

Payment accepted

The types of payment accepted by an establishment are listed in the payment accepted section. If you plan to pay by card, check that the establishment will take your particular card before you book. Some proprietors will charge you a higher rate if you pay by credit card rather than cash or cheque. The difference is to cover the percentage paid by the proprietor to the credit card company. When you book by telephone, you may be asked for your credit card number as confirmation. But remember, the proprietor may then charge your credit card account if you cancel your booking. See under Cancellations on page 415.

Rating Applied For

At the time of going to press some establishments featured in this guide had not yet been assessed and so their new rating could not be included. Rating Applied For indicates this.

Essential information

Customs and immigration

On arrival in the United Kingdom, you must show a valid national passport or equivalent document that satisfactorily establishes your identity and nationality. You may need a visa – entry clearance certificate – before you travel to Britain, if you are not a British citizen or a citizen of one the European Economic Area (EEA) countries.

Money and currency

Britain's unit of currency is the Great British Pound (sterling) – GBP. The symbol for the pound sterling is £. British money is based on the decimal system – there are one hundred pence to each pound. Coins have the values of 1p, 2p, 5p, 10p, 20p, 50p, £1 and £2. Notes have the values of £5, £10, £20 and £50. Scottish £1 notes are still in circulation in Scotland. The Channel Islands and the Isle of Man have some different coins and notes from the mainland but the monetary system is the same.

Communication

Public payphones
Public payphones are widely available throughout the UK. Many provide additional services including email, mobile phone text messaging, and internet services.

Mobile phones
Most mobile phones will work via 'roaming' in Britain. Check with your mobile phone provider before you leave that the roaming function is activated on your phone. You can buy a British prepay mobile phone including phone number and SIM card in many high street shops. You do not need to provide identification to purchase a prepay phone, but you will need to provide identification and proof of address in Britain to set up a mobile phone contract.

Medicine and health

Medical insurance
You are strongly advised to take out adequate insurance before travelling to Britain. Your travel agent will be able to suggest a suitable policy.

Bringing medicine into the UK
If you want to bring medicine into the UK, first check that it is licensed for use. Always carry medicines in a correctly labelled container as issued by the pharmacist. Otherwise, bring a letter from your doctor or a personal health record card giving details of the drug prescribed, in case it is queried by customs or you require additional supplies. Remember that some medicines available over-the-counter in other countries may be controlled in Britain, and vice versa.

For further information please call HM Customs and Excise Advice Centre on +44 (0) 20 8929 0152.

Pharmacies and chemists
In Britain you can obtain prescription and over-the-counter (non-prescription) medications, as well as expert medical advice, at pharmacies – often called chemists. We recommend you carry a letter from your doctor stating your prescription and dosage if you are taking any medication.

Pharmacy opening hours
Pharmacies are usually open from 09.00 to 18.00 Monday to Friday, 09.00 to 13.00 on Saturdays and limited availability on Sundays. However, in larger cities and some supermarkets you will find a number of pharmacies open late during the week and on the weekend. For more information and to find a pharmacy near you, visit the National Health Service pharmacy information website (nhs.uk/servicedirectories).

Vaccinations and inoculations
You do not require an International Certificate of Vaccination when travelling to the UK, but you should check if one is needed on re-entry into your own country.

Food and water

The level of food hygiene in the UK is very high, so you should simply observe normal precautions such as ensuring food is thoroughly cooked or that it is within the expiry date. The standard of water cleanliness is also very high and you can usually drink from all taps that supply water to kitchens. Tap water in restaurants and ice cubes are also generally safe. You can find bottled water in most grocery shops and supermarkets.

Time zone and holidays

British summer time

British summer time starts on the last Sunday in March when clocks go forward one hour at 01.00, and ends on the last Sunday in October when they go back one hour at 01.00. The time for the rest of the year is Coordinated Universal Time.

Public holidays

For a list of 2009 public holidays in the UK, see page 395.

School holidays

The main summer holiday is about six weeks from mid-July to early September. Children also have two weeks holiday at Christmas and at Easter, plus a week in mid-October and in mid-February. Exact dates vary between each education authority.

Utilities and services

Electricity

The voltage used in Britain is 240 Volts AC at 50HZ. Most power sockets are designed for standard three-pin square plugs. Electrical appliances in Britain generally use the British standard plug with three square pins. Plug socket adaptors and power transformers are widely available; you can buy them at most airports, electrical shops and hardware stores.

Gas

Gas is often used in homes for cooking, central heating and to heat water. Some cookers may use both gas and electricity, for example they may use gas for the hob and electricity for the oven.

Car fuel

Most cars in Britain run off petrol or diesel. Petrol is usually sold as either Four Star (usually a red pump) or Unleaded (usually a green pump) – both available from most petrol stations. There are an increasing number of electric, or electric-petrol combined and liquefied petroleum gas (LPG) cars on the road.

Weather and what to wear

Weather overview

Britain has a fairly temperate climate and can sometimes be overcast. There are long summer evenings due to the northerly latitude and periods of fine weather can happen in all seasons. The weather can vary greatly from day to day, but generally summer (June-August) is hot 14-30°C, and winter (December-February) is a cool 1-5°C. There is quite a difference in temperature between Scotland and Southern England – generally, the further south, the warmer it is likely to be.

What to wear

Whatever the season, the British weather is liable to change from day to day. It is a good idea to bring a selection of items including some light clothes, items you can layer (that way you can add or remove layers depending on temperature), at least one warm pullover and a waterproof coat or umbrella.

Tourist Information Centres

There is a network of Tourist Information Centres across Britain. Knowledgeable staff will be happy to offer help and advice. Many centres can also provide maps and guides and it is often possible to book accommodation and travel tickets. Please refer to the regional sections of this guide for lists of local Tourist Information Centres.

Getting around Britain

London transport

London Underground (also called the Tube) has 12 lines, each with its own unique colour, so you can easily follow them on the Underground map. Most lines run through central London, and many serve parts of Greater London.

Buses are a quick, convenient way to travel around London, providing plenty of sightseeing opportunities on the way. There are over 6,500 buses in London operating 700 routes every day. You will need to buy a ticket before you board the bus – available from machines at the bus stop – or have a valid Oyster card (see below).

London's National Rail system stretches all over London. Many lines start at the main London railway stations (Paddington, Victoria, Waterloo, Kings Cross) with links to the Tube. Trains mainly serve areas outside central London, and travel over ground.

Children usually travel free, or at reduced fare, on all public transport in London.

Oyster cards

Oyster cards can be used to pay fares on all London Underground, buses, Docklands Light Railway and trams; they are generally not valid for National Rail services in London.

Oyster cards are very easy to use – you just touch the card on sensors at stations or on buses and it always charges you the lowest fare available for your journey. You buy credit for your journey and when it runs out you simply top up with more.

Oyster is available to adults only. Children below the age of 11 can accompany adults free of charge. Children between the ages of 11 and 15 should use the standard child travel card. You can get an Oyster card at any underground station, at one of 3,000 Oyster points around London displaying the London Underground sign (usually shops), or from visitbritaindirect.com.

Rail and train travel

Britain's rail network covers all main cities and smaller regional towns. Trains on the network are operated by a few large companies running routes from London to stations all over Britain, and smaller companies running routes in regional areas. You can find up-to-the-minute information about routes, fares and train times on National Rail Enquiries (nationalrail.co.uk). For detailed information about routes and services, refer to the train operators' websites (see page 428).

Railway passes

BritRail offers a wide selection of passes and tickets giving you freedom to travel on all National Rail services. Passes can also include sleeper services, city and attraction passes and boat tours. Passes can normally be bought from travel agents outside Britain or by visiting the Britrail website (britrail.com).

Bus and coach travel

Public buses

Every city and town in Britain has a local bus service. These services are privatised and run by separate companies. The largest bus companies in Britain are First (firstgroup.com/bustravel.php), Stagecoach (stagecoachbus.com), and Arriva (arrivabus.co.uk), which run buses in most UK towns. Outside London, buses usually travel to and from the town centre or busiest part of town. Most towns have a bus station, where you'll be able to find maps and information about routes. Bus route information may also be posted at bus stops.

Tickets and fares

The cost of a bus ticket normally depends on how far you're travelling. Return fares may be available on some buses, but you usually need to buy a 'single' ticket for each individual journey.

You can buy your ticket when you board a bus, by telling the driver where you are going. One-day and weekly travel cards are available in some towns, and these can be bought from the driver or from an information centre at the bus station. Tickets are valid for each separate journey rather than for a period of time, so if you get off the bus you'll need to buy a new ticket when getting on another bus.

Travelling to the UK by coach
There are coach routes to Britain from numerous European destinations. Although it may take much longer, coach travel is a cheap alternative to flying. One of the largest operators to the UK is Eurolines, which offers routes to Britain from over 500 destinations. For more information visit the Eurolines website at nationalexpress.com/eurolines/home/hp.cfm.

Car and vehicle hire
Hiring a car is a good way to travel around Britain at your own pace. You can use one for your whole visit, or for a short part of it. There are hundreds of car hire companies around Britain with many of them offering competitive prices.

What documents do I need?
You'll need to have a full, valid licence issued in your country of residence and held for at least a year (some companies ask for two years). If your licence is not issued by an EC/ECA country, an International Driver's Permit may be required.

Regulations
The average minimum car hire age is 23 (21 with some companies), and the average maximum age is 70 (80 in some companies). There may be restrictions on the type and size of car younger drivers can hire. Rental rates may also be higher for younger drivers. Most car hire companies provide emergency roadside assistance from the AA (theaa.com) or RAC (rac.co.uk) in case of a breakdown, but it is advisable to check this when booking.

Driving in Britain
Here are a few of the most important rules to remember when driving in Britain:
* Drive on the left-hand side of the road
* It is illegal to use a mobile phone when driving – if you need to make a call, find a safe place to stop first
* Seat belts must be worn and the correct child restraints used.

If you plan to drive during your trip to Britain, you should read the Highway Code before you get in a car. For more information visit direct.gov.uk.

London congestion charge
The congestion charge is an £8 daily charge to drive in central London at certain times. Check whether the congestion charge is included in the cost of your car when you book. If your car's pick up point is in the congestion-charging zone, the company may pay the charge for the first day of your hire.

Low Emission Zone
The Low Emission Zone is an area covering most of Greater London, within which the most polluting diesel-engine vehicles are required to meet specific emissions standards. If your vehicle does not, you will need to pay a daily charge.

Vehicles affected by the Low Emission Zone are older diesel-engine lorries, buses, coaches, large vans, minibuses and other heavy vehicles such as motor caravans and motorised horse boxes. This includes vehicles registered outside of Great Britain. Cars and motorcycles are not affected by the scheme.

For more information visit tfl.gov.uk/roadusers/lez.

Domestic flights
Flying is a time-saving alternative to road or rail when it comes to travelling around Britain. Domestic flights are fast and frequent and there are 33 airports across Britain operating domestic routes. You will find airports marked on the maps at the front of this guide.

Domestic flight advice
Photo ID is required to travel on domestic flights. It is advisable to bring your passport, as not all airlines will accept other forms of photo identification.

There are very high security measures at all airports in Britain. These include restrictions on items that may be carried in hand luggage. It is important that you check with your airline prior to travel, as these restrictions may vary over time. Make sure you allow adequate time for check-in and boarding.

Ferries
All major ferry companies are represented around Britain. For larger destinations, departure points include the cities of Southampton, Dover and Harwich, all within easy reach of London. If you prefer to travel on a smaller ship, many companies offer a range of itineraries to suit your requirements.

Cycling
Cycling is a good way to see some of Britain's best scenery and there are many networks of cycling routes. The National Cycle Network offers over 10,000 miles of walking and cycling routes connecting towns and villages, countryside and coast across the UK. For more information and routes see opposite or visit Sustrans at sustrans.co.uk.

National cycle network

Sections of the National Cycle Network are shown on the maps in this guide. The numbers on the maps will appear on the signs along your route **3**. Here are some tips about finding and using a route.

- **Research and plan your route online**
  Log on to **sustrans.org.uk** and click on 'Get cycling' to find information about routes.

- **Order a route map**
  Useful, easy-to-use maps of many of the most popular routes of the National Cycle Network are available from Sustrans, the charity behind the Network. These can be purchased online or by mail order – visit **sustransshop.co.uk** or call **+44 (0) 845 113 0065**.

- **Order Cycling in the UK**
  This official guide to the National Cycle Network gives details of rides all over the UK.

ROUTE NUMBER	ROUTE/MAP NAME	START/END OF ROUTE
South West England		
3 & 32	The Cornish Way	Land's End – Bude
South East England		
4 & 5	Thames Valley	London – Oxford via Reading
Northern England		
1	Coast & Castles South	Newcastle – Berwick-upon-Tweed – Edinburgh
7, 14 & 71	Sea to Sea (C2C)	Whitehaven/Workington – Sunderland/Newcastle upon Tyne
14	Three Rivers	Middlesbrough – Durham – South Shields
65 & Regional 52 (W2W)	Yorkshire Moors & Coast	Middlesbrough – Easingwold & Barnard Castle – Whitby
65 & 66	Yorkshire Wolds, York & Hull	Easingwold – York – Hull
68	Pennine Cycleway (South Pennines & the Dales)	Holmfirth – Appleby-in-Westmorland/Kendal
72	Hadrian's Cycleway	Ravenglass – South Shields
Wales		
4 & 47	Celtic Trail East	Chepstow – Cardiff – Swansea
4 & 47	Celtic Trail West	Swansea – Fishguard
81 & 82	Lôn Cambria & Lôn Teifi	Fishguard – Aberystwyth – Shrewsbury
8 & 42	Lôn Las Cymru (South)	Chepstow or Cardiff – Builth Wells
8	Lôn Las Cymru (North)	Builth Wells – Machynlleth – Holyhead
Scotland		
7	Lochs & Glens South	Carlisle – Ayr – Glasgow
7	Lochs & Glens North	Glasgow – Inverness
76	Round the Forth	Edinburgh – Stirling
78	Oban to Campbeltown	Oban – Campbeltown
Northern Ireland		
91	Kingfisher Trail	Enniskillen – Carrick-on-Shannon
91 & 92	The North West Trail	Strabane – Sligo

Distance chart

The distances between towns on the chart below are given to the nearest mile, and are measured along routes based on the quickest travelling time, making maximum use of motorways or dual-carriageway roads. The chart is based upon information supplied by the Automobile Association.

To calculate the distance in kilometres multiply the mileage by 1.6

For example: Brighton to Dover
82 miles x 1.6 =131.2 kilometres

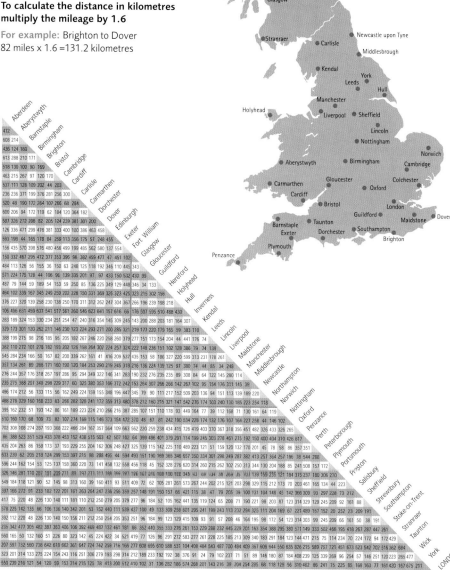

Diagonal headings (top-left to bottom-right):
Aberdeen, Aberystwyth, Barnstaple, Birmingham, Brighton, Bristol, Cambridge, Cardiff, Carlisle, Carmarthen, Dorchester, Dover, Edinburgh, Exeter, Fort William, Glasgow, Gloucester, Guildford, Hereford, Holyhead, Hull, Inverness, Kendal, Leeds, Lincoln, Liverpool, Maidstone, Manchester, Middlesbrough, Newcastle, Northampton, Norwich, Nottingham, Oxford, Penzance, Perth, Peterborough, Plymouth, Portsmouth, Preston, Salisbury, Sheffield, Shrewsbury, Southampton, Stoke-on-Trent, Stranraer, Taunton, Wick, York, LONDON

```
472
608 214
436 124 180
613 288 210 171
518 130 100 90 169
463 215 267 97 120 170
537 111 128 109 202 44 203
236 236 371 199 376 281 256 300
520 48 190 172 264 107 266 68 284
600 206 94 172 119 62 184 120 364 182
587 326 272 208 82 205 124 239 381 301 200
126 336 471 299 476 381 333 400 100 386 463 458
593 198 44 165 178 84 259 113 356 175 57 248 455
156 435 570 398 576 480 456 499 199 485 562 580 137 554
150 332 467 295 472 377 353 396 96 382 459 477 47 451 102
484 113 126 56 155 36 150 63 248 125 118 192 346 110 445 343
571 224 175 128 44 106 96 139 335 201 97 97 433 150 532 430 98
487 79 144 59 189 54 153 59 250 85 136 225 349 129 448 346 34 133
464 102 339 167 345 249 259 202 228 150 331 369 326 323 425 323 215 302 156
376 227 320 139 258 230 138 250 170 311 312 262 247 304 367 266 196 239 198 218
106 496 631 459 637 541 517 561 260 546 623 641 157 616 66 176 507 595 510 488 430
283 189 324 153 330 234 251 254 47 240 316 354 145 309 245 143 200 288 203 181 164 307
329 173 301 120 262 211 146 230 123 224 293 271 200 285 321 219 177 220 179 165 59 383 110
388 199 275 98 216 185 95 205 182 267 246 220 258 260 379 277 151 173 154 204 44 441 176 74
362 110 272 101 279 182 193 202 126 158 264 302 224 257 324 222 148 236 151 102 128 386 79 74 139
545 284 234 166 50 167 82 200 339 262 161 41 416 209 537 435 153 58 186 327 220 599 313 231 178 261
357 134 261 89 266 171 160 190 120 184 253 290 219 245 318 216 136 224 125 97 380 74 44 85 34 248
276 244 357 176 318 267 197 286 95 294 349 322 146 341 283 190 232 276 235 89 308 84 64 122 145 280 114
235 275 388 207 349 298 229 317 60 325 380 353 106 372 242 153 264 307 266 262 902 95 154 76 311 165 39
486 174 212 56 133 115 56 162 249 224 159 155 348 196 447 345 79 90 111 217 152 509 203 136 94 151 113 139 189 220
488 278 329 160 168 233 63 266 282 328 241 170 378 212 360 315 321 167 174 103 240 130 185 223 254 118
395 162 232 51 193 142 86 161 189 223 224 210 266 216 387 285 107 151 110 178 71 430 164 77 39 112 168 71 130 161 64 119
510 160 170 68 109 73 82 107 274 169 115 146 373 154 472 370 48 67 81 242 190 534 228 174 132 176 107 164 227 258 44 146 102
702 308 108 274 287 193 368 222 466 284 167 357 564 109 663 562 220 259 238 434 415 726 419 403 370 367 318 356 451 482 326 433 326 265
86 388 523 351 529 433 378 453 152 438 515 503 42 507 102 64 399 486 401 379 291 114 199 245 303 278 461 275 192 150 400 404 310 426 617
435 204 263 86 158 173 37 193 229 255 204 162 306 248 427 325 139 115 142 225 110 489 223 121 51 159 120 132 170 201 45 78 58 86 357 351
633 239 62 205 218 124 299 153 397 215 98 288 495 44 594 493 151 190 243 437 400 713 309 398 393 345 340 378 483 514 287 382 382 472 37 537 282
596 244 162 154 53 125 137 158 360 222 73 141 458 132 558 456 118 45 152 328 276 620 314 260 215 262 102 250 313 344 130 204 188 85 241 508 157 172
417 75 220 48 226 130 140 111 181 110 212 250 279 205 379 277 96 184 52 105 162 441 135 119 124 65 208 71 190 221 98 203 87 123 314 329 129 245 209 92 161 88
323 201 314 133 275 224 154 243 116 251 306 279 193 298 314 212 189 233 192 38 376 91 24 79 102 237 71 51 89 146 180 87 184 408 239 125 339 269 96 254 57 146 251 120 223 265 477
560 165 50 132 160 51 226 80 323 142 45 224 421 34 521 419 71 126 96 297 272 583 277 261 228 215 213 309 340 183 291 184 123 144 471 215 75 114 234 70 224 172 94 172 429
207 597 732 560 738 642 618 662 361 647 724 742 258 716 166 277 608 695 610 588 531 104 408 484 543 487 700 484 409 367 609 644 550 635 835 234 589 757 721 451 673 523 542 702 516 362 684
550 239 216 121 54 120 59 153 314 215 125 78 413 200 512 410 102 31 136 282 186 574 268 201 143 216 39 204 254 285 68 118 129 56 310 462 86 241 75 225 85 169 163 77 161 420 167 675 211
```

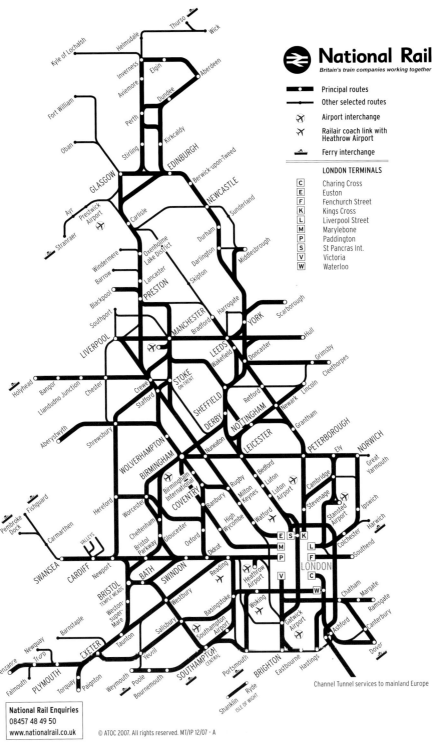

National Rail
Britain's train companies working together

Principal routes
Other selected routes
Airport interchange
Railair coach link with Heathrow Airport
Ferry interchange

LONDON TERMINALS

C	Charing Cross
E	Euston
F	Fenchurch Street
K	Kings Cross
L	Liverpool Street
M	Marylebone
P	Paddington
S	St Pancras Int.
V	Victoria
W	Waterloo

Channel Tunnel services to mainland Europe

National Rail Enquiries
08457 48 49 50
www.nationalrail.co.uk   © ATOC 2007. All rights reserved. MT/IP 12/07 · A

08/NRE/1320

Transport contacts

General travel information

Streetmap	streetmap.co.uk	
Transport Direct (a journey planner)	transportdirect.info	
Transport for London	tfl.gov.uk	+44 (0) 20 7222 1234
Travel Services	departures-arrivals.com	
Traveline (public transport information)	traveline.org.uk	+44 (0) 870 200 2233

Bus & coach

Megabus	megabus.com	+44 (0) 870 550 5050
National Express	nationalexpress.com	+44 (0) 870 580 8080
WA Shearings	washearings.com	+44 (0) 1942 823371

Car & car hire

AA	theaa.com	+44 (0) 161 495 8945
Green Flag	greenflag.co.uk	+44 (0) 845 246 1557
RAC	rac.co.uk	+44 (0) 870 572 2722
Alamo	alamo.co.uk	+44 (0) 870 400 4562*
Avis	avis.co.uk	+44 (0) 844 581 0147
Budget	budget.co.uk	+44 (0) 1344 484100
Easycar	easycar.com	0906 333 3333**
Enterprise	enterprise.com	+44 (0) 870 350 3000*
Hertz	hertz.co.uk	+44 (0) 870 844 8844*
Holiday Autos	holidayautos.co.uk	+44 (0) 1483 909697
National	nationalcar.co.uk	+44 (0) 870 400 4581
Thrifty	thrifty.co.uk	+44 (0) 1494 751500

Air

Air Southwest	airsouthwest.com	+44 (0) 870 043 4553
Blue Islands (Channel Islands)	blueislands.com	+44 (0) 845 620 2122
BMI	flybmi.com	+44 (0) 1332 648181
BMI Baby	bmibaby.com	+44 (0) 870 126 6726
British Airways	ba.com	See website for details
British International (Isles of Scilly to Penzance)	islesofscillyhelicopter.com	+44 (0) 1736 363871*
Eastern Airways	easternairways.com	+44 (0) 870 366 9989
Easyjet	easyjet.com	See website for details
Flybe	flybe.com	+44 (0) 1392 268500*
Flyglobespan	flyglobespan.com	+44 (0) 871 271 0415*
Jet2.com	jet2.com	See website for details
Manx2	manx2.com	+44 (0) 871 200 0440*
Ryanair	ryanair.com	See website for details
Skybus (Isles of Scilly)	islesofscilly-travel.co.uk	+44 (0) 1736 334220
Thomsonfly	tomsonfly.com	+44 (0) 871 231 4869
VLM	flyvlm.com	See website for details

Train

National Rail Enquiries	nationalrail.co.uk	+44 (0) 20 7278 5240
		0845 748 4950***

Consult National Rail Enquiries for up-to-the-minute advice on journey planning, train times and service updates.

The Trainline (online booking)	trainline.co.uk	
UK train operating companies	rail.co.uk	
Arriva Trains	arriva.co.uk	+44 (0) 191 520 4000
c2c	c2c-online.co.uk	+44 (0) 845 601 4873
Chiltern Railways	chilternrailways.co.uk	+44 (0) 845 600 5165
CrossCountry	crosscountrytrains.co.uk	+44 (0) 870 010 0084
East Midlands Trains	eastmidlandstrains.co.uk	+44 (0) 845 712 5678
Eurostar	eurostar.com	+44 (0) 1233 617575
First Capital Connect	firstcapitalconnect.co.uk	+44 (0) 845 026 4700
First Great Western	firstgreatwestern.co.uk	+44 (0) 845 700 0125
Gatwick Express	gatwickexpress.com	+44 (0) 121 410 5015
Heathrow Connect	heathrowconnect.com	+44 (0) 845 678 6975
Heathrow Express	heathrowexpress.com	+44 (0) 845 600 1515
Hull Trains	hulltrains.co.uk	+44 (0) 845 071 0222
Island Line	island-line.co.uk	+44 (0) 845 600 0650
London Midland	londonmidland.com	+44 (0) 844 811 0133
Merseyrail	merseyrail.org	+44 (0) 151 702 2071
National Express East Anglia	nationalexpresseastanglia.com	+44 (0) 845 600 7245
National Express East Coast	nationalexpresseastcoast.com	+44 (0) 845 722 5333
Northern Rail	northernrail.org	+44 (0) 845 000 0125
ScotRail	firstgroup.com/scotrail	+44 (0) 845 601 5929
South Eastern Trains	southeasternrailway.co.uk	+44 (0) 845 000 2222
South West Trains	southwesttrains.co.uk	+44 (0) 845 600 0650
Southern	southernrailway.com	+44 (0) 845 127 2920
Stansted Express	stanstedexpress.com	+44 (0) 845 600 7245
Translink	nirailways.co.uk	+44 (0) 28 9066 6630
Transpennine Express	tpexpress.co.uk	+44 (0) 845 600 1671
Virgin Trains	virgintrains.co.uk	+44 (0) 845 722 2333*

Ferry

Ferry information	sailanddrive.com	
Condor Ferries (Channel Islands)	condorferries.co.uk	+44 (0) 845 609 1024*
Steam Packet Company (Isle of Man)	steam-packet.com	+44 (0) 1624 661661
Isles of Scilly Travel	islesofscilly-travel.co.uk	+44 (0) 1736 334220
Red Funnel (Isle of Wight)	redfunnel.co.uk	+44 (0) 845 155 2442
Wight Link (Isle of Wight)	wightlink.co.uk	+44 (0) 23 9285 5230

Phone numbers listed are for general enquiries unless otherwise stated.

* Booking line only ** UK number only, charged at premium rate

*** UK number only

Britain at a glance

with Northern Ireland and the Channel Islands

SCOTLAND

NORTHERN ENGLAND
Cheshire, Cumbria, Durham, East Yorkshire, Greater Manchester, Lancashire, Merseyside, North Yorkshire, Northumberland, South Yorkshire, Tees Valley, Tyne and Wear, West Yorkshire

CENTRAL ENGLAND
Bedfordshire, Cambridgeshire, Derbyshire, Essex, Herefordshire, Hertfordshire, Leicestershire, Lincolnshire, Norfolk, Northamptonshire, Nottinghamshire, Rutland, Shropshire, Staffordshire, Suffolk, Warwickshire, West Midlands, Worcestershire

NORTHERN IRELAND   **WALES**

LONDON

SOUTH WEST ENGLAND
Bristol, Cornwall, Devon, Dorset, Gloucestershire, Isles of Scilly, Somerset, Wiltshire

SOUTH EAST ENGLAND
Berkshire, Buckinghamshire, East Sussex, Hampshire, Isle of Wight, Kent, London, Oxfordshire, Surrey, West Sussex

THE CHANNEL ISLANDS
Guernsey and Jersey are not drawn to scale

Guernsey

Jersey

A guide to English counties

If you know what county you wish to visit you'll find it in the regional section shown below.

County	Region	County	Region
Bedfordshire	Central England	Leicestershire	Central England
Berkshire	South East England	Lincolnshire	Central England
Bristol	South West England	Merseyside	Northern England
Buckinghamshire	South East England	Norfolk	Central England
Cambridgeshire	Central England	North Yorkshire	Northern England
Cheshire	Northern England	Northamptonshire	Central England
Cornwall	South West England	Northumberland	Northern England
Cumbria	Northern England	Nottinghamshire	Central England
Derbyshire	Central England	Oxfordshire	South East England
Devon	South West England	Rutland	Central England
Dorset	South West England	Shropshire	Central England
Durham	Northern England	Somerset	South West England
East Yorkshire	Northern England	South Yorkshire	Northern England
East Sussex	South East England	Staffordshire	Central England
Essex	Central England	Suffolk	Central England
Gloucestershire	South West England	Surrey	South East England
Greater Manchester	Northern England	Tees Valley	Northern England
Hampshire	South East England	Tyne and Wear	Northern England
Herefordshire	Central England	Warwickshire	Central England
Hertfordshire	Central England	West Midlands	Central England
Isle of Wight	South East England	West Sussex	South East England
Isles of Scilly	South West England	West Yorkshire	Northern England
Kent	South East England	Wiltshire	South West England
Lancashire	Northern England	Worcestershire	Central England

To help readers we do not refer to unitary authorities in this guide.

Index by property name

Accommodation with a detailed entry in this guide is listed below.

Index by place name

The following places all have detailed accommodation entries in this guide. If the place where you wish to stay is not shown, the location maps (starting on page 30) will help you to find somewhere to stay in the area.

Turn to the pages indicated for detailed accommodation entries in these places.

Published by: Heritage House Group (Ketteringham Hall, Wymondham, Norfolk NR18 9RS; t +44 (0) 1603 819420; f +44 (0) 1603 814325; hhgroup.co.uk) on behalf of VisitBritain, Thames Road, Blacks Road, London W6 9EL
Publishing Manager: Tess Lugos
Production Manager: Iris Buckley
Compilation, design, copywriting, production and advertisement sales: Jackson Lowe Marketing, 3 St Andrews Place, Southover Road, Lewes, East Sussex BN7 1UP
t +44 (0) 1273 487487 jacksonlowe.com
Cover design: Jamieson Eley, Nick McCann
Typesetting: Marlinzo Services, Somerset and Jackson Lowe Marketing
Accommodation maps: Based on digital map data © ESR Cartography, 2008
Touring maps: © VisitBritain 2005. National Parks, Areas of Outstanding Natural Beauty, National Trails and Heritage Coast based on information supplied by Natural England, the Countryside Council for Wales and Scottish Natural Heritage. Cycle Networks provided by Sustrans
Printing and binding: 1010 Printing International Ltd, China

Front cover (from top): Combe House Hotel & Restaurant, Honiton, Devon; Three Cliffs Bay Caravan Park, Penmaen, Gower, Swansea (britainonview/Rod Edwards); Dunalastair Holiday Houses, Kinloch Rannoch, Perth and Kinross
Back cover: Plas Dinas Country House, Caernarfon, Gwynedd

Photography credits: © Crown copyright (2008) Visit Wales; britainonview/David Angel/ANPA/Daniel Bosworth/Martin Brent/brightonview/Caravan Club/Alan Chandler/East Midlands Tourism/East of England Tourism/Eden Project/Rod Edwards/Damir Fabijanic/FCO/Klaus Hagmeier/Joanna Henderson/Adrian Houston/Kent Tourism Alliance/Simon Kreitem/Lee Valley Regional Park/Pawel Libera/James McCormick/McCormick-McAdam/Eric Nathan/David Noton/NWDA/Tony Pleavin/Grant Pritchard/Ingrid Rasmussen/Olivier Roques-Ro/David Sellman/Andy Sewell/Jon Spaull/Troika/Visit Chester & Cheshire/Wales Tourist Board Photo Library/Michael Walter/Juliet White/Worcestershire County Council; Iris Buckley; Caravan Club; The Deep; Imperial War Museum North; Michael Jackson; Jersey Tourism; Allan McPhail; Northern Ireland Tourist Board; NTPL/Rob Judges; One NorthEast Tourism; Mark Passmore; South West News Service; Thermae Bath Spa/Matt Cardy; P Tomkins/VisitScotland/Scottishviewpoint; Visit Bristol; Visit Wales; VisitGuernsey; visitlondonimages/britainonview; VisitScotland/Scottishviewpoint

A VisitBritain Publishing guide